HARDPRESS.NET
HOME OF HARD-TO-FIND BOOKS

The Critical Review, Or, Annals of Literature
by Tobias George Smollett

THE
CRITICAL REVIEW:
OR,
Annals of Literature.

BY
A SOCIETY of GENTLEMEN.

VOLUME the FIFTY-SECOND.

———— *Nothing extenuate,*
Nor set down aught in malice.   SHAKSPEARE.

Ploravere suis non respondere favorem
Speratum meritis————   HOR.

LONDON,
Printed for A. HAMILTON, in Falcon-Court, Fleet-Street.
MDCCLXXXI.

CONTENTS.

A 2

Poems,

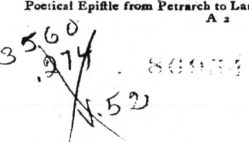

CONTENTS.

Palmer's

CONTENTS.

Biblio-

CONTENTS.

Ode

CONTENTS.

2   Crowe's

CONTENTS.

THE

THE

CRITICAL REVIEW.

For the Month of *July*, 1781.

The History of the Isle of Wight.   4to.   1l. 7s. *in boards.*
Robinson.

THE situation of Hampshire, and the number of places of note which it contains, might have justly entitled this county much earlier to the attention of topographical writers.   But though histories of many other parts of England, of less consideration, have preceded, it now enjoys, as a reparation for long neglect, the honour of having a portion of it illustrated, in the present work, by sir Richard Worsley, baronet.——Of the origin and publication of this work, we meet with the following ingenuous account in the Preface.

'Notwithstanding the favourable reception given by the public, to descriptive histories of counties, and other districts of England, a History of Hampshire is yet wanting; the present publication is intended, in some degree, to supply that deficiency.

'The Isle of Wight, though a portion of that county, is so detached by nature, and discriminated by peculiar circumstances, as to be pointed out for an object of separate description.   This indeed appears to have been the opinion of some learned men in former times; as we find, in Bishop Nicholson's Historical Library, that there existed, in the last century, in the library of Arthur, earl of Anglesea, a manuscript, intitled, A General Survey of the Isle of Wight, written by sir Francis Knollis, privy counsellor to queen Elizabeth.   A History and Description of the Isle of Wight was also planned, early in the seventeenth century, by Dr. Richard James, of Corpus Christi College, Oxford,

a naa native of the island, and nephew of the first keeper of the Bodleian Library, where his manuscript, intitled, Antiquitates Insulæ Vectæ, is still preserved. It contains little more than extracts from our early histories, for the beginning of his work; but, from a summary prefixed to them, it appears that his plan was very comprehensive.

' About the same period, sir John Oglander, a gentleman of one of the most ancient families of the island, employed himself in collecting miscellaneous observations relative to it, mostly such as came within his own knowlege. His notes, beginning with the year one thousand six hundred and fifteen, and continued to the year one thousand six hundred and forty-nine, remain in the possession of his worthy successor, sir William Oglander, baronet. They contain a great variety of very valuable, though unmethodised, materials.

' The History now offered to the public, owes its origin to sir James Worsley, baronet, of Pilewell, in Hampshire, who began to prepare materials for it early in the present century, and prosecuted the work till the time of his death, which happened in the year one thousand seven hundred and fifty-seven. An unusual length of life afforded him the means of much observation, and extensive enquiry; he bestowed no small labour in searching and examining records; he had access to sir John Oglander's manuscript, and made considerable use of it. Little, either of description or of natural history, is found in his papers; but he had made some progress in digesting the civil history of the island, and he evidently intended it for publication. Yet, notwithstanding all the advantages he enjoyed, he left his design incomplete. His manuscript, with considerable additions by his son sir Thomas Worsley, has descended to his grandson; who considers this publication as the discharge of a filial duty.'

The volume begins with a general description of the Isle of Wight, its situation, extent, soil, produce, trade, parochial divisions, and number of inhabitants. The historian observes, that many writers represent the Isle of Wight as having been formerly attached to the main land, from which it was separated by the encroachments of the sea. This opinion, it is remarked, has probably been adopted upon the authority of Diodorus Siculus, who mentions a peninsula, called Vectis, as the mart to which the Cornish merchants used to bring their tin in carts. Several circumstances, however, among which is the distance of the place, have inclined some antiquaries to question, whether by Vectis, Diodorus Siculus really meant the Isle of Wight. In treating of this subject, sir Richard Worsley recites the opinions and arguments of Mr. Borlase, in his Natural History of Cornwall, and of Mr. Whitaker, in the History of Manchester; to which are subjoined the following remarks made by a gentleman of the island. Those are,

' That,

' That, at each extremity of the channel between the island and Hampshire, the tide rushes in and out with such impetuosity as to render these parts the deepest and most dangerous, whereas, near the midway, where the tides meet, though the conflict makes a rough water, according as the wind may assist the one or the other, there is no rapidity of current to carry away the soil and deepen the bottom ; accordingly we discover a hard gravelly beach there, extending a great way across the channel, a circumstance not to be found in any other part of it. Corresponding with this, on the Hampshire side, is a place called Leap, possibly from the narrowness of the pass, and on the Isle of Wight, opposite this, is a strait open road, of at least two miles in length, called Rew-street, probably from the French word Rue, to which the translation of it might afterwards be added : this road, after having crossed the forest, may be traced by an observant eye from St. Austin's Gate to the west of Carisbrook castle, over a field called North Field, by Sheat, and so on to the south side of the island. Many parts of this road are of little or no use at this time, and, unless it was heretofore used for the purpose of conveying tin, it is not easy to conjecture what purpose it was to answer.'

The argument drawn from the apparent design of the road above mentioned, carries with it great force in determining this controversy ; nor is the want of historical evidence, respecting the disjunction of the Isle of Wight from the main land of Britain, sufficient reason for questioning the existence of the event, when we know of many such instances in the natural history of the world.

The second chapter treats of the military history of the island ; the several descents made by the Romans, Saxons, Danes, and French ; the ancient feudal military force, and present state of the militia ; with an account of the castles and forts. The narrative recites the various descents which have been made on the Isle of Wight, from the year 43, when it was conquered by the Romans, to the invasion of the French in 1545. In detailing those transactions, the author has had recourse chiefly to the Saxon Chronicle ; and in what respects the ancient military force of the island, to authentic records, of which copies are given in an Appendix. To induce people to settle in the Isle of Wight, several privileges and immunities were conferred on the inhabitants by a grant of Edward the Third. They were not to be charged with the aid granted to the king ; and no inhabitant of the island could be compelled to serve on any jury or inquest out of it.

The description of the castle of Carisbrooke is drawn with great accuracy. It appears that at the south-east angle of this fort there are the remains of a tower, the walls of which were in some places no less than eighteen feet thick. Here is a well, said to be three hundred feet deep ; but it has been partly filled up as useless and dangerous. Under a small building in the castle-yard is another well, more than two hundred feet deep, whence the water for the use of the garrison was drawn by means of a large wheel, turned by an ass. This duty, we are told, was for forty years performed by the same animal, not long since dead. Down this well, the historian informs us, it is usual to drop a pin, which after a lapse of about three seconds of time, produces a greater sound than can well be conceived by those who have not heard it.

Carisbrooke Castle is remarkable for the confinement of Charles the First, who was detained in it a prisoner from November 1647, to September the following year. All the other forts, of which are several in the island, were erected in the reign of Henry VIII.

The third chapter recites the succession of the lords of the island, with their franchises. The historian observes, that the lordship of the Isle of Wight does not appear to have been granted to any subject before the Norman conquest. The first that held this honour was William Fitz Osborne, kinsman to William the Conqueror, from whom he obtained a grant of it. Fitz Osborne founded two abbeys in Normandy, one at Lyra, the other at Cormeilles, and also a priory at Carisbrook, which, with six churches in the Isle of Wight, besides several others, he gave to the abbey at Lyra. He survived the conquest only four years, being slain in battle, and was buried in the abbey of Cormeilles.

The second lord of the Isle of Wight was Roger de Breteville, or de Bristolis, earl of Hereford. This nobleman having entered into a conspiracy against the king, was tried and found guilty of treason, for which his lands were confiscated, and he was sentenced to perpetual imprisonment.

The lordship of the island being forfeited on this event, continued in the crown until Henry the First granted it to Richard de Redvers, Ripariis, or Rivers, a descendant of Richard, first duke of Normandy, by an illegitimate son. Richard de Redvers dying in the first year of the reign of Stephen, was succeeded in the lordship of the Isle of Wight by his son Baldwin. The lordship of the island continued in this family for several generations, till Edward the First obtained it by purchase from Isabella de Fortibus: It was again separated from the crown by Edward the Second, who granted it to his favourite Piers Gaveston ; but on a remonstrance of the nobility, the king resumed the grant the following year, and con-

conferred the lordship of the island on his eldest son Edward, afterwards king Edward the Third. This prince retained it in his possession till his death; but Richard the Second afterwards granted it to William Montacute, earl of Salisbury, for life. He dying without issue, the lordship was next conferred on Edward, earl of Rutland, afterwards duke of York. On his death, the duchess of York obtained a grant of the Isle of Wight, for her life; at the expiration of which it devolved, by a reversionary grant, on Humphrey, duke of Gloucester, son of Henry the Fourth. He is supposed to have held the island to the time of his death, notwithstanding two years before that event, Henry Beauchamp, duke of Warwick, was crowned king of the Isle of Wight; king Henry the Sixth, in person, assisting at the ceremonial, and placing the crown on his head. This, the historian observes, though a very honourable mark of the royal favour, conveyed no regal authority, the king having no power to transfer the sovereignty of any part of his dominions. There is reason to conclude, that, though titular king, he did not even possess the lordship of the island; no surrender appearing from duke Humphrey, who was then living, and had a grant for the term of his life. Under those circumstances, the honour conferred on the duke of Warwick must appear very whimsical.

For an account of the subsequent lords of the Isle of Wight, we shall present our readers with an extract from the work.

' Among the records in the Tower of London are found two petitions from the inhabitants of the island, dated the twenty-eighth of Henry the Sixth, one to the king, and the other to the parliament, complaining of the bad government, and defenceless state of the island at that time; and, though the particulars are not clearly stated, nor, perhaps from the confusion of affairs, illustrated by any contemporary records, yet they nevertheless afford sufficient evidence to rank Richard Plantagenet, duke of York, father of king Edward the Fourth, among the lords of the island. He is not indeed expresly so termed, but is mentioned in the second petition as exercising such acts of government there, as could only be performed by one vested with that authority: for he had appointed one John Newport his lieutenant, and steward of the island; and, on his misbehaviour, displaced him, and conferred that employment on Henry Bruin. Newport, after his dismission, although negotiating with the king for his re-establishment, took advantage of the relaxed state of government, and committed great outrages on the inhabitants, both by land and sea, which are pathetically set forth in the petition; but the king and parliament, as well as the duke of York, were then too much engaged to afford them relief.

' The

' The history of the duke is well known ; the king's constitutional imbecility increasing, he was invested with the administration of government, under the title of protector : his birth, influence, and connexions inspired him with the hopes of ascending the throne, but his conduct in the attempt was too mild and cautious for the turbulence of those times, though sufficiently explicit to drive him into measures that terminated in his destruction. He lost his life at the battle of Wakefield, leaving his more daring son to reap the fruit of his pretensions.

' In the thirty-first year of Henry the Sixth, Edmund, duke of Somerset, who married the sister and coheir of Henry, duke of Warwick, before mentioned as king of the island, having some time before supplanted the duke of York in the regency of France, obtained a grant of this island, and the castle of Carisbrooke, to him and the heirs male of his body, in satisfaction, as it was alleged, for certain sums of money due to him from the king's exchequer, and for the duties of petty customs in the port of London, which were part of his inheritance. This duke was slain at the first battle of St. Alban's, in the thirty-third year of Henry the Sixth.

' Henry, duke of Somerset, his son, succeeded him in the lordship of this island : on some disgust he quitted the royal party, and went over to that of the duke of York, but afterwards returning to the king's service, he was taken prisoner by the Yorkists, at the battle of Hexham, and by them beheaded.

' In the sixth year of Edward the Fourth, Anthony de Wydeville, or Woodville, lord Schales, and after his father's demise, earl Rivers, had a grant of this island, with the castle of Carisbrooke, and all other rights appertaining to the lordship, to him and his heirs male ; after the decease of that king, he, standing in the way of the ambitious views of Richard, duke of Gloucester, was seized, and, without any legal process, beheaded in Pontefract castle.

' Sir Edward Wydeville, brother of the afore mentioned Anthony, earl Rivers, was, in the first year of Henry the Seventh, made captain of the Island. Sir William Dugdale supposes him to have been the brother of the first earl Rivers ; but in that he is mistaken, as well as in terming him governor of the Isle of Wight, a title not assumed till many years after, by the captain of the island. This sir Edward Wydeville, in the fourth year of Henry the Seventh, undertook, with a force raised in this island, to assist the duke of Brittany, against the king of France, conceiving it would be pleasing to his master, who was supposed secretly to favour the duke's interest, though then acting as a mediator between the contending parties. Sir Edward, therefore, first asked permission to engage in that cause, and receiving a denial, imagined it was only given to save appearances, and that the king would not be displeased with a private attempt in the duke's favour ; he therefore repaired to the Isle of Wight, and,

con-

convening the inhabitants by a general muster, he then proposed the business to the gentlemen, telling them how acceptable it would be to the king, how honourable to themselves, and how greatly demonstrative of their regard to him, which he should ever gratefully retain in his memory; and that to requite them, he would not only employ his whole fortune, but also all his interest with his sovereign. He farther expatiated on the justice of the cause, informing them that the king of France was not only endeavouring to possess himself of the dukedom of Brittany, but also the duke's daughter, the lawful wife of Maximilian, king of the Romans; and that if these designs were suffered to succeed, they would have a very disagreeable neighbour, instead of their ancient and good allies the dukes of Brittany. This harangue had but too good success, great numbers flocking to his standard; out of these he selected about forty gentlemen, and four hundred of the stoutest from the commonalty, who embarked at St. Helen's in four vessels; they were clothed in white coats, with red crosses, and were joined by fifteen hundred of the duke's forces, dressed in the same uniform, to make the auxiliaries appear the more numerous. Unfortunately, at the battle of St. Aubin's, in Brittany, the duke was defeated, and sir Edward, with all the English slain, except one boy, who brought home the melancholy tidings, particularly so to this island, as there was scarce a family but what lost a relation in this expedition. Sir Edward died unmarried.

' It was this tragical event that occasioned an act of parliament to be passed, intended to promote the population of the island, by prohibiting any of its inhabitants from holding farms, lands, or tithes, exceeding the annual rent of ten marks. A regulation that could not, from the constant decrease of the value of money, remain long in force: to make a law of this nature permanent, the quantity of land, and not of rent, should be ascertained; but political writers are by no means agreed as to the effects of such restrictions.

' It is not certain whether sir Edward was lord of the island, or, as his title imported, only captain thereof, though, from the great influence he appears to have had over the inhabitants, instanced in their engaging in his ill-fated expedition, the former seems most probable. After his decease, Henry the Seventh, intent upon lessening the power of the barons, never granted away the lordship of this island, which has ever since remained in the crown: thus its government was changed into a more military appointment; and though the captain, or governor, might hold some lands, that remained to the castle, they are annexed to the charge of it, and were enjoyed, jure officii only.'

The detail of the lords of the Isle of Wight is illustrated by several plates, exhibiting chiefly the seals of the different families; an embellishment which shews the great attention paid by sir Richard Worsley to the splendor of the work.

B 4

The

The chief privilege enjoyed by the lord of the Isle of Wight, as the historian remarks, was that of holding a judicial tribunal, called the Knighten Court, properly the Knight's Court, the nature of which is afterwards distinctly delineated in the work.

We shall delay the farther prosecution of this History till our next Review; observing only at present that it is distinguished by such accuracy as might be expected in a work which has been digested with so much deliberation and care. It is impossible to discriminate the materials collected by the father and son; but from observations of recent date, we may ascribe no small share of the researches, as well as the arrangement, to the right honourable editor, who appears to be every way well qualified for the discharge of the filial duty which he has so piously fulfilled.

[*To be continued.*]

The History of Great Britain, *from the first Invasion of it by the* Romans *under* Julius Cæsar. *By* Robert Henry, D. D. *Vol. IV.* 4to. 1l. 1s. *in boards.* Cadell.

DR. Henry seems to prosecute, with unabating ardour, the extensive plan of this work. The present volume comprises the period of history from the death of king John to the accession of Henry the Fourth; an interval of more than a hundred and eighty years. The authorities on which the narrative is founded have been so often cited by preceding writers, that few remarks are to be made on the detail of transactions. It is chiefly the style, and the description of characters, which can, in so late an age, render an author of English history conspicuous for originality in the manner of treating his subject. We shall therefore lay before our readers Dr. Henry's character of the earl of Leicester, who was killed in a battle near Evesham, in the year 1265.

' Thus fell Simon de Montfort, the great earl of Leicester, who raised himself to a degree of greatness hardly inferior to royalty, and of wealth superior to that of some of our monarchs. Nothing is more difficult than to form a just idea of the real character of this illustrious person, who was abhorred as a *devil* by one half of England, and adored as a *saint* and guardian *angel* by the other. He was unquestionably one of the greatest generals and politicians of his age; bold, ambitious, and enterprising; ever considered, both by friends and enemies, as the very soul of the party which he espoused. He was fierce and clamorous in the cause of liberty, till he arrived at power, which he employed in aggrandising and enriching his own family. But whether
ther

ther he did this in order to enable him to establish the liberties of his country on a solid foundation, or only to gratify his
own avarice and ambition, is perhaps impossible to be determined.'

In this passage, the antithesis of *devil* and *saint* appears to
be an unnecessary amplification ; at least, the former of those
epithets might, we think, have been omitted with propriety.

The following is the character which he draws of Henry
the Third.

' Henry III. surnamed of Winchester, was in his person of
middle stature, of a robust constitution, but unpleasing countenance ; his left eye-brow hanging down and almost covering his
eye. This prince was certainly not possessed of great intellectual
abilities, much less of true wisdom, and the right art of governing ; yet his understanding does not seem to have been remarkably defective, but had unhappily taken a turn towards low
dishonest cunning. As the ends which he had in view were often
bad, and such as could not be openly avowed, he endeavoured
to attain them by the winding ways of treachery and deceit.
Some of Henry's repartees are preserved in history, which do
not bespeak him to have been that simple fool he is often represented. When the archbishop of Canterbury, with the bishops
of Winchester, Salisbury, and Carlisle, were sent by parliament,
in 1253, to present a very strong remonstrance against uncanonical
and forced elections to vacant sees : " It is true, replied he, I
have been somewhat faulty in that particular : I obtruded you,
my lord of Canterbury, upon your see : I was obliged to employ both entreaties and menaces, my lord of Winchester, to get
you elected, when you should have been rather sent to school :
my proceedings were indeed very irregular and violent, my lords
of Salisbury and Carlisle, when I raised you from the lowest stations to your present dignities. It will become you therefore,
my lords, to set an example of reformation, by resigning your
present benefices, and try to obtain preferment in a more regular
manner." But this prince was much more defective in personal
courage than in understanding ; and, as appears from the whole
course of his history, as well as from many anecdotes, was of a
very cowardly and timorous nature. In the year 1258, when
the royal authority was much eclipsed, and the earl of Leicester
was in his glory, the king, in going to the Tower by water, was
overtaken in a storm of thunder and lightning, with which he was
greatly terrified, and ordered his barge to be put a shore at the
first landing place. But being met by the earl of Leicester at his
landing, his terrors redoubled, and he exhibited all the marks of
the greatest consternation in his countenance, which made the
earl observe, that the storm was now over, and he had no further
reason to be afraid ; to which the king replied, " I am indeed beyond measure afraid of thunder and lightning ; but, by God's
head,

head, I fear thee more than all the thunder in the universe." Henry was still more destitute of the noble virtues of sincerity in making, and fidelity in observing his engagements, than he was of courage. Whenever he was hard pushed by the discontented barons, he submitted to any terms they thought fit to prescribe, and confirmed them by all the most awful oaths and solemnities they could devise: but the moment he thought he could do it with safety, he violated all his promises and oaths without hesitation, satisfying himself with the absolution of his good friend the pope, which he easily obtained. This wicked prevarication was not more odious than it was pernicious to his affairs, and obliged the barons to proceed to much greater extremities than otherwise they would have done, plainly perceiving that nothing could make him keep his promises, but putting it out of his power to break them. But the most singular feature in this prince's character was his incorrigible partiality and affection to foreigners, which attended him through his whole life, and occasioned infinite vexations to himself and his subjects. No sooner was one set of these foreign favourites driven from the royal presence, by attacks which shook the throne itself, than others took their place, and were cherished with equal fondness, and displaced with equal difficulties and dangers. It is highly probable, that these foreigners, having their fortunes to make, were much more supple and insinuating, and more ready to comply with all his humours, than the English barons, conscious of their own power and importance. The piety of this prince is much extolled by the monkish writers of those times. He was no doubt a very useful and liberal son to his holy father the pope, whom he assisted with all his might in fleecing his unhappy subjects. He was also a most devout worshipper of rusty nails and rotten bones, particularly those of his favourite St. Edward the Confessor, which he placed in a shrine of gold, adorned with precious stones. One of the most commendable parts of this prince's character is hardly ever mentioned by our historians, his love of the arts; for the encouragement of which he expended great sums of money. It must further be owned, that he was a very warm and generous, though not a very constant friend, a faithful husband, and an affectionate parent.'

In mentioning the instances of this king's piety, our author seems to affect the sarcastic style of Voltaire, without the vivacity of that agreeable writer.

In general, Dr. Henry gives a plain and faithful narrative of transactions, in a style which is sometimes careless, but for the most part conducted with a decent attention to mediocrity of embellishment; and where his subject admits of any striking anecdote, he fails not to lay hold of the opportunity to introduce it.

The second chapter contains the history of religion in Great Britain, during the period which forms the subject of this volume. The following anecdote relative to the courage of the bishop of Lincoln, in resisting the imperious dictates of papal despotism, affords a memorable instance of the exertion of religious liberty amidst the general superstition of those times.

' While the pope was thus trampling upon the church and kingdom of England, a private prelate had the courage to oppose him ; and, which is more wonderful, to oppose him with success. This ecclesiastical hero was Robert Grosted, bishop of Lincoln, a person of uncommon learning for the age in which he lived ; and of such unfeigned piety, untainted probity, and undaunted courage, as would have rendered him an ornament to any age. When this bishop received bulls from Rome, he examined them with great attention ; and if he found that they commanded any thing contrary to the precepts of the gospel, and the interests of religion, (which was very often the case), he tore them in pieces, instead of putting them in execution. Innocent IV. one of the most imperious pontiffs that ever filled the papal chair, sent this bishop a bull, which contained in it the scandalous clause of *Non obstante,* so much and so justly exclaimed against in that age ; and besides, commanded him to bestow a considerable living in his gift upon the pope's nephew, who was an infant. The bishop was so far from complying with this bull, that he sent the pope a letter, in which he exposed the injustice and impiety of it, with the greatest freedom and severity. With regard to the clause of *Non obstante,* lately introduced into the papal bulls, the good bishop used these expressions in his letter : " That it brings in a deluge of mischief upon Christendom, and gives occasion to a great deal of inconstancy and breach of faith ; it even shakes the very foundations of truth and security amongst mankind, and makes language and letters almost insignificant." With respect to that part of the bull which required him to bestow a benefice upon an infant, he says,—" Next to the sins of Lucifer and Antichrist, there cannot be a greater defection, or which carries a more direct opposition to the doctrine of our Saviour and his apostles, than to destroy peoples souls, by depriving them of the benefits of the pastoral office : and yet those persons are guilty of this sin, who undertake the sacerdotal function, and receive the profits, without discharging the duty. From hence it is evident, that those who bring such unqualified persons into the church, and debauch the hierarchy, are much to blame ; and that their crimes rise in proportion to the height of their station." These were strains of truth and freedom to which his holiness had not been accustomed. He fell into a furious passion, and swore by St. Peter and St. Paul, that he would utterly confound that old, impertinent, deaf, doting fellow, and make him a talk, and astonishment, and example to all the world. " What !" said he, " is not the king of England, his master, our vassal, or rather our slave ? and will he not, at

the

the least sign of ours, caft him into prifon?" When his holiness had a little spent his rage, the cardinals represented to him; " That the world began to discover the truth of many things contained in the bishop's letter; and that if he persecuted a prelate so renowned for piety, learning, and holiness of life, it might create the court of Rome a great many enemies." They advised him therefore to let the matter pass, and make as if he had never seen this provoking letter.   What honour is due to the memory of the noble Grosted, who made so bold a stand against the tyranny of the court of Rome, in an age when it trampled upon kings and emperors!'

The third chapter treats of the history of the constitution, government, and laws of Great Britain, during the period above mentioned.   Our author shews that the common, as well as the statute law of England received considerable improvements in the reign of Henry the Third.   To promote this reformation, several circumstances contributed; viz. the establishment of the court of Common Pleas at Westminster; the retreat of the clergy, who were great enemies to the common law, both from the bench and from the bar, in obedience to a canon made A. D. 1217; the establishment of the inns of court; the decline of trials by ordeals and single combat, with some other regulations.   Dr. Henry has traced with great perspicuity the changes which took place in the constitution, government, and laws of Great Britain, during the several reigns in the period which forms the subject of the present volume; and he has occasionally accompanied the recital with sensible remarks.

The fourth chapter comprises the history of learning in Great Britain, during the thirteenth and fourteenth centuries. Dr. Henry observes, that, though the state of learning in this period was fluctuating, and some parts perhaps declined a little; yet, upon the whole, the circle of the sciences was enlarged, and some of them were considerably improved.   This he endeavours to evince from a view of the sciences that were cultivated; of the most learned men who flourished; and of the most considerable seminaries of learning that were established in Britain.

In the fifth chapter the author gives a history of the arts in Great Britain, during the period of his present enquiry; first of the necessary arts, and afterwards of the fine arts.   It does not appear that any new operations of great importance in agriculture were introduced in this period; but those which had before been in use were now practised more universally, and with greater dexterity than in former times.   Dr. Henry remarks, as a curious circumstance, that not only treatises

com-

compofed for the inftruction of farmers, and their fervants, down to the fwine-herd, were written in Latin ; but even the accounts of the expences and profits of farms and dairies were kept in that language. That the Latin of thofe accounts was not claffical, he gives the following inftances from Fleta : ' Et pro uno *feedcod* empto iiid.——Et pro uno *cartfadel* uno colero cum uno pari tractuum emptis xivd.——Et pro factura de *drawgere* iiid.——Et pro uno *dungecart* empto xivd.——Et pro farratione & dolatione unius *cartbody* vi d.'

Architecture, our author obferves, continued nearly in the fame ftyle with that which was introduced towards the end of the preceding period, and which he has formerly defcribed. Prodigious numbers, both of churches and monafteries were built in Britain, in the thirteenth and fourteenth centuries. The ftyle was what is commonly called the lighter Gothic, with fome variations. In the thirteenth century were introduced lofty fteeples, with fpires and pinnacles. The following paffage accounts for the attention which was paid to the Society of Mafons in thofe times.

' The opulence of the clergy, and zeal of the laity, furnifhed ample funds for building fo great a number of magnificent churches, monafteries, and religious houfes, that it was with great difficulty workmen could be procured to execute thofe pious works. The popes, for very obvious reafons, favoured the erection and endowment of churches and convents ; and granted many indulgences, by their bulls, to the fociety of mafons, in order to increafe their numbers. Thefe indulgences produced their full effect in thofe fuperftitious times ; and that fociety became very numerous, and raifed a prodigious multitude of magnificent churches about this time in feveral countries. " For (as we are told by one who was well acquainted with their hiftory and conftitution) the Italians, with fome Greek refugees, and with them French, Germans, and Flemings, joined into a fraternity of architects, procuring papal bulls for their encouragement, and particular privileges ; they ftyled themfelves Free-mafons, and ranged from one nation to another, as they found churches to be built, (for very many in thofe ages were every where in building, through piety or emulation) : their government was regular ; and where they fixed near the building in hand, they made a camp of huts. A furveyor governed in chief ; every tenth man was called a warden, and overlooked each nine. The gentlemen in the neighbourhood, either out of charity or commutation of penance, gave the materials and carriages. Thofe who have feen the accounts in records of the charge of the fabrics of fome of our cathedrals, near four hundred years old, cannot but have a great efteem for their economy, and admire how foon they erected fuch lofty ftructures."

Dr.

Dr. Henry juftly remarks, that the keen purfuit of the philofopher's ftone, in which many ingenious men were at this time engaged, contributed not a little to make them better acquainted with the nature and compofition of metals, and with the arts of compounding, melting, and refining them. Of copper they not only made many ufeful utenfils, but even ftatues. It appears from an authority cited, that the fum of four hundred pounds was paid, in the year 1395, to Nicolas Broker and Godfrey Preft, citizens of London, copperfmiths, for two ftatues, one of the king, and another of the queen, made of copper, and gilt.

Rude as we confider thofe times, rich and magnificent furniture feems not to have been uncommon.

‘ It is, fays our author, impoffible to perufe the defcription of the gold and filver plate and jewels taken from Piers Gavefton, the unfortunate favourite of Edward II. by the earls of Lancafter and Warwick, without admiring both the quantity and workmanfhip. Some pieces of the filver plate in that collection are faid to have been worth four times the quantity of filver which they contained. At the triumphant entry of Richard II. and his good queen Anne, into London, A. D. 1392, the citizens, befides many other gifts, prefented a crown of gold to the king, and another to the queen, both of great value, at the Fountain in Cheapfide ; and when the proceffion had advanced a little further, they prefented a table of gold, with a reprefentation of the Trinity upon it, worth eight hundred pounds, equivalent to eight or ten thoufand pounds of our money, to the king ; and another table of gold, with the figure of St. Anne upon it, of equal value, to the queen. There is the fulleft evidence, that England was very rich in gold and filver plate in this period ; for, befides the immenfe maffes of thofe precious metals in the cathedral, conventual, and other churches, made into images, altar-tables veffels and utenfils of various kinds, fome of the nobles had greater quantities of plate than we could imagine. When the palace of the Savoy, belonging to John of Gaunt duke of Lancafter, was burnt, with all its rich furniture, in the great infurrection A. D. 1381, the keeper of the duke's wardrobe declared, upon oath, that the filver, filver gilt, and gold plate, in that palace, would have loaded five carts.’

Both fculpture and painting appear to have been greatly cultivated. So fafhionable, we are told, was the ftudy of the latter, that it was efteemed as neceffary a part of the education of a young gentleman as writing.

The fixth chapter contains the hiftory of commerce, coin, and fhipping, of the period above fpecified. Internal trade was at this time burdened with a variety of taxes and impofitions, which were demanded by every town, and by every baron
through

through whose boundaries traders conveyed their goods, as well as at every place where they exposed them to sale. The foreign trade of England, however, our author is of opinion, was more considerable and extensive than is commonly imagined. This he infers from a review of the several countries with which the people of England had commercial intercourse, and of the several sovereigns and states with which the kings of England had commercial treaties.

The seventh and last chapter treats of the manners, vices, remarkable customs, language, dress, diet, and diversions. The author has added an Appendix, containing, 1. A copy in Latin of the Magna Charta granted by Henry the Third. 2. A translation of the preceding Magna Charta. 3. A catalogue of provisions, &c. at the installation-feast, in 1309, of Ralph de Borne, abbot of St. Austin's Abbey, Canterbury, with their prices. 4. A charter of Henry the Third, in the vulgar English of that time, with a literal translation interlined.

The same general remarks which were made on the execution of the preceding parts of this work, are equally applicable to the present volume ; where Dr. Henry continues to discover great industry in researches, and where he has amassed much historical and antiquarian information, relative to various subjects which interest the curiosity of a reader.

The History of English *Poetry.* *Vol. III.* *By* Thomas Warton, B. D. [*Continued from Vol.* LI. *p.* 330.]   27. 375

IN the twenty-second section, Mr. Warton introduces to the reader's acquaintance a name that has never before appeared in poetical biography. It is that of Nicholas Grimoald, a native of Huntingdonshire, who flourished about the middle of the sixteenth century. Our author observes, that after lord Surrey, he is the second English poet who wrote in blank-verse ; to which he added new strength, elegance, and modulation. As a writer of verses in rhyme, it is Mr. Warton's opinion that he yields to none of his contemporaries, for chasteness of expression, and the concise elegancies of didactic versification. In support of those remarks, the historian adduces several specimens, for which we refer our readers to the work.

In section twenty-third, Mr. Warton gives farther proof of his researches, and accurate examination of the writers subjected to his view. He observes that all the poets of the reign of Henry VIII. were not educated in the school of Petrarch.
The

The graces of the Italian muse, which had been taught by Surrey and Wyat, were confined to a few. Nor were the beauties of the claffics yet become general objects of imitation. He afterwards delivers an account of the inferior poets of this period. The person first mentioned is Andrew Borde, who, says Mr. Warton, writes himself ANDREAS PERFORATUS, with as much propriety and as little pedantry as Buchanan calls one Wifehart SOPHOCARDIUS. He was a physician, and practised chiefly in Hampshire. Hearne is of opinion that he gave rise to the name of Merry Andrew, the fool on the mountebank's stage. He is also supposed to have compiled or composed the *Merry Tales of the Mad Men of Gotham.* Next follow the names of John Bale, promoted to the bishoprick of Offory by king Edward the Sixth; Brian Anflay, or Annefley, yeoman of the wine-cellar to Henry the Eighth; Wilfrid Holme, a gentleman of Huntington in Yorkshire; and a few others. Of the writings of thofe fubordinate poets our author gives an adequate account.

The twenty-fourth fection is occupied with an account of John Heywood, commonly called the epigrammatift, who was favoured and rewarded for his buffooneries by Henry the Eighth; and in the twenty-fifth fection we are prefented with fome juvenile pieces, the very early productions of fir Thomas More, whofe character, without the fame of poetical talents, will always be revered.

In the twenty-fixth fection our author retracts his opinion relative to the date of the *Notbrowne Mayde,* which he now, on probable reafons, concludes to have been written in the reign of Henry the Eighth, a hundred years later than Prior had fixed its origin. On mature confideration of the fubject, Mr. Warton makes the following judicious remarks on the conduct both of the original author and Mr. Prior.

' Whoever was the original inventor of this little dramatic dialogue, he has fhewn no common fkill in contriving a plan, which powerfully detains our attention, and interefts the paffions, by a conftant fucceffion of fufpence and pleafure, of anxiety and fatisfaction. Betwixt hopes perpetually difappointed, and folicitude perpetually relieved, we know not how to determine the event of a debate, in which new difficulties ftill continue to be raifed, and are almoft as foon removed. In the midft of this viciffitude of feelings, a ftriking contraft of character is artfully formed, and uniformly fupported, between the feeming unkindnefs and ingratitude of the man, and the unconquerable attachment and fidelity of the woman, whofe amiable compliance unexpectedly defeats every objection, and continually furnifhes new matter for our love and compaffion. At length, our fears fubfide in in the triumph of suffering innocence and patient sincerity. The man, whose hard speeches had given us so much pain, suddenly surprises us with a change of sentiment, and becomes equally an object of our admiration and esteem. In the disentanglement of this distressful tale, we are happy to find, that all his cruelty was tenderness, and his inconstancy the most invariable truth ; his levity an ingenious artifice, and his perversity the friendly disguise of the firmest affection. He is no longer an unfortunate exile, the profligate companion of the thieves and ruffians of the forest, but an opulent earl of Westmoreland ; and promises, that the lady, whe is a baron's daughter, and whose constancy he had proved by such a series of embarrassing proposals, shall instantly be made the partner of his riches and honours. Nor should we forget to commend the invention of the poet, in imagining the modes of trying the lady's patience, and in feigning so many new situations : which, at the same time, open a way to description, and to a variety of new scenes and images.

' I cannot help observing here, by the way, that Prior has misconceived and essentially marred his poet's design, by softening the sternness of the man, which could not be intended to admit of any degree of relaxation. Henry's hypocrisy is not characteristically nor consistently sustained. He frequently talks in too respectful and complaisant a style. Sometimes he calls Emma my *tender maid*, and my *beauteous Emma* ; he fondly dwells on the ambrosial plenty of her flowing ringlets gracefully wreathed with variegated ribbands, and expatiates with rapture on the charms of her snowy bosom, her slender waist, and harmony of shape. In the ancient poem, the concealed lover never abates his affectation of rigour and reserve, nor ever drops an expression which may tend to betray any traces of tenderness. He retains his severity to the last, in order to give force to the conclusion of the piece, and to heighten the effect of the final declaration of his love. Thus, by diminishing the opposition of interests, and by giving too great a degree of uniformity to both characters, the distress is in some measure destroyed by Prior. For this reason, Henry, during the course of the dialogue, is less an object of our aversion, and Emma of our pity. But these are the unavoidable consequences of Prior's plan, who presupposes a long connection between the lovers, which is attended with the warmest professions of a reciprocal passion. Yet this very plan suggested another reason, why Prior should have more closely copied the cast of his original. After so many mutual promises and protestations, to have made Henry more obdurate, would have enhanced the sufferings and the sincerity of the amiable Emma.'

Mr. Warton thinks it probable, that the metrical romances of *Richard Cœur de Lyon, Guy Earl of Warwick*, and *Syr Bevys of Southampton,* were modernised in the reign of Henry VIII. from more ancient and simple narratives. Among the poetry of this reign, he has feen fome Chriftmas Carols, intended for enlivening the feftivity of that feafon, and not fuch as are now current with the common people under the fame title.   He obferves that the boar's head fonfed, was anciently the firft difh on Chriftmas day, and was carried up to the principal table in the hall with great folemnity.   It appears from Hollinfhead, that in the year 1170, on the day of the young prince's coronation, king Henry the Firft ' ferved his fonne at the table as fewer, bringing up the boar's head with trumpets before it according to the manner.'   This annual ceremony was accompanied with a carol, of which the following fpecimen is preferved.

> ' *Caput Apri defero,*
> *Reddens laudes Domino.*
> The bores head in hande bringe I,
> With garlandes gay and rofemary.
> I pray you all fynge merely,
>   *Qui eftis in convivio.*

> ' The bores head, I underftande,
> Is the chefe fervyce in this lande :
> Look wherever it be fande
>   *Servite cum cantico.* .

> ' Be gladde lordes, both more and laffe,
> For this hath ordayned our ftewarde
> To chere you all this chriftmaffe,
> The bores head with muftarde.'

This carol, yet with many innovations, is retained at Queen's College in Oxford.

Our author remarks, that the public pageantries of Henry the Eighth's reign evince a confiderable progrefs of claffical learning in England.   As an inftance, he defcribes the fhews exhibited with great magnificence at the coronation of queen Anne Boleyn, in the year 1533.   Towards the latter part of Henry's reign, much of the old cumberfome ftate began to be laid afide.   This our author infers from a fet of new regulations given to the royal houfhold by cardinal Wolfey, about the year 1526.   At this period alfo, the fine arts, in general, began to receive great improvement.

The twenty-feventh fection opens with a new epoch in the hiftory of Englifh poetry.   The reformation of the church, as our author obferves, produced, for a time, an alteration in the general fyftem of ftudy, and changed the character and fubjects of our poetical compofitions.   Metrical tranflations of various parts of the facred fcripture, were now made ; the chief of which is the verfification of the Pfalter by Sternhold
                                                                    and

and Hopkins. Wyat and Surrey had before made translations of the Psalms into metre; but Sternhold was the first whose metrical version was used in the church of England. He was a native of Hampshire, and became groom of the robes to Henry the Eighth; in which department, we are told, either his diligent services or knack at rhyming so pleased the king, that his majesty bequeathed him a legacy of one hundred marks. He continued in the same office under Edward the Sixth, and is said to have acquired some degree of reputation about the court for his poetry. Contemporary with Sternhold, and his coadjutor, was John Hopkins, a clergyman and schoolmaster of Suffolk. He translated fifty-eight of the Psalms, distinguished by the initials of his name. Among the other contributors to this undertaking, the chief, at least in point of rank and learning, was William Whyttingham, promoted by the earl of Leicester to the deanery of Durham.

At the beginning of the Reformation, the spirit of versifying the Psalms, and other parts of the Bible, appears to have been extremely prevalent. The practice was originally introduced into France by Clement Marot, a valet of the bed-chamber to king Francis the First, and a favourite poet of that country. The following anecdotes place in a strong light the extraordinary regard in which this species of composition was held at the court of France.

'They were the common accompaniments of the fiddle. They were sold so rapidly, that the printers could not supply the public with copies. In the festive and splendid court of Francis the First, of a sudden nothing was heard but the psalms of Clement Marot. By each of the royal family and the principal nobility of the court, a psalm was chosen, and fitted to the ballad-tune which each liked best. The dauphin prince Henry, who delighted in hunting, was fond of Ainsi qu'on oit le cerf bruire, or, Like as the hart desireth the water-brooks, which he constantly sung in going out to the chace. Madame de Valentinois, between whom and the young prince there was an attachment, took Du fond de ma pensée, or, From the depth of my heart, O Lord. The queen's favourite was, Ne vueilles pas, O Sire, that is, O Lord, rebuke me not in thine indignation, which she sung to a fashionable jig. Antony king of Navarre sung, Revenge moy, pren le querelle, or, Stand up, O Lord, to revenge my quarrel, to the air of a dance of Poitou. It was on very different principles that psalmody flourished in the gloomy court of Cromwell. This fashion does not seem in the least to have diminished the gaiety and good humour of the court of Francis.

In the two subsequent sections our author takes notice of other metrical compositions, founded on different parts of

scrip-

scripture.   The principal of thofe are archbifhop Parker's Pfalms, Crowley's puritanical Poetry, and Tye's Acts of the Apoftles, in rhyme.   Mr. Warton very juftly depreciates this heterogeneous fpecies of compofition; which by mixing the ftyle of profe with verfe, and of verfe with profe, deftroys the character and effect of both.

Our author informs us that the firft Chanfon à boire, or drinking-ballad, of any merit, in our language, appeared in the year 1551.   He remarks that it has a vein of eafe and humour, which we fhould not expect to have been infpired by the fimple beverage of thofe times.   For the entertainment of our readers we fhall give it at full length.

‘ I cannot eat, but little meat,
    My ftomach is not good ;
But fure I think, that I can drink
    With him that weares a hood.
Though I go bare, take ye no care,
    I nothing am a colde ;
I ftuffe my fkin fo full within,
    Of joly good ale and olde.
Backe and fide go bare, go bare,
    Both foot and hand go colde ;
But, belly, God fend thee good ale inoughe,
    Whether it be new or old !

‘ I love no roft, but a nut-browne tofte,
    And a crab laid in the fire ;
A little bread fhall do me ftead,
    Moche bread I noght defire.
No froft no fnow, no winde, I trowe,
    Can hurt me if I woide,
I am fo wrapt, and throwly lapt
    Of joly good ale and olde.
Backe and fide, &c.

‘ And Tib my wife, that as her life
    Loveth well good ale to feeke,
Full oft drinkes fhee, till ye may fee
    The teares run downe her cheeke.
Then doth fhe trowle to me the bowle
    Even as a mault-worm fholde ;
And, ‘‘ faith, fweet heart, I tooke my part
    Of this joly good ale and olde.’’
Backe and fide, &c.

‘ Now let them drinke, till they nod and winke,
    Even as good fellows fhould do :
They fhall not miffe to have the bliffe
    Good ale doth bringe men to.

And

.And al goode fowles that have fcoured bowles,
  Or have them luftely trolde,
God fave the lives, of them and their wives,
  Whether they be yong or olde !
Backe and fide, &c.'

In fections thirty, thirty-one, thirty-two, and thirty-three, we are prefented with an account of various poetical compofitions, the chief of which is the Mirrour of Magiftrates. This piece is faid to be the production of feveral authors ; but its principal inventor, and moft diftinguifhed contributor was Thomas Sackville, the firft lord Buckhurft, and the firft earl of Dorfet.

Section thirty-fourth is chiefly occupied with an account of the life and writings of Richard Edwards, principal poet, player, mufician, and buffoon, to the courts of Mary and Elizabeth ; and the thirty-fifth fection gives a detail of remarkable circumftances in the life of Tuffer, with an examination of his Hufbandrie, one of our earlieft didactic poems. The hiftorian obferves, that

  ' This author's general precepts have often an expreffive brevity, and are fometimes pointed with an epigrammatic turn and a fmartnefs of allufion. As thus,

  ' Saue wing for a threfher, when gander doth die ;
Saue fethers of all things, the fofter to lie :
Much fpice is a theefe, fo is candle and fire ;
Sweet faufe is as craftie as euer was frier.

' Again, under the leffons of the houfewife.

  ' Though cat, a good moufer, doth dwell in a houfe,
Yet euer in dairie haue trap for a moufe :
Take heed how thou laieft the bane for the rats,
For poifoning thy fervant, thyfelf, and thy brats.

' And in the following rule of the fmaller economics.

  ' Saue droppings and fkimmings, however ye doo,
For medcine, for cattell, for cart, and for fhoo.

' In thefe ftanzas on haymaking, he rifes above his common manner.

  ' Go mufter thy feruants, be captain thyfelfe,
Prouiding them weapons, and other like pelfe :
Get bottels and wallets, keepe fielde in the heat,
The feare is as much, as the danger is great.

  ' With toffing, and raking, and fetting on cox,
Graffe latelie in fwathes, is haie for an oxe.
That done, go to cart it, and haue it awaie :
The battel is fought, ye haue gotten the daic.'

In

In the thirty-fixth fection the author gives an account of
the poems of William Forreft.   One of thofe, a MS. in
the Bodleian Library at Oxford, is a panegyrical hiftory in
octave rhyme, of the life of queen Catherine, the firft queen
of Henry the Eighth.   Mr. Warton informs us, that this
poem, which confifts of twenty chapters, contains a zealous
condemnation of Henry's divorce ; and, he believes, preferves
fome anecdotes, yet apparently mifreprefented by the writer's
religious and political bigotry, not extant in any of our printed
hiftories.

About the middle of the fixteenth century, there appears
to have exifted in England a great prejudice againft the ftudy
of the claffics.   Mr. Warton mentions a poem of two fheets,
entitled, The Ungodlineffe of the Hethnicke Goddes; or the
Downfall of Diana of the Ephefians, the writer of which,
whofe arguments and poetry are equally weak, attempts to
prove, that the cuftom of training youths in the Roman poets
encouraged idolatry and pagan fuperftition.

' But, fays our author, the claffics were at length condemned
by a much higher authority.   In the year 1582, one Chriftopher Ocland, a fchoolmafter of Cheltenham, publifhed two poems
in Latin hexameters, one entitled Anglorum Prælia, the other
Elizabetha.   To thefe poems, which are written in a low ftyle
of Latin verfification, is prefixed an edict from the lords of
privy council, figned, among others, by Cowper bifhop of Lincoln, lord Warwick, lord Leicefter, fir Francis Knollys, fir
Chriftopher Hatton, and fir Francis Walfingham, and directed to
the queen's ecclefiaftical commiffioners, containing the following
paffage.   "Forafmuche as the fubject or matter of this booke is
fuch, as is worthie to be read of all men, and efpecially in
common fchooles, where diuers heathen poets are ordinarily read
and taught, from which the youth of the realme doth rather
receiue infection in manners, than aduancement in uertue : in
place of fome of which poets, we think this booke fit to read
and taught in the grammar fchooles : we haue therefore thought,
as wel for the encouraging the faid Ocklande and others that are
learned, to beftowe their trauell and ftudies to fo good purpofes,
as alfo for the benefit of the youth and the removing of fuch
lafciuious poets as are commonly read and taught in the faide
grammar-fchooles (the matter of this booke being heroicall and
of good inftruction) to praye and require you vpon the fight
hereof, as by our fpecial order, to write your letters vnto al the
bifhops throughout this realme, requiring them to giue com-
maundement, that in al the gramer and free fchooles within
their feuerall diocelfes, the faid booke de Anglorum Prælijs, and
peaceable gouernment of hir majeftie, [the Elizabetha,] may be
in place of fome of the heathen poets receyued, and publiquely
                                                          read

read and taught by the fcholemafters." With fuch abundant
circumfpection and folemnity, did thefe profound and pious politicians, not fufpecting that they were acting in oppofition to
their own principles and intentions, exert their endeavours to
bring back barbarifm, and to obftruct the progrefs of truth and
good fenfe.'

[*To be continued.*]

Philological Inquiries in Three Parts by James Harris, *Efq.* 51.401
[*Concluded from vol.* LI. *p.* 407.]

IT is with great pleafure we refume the confideration of this
work, and accompany the learned and amiable writer
through the fecond volume, and third part of his Philological
Inquiries. The third part comprehends a general view of the
learning and character of the middle age ; that is, as Mr.
Harris defines it, the interval between the fall of the Weftern
empire in the fifth century, and of the Eaftern in the fifteenth.

' This was the age (to ufe his own words) of monkery and legends ; of Leonine verfes, (that is of bad Latin put into rhime) ;
of projects to decide truth by plough-fhares and batoons ; of
crufades to conquer Infidels, and extirpate heretics ; of princes
depofed, not as Croefus was by Cyrus, but by one who had no
armies, and who did not even wear a fword.'

Our author modeftly ftyles this part of his work, *a curfory
difquifition, illuftrated by a few felect inftances.* However curfory, it bears evident marks of a mafterly hand ; and will
contribute to the improvement of critical knowlege. A good tafte
muft certainly be formed by a careful ftudy of the beft writers ;
but fome advantages may be derived from obferving the defects
of bad ones. This hiftory of the middle age proves, that true
genius will produce fine writing, and fine fentiment, amidft
the greateft cloud of ignorance, or depravity of tafte ; and
our author teaches us, that real beauties, wherever they are
found, are always referable to the genuine principles of criticifm. But Philology is not the only object in view ; Mr.
Harris directs us from the examples here given to acknowlege

' For the honour of humanity, and of its great and divine
Author, who never forfakes it, that fome fparks of intellect were
at all times vifible, through the whole of this dark and dreary
period.'

Three claffes of men were, during this interval, confpicuous ; the Byzantine Greeks, the Saracens or Arabians, and
the Latins or Franks, inhabitants of Weftern Europe. The
account of the Byzantine Greeks begins with the following
remarks upon the rife of commentators.

' Sim-

' Simplicius and Ammonius were Greek authors, who flourished at Athens during the sixth century ; for Athens, long after
her trophies at Marathon, long after her political fovereignty
was no more, still maintained her empire in philofophy and the
fine arts.

' Philofophy, indeed, when thefe authors wrote, was finking
apace. The Stoic fyftem, and even the Stoic writings, were the
greater part of them loft. Other fects had fhared the fame fate.
None fubfifted but the Platonic and the Peripatetic ; which, being both derived from a common fource (that is to fay, the Pythagorean) were at this period blended, and commonly cultivated
by the fame perfons.

' Simplicius and Ammonius, being bred in this fchool, and
well initiated in its principles, found no reafon, from their education, to make fyftems for themfelves ; a practice, referrable
fometimes to real genius, but more often to not knowing, what
others have invented before.

' Confcious therefore they could not excel their great predeceffors, they thought, like many others, that the commenting
of their works was doing mankind the moft effential fervice.

' 'Twas this, which gave rife, long before their time, to that
tribe of commentators, who, in the perfon of Andronicus the
Rhodian, began under Auguftus, and who continued, for ages
after, in an orderly fucceffion.'

Mr. Harris continues his narrative of the Byzantine Greeks,
with doing great juftice to the characters of Suidas, Stobæus,
and Photius, who were really men of confiderable learning and
abilities. It is a curious fact, that Michael Pfellus, of the
eleventh century, actually commented upon and explained
twenty-four comedies of Menander ; which fhews, that thofe
excellent compofitions were extant at that period.

' And why (demands our author) fhould not the polite Menander have had his admirers in thefe ages, as well as the licen-
tious Ariftophanes ? — Or rather, why not as well as Sophocles,
and Euripides ? The fcholia upon thefe (though fome perhaps
may be more ancient) were compiled by critics, who lived long
after Pfellus.

' We may add with regard to all thefe fcholiafts (whatever
may have been their age) they would never have undergone the
labours of compilation and annotation, had they not been encouraged by the tafte of their contemporary countrymen. For who
ever publifhed, without hopes of having readers ?

' The fame may be afferted of the learned bifhop of Theffalo-
nica, Euftathius, who lived in the twelfth century. His admiration of Homer muft have been almoft enthufiaftic, to carry him
through fo complete, fo minute, and fo vaft a commentary, both
upon the Iliad and the Odyffey, collected from fuch an immenfe
number both of critics and hiftorians.'

                                                              Eu-

Euftathius, the commentator of Ariftotle, and feveral others, are afterwards mentioned with great commendation. But Mr. Harris particularly dwells upon the defcription given by Nicetas, the Choniate of the ftatues, which were deftroyed at Conftantinople by the crufaders,

‘ Not only becaufe the facts, related by this hiftorian, are little known, but becaufe they tend to prove, that even in thofe dark ages (as we have too many reafons to call them) there were Greeks ftill extant, who had a tafte for the finer arts, and an enthufiaftic feeling of their exquifite beauty.’

Nicetas was prefent at the facking of Conftantinople in the year 1205.

The third chapter contains an hiftorical account of Athens, from the time of her Perfian triumphs to that of her becoming fubject to the Turks. This is an interefting chapter ; and is written with judgement and accuracy ; but we cannot felect a detached part without injuftice to the reft, and the whole is too long to lay before our readers.

We have, under the fecond head a general view, not only of the learning of the Arabians, but of their character, and manners ; and a variety of anecdotes are introduced, which are curious in themfelves, and illuftrate or confirm the favourable opinion which Mr. Harris appears to have entertained of this people. He obferves, indeed, that they began ill ; (alluding to the deftruction of the Alexandrian library by the Caliph Omar) but then by degrees they recurred to their ancient character, which they boafted to imply three capital things, hofpitality, valour, and eloquence. He therefore haftens to the time when the Abaffidæ reigned, whofe dominion lafted for more than five centuries. The former part of this period was the æra of the grandeur and the magnificence of the caliphate.

Several extracts are here given from the life of the great Saladin, as written by Bohadin, who was his conftant attendant. It feems the object of our author to prove, from the example of the Arabians, that learning and virtue, elegance of tafte, and greatnefs of mind, naturally flourifh at the fame time, and rife and fall together. By way of fpecimen of the *fentiments* and *manners* of the Arabians at the period when they moft cultivated letters, the following ftory is related from Abulpharagius, an Arabian hiftorian of the thirteenth century, whofe works were publifhed in Arabic and Latin by the learned Pococke, at Oxford, A. D. 1663.

‘ The caliph, Mottawakkel, had a phyfician belonging to him, who was a Chriftian, named Honaïn. One day, after fome

other

other incidental conversation, I would have thee, says the caliph, teach me a prescription, by which I may take off any enemy I please, and yet at the same time it should never be discovered. Honaïn, declining to give an answer, and pleading ignorance, was imprisoned.

' Being brought again, after a year's interval, into the caliph's presence, and still persisting in his ignorance, though threatened with death, the caliph smiled upon him and said, Be of good cheer, we were only willing to try thee, that we might have the greater confidence in thee.

' As Honaïn upon this bowed down and kissed the earth, What hindered thee, says the caliph, from granting our request, when thou sawest us appear so ready to perform what we had threatened ? Two things, replied Honaïn, my religion, and my profession : my religion, which commands me to do good to my enemies ; my profession, which was purely instituted for the benefit of mankind. Two noble laws, said the caliph, and immediately presented him (according to the Eastern usage) with rich garments and a sum of money.'

When our author proceeds, under the third head, to the Latins or Franks, we find with pleasure the names of many of our countrymen ; and we believe that this island may justly boast a far greater proportion of learned men than could have been expected, when we consider how few they were at that time in Europe.

Mr. Harris expresses a more favourable opinion of the schoolmen, than is generally entertained of them. They were in their day ridiculously extolled, and perhaps are now too much despised. After mentioning the schoolmen, he takes notice of John of Salisbury, whom he seems well pleased to call his countryman ; and who appears, by the several extracts given from his works, to have been a man of considerable science. It is well observed, that some knowlege of the fine arts existed, during the middle age, in Italy and Greece ; and that Italy deriving them from Greece, communicated them to the rest of Europe. Mr. Harris in all his works is fond of expressing his admiration of the Greeks. It is indeed an extraordinary fact, and affords subject for curious speculation, that Greece, at a very remote period, attained an eminence in learning and the arts, in eloquence and in taste, which succeeding ages have rarely equalled, and never excelled. Europe has twice derived its literature and its politeness from this source : for we all know the effects which the conquest of Greece produced in ancient Rome ; and the fugitives, who escaped from Constantinople, after it was taken by Mahomet the Second, were the principal cause of the restoration of learning. Our author too remarks,

' A few

' A few Greek painters, in the thirteenth century, came from Greece into Italy, and taught their art to Cimabue, a Florentine. Cimabue was the father of Italian painters, and from him came a succession, which at length gave the Raphaels, the Michael Angelo's, &c.

' The statues, and ruined edifices, with which Italy abounded, and which were all of them by Greek artists, or after Grecian models, taught the Italians the fine arts of sculpture and architecture.'

The degeneracy of the Greeks in modern times prevents our ascribing their ancient superiority to natural causes. If we allow the activity of their genius, and the delicacy of their feelings to have been native advantages, we must attribute the exertions which they made, and the wonderful success of those exertions in the various improvement of the human faculties, to their education and government, to the great occasions, which called forth their talents, and to the spirit of emulation, which was universally diffused among them.

The eleventh chapter contains a history of the origin of rhyme, and the progressive deviations from *the harmonious simplicity of the syllabic measure,* (as Mr. Harris styles it) which was confined to the purest ages of Greek and Roman poetry.

From the twelfth chapter it appears that the spirit of adventure, and a zeal to make new discoveries, were not confined to the more enlightened ages; for in the thirteenth and fourteenth centuries Paul the Venetian, and sir John Mandeville, traversed Asia and some part of Africa; the former visited China at an earlier period than is generally assigned for the intercourse of European travellers with that great empire. Next follows the character of sir John Fortescue, whose memory was highly revered by our author, both as a scholar and an Englishman. Speaking of the reign of Henry the Sixth, it is observed,

' This was a period, disgraced by unsuccessful wars abroad, and by sanguinary disorders at home. The king himself met an untimely end, and so did his hopeful and high spirited son, the prince of Wales. Yet did not even these times keep one genius from emerging, though plunged by his rank into their most tempestuous part. By this I mean sir John Fortescue, chancellor of England, and tutor to the young prince, just mentioned. As this last office was a trust of the greatest importance, so he discharged it not only with consummate wisdom, but (what was more) with consummate virtue.

' His tract in praise of the laws of England, is written with the noblest view that man ever wrote; written to inspire his pupil with a love of the country he was to govern, by shewing him

him that, to govern by thofe admirable laws, would make him a far greater prince than the moft unlimited defpotifm.

' This he does not only prove by a detail of particular laws, but by an accurate comparifon between the ftate of England and France, one of which he makes a land of liberty, the other of fervitude. His thirty-fifth and thirty-fixth chapters upon this fubject are invaluable, and fhould be read by every Englifhman, who honours that name.

' Through thefe and the other chapters, we perceive an interefting truth, which is, that the capital parts of our conftitution, the trial by juries, the abhorrence of tortures, the fovereignty of parliament as well in the granting of money, as in the making and repealing of laws, I fay, that all thefe, and many other ineftimable privileges, exifted then, as they do now; were not new projects of the day, but facred forms, to which ages had given a venerable fanction.

' As for the literature of this great man (which is more immediately to our purpofe), he appears to have been a reader of Ariftotle, Diodorus Siculus, Cicero, Quinctilian, Seneca, Vegetius, Boethius, and many other ancients; to have been not uninformed in the authors and hiftory of later ages; to have been deeply knowing not only in the laws of his own country (where he attained the higheft dignity they could beftow) but in the Roman or civil law, which he holds to be far inferior; we muft add to this a mafterly infight into the ftate and policy of the neighbouring nations.'

We thought this extract ought to be laid before our readers; for fir John Fortefcue is here evidently propofed, as an example to our age; which, however enlighted, is not diftinguifhed for the more manly and exalted virtues.

' The excellent treatife *de Laudibus Legum Angliæ*, certainly proves the antiquity of our free government; it contains a complete refutation of the fuperficial conceits of fome modern writers, among whom it hath been fafhionable to maintain, that this country had no fettled fyftem of liberty, till the Revolution; and that in the days of feudal tyranny, all Europe was equally in a ftate of vaffalage. Such opinions detract from the refpect which is due to the venerable fabrick of our conftitution: whilft, on the other hand, a juft notion of the wifdom and fpirit of our anceftors will encourage us to adhere inflexibly to thofe principles, which the experience of ages hath fhewn to be the true fobrce of our national glory and happinefs.

The architecture of this period produced, as Mr. Harris obferves, thofe admirable ftructures of Salifbury Cathedral, and King's College Chapel at Cambridge; works, which, if they ftood fingle, would redeem the times in which they were conftructed, from the imputation of barbarifm.

In

In the thirteenth chapter our author, to use his own ex-pression, *passes from the elegant works of art to the more elegant works of nature.* This chapter begins with shewing that men of genius have always admired the beauties of nature. Some fine passages are cited from Horace, Virgil, and Milton, from whence it appears, that the great elements of this species of beauty were understood by those excellent poets to consist in water, wood, and uneven ground, to which may be added, lawn. The observations which follow are so interesting to most of our readers, that we shall give them at length.

' The painters seem to have felt the power of these elements, and to have transferred them into their landscapes with such amazing force, that they appear not so much to have followed, as to have emulated nature. Claude de Lorraine, the Poussins, Salvator Rosa, and a few more, may be called superior artists in this exquisite taste.

' Our gardens in the mean time were tasteless and insipid. Those, who made them, thought the farther they wandered from nature, the nearer they approached to the sublime. Unfortunately, where they travelled, no sublime was to be found; and the farther they went, the farther they left it behind.

' But perfection, alas! was not the work of a day. Many prejudices were to be removed; many gradual ascents to be made; ascents from bad to good, and from good to better, before the delicious Amenities of a Claude or a Poussin could be ri-valled in a Stour-head, a Hagley, or a Stow; or the tremendous charms of a Salvator Rosa be equalled in the scenes of a Piercefield or a Mount Edgecumb.'

But the principal design of this chapter is to prove, that a taste for natural beauty was not wanting to the enlightened few of the middle age; which position is chiefly illustrated by an extract from Leland, by the situation of Vaucluse, the fa-vourite retreat of Petrarch; and by several charming descrip-tions from Sannazarius, of his villa of Margillina in the Bay of Naples.

After these reflections upon the taste and genius, the lite-rature, the spirit of adventure, and the works of art, which appear from this enquiry to have belonged to the middle age, our author draws a melancholy picture of the ignorance and savageness of the laity; for he had before observed, that al-most all who were distinguished for their learning during this period, were ecclesiastics. Some causes are assigned for this general barbarism; the most material one is the want of edu-cation.

' Nothing, Mr. Harris observes, mends the mind more than culture, to which these emigrants had no desire, either from ex-ample or education, to lend a patient ear.'

The

The following remark occurs in this place.

'Though the darkness in Weſtern Europe, during the period here mentioned, was (in ſcripture language) a darkneſs that might be felt, yet is it ſurpriſing that, during a period ſo obſcure, many admirable inventions found their way into the world; I mean ſuch as clocks, teleſcopes, paper, gunpowder, the mariner's needle, printing, and a number here omitted *.'

Upon this ſubject a query is ſubmitted to the reader.

'If the human mind be as truly of divine origin, as every other part of the univerſe; and if every other part of the univerſe bear teſtimony to its author: do not the inventions above mentioned give us reaſon to aſſert, that God in the operations of man, never leaves himſelf without a witneſs ?'

In the concluſion of this volume we have our author's opinion of his contemporaries; an opinion which does great honour to the liberality of his ſentiments, and the benevolence of his heart. Serious men, particularly in the decline of life, are fond of declaiming againſt the degeneracy of the age in which they live. Mr. Harris, on the contrary, not only vindicates the preſent times, but expoſes the injuſtice and the unreaſonableneſs of theſe melancholy declaimers, and the miſchievous tendency of their aſſertions. The following reflections, which ariſe upon this occaſion, are of conſiderable importance.

'As man is by nature a ſocial animal, good humour ſeems an ingredient highly neceſſary to this character. 'Tis the ſalt, which gives a ſeaſoning to the feaſt of life; and which, if it be wanting, ſurely renders the feaſt incomplete. Many cauſes contribute to impair this amiable quality, and nothing perhaps more, than bad opinions of mankind. Bad opinions of mankind naturally lead us to miſanthropy. If theſe bad opinions go farther, and are applied to the univerſe, then they lead to ſomething worſe, for they lead to Atheiſm. The melancholy and moroſe character being thus inſenſibly formed, morals and piety ſink of courſe; for what equals have we to love, or what ſuperior have we to revere, when we have no other objects left, than thoſe of hatred, or of terror?

'It ſhould ſeem then expedient, if we value our better principles, nay, if we value our own happineſs, to withſtand ſuch dreary ſentiments.'

It is indeed a very falſe idea, that piety ariſes from a gloomy temper. A chearful mind naturally produces good-will towards men, and gratitude to God. It inclines us to receive

* 'See two ingenious writers on this ſubject, Polydore Virgil, De Rerum Inventoribus; and Pancirollus, De Rebus perditis et inventus.'

pleafure from all the objects which furround us, and to dwell upon what is moft beautiful, and moft excellent ; from whence we are led to the contemplation of the Divine Being, who is the fource of all perfection.

Upon the whole, this work impreffes upon our minds a very pleafing idea of Mr. Harris's character ; and raifes a high veneration for it.   He feems to have defigned this publication, not only as a retrofpective view of thofe ftudies, which exercifed his mind in the full vigour of life ; but likewife as a monument of his affection to his numerous friends, and a teftimony of his general candour and benevolence.   We cannot take our leave of it without felecting the following paffage, as a fpecimen of many other encomiums upon diftinguifhed perfons of the prefent age, which are interfperfed in feveral parts of this work.

‘ Nor muft I forget Dr. Taylor, refidentiary of St. Paul's, nor Mr. Upton, prebendary of Rochefter.   The former, by his edition of Demofthenes (as far as he lived to carry it), by his Lyfias, by his comment on the Marmor Sandvicenfe, and other critical pieces ; the latter, by his correct and elegant edition, in Greek and Latin, of Arrian's Epictetus (the firft of the kind that had any pretenfions to be called complete), have rendered themfelves, as fcholars, lafting ornaments of their country.   Thefe two valuable men were the friends of my youth ; the companions of my focial, as well as my literary, hours.   I admired them for their erudition ; I loved them for their virtue ; they are now no more——

‘ His faltem accumulem donis, et fungar inani

　　Munere—— ——   Virg.’

To this work is fubjoined an Appendix of four different pieces :

‘ The firft, containing an account of the Arabic manuftripts, belonging to the Efcurial Library in Spain.

‘ The fecond, containing an account of the manufcripts of Livy, in the fame library.

‘ The third, containing an account of the manufcripts of Cebes, in the Library of the king of France, at Paris.

‘ The fourth, containing fome account of literature in Ruffia, and of its progrefs towards being civilized.’

✓ *The History of the Legal Polity of the* Roman *State.*   [*Continued from vol.* LI. *p.* 416.]

IN the fourth chapter of the fecond book, Dr. Bever proceeds to deliver an account of the various fources of interpretation by which the laws of the twelve tables, originally

ob-

obfcure in their compofition, were elucidated and afcertained. Thofe fources were, the 'Fori Difputationes,'—'Refponfa Prudentum,'—Legis Actiones,'—'Jus Civile Flavianum,'—'Jus Civile Ælianum.' Befide the college of the 'Pontifices,' many perfons of the firft rank for their experience and political knowlege, formed themfelves into private focieties, to debate on fuch ambiguous queftions of law as were occafionally referred to their confideration, until they could agree to determine the fenfe in which thofe doubtful ftatutes ought in future to be underftood. Though in this employment they acted under no public authority, yet the reputation of their wifdom and integrity gave fuch weight to their decifions, that thefe were, from time to time, adopted by the courts of juftice, and received, by a kind of general acquiefcence, into the body of the unwritten, or common law, under the name of 'Fori Difputationes,' and fometimes of 'Jus Civile.'.

In the earlier times of the Roman ftate, the great fages of the law contented themfelves with delivering their opinions in private, to fuch only as had immediate occafion to confult them. But afterwards men of the greateft diftinction taught the law publicly in their own houfes, to all who were defirous of becoming their pupils; a proficiency in legal knowlege being then confidered as a principal ornament of a ftatefman, and the fureft road to the moft honourable offices in the republic. From the interpretation given by thofe refpectable authorities, arofe that fpecies of law, particularly known by the title of 'Refponfa Prudentum.'

Our author obferves, that the cuftom of interpreting the laws in the manner above mentioned, had been of great fervice in clearing away many of their difficulties, and afcertaining their true fenfe. Something, however, was ftill wanted to fuit them to juridical practice. For this purpofe thofe learned interpreters contrived certain writs or forms, by the help of which, a more regular method of proceeding was introduced into the courts of law. Thefe writs obtained the name of 'Legis,' or 'Legitimæ Actiones.'

Notwithftanding the acknowleged ufefulnefs of thofe forms, they lay in a very confufed ftate, for more than a century after their introduction, till Appius Claudius Cæcus reduced them into one collection. The 'Pontifices,' however, from a defire of preferving their own confequence, ftill kept this ufeful work clofely locked up with their own archives, fo that a fight of it could not be obtained without their exprefs permiffion. This being a fubject of univerfal complaint, Cneius Flavius, who was the fecretary of Appius, and had free accefs

cess to his papers, made a transcript of this valuable work, which he afterwards published. It received the name of ' Jus Civile Flavianum ;' and was followed, in a few years, by a second work of the same kind, which was, from its author, Caius Ælius, denominated ' Jus Civile Ælianum.'

Dr. Bever remarks, that the ' Legis Actiones,' and several other forms in the system of Roman jurisprudence, deserve the attention of the English lawyers, much more than might be imagined ; because they bear a strong analogy to many of those legal forms, so much used in the earlier times of our constitution, more immediately succeeding the Norman Conquest ; which are preserved in that venerable collection, the ' Registrum Omnium Brevium.'

The fifth chapter delineates the principal legislative powers of the Roman state ; the methods of voting, and of enacting laws ; with the ' Leges,'—' Plebiscita,'—and ' Senatus Consulta.' Those comprehend the various laws enacted in the later ages of the republic, when the system of ancient jurisprudence had become insufficient for the exigencies of the state.

From the conclusion of this chapter, we shall lay before our readers the author's judicious observations on the Roman government.

' Great and prosperous as it actually became in the course of time, it owed very little of that grandeur to any regular chain of political reasonings, or to the prophetic deductions of deep-sighted philosophy ; but rather, to a diligent and unremitting attention to the various incidents, that occasionally offered themselves, in the several struggles and difficulties, in which this active people were so frequently involved. By taking a proper advantage of these, as they happened, and by always chusing the most promising and beneficial, they arrived, says Polybius, at the very same end that Lycurgus attained, and formed the most beautiful system of government then existing.

' In contemplating, therefore, its rapid increase ; its unexampled success ; the profound awe and veneration which it impressed upon the whole ancient world ; we may be tempted to believe, that the various parts of it were so ingeniously contrived, and the respective powers of each order so equally poised, as to secure to it an uninterrupted state of union and stability ; and, from hence, to accede to the opinion of the same writer, that " it was not possible for human wisdom to invent a more perfect scheme of civil policy."

' It is to be feared, however, that this eminent author was too much dazzled by the lustre of the period in which he wrote ; and that he gave a higher colouring to his picture, than could be well justified from a view of the original. By the final subjection of her moft potent and formidable rival, the republic was then advanced to the brighteft æra of her glory; when fhe might, indeed, beft deferve fo flattering a compliment, at the leaft expence of fincerity and truth. But, with all his knowlege of Roman affairs, the fidelity of the hiftorian feems to have yielded too much to the partiality of the panegyrift, in favour of that ftate, which had atchieved fuch wonders, by the hand, efpecially, of his pupil, friend, and patron.

' In the cooler moments of his reflection, he well knew, that the moft valuable productions, both of the political and phyfical world, carried within themfelves their own congenial defects ; infomuch, that, though they might chance to efcape external injuries, they were liable to be corroded and deftroyed by certain internal principles of corruption, implanted in their vitals by the hand of Nature. Such was the contexture of the Roman conftitution, which, even in the fummit of its felicity, was plentifully ftored with the feeds of its own diffolution. The fame powers, that, by an amicable co-operation with each other, cemented its various parts in one firm bond of union and friendfhip, by any wilful abufe or mifapplication, became, with the fame facility, the caufes of the moft ruinous difcord.

' The time was not very far diftant, when the pride of victory, and the deceitfulnefs of profperity, were to extinguifh that patient bravery, that unaffected purity of manners, which had hitherto directed her feet in the paths of true glory. The meek fpirit of obedience, which is the foul of political order, was now to give way to a turbulent impatience of legal reftraint, and to an overweening conceit of felf-confequence ; when every pert demagogue was to think himfelf at liberty to difturb the decorum of popular affemblies, by his feditious declamations ; as if effrontery of face, and volubility of tongue, were the only neceffary accomplifhments of an orator and a ftatefman.

' When, therefore, we confider this celebrated conftitution, with all thefe precarious and uncertain effects ; there will be no injuftice in faying, that, in almoft every period of its exiftence, it was more excellent in its parts, than in the whole. Though the materials of which it was compofed were good in their kind, yet they wanted the hand of one able architect, to give them that uniformity and harmony, which are effential both to the ftrength and beauty of the edifice. The numerous conftituents of this vaft and complex body were generally much too independent of each other : they too often neglected, or even purpofely avoided, that mutual communication of fentiments, which the nature of legiflation always requires ; confequently, the laws made by each refpectively, bore too partial a relation to the intereft of their own order, to be of any extenfive ufe to the whole community. This was particularly the cafe in the more unfettled and diftracted times of the republic ; when laws were frequently paffed, even as it were in fpite ; and were dictated by a jealoufy of each other's fuperiority, rather than by a difinterefted zeal

for

for the common caufe of focial tranquillity. Thus, the ba-
lance of orderly policy could never fettle into its due equilibrium ; but was kept in a continued ftate of ofcillation between both extremes, till it finally preponderated in favour of
one great leviathan of power, who became, of himfelf, more than
equal to all the reft together ; a fatal confequence, that will ever
refult from popular liberty, when more eagerly coveted, than
well underftood ; and more tumultuoufly afferted, than tempe-
rately enjoyed.

' Under the prefent view, therefore, of the legal polity of this
illuftrious ftate, it may be well compared to a plentiful magazine of heterogeneous merchandizes, which, when thrown together in one undiftinguifhed mafs, difgufts the eye with its confufed and fhapelefs appearance ; but, when the feveral parts are
judicioufly felected, and diffufed through their regular channels,
makes glad the heart of man, and enriches the univerfe with the
abundance of its treafures.'

In the fixth chapter the author relates the hiftory of the
' Jus Honorarium.' This branch of jurifprudence was founded
upon the edicts of the magiftrates, the prætors, ædiles, and
cenfors. The author concludes the chapter with fome pertinent reflections on falfe ideas concerning liberty, for which we
refer our readers to the work.

The third book is employed on the imperial government,
fo long as the feat of empire continued at Rome. The author fets out with enquiring into the caufes of this great revolution ; among which he particularly confiders the origin
and progrefs of the Agrarian Laws, the decline of the de-
mocracy, and the increafe of the ariftocracy. In this part of
the work, we meet with many juft obfervations on fome of the
moft diftinguifhed characters in thofe times. In the fecond
chapter, Dr. Bever difplays the origin of the imperial government under Julius Cæfar ; whofe conduct he vindicates, by ftrong arguments, from the reprefentation of thofe
writers, who have placed it in an unfavourable light.

The third chapter contains general obfervations upon the
ftate of the conftitution at the above period ; an account of
the fecond triumvirate, and the progrefs of the imperial
power under Octavius. The fourth defcribes the nature of
the imperial government, with the ftate of it under Tiberius ; and the fifth affords a general view of the political characters of the fucceeding emperors, to the reign of Alexander
Severus.

The fixth chapter contains an enquiry into the nature and
extent of the ' Lex Regia,' or declarative act of the ftate, by
which it has been imagined that the conftitution was rendered
D 2   defpotic.

despotic.   We shall present our readers with part of the historian's remarks on this subject.

'The origin of this law is, by most modern writers, referred to the age of Augustus ; though it is a circumstance well worthy of observation, that no such law either now does, or was ever known to have existed ; and that neither the name of Augustus, nor of any other particular prince, is once mentioned by Justinian in the passages here cited ; so as to enable us to determine, with any degree of certainty, in whose favour, or upon what occasion, it was enacted. A law, which at once would have totally changed the face of the, Roman constitution, and have annihilated a power, that, with little interruption, had resided in the collective body of the people, for the five centuries immediately preceding, must have been a phænomenon in politics, too remarkable to have escaped the notice of the most inattentive and superficial annalist. And yet it is certainly true, that not even the most accurate and best informed historians, who lived the nearest to those times, have left us any reason to suppose that they ever had the least knowlege of such an act of the legislature.

'As it has so little foundation in fact, it has still less in probability. Augustus, with all his moderation, would hardly have rejected so substantial a compliment, when unanimously made him by the whole people ; or have failed to cause a law, which would at once have secured independency to himself and his successors, to be recorded as speedily as possible, and to be authenticated with every public mark of notoriety. But, in truth, it was contrary to the professed policy of this wise prince ever to aspire to any such state of dangerous pre-eminence. His uniform principle was to avoid all invidious marks of sovereignty, and to preserve (as we have already abundantly seen) every exterior appearance of the ancient commonwealth. The old republican spirit was now indeed much broken and depressed ; but the lion, though aged and infirm, might awake from his slumbers ; and had still vigour and courage enough remaining, to startle and revolt at the name of king, and to betray his natural antipathy to every thing that favoured of the regal dignity. Mæcenas indeed advised him to assume a share of legislative power to himself ; but still upon condition of not exercising that power, without consulting with the first persons of the senate : which advice he always very carefully followed.

'His successors, though of characters too often the direct reverse of his own, and with very little concern for the real interests of the people, wanted not penetration to discern, that the genius of Rome, even in the state of debasement she then was, would not look with patience upon the gaudy pageantry of absolute monarchy. They contented themselves therefore with the more modest appellation of Imperator, which they were at
li-

liberty to affume and repeat as often as they pleafed; and by thus appearing to prefer military glory to civil power, they flattered the high fpirit of a warlike people, without alarming their apprehenfions; they even affected to be worfhipped as gods, when they declined the title of kings. If then there was fuch magic in a fingle word, as to diffufe terror and difguft through the minds of fo many millions, it is not to be fuppofed that a law, bearing fo invidious a mark, could ever have been received by them with any degree of approbation, much lefs of obedience.

' The moft rational way, therefore, of accounting for the rife and growth of this very univerfal error, is from that furprifing concurrence of fortunate circumftances, which placed Octavius at the head of the Roman world. The people, wearied out with the ftruggles of oppofite factions, and with the oppreffions of an infolent and overbearing ariftocracy, were eager to fly for protection to the arms of a young conqueror, who, by his wifdom, prowefs, or good fortune, had obtained a decifive fuperiority over all his competitors; who was now able to quell thefe tumultuous fpirits, and to reduce them all to a more reafonable level. Finding that he had both the will and the power to infure to them the bleffings of peace, which their diftracted ftate had fo long panted after, they were, perhaps, not lefs glad to throw the burden of the government upon his fhoulders, than he might be to take it up. He became their fovereign, therefore, even by the very exigencies of the times; and by prudently affociating himfelf with all the other public magiftrates in their turns; by treating them as his colleagues in office, and by affecting no greater fhare in the adminiftration than themfelves, he was in fact a king, without affuming any determinate title whatever. Thus by coveting nothing, he obtained all; and made it the intereft of the people to grant, what would have been very impolitic in himfelf to demand. Well convinced that he was not difpofed to abufe their confidence, they daily ftrengthened his hands by new conceffions, till they had hardly left themfelves any further favours to beftow.'

The feventh chapter comprifes an account of the confiftory of the emperors, a council compofed of the officers of ftate, the moft refpectable patricians, and the moft eminent profeffors of the law. The author explains the nature of the imperial conftitutions, known by the names of refcripts, decrees, and edicts.

In the eighth chapter Dr. Bever delineates the ftate of the ' Refponfa Prudentum,' and of the profeffion of law under the emperors; with the different fects of the lawyers; of all of which he has given a clear and accurate account.

The ninth chapter contains a general view of the ftate of the Roman government, from the death of Alexander Severus, to the abdication of the imperial power by Dioclefian.

The fourth book treats of the imperial government, from the removal of the feat of empire to Byzantium by Conftantine, to the revival and diffufion of the Roman laws over Europe in the twelfth century. The firft chapter contains a view of the ftate of the Roman government and laws, from Conftantine to Juftinian. The next exhibits the ftate of the laws after Theodofius II. with the reformation of them by Juftinian. In this chapter the hiftorian relates the origin of the Inftitutes, Digeft or Pandeats, the Code, and the New Couftitutions; all which conftitute the body of the Civil Law.

' Upon an impartial review of this princely colleaion, fays our author, which contains the quinteffence of whatever is ufeful and excellent among the accumulated produations of fourteen centuries, inftead of envioufly dwelling upon its defeas, or complaining of its magnitude, we fhould rather admire the judgment and perfeverance of thofe learned perfonages who had courage to undertake this more than Herculean labour; and reduced the whole into fo reafonable and moderate a compafs, as that in which it is now extant.'

The laft chapter of the volume delineates the ftate of Juftinian's laws in the Eaft; the alterations by Bafilius Macedo. and Leo the philofopher; the progrefs and decline of thofe laws in the Weft; with their revival in the twelfth century, and a particular enquiry into that event.

In this Hiftory Dr. Bever has, with great perfpicuity, traced the progrefs of the celebrated fyftem of civil law through a feries of near two thoufand years. He difcovers the ftrongeft marks of accurate enquiry, as well as judicious reflexion. Having fo much enriched the prefent volume with hiftorical detail, and pertinent remarks, we may expea a yet more interefting fund of obfervation in the fecond; which will not only relate the connexion of the civil with the feudal and canon laws, but their joint effea on the refpeaive governments of thofe countries where they have been adopted. Due attention, we are informed, will be paid to the various operations of thofe laws in the different parts of the Britifh empire, efpecially in the maritime and ecclefiaftical courts. We cannot help expreffing a defire, that Dr. Bever's profeffional engagements may afford him leifure to complete a work, which cannot fail of proving highly acceptable to every enquirer into the hiftory of our conftitution and juridical fyftem.

Theatre

Theatre of Education. Translated from the French *of the Countess* de Genlis. *4 Vols. 8vo. 1l. in boards.* Cadell.

AS the formation of the minds of youth is a matter of the utmost confequence and importance in every ftate, thofe who direct their ftudies towards it, are doubtlefs highly deferving both of attention and applaufe: the tafk, however, is by no means an eafy one; nothing is more difficult to a good writer than to adapt himfelf to the capacity of his inferiors, and to lead the young readers into a knowlege of men and manners, without, at the fame time, running the hazard of depraving their tafte or corrupting their manners: this arduous tafk Mademoifelle de Genlis, the original author of the work before us, has performed with fingular judgment and fuccefs.

' The work, as the tranflator has obferved, is equally adapted to the inftruction of both fexes, who will find engaging defcriptions of characters well worth their imitation, and meet with inftructive examples to deter them from thofe vices and follies which are moft incident to an early period of life. Though the Comedies of the countefs de Genlis, in which fhe has fhewn extenfive knowlege, fine tafte, exquifite fenfibility, and the moft exalted virtue, were written for the ufe of youth, they are not confined to the improvement of the young; perfons of all ages, of all ranks and profeffions, may difcover ufeful hints for the regulation of their conduct in the moft important fituations of life: where they meet not with inftruction, they will always find amufement, but in general, it has been the aim of this refpectable lady to unite thefe objects, in which fhe has fo happily fucceeded, that her work is confidered as an agreeable domeftic monitor in moft families on the continent.'

The four volumes contain twenty-four little comedies, of one, two, or three acts, each of which reprefents fome interefting domeftic circumftance, and inculcates fome particular moral, or focial duty. The dialogue is, in general, eafy, fprightly, and fenfible, conveying many judicious reflections on men and things; fuch as may be peculiarly ferviceable to young women, whom they were principally calculated to inftruct.

In a prefatory advertifement to one of thefe comedies, which is called the Queen of the Rofe, we meet with an entertaining account of a fingular cuftom kept up for many years, and ftill prevailing in Picardy, which we fhall here fubjoin for the amufement of our readers.

" There is ftill (fays the author of the memorial) a part of the world where fimple genuine virtue receives public honours.

It is in a village of Picardie, a place far diftant from the politenefs and luxury of great cities. There, an affecting ceremony, which draws tears from the fpectators, a folemnity, awful from its venerable antiquity, and falutary influence, has been preferved notwithftanding the revolutions of twelve centuries; there, the fimple luftre of the flowers with which innocence is annually crowned, is at once the reward, the encouragement, and the emblem. Here, indeed, ambition preys upon the young heart, but it is a gentle ambition; the prize is a hat, decorated with rofes. The preparations for a public decifion, the pomp of the feftival, the concourfe of people which it affembles, their attention fixed upon modefty, which does itfelf honour by its blufhes, the fimplicity of the reward, an emblem of thofe virtues by which it is obtained, the affectionate friendfhip of the rivals, who, in heightening the triumph of their queen, conceal in the bottom of their worthy hearts, the timid hope of reigning in their turn: all thefe circumftances united, give a pleafing and affecting pomp to this fingular ceremony, which makes every heart to palpitate, every eye to fparkle with tears of true delight, and makes wifdom the object of paffion. To be irreproachable is not fufficient, there is a kind of noblenefs, of which proofs are required; a noblenefs, not of rank and dignity, but of worth and innocence. Thefe proofs muft include feveral generations, both on the father and mother's fide; fo that a whole family is crowned upon the head of one; the triumph of one, is the glory of the whole; and the old man in grey hairs, who fheds tears of fenfibility on the victory gained by the daughter of his fon, placed by her fide, receives, in effect, the reward of fixty years, fpent in a life of virtue.

" By this means, emulation becomes general, for the honour of the whole; every one dreads, by an indelicate action, to dethrone either his fifter or his daughter. The Crown of Rofes, promifed to the moft prudent, is expected with emotion, diftributed with juftice, and eftablifhes goodnefs, rectitude, and morality, in every family; it attaches the beft people to the moft peaceful refidence.

" Example, powerful example, acts even at a diftance; there, the bud of worthy actions is unfolded, and the traveller, in approaching this territory, perceives, before he enters it, that he is not far from Salency. In the courfe of fo many fucceffive ages, all around them has changed; they alone will hand down to their children, the pure inheritance they received from their fathers: an inftitution truly great, from its fimplicity; powerful, under an appearance of weaknefs; fuch is the almoft unknown influence of honours; fuch is the ftrength of that eafy fpring, by which all men may be governed: fow honour, and you will reap virtue.

" If we reflect upon the time the Salencians have celebrated the feftival, it is the moft ancient ceremony exifting. If we attend to its object, it is, perhaps, the only one which is dedicated

I   dicated

dicated to the service of virtue. If virtue is the most useful and estimable advantage to society in general, this establishment, by which it is encouraged, is a public national benefit, and belongs to France.—

" According to a tradition, handed down from age to age, Saint Medard, born at Salency; proprietor, rather than lord, of the territory of Salency (for there were no fiefs at that time), was the institutor of that charming festival, which has made virtue flourish for so many ages. He had himself the pleasing consolation of enjoying the fruit of his wisdom, and his family was honoured with the prize which he had instituted, for his sister obtained the Crown of Roses.

" This affecting, and valuable festival, has been handed down from the fifth century to the present day. To this rose is attached a purity of morals, which, from time immemorial, has never suffered the slightest blemish ; to this rose are attached the happiness, peace, and glory of the Salencians.

" This rose is the portion, frequently the only portion which virtue brings with it ; this rose forms the amiable and pleasing tie of a happy marriage. Even fortune is anxious to obtain it, and comes with respect, to receive it from the hand of honourable indigence. A possession of twelve hundred years, and such splendid advantages, is the fairest title that exists in the world.

" An important period for the Festival of the Rose, was, when Louis the Thirteenth sent the marquis de Gordes, the captain of his guards, from the castle of Varennes to Salency, with a blue ribbon, and a silver ring, to be presented from him to the Queen of the Rose. It is from that honourable epocha that a blue ribbon, flowing in streamers, surrounds the crown of roses ; that a ring is fastened to it, and the young girls of her train, wear over their white robes, a blue ribbon, in the manner of a scarf.

" In 1766, Mr. Morfontaine settled a yearly income of one hundred and twenty livres upon the girl then elected queen. This income to be enjoyed by her during life, and, after her death, each succeeding girl, who should be crowned queen, to have one year's income on the day of her election. This noble generosity can only be rewarded by the homage of the public, and honour alone is the worthy recompence.

" Some days before the feast of Saint Medard, the inhabitants assemble in presence of the officers of justice, where this worthy company deliberate upon the important business of making a choice ; in doing which, they have no object in view but equity. They know all the merits that give a title to the crown ; they are acquainted with all the domestic details of their peaceful village ; they have not, nor cannot have, any other intention, but to be just : enthusiasm and respect for the memory of the holy institutor, and the excellence of the institution, are still in full force among

among them. They name three girls, three virtuous Salencians; of the moſt eſteemed and reſpectable families.——

" The nomination is immediately carried to the lord of Salency, or to the perſon appointed to repreſent-him, who is free to decide between the three girls, but obliged to chooſe one of them, whom he proclaims queen of the year.

" Eight days before the ceremony, the name of the ſucceſsful candidate is declared in church.——

" When the great day of the feſtival arrives, which is always the eighth of Jnne, the lord of Salency may claim the honour of conducting the queen to be crowned. On that grand day, ſhe is greater than all by whom ſhe is ſurrounded; and that greatneſs is of a nature which has nothing in common with the uſual diſtinctions of rank.

' The lord of Salency has the privilege of going to take virtue from her cottage, and lead her in triumph. Leaning upon his arm, or the arm of the perſon whom he has ſubſtituted in his place, the queen ſteps forth from her ſimple dwelling, eſcorted by twelve young girls, dreſſed in white, with blue ſcarfs; and twelve youths, who wear the livery of the queen; ſhe is preceded by muſic and drums, which announce the beginning of the proceſſion: ſhe paſſes along the ſtreets of the village, between rows of ſpectators, whom the feſtival has drawn to Salency, from the diſtance of four leagues. The public admire and applaud her; the mothers ſhed tears of joy, the old men renew their ſtrength to follow their beloved queen, and compare her with thoſe whom they have ſeen in their youth. The Salencians are proud of the merits of her to whom they give the crown; ſhe is one of themſelves, ſhe belongs to them, ſhe reigns by their choice, ſhe reigns alone, and is the only object of attention.

" The queen, being arrived at the church, the place appointed for her is always in the midſt of the people, the only ſituation could do her honour; where ſhe is, there is no longer any diſtinction of rank, it all vaniſhes in the preſence of virtue. A pew, placed in the middle of the choir, in ſight of all the people, is prepared to receive her: her train range themſelves in two lines by her ſide; ſhe is the only object of the day, all eyes remain fixed upon her, and her triumph continues.

" After veſpers the proceſſion begins again; the clergy lead the way, the lord of Salency receives her hand, her train join, the people follow, and line the ſtreets, while ſome of the inhabitants, under arms, ſupport the two rows, offering their homage by the loudeſt acclamations, until ſhe arrives at the chapel of St. Medard, where the gates are kept open: the good Salencians do not forſake their queen at the inſtant when the reward of virtue is going to be delivered; it is at that moment in particular, that it is pleaſing to ſee her, and honourable for her to be ſeen.

" The officiating clergyman bleſſes the hat, decorated with roſes, and its other ornaments; then turning towards the aſſembly,

fembly, he pronounces a difcourfe on the fubject of the feftival. What an affecting gravity, what an awful impreffion does the language of the prieft (who in fuch a moment celebrates the praifes of wifdom,) make upon the minds of his hearers! he holds the crown in his hand, while virtue waits kneeling at his feet; all the fpectators are affected, tears in every eye, perfuafion in every heart; then is the moment of lafting impreffions; and at that inftant he places the crown upon her head.

" After this begins a Te Deum, during which the proceffion is refumed.

" The queen, with the crown upon her head, and attended in the fame manner as fhe was when going to receive it, returns the way fhe came; her triumph ftill increafing as fhe paffes along, till fhe again enters the church, and occupies the fame place in the middle of the choir, till the end of the fervice.

" She has new homage to receive, and, going forth, is attended to a particular piece of ground, where crowned innocence finds expecting vaffals prepared to offer her prefents. They are fimple gifts, but their fingularity proves the antiquity of the cuftom; a nofegay of flowers, a dart, two balls, &c. &c.

" From thence fhe is conducted, with the fame pomp, and led back to her relations, and, in her own houfe, if fhe thinks proper, gives a rural collation to her conductor and her retinue.

" This feftival is of a fingular kind, of which there is no model elfewhere. It is intended to encourage wifdom, by beftowing public honours, and for fuch a purpofe they ought to be boundlefs. Where virtue reigns there is no rival, and whoever wifhes for diftinction in her prefence, cannot be fufficiently fenfible of what is due to her triumph.

" The diftinguifhing characteriftic of this feftival is, that every part of it is referable to the queen, that every thing is eclipfed by her prefence; her fplendour is direct, not reflected; her glory borrows nothing from diftinction of ranks; fhe has no need of any one to make her great and refpectable; in one word, it is the image of virtue which fhines, and every thing difappears before her."

This is a curious little hiftory, and exhibits a pleafing paftoral fcene that carries with it a dramatic air, and feems to promife a good foundation for that fpecies of the comic opera which has lately been fo well received amongft us. If properly executed it would probably meet with fuccefs on our own ftage. Mad. de Genlis has made that ufe of the fable which was moft fuitable to her plan, and drawn fome ufeful inftructions from it in a few ferious fcenes that may be of fervice to her young female pupils. The following extract may ferve as a fpecimen of this ingenious author's manner of treating

ing

ing her subject, which, though it does not abound in that laboured wit and studied repartee which are to be found in some of our modern comedies, is, notwithstanding, replete with good sense and morality.

After premising that Helen is the heroine of the piece, the Prior (the judge appointed to bestow the crown of roses) and Monica, a very old woman, a peasant of Salency, we shall present our readers with the last scene of the first act of this little piece.

'SCENE VI.

' The Prior, Mrs. Dummer, Mary, Monica, Helen, Theresa.

(Monica supported by Helen, who has hold of Mary by the hand on the other side.)

' *The Prior.* Good day, Mother Monica ; how do you do ?

' *Monica.* Thank you, Mr. Prior, e'en but so so. —— Marry, by next Louis's day, I shall be fourscore, and that is an age to make one feel ; my limbs fail me, and I can scarce walk.

' *Mrs. Dummer.* Set a chair for her.

' *Mon.* Thank you, Madam, I'll e'en sit down then with your good leave. *(Helen places a chair near the press. Monica sits down.)*

' *Prior.* Mother Monica, we sent Helen to beg the key of your press.

' *Mon.* Why, truly, I don't give the key of our treasure so readily to such young folks ; it will be time enough when she is Queen of the Rose, if it please God that I live to see that day ; but I have brought you the key ; here it is, Mr. Prior.

' *Prior.* Now, Mrs. Dummer, you shall see the fairest family-titles that exist in the world ; look here.

' *Mrs. Dum.* *(looking into the press.)* Ha ! what is that under all these little niches of glass ?

' *Prior.* Dried Crowns of Roses.

' *Mon.* O yes, they are dry, for some of them have been there much more than a hundred years !

' *Mary.* O, Mama, it is pretty —— they are just like a shrine for relics.

' *Prior.* Well, Mrs. Dummer, you don't say any thing.

' *Mrs Dum.* I am quite confounded ! —— How is this ! Have there been as many Queens of the Rose in this family, as I see crowns here ?

' *Mon.* Ah, Madam, there are many more ; I had another daughter, who is dead, who had a number of daughters ; all the crowns of that side of the house are wanting ; and then, my father married again, and his children, as was but right, have inherited some of the crowns ; we have only those of the direct line.

' *Mrs. Dum.* *(still looking in the press.)* They all have labels.

' *Prior.* Yes, the names of the Queens are written upon these labels.

' *Mrs.*

' *Mon.* Mr. Prior, you, who know all this as well as your Pater-noſter, ſhew Madam the crown of Mary-Jean Bocard ; it is the oldeſt, I believe.

' *Prior.* Is it not at the top of the preſs ?

' *Mon.* Yes. Can you reach it ?

' *Prior.* Yes, yes, I have it.———Let us ſee the date.——— *(He reads.)* fifteen hundred and twenty.

' *Mrs. Dum. holding the Crown, which is under a glaſs.* One thouſand five hundred and twenty !———

' *Mon.* This is a valuable piece, is it not ?

' *Mary, looking at the Crown.* What is that a Roſe ? How it is changed !

' *Mon.* Helen, ſhew that of Catharine Javelle ; it ſtands be-low———

' *Helen.* Yes, grandmother———

' *Mon.* Catharine Javelle was my mother's ſiſter, and died very young : her ſtory is comical.

' *Prior.* Tell it us, mother Monica.

' *Mon.* You muſt know then, ſhe was waſhing linen at the great pond ; ſhe had no body with her but a little boy of ſeven years old, to carry the linen ; when, all of a ſudden, little John-ny —— (his name was Johnny, he was the ſon of poor Michael.)

' *Prior.* He is ſtill living ; that Johnny, is now goodman Ruſſel ?

' *Mon.* Juſt ſo———But, Mr. Prior, you know the whole hiſtory !

' *Prior.* No matter, go on mother Monica.

' *Mrs. Dum.* I pray you do, Mrs. Monica.

' *Mon.* Well then———I forget where I left off———

' *Helen.* Grandmother, you was at, *when all of a ſudden, and at the brink of the pond.*

' *Mon.* Ay——behold, all of a ſudden, Johnny fell into the pond head foremoſt, *flounce,* there he was in the water———upon which, by my troth, my aunt Catharine Javelle did not make two ſteps of it, but threw herſelf headlong after him, and then fiſhed up Johnny, like a gudgeon, and brought him ſafe to the ſhore.

' *Mrs. Dum.* O heavens !

' *Prior.* You muſt know this pond is exceſſively deep.

' *Mon.* O it is an abyſs —— In ſhort ſhe laid him upon the graſs ; but Johnny had ſwallowed ſo much water, ſo very much, that he was in a ſwoon———My Aunt ſaid to herſelf, what ſhall I do with this child, and likewiſe with my linen ?———It was late, ſhe muſt return home, ſhe had a mile and a half to go, and nobody to help her, ſhe was trembling, and all in confuſion ; but, however, ſhe took Johnny aſtraddle on her ſhoulders, and, leaving all her linen behind her, came back in that manner to the village.

' *Mrs. Dum.* I hope ſhe was Queen that year ?

' *Mon.* O, my God, yes. It is an ill wind that blows nobody good, as the ſaying is ; it is very fortunate for a young girl to find

And fuch opportunities; marry, the like don't happen every day.

' *Mrs. Dum.* Ah, Mr. Prior, what is moft curious in Salency, is not the proceffion of the feftival, but to fee and to hear thefe things.

' *Prior.* I told you fo ———— (*He looks at his watch.*) But it is twelve o'clock; we muft go.

' *Mrs. Dum.* I can't take my eyes off that prefs.

' *Prior.* To be fure, thefe refpectable titles, thofe proofs of merit, are as valuable as the pieces of old parchment, of which fome people are fo vain.

' *Mrs. Dum.* Upon my life, I could fee all the parchments in the world with a dry eye, though I have fome; but in looking at thefe dried Rofes, I find the tears ftart!——Ah, how forry am I that Mary is not five or fix years older!——She would have been fenfible of this.

' *Mary.* Mama, you muft bring me back when I grow bigger.

' *Prior.* She is right; it is very good for a young girl to breathe the air of Salency.—Farewell, mother Monica.

' *Mon.* My God, Mr. Prior, Gertrude will be very forry.——

' *Prior.* I fhall return.

' *Mon.* Mr. Prior, the declaration, however, is to be at five o'clock?

' *Prior.* Yes, mother Monica. (*He takes her by the hand.*) My worthy woman, be perfectly eafy——I beg of you——

' *Mon.* O good Lord!——

' *Prior.* Farewell—till by and by.

' *Mrs. Dum.* Farewell, my dear Mrs. Monica.

' *Mon.* Your fervant, Madam.

(*Mrs. Dummer and the Prior go out.*

Helen goes to open the door for them, and makes feveral courtefies, which Mrs. Dummer returns, after having embraced her. In the mean time, Monica remains alone at the front of the ftage.

' *Mon.* Mr. Prior bid me *be perfectly cafy*; that is a good fign! May God Almighty grant it!—(*to Helen, who returns.*) Helen, did you hear what Mr. Prior faid?——

' *Helen.* O God, yes, grandmother; I am ftill all in confufion.—He took hold of your hand.——

' *Mon.* And he fqueezed it, my child——I dared not fpeak to him of you, becaufe of the lady being prefent.——

' *Helen.* O grandmother—I have very agreeable forebodings!

' *Mon.* And fo have I.—O Lord, I fhall fee you this very day, in five hours, with the crown of rofes!—After that I fhall die content.—But heark'ee child, don't go to be vain of this; don't therefore fancy yourfelf better than Therefa or Urfula; that would fpoil all.

' *Helen.* Why fhould I be vain of it? If I am crowned, I fhall owe it to you and my mother; I am only vain of being both your daughter and hers —

' *Mon.*

' *Mon.* Poor little dear !——come and kifs me—God will blefs you, you deferve it.——But what is the matter !——you feem to be in tears ?

' *Helen.* It is very true——I am thinking now, that if you fhould flatter yourfelf with the hope of my getting the crown, and unhappily I do not gain it——you will be fo uneafy, fo forely vexed——

' *Mon.* Do not fob fo for that.——Well, my child, if you do not get it, we muft fubmit ; that is no reafon for murmuring againft Providence. But the Prior bid me be perfectly eafy ; I promife you he did not fay that for nothing.——Come, my girl, and fhut the prefs, for you muft go and get dinner ready.—Is not your brother come back yet ?——

' *Helen.* No, grandmother, he is always at the other end of the village with poor Robert, who is very fick, and knows no comfort but when Bafil is with him ; and my brother, who loves Robert as he does his eyes, wifhes to remain with him till the time of the ceremony.

' *Mon.* That is very right, very right, indeed. Give me my key—I hope I fhall open that prefs this night yet, to lock up your crown in it.

' *Helen.* O dear grandmother !

' *Mon.* Give me your arm, my girl. Come, let us go. (*They go out.*)'

Though this is by no means the moft fhining part of the performance before us, the reader will perceive in it a great deal of nature and fimplicity ; which, together with a peculiar elegance of fentiment and diction, runs through the whole work. We would recommend it, therefore, to the few parents and guardians left amongft us, who, in the education of their children and pupils, have a regard for their moral character, and above all to the fchool-miftreffes in this metropolis and its environs, who, we think, cannot employ their fcholars better than in reading and repeating thefe entertaining and inftructive comedies.

The private Life of Lewis XV. *Tranflated from the* French *by* J. O. Juftamond, *F. R. S.* 4 *vols.* 8*vo.* 1*l. in boards.* Dilly.

THIS hiftory, as the original editor obferves, performs much more than it promifes : for while we might expect from it only anecdotes of a private nature, it prefents us chiefly with a narrative of the public tranfactions in the reign of Lewis the Fifteenth. It appears that this prince, in the early part of his life, was of a delicate conftitution ; on which account he was prevented from applying to such studies as require much attention. Before he was ten years of age, however, a book was printed under his name, describing the courses of the principal rivers in Europe. It is said that M. De Lisle, his instructor in geography, had given him considerable assistance. But, as the editor remarks, the pupil must have had some share in it, to have given reason to the courtiers for so much flattery on this subject.

The sending back, in 1725, the Infanta of Spain, who had been destined for consort to the young king of France, was vindicated by the French court upon principles of policy : but if we may credit the present history, this measure was the effect of an intrigue, in which the person principally concerned, was the duchess of Bourbon.

In the history of the year 1726, we find the following character of the young king, and cardinal Fleuri, formerly his preceptor, but who became prime minister, on the death of the regent.

‘ Lewis XV. when he undertook to free himself from the tutelage of the duke of Bourbon, was entering into the age of adolescence, being between sixteen and seventeen years of age. His cotemporaries describe him as being handsome, of a proper stature, with a leg perfectly well made, a noble mein, his eyes large, his look rather mild than fierce, his eye-brows dark ; and his appearance all together seeming to bespeak that delicate habit of body, which he afterwards fortified so much by exercise, that he was able to bear the greatest fatigues. It is to this tardy progress of nature in him, that we are undoubtedly to attribute the calmness of those passions, which are so active at that age in most individuals of strong constitutions, and especially among princes, with whom every thing contributes to awaken these passions early. He then appeared indifferent for women, for play, and for high living, all of which he was much addicted to after. Hunting was his only pleasure, whether it were that a secret instinct led him to this salutary exercise, or that want of employment prompted him to it, from the apprehension of that tædium, which already began to embitter his best days : for his education having been much neglected, from the fear of fatiguing him in his infancy, his mind was but little embellished, and he had not acquired that taste for study, which is of so great resource at all times, and in every station. He had an invincible aversion for business, so that he could scarce bear to hear it spoken of. Having no thirst of glory, he wanted that energy, which, in his great-grandfather, had corrected the defects of education, and made up for his ignorance. In a word, being of an easy, indolent, and timid disposition, he was calculated to be governed by the first person who should gain an ascendant over him. This circumstance the preceptor of the prince soon

per-

perceived, and he availed himself of it, to lay the foundation of his grandeur.

' The preceptor was, in many points, of a character similar to that of his royal pupil. Hence that sympathy between them, which made the one so much attached to the interests of his master, and the other so obedient to the counsels of his preceptor. Simplicity, modesty, prudence, and circumspection, were, in some sort, the safeguards of the ambition of the ancient bishop of Frejus; his ambition partook of those qualities; it made its way by patience and insinuation, and had nothing in it of that active and turbulent progression which marks this passion in other men. It had already, undoubtedly, arrived to a great height, but by slow degrees. The cardinal was seventy-three years old when he was appointed to the ministry. Born in a southern province of France, of parents, if not obscure, at least little known, he was designed for the church, and instructed in the sciences suitable to that profession, which he entered into early. It is the profession the best calculated to promote those who are not called up to high employments by their birth.

' The abbé Fleuri had an ardent desire to appear at court, being certain that his youth and his person would be of wonderful advantage to him; he managed so well, that he came furnished with pretty good recommendations, which he supported by his merits among the women, but always with that reserve and discretion which guided all his conduct, and which even the ladies were not able to remove. He obtained the post of king's chaplain, and a few years after was named to a bishopric. Thus he was again sent back into a province, and even at a great distance from the scene on which he had but just shewn himself; but hypocrisy was to be the principal spring of his elevation. His exactness in the performance of his duty made him be taken notice of by Lewis XIV. and chosen to superintend the education of Lewis XV. He soon flattered himself, that he should realize in his person the great predictions of the astrologers, in which he had much confidence; for although he had a great share of understanding, yet he was not possessed of that genius, which being superior to events, feels itself capable of commanding them, and expects its fortune from itself alone. This weakness, however, was very useful to him, inasmuch as, relying on that happy fatality in which he believed, he accustomed himself early to his elevation, which did not appear strange to him; and inasmuch as the assurance of success, without ever making him presumptuous, inspired him with that perseverance which supplied the place of energy, and enabled him to undertake a plan of fortune, which otherwise he would never have conceived. The ascendant which he found he had over his pupil, in proportion as he discovered his inclinations and qualities, persuaded him, that in time he might aspire to the highest pitch of power ; and the death of the regent opened the moſt extenſive career to his ambition.'

The circumſtance which will render the adminiſtration of cardinal Fleuri ever memorable in the hiſtory of the ſciences, is the execution of that great deſign of determining the figure of the earth ; a point of great importance to navigation.

The private life of Lewis XV. after his arrival at manhood, affords an almoſt uninterrupted ſcene of voluptuouſneſs ; with no other diverſity than the caſual ſucceſſion of the objects of royal favour ; which ſeems to have been always attracted by artifice, and to have been carried to an exceſs that betrayed infatuation. We are informed, however, that in the midſt of his debaucheries, he never failed of ſaying his prayers morning and evening ; that he heard maſs ſaid regularly every day ; and attended at every office of divine worſhip. It is farther ſaid, that he abhorred irreligious perſons ; and for that reaſon, notwithſtanding all the adulation laviſhed upon him by Voltaire, the king could never endure him.

We ſhall conclude with obſerving, that theſe volumes afford conſiderable information reſpecting the reign of Lewis XV. But though they may gratify, in ſome degree, the lovers of anecdote, they are void of the dignity of hiſtorical compoſition.

Free Examination of the Socinian *Expoſition of the prefatory Verſes of* St. John's *Goſpel. By the Rev.* R. Shepherd, *B. D.* 8vo. 2s. 6d. Flexney.

THE doctrines, which are uſually termed Socinian, have been lately propagated by ſeveral writers with great zeal ; and are at preſent ſuppoſed to be gaining ground, under the more faſhionable and ſpecious appellation of unitarian principles. But the author of this tract conſiders them as founded on arbitrary and irrational interpretations of ſcripture ; and their advocates as apoſtates, and as much the enemies of Chriſtianity as the Deiſts.

The preface to St. John's Goſpel is of great importance in this controverſy. Abauzit and others have ſuppoſed the firſt verſe to have been levelled againſt the worſhippers of the goddeſs Minerva ; the third to have been written with a view to obviate the doctrines of the Epicurean philoſophy, &c.

But, ſays our author, ' if thoſe critics had conſidered St. John's character, the nature of his miniſtry, and the object of his goſpel, they muſt have been convinced, that it was much

out

out of his character, and beside his purpose, to have employed himself in confuting the vague and difcordant doctrines of heathen philofophy.

'John was by education a fifherman, the fon of a fifherman, and confequently out of the way of acquaintance with the philofophy of the Gentiles, or the abftrufe learning of the Jewifh doctors : but, writing to his own people, he chofe the moft familiar terms, and common phrafes. His gofpel was not calculated for philofophers and doctors only, that he fhould confine himfelf to their terms : it was adapted to common capacities, after the pattern of Chrift's preaching, of which this is one characteriftic, " the poor have the gofpel preached unto them."

This is a very proper remark ; for every commentator ought, above all things, to confider the character, fituation, circumftances, and views of his author, before he can undertake to explain his meaning in any difficult paffage. Yet in the prefent cafe, it may be obferved by the Socinians, that if St. John defigned to teach his illiterate countrymen the doctrines maintained by the Athanafians, he might have expreffed himfelf in much lefs obfcure and ambiguous terms.

Our author however infifts, that the Socinian interpretation is forced and unnatural.

' St. John's frequent allufions to the pre-exiftence of Chrift, and direct affertions of it, if they are all to be underftood, not in their plain and obvious, but in an allegorical and figurative fenfe ; muft be acknowledged as calculated only for profound fcholars, acute and fubtle critics. And even among thofe there muft be an eternal difagreement ; and tropes and figures muft be varioufly admitted, according to the tafte and imagination of the critic. Or if, in reply to this reflection it be urged, that fuch tropes and figures are frequent with the Eaftern writers, however harfh and unnatural they may found in the Weftern languages ; yet we are to confider that the religion of Chrift was an univerfal religion, and the doctrines of the gofpel were calculated for the Weftern, as well as the Eaftern hemifphere.

' But, fay the Socinians, allow nothing to be figurative that is afferted in the New Teftament, and you will find there is no way of evading any papiftical arguments in fupport of the groffeft errors: fuch particularly as tranfubftantiation. Is there then no difference between refolving every thing, that has the appearance of a difficulty, into tropes and figures, and never admitting them ? If expreffions in their plain and obvious fenfe imply an impoffibility, from which a figurative interpretation will free them ; there, and there only, we are to admit the figure. But we are to confider, that nothing

E 2

im·

implies an impoffibility with God, that does not imply a contradiction; fuch as that the fame thing be round and fquare, exift and not exift, at the fame, &c.

'Socinus himfelf was little acquainted with antiquity; and therefore he affected to treat the writings of the fathers with contempt. His difciples have followed the example of their great mafter; they feldom cite the fathers, but in affectation of ridiculing them; and in the attempt have generally evinced, how little they underftood them. That their opinions in points of doctrine, are infallible, is not pretended: but as being nearer the apoftolic age, and therefore having better opportunities of being well informed in cafes of teftimony, and matters of fact, the fathers do fo far undoubtedly deferve our attention.

'No men are more acute than the Socinian writers, in difcovering difficulties in doctrines, to which their own opinions are oppofed: none more blind to the inconfiftencies, which the notions they have themfelves adopted, involve. Difficulties have been ftarted in the doctrine of Chrift's pre-exiftence and divinity; how unjuftly, I mean not in this place to confider: my prefent defign being only to enquire whether there be no difficulties, no error, no inconfiftency in the oppofite doctrine of Socinus.

'Does the idea, for inftance, of a being produced without the inftrumentality of man, by the energetic influence of the Holy Spirit, coincide with our idea of a mere and abfolute man: or does it not fuggeft to us the notion of a being fomewhat allied in nature to that fuperior exiftence, from whence it was immediately derived?

'Is there no difficulty, in fuppofing a man, divinely commiffioned to inftruct the world in the pure worfhip of the Deity: while at the fame time his inftructions were fo enigmatically delivered, that inftead of promoting fuch purity of worfhip, even amidft thofe who embraced his religion, they produced nothing, in the courfe of fourteen or fifteen hundred years, but a fcheme of religion both in principle and practice grofsly idolatrous?

'Is there no difficulty in conceiving one man, in compenfation for three years miniftry and the example of an innocent life, to be raifed in honour, power, and dignity, not only infinitely beyond the reft of the human race; but above all other fyftems of fuperior beings: angels, and powers, being not only made inferior, but fubject, to him?

'Is there no inconfiftency in the idea of a man, being conftituted mediator between God and man; that is, between God and himfelf?'

This

This laſt argument recoils upon the *orthodox.* For ſuppoſing Chriſt to be God, he is by *himſelf* conſtituted mediator between *himſelf* and man.

In this tract the author examines, firſt, the expoſition which Socinus has given of the beginning of St. John's goſpel; and afterwards the interpretation of his followers.

We do not perceive, by any direct aſſertions, that this writer is an Athanaſian; yet we cannot underſtand the following paſſage, upon any other ſuppoſition.

' If Chriſt, as the Socinians aſſert, was merely and abſolutely man, the Perſians are not greater idolators than the Chriſtian world; that ſmall part of it excepted, which has been enlightened by the doctrines of Socinus. If he were of a ſuperior nature, and declared ſuch, the Socinian is as great an apoſtate from Chriſtianity as Julian himſelf.'

This argument affects every hypotheſis, but that of Athanaſius: becauſe no *created being* whatever can be the proper object of divine worſhip.

In this writer the Socinians have met with an antagoniſt, who has repelled the darts of his apponents with dexterity, and given them ſome ſevere and unexpected ſtrokes.

Journal of Captain Cook's *laſt Voyage to the* Pacific Ocean, *on Diſcovery*; *Performed in the Years* 1776, 1777, 1778, 1779. *8vo.* 6s. *in boards.* Newbery.

THE ſeveral voyages lately performed round the world have been objects of public curioſity: but the laſt, in particular, on account of the important view with which it was projected, excited uncommon expectation. The hope of diſcovering a north-weſt paſſage from the Atlantic to the Pacific Ocean, ſeems now to be for ever extinguiſhed. We have only to regret, that ſo valuable a navigator as captain Cook, with whom we may join his ſucceſſor, captain Clarke, ſhould have been added to the other victims which, ſince the fifteenth century, have periſhed in the proſecution of this enterprize.

Of the name of the author or editor of this Journal we are not informed; and cannot, therefore, determine in reſpect of its authenticity. The editor, however, affirms, that what immediately relates to the object of the voyage, the places the ſhips viſited, and the reception of Omai at Otaheite, are, in general, related with fidelity, though the colouring, on ſome occaſions, be perhaps a little heightened. We doubt not, that many readers, in reliance on this declaration, will have re-

courſe

courſe to the preſent narrative, until the account by authority ſhall be publiſhed.

The two ſhips employed in this voyage were the Diſcovery and the Reſolution, which ſailed in the ſummer of 1776. The firſt object of the expedition was to carry back Omai to Otaheite; and the next, to proceed on the diſcovery of the north-weſt paſſage. The editor of the Journal gives the following account of Omai, from Mr. Foſter.

" Omai has been conſidered either as remarkably ſtupid or very intelligent, according to the different allowances which were made by thoſe who judged of his abilities. His language, which is deſtitute of every harſh conſonant, and where every word ends with a vowel, had ſo little exerciſed his organs of ſpeech, that they were wholly unfit to pronounce the more complicated Engliſh ſounds; and this phyſical or rather habitual defect, has too often been miſconſtrued. Upon his arrival in England, he was immediately introduced into general company, led to the moſt ſplendid entertainments, and preſented at court amidſt a brilliant circle of the firſt nobility. He naturally imitated that eaſy and elegant politeneſs which is ſo prevalent in all thoſe places; he adopted the manners, the occupations, and amuſements of his companions, and gave many proofs of a quick perception and lively fancy. Among the inſtances of his intelligence, I need only mention his knowlege of the game of cheſs, in which he had made an amazing proficiency. The multiplicity of objects which crowded upon him, prevented his paying due attention to thoſe particulars, which would have been beneficial to himſelf and his countrymen at his return. He was not able to form a general comprehenſive view of our whole civilized ſyſtem, and to abſtract from thence what appeared moſt ſtrikingly uſeful and applicable to the improvement of his country. His ſenſes were charmed by beauty, ſymmetry, harmony, amd magnificence; they called aloud for gratification, and he was accuſtomed to obey their voice. The continued round of enjoyments left him no time to think of his future life; and being deſtitute of the genius of a Tupaïa, whoſe ſuperior abilities would have enabled him to form a plan for his own conduct, his underſtanding remained unimproved   After having ſpent near two years in England, Mr. Foſter adds, that his judgment was in its infant ſtate, and therefore (when he was preparing to return) he coveted almoſt every thing he ſaw, and particularly that which amuſed him by ſome unexpected effect: to gratify his childiſh inclinations, as it ſhould ſeem, rather than from any other motives, he was indulged with a portable organ, an electrical machine, a coat of mail, and a ſuit of armour."

We are informed, that on the arrival of the veſſels at Otaheite, the riches of Omai, and the favour ſhewn him by
cap-

captain Cook, excited much envy and jealousy among the chiefs of that island. The several officers, and Omai, were soon invited to dine with king Ottoo. The dinner confisted of fish and fowl of various kinds, dressed after their manner; barbicued pigs, stewed yams, and fruits of the most delicious flavour, all served with an ease and regularity that is seldom to be found at European tables, when the ladies are excluded from making part of the company. As soon as dinner was over, the guests were conducted to the theatre, where was in readiness a company of players to perform a dramatic entertainment.

'The drama, says the editor, was regularly divided into three acts: the first consisted of dancing and dumb-shew; the second, of comedy; which to those who understood the language was very laughable, as Omai and the natives appeared highly diverted the whole time; the last was a musical piece, in which the young princesses were the sole performers. There were between the acts some feats of arms exhibited. The combatants were armed with lances and clubs. One made the attack, the other stood upon the defensive. He who made the attack brandished his lance, and either threw, pushed or used it in aid of his club. He who was upon the defensive, stuck the point of his lance in the ground, in an oblique direction, so that the upper part rose above his head, and by observing the eye of his enemy, parried his blows or strokes by the motion of his lance. By his dexterity at this manœuvre he turned aside the lance, and it was rare that he was hurt by the club. If his antagonist struck at his legs, he shewed his agility by jumping over the club; and if at his head, he was no less nimble in crouching under it. Their dexterity consisted chiefly in the defence, otherwise the combat might have been fatal, which always ended in good humour.'

On the arrival of Omai's mother, and several of his relations, they testified their joy at his return by striking their face and arms with sharks teeth, till they were all over besmeared with blood.

The following are the particulars relative to the death of captain Cook; who was unfortunately killed by the savages, at O-why-ee, in February, 1779.

' On the morning of the 14th, our great cutter, which was moored to the buoy, was missing from her moorings, and, upon examination, the boat's painter was found cut two fathoms from the buoy, and the remainder of the rope gone with the boat.

' This gave cause to suspect that some villainy was hatching, and, in order to prevent the ill consequences that might follow, both captains met on board the Resolution, to consult what was best to be done on this critical occasion. The officers from both

E 4

ships were present at this council, where it was resolved to seize the king and to confine him on board till the boat should be returned

' With this view, early on the morning of the 14th, captain Cook, with twenty marines, went on shore under cover of the guns of both ships. The Indians observing our motions, and seeing the ships warping towards the towns, of which there were two, one on each side the harbour's mouth, they concluded that our design was to seize their canoes. In consequence of which most of their large war canoes took the alarm, and were making off, when our guns, loaded with grape and canister shot, drove them back; and the captain and his guard landed without opposition. We observed, however, that their warriors were cloathed in their military dress, though without arms, and that they were gathering together in a body from every direction, their chiefs assuming a very different countenance to what they usually wore upon all former occasions. However, captain Cook, attended by Mr. Philips, lieutenant of marines, a serjeant, and ten privates, regardless of appearances, proceeded directly to the king's residence, where they found him seated on the ground, with about twelve of his chiefs round him, who all rose in the utmost consternation on seeing the captain and his guard enter. The captain addressed the king in the mildest terms, assuring him that no violence was intended against his person or any of his people, except against those who had been guilty of a most unprecedented act of robbery, by cutting from her moorings one of the ship's boats, without which they could neither conveniently water the ships, nor carry on the necessary communication with the shore; calling upon the king, at the same time, to give orders for the boat to be immediately restored; and insisting upon his accompanying him to the ships, till his orders should be carried into execution. The king protested his total ignorance of the theft; said he was very ready to assist in discovering the thief, and should be glad to see him punished; but shewed great unwillingness to trust his person with strangers, who had lately exercised very unusual severities against his people. He was told that the tumultuous appearance of the people and their repeated robberies made some uncommon severities necessary; but that not the least hurt should be done to the meanest inhabitant of his island by any person belonging to the ships, without exemplary punishment; and all that was necessary for the continuance of peace was, to pledge himself for the honesty of his people. With that view, and that view only he came to request the king to place confidence in him, and to make his ship his home, as the most effectual means of putting a stop to the robberies that were now daily and hourly committed by his people, both at the tents and on board the ships, and were now so daring as to become insufferable. The king, upon this remonstrance, was preparing to comply; but the chiefs, taking the alarm, began to steal away one after another, till they were stopped by the guard. In about half

half an hour the king was ready to accompany captain Cook on board ; but by that time fo great a body of Indians were got together and lined the fhore, that it was with difficulty they could break through the multitude, who now began to behave outrageoufly, and to infult the guard. Captain Cook, obferving their behaviour, gave orders to the officer of marines to make way, and if any one oppofed, to fire upon and inftantly difpatch him. This order lieutenant Philips endeavoured to carry into execution, and a lane was made for the king and his chiefs to get to the boats, but they had fcarce reached the water-fide, when the word was given, that Tu-tee was about to carry off their king to kill him. In an inftant a number of their fighting men broke from the crowd, and with clubs rufhed in upon the guard, four of whom were prefently difpatched. A ruffian making a ftroke at captain Cook, was fhot dead by the captain himfelf, who, having a double barrelled gun, was aiming at another, when a favage came behind him and ftriking him on the head with his club felled him to the ground ; and then thruft his pa-ha-he (a kind of poignard made by our armourers at the requeft of the king, the day before) through his body with fuch force that, entering between his fhoulders, the point of it came out at his breaft. The quarrel now became general. The guns from the fhips began to pour in their fire upon the crowd, as did likewife the marine guard, and the marine from the boats ; and though the flaughter among the favages was dreadful, yet, enraged as they were, they ftood our inceffant fire with aftonifhing intrepidity, infomuch that, in fpite of all our efforts, they carried off the bodies of the dead, as a mark of triumph.'

The volume, which is not deftitute of information and entertainment, befides fome plates, is decorated with a chart reprefenting the courfe of the voyage.

Sea Sermons : or, a Series of Difcourfes for the Ufe of the Navy. By the Rev. James Ramfay. *8vo.* 4s. *fewed.* Rivington.

THE author of thefe difcourfes, finding that common ones were not fitted for the circumftances of a fhip of war, drew up thefe for the ufe of his majefty's fhip the Prince of Wales, and adapted his inftructions to the particular fituation of feamen.

They are offered to the public, not as finifhed effays, or accurate difcuffions of particular points of doctrine, but as helps to reflection. Men are not ignorant, but carelefs of their duty ; and therefore the preacher very juftly thought it more neceffary to give his hearers a right turn, than to inform their underftanding.

The

The fubjects, which he treats of are the following : Virtue the Foundation of fuccefs (preached after the taking of St. Lucia) ; the Duty of exerting ourfelves in the Caufe of our Country ; the Sinfulnefs of Mutiny, of Defertion, Drunkennefs, and common Swearing ; on the Value of the Soul ; our Duty to God, to ourfelves, to our Neighbour, and to our Country ; and, laftly, of Man's Duty, as laid down in the Gofpel.

To thefe difcourfes the author has prefixed an Addrefs to the Seamen ferving in the Royal Navy. In this introduction, as well as in the fubfequent Sermons, he very properly confiders them as fuftaining the moft refpectable characters. Having reprefented to them the neceffity of fubordination, and of moral and religious reftraints, he thus proceeds :

' When you are confidered as being loofed from obligations that bind other men, by that fuppofition you are degraded below the rank of other men. And does this fuit your ambition ? Can you, who are the inftruments of your country's wealth, the guardians of her laws, the avengers of her wrongs, bear to be confidered in fuch an humiliating light, to be fet below the loweft of the helplefs people, whom you protect, defend, and enrich ?

' And as doubtlefs you will conclude with me, that nothing in your ftation debafes you below the rank of other men, fo there is nothing in your cuftoms or way of life that fhould produce the effect. Travelling is a great means of acquiring knowlege ; but you are travellers by profeffion. Your art draws its principles from the knowlege of nature, an acquaintance with aftronomy, the winds, the feafons, the produce of the various countries, the wonders of the deep, the peculiarities of climates and kingdoms. You cannot therefore plead ignorance ; for by only keeping open your eyes and ears, you muft draw in knowlege and information beyond the bulk of mankind. You want nothing but a little difcreet reflection to fet you above the greater part of your brethren in the fcale of reafon and improvement. To produce that is the defign of the following difcourfes.

' And, my brethren, ought reflection to be wanting among you, whofe way of life is one fcene of filent attention and fober obfervation ? When that noble machine which you direct in your country's fervice is once fitted by your induftry, and put in motion by your fkill, your employment becomes then confined to an obfervation of the heavens, and an attendance on their movements. This muft naturally be accompanied with a reference to, and a dependence on that Being, in whofe hands the winds and feafons are, who alone can forward or protect you. And fhall we, notwithftanding, find a greater neglect of God, and a more univerfal profanation of his name among you than other men? For fhame, brethren, this ought not fo to be.

                                      ' Again,

'Again, the conducting of the ship depends on the vigour and strength which you are able to exert in working her. But these are not to be acquired in the ways of drunkenness or debauchery, or to be preserved in the arms of a strumpet. Health and strength are the property only of the chaste and sober. As you therefore value your profession, you will guard against excess of every kind, and lead sober regular lives.

'You and your comrades are brought together for one purpose of mutual assistance and exertion. Your success depends on your joint efforts. Your brother's interest and welfare then become your's. You rise and fall together. And here far be it from me to fix indiscriminate censure You are an open, free-hearted people, and only need to have your generosity directed to its proper object When therefore you indulge the natural benevolence of your hearts in doing good offices to your neighbour, consider God as commanding the duty, and prescribing his love to you as the measure of it.

'Lastly, the purpose of your profession is a public purpose: it is either to enrich, or to protect your country. Hence the unlawfulness of mutiny, desertion, drunkenness, and disobedience of orders, as destructive of the very end of your profession. Hence diligence, assiduity, ready obedience, and their foundation industry and sobriety, become necessary qualifications in the public service.'

At sea oaths having been considered as a necessary appendage to command, the author takes some pains to answer this and every other argument in defence of common-swearing, in three sermons.

In the Sermon on Desertion he gives his auditors this interesting view of the deserter, and the faithful seaman.

'From some capricious dislike to some officer, or the service, or more frequently a capricious desire of roving, the inconsiderate man has resolved to desert, to abandon the service, to leave behind him his pretensions to preferment, to a retreat in Greenwich, perhaps to two or three years hard earned wages. In order to get an opportunity to steal away, he must feign an hypocritical assiduity in his duty, that he may be trusted in a boat; or he forges some lie of a friend, or business that requires his presence on shore; or he takes advantage of a dark night, like a coward to abandon his station, in swimming to land at the risk of his life. Thus the very act of desertion is not only an act of base perfidy, a breach of duty to our country, but it is a mean, pitiful lie before God, the God of truth: and the circumstance in which the lie is framed or acted, will enhance its criminality, and heighten its punishment.

'When he goes ashore he dares not shew his face as an honest man: he lurks in corners ashamed of himself, blushing for his conduct; he is obliged to associate with the most worthless diseased

eaſed wretches of both ſexes, from whom he catches every profligate habit, and contracts every loathſome diſeaſe ; while he is
forced to live on unwholeſome ſcraps, or to riſk his life in ſteal-
ing to ſatisfy his hunger. But he ſoon meets with ſome kid-
napper who ſells him to a cruel ſavage of a ſhipmaſter, perhaps
a foreigner, perhaps the enemy of his country, who works him
beyond his ſtrength, and then turns him aſhore in a ſtrange
country, cheated of his wages, unable to work for ſubſiſtence.
Perhaps a loathſome ditch receives his emaciated carcaſe, or he
wanders a bloated, diſeaſed vagabond, kept from day to day alive
by the reluctant hand of modern charity, an out-caſt from ſociety. Thus (for this is no feigned caſe) the deſerter is equally
a compound of iniquity and folly : he is falſe to his country,
cruel to himſelf, miſerable while he lives from dread of detection,
and abandoned in his diſtreſs by that ſociety which he refuſed to
ſerve.

    ' Set againſt him the ſober man, who chearfully ſerves his
country, and ſee if the different conditions will bear a compariſon. Firſt, the ſeaman's duty in a king's ſhip is in general
eaſier and better' timed than in the merchant ſervice, for which
the public is deſerted. In the navy, officers take a pride in exerting themſelves to get an healthy, vigorous ſhip's company.
Your health is conſulted, your ſickneſs is provided for. Though
your wages be nominally ſmaller than in the merchant ſervice,
yet you ſave moſt for your families in the public ſervice. If
you have any ambition to raiſe yourſelves in your profeſſion, there
are various offices to which, according to your qualifications,
you may be preferred, which give you eaſe in your duty, and
conſideration among your fellows : particularly a ſober, diligent
conduct recommends you to the confidence and good-will of your
officers ; and from my acquaintance with the ſervice, I think I
can with hardly a ſingle exception ſay, that I never knew a
quiet, diligent ſeaman, who was ill treated by any officer, or
who indeed was not a favourite with the officers in general. We
now and then meet with a crabbed, implacable officer : but it
muſt be confeſſed, that generally there are turbulent, diſobedient,
worthleſs men, ſufficient for the exerciſe of their ill-nature, to
be found in every ſhip, whom that love of juſtice that is inherent in even the moſt unfeeling hearts, points out as objects of
their ſeverity : as if both were brought together by Providence,
for the mutual puniſhment and plague of each other's reſtleſs, diſ-
agreeable qualities.

    ' If we take into account that very noble retreat which is pro-
vided for you in Greenwich Hoſpital, a chearful perſeverance in
the ſervice of your country is equally your intereſt and your
duty. You have applied yourſelves to a ſea-life. To paſs by
the conſideration of your country's having a claim to your ſervice which cannot be extinguiſhed, and of your obligation
when called on to defend her cauſe. The merchant ſervice cannot

not contend with the navy in eafineſs of duty, in opportunity of preferment, in real profit, in care when ſick, in a retreat for old age. Therefore the ſeaman who chearfully perſeveres in ferving his country, is both prudent and virtuous : in his country he has ſecured a protector and nurſe for his latter days ; he has made good men his benefactors, and God his friend.

' We have confidered the deſerter's guilt as a crime againſt thoſe fundamental laws of ſociety, which have God for their author, and certainly will have him for their avenger. But he who withdraws from the ſervice of his country, as far as in him lies, abandons her to the violence of the enemy, and is anſwerable in equity for every loſs and defeat which he might have helped to have prevented. He therefore is to be ſhunned, to be held in abhorrence by every honeſt man, as the deſtroyer of his country. The laws of every ſtate make his puniſhment death, and juſtly ; for in him you puniſh an enemy to his country, a diſobedient child, an unnatural parent, an unfeeling relation, a cruel neighbour : and ſuch a man's preparation to meet his God in judgment, ſhall be left to your own reflections.'

We have been more particular in our account of theſe diſcourſes, than we otherwiſe ſhould have been, as they are the firſt we have ſeen upon the ſubject, and have a confiderable ſhare of merit. We are ſorry however to reflect, that they certainly had more efficacy, when delivered by the preacher, than they are likely to have, when they are only ſubmitted to the peruſal of ſeamen.

Runic *Odes.* *Imitated from the* Norfe *Tongue.* *In the manner of* Mr. Gray. *By* Thomas James Mathias. 4to. 1s. 6d. T. Payne.

TO thoſe who are deeply ſkilled in the *Norfe* tongue, thoſe who prefer Oſſian to Homer, and Telieſſin to Milton, to thoſe who love *Runic* odes becauſe they are *Runic*, to all thoſe who are fond of the marvellous, the romantic, and the unintelligible, we recommend theſe poems, which, we doubt not, will give them the greateſt pleaſure, and afford the higheſt entertainment : at the ſame time we acknowlege ourſelves totally incapable of reliſhing ſuch ſublime beauties. The firſt Ode which we meet with in this collection carries us *beyond the viſible diurnal ſphere,* into regions, ideas, and manners far removed from this world and all that belongs to it. It is called the *Twilight of the Gods,* which, it ſeems, ' in the northern mythology is that period when the evil being ſhall break his confinement ; the human race, the ſtars, and the ſun ſhall diſappear ; the earth ſink in the ſeas, and fire conſume the ſkies ; even Odin himſelf and all his kindred gods ſhall periſh.'

1   *To*

To support this strange mythology, strange personages and strange ideas are introduced by the poet.

> ' From the regions of the south
> Surtur bursts with fiery mouth :
> High o'er yonder black'ning shade
> Gleams the hallow'd sun-bright blade,
> Which, in star-bespangled field,
> Warrior gods encount'ring wield.
> From vengeance' red celestial store,
> Ministers of ruin pour ;
> Caverns yawning, mountains rending :
> Conscious of the fate impending,
> Ydrasils prophetic ash
> Nods to the air with sudden crash :
> Monstrous female forms advance,
> Stride the steed, and couch the lance ;
> Armed heroes throng the road,
> All from Hela's dark abode ;
> And see, from either verge of heav'n,
> That concave vast asunder riv'n.
>   ' Why does beauteous Lina weep ?
> Whence those lorn notes in accent deep ?
> For battle Odin 'gins prepare ;
> Aloft in distant realms of air,
> Mark the murd'rous monster stalk,
> In printless majesty of walk.
> Odin kens his well-known tread ;
> The fatal sisters clip the thread :
> To the mansion cold he creeps—
> In vain the beauteous Lina weeps.'

The *printless majesty of walk* appears, at least to a mere English ear, rather uncouth ; but we do not understand *Norse*, from which it may, for aught we know, be a literal translation, as well as *creeping to the cold mansion*, which, we suppose is meant as a new phrase for *dying*.

The first Ode ends thus,

> ' No more this *pensile mundane* ball
> Rolls thro' the wide aereal hall ;
> Ingulphed sinks the vast machine.
> Who shall say, the things have been ?
> For lo ! the curtain close and murk
> Veils creation's ruin'd work.'

Here the translator must again have recourse to the Norse tongue, and plead his strict attachment to, and close imitation of the original, as he will not otherwise reconcile us to his *pensile mundane* balls, and *murk* curtains. The second Ode is called the Renovation of the World : the third, a Dialogue at the Tomb of Argantyr, between Hirvor and Argantur; the fourth is intituled, the Battle; the fifth, Tudor; and the sixth and laſt, an Incantation; all written in the ſame ſtrain. If any of our readers chuſe ſuch kind of ‘ Lenten entertainment,’ let them ſit down to it

> ‘ with what appetite they may.’

For our own parts, with all due deference to Norſe and Welch dainties, we muſt own a little plain ſolid Engliſh food is more ſuitable to our palates.

FOREIGN ARTICLES.

Mémoire hiſtorique ſur la Maladie ſingulière de la Veuve Mélin, dite la Femme-aux Ongles. Lû à la Faculté. Par M. Saillant. *8vo. Paris.*

THE diſeaſe here deſcribed, is by the author of this Memoir ſuppoſed to have been *a plica Polonica non explicata* ; it took its firſt riſe from the ſecond lying-in of the patient. A patient, indeed, ſhe was in every poſſible ſenſe of the word ; for it may juſtly be queſtioned whether all the records of human life and human miſeries, could produce one inſtance of ſufferings of any human creature, more multifarious and complicated, more acute, longer, and yet ſupported by a perſon of a delicate conſtitution, and uncommon ſenſibility, with ſuch a degree of fortitude, conſtancy, patience, and even ſerenity of mind, and reſignation to the will of her Creator.

The whole account of this complication of ſufferings cannot poſſibly be read without a mixture of the deepeſt compaſſion, of horror, diſguſt, and amazement. Phyſicians, however, philoſophers, and divines ought to read the whole of it : though we muſt confine ourſelves to a mere tranſient glance on this ſpectacle of human woes. On a whole human body miſerably diſtorted in all its parts from its natural frame, and entirely helpleſs : inſtead of nails on hands and feet, a ſpecies of loathſome claws, continually ſuppurating, and inhabited by neſts of excruciating and indeſtructive inſects ; fingers contracted, monſtrouſly thick, and inflamed : a mouth without teeth, full of ulcers, and inceſſantly ſalivating, &c. From the firſt beginning of the diſeaſe the patient became totally blind, and her hearing too ſeemed frequently endangered. For twenty-two years together, ſhe could hardly change the excruciating poſture of her body, for an inſtant. Add to this, frequent itchings, and anxieties, a quick ſenſibility of temper, a delicate frame ; once a *total want of ſleep for three years together !* during the courſe of this diſeaſe ſeveral attacks by other acute diſeaſes ; this ſcene of miſery protracted through twenty-four years ſucceſſively, amidſt the preſſure of poverty, ſupported by alms, and at laſt concluded, not by the natural reſult of the diſeaſe itſelf, but by ſome ſpoonfuls of ſtrong liquors given to the patient.

In all this immenſe and unutterable miſery, ſays the author, the patient preſerved ſuch a patience, tranquillity, reſignation, and even a chearfulneſs, as could not poſſibly ſpring from any other ſource than a beneficent and enlightened religion : it is alſo remarkable
that

that her face has continued rather handsome, and preserved the signs of virtuous serenity.   She died in the forty seventh year of her age; her corpse was dissected: the skeleton, with an arm, preserved in spirits, were by Mr. Saillant presented to the College of Physicians at Paris, who preserve the whole, with her portrait, and a suitable instruction: and have ordered this Memoir to be printed and published.

Précis d'une Histoire générale de la Vie privée des François dans tous les tems et dans toutes les Provinces de la Monarchie.   1 vol. 8vo. Paris.

THIS volume is intended only for a short abstract of the contents of a much larger work, which the authors propose to publish in four volumes in quarto, illustrated with a great number of copper plates: and of which the first will treat of viands and food; the second of dwellings; the third of dresses and fashions; and the fourth of entertainments, amusements, games, &c. The present summary abstract of the subjects of each respective section of the future work, is well calculated to inspire its readers with a favourable opinion of the work, and with an eager desire of seeing the whole published, and supported throughout with the necessary proofs; which are here promised. The authors have the use of a large library, and of a number of scarce MSS. they often appeal to old pictures, and to other monuments.

They will begin with an history of the culture of the various species of corn, of culinary plants, &c. in France. The invention of the art of refining sugar is here placed in the year 1420. Chocolate was introduced by the queen of Lewis XIV. A section will treat of the various kinds of furniture. Table cloths have for a long time been of woollen; table linen is said to have been first fabricated at Rheims. The use of forks was not yet known under the Merovingian kings. Stoves were already used in 1338 in the king's palace; the various revolutions of the head-dresses will be described from ancient paintings. Perfumed gloves were introduced in France by an Italian, count Frangipani, in the times of Catherine de Medicis. The first lace was imported from Venice and Genoa; as it drained the kingdom of considerable sums. a prohibition was issued in 1629. to wear any lace of a higher price than three livres per French ell: and as none of so low a price were to be got, this prohibition gave rise to the lace-manufactories in Picardy. Many fashions have been obtruded on the French by foreigners: who, however, have the comfort of boasting their improvements on foreign inventions: ' Nous adoptons, say they, quelquefois les modes de nos voisins: mais bientôt après nous les leur renvoyons perfectionnés, et après leur avoir donné le bon tour et le bon air qu'on ne trouve qu'en France.'

The origin of card-playing is here placed, as usual, in the reign of Charles VI. and piquet is said to be one of the most ancient games. Whist is thought to be an English invention, ill calculated for the vivacity of French men; and, on that account, already supplanted by the sprightlier game of trisette.

De

De prima Expeditione Attilæ, *Regis* Hunnorum, *in* Gallias, *ac de Rebus geftis* Waltharii Aquitanorum *Principis, Carmen Epicum Seculi VI. ex Cod. MS. Membranaceo optimæ notæ, fummâ Fide defcriptum, nunc primum in Lucem produ&um, et omni Antiquitatum genere, imprimis vero Monumentis coævis, illuftratum et adau&um a* Frid. Chriftoph. Jonath. Fifcher, J. C. Haienfi. 10 *Sheets large Quarto.* Leipzig.

THIS poem was difcovered by M. de Moſheim, in a MS. of the thirteenth century, which had been fent him from a certain convent in Bavaria. He copied it, and gave his copy with the original to the editor, who has publiſhed it with a learned commentary. His notes were then examined by Dr. Biefter, who fubjoined his corrections of the readings of fome paffages.

Dr. Fifcher concludes from the firſt line,

' Tertia pars orbis *fratres,* Europa vocatur,'

that the author of this poem was a monk. The age of the poem he appears to determine by the analogy of its ſtyle to that of fome other poems of the fixth century, and by the manners delineated in it. Some paffages of it are borrowed from Virgil; others feem to bear fome relation to paffages from Homer. The language is often mixed with Celtic and German words: and the contents, efpecially thofe relating to Attila, coincide with the accounts given of him by Prifcus, Jornandes, and other contemporary writers.

The editor has been at great pains in his preface to prove the uſe of this *fragment,* for hiſtory, politics, and jurifprudence: for it is but a fragment, broke off with the 1333d verfe in the midſt of a fight between three of its perfonages.

FOREIGN LITERARY INTELLIGENCE.

Om gamle Danſke *Gilder og deres Undergang;* or, *on the ancient* Daniſh *Guilds, and their Extinction.* 8vo. Copenhagen. (Daniſh.)

THIS treatife confiders the conſtitution of the ancient Daniſh guſlds, only with regard to its influence on the adminiſtration of juſtice: though the author has, in his preface, gratified thofe who are defirous of more ample and more complete information, with an enumeration of many German and all the Daniſh works on this fubject; and given fome curious accounts of the origin and conſtitution of all guilds and fraternities.

Statiftica Ecclefiæ Germanicæ. *Edidit in Ufum Auditorum fuorum* Franc. Xaver. Holl. *SS. Th. et J. V. D. Juris Eccl. in Univ.* Heidelbergenfi *Pr. P. O. Tom. I.* 8vo. Heidelberg.

A learned and ufeful performance, though not entirely free from partiality.

Ifaac *et* Rebecca, *ou les Nôces Patriarchales, Poëme en Profe en cinq Chants.* 12mo. Paris.

A new edition of a poem in which M. le Suire has attempted, with fome fuccefs, to imitate Mr. Gefner's poem, the Death of Abel.

Histoire générale et particulière de la Grèce ; contenant l'Origine, le Progrès, et la Décadence des Loix, des Sciences, des Arts, des Lettres, de la Philosophie, &c. Précédée d'une Déscription Géographique, &c. et terminée par le Parallele des Grecs anciens avec les Grecs modernes. Par M. Cousin Despréaux, *&c.* 4 *vols.* 12mo. Paris.

These four first volumes bring the history of the Greeks down to the times of the Trojan war. They are therefore only the beginning of a voluminous, but, at the same time, a valuable work.

Théorie de l' Intérêt de l'Argent, tirées des Principes du Droit naturel, de la Théologie, et de la Politique, contre l'Abus de l'Imputation de l' Usure. 12mo. Paris.

A judicious performance, in which the author appears to have steered the middle course between two extremes.

Poëme sur la Mort de l'Impératrice-Reine Marie-Thérése d'Autriche. *Par M.* de Rochefort, *&c.* 4to. Paris.

The best and only valuable panegyric on virtuous sovereigns is an impartial history of their lives and reigns. To feel all the merit of the late empress-queen, we need only recollect in what a situation she found her dominions at her accession, and contrast it with the state of prosperity in which she left them, when she breathed her last vows and sighs for their happiness, and that of mankind.

'Absint inani funere Næniæ,
Luctusque turpes et querimoniæ!
Compesce clamorem, ac sepulchri.
Mitte supervacuos honores l'

Analyse des Infiniment petits pour l'Intelligence des Lignes Courbes. Par M. le Marquis de l'Hopital. 4to. Paris.

The merit of this classical work is well known. It has run through several editions. The present one is illustrated and improved with many excellent notes by M. le Fevre.

Analyse sur l'Ame des Bêtes. Lettres Philosophiques. 8vo. Paris.

This writer proposes a new system on the souls of brutes. He allows them a spiritual and intelligent soul; but limits their knowlege to physical good and evil only; and endeavours to make his theory agree with the Bible.

*Lettere Odeporiche d'*Angelo Gualandris. 8vo. *in* Venezia.

The result of travels undertaken by the command of the republic of Venice, and at the expence of the univerfity of Padua, through Italy, Swifferland, France, and England. They relate to natural history, mineralogy, botany, &c. and though the greater part of the objects are merely enumerated, they may yet prove useful to future travelling naturalists.

Monitum ad Observatores, Societatis Meteorologicæ Palatinæ *a Serenissimo Electore* Carolo Theodoro *recens institutæ.* 4to. Manheim.

Containing a plan of the meteorological observations undertaken by the society lately established for that purpose by the elector Palatine. This society wishes for correspondents willing to contribute observations, made with similar instruments, which he offers, on the part of his electoral highness, to furnish to those who would assiduously employ themselves on such enquiries.

Assemblée publique de la Société Royale des Sciences, tenue en Présence des Etats de la Province de Languedoc. 4to.

A collection containing the eulogies of the late chevalier Linnæus, and of the cardinal de la Roche-Aymon; with some useful memoirs and observations on various subjects.

La Découverte australe par un Homme volant ; ou, le Dédale François : *Nouvelle très-philosophique : suivie de la Lettre d'un Singe, &c. Avec une Estampe à chaque fait principal.* 4 *vols.* 12mo. Paris.

A very strange, fanciful, and grotesque performance, by that fertile writer, M. Rétif de la Bretonne.

MONTHLY CATALOGUE.

✓ POLITICAL.

Principles of Law and Government, with an Inquiry into the Justice and Policy of the present War, and most effectual Means of obtaining an honourable, permanent, and advantageous Peace. 4to. 7s. 6d. Murray.

SINCE the commencement of the present dispute with America, the partizans for the colonies have frequently resorted to abstract principles, in justification of the revolt. For the same purpose have been invented systems of government, equally ideal and inconformable to the most established rules of political administration. The treatise now before us appears to have been written with a similar view. It is divided into two parts: in the former of which the author treats of the origin of law and government; of different forms of government; and of the dissolution of law and government. The latter part consists of an inquiry into the justice and policy of the present war, and the most effectual means of obtaining an honourable, permanent, and advantageous peace. It were superfluous to prosecute an inquiry which has so often undergone examination, both in literary controversy and public debate. We shall, therefore, only observe, that this writer, however systematic his theory, deviates in nothing essentially from the commonly received notions of law and government; but endeavours to adapt them to an extension of American privileges, which, in the present stage of the dispute, cannot admit, on the side of Great Britain, to become the subject of deliberation.—The author has subjoined an Appendix, containing some extracts relative to criminal justice, and the laws of imprisonment, from Mr. De Lolme's account of the English government.

Two additional Letters to Count Welderen *on the present Situation of Affairs between* Great Britain *and the* United Provinces. *By* John Andrews, *LL.D.* 8vo. 2s. White.

In our Review for February, we gave an account of Dr. Andrews' two former Letters; where he placed in the strongest

light

light the impolitic and unjustifiable conduct of the Dutch, in uniting with the enemies of Great Britain, against a nation which has so long been the faithful ally of Holland, and the surest defence of the states against the dangerous power of the house of Bourbon. In the Letters now before us, he continues to paint, with the same force of argument, the pernicious consequences of those measures; not only hazardous to Great Britain, considering the extent of the war which she has at present to maintain, but ultimately, perhaps, destructive of the independence of the Dutch. These Letters are no less distinguished by the just and sensible observations with which they abound, than by the author's candour and liberality, so conspicuous even amidst the indignation which the subject cannot but frequently suggest.

Dissertation on National Assemblies under the Saxon *and* Norman *Governments. With a Postscript addressed to the Dean of Glocester. By* James Ibbetson, *Esq.* 4to. 2s. Faulder.

This treatise is the production of James Ibbetson, esq. barrister at law, who investigates the constitution of parliament with great perspicuity. The Dissertation is divided into two sections, the former of which relates to the Saxon, and the latter to the Norman government. Mr. Ibbetson explodes the opinion of those who maintain that the general assemblies, in their original state, were composed entirely of the feudal vassals. He observes, that at the establishment of the fiefs in England, as well as in France, the allodial property was extensively diffused, and of the freest and most independent nature; though, in the advanced state of the feudal government, the immediate vassals of the crown had a decided superiority. On taking a short view of the Saxon constitution, Mr. Ibbetson admits in it a degree of imbecility; but the idea of its total inefficacy he utterly disapproves.

From the remarks which the author has made in the course of his enquiry, he concludes that the national assembly of the Saxons asserted the right of electing its supreme magistrate: that it possessed the legislative, the judicial, and the fiscal powers; and that the people had a considerable share in the direction of its councils, and the confirmation of its decrees.

Mr. Ibbetson observes that the Norman conquest is the epoch whence we justly date the perfection and the corruption of the feudal establishment; but that the tyranny which succeeded this period, conduced afterwards to essential improvements of the constitution. In this Dissertation, the author has greatly elucidated the ranks of the different members of the ancient parliaments, with their legislative and political authority. A Postscript is added, in which Mr. Ibbetson, in support of his own observations, makes some remarks, relative to the Gothic constitution, on the Dean of Gloucester's Treatise on Civil Government.

Plan

Plan for the better Relief and Employment of the Poor; for enforcing and amending the Laws respecting Houses of Correction, and Vagrants; and for improving the Police of this Country. Together with Bills offered to Parliament for those Purposes. By Thomas Gilbert, *Esq.* 8vo. 2s. 6d. Wilkie.

The author of this Plan is a member of parliament, who appears to have considered the subject with great attention. Mr. Gilbert observes, that the distressed state of the poor, notwithstanding the great amount of the poor-rates, calls for the speedy and effectual interposition of the legislature. With this view he judiciously investigates the causes, and points out the remedy, of the above mentioned evil. The causes he assigns are, idleness, profligacy, and a relaxation of the laws; and the remedy he proposes is labour and industry, enforced by a vigorous and spirited execution of the acts of parliament, rendered more effectual by a few amendments. To facilitate the accomplishment of this purpose, Mr. Gilbert has drawn up three bills; the first of which is for the better relief and employment of the poor; the second, to amend, and render more effectual, the laws in being relative to houses of correction; and the third, to amend and make more effectual the laws relative to rogues, vagabonds, and other idle and disorderly persons. To the several bills are subjoined rules, orders, and regulations, well calculated to promote the laudable reformation which the author proposes.

The Irenarch: or Justice of Peace's Manual. II. Miscellaneous Reflections upon the Laws, Policy, Manners, &c. III. An Assize Sermon, preached at Leicester, 12 August, 1756. *By* Ralph Heathcote, *D. D.* 8vo. 3s. T. Payne.

A considerable part of this publication consists of miscellaneous reflections on laws, policy, manners, &c. in a dedication to lord Mansfield.

One great object of the author is ' to oppose and check that outrageous, indiscriminate, and boundless invective, which has been repeatedly levelled at this illustrious character: that cruel, injurious, unrelenting malignity, which overlooking or misrepresenting the great and good in a character, and fastening upon foibles, imperfections, and infirmities, delights to worry down, and tear it to pieces.'—This dedication was first printed in 1774.

The Irenarch is a small tract on the office of a justice of the peace, its origin, nature, extent, and limits; and the qualifications necessary to discharge it laudably.

The primary qualifications, which, he says, are necessary to make a wise and good magistrate, are these: a quick, clear, and sound understanding, a perfect knowlege of the world, a competent acquaintance with the laws and constitution of his country, a love of justice, and a spirit of moderation. But he observes, there are several secondary or inferior qualities, which

ar

are neceſſary to render this magiſtrate as perfect as he means to repreſent him. The grand point, therefore, to which all his endowments muſt be directed, is to decide, according to right, with preciſion and accuracy. For this purpoſe he muſt hear with affability, examine with deliberation, keep within the bounds of his office, be of a compoſing, and pacific ſpirit, and ſtrictly abſtain from every thing, that bears even the moſt diſtant appearance of profit to himſelf.—This tract was printed in 1771.

In a poſtſcript to this piece, he grounds an apology for a ſuppoſed neglect in juſtices to execute the laws as they ought, upon this ſuppoſition, that manners will always controul and govern laws, and that juſtices muſt therefore be content to execute laws, as they can. This poſition he endeavours to evince by an appeal to the experience of ages, to the teſtimonies of legiſlators and ſtateſmen, and to the laws againſt ſwearing, drinking, duelling and bribing at elections.—This poſtſcript was printed with the dedication in 1774.

The obſervations, which the author has advanced on the foregoing ſubjects, are illuſtrated by notes, and extracts from the moſt eminent writers, ancient and modern.

At the concluſion is ſubjoined an Aſſize-Sermon on the words of Micah, ' What doth the Lord require of thee,' &c. ſhewing, that to do juſtly and to love mercy includes our civil, and to walk humbly with God, our religious duty ; or, in other words, that morality and religion are eſſential to ſociety.

By theſe tracts our author appears to be no enthuſiaſt in his views of reformation ; but to be actuated by proper notions of human nature, and the principles of calm and deliberate reaſon.

D I V I N I T Y.

Ethics, rational and theological, with curſory Reflections on the general Principles of Deiſm. By John Groſe, *F. A. S. 8vo. 6s. ſewed.* Faulder.

This volume contains about thirty eſſays on happineſs, religion, friendſhip, truth, wiſdom, virtue, vice, and other moral ſubjects. The author poſſeſſes a lively imagination ; but writes in ſuch a flowery ſtyle, that one of his deſcriptions is like a picture, ſet off with all the colours of the rain-bow.

Two or three ſentences from this volume will be ſufficient.

' Envy in its ſable garb, with piteous and diſtreſſing mein, that fain would veil the glittering orb of bliſs, with dark tempeſtuous clouds, is now transformed into a beam of love, that penetrates the remoteſt corners of the earth. Pride, that devouring locuſt, which preys on intellective reaſon,—contaminates the ſenſes,—debilitates the will, is changed into the admired flower of humility, and tranſplanted into the garden of eternal love.'

The reader may probably imagine, that this ſentence appears to diſadvantage, by being detached from the context. We ſhall therefore preſent him with the firſt paragraph from our author's Eſſay on Vice.

' At

' At the earlieſt period of time, when innocence ornamented humanity,—and purity wore an earthly form, extatic bliſs reigned with uninterrupted ſway, and illuminated every trace of being — Danger was hitherto unknown,—fear had never ſhewn its affrighted aſpect,—nor diſtreſs its armed hoſt. Reflection yielded a ſucceſſion of increaſing joys—thought was the ſeed-time of apparent eaſe, and revolving moments as the harveſt of complete fruition.—Encircled by the chearing rays of unremitting bliſs, nature exhilarated the happy pair with continual delights, and proved, in majeſtic luſtre, its author to be divine.—But ſad to relate,—the fatal hour arrived when ſpotleſs innocence exchanged its beauteous garb, for that of vice. A midnight gloom pervades the tragic ſcene,—and ſhame veils guilt with awe. Horror ſtalks into the maze of life, and ſonorous vengeance is in idea heard,—reſentment is the expected meſſenger of woe, and injured juſtice the executioner of man.—What conſcious innocence had emboldened to enjoy, guilt with acrimony forbids,—and flight proves the fancied refuge of an enfeebled—fallen creature.'

This glittering, gaudy, and fantaſtic language can only be agreeable to thoſe, who have no taſte for natural ſimplicity.

A ſtrict Conformity between our Prayers and Actions earneſtly recommended, in a Sermon preached at Whittingham, Northumberland, Feb. 10, 1779, *being the General Faſt. By the rev.* J. Twentyman. *Small 8vo. 6d.*

A plain, practical diſcourſe, on Iſaiah i. 19, 20. ' If ye be willing and obedient, &c.' ſuited to the capacities of a country congregation.

Grace without Enthuſiaſm. A Sermon preached at the Pariſh Church of All Saints, Colcheſter, *on* Trinity Sunday, 1781. *By* Nathaniel Forſter, *D. D. 2vo. 6d.* Robinſon.

A rational and uſeful diſcourſe, in which the author, in oppoſition to the Methodiſts and other enthuſiaſts, very clearly ſhews, that the Holy Spirit may be properly ſaid to aſſiſt all Chriſtians, as well in the knowlege, as in the practice of their duty, without any infringement on the freedom of their rational powers, by the plain rule of life, which is laid before them in the goſpel ; and that neither the ſcriptures, nor the articles or the liturgy of our church, authorize us to ſay, that it is neceſſary for us to *feel*, to *know*, to have *experimental conviction* of the divine operation on the mind, before we have any ground to hope that we are in a ſtate of ſalvation.

CONTROVERSIAL.

Whiſpers for the Ear of the Author of Thelyphthora, *in favour of Reaſon and Religion, aſperſed through that Work. By* E. B. Greene, *Eſq. 8vo. 2s. 6d.* H. Payne.

In romance we read of giants, inhabiting enchanted caſtles, deflowering virgins, and committing depredations on the adjacent country. The author of Thelyphthora is one of this class. Under the specious pretence of protecting innocent and helpless maidens, he seizes them by dozens, and conveys them to a dungeon, called the Castle of Polygamy; where he shuts them up for life, and consigns them to the demons of lust, envy, spleen, vexation, and discord. Several knights-errant have already encountered the giant, and given him many furious blows. But he still maintains his ground, and defends himself by *three brazen* walls, which he thinks impregnable. His present antagonist is styled the knight of the *Green* armour. On former occasions he has distinguished himself by feats of chivalry in Greece and Latium, where he paraded in a *glittering* coat of mail, on a snow-white palfry, *richly caparisoned*; and, mistaking his friends for his foes, laid many an ancient hero at his feet. This attack upon the giant is only the prelude to a more serious and determined onset: for hitherto he has only reconnoitred the enemy, brandished his flaming sword, and displayed some manoeuvres of a mysterious nature. In his second engagement, he is to meet him on sacred ground, ' with the Bible in one hand, and Thelyphthora in the other;' when the caitiff, we make no doubt, will be completely defeated, the captive damsels restored to liberty, and the enchanted castle levelled with the ground.

P O E T R Y.

Poems on various Subjects. Small 8vo. 2s. 6d. Richardson *and* Urquhart.

In this volume of poems, written, as we learn from a copy of verses inserted amongst them, by a young gentleman lately of the Marischal College of Aberdeen, there is little to be blamed, and still less to be commended; they flow on in an easy strain of mediocrity, and neither awaken contempt and resentment, or command attention and applause.

There are, however, some parts of it not without poetical merit, particularly the Ode to Sensibility, the Ode to Friendship, and the Ode to Simplicity; the last of which, as a specimen of our author's manner, we shall lay before our readers.

' O D E to SIMPLICITY.

' Thou heart-commanding, modest power !
Of nature born in sylvan bower;
More sweet art thou in native grace,
Than gayest Art with fashion'd face,
That tries, with tints and rich perfume,
To emulate thy breath and bloom.
Simplicia see all form'd to please,
With untaught elegance and ease;
But school'd by Affectation's care,
She struts with stiff pedantic air,

With

With ftrained fmile and tortur'd eye,
That fparely throws the glance from high.
How impotent fuch efforts prove,
To warm the tender heart to love !
It fcorns the glofs, and cold recoils
From fuch prepofterous, wreathed wiles.
—O fweet Simplicity ! what art
Can thee forego and catch the heart ?
How vain the lifelefs, flowery lays
Bedaub'd with cumbrous foreign phrafe,
By foppifh Fancy trimly wrought,
To hide her want of burning thought !
  ' Difdaining now thy precepts plain,
How rambles rude th' Hefperian ftrain,
That once, when owning thy control,
With fimple note could melt the foul !
Now rais'd aloud, with trilling pride,
Of paffion and expreffion void,
It drives with idle, mad career,
Grates harfhnefs on the tingling ear.
How loft the artlefs powers of fong,
Unknown fave woods and vales among !
  ' Yet oft, by Art's fubmiffive aid,
Thy charms more pleafing are difplay'd ;
When by thy rule, fhe works unknown,
Nor claims the merit as her own.
Thou, deck'd by her, art more admir'd
She pleafes more, as more retir'd.
Thy manner fpeaks the noble mind :
And hollow Art, the little foul confin'd.'

This Ode ends rather abruptly : and *void* and *pride* are bad rhymes. We would advife this young author, whofe faults his age will in fome meafure excufe, and which, therefore, we fhall not point out, not to publifh every thing which he writes; but, for the future, notwithftanding what a circle of flattering friends may fay, to remember that a few verfes well-written, and carefully correfted, will give him more reputation than half a dozen fuch volumes as that which he has already produced.

A Poetical Epiftle from Petrarch *to* Laura. 4to. 1s. Walter.

The author of this Epiftle has rather imprudently taken upon him the name of *Petrarch*, one of the moft elegant Italian writers ; and, in confequence of fo bold an attempt, has addreffed his *Laura* in a ftyle very different from that which fhe had been fo long ufed to from the pen of her enraptured poet. When a gentleman, inftead of fculking in a domino at a mafquerade, chufes to affume a *character*, he fhould always confider whether he has parts and genius to fupport it. That our poetical incognito could never be miftaken for *Petrarch*, will appear from
the

the following lines, which we meet with in the beginning of the Epiftle.

'Say, lovely Laura, can my foul forget
Thy fplendid form in this ferene retreat?
Can Reafon's voice my ardent love reftrain?
Can Reafon teach me that my love is vain?
Not all the powers of abfence can impart
Relief, or foothe to reft my wounded heart:
Thy beauteous image haunts this ftill abode,
And fighs for Laura mix with prayers to God.
'Yet, why fhould I the glittering pile deftroy
Of fond illufions which my foul employ?
From memory's tablet raze the form divine,
Where winning grace and rigid virtue fhine?
No, in the deep recefles of my heart,
With joy I'll cherifh each deftructive dart;
Recall each dear idea of my love,
And all the fweets of meditation prove.
'Within thofe walls where Clara's virgin choir
With warbled ftrains the facred flame infpire,
And each glad heart its thankful tribute pays
Of hymn, harmonious in its Maker's praife:
There (whilft I liften'd to the mattin lay,
That feem'd to gratulate the dawn of day)
I firft beheld the fource of each delight;
There firft my Laura blefs'd my ravifh'd fight.
Wild, as a ftag untam'd, I erft had rov'd,
And often thought, but never found I lov'd;
Defires compos'd each cold affection rear'd,
Whofe gelid influence banifh'd warm regard:
But every nerve, in that propitious hour,
Qwn'd in reality love's mighty power;
That heart then felt the force of each bright charm,
Which long had baffled every foft alarm.
What keen emotions then awak'd my foul!
My eyes entranc'd alternate glances ftole;
They now devour'd the beauteous fmiles that grac'd
Each lovely feature:—now with rapture trac'd
The lines expreffive of a fofter fenfe,
And looks that beam'd with fweet benevolence.
The auburn treffes love had wove to warm,
With nature's fhade adorn'd each glowing charm.
The violet form, in richeft purple dreft,
With pleafing luftre deck'd the verdant veft;
Whilft every elegance of air, betray'd
Celeftial limbs in heavenly robes array'd.'

In thefe lines the reader will be able to find very little refemblance of the tender, pathetic, and ingenious Italian bard; as they are all

feeble,

feeble, languid, and miserably inferior to the great exemplar in diction, sentiment, and every requisite of true poetry : the idea of *cherishing a dart*, and *baffling soft alarms*, even borders on the burlesque and ridiculous ; and the phrase which our author introduces of *in reality*, is certainly, to say no worse of it, very *unpoetical*. We must beg leave also to observe, that this writer's rhymes are extremely incorrect and unwarrantable, as there is very little similarity of sound in *wild* and *fill'd*, *beam* and *flame*, *good* and *road*, with many others, which seem as cross to each other, and to answer as unkindly, as Laura did to her faithful Petrarch. We should advise this gentleman therefore, who, in our opinion, has not enough in him either of the lover or the poet to pass for a *Petrarch*, to assume, at the next literary masquerade, some character which will suit him better ; and in which we heartily wish him more success.

Poems, by the rev. Mr. Logan, *one of the Ministers of* Leith. 8vo. 2s. 6d. Cadell.

In these Poems, written by the ingenious Mr. Logan, there is a fine flow of numbers, and great command of language ; the verse is, in general, very correct ; and the sentiments and reflections much superior to what we generally meet with in love sonnets. The following lines, extracted from an Ode on the Death of a young Lady, are remarkably elegant and pathetic.

‘ O from thy kindred early torn,
And to thy grave untimely borne !
Vanish'd for ever from my view,
Thou sister of my soul, adieu !

‘ Fair with my first ideas twin'd,
Thine image oft will meet my mind ;
And, while remembrance brings thee near,
Affection sad will drop a tear.

‘ How oft does sorrow bend the head,
Before we dwell among the dead !
Scarce in the years of manly prime,
I've often wept the wrecks of time.

‘ What tragic tears bedew the eye !
What deaths we suffer ere we die !
Our broken friendships we deplore,
And loves of youth that are no more !

‘ No after-friendship e'er can raise
Th' endearments of our early days ;
And ne'er the heart such fondness prove,
As when it first began to love.’

This is the voice of nature, and the language of the heart. The Ode to Women has great merit. Our readers will be obliged to us for the two last stanzas ; where the poet, after advising the ladies to trust to nature, and despise the fashionable assistance of art, thus illustrates his doctrine.

‘ The

' The midnight minstrel of the grove,
Who still rehews the hymn of love,
   And woes the wood to hear;
Knows not the sweetness of his strain,
Nor that, above the tuneful train,
   He charms the lover's ear.
' The zone of Venus, heavenly-fine,
Is Nature's handy-work divine,
   And not the web of art;
And they who wear it never know
To what enchanting charm they owe
   The empire of the heart.'

The poem in this collection called the Lovers, is extremely well written, as well as the Tale which follows it; but they are both too long. The hymns at the end are, like all other hymns, dull and tiresome.—From the specimen, notwithstanding, which we have given of Mr. Logan's poetry, our readers will perceive that his Pegasus has fire and spirit; and that when he comes hereafter to take longer journies, and mend his pace, he will make no inconsiderable figure in the regions of Parnassus.

✓ N O V E L.

The Revolution, a Novel, in four Volumes. Vol. I. Small 8vo. 2s. 6d. Fielding.

We are informed by an advertisement, that the author of this production, who died in 1774, was a youth under eighteen; that he never had a classical education; and that at the time he composed this work, he earned his bread by hard labour. In such circumstances, it cannot be suprising, if he should not attain that fame, which, we are told, was the object of his ambition. He had, it seems, designed the work on the plan of an epic poem, and had at first introduced machinery; but afterwards altered those parts. The manuscript, it is said, would make four such volumes as the present; and the whole was completed in the space of eight or nine months. A work the production of so young a man, composed under so great disadvantages, and deprived of his corrections, it would be hard to judge with any degree of severity. Suffice it to say, that the work discovers an invention far beyond what might be expected from the youth and situation of the author; and which, if employed on a more interesting subject, under the judgment of maturer age, might have procured his name a monument among those who have been distinguished by genius.

✓ M E D I C A L.

An Account of a Method of preserving Water at Sea from Putrefaction, &c. By Thomas Henry, F. R. S. 8vo. 2s. Johnson.

A method of preserving water free from putrefaction was some years since proposed by the late Dr. Alston of Edinburgh. It con-

consisted in adding to each cask of water a quantity of lime, which by its antiseptic property produced the desired effect. To free the water, at the time of using it, from the lime, Dr. Alston proposed the precipitation of the latter, by adding a quantity of magnesia alba. The expence attending this process, however, having prevented the doctor's proposal from being carried into execution, Mr. Henry has contrived a method of precipitating the lime by means of calcareous earth and the vitriolic acid, which may be afforded at a very trifling expence. He describes with great accuracy, as well as illustrates by plates, both the process and the vessels for conducting it; subjoining likewise a method of impregnating water in large quantities with fixed air, for the use of the sick on board of ships, and in hospitals; besides a process for obtaining artificial yeast, Pyrmont water, and Seltzer water; with the following method of preserving Mr. Bewly's julep.

'Dissolve three drams of fossil alkali in each quart of water, and throw in streams of fixed air, till the alkaline taste be destroyed, and the water have acquired an agreeable pungency. This julep should not be prepared in too large quantities; and should be kept in bottles very closely corked and sealed. Four ounces of it may be taken at a time, drinking a draught of lemonade, or water acidulated with vinegar, or weak spirit of vitriol, by which means the fixed air will be extricated in the stomach.'

Mr. Henry has added a Postscript, containing an answer to such objections as may be made to the method of preserving water from putrefaction. The assiduity with which he has prosecuted the subject, deserves great commendation; and we should be extremely glad to find that his laudable efforts for preserving the health of our seamen, have been seconded by those who have the direction of the naval department.

The Conductor and Containing Splints; or, a Description of Two Instruments for the safer Conveyance and more perfect Cure of Fractured Legs. Third Edition. By Jonathan Wathen, *F. R. S. 8vo. 1s. 6d.* Cadell.

Some years ago, the author of this pamphlet, Mr. Wathen, published a description of two machines: one for carrying, and the other for the more easy cure of a fractured leg. In the present edition, he relates some improvements which he has made on his former invention. We are now also presented with the representation of two new invented tourniquets; constructed in such a manner as to be easy of application, and capable of being instantly slackened, tightened, or removed at pleasure. The invention discovers mechanical ingenuity, and merits the attention of surgeons.

Account

Account of an Elaſtic Trochar, conſtructed on a new Principle of Tapping the Hydrocele. By John Andree. 8vo. 1s. L. Davis.

This inſtrument conſiſts of two parts, viz. the ſtilet, or perforator, and the canula. The whole of the ſtilet, excepting its point, is contained within the canula, which is a flat tube, but ſomewhat convex on each ſurface, and has two ſharp edges. The canula is formed of two pieces of well-tempered elaſtic ſteel, accurately fitted together at their edges. When the inſtrument has been paſſed into the body, on withdrawing the ſtilet with the ſmalleſt degree of force, the canula opens juſt wide enough to allow of its exit, and cloſes immediately after, by its own elaſticity. Previous to the account of this trochar, Mr. Andree ſhews the inconvenience of that which has hitherto been uſed; clearly evincing the ſuperiority of the new trochar from two conſiderations. One is, that it gives much leſs pain in the operation; and the other, that it may be uſed with perfect ſafety in an early ſtage of dropſical ſwellings. This inſtrument appears to be a great improvement on the former trochar; and will, we doubt not, be generally adopted in practice.

An Addreſs to the Nobility and Gentry of both Sexes, on the great and good Effects of the Univerſal Medicine of the ancient Magi; being the grand and inviolable Secret of Maſonry. By S. Freeman, M. D. 8vo. 6d.

The title of this pamphlet is, we preſume, ſufficient to give our readers a juſt idea of its futility. It is a rhapſody of jargon, calculated to impoſe upon the ignorant under the ſemblance of abſtruſe knowlege; equally deſtitute of ſcience and of truth, and myſterious only by its own abſurdity.

Obſervations on the Diſeaſes which appeared in the Army on St. Lucia, *in* 1778, *and* 1779. *Small* 8vo. 2s. ſewed. Dilly.

Mr. Rollo, the author of this treatiſe, beſide a general account of St. Lucia, gives a deſcription of the ſeveral places in that iſland which were occaſionally occupied by the army during the ſickly ſeaſons in 1778 and 1779. The diſeaſes then moſtly prevalent were intermittents, remitting fevers, and the dyſentery; which Mr. Rollo imputes principally to the putrid air of the marſhes. Reſpecting the treatment of the tertian, the author informs us, that having cleared the firſt paſſages, they always gave a combination of tartar emetic and opium in ſolution, after the cold ſtage began to diſappear. In the remittent, the moſt effectual means for procuring a diſtinct remiſſion, was found to be nauſeating doſes of tartar emeric; giving, at the time of the uſual exacerbation of the fever, an opiate by itſelf, or combined with an antimonial, according to the ſtate of the ſtomach, in the ſame manner as after the cold ſtage of an intermittent. In the dyſentery, after diſcharging the vitiated contents of the ſtomach and

bowels,

bowels, the best remedy was found to be opium, assisted by diet, air, and cleanliness The treatise contains many observations which may be highly useful to practitioners in the West Indies ; and the author has added a short and judicious address to military gentlemen, on the means of preserving health in those climates.

✓MISCELLANEOUS.

The Ancient and Modern History of Gibraltar, *and the Sieges and Attacks it hath sustained, &c.* By J. S. Dodd. 8vo. 3s. Murray.

This production commences with a short description, and historical account, of Gibraltar ; extracted, it is probable, from a large work on the same subject, published a few years since, by an officer of the army. So far the author might entertain some hope of gratifying curiosity : but more than the half of the volume consists of a minute, uninteresting journal of the siege of Gibraltar by the Spaniards, in 1727. What purpose such a narrative can answer, we are quite at a loss to determine.

A Month's Tour in North Wales, Dublin, *and its Environs.* Small 8vo. 2s. Kearsly.

The author of this little Tour seems well qualified for making the most of his subject. Though the scenes be not very interesting, they are so delineated as to afford gratification to the reader. The description is richly interspersed with incidents, and not unfrequently with remarks on manners and customs ; all which are blended in an agreeable and lively manner.

A Genealogical History of the present Royal Families of Europe : *Illustrated with Tables of Descent.* By Mark Noble, *F. A. S.* Small 8vo. 3s. sewed. Baldwin.

This small volume, the author informs us, was compiled for his own private use ; but thinking that it might be serviceable to others, he at length committed it to the press. The volume begins with the history of the Imperial family, from Frederick the third, arch-duke of Austria, elected emperor in 1440, to the present time. Next follow the families of Russia, Turkey, Great Britain, France, Spain, Portugal, Denmark, Sweden, Poland, Prussia, Naples, Sicily, and Sardinia. To these is added the succession of the Stadtholders ; and of the Popes, from 1417 to the present time, with their family-names and characters. The different articles are introduced with a general account of the government, and the religion of each country ; and the descent of all the sovereign families is illustrated by particular tables. The whole forms a useful compendium of genealogical history, from the foundation of the various families, whose descendants are potentates in Europe.

The

The Phœnix, an Essay. By John Goodridge. 8*vo*. 3*s*. Wells *and* Grosvenor.

The author of this work is captain John Goodridge, late commander of one of his majesty's packet boats, stationed at Falmouth. The captain, if he is yet alive, is seventy-one, and this is probably the child of his old age.

Some of the notions, which he endeavours to maintain, are these : that the six days of the creation were equal to six years ; that the earth did not move round its own axis till the Fall ; that its diurnal motion took place on Adam's transgression, and was occasioned by the collision or near approach of a comet, which gave a terrible shock to the earth ; that the same comet, which returns after a period of about 575 years, likewise occasioned the deluge ; that its last appearance was in 1680 ; that at its next return it will occasion the conflagration and the millenium ; and, lastly, that this comet is the phœnix of the ancients.

The circumstances, which chiefly induce him to believe, that this comet is the phœnix, are these : ' Its periods are upon an average about 575 years : this certainly agrees with the return of the phœnix, which is said to be about 600 years ; secondly, the comet's flight and quick passage through the heavens ; thirdly, its tail, both which are common to birds in general ; lastly, the comet's going down to the sun, where, by the violence of the sun's heat, it is terribly burnt, and when it returns, in flying off again it is then called the young phœnix.'—

—' As to the time, he says, when the conflagration is to take place, I have not in the least *hinted* either the *day* or the month, in which it may happen, nor have I attempted to confine the time to a single year ; but (unless it should please God to alter the course of the comet) I am *confid nt*, it will happen some time in the year 2255 or 6.'

The captain's calculation is particular enough in all reason : prophets should not be pressed too closely ; and no body will desire him to limit either the day or the month, as he has determined the year with so much confidence.

The reader is not to imagine that this is a fugitive piece, like many of our modern productions. The author makes no doubt, but that it will ' exist till the next return of the phœnix,' and if hereafter any patriotic bookseller, or generous philanthropist, should think proper to give the world a new impression of thirty thousand copies, he will do an essential service to mankind: for, as the author says, ' the more general it may be at that time, of the more benefit it will prove to the then inhabitants of the earth.'

THE
CRITICAL REVIEW.

For the Month of *August*, 1781.

Prefaces biographical and critical to the Works of the English *Poets.*
By Samuel Johnson, *LL.D.* *Vol. V, VI, VII, VIII, IX,* 47. 354
and X. small 8*vo.* Printed for the principal Bookfellers.
[*Concluded.*]

THESE volumes are a continuation, of a most learned
and ingenious work, of which we gave an account in
a former volume *, and complete the elegant edition of
English poets publifhed by the Bookfellers of London.

The character both of the author and his performance
are already too well known and eftablifhed in the republic
of letters, to make any farther recommendation neceffary;
it may be fufficient, therefore, to obferve, that in thefe
Lives of the Poets we meet with the fame critical penetration and fagacity, the fame accurate knowlege of men
and manners, judicious reflections, nervous ftyle, and manly
fentiments, that diftinguifhed the former volumes.——This
part of the work is, at the fame time, more interefting, as it
contains the lives, and difplays the characters, of perfons living nearly in our own times; and whom fome of us were, perhaps, perfonally acquainted with, Pope, Swift, Gay, Thom-
fon, Young, Collins, Gray, Dyer, Akenfide, &c.——Amongft
thefe, the life of the celebrated Dr. Young is not written by Dr. Johnfon, but by a gentleman, who, the Dr.
informs us, had better information concerning it than he

---

* See Crit. Rev. vol. xlvii. p. 354, 450.

could obtain.—We could have wished, however, that Mr/ Herbert Croft, of Lincoln's-Inn, who writes this life for his friend Dr. Johnson, had himself received . more information, with regard both to the public and private character of Dr/ Young, than we here meet with.

' Of the domestic manners and petty habits (says Mr. Croft) of the author of the Night Thoughts, I hoped to have given you an account from the best authority ; — but who shall dare to say, To-morrow I will be wise or virtuous, or to-morrow I will do a particular thing ? Upon enquiring for his housekeeper, I learned that she was buried two days before I reached the town of her abode.'

Mr. Croft, we observe, has taken no small pains to vindicate the character of Dr. Young's son, (a worthy man, and, we believe, now living) from the misrepresentations of the Biographia Britannica, which, he tells us,

' Not satisfied with pointing out the son of Young, in that son's life-time, as his father's Lorenzo, travels out of its way into the history of the son, and tells of his having been forbidden his college at Oxford for misbehaviour, and of his long labouring under the displeasure of his father. How such anecdotes, were they true, tend to illustrate the Life of Young, it is not easy to discover. If the son of the author of the Night Thoughts was indeed forbidden his college for a time at one of our universities, the author of Paradise Lost was disgracefully ejected from the other, with the additional indignity of public corporal correction. From juvenile follies who is free ? Were nature to indulge the son of Young with a second youth, and to leave him at the same time the experience of that which is past, he would probably pass it differently (who would not ?) ; he would certainly be the occasion of less uneasiness to his father ;—but, from the same experience, he would as certainly be treated in a different manner by his father. Young was a poet ; poets (with reverence be it spoken) do not make the best parents. Fancy and imagination seldom deign to stoop from their heights ; always stoop unwillingly to the low level of common duties. Aloof from vulgar life, they pursue their rapid flight beyond the ken of mortals, and descend not to earth but when obliged by necessity. The prose of ordinary occurrences is beneath the dignity of poetry. Yet the son of Young would almost sooner, I know, pass for a Lorenzo, than see himself vindicated, at the expence of his father's memory, from follies which, if it was blameable in a boy to have committed them, it is surely praise worthy in a man to lament, and certainly not only unnecessary but cruel in a biographer to record.'

This

This extract, our readers will observe, is not very favourable to Dr. Young.—Poets, Mr. Croft tells us, ' do not make the best parents :' we cannot, however, subscribe to the truth of this observation, as no satisfactory reason can, perhaps, be assigned why poets should not be as good parents as other men.—This gentleman informs us, that Philander and Narcissa, in the Night Thoughts, are Mr. and Mrs. Temple ; and that the poet seems to dwell with more melancholy on *their* deaths than that of his *wife.*

In justice to Mr. Croft it is necessary to observe, that he has endeavoured to assimilate his part of the work with the rest, . by a careful and studious imitation of Dr. Johnson's style and manner, which he seems to have hit off with some degree of success.

Our readers, however, are, by this time, we suppose, rather impatient for an extract from the great biographer himself. In a work of this nature, where every part has nearly an equal share of merit, it is difficult to select those which may lay claim to our superior admiration. If a preference, however, must be given, we should bestow it on the lives of Pope, Addison, and Thomson, which seem to have been written *con amore,* and to shine in this collection with peculiar lustre.

The following character of Addison, which we find at the conclusion of his life, is equally just and delicate.

' As a describer of life and manners, he must be allowed to stand perhaps the first of the first rank. His humour, which, as Steele observes, is peculiar to himself, is so happily diffused as to give the grace of novelty to domestick scenes and daily occurrences. He never outsteps the modesty of nature, nor raises merriment or wonder by the violation of truth. His figures neither divert by distortion, nor amaze by aggravation. He copies life with so much fidelity, that he can be hardly said to invent ; yet his exhibitions have an air so much original, that it is difficult to suppose them not merely the product of imagination.

' As a teacher of wisdom he may be confidently followed. His religion has nothing in it enthusiastick or superstitious : he appears neither weakly credulous nor wantonly sceptical ; his morality is neither dangerously lax, nor impracticably rigid. All the enchantment of fancy and all the cogency of argument are employed to recommend to the reader his real interest, the care of pleasing the author of his being. Truth is shewn sometimes as the phantom of a vision, sometimes appears half-veiled in an allegory : sometimes attracts regard in the robes of fancy, and sometimes steps forth in the confidence of reason. She wears a thousand dresses, and in all is pleasing.

' Mille habet ornatus, mille decenter habet.

G 2

' His

'His prose is the model of the middle stile; on grave subjects not formal, on light occasions not grovelling; pure without scrupulosity, and exact without apparent elaboration; always equable, and always easy, without glowing words or pointed sentences. Addison never deviates from his track to snatch a grace; he seeks no ambitious ornaments, and tries no hazardous innovations. His page is always luminous, but never blazes in unexpected splendour.

'It seems to have been his principal endeavour to avoid all harshness and severity of diction; he is therefore sometimes verbose in his transitions and connections, and sometimes descends too much to the language of conversation; yet if his language had been less idiomatical, it might have lost somewhat of its genuine Anglicism. What he attempted, he performed; he is never feeble, and he did not wish to be energetick; he is never rapid, and he never stagnates. His sentences have neither studied amplitude, nor affected brevity: his periods, though not diligently rounded, are voluble and easy. Whoever wishes to attain an English stile, familiar but not coarse, and elegant but not ostentatious, must give his days and nights to the volumes of Addison.'

To this we will subjoin what our author has said of that amiable man and excellent poet, James Thomson.

'Thomson, (says Dr. Johnson) as a writer, is entitled to one praise of the highest kind; his mode of thinking, and of expressing his thoughts, is original. His blank verse is no more the blank verse of Milton, or of any other poet, than the rhymes of Prior are the rhymes of Cowley. His numbers, his pauses, his diction, are of his own growth, without transcription, without imitation. He thinks in a peculiar train, and he thinks always as a man of genius; he looks round on Nature and on Life, with the eye which Nature bestows only on a poet; the eye that distinguishes, in every thing presented to its view, whatever there is on which imagination can delight to be detained, and with a mind that at once comprehends the vast, and attends to the minute. The reader of the Seasons wonders that he never saw before what Thomson shows him, and that he never yet has felt what Thomson impresses.

'His is one of the works in which blank verse seems properly used; Thomson's wide expansion of general views, and his enumeration of circumstantial varieties, would have been obstructed and embarrassed by the frequent interfections of the fense, which are necessary effects of rhyme.

'His descriptions of extended scenes and general effects bring before us the whole magnificence of Nature, whether pleasing or dreadful. The gaiety of Spring, the splendour of Summer, the tranquillity of Autumn, and the horror of Winter, take in their turns possession of the mind. The poet leads us through the appearances of things as they are successively varied by the vi-

viciffitudes of the year, and imparts to us fo much of his own enthufiafm, that our thoughts expand with his imagery, and kindle with his fentiments. Nor is the naturalift without his part in the entertainment; for he is affifted to recolleft and to combine, to arrange his difcoveries, and to amplify the fphere of his contemplation.

'The great defeft of the Seafons is want of method; but for this I know not that there was any remedy. Of many appearances fubfifting all at once, no rule can be given why one fhould be mentioned before another; yet the memory wants the help of order, and the curiofity is not excited by fufpenfe or expeftation.

' His diftion is in the higheft degree florid and luxuriant, fuch as may be faid to be to his images and thoughts both their luftre and their fhade; fuch as invefts them with fplendour, through which perhaps they are not always eafily difcerned. It is too exuberant, and fometimes may be charged with filling the ear more than the mind.

' Thefe Poems, with which I was acquainted at their firft appearance, I have fince found altered and enlarged by fubfequent revifals, as the author fuppofed his judgement to grow more exaft, and as books or converfation extended his knowledge and opened his profpefts. They are, I think, improved in general; yet I know not whether they have not loft part of what Temple calls their race; a word which, applied to wines, in its primitive fenfe, means the flavour of the foil.'

This criticifm is elegant, candid, and judicious; the praife beftowed is not (as praifes often are) vague, general, and indifcriminate, but founded on true tafte and reafon; nor is the cenfure lefs juft.

Though Dr. Johnfon's critical determinations will always be received with deference and refpeft, we much doubt whether they will be implicitly fubmitted to with regard to that great favourite of the ladies Matthew Prior, whom our biographer feems to have placed in a lower fcale of merit than is generally allotted to him.—Of this poet, Dr. Johnfon has taken the liberty to fay, that his love-verfes are not diftated by nature, and have neither gallantry nor tendernefs; that his mythological allufions are defpicable; and that when he tries to aft the lover without the help of his gods and goddeffes, his thoughts are unaffefting or remote; that his Henry and Emma is a dull tedious dialogue.

' His Poem (fays our author) on the Battle of Ramilies is neceffarily tedious by the form of the ftanza: an uniform mafs of ten lines, thirty-five times repeated, inconfequential and

flightly

slightly connected, must weary both the ear and the understanding. His imitation of Spenser, which consists principally in *I ween* and *I weet*, without exclusion of later modes of speech, makes his poem neither ancient nor modern. His mention of Mars and Bellona, and his comparison of Marlborough to the Eagle that bears the thunder of Jupiter, are all puerile and unaffecting; and yet more despicable is the long tale told by Lewis in his despair, of Brute and Troynovante, and the teeth of Cadmus, with his similes of the raven and eagle, and wolf and lion. By the help of such easy fictions, and vulgar topicks, without acquaintance with life, and without knowledge of art or nature, a poem of any length, cold and lifeless like this, may be easily written on any subject.'

He tells us afterwards, that Prior's Alma has no plan, and that his Solomon is tedious and uninteresting; and that whatever he claims above mediocrity, seems the effort of struggle and of toil.

' He has (says he) many vigorous but few happy lines; he has every thing by purchase, and nothing by gift; he had no nightly visitations of the Muse, no infusions of sentiment or felicities of fancy.'

The legality of this severe sentence against poor Matt. will probably be disputed in the court of criticism by some of his warm friends and admirers.—We shall not, however, enter into the contention, but proceed to observe, that our biographical legislator, in another part of this work, has again boldly steered against the tide of popular opinion, by calling in question the transcendent excellence of our modern Pindar, Mr. Gray, whom he has dethroned and degraded, in the following terms.

' Gray's Poetry (says he) is now to be considered; and I hope not to be looked on as an enemy to his name, if I confess that I contemplate it with less pleasure than his life.

' His ode on Spring has something poetical, both in the language and the thought; but the language is too luxuriant, and the thoughts have nothing new. There has of late arisen a practice of giving to adjectives, derived from substantives, the termination of participles; such as the *cultured* plain, the *daisied* bank; but I was sorry to see, in the lines of a scholar like Gray, the *honied* Spring. The morality is natural, but too stale; the conclusion is pretty.

' The poem on the Cat was doubtless by its author considered as a trifle, but it is not a happy trifle. In the first stanza *the azure flowers* that *blow*, shew resolutely a rhyme is sometimes made when it cannot easily be found. Selima, the Cat, is called a nymph, with some violence both to language and sense;

fenfe; but there is good ufe made of it when it is done; for of the two lines,

> " What female heart can gold defpife ?
> What cat's averfe to fifh !"

the firft relates merely to the nymph, and the fecond only to the cat. The fixth ftanza contains a melancholy truth, that *a favourite has no friend*; but the laft ends in a pointed fentence of no relation to the purpofe; if *what gliftered* had been *gold*, the cat would not have gone into the water; and, if fhe had, would not lefs have been drowned.

'The *Profpect of Eaton College* fuggefts nothing to Gray, which every beholder does not equally think and feel. His fupplication to father Thames, to tell him who drives the hoop or toffes the ball, is ufelefs and puerile. Father Thames has no better means of knowing than himfelf. His epithet *buxom health* is not elegant; he feems not to underftand the word. Gray thought his language more poetical as it was more remote from common ufe: finding in Dryden *honey redolent of Spring*, an expreffion that reaches the utmoft limits of our language, Gray drove it a little more beyond common apprehenfion, by making *gales* to be *redolent of joy and youth*.

'Of the *Ode on Adverfity*, the hint was at firft taken from *O Diva, gratum quæ regis Antium*; but Gray has excelled his original by the variety of his fentiments, and by their moral application. Of this piece, at once poetical and rational, I will not by flight objections violate the dignity.

'My procefs has now brought me to the *wonderful wonder of wonders*, the two Sifter Odes; by which, though either vulgar ignorance or common fenfe at firft univerfally rejected them, many have been fince perfuaded to think themfelves delighted. I am one of thofe that are willing to be pleafed, and therefore would gladly find the meaning of the firft ftanza of the *Progrefs of Poetry*.

'Gray feems in his rapture to confound the images of *fpreading found* and *running water*. A *ftream of mufick* may be allowed; but where does *mufick*, however *fmooth and ftrong*, after having vifited the *verdant vales*, *rowl down the fteep amain*, fo as that *rocks and nodding groves rebellow to the roar*? If this be faid of *mufick*, it is nonfenfe; if it be faid of *water*, it is nothing to the purpofe.

'The fecond ftanza, exhibiting Mars's car and Jove's eagle, is unworthy of further notice. Criticifm difdains to chafe a fchool-boy to his common places.

'To the third it may likewife be objected, that it is drawn from mythology, though fuch as may be more eafily affimilated to real life. Idalia's *velvet-green* has fomething of cant. An epithet or metaphor drawn from nature ennobles art; an epithet or metaphor drawn from art degrades nature. Gray is too fond of words arbitrarily compounded. *Many-twinkling* was formerly

cenfured

censured as not analogical; we may say *many-spotted,* but scarcely *many-spotting.* This stanza, however, has something pleasing.

'Of the second ternary of stanzas, the first endeavours to tell something, and would have told it, had it not been crossed by Hyperion: the second describes well enough the universal prevalence of poetry; but I am afraid that the conclusion will not rise from the premises. The caverns of the North and the plains of Chili are not the residences of *Glory* and *generous Shame.* But that poetry and virtue go always together is an opinion so pleasing, that I can forgive him who resolves to think it true.

'The third stanza sounds big with *Delphi,* and *Egean,* and *Ilissus,* and *Meander,* and *hallowed fountain* and *solemn sound;* but in all Gray's odes there is a kind of cumbrous splendor which we wish away. His position is at last false; in the time of Dante and Petrarch, from whom he derives our first school of Poetry, Italy was over-run by *tyrant power* and *coward vice;* nor was our state much better when we first borrowed the Italian arts.

'Of the third ternary, the first gives a mythological birth of Shakspeare. What is said of that mighty genius is true; but it is not said happily: the real effects of his poetical power are put out of sight by the pomp of machinery. Where truth is sufficient to fill the mind, fiction is worse than useless; the counterfeit debases the genuine.

'His accounts of Milton's blindness, if we suppose it caused by study in the formation of his poem, a supposition surely allowable, is poetically true, and happily imagined. But the *ear* of Dryden, with his *two coursers,* has nothing in it peculiar; it is a car in which any other rider may be placed.

'The Bard appears, at the first view, to be, as Algarotti and others have remarked, an imitation of the Prophecy of Nereus. Algarotti thinks it superior to its original; and, if preference depends only on the imagery and animation of the two poems, his judgement is right. There is in the Bard more force, more thought, and more variety. But to copy is less than to invent, and the copy has been unhappily produced at a wrong time. The fiction of Horace was to the Romans credible; but its revival disgusts us with apparent and unconquerable falsehood. *Incredulus odi.*

'To select a singular event, and swell it to a giant's bulk by fabulous appendages of spectres and predictions, has little difficulty, for he that forsakes the probable may always find the marvellous; and it has little use, we are affected only as we believe; we are improved only as we find something to be imitated or declined. I do not see that the Bard promotes any truth, moral or political.

'His stanzas are too long, especially his epodes; the ode is finished before the ear has learned its measures, and consequently

ly before it can receive pleasure from their consonance and recurrence.

Dr. Johnson then enters into a minute examination of the several stanzas of the Bard, and concludes his criticism on the Odes by observing that they

'Are marked by glittering accumulations of ungraceful ornaments; they strike rather than please; the images are magnified by affectation; the language is laboured into harshness. The mind of the writer seems to work with unnatural violence. *Double, double, toil and trouble.* He has a kind of strutting dignity, and is tall by walking on tiptoe. His art and his struggle are too visible, and there is too little appearance of ease or nature.

Whether the whole of this free censure is strictly just and well founded, we will not pretend to determine. Certain it is, however, at least in our opinion, that no man ever acquired a high reputation at so easy a rate, or received such *great wages* for *so little work*, as Mr. Gray.—On his Elegy in a Country Church-Yard, we agree with Dr. Johnson, that too much praise cannot well be lavished; at the same time we think with him, that Gray's Odes, as well as his other little performances, have been much over-rated. The reputation of a poet in this country is, indeed, a matter very fluctuating and uncertain. Whilst he lives, and perhaps many years afterwards, a proper and unbiassed judgment of his real merit is seldom found. It is a long time before whim and caprice, prejudice and partiality subside; and the true character is not often ascertained, till that of the man is entirely forgotten. Gray has been placed by his sanguine admirers by the side of Dryden and Pope. Dr. Johnson seems to have levelled him with the minor bards of a much inferior rank: half a century hence he may, perhaps, be fixed in his right and proper station,

'Behind the foremost, and before the last.'

In the mean time, as the twig inclined too much one way, we are obliged to Dr. Johnson for bending strongly towards the other, which may make it strait at last.

We cannot dismiss this article without congratulating the public, on the extraordinary pains and industry which our excellent biographer has bestowed on the life of Pope. Much more is said of *him*, (though not more than he deserves) than of any other writer: every part of his character is delineated with the greatest accuracy, and every part of his writings criticised by the nice hand of taste, judgment, and impartiality. What is

said

said of Pope's Letters is so just and sensible, that we cannot withhold from our readers the following quotation.

" Of his social qualities (says Dr. Johnson), if an estimate be made from his Letters, an opinion too favourable cannot easily be formed ; they exhibit a perpetual and unclouded effulgence of general benevolence, and particular fondness. There is nothing but liberality, gratitude, constancy, and tenderness. It has been so long said as to be commonly believed, that the true characters of men may be found in their letters, and that he who writes to his friend lays his heart open before him. But the truth is, that such were simple friendships of the golden age, and are now the friendships only of children. Very few can boast of hearts which they dare lay open to themselves, and of which, by whatever accident exposed, they do not shun a distinct and continued view ; and, certainly, what we hide from ourselves we do not shew to our friends. There is, indeed, no transaction which offers stronger temptations to fallacy and sophistication than epistolary intercourse. In the eagerness of conversation the first emotions of the mind often burst out, before they are considered ; in the tumult of business, interest and passion have their genuine effect ; but a friendly letter is a calm and deliberate performance, in the cool of leisure, in the stillness of solitude, and surely no man sits down to depreciate by design his own character.

" Friendship has no tendency to secure veracity ; for by whom can a man so much wish to be thought better than he is, as by him whose kindness he desires to gain or keep ? Even in writing to the world there is less constraint ; the author is not confronted with his reader, and takes his chance of approbation among the different dispositions of mankind ; but a letter is addressed to a single mind, of which the prejudices and partialities are known ; and must therefore please, if not by favouring them, by forbearing to oppose them.

" To charge those favourable representations, which every man gives of himself, with the guilt of hypocritical falshood, would show more severity than knowledge. The writer commonly believes himself. Almost every man's thoughts, while they are general, are right ; and most hearts are pure, while temptation is away. It is easy to awaken generous sentiments in privacy ; to despise death when there is no danger ; to glow with benevolence when there is nothing to be given. While such ideas are formed they are felt, and self-love does not suspect the gleam of virtue to be the meteor of fancy.

" If the Letters of Pope are considered merely as compositions, they seem to be premeditated and artificial. It is one thing to write because there is something which the mind wishes to discharge ; and another, to solicit the imagination because ceremony or vanity requires something to be written. Pope confesses his early Letters to be vitiated with *affectation and ambition*; to know whether he disentangled himself from these per-
verters

verters of epiftolary integrity, his book and his life muft be fet in comparifon.'

Thefe obfervations are the refult of good fenfe, and a know-lege of mankind, and may be ufeful by cautioning us againft form-ing any decifive opinion of real characters merely from the let-ters of our friends; for, as Dr. Johnfon very properly obferves,

' In the Letters both of Swift and Pope there appears fuch narrownefs of mind, as makes them infenfible of any excel-lence that has not fome affinity with their own, and confines their efteem and approbation to fo fmall a number, that who-ever fhould form his opinion of the age from their reprefentation, would fuppofe them to have lived amidft ignorance and barba-rity, unable to find among their contemporaries either virtue or intelligence, and perfecuted by thofe that could not under-ftand them.'

In that part of the life of Pope, where mention is made of his friend bifhop Warburton, we meet with the character of that learned and ingenious prelate, which is drawn, as our readers will fee, by a mafterly hand; and which, we think, might ftand with propriety at the head of his works, in all fu-ture editions of them.

' About this time (fays our author) Warburton began to make his appearance in the firft ranks of learning. He was a man of vigorous faculties, a mind fervid and vehement, fupplied by inceffant and unlimited enquiry, with wonderful extent and variety of knowledge, which yet had not oppreffed his imagin-ation, nor clouded his perfpicacity. To every work he brought a memory full fraught with a fancy fertile of original combina-tions, and at once exerted the powers of the fcholar, the rea-foner, and the wit. But his knowledge was too multifarious to be always exact, and his purfuits were too eager to be always cautious. His abilities gave him an haughty confidence, which he difdained to conceal or mollify; and his impatience of oppo-fition difpofed him to treat his adverfaries with fuch contemptu-ous fuperiority as made his readers commonly his enemies, and excited againft him the wifhes of fome who favoured his caufe. He feems to have adopted the Roman Emperor's determination, *oderint dum metuant*; he ufed no allurements of gentle language, but wifhed to compel rather than perfuade.

' His ftyle is copious without felection, and forcible without neatnefs; he took the words that prefented themfelves: his diction is coarfe and impure, and his fentences are unmea-fured.'

In a page or two beyond this, Dr. Johnfon tells us, that Warburton was obliged to Pope for introducing him to Mr. Allen, ' who gave him his niece and his eftate, and by confequence a bishopric.'—Here we believe Dr. Johnson has attributed more power and influence to Allen than he ever possessed; as Warburton's preferment, we have always understood, did not arise from his succeeding to Allen's estate, but to his own literary merit, which was taken notice of and rewarded by lord Chatham, then Mr. Pitt and prime minister, who made him a bishop.

The comparison drawn between Pope and Dryden, which our readers will find towards the conclusion of his life (too long to be here inserted) is finely executed, and the merits of the two writers excellently discriminated. The beauties of Pope's Essay on Criticism are judiciously illustrated; and the Rape of the Lock honoured with that praise and admiration which it so justly deserves.—The translation of Homer has, perhaps, great as it is, more than a sufficient portion of commendation bestowed upon it by our sagacious critic, who endeavours strenuously to defend Pope against those who objected that his version of Homer was not Homerical; that it exhibits not any resemblance of his original and characteristic manner, and wants his artless grandeur and unaffected majesty.

' To a thousand cavils (says Dr. Johnson) one answer is sufficient; the purpose of a writer is to be read, and the criticism which would destroy the power of pleasing must be blown aside. Pope wrote for his own age and his own nation: he knew that it was necessary to colour the images and point the sentiments of his author; he therefore made him graceful, but lost him some of his sublimity.'

Here what our author has urged does by no means remove the objection. Allowing all Pope's merit, it is certainly possible to produce a better and more faithful translation of Homer than he has given us; but it must be in blank verse, which is more suitable to the nature of an epic poem: though, after all, we believe with Dr. Johnson, that such a translation would not have so many readers.

The quotations above given, and the remarks already made, renders it almost needless to say what justice demands of us, that this performance is one of the most acute, agreeable, and entertaining works that has passed under our inspection: and we lament that the collection is not larger, as we should then have had more lives of the English poets by Dr. Johnson.

The Journey to Snowdon. 4to. 10s. 6d. boards. White.

THIS is a continuation of a Tour to Wales * by Mr. Pennant, a gentleman well known in the literary world by his account of Scotland, and other ingenious performances. As Wales is a part of the kingdom abounding in the finest prospects, and most beautiful scenery, and where nature appears in all her sublimity and magnificence, affording, at the same time, an ample field for the curiosity of the naturalist, and food sufficient for the antiquary, an accurate description of it cannot but be acceptable to the public, especially when given by so careful an observer as Mr. Pennant, who has omitted nothing which the information of preceding writers, or which oral or traditional knowlege could procure with regard to every place through which he paffed, and every person or circumstance which he has occasion to mention. To a native of this country, whose honest prejudices warmly interest him in every thing that concerns it, the work before us must be doubly agreeable, as the author who is himself, we believe, both a native and inhabitant, takes every opportunity, in his relation of different occurrences, to celebrate the virtues of his countrymen. If the reader, indeed, has not some knowlege of Welch, he will not so well relish the beauties of it. A mere Englishman would even sometimes be puzzled to decypher the following formidable letters,

BWLCH OER —DDRWS,

which, notwithstanding, form the running title of page 16, with several others equally illegible.

- Impartiality obliges us here to remark, that there is not that ease, terseness, and perspicuity in the style of this performance which we could wish to have met with ; the facts and occurrences recounted, and the observations made, are not well ranged and digested ; add to this, that the diary-manner in which the narrative of the Journey is continued, has something very aukward and uncouth in it.

' Return along the ridge of the hill—see beneath me the little church of Gwaen-ysher—descend to the church and village Llanasa—quit the turnpike road on the left—ford the Wheler, and after crossing the Clwyd, reach Llewinni, &c.' This method of reciting what happened, may be useful in a memorandum book, and of service to travellers who are to go the same road; but a frequent repetition of it in a printed book, is rather tedious and disgusting. We mean

---

* See Crit. Rev. vol. xlv. p. 268.

not,

not, however, by this remark, to derogate from the general merit and utility of this performance, which is, upon the whole, confidered as part of a hiftory of the country, both inftructive and entertaining, as our readers will perceive by the following extracts, which we have felected as fome of the moft ftriking and agreeable.

' In the year 1572, fays our author, the refiant burgeffes who are voters for a member for the borough of Denbigh, had the courage to withftand the infinuations, the promifes, and the threats, of as unprincipled a lord as this kingdom was ever afflicted with; who had power to inflict, and will to execute, any vengeance that oppofition to his arbitrary inclinations might excite. In that year it was his pleafure that one Henry Dynne fhould reprefent this borough in parlement; the burgeffes were refractory, and cho'e another perfon; which gave rife to the following letter, which I print, as a *fans pareille*.

' A l · fent from the earl of Leicefter to the bayliffe, aldermen, and burgeffes, greatlie blaminge them for making choife of the burges of the parliament without his lordfhip's confente, and commanding them to aliter their electione, and to chofe Henrie Dynne.

' I have bene latlie advertifed how fmall confideration youe have had of the l^{re} I wrote unto you, for the nomynafion of yor burgefs, whereat as I cannot but greatlie mervayle (in refpect I am yor l. and you my tenaunts, as alfo the manie good tournes and comodities wch I have bene allwayes willinge to procure youe, for the benefitte of yor whole ftate) fo do I take the fame in fo——, and vill yte fo unthankfullie, as yf youe do not uppon receite hereof prefentlie revoke the fame, and appointe fuche one as I fhall nominate, namelie, Henrie Dynne, be ye well affured never to loke for any ffriendfhipe or favo' at my hande, in any yo' affayres hereafter; not for any great accompt I make of the thinge, but for that I would not it fhou'd be thought that I have fo fmall regard borne me at yo' hands, who are bounden to owe (as yo' L.) thus much dutie as to know myne advice and pleafure; that will haplie be aleadged, that yo' choice was made before the receipt of my l^{res} (in relic I would litle have thoughte that youe would have bene fo forgetfull, or rather careleffe of me, as before yor elecion not to make me privie therto, or at the leaft to have fome defire of myne advife therein (having tyme ynoughe fo to do) but as you have of yo' felfes thus rafhlie proceded herein, without myne affent, foe have I thought good to fignifie unto youe, that I mean not to take it in any wife at yo' hands, and therefore wyfh you more advifedlie to confider hereof, and to deale with me as maye continue my favo' towards you, otherwife loke for no favo' at my hands: and fo fare ye well. From the court, this laft day of April, 1572.

R. LEYCESTER.

' This

' This doughty letter had no effect: the burgesses adhered to their own choice, and Richard Candishe, gent. stands as member for Denbigh in that year.'

This is a curious letter, and may serve to shew that the custom of peers interfering in elections, has at least the plea of antiquity in its favour.

There is something droll in the following confession of Mr. Pennant, and the little history annexed to it,

' I hope my *countrymen* (says he) will not grow *indignant*, when I express my fears, that in very early times we were as fierce and savage as the rest of Europe: and they will bear this the better, when they reflect, that they keep pace with it in civilization, and in the progress of every fine art. We cannot deny but that we were, to the excess,

' Jealous in honor, sudden and quick in quarrel.

' Two gentlemen of this house exemplify the assertion. Meiric ap Bleyddyn, resentful of the injuries which he and his tenants received from the English judges and officers, slew one of the first, and hanged several of the latter on the oaks of his woods; by which he forfeited to the crown the lands, still known in these parts by the name of Tèr Meiric Llwyd, or the estate of Meiric Llwyd. As to his person, he secured it within the sanctuary at Hulston; and marrying, founded in that neighbourhood the house of Llwyd y Maen.

' Bleyddyn Vychan, another of this race, fell out with his tenants, and in a fit of fury chased them from his estate, and turned it into a forest; a pretty picture of the manners of the times! The place lies in the parish of Llansanan, and bears the name of Forest to this day.'

From the story, as above related, we have reason to suppose that Mr. Pennant's countrymen are apt to be a little *quarrelsome*. From an inscription which we meet with a little after, a suspicion arises, that they are liable to another weakness also. Mr. Pennant indeed insinuates as much, where he tells us that

' In Llenrhaider, a village near Denbigh castle, in the churchyard is a common altar-tomb of a gentleman, who chose to build his fame on the long series of ancestors which distinguished his from vulgar clay. It tells us, that

HEARE LYETH THE BODY OF
JOHN, AP ROBERT, OF PORTH, AP
DAVID, AP GRIFFITH, AP DAVID
VAUCHAN. AP BLETHYN, AP
GRIFFITH, AP MEREDITH,
AP JERWORTH, AP LLEWELYN,
AP JERORH, AP HEILIN, AP
COWRYD, AP CADVAN, AP
ALAWGWA,

ALAWGWA, AP CADELL, THE
KING OF POWYS, WHO
DEPARTED THIS LIFE THE
XX DAY OF MARCH, IN THE
YEAR OF OUR LORD GOD
1642, AND OF
HIS AGE XCV.'

For the infertion of this epitaph our author's countrymen have perhaps more reafon to be *indignant,* than for the quotation before given.

When our traveller gets to a place called Bar-mouth, in Meirionydfhire, he tells us a very extraordinary ftory, which he attefts, of a fafting woman, and which, for its fingularity, we fhall infert.

' My curiofity (fays he) was excited to examine into the truth of a furprizing relation of a woman in the parifh of Cylynin, who had fafted a moft fupernatural length of time. I took boat, had a moft pleafant paffage up the harbour, charmed with the beauty of the fhores, intermixed with woods, verdant paftures, and corn fields. I landed, and, after a fhort walk, found in a farm called Tydden Bach, the object of my excurfion, Mary Thomas, who was boarded here, and kept with great humanity and neatnefs. She was of the age of forty-feven, of a good countenance, very pale, thin, but not fo much emaciated as might be expected, from the ftrangenefs of the circumftances I am going to relate; her eyes weak, her voice low, deprived of the ufe of her lower extremities, and quite bedridden; her pulfe rather ftrong, her intellects clear and fenfible.

' On examining her, fhe informed me, that at the age of feven, fhe had fome eruptions like the meafles, which grew confluent and univerfal; and fhe became fo fore, that fhe could not bear the left touch: fhe received fome eafe by the application of a fheep's fkin, juft taken from the animal. After this, fhe was feized, at fpring and fall, with fwellings and inflammations, during which time fhe was confined to her bed; but in the intervals could walk about; and once went to Holy-well, in hopes of cure.

' When fhe was about twenty-feven years of age, fhe was attacked with the fame complaint, but in a more violent manner; and during two years and a half, remained infenfible, and took no manner of nourifhment, notwithftanding her friends forced open her mouth with a fpoon to get fomething down; but the moment the fpoon was taken away, her teeth met, and clofed with vaft fnapping and violence: during that time, fhe flung up vaft quantities of blood.

' She well remembers the return of her fenfes, and her knowledge of every body about her. She thought fhe had flept but a night, a night, and afked her mother whether fhe had given her any thing the day before, for fhe found herfelf very hungry. Meat was brought to her; but fo far from being able to take any thing folid, fhe could fcarcely fwallow a fpoonful of thin whey. From this, fhe continued feven years and a half without any food or liquid, excepting fufficient of the latter to moiften her lips. At the end of this period, fhe again fancied herfelf hungry, and defired an egg; of which fhe got down the quantity of a nut kernel. About this time, fhe requefted to receive the facrament; which fhe did, by having a crum of bread fteeped in the wine. After this, fhe takes for her daily fubfiftence a bit of bread, weighing about two penny-weights feven grains, and drinks a wine glafs of water: fometimes a fpoonful of wine, but frequently abftains whole days from food and liquids She fleeps very indifferently: the ordinary functions of nature are very fmall, and very feldom performed. Her attendant told me, that her difpofition of mind was mild; her temper even; that fhe was very religious, and very fervent in prayer: the natural effect of the ftate of her body, long unembarraffed with the groffnefs of food, and a conftant alienation of thought from all worldly affairs.'

Snowdon, the great object of curiofity, for a view of which the journey was undertaken, is thus defcribed.

' The top of Snowdon, which by way of pre-eminence is ftyled Y WYDDEA or the *Confpicuous*, rifes almoft to a point, the mountain from hence feems propped by four vaft buttreffes; between which are four deep Cwms, or hollows: each, excepting one, had one or more lakes, lodged in its diftant bottom. The neareft was Ffynnon Lâs, or The Green Well, lying immediately below us. One of the company had the curiofity to defcend a very bad way to a jutting rock, that impended over the monftrous precipice; and he feemed like Mercury ready to take his flight from the fummit of Atlas. The waters of Ffynnon Lâs, from this height, appeared black and unfathomable, and the edges quite green. From thence is a fucceffion of bottoms, furrounded by the moft lofty and rugged hills, the greateft part of whofe fides are quite mural, and form the moft magnificent amphitheatre in nature. The Wyddfa is on one fide; Crib y Diftill, with its ferrated tops, on another; Crib Coch, a ridge of fiery rednefs, appears beneath the preceding; and oppofite to it is the boundary called the Lliwedd. Another very fingular fupport to this mountain is Y Clawdd Coch, rifing into a fharp ridge, fo narrow, as not to afford breadth even for a path.

' The view from this exalted fituation is unbounded. In a former tour, I faw from it the county of Chefter, the high hille of Yorkfhire, part of the north of England, Scotland, and Ireland: a plain view of the Ifle of Man; and that of Anglefea lay extended like a map beneath us, with every rill vifible. I took much pains to fee this profpect to advantage; fat up at a farm on the weſt till about twelve, and walked up the whole way. The night was remarkably fine and ſtarry : towards morn, the ſtars faded away, and left a ſhort interval of darkneſs, which was ſoon diſperſed by the dawn of day. The body of the ſun appeared moſt diſtinct, with the rotundity of the moon, before it roſe high enough to render its beams too brilliant for our ſight. The ſea which bounded the weſtern part was gilt by its beams, firſt in ſlender ſtreaks, at length glowed with redneſs. The proſpect was diſcloſed to us like the gradual drawing up of a curtain in a theatre. We ſaw more and more, till the heat became ſo powerful, as to attract the miſts from the various lakes, which in a ſlight degree obſcured the proſpect. The ſhadow of the mountain was flung many miles, and ſhewed its bicapitated from ; the Wyddfa making one, Crib y Diſtill the other head. I counted this time between twenty and thirty lakes, either in this county, or Meirionyddſhire. The day proved ſo exceſſively hot, that my journey coſt me the ſkin of the lower part of my face, before I reached the reſting-place, after the fatigue of the morning.

' On this day, the ſky was obſcured very ſoon after I got up. A vaſt miſt enveloped the whole circuit of the mountain. The proſpect down was horrible. It gave an idea of numbers of abyſſes, concealed by a thick ſmoke, furiouſly circulating around us. Very often a guſt of wind formed an opening in the clouds, which gave a fine and diſtinct viſto of lake and valley. Sometimes they opened only in one place ; at others, in many at once, exhibiting a moſt ſtrange and perplexing ſight of water, fields, rocks, or chaſms, in fifty different places. They then cloſed at once, and left us involved in darkneſs ; in a ſmall ſpace, they would ſeparate again, and fly in wild eddies round the middle of the mountains, and expoſe, in parts, both tops and baſes clear to our view. We deſcended from this various ſcene with great reluctance ; but before we reached our horſes, a thunder ſtorm overtook us. Its rolling among the mountains was inexpreſſibly awful : the rain uncommonly heavy. We re-mounted our horſes, and gained the bottom with great hazard. The little rills, which on our aſcent trickled along the gullies on the ſides of the mountain, were now ſwelled into torrents ; and we and our ſteeds paſſed with the utmoſt riſque of being ſwept away by theſe ſudden waters. At length we arrived ſafe, yet ſufficiently wet and weary, to our former quarters.

' It is very rare that the traveller gets a proper day to aſcend the hill ; for it often appears clear, but by the evident attraction of the clouds by this lofty mountain, it becomes ſuddenly and unexpectedly enveloped in miſt, when the clouds have juſt become appeared very remote, and at great heights. At times, I have obſerved them lower to half their height, and notwithſtanding they had been diſperſed to the right and to the left, yet then have met from both ſides, and united to involve the ſummit in one great obſcurity.

                                                        ' The

' The quantity of water which flows from the lakes of Snowdonia, is very confiderable; fo much, that I doubt not but collectively they would exceed the waters of the Thames, before it meets the flux of the ocean.

' The reports of the height of this noted hill have been very differently given. A Mr. Cafwell, who was employed by Mr. Adams, in 1682, in a furvey of Wales, meafured it by inftruments made by the directions of Mr. Flamftead; and afferts its height to have been twelve hundred and forty yards: but for the honor of our mountain I am forry to fay, that I muft give greater credit to the experiments made of late years, which have funk it to one thoufand one hundred and eighty-nine yards and one foot, reckoning from the quay at Caernarvon to the higheft peak.'

This work is adorned with a frontifpiece and eleven plates, fome of which are well executed, particularly the head of fir Richard Wynne, by Cornelius Janfen, finely engraved by Bartolozzi. There is likewife given with this volume a fmall fet of fupplemental plates, etched by Mofes Griffiths, whom our author recommends to the public as a worthy, fober, and ingenious man, and an almoft felf-taught genius. Thefe etchings are faithfully performed, and, confidered as firft efforts, have no inconfiderable merit.

Remarks on the Influence of Climate, Situation, Nature of Country, Population, Nature of Food, and Way of Life, on the Difpofition and Temper, Manners and Behaviour, Intellects, Laws and Cuftoms, Form of Government, and Religion, of Mankind. By William Falconer, M. D. F. R. S. 4to. 18s. boards. Dilly.

IN a preface to this work, Dr. Falconer defires the reader would obferve, that he has not given it the name of a treatife, or effay, but of Remarks; as he means not to infinuate that it affords a complete difcuffion of the fubject, but only a collection of fuch obfervations as occurred to him on a general view of the influence of phyfical caufes on the moral world. In regard to thofe who have treated of this fubject, he mentions, as a common miftake, the making their pofitions too univerfal. The effects of climate, &c. he farther obferves, are all of them general, and not particular; and if a confiderable majority of the nations, as well as the individuals, that live under a certain climate, are affected in a certain manner, we may pronounce decifively on its influence, notwithftanding there may be fome exceptions. It muft alfo, he remarks, be taken into confideration, that the influence of

one of the above caufes often corrects the other ; a circumftance which he illuftrates by a few examples.   Numerous as
are the caufes of phyfical influence mentioned by Dr. Falconer,
he means not to have it underftood, that he has comprehended
the whole which can be fuppofed to operate on the human
character ; but though they may be only a fmall part, he
believes them to be among the moft powerful and important.

The work is divided into fix books, and thofe into chapters and fections.   The author begins with the confideration
of climate ; fhewing the firft effects of heat upon the living
human body, and afterwards thofe of cold.   To give our
readers an idea of the principles upon which he proceeds, we
fhall lay before them the fecond and third chapters of this
book.

' *On the Effects of Heat upon the living Human Body.*

' Heat is perhaps the moft univerfal ftimulus with which we
are acquainted ; when applied in any great degree to the human
body, it excites the action of the nervous fyftem in general, and
of the cutaneous nerves efpecially, which are moft expofed to its
influence, and renders them more fufceptible of any impreffion.
If the heat be long continued, it produces a moifture upon the
fkin, called perfpiration, which, by relaxing the cuticle, keeps
the fubjacent nervous papillæ in a fupple ftate, and obvious to
every impulfe.   It likewife expofes the extremities of the nerves
to external impreffions, by keeping the fkin in a fmooth ftate, and
void of corrugation.   Heat alfo, by increafing the fecretion of
perfpiration, caufes the perfpirable matter (fimilar to what occurs in other increafed glandular difcharges, as the faliva, the
mucus of the nofe, &c.) to be very much attenuated, and confequently fit for being eafily and quickly evaporated, without the
fame portion of it remaining long upon the fkin, or leaving much
refiduum ; which renders the cuticle very thin and fine, and of
confequence fit for tranfmitting fenfations through its fubftance.
By increafing the perfpiration, heat diminifhes the other evacuations, and even the fecretions.   The urine is feparated but in
fmall quantity, and the alvine evacuation is very flow.   The bile
however muft be excepted, which is confiderably increafed in quantity, and as fome think rendered more acrimonious in quality.
The difpofition of the body and juices to putrefaction is alfo
much augmented.

' *Effects of Cold on the living Human Body.*

' Cold, on the contrary, in fimilar circumftances, corrugates or
wrinkles the cuticle, and caufes the cutaneous papillæ to contract,
and to retire deeper into the fkin.   It alfo clofes the orifices of
the cutaneous glands, and thus prevents the accefs of any irri-
tating fubftance.   By contracting the nervous papillæ, it diminifhes

nishes perspiration, and probably makes the perspirable matter more viscid, which renders the cuticle more dry and rigid, and even considerably thicker ; by all which the accuracy of sensation or feeling is much diminished. Perhaps too, as Mr. Montesquieu observes, the constriction on the miliary glands may render the nerves of the skin in a degree paralytic ; and this I am inclined to believe may be in some measure the case, from that insensibility which occurs in the access of fevers, especially intermittents, where the cold fit is the most strong and distinguishable.

' The secretion of the bile is diminished by cold, and its quality rendered less acrimonious. The urinary and alvine evacuations are more regular, and more proportioned to the quantity of food taken in. The bodily strength is also greater, the bulk of the body larger, and its humours less disposed to putrefaction.'

In the fourth chapter the author examines the effects of heat on the temper and disposition. Having observed that heat increases the faculty or power, as well as the accuracy, of sensation or feeling, he next remarks that this sensibility of the body is by sympathy communicated to the mind ; producing that almost incredible degree of mental sensibility which prevails in hot climates. Hence, he observes, arises, among the inhabitants of those climates, their passionate temper, remarked by Hippocrates, and their impatience under several circumstances of behaviour, which never affect people of a more phlegmatic temperament. He adds, that this is particularly observable in Europe among the Italians, and in America among the inhabitants of the West India Islands.

The author observes, that to the same sensibility is owing the amorous disposition of the people of hot climates ; which disposition, in its turn, increases the sensibility that produced it. This, as well as the jealousy attendant on love, has been always remarked as a part of the character of the people in those countries.

Concerning the vindictive disposition, we meet with the following observations.

' From what has been said of the sensibility of the people of hot climates, we might be inclined to think that their disposition would be exceedingly mild and tender ; but this I do not believe to be the general character of the people. The sensibility with which they are endued, however it may teach them to feel for others, causes them to have very quick sensations on their own account. Thus many circumstances, which are overlooked in cold climates, are construed into irreparable affronts in Japan, and such as nothing but death can expiate. Even the Chinese, who, as a commercial people, are obliged to have some com-

H 3

mand

mand of temper, are, when much provoked, violent and vindictive. The same difference is, in some measure, observable between Spain and Italy, and England. The cruel revenges likewise, such as by the dagger and by poison, so frequent in hot climates, with the inhuman treatment of prisoners which generally prevails there, prove evidently their disposition to be of this nature.'

On the principle of sensibility the author also accounts for the levity or inconstancy, so remarkable among the inhabitants of warm climates.

Another characteristic disposition generally imputed to the inhabitants of hot climates is timidity. Dr. Falconer observes that this likewise is partly owing to the sensibility of the people ; but that other causes concur. For instance, the great perspiration to which they are subject, weakening the body, the languor is communicated to the mind.

In respect of indolence, which constitutes an ingredient in the character of the inhabitants of hot climates, Dr. Falconer observes that it proceeds from several causes, such as heat, languor, and great perspiration.

' I am likewise inclined to believe, says he, that the bilious disposition of the inhabitants of these countries, has some share in causing their indolence of disposition. Hot climates, I have before remarked, tend to increase the generation of bile, which also is often obstructed in its passage into the intestines, and regurgitated into the system ; and this takes place so frequently there, as to form, in some measure, a characteristic of the people. Now the bile, although intended by nature to be an active stimulus to the intestines, exerts an effect totally different when absorbed into the circulatory system. It there produces an aversion to motion, or exertion of any of the faculties of either mind or body ; from which effect, it may reasonably be supposed to contribute towards forming this part of their character. The tendency, likewise, of the animal fluids to putrefaction, which is almost always the case in such climates, and is probably owing to the constant perspiration, has likewise, I imagine, some effect in producing this inactivity of disposition, as nothing so much or so quickly debilitates the human body. This we see instanced in the case of putrid fevers, a sudden and remarkable prostration of strength being one of their most distinguishing symptoms. Even the cowardice of the people operates as a cause of their indolence ; which last favours the other again in its turn.'

In the fifth chapter, our author considers the effects of a cold climate on the temper and disposition. He observes that cold, by blunting the power of feeling, tends greatly to diminish the sensibility of the system in general ; and that the cir-

circumſtances of the greater bulk and bodily ſtrength of the people of cold climates, likewiſe afford reaſons why they are endowed with leſs ſenſibility. The inhabitants of cold countries, he remarks, have little diſpoſition to the tender paſſions, which are connected with great ſenſibility ; and that enthuſiaſtic friendſhip, for the ſame reaſon, is alſo little known among them. In making this remark, our author means not to inſinuate, that people in cold climates are deſtitute of that bond of ſociety, but that their attachment is derived from other, and perhaps more laudable motives, ſuch as eſteem and gratitude, and ſeldom arrives at that height of fondneſs and partiality which diſtinguiſhes the other.

Dr. Falconer is of opinion, that the inhabitants of cold countries are far from being deſtitute of benevolence and kindneſs of diſpoſition ; the impreſſion of which, he thinks, is more permanent, and attended with greater effect, than in the inhabitants of hot climates. In ſupport of this character he mentions their charity to the poor, and their mild treatment of priſoners taken in war. It may be queſtioned, however, whether thoſe two virtues are not more owing to civilization than the influence of climate.

The qualities next aſcribed by our author to the inhabitants of cold climates are, ſteadineſs of conduct, and bravery ; the latter of which, according to his principle, ariſes from the diminution of ſenſibility.

‘ The courage, however, of theſe people, ſays Dr. Falconer, appears to be rather of the paſſive kind ; though to a great degree inſenſible of fear, they are from the ſame inſenſibility leſs capable of briſk exertion. At this diſpoſition Strabo ſeems to hint, who remarks, that the northern nations were famous in cloſe fights, and for perſevering courage. This appears too from the circumſtances in general attending the wars in which the Ruſſians have been engaged. Though frequently victorious over the beſt-diſciplined troops, even thoſe of the king of Pruſſia, by their intrepidity and ſteadineſs, they were leſs able to improve a victory, or to reap all the concurrent advantages from it, than their more ſoutherly neighbours.’

The inſtance above adduced by our author in confirmation of his doctrine, ſeems not to be entirely ſatisfactory. To improve a victory depends rather on the commander than the army ; and the former may be actuated by different conſiderations, excluſive of any which can be ſuppoſed to ariſe from inſenſibility. The doctor is of opinion, that the courage of the inhabitants of cold countries is alſo partly derived from the habit of labour, exerciſe, and induſtry, inſpired by the

H 4

cli-

climate.   Different caufes mentioned in other parts of the work, he thinks, likewife concur.

The fixth chapter treats of the effect of moderate climates on the temper and difpofition.   To the inhabitants of fuch climates the author afcribes a degree of fenfibility and a temper of mind equally remote from thofe which characterize the people in hot or cold countries.   Love, he thinks, undoubtedly appears to the greateft perfection in moderate climates. It is there united with a degree of fenfibility and paffion on one hand, and efteem and attachment on the other.

In refpect of friendfhip, and moderation of conduct, he alfo gives the preference to the inhabitants of temperate climates.   He is of opinion, however, that they are particularly liable to ficklenefs of difpofition.

'Ficklenefs alfo, fays he, or uncertainty of temper, is another mark of the inhabitants of moderate climates.   This might naturally be expected from fuch a medium of temperature, where neither of the two extremes prevail in a degree fufficient to imprefs the mind with the peculiar effects of either.   This difpofition is very obfervable amongft our own countrymen, and begets a habit of impatience, which makes them incapable of bearing even the happieft and moft fortunate train of affairs for any long time together.   This is remarkably inftanced in political matters.   The prefent ftate of which is almoft always reprefented in the common difcourfe of the people to be the worft that is poffible to be imagined.   This increafes often to fuch a degree, as to caufe an alteration of public meafures, and fometimes of minifters; which at firft gives fatisfaction, but foon a frefh fubject of complaint is ftarted, and a new mode of conduct becomes neceffary; which alfo in its turn is changed in like manner.   Nor is this confined to public affairs only, although in them it is moft confpicuous, as being fubjects of the moft general and public debate; but daily appears in private life, in which we fee people, whofe fituation in almoft every refpect would appear to a ftranger nearly as happy as the condition of human nature admits, complaining of their unhappinefs, depreciating every good, and magnifying every frivolous misfortune; and this with fuch eagernefs, that they often feem, when intent on demonftrating the miferies of their lives, to efcape from their forrows, and to find a tolerable paftime in proving that they are unhappy.   Nor are the effects of this difpofition confined to mere declamation, or verbal complaint; it often produces the moft terrible confequences, by inducing the fufferers to put an end to their miferies by a voluntary death.

'This often happened among the Greeks and Romans; but we never hear of any of them deftroying themfelves without fome apparent caufe.   But the Englifh, and indeed fome other nations

tions in nearly the same latitude, often put an end to their lives in the bofom of happinefs. This feems to refemble a diforder of the climate, and to be interwoven into the conftitution of the people. With them, labour and pain are in general more tolerable than a wearinefs of life, or an uneafinefs in exiftence. Pain is a local thing, which leads us to a defire of feeing an end of it. The burthen of life is an evil confined to no particular place, which prompts us to the defire of ceafing to live. This impatience is totally different from the levity of hot climates. The latter, I have before obferved, is of the nature of a tranfitory attachment, which is effaced by a fubfequent ; but the former is generally a fettled difguft. In the one cafe, the change happens from a new impreffion ; in the other, from diflike of the prefent fituation.

' The levity of hot climates differs alfo from the impatience of the Englifh, in being more perfonal. In the former, they are variable in their perfonal attachments, whilft their manners and cuftoms remain unchanged through ages.

' With us, the manners and cuftoms are perpetually varying, whilft our perfonal regards are fteady and permanent. This difpofition appears very remarkably in political affairs. In England, the chief complaint againft any particular adminiftration is on account of certain meafures which they have adopted ; and if thefe be altered, the people feldom fail of being fatisfied, at leaft for a time.

' But the infurrections in the Eaft, are directed chiefly againft the perfon of fome particular minifter or favourite ; and, provided he be but removed, the complaints of the people are generally appeafed, though the meafures and ftyle of government remain as before.'

In the foregoing extract. Dr. Falconer imputes to temperature entirely an effect which feems rather to proceed from the variation of temperature, or from the frequent humidity of the atmofphere in an infular fituation. His remarks on the different difpofition of the Englifh, and the inhabitants of the Eaftern countries are alfo liable to objection. If, in England, there fhould arife a complaint againft any particular adminiftration, on account of certain meafures which they have adopted, what can be more natural, in any climate, than that upon an alteration of the obnoxious meafures, the people feldom fail of being fatisfied ? The fatisfaction of the inhabitants of the Eaft, according to the propofition which our author has ftated, is equally conformable to nature. Both the Englifh and Eaftern nations are fuppofed to have obtained a redrefs of their grievances ; and each, from the want of motive, or from an attachment to the government of the refpective country, ceafes all farther complaint.

I   Ac-

According to this writer, the inhabitants of temperate climates, although inferior in paſſive courage to thoſe of the cold, have more courage of the active kind, and are more enterpriſing. He is alſo of opinion, that temperate climates produce a much greater variety of character and diſpoſition, than either of the two extremes of heat or cold.

In the ſeventh chapter, which relates to climates ſubject to great variety of temperature, we meet only with a few obſervations from the writings of Hippocrates.

The eighth chapter treats of the effects of climate on the manners; reſpecting which our author makes the following obſervations.

' In point of morality in general, it is, I believe, that the manners of cold climates far exceed thoſe of warm; in the latter, the paſſions are naturally very ſtrong, and likewiſe kept in a perpetual ſtate of irritation from the high begree of ſenſibility that prevails, which cauſes a great multiplication of crimes, by multiplying the objects of temptation. Many deſires and paſſions ariſe there, from cauſes that would either never occur in a cold climate, or be eaſily reſiſted; but in a warm one, the paſſion or inclination is ſtronger, and the power of reſtraint leſs. In cold climates, the deſires are but few, in compariſon, and not often of a very immoral kind; and thoſe repreſſed with leſs difficulty, as they are ſeldom very violent. In temperate climates, the paſſions are in a middle ſtate, and generally inconſtant in their nature; ſufficiently ſtrong, however, to furniſh motives for action, though not ſo powerful as to admit of no reſtraint from conſiderations of prudence, juſtice, or religion.'

Dr. Falconer remarks, that the moral qualities of a people, depending in a great meaſure on ſenſibility, the inhabitants of hot climates are particularly liable to be influenced from an exceſs of this principle.

He illuſtrates his doctrine by obſervations on emotions of paſſion, gallantry and intrigue, jealouſy, cowardice, ſuſpicion, fraud and knavery, perfidy and inconſtancy, idleneſs, luxury, exceſs in diet, and gaming.

The ninth chapter treats of the effects of a cold climate on the morals. The characteriſtic vices of thoſe who inhabit ſuch climates, in the opinion of our author, are proneneſs to acts of violence, drunkenneſs, gaming; and their virtues, decency of conduct and behaviour, candour and openneſs, conſtancy and reſolution, activity and induſtry; the two laſt of which, he thinks, are confined chiefly to bodily exertion, and have little reference to mental employments.

We

We shall present our readers with the tenth chapter, which relates to the moral character of the people of temperate climates.

' The moral character of the people of temperate climates is of a mixed kind, though considerably more inclinable to virtue, at least the practical part of it, as far as regards external actions, than those of hot ones. Their greater acquaintance with the nature of trade, and the necessity of a mutual confidence, especially in large concerns, renders them less knavish and deceitful. Their consciousness of superiority, both in courage and in military science, renders them less cruel ; and their sense of the necessity of decency of conduct and behaviour, in order to preserve the police and form of government, prevents scandalous or open violations of morality.

' The confidence in their power and abilities, of which I have just spoken, is, I imagine, productive of another good effect, in rendering the people less selfish and interested, and in infusing into them a degree of public spirit and regard for their country, and mankind in general. When a man lives in daily fear for his person or property, all his regards are centered in himself, or confined to his nearest connections ; and the farther he enlarges his views, the more he thinks he increases his danger. But when a man esteems himself and his connections to be in a reasonable state of security, the human mind, naturally active, seeks for employment elsewhere ; and in those, whose dispositions are inclined to virtue, settles in promoting the good of their country, or the interests of mankind in general.

' This is a circumstance highly advantageous to the public ; and accordingly we see, in the temperate climates of Europe, that the interests of every state are better understood, and more attended to, both in their commercial and political capacity, than in any of the other quarters of the world ; and that, accordingly, they formerly had, and still retain, the pre-eminence.'

From the account and specimens already given of this work, our readers will observe, that Dr. Falconer delineates with great minuteness the operation of those causes, both physical and moral, which he supposes to have an influence on the characters of different nations. The subject has been treated by other writers, particularly Mr. Hume and baron Montesquieu ; the former of whom has perhaps ascribed too little, and the latter too much, to the influence of climate. Dr. Falconer appears to tread chiefly in the steps of the French author ; whose theory he has extended, and ingeniously applied, through a variety of complicated speculations. If he has given such a scope to detail as may be thought by some readers unnecessary, we must impute his conduct to the desire of unfolding the principles of his enquiry in the clearest and fullest view.

[*To be continued.*]

The History of English *Poetry.* *Vol. III.* *By* Thomas Warton, B. D. [*Concluded from Vol.* LI. *p.* 330.].

MR. Warton justly observes that, at the revival of learning, the progress of our language was greatly retarded by the custom of writing in Latin. The first that set the example of cultivating their vernacular tongue, were sir Thomas More, and Roger Ascham ; the former of whom wrote in it a Dialogue on Tribulation, and a History of Richard the Third ; and the latter composed his Toxophilus, chiefly with a view of giving a correct model of English composition. The example of those writers was soon followed by other learned men, particularly by Thomas Wilson, who published a system of Logic and Rhetoric ; in the latter of which he delivers explicit rules for composing in the English language.

The first poem the historian mentions at the commencement of the reign of queen Elizabeth, is the play of Gordobuc, written by Thomas Sackville, lord Buckhurst ; of which, though foreign to our author's plan, yet as being the earliest specimen in our language of a regular tragedy, he delivers a particular account. It was first exhibited in the great hall of the Inner Temple, by the students of that society, as part of a Christmas entertainment, and afterwards before queen Elizabeth at Whitehall, in January 1561. Every act is introduced, as was the custom in our old plays, with a piece of machinery, called the dumb show, shadowing by an allegorical exhibition, the matter that was immediately to follow. In treating of the nature of this entertainment, Mr. Warton makes the following remark.

' I take this opportunity of expressing my surprise, that this ostensible comment of the dumb shew should not regularly appear in the tragedies of Shakspeare. There are even proofs that he treated it with contempt and ridicule. Although some critics are of opinion, that because it is never described in form at the close or commencement of his acts, it was therefore never introduced. Shakspeare's aim was to collect an audience, and for this purpose all the common expedients were necessary. No dramatic writer of his age has more battles or ghosts. His representations abound with the usual appendages of mechanical terror, and he adopts all the superstitions of the theatre. This problem can only be resolved into the activity or the superiority of a mind, which either would not be entangled by the formality, or which saw through the futility, of this unnatural and extrinsic ornament. It was not by declamation or by pantomime that Shakspeare was to fix his eternal dominion over the hearts of mankind.'

Our

Our author obſerves, that this appearance of a regular tragedy, with the diviſion of acts and ſcenes, and the accompaniment of the ancient chorus, ſeems to have directed the attention of our more learned poets to the ſtudy of the old claſſical drama, and in a ſhort time to have produced Engliſh verſions of the Jocaſta of Euripides, and of the ten tragedies of Seneca ; but he does not find that it was ſpeedily foHowed by any original compoſitions on the ſame legitimate model. Many more of the ancient poets, however, ſoon after appeared in Engliſh verſe. Before the year 1600, Homer, Muſæus, Virgil, Horace, Ovid, and Martial, were tranſlated : of which verſions Mr. Warton gives ſeveral ſpecimens, accompanied with critical remarks, and anecdotes of the reſpective authors. For the gratification of our readers we ſhall lay before them the two following extracts.

From the tranſlation of Ovid's Metamorphoſis, by Arthur Golding.

‘ The princely pallace of the Sun, ſtood gorgeous to behold,
On ſtately pillars builded high, of yellow burniſht gold ;
Beſet with ſparkling carbuncles, that like to fire did ſhine,
The roofe was framed curiouſly, of yuorie pure and fine.
The two-doore-leves of ſiluer clere, a radiant light did caſt :
But yet the cunning workemanſhip of thinges therein far paſt
The ſtuffe whereof the doores were made : for there a perfect plat,
Had Vulcane drawne of all the world, both of the ſourges that
Embrace the earth with winding waves, and of the ſtedfaſt
    ground,
And of the heauen itſelf alſo, that both encloſeth round.
And firſt and foremoſt of the ſea, the gods thereof did ſtand,
Loude-ſounding Tryton, with his ſhrill and writhen trumpe in
    hand,
Unſtable Protew, changing aye his figure and his hue,
From ſhape to ſhape a thouſand ſights, as liſt him to renue.——
In purple robe, and royall throne of emerauds freſhe and greene,
Did Phœbus ſit, and on each hand ſtood wayting well beſeene,
Dayes, Months, Yeeres, Ages, Seaſons, Times, and eke the equall
    Houres ;
There ſtood the Springtime, with a crowne of freſh and fragrant
    floures :
There wayted Summer naked ſtarke, all ſaue a wheaten hat :
And Autumne ſmerde with treading grapes late at the preſſing
    vat :
And laſtly, quaking for the colde, ſtood Winter all forlorne,
With rugged head as white as doue, and garments al to torne ;
Forladen with the iſycles, that dangled vp and downe,
Upon his gray and hoarie beard, and ſnowie frozen crowne.
The Sunne thus ſitting in the midſt, did caſt his piercing eye, &c.’

Horace's

Horace's Epistle to Albius Tibullus, by Thomas Drant.

' Tybullus, frend and gentle iudge
 Of all that I do clatter,
What doft thou all this while abroade,
 How might I learne the matter?
Doft thou inuente fuch worthy workes
 As Caffius' poëmes paffe?
Or dofte thou clofelie creeping lurcke
 Amid the wholfom graffe?
Addicted to philofophie,
 Contemning not a whitte
That's feemlie for an honeft man,
 And for a man of witte.
Not thou a bodie without breaft!
 The goddes made thee t'excell
In fhape, the gods haue lent thee goodes,
 And arte to vfe them well.
What better thing vnto her childe
 Can wifh the mother kinde?
Than wifedome, and, in fyled frame,
 To vtter owte his minde:
To haue fayre fauoure, fame enoughe,
 And perfect ftaye, and health;
Things trim at will, and not to feele
 The emptie ebb of wealth
Twixt hope to haue, and care to kepe,
 Twixt feare and wrathe, awaye
Confumes the time: eche day that cummes,
 Thinke it the latter daye.
The hower that cummes unlooked for
 Shall cum more welcum aye.
Thou fhalt me fynde fat and well fed,
 As pubble as may be;
And, when thou wilt, a meric mate,
 To laughe and chat with thee.'

Tranflation was not at this time confined to the Greek and Roman writers, but included Italian books, efpecially fuch as were written on fictitious and narrative fubjects; a circumftance which had great influence on Englifh literature, and, in particular, on poetry. Mr. Warton prefents us with a full view of the chief of thofe tranflations from the Italian, which appeared in England before the year 1600. From his minute and accurate enquiry we learn, that the beft ftories of the early and original Italian novelifts, either by immediate tranflation, or through the mediation of Spanifh, French, or Latin verfions, by paraphrafe, abridgement, imitation, or with the change of names, incidents, and characters, were generally known in England before the clofe of the reign of Elizabeth.

After

After deducing and delineating by a number of examples, accompanied with judicious remarks, the hiftory of Englifh poetry during part of the adminiftration of Elizabeth, Mr. Warton favours us with fome general reflexions on the poetical genius of this reign. Thefe are comprifed in the laft fection of the volume, which is replete with a variety of ingenious and philofophical obfervations; fo interefting to every reader of tafte, that, were it compatible with the plan of our Review, we fhould with pleafure extract the whole fection: but we cannot refrain from availing ourfelves of the following fpecimen.

' The age of queen Elizabeth is commonly called the golden age of Englifh poetry. It certainly may not improperly be ftyled the moft poetical age of thefe annals.

' Among the great features which ftrike us in the poetry of this period, are the predominancy of fable, of fiction, and fancy, and a predilection for interefting adventures and pathetic events. I will endeavour to affign and explain the caufe of this characteriftic diftinction, which may chiefly be referred to the following principles, fometimes blended, and fometimes operating fingly: the revival and vernacular verfions of the claffics, the importation and tranflation of Italian novels, the vifionary reveries or refinements of falfe philofophy, a degree of fuperftition fufficient for the purpofes of poetry, the adoption of the machineries of romance, and the frequency and improvements of allegoric exhibition in the popular fpectacles.

' When the corruptions and impoftures of popery were abolifhed, the fafhion of cultivating the Greek and Roman learning became univerfal: and the literary character was no longer appropriated to fcholars by profeffion, but affumed by the nobility and gentry. The ecclefiaftics had found it their intereft to keep the languages of antiquity to themfelves, and men were eager to know what had been fo long injurioufly concealed. Truth propagates truth, and the mantle of myftery was removed not only from religion but from literature. The laity, who had now been taught to affert their natural privileges, became impatient of the old monopoly of knowlege, and demanded admittance to the ufurpations of the clergy. The general curiofity for new difcoveries, heightened either by juft or imaginary ideas of the treafures contained in the Greek and Roman writers, excited all perfons of leifure and fortune to ftudy the claffics. The pedantry of the prefent age was the politenefs of the laft. An accurate comprehenfion of the phrafeology and peculiarities of the ancient poets, hiftorians, and orators, which yet feldom went farther than a kind of technical erudition, was an indifpenfable and almoft the principal object in the circle of a gentleman's education. Every young lady of fafhion was carefully inftituted in claffical letters: and the daughter of a duchefs was taught, not only to diftil ftrong waters, but to conftrue Greek. Among the learned

fe-

females of high diftinction, queen Elizabeth herfelf was the moft confpicuous. Roger Afcham, her preceptor, fpeaks with rapture of her aftonifhing progrefs in the Greek nouns ; and declares with no fmall degree of triumph, that during a long refidence at Windfor-caftle, fhe was accuftomed to read more Greek in a day, than " fome prebendary of that church did Latin, in one week." And although perhaps a princefs looking out words in a lexicon, and writing down hard phrafes from Plutarch's Lives, may be thought at prefent a more incompatible and extraordinary character, than a canon of Windfor underftanding no Greek and but little Latin, yet Elizabeth's paffion for thefe acquifitions was then natural, and refulted from the genius and habitudes of her age.

' The books of antiquity being thus familiarifed to the great, every thing was tinctured with ancient hiftory and mythology. The heathen gods, although difcountenanced by the Calvinifts on a fufpicion of their tending to cherifh and revive a fpirit of idolatry, came into general vogue. When the queen paraded through a country-town, almoft every pageant was a pantheon. When fhe paid a vifit at the houfe of any of her nobility, at entering the hall fhe was faluted by the Penates, and conducted to her privy chamber by Mercury. Even the paftry-cooks were expert mythologifts. At dinner, felect transformations of Ovid's Metamorphofes were exhibited in confectionary : and the fplendid iceing of an immenfe hiftoric plumb-cake, was emboffed with a delicious baffo-relievo of the deftruction of Troy. In the afternoon, when fhe condefcended to walk in the garden, the lake was covered with Tritons and Nereids : the pages of the family were converted into wood-nymphs who peeped from every bower : and the footmen gamboled over the lawns in the figure of fatyrs. I fpeak it without defigning to infinuate any unfavourable fufpicions, but it feems difficult to fay, why Elizabeth's virginity fhould have been made the theme of perpetual and exceffive panegyric : nor does it immediately appear, that there is lefs merit or glory in a married than a maiden queen. Yet, the next morning, after fleeping in a room hung with the tapeftry of the voyage of Eneas, when her majefty hunted in the park, fhe was met by Diana, who pronouncing our royal prude to be the brighteft paragon of unfpotted chaftity, invited her to groves free from the intrufions of Acteon. The truth is, fhe was fo profufely flattered for this virtue, becaufe it was efteemed the characteriftical ornament of the heroines, as fantaftic honour was the chief pride of the champions, of the old barbarous romance. It was in conformity to the fentiments of chivalry, which ftill continued in vogue, that fhe was celebrated for chaftity : the compliment, however, was paid in a claffical allufion.

' Queens muft be ridiculous when they would appear as women. The fofter attractions of fex vanifh on the throne. Elizabeth fought all occafions of being extolled for her beauty, of which indeed in the prime of her youth fhe poffeffed but a fmall fhare,
what-

whatever might have been her pretensions to absolute virginity. Notwithstanding her exaggerated habits of dignity and ceremony, and a certain affectation of imperial severity, she did not perceive this ambition of being complimented for beauty, to be an idle and unpardonable levity, totally inconsistent with her high station and character. As she conquered all nations with her arms, it matters not what were the triumphs of her eyes. Of what consequence was the complexion of the mistress of the world? Not less vain of her person than her politics, this stately coquet, the guardian of the protestant faith, the terror of the sea, the mediatrix of the factions of France, and the scourge of Spain, was infinitely mortified, if an embassador, at the first audience, did not tell her she was the finest woman in Europe. No negociation succeeded unless she was addressed as a goddess. Encomiastic harangues drawn from this topic, even on the supposition of youth and beauty, were surely superfluous, unsuitable, and unworthy; and were offered and received with an equal impropriety. Yet when she rode through the streets of the city of Norwich, Cupid, at the command of the mayor and aldermen, advancing from a groupe of gods who had left Olympus to grace the procession, gave her a golden arrow, the most effective weapon of his well-furnished quiver, which under the influence of such irresistible charms was sure to wound the most obdurate heart. " A gift, says honest Hollinshed, which her majesty, now verging to her fiftieth year, received very thankfullie." In one of the fulsome interludes at court, where she was present, the singing-boys of her chapel presented the story of the three rival goddesses on mount Ida, to which her majesty was ingeniously added as a fourth : and Paris was arraigned in form for adjudging the golden apple to Venus, which was due to the queen alone.

‘ This inundation of classical pedantry soon infected our poetry. Our writers, already trained in the school of fancy, were suddenly dazzled with these novel imaginations, and the divinities and heroes of pagan antiquity decorated every composition. The perpetual allusions to ancient fable were often introduced without the least regard to propriety. Shakspeare's Mrs. Page, who is not intended in any degree to be a learned or an affected lady, laughing at the cumbersome courtship of her corpulent lover Falstaffe, says, " I had rather be a giantess and lie under mount Pelion." This familiarity with the pagan story was not, however, so much owing to the prevailing study of the original authors, as to the numerous English versions of them, which were consequently made. The translations of the classics, which now employed every pen, gave a currency and a celebrity to these fancies, and had the effect of diffusing them among the people. No sooner were they delivered from the pale of the scholastic languages, than they acquired a general notoriety. Ovid's Metamorphoses just translated by Golding, to instance no farther, disclosed a new world of fiction, even to the illiterate. As we had now all the ancient fables in English, learned allusions, whether in a poem or a pageant, were no longer obscure and unintelligible

intelligible to common readers and common spectators. And here we are led to observe, that at this restoration of the classics, we were first struck only with their fabulous inventions. We did not attend to their regularity of design and justness of sentiment. A rude age, beginning to read these writers, imitated their extravagancies, not their natural beauties. And these, like other novelties, were pursued to a blameable excess '—

' — Another capital source of the poetry peculiar to this period, consisted in the numerous translations of italian tales into English. These narratives, not dealing altogether in romantic inventions, but in real life and manners, and in artful arrangements of fictitious yet probable events, afforded a new gratification to a people which yet retained their ancient relish for taletelling, and became the fashionable amusement of all who professed to read for pleasure. They gave rise to innumerable plays and poems, which would not otherwise have existed ; and turned the thoughts of our writers to new inventions of the same kind. Before these books became common, affecting situations, the combination of incident, and the pathos of catastrophe, were almost unknown. Distress, especially that arising from the conflicts of the tender passion, had not yet been shewn in its most interesting forms. It was hence our poets, particularly the dramatic, borrowed ideas of a legitimate plot, and the complication of facts necessary to constitute a story either of the comic or tragic species. In proportion as knowlege encreased, genius had wanted subjects and materials. These pieces usurped the place of legends and chronicles. And although the old historical songs of the minstrels contained much bold adventure, heroic enterprise, and strong touches of rude delineation, yet they failed in that multiplication and disposition of circumstances, and in that description of characters and events approaching nearer to truth and reality, which were demanded by a more discerning and curious age. Even the rugged features of the original Gothic romance were softened by this sort of reading : and the Italian pastoral, yet with some mixture of the kind of incidents described in Heliodorus's Ethiopic history now newly translated, was engrafted on the feudal manners in Sydney's Arcadia.'

In the three volumes now published of this work, the ingenious author has traced only the rudest efforts of poetical genius in England. He is, at length, however, arrived at a period when the British Muse begins to assume a nobler and more classical appearance, when refinement of taste corrects the extravagance of imagination, and a prospect opens to the attainment of perfection in English poetry. We congratulate Mr. Warton on an epoch that offers for his investigation the most beautiful productions in our language, and which will afford subjects more worthy the exertion of those critical talents, so eminently displayed in this history ; a history abounding with the strongest proofs of attentive enquiry, of the most polished taste, and most judicious observation.

Two

Two Letters to Dr. Newcome, *Bishop of* Waterford. *On the Duration of Our Saviour's Ministry. By* Joseph Priestley, *LL.D. F. R. S.* 8vo. 2s. 6d. sewed. Johnson.

THIS publication consists of two letters. The first was annexed to the author's English Harmony of the Evangelists; but not being large, is now reprinted, that the reader may have the whole correspondence, in a more convenient form.

The second contains an answer to the arguments advanced by the bishop of Waterford, in his tract on the Duration of our Lord's Ministry *.

The Christian fathers, in general, supposed, that our Lord's public ministry extended no farther than one complete year. Their testimony, our author conceives, is of great importance. And he observes, that even Eusebius, the first who extended our Lord's ministry beyond two years and a half, and, as far as appears, all other writers, till the very moderns, supposed, that the three first evangelists related only the events of one year; that is, they go upon the idea, that only one year intervened between the imprisonment of John, and the death of Christ. ' But this space, says he, by your lordship's own confession, includes all the events, that Mr. Mann and myself endeavour to bring within the compass of a year. So that whatever the ancients thought of that part of our Lord's ministry, which preceded the imprisonment of John the Baptist (which they suppose to be recorded by John) they all agreed with me in every thing, that your lordship finds the hardest to be reconciled to, in my hypothesis. —

' —— Admitting what Eusebius and all the ancients supposed (and on what good authority can we dispute it) that the three first evangelists related the events of only one year of our Lord's life, can your lordship think it credible, that they should all confine themselves to the last of three or four, when the whole was equally before them? Was there no event in the whole compass of the two or three preceding years, that they thought worth singling out and recording? This would be more especially extraordinary in the case of Luke, who relates the circumstances of our Saviour's birth so very minutely, and his visits to Jerusalem at twelve years of age. A total silence in such a writer as this, to the two or three first years of the opening of our Lord's ministry, is altogether unaccountable.'——

* See Crit. Rev. vol. l. p. 181.

' —— It

' — It is observable, that long after the opinion began to be formed, that our Saviour's ministry must have continued at least two years, all the fathers, even so late as Jerom, still speak of our Lord's suffering in the fifteenth of Tiberius, which is really inconsistent with it. For what could Christian writers mean by the fifteenth of Tiberius, but the same year that Luke meant by it? In fact, it must have been copied from Luke. But this is the very year, in which that evangelist says, that John began to preach. There is no room therefore for the extension of our Lord's ministry beyond one year.

' It cannot indeed be strictly true, that our Saviour died in the same year, in which John began to preach. But the early Christians, having a general idea, that the whole subject of Luke's gospel, beginning with the preaching of John, was comprized within the space of little more than a year, they might, writing not as chronologers, but only mentioning facts incidentally, give the date, that Luke begins with, to all the events comprised within it promiscuously.

' Or, since all the most early writers, who mention any date of the death of Christ according to the consuls, say that it happened when the Gemini were in that office, and their consulship was the fifteenth of the complete years of Tiberius *, they might omit that part of the year after August, in which Augustus died, and give it to Augustus.—Either of these suppositions will tolerably well account for the slight inaccuracy.'

There is something remarkable in the conduct of Luke's fixing with great circumstantiality the time of the commencement of John's preaching ; but assigning no date to the death of Christ, an event of much more consequence. Our author thinks, that his conduct is not consistent, but on the supposition of one of these events being in his idea, so connected with the other, in the course of his narrative, as that the date of it might easily be inferred from the date of the other, which he asserts, from the tenor of his gospel, to be the case : and in this, he presumes, he has the sanction of all the ancients.

It was, he observes, their unanimous opinion, that only one year intervened between the imprisonment of John and the death of Jesus. And what is there, he asks, in the history of Luke, from the commencement of the preaching of

---

* That is, from the time of his being sole emperor, not from the time when he was admitted partner in the empire by Augustus.

John

John to his imprifonment, that is, to Jefus's journey to Galilee, which followed immediately upon it, that can be fuppofed by any reafonable conftruction, to take up more than a few months ? It is all related in his third chapter, and the thirteen firft verfes of the fourth, which contains an account of nothing more than the preaching of John before the baptifm of Jefus, and the temptation.

In the next fection the author reconfiders and corroborates his argument, derived from the ignorance of Herod concerning Jefus, at the time of the death of John the Baptift.

Upon the bifhop's hypothefis, Jefus had preached publicly almoft two years, and the greateft part of the time alone, John being in prifon ; and this ignorance of Herod, our author thinks, is unaccountable. But upon his own hypothefis, Jefus had not been fo much expofed to public notice, more than between four and five weeks ; and therefore he fuppofes, that Herod being probably, like other kings and great men, engaged in a multiplicity of bufinefs or pleafure, he might not have heard of Jefus.

In the fourth fection the author fhews, that the word πασχα, John vi. 4. is an interpolation, and does not appear to have been in the text, in the time of Irenæus, nor probably in that of Eufebius, nor yet in that of Epiphanius ; as thefe writers take no notice of that expreffion, though it was of importance to them in fome of their writings.

The bifhop, in order to reprefent the hurry, which he thinks our Saviour muft have been in, on Dr. Prieftley's hypothefis, has drawn a plan of all his journeys from the firft paffover to the next pentecoft, and then computes the number of miles he muft have travelled every day. Our author reviews this computation, and finds, that there is no occafion, on his hypothefis, to have fuppofed our Lord to have travelled quite four miles per day ; ' and where, fays he, is the great improbability in this ? Few men of an active life walk lefs, and many perfons three or four times as much the whole year through. It is befides by no means certain, though it feems to be generally taken for granted, that our Saviour always travelled on foot.'

In the remaining part of this letter, the author confiders the fuppofed references to more than two paffovers in the gofpels of the three firft evangelifts, the argument for the probable duration of our Saviour's miniftry from the objects of it, the transactions at the firft paffover, his various journeys, the harmony of the gofpels according to the ancients, with feveral incidental circumftances.

I 3

. In this enquiry he has displayed his usual ingenuity and penetration, and given his hypothesis a very great appearance of probability. Yet, we do not suppose, that the controversy will be determined by this letter.

The History of the Isle of Wight. [*Concluded from p. 8.*]

IN our last Review we traced the progress of the historian through the three first chapters of this work. The fourth contains an account of the wardens, captains, and governors of the island, with the principal events under their administration. The author observes, that the persons honoured with this charge were generally selected from among the principal gentlemen of the island, and usually commissioned by the crown, though sometimes appointed by by the lord of the island, or, with especial permission, elected by the inhabitants. The first institution of this office was during the minority of Baldwin the Third, grandson of William de Vernun, earl of Devon, soon after the accession of Henry the Third. The person entrusted with it was Walleran de Ties, famous for his defence of the castle of Berkhemstead against Lewis, the eldest son of Philip, king of France.——We cannot pass over this part of the work without remarking the extraordinary pains which have been taken to supply it with materials from ancient records : for the only evidence that proves this Walleran to have been warden of the island, is his appearing a subscribing witness to a grant made to the Abbey of Quarr, which is thus signed, *Teste Wallerano Teutonico custode insulæ.* He lived till the reign of Edward the First, when dying without issue, his manor of Ringwood, in Hampshire, escheated to the king.

The historian observes, that

' The office of warden appears not to have been incompatible with the monastic profession, as in the thirteenth of Edward the Third, it appears to have been held by the abbot of Quarr, who received instructions to array all the able men, and to supply them with arms, and also to cause beacons and other signals to be erected on the hills, to convey speedy notice of the approach of an enemy.

' The office was also occasionally elective, as is instanced in an order entered on the rolls of parliament, in the fourteenth of Edward the Third, when an invasion being apprehended, the sheriff of Hampshire, together with the constable of Carisbrooke castle, were directed to convene the inhabitants of the island to elect a warden, who should take charge of the defence of the island

island during the king's pleasure; instead of one, three were elected, sir Bartholomew Lisle, John de Langford, lord of Chale, sir Theobald Russel, lord of Yaverland.'—

' — Three other wardens are found in the sixteenth year of the same king, when a precept was directed to Bartholomew Lisle, John de Kingston, and Henry Romyn, custodes of the island, commanding them to make inquisition what services were due from the inhabitants in time of war, of what nature, and from what lands and tenements.'

On the death of Humphrey, duke of Gloucester, lord of this island, in the twenty-fifth year of Henry the Sixth, the king appointed Henry Trenchard to the office of constable of the Castle of Carisbrooke, with a salary of *twenty pounds per annum*, as keeper of the forest of Parkhurst, and *four pence per day* for the pay of the porter of the castle.

In the third year of Henry the Eighth, the government of the island was conferred on sir James Worsley, keeper of the king's wardrobe, and master of the robes.

This gentleman being probably an ancestor of the respectable family to which the public is indebted for the present work, we think he has a just title to be particularly noticed in the history of the island, and shall therefore present our readers with the following part of the narrative.

' He was the younger brother of a very ancient family of that name in Lancashire, and had been many years page to Henry the Seventh; he was constituted captain of the island for life, with a salary of six shillings and nine pence per diem for himself, two shillings for his deputy, and six pence each for thirteen servants; he had besides a reversionary grant of the office of constable of Carisbrooke castle, when it should become vacant, and was by the same commission made captain of all the forts in the island. He was steward, surveyor, receiver, and bailiff of all the crown lands; and was either to retain his salary and allowances out of the moneys he received, or to take the same from the king's receiver in the county of Southampton. He was likewise constituted keeper of Carisbrooke Forest and Park, with a fee of two shillings per diem; and warden and master of the duckcoy of wild fowl, as well within the said park and forest there, as within and throughout the whole island. He was empowered to lease any of the king's houses, demesne lands, and farms, either by lease of years, or by copy of court roll for lives, where the lands have usually been passed in that manner: the old rent being reserved by such lease or copy. He had the return of all writs, the execution of process, and the office of sheriff within the said island, the sheriff of the county, or his officer, being excluded from acting there, unless in default of the captain; he was also clerk of the market, and coroner in the island.

I 4   ' Ri-

' Richard Worsley, esq. on the death of sir James his father, in the twenty-ninth of Henry the Eighth, succeeded him in the office of captain, and soon after had the honour of entertaining the king at his seat at Appuldurcombe. The king was attended by his favourite the lord Cromwell, then constable of Carisbrooke castle, which office was, on his lordship's attainder and execution, conferred on Mr. Worsley.

' Five years after, the French, having failed in an attempt against our fleet, notwithstanding their superiority at sea, made a descent on the island, which they intended to take possession of; but were, by the bravery of the islanders, and good conduct of their captain, soon driven back to their ships, with the loss of their general, and a great many of their men. It was on this occasion that new forts were ordered to be erected for the protection of the island, which were executed under the direction of the captain; one of them was called Worsley's Tower: by his representations the inhabitants were prevailed on to provide a train of artillery for the defence of the island, at their own charges. He continued in office till the death of Edward the Sixth; but being zealous in promoting the Reformation, as appears by his acting as a commissioner for the sale of church plate on the suppression of religious houses, at the accession of queen Mary he resigned his offices, and Mr. Girling, a man of low extraction, succeeded him; of whom, although no particulars are recorded, yet it is to be presumed, that he was no ways unfavourable to a restoration of the Romish religion. On the queen's death, Richard Worsley was again reinstated. He was previously sent with lord Chidiock Paulet, son of the marquis of Winchester, and governor of Portsmouth, with a commission to survey and repair the fortifications there, and was joined with a gentleman of the name of Smith, in a like commission to put the forts in the Isle of Wight in a state of defence, as a French invasion was then apprehended; four months after this he received his commission as captain of the island, and among other instructions was ordered to introduce the use of harquebusses among the people; he was also to signify to the queen and council, wherein his legal authority proved deficient, that it might be taken into consideration: but this was unnecessary, he conducting himself with such affability and prudence, that the people readily complied with his directions, in whatever appeared to him necessary to guard them against an enemy; as is instanced by their providing the field pieces before mentioned, which were supplied by several of the parishes. He was likewise employed by the queen in fortifying the sea-coasts, being afterwards sent with sir Hugh Paulet, captain of the Isle of Jersey, and others, to survey and order forts for the protection of Jersey and Guernsey. In conformity with his instructions, he introduced the use of fire-arms in the Isle of Wight, and an armourer was settled in Carisbrooke castle, to make harquebusses, and to keep them in order.'

The government of the Isle of Wight seems to have been usually considered as an office of great trust, and to have been

ob-

obtained only by particular access to the favour of the court. On the death of the former captain, the command of the island was bestowed on Edward Horsey, esq. soon afterwards knighted, a gentleman of an ancient family in Dorsetshire, and the great confidant of the earl of Leicester. We are informed, that the great plenty of hares and other game, with which the island is stored, is owing to his care: he is reported to have given a lamb for every hare that was brought to him from the neighbouring countries.

Sir Edward Horsey was succeeded by sir George Carey, afterwards lord Hunsdon, nearly related to queen Elizabeth; Henry, lord Hunsdon, his father, being nephew of queen Anne Boleyn. He was lord chamberlain of the household, one of the privy council, and a knight of the garter. He is the first captain, or warden, of the island that assumed the title of governor. It was suspected, from this alteration in his style, and from his general behaviour, that his intention was to subject the inhabitants of the island to the military power; but perhaps it may have proceeded entirely from the haughtiness of his disposition, by which he appears to have given general disgust to the gentlemen of the island. The historian justly observes, that his consciousness of support from government made him adopt the prudent orders given for the defence of the island in the reign of Edward the Third, not considering that those orders were issued with the consent of the inhabitants. On this occasion, the latter laid before the lords of council a representation, which, as our author remarks, may be considered as a little bill of rights of the island. It is entitled, Demands by the Gentlemen of the Isle of Wight for Reformation of a certain absolute Government lately assumed by the Captain there, tending to the Subversion of the Law, and to the taking away of the natural Freedom of the Inhabitants. This is said to be the first instance of any complaint exhibited by the inhabitants of the island against their captain, for exerting his authority in the cause of their protection. The remonstrance, however, procured the desired effect; for we are informed that the obnoxious powers, to which the inhabitants objected, were never afterwards claimed by any governor.

We are informed by sir Richard Worsley, that sir John Oglander, in his Memoirs, commends sir George Carey for residing in the castle of Carisbrooke, and for his great hospitality there; speaking also of the time of his government as the period when the island was in its most flourishing state. From those Memoirs we are favoured, in a note,

note, with the following extract, exhibiting a very striking description of the manners of the times.

"I have heard, says sir John, and partly know it to be true, that not only heretofore there was no lawyer nor attorney in owre island, but in sir George Carey's time, an attorney coming in to settle in the island, was, by his command, with a pound of candles hanging att his breech lighted, with bells about his legs, hunted owte of the island : insomuch that oure ancestors lived here so quietly and securely, being neither troubled to London nor Winchester, so they seldom or never went owte of the island ; insomuch as when they went to London (thinking it an East India voyage), they always made their wills, supposing no trouble like to travaile."

'Sir John, in another part of his Memoirs, observes, that

"The Isle of Wight, since my memory, is infinitely decayed ; for either it is by reason of so many attorneys that hath of late made this their habitation, and so by sutes undone the country, (for I have known an attorney bring down after a tearm three hundred writts, I have also known twenty nisi prius of our country tried at our assizes, when as in the queen's time we had not six writts in a yeare, nor one nisi prius in six yeares) or else, wanting the good bargains they were wont to buy from men of war, who also vented our commoditys at very high prices ; and readie money was easie to be had for all things. Now peace and law hath beggered us all, so that within my memorie many of the gentlemen, and almost all the yeomanry are undone.

"Be advised by me, have no suites at lawe, if it be possible : agree with thine adversary although it be with thy losse : for the expence of one tearme will be more than thy losse. Besides the neglect of thy time at home, thy absence from thy wife and children, so manie inconveniences hangeth upon a suite in lawe, that I advise thee, although thou has the better of it, let it be reconciled without law : at last twelve men or one must end it, let two honest ones do it at firste. This country was undone with it in king James his reign. Hazard death and all quarrels rather than let thy tongue make his master a slave." MSS. Memoirs.'

Sir John Oglander also relates, that in the government of the earl of Southampton, who immediately succeeded sir George Carey, and was universally esteemed for his affable and obliging behaviour, he had seen thirty or forty knights and gentlemen at bowls with his lordship on St. George's Down, where they had an ordinary twice every week.

In that part of the history which treats of the confinement of Charles the First in Carisbrooke Castle, we are presented with several interesting anecdotes not generally known ; but for which we refer our readers to the work. We shall only in-

form

form them, that the unfortunate monarch's watch is now in the possession of James Worsley, esq. of Stenbury; the king having, on his journey to Hurst Castle, whither he was removed by the parliament, given it to Mr. Edward Worsley, as a token of his remembrance.

The fifth chapter contains an account of the boroughs of Newport, Newtown, and Yarmouth. The first charter of immunities granted to the borough of Newport, was from Richard de Redvers, earl of Devon, the son of earl Richard. Its exact date is not known; but the historian observes, that it must have been in the time of Henry the Second, as the earl died in the thirtieth year of that reign. This charter, we are informed, like most of that early period, is very concise, expressing no more than a grant of liberties in general terms. A second charter, which is in the usual style, was granted to this town by Isabella de Fortibus, countess of Devon. The latter of those afterwards received several royal confirmations. A charter of incorporation was granted to this borough by James the First, and another by Charles the Second. Newport stands nearly in the centre of the island, of which it is the capital; and is a well-built, neat town, lately paved in the modern manner, with footways on each side. Here is a considerable manufactory of starch, the duty of which annually amounts to at least one thousand pounds. Of this town, as well as of the boroughs of Newtown and Yarmouth, we are presented with a particular account, which seems to be drawn up with great correctness and precision.

The sixth chapter treats of the religious houses, their foundations, and endowments; and the seventh, of the parish-churches and chapels; their founders and endowments; besides the most considerable manors and seats, with their ancient lords and present proprietors.

This part of the work, distinguished also by great minuteness, and lively description, contains many particulars of historical and genealogical information, which have been collected from a variety of sources relative to British antiquities.—Whether this writer recites an anecdote, or delineates the beauties of a country seat, his narrative is generally clear, easy, and expressive; conveying an accurate idea of the object, without either the disgust which arises from uninteresting description, or from ostentatious amplification.

The various parts of the book are illustrated with a great number of copper-plates, particularly of ancient seals, and of gentlemen's seats, exclusive of an accurate map of the island, prefixed to the volume. But in a work conducted with so much perspicuity, and enriched with such materials

of

of antiquarian research, those embellishments, however beautiful, are but secondary objects of regard.

The work is furnished with a valuable Appendix, containing no less than ninety different articles, relative either to the history or antiquities of the island. The first article, in this miscellaneous collection, is a list of the landholders in the Isle of Wight, with the valuation of the lands; extracted from Domesday Book. The following note, at the beginning of this article, is highly worthy of attention.

'Most of the writers on antiquity, as well as the lawyers, having been mistaken in the hide, which they all conclude to be a measure of land; it may be necessary to examine more particularly what is meant by a hide of land. If lord Coke and others, who think it was the same with a carucate, had considered duly how the hides and carucates appear in Domesday book, they never could have been betrayed into that error: it being obvious that hides and carucates are there distinguished from each other. The order of that book is, 1. To note the possessor. 2. The name of the lands. 3. The rate or value of the lands in hides. 4. The quantity in carucates, or plough lands, virgates, or yard lands, bovates, &c. After these particulars, we see the houses, servants, cottagers, woods, &c. The number of carucates almost always exceeds that of the hides; in one place more carucates make the hide than another, which difference arises either from the quality of the land, or perhaps sometimes from the favour of the commissioners in making the rates. We find also, that several manors are rated lower, or at a less number of hides, in this tax book, than they had been rated in the time of Edward the Confessor: and some are said not to be rated, because they were in the king's hands. For instance, the manor of Boucomb, one of the most considerable manors in the island, which had paid for four hides in the Confessor's time, is here not rated at all; and yet it is said to contain fifteen carucates of land. From hence the hide plainly appears to be the discretional rate, or valuation fixed to ascertain the Danegeld, which tax was also termed hidage; and the carucate, to be the content of the land in acres.'

From a subsequent passage in this article, relative to Watchingwood, sir Richard Worsley remarks the mistake of some historians, who affirm that Woodstock Park, made by king Henry I. was the first park in England.

We shall conclude our account of this work with observing, that it discovers an extent of researche, not only seldom to be met with in the most copious productions of this kind, but such as is both suitable and sufficient for elucidating the history of an island, that has hitherto been so imperfectly treated

treated by any topographical writer. Several subjects, relative to history and antiquity, are ascertained with great judgment, as well as accurate information ; and the whole is founded upon authorities of the most satisfactory nature.

Loose Hints upon Education, chiefly concerning the Culture of the Heart. 8vo. 5s. boards. Murray.

AS this volume is avowedly the production of lord Kaims, author of the Elements of Criticism, and Sketches of the History of Man, works of acknowledged merit, we sat down to the perusal of it with much prepossession in its favour, and entertained the most sanguine hopes of being both amused and instructed. Sorry we are to say, that we were grievously disappointed, as it appeared, on an impartial examination, that the work contained nothing new, solid, entertaining, or satisfactory ; the whole being only a collection of vague, and desultory hints, common-place reflections, trifling advice, and old stories, heaped together without order or precision, in a coarse and slovenly style. Never, indeed, do we remember to have seen a subject so serious and important as the education of children, treated in a manner so careless and uninteresting.

In our author's second section on the management of children in the first stage of life, we meet with the following deep and most sagacious reflection.

' Some children are by nature rash and impetuous : a much greater number are shy and timid. The disposition of a child appears early ; and both extremes ought to be corrected whenever an opportunity occurs. Fear is a passion implanted in our nature to warn us of danger, in order to guard against it. When moderate so as to raise our activity only, without overwhelming us, it is a most salutary passion : but when it swells to excess, which it is apt to do in a timid disposition, far from contributing to safety, it stupifies the man, and renders him incapable of action.'

Surely there wants no ghost, nor lord Kaims, to tell us this ; to dwell upon such trite and obvious truths, with an air of consequence and importance, is truly ridiculous : nothing can be more puerile than the following passage.

' *Will I* be thought to refine too much when I maintain, that a habit of cheerfulness acquired during infancy, will contribute to make a face beautiful ? A savage mind produces savage manners ; and these in conjunction produce a harsh and rugged coun-

countenance. Hence it is that a national face improves gradually, with the manners of the people. Listen to this ye mothers, with respect especially to your female children : you will find that cheerfulness is a greater beautifier than the finest pearl powder.'

If any of our readers are fond of pretty little stories, to repeat to their children, we recommend to them the following.

' A boy about the age of ten, says to his father, " Papa, give me some money. There is a shilling, will that do? No." " There's a guinea Thank you papa." The gentleman discovered, that it was given to a woman who had been delivered of twins, and was obliged to hire a nurse for one of them. A boy of five years, observing that a gentleman playing at cards did not pay what he lost, and concluding that he had no money, begged some from his father to give to the gentleman. A boy between seven and eight, of a noble family, strayed accidentally into a hut where he saw a poor woman with a sick child on her knee. Struck with compassion, he instantly gave her all the money he had ; carried to her from the herb market, turnips and potatoes, with bread and scraps from his father's kitchen. The parents enchanted with their son, took the poor family off his hand. Two or three years after, he saved the whole of his weekly allowance, till it amounted to eleven or twelve shillings, and purchased a Latin dictionary, which he sent to a comrade of his at the grammar school. Many other acts of goodness are recorded of this boy in the family. Can there be conceived a misfortune that will sink deeper into the heart of affectionate parents, than the death of such a child? It wrings my heart to think of it.

' Ostendent terris hunc tantum fata, neque ultra.
Esse sinent.
Heu, miserande puer ! si qua fata aspera rumpas,
Tu Marcellus eris.'

Here, gentle reader, you see a proof of the author's great learning? Was ever this celebrated passage in Virgil so happily quoted, and so well applied?—Immediately after this, we are presented with a new method of paying the poor's rates.

' There is no branch, says he, of education more neglected than the training of young persons to be charitable. And yet were this virtue instilled into children, susceptible of deep impressions, a legal provision for the poor would be rendered unnecessary: it would relieve England from the poor rates, a grievous burden that undermines both industry and morals.'

This

This convenient mode of paying the poor's rates, will, we hope, meet with encouragement from the prime minister; we know not whether, if properly attended to and improved upon, it might not, in time, discharge the national debt.

To those who are fond of good instruction and genteel compliment, we recommend the following lines.

' Exercise is not more salutary, to the body than to the mind' (this observation is shrewd, no doubt, and perfectly new) what then? Why, then—' When your little boy wants to have any thing done, let him first try what he can do himself. A savage having none to apply to for advice or direction, is reduced to judge for himself at every turn: he makes not a single step without thinking before hand what is to follow; by which means, a young savage is commonly endued with more penetration, than an Oxford or Cambridge scholar.'

Nothing can be more obliging than the high opinion which our author, in his last sentence, seems to entertain of the two universities.

In page 97 this discerning writer informs us, that

' If it were the fashion among people of rank to dress their children plain, it would have a wonderful good effect, not only on themselves, but on their inferiors. Young people would learn to despise fine cloaths, and to value themselves on good behaviour: neatness and elegance would be the sole aim in dress.'

This is most indisputably true; but how shall we ever persuade them to it? not, we fear, by the following rule:

' As soon, says our author, as children are susceptible of verbal instruction, let them know that the chief use of cloaths is to keep them warm; and that to be distinguished by their finery, will make them either be envied or ridiculed.'

And does lord Kaims really think that children in the *third* stage (for this is amongst his instructions for *them*) will be so foolish as to believe us when we tell them that the only *use of cloaths is to keep them warm?*

Of such remarks, and of such instructions, consists the whole of this performance, which, instead of that good sense and penetration, that critical sagacity and elegant taste, which distinguished our author's former works, presents us with nothing but a melancholy instance of intellectual decay, and the vapid dregs of exhausted genius.

Ele-

Elements of Elocution. **By** J. Walker. *Two Volumes.* 8vo. 12s. Robinson.

THIS work is the substance of a course of lectures on the art of reading, delivered at several colleges in the university of Oxford.

It is not merely a collection of sentences, and independent observations; but a regular system, founded on certain principles, which the author has illustrated and supported with great industry, modesty, and ingenuity.

The elocution, which is the object of this essay, is the pronunciation, which is given to words, when they are arranged into sentences, and form a discourse. The mode of pronouncing single words, independently on one another, is no part of his plan.

As the sense of an author is the first object of reading, he finds it necessary to enquire into those divisions and subdivisions of a sentence, which are employed to fix and ascertain its meaning. This leads him to consider the doctrine of punctuation. The use of the comma, being perhaps attended with more difficulty, than that of the other points, he has considered it with particular attention, and laid down a great variety of rules for its proper application. The greatest part of these directions are undoubtedly right; but, we apprehend, that if certain *general* rules could be adopted, the business of punctuation, or, which is the same thing, that of pausing in reading, would be more easily understood, and more regularly observed.

Sentences, in general, require a comma, or a pause, where there is a *connective* particle, or a word, *introducing* a new member, which may be separated from the preceding part.

1. All conjunctions are, as it were, the joints, where the body of a sentence ought to be divided. For instance:

I am convinced, *that* it is a mistake. I am informed, *that* you are the author. I wish to know, *whether* you intend to go to Italy, or not. I shall be satisfied, *when* I have seen the original. I shall keep it, *if* you please. I shall stay, *but* you may return. He has finished it, *as* you directed. I will set out immediately, *lest* I should be too late. He will continue there, *till* the end of August, &c.

2. Personal pronouns may generally admit a comma, or a small pause, before them: as, the author, *who* wrote on that subject. The tree, *which* grows in the garden. The lady, *whom* I saw at Paris. The fruit of that forbidden tree, *whose* mortal taste. The folio volume, *that* lies on the table, &c.

3. If

3. If a prepofition is prefixed to the pronoun, the paufe is before the prepofition. For inftance : the room, *in which* I am fitting. The gentleman, *with whom* I am acquainted. The country, *from which* he came. The prize, *for which* he contends, &c.

There are many rules, mentioned by this writer, which deferve attention, and to which we muft refer thofe readers, who wifh to form a competent idea of punctuation. We have fuggefted thefe three as hints only, which may open the way to a farther inveftigation of the fubject.

Befides the paufes, which indicate a greater or lefs feparation of the parts of a fentence, and a conclufion of the whole, there are certain inflections of voice, accompanying thofe paufes, which are as neceffary to the fenfe of the fentence, as the paufes themfelves. Any method therefore, which can afcertain thofe inflections, and convey them to the underftanding of the reader, by certain written marks and diftinctions, cannot fail of being acceptable to thofe, who wifh to become proficients in the art of elocution.

A laudable attempt to difcover fomething of this nature has led our author into a diftinction of the voice, which, though often mentioned by muficians, has been but little noticed by teachers of reading ; which is, that diftinction of the voice into the upward and downward flide, into which all fpeaking founds may be refolved. The moment, fays he, I admitted this diftinction I found I had poffeffion of the quality of the voice I wanted.

' Thefe two flides, or inflexions of voice are the axes, as it were, on which the force, variety, and harmony of fpeaking turns. They may be confidered as the great outlines of pro nunciation ; and if thefe outlines can be tolerably conveyed to a reader, they muft be of nearly the fame ufe to him, as the rough draught of a picture is to a pupil in painting. This then we fhall attempt to accomplifh, by adducing fome of the moft familiar phrafes in the language, and pointing out the inflexions which every ear, however unpractifed, will naturally adopt in pronouncing them. Thefe phrafes, which are in every body's mouth, will become a kind of *data*, or principles, to which the reader muft conftantly be referred, when he is at a lofs for the precife found, that is underftood by thefe different inflexions ; and thefe familiar founds, it is prefumed, will fufficiently inftruct him.'—

' — Much of that force, variety, and harmony which we hear in fpeaking arifes from two different modes of uttering the words of which a fentence is compofed ; the one, that which terminates the word with an inflexion of voice that rifes, and the other, that which terminates the word with an inflexion of voice that falls.   By rifing, or falling, is not meant the pitch of voice in which the whole word is pronounced, or that loudnefs or foftnefs which may accompany any pitch ;   but that upward or downward flide which the voice makes when the pronunciation of a word is finifhing ; and which may, therefore, not improperly be called the rifing and falling inflexion.

‘ So important is a juft mixture of thefe two inflexions, that the moment they are neglected, our pronunciation becomes forcelefs and monotonous ;   if the fenfe of a fentence requires the voice to adopt the rifing inflexion, on any particular word, either in the middle, or at the end of a phrafe, variety and harmony demand the falling inflexion on one of the preceding words ;   and on the other hand, if emphafis, harmony, or a completion of fenfe requires the falling inflexion on any word, the word immediately preceding, almoft always demands the rifing inflexion ; fo that thefe inflexions of voice are in an order nearly alternate.

‘ This is very obfervable in reading a fentence, when we have miftaken the connexion between the members, either by fuppofing the fenfe is to be continued, when it finifhes, or fuppofing it finifhed when it is really to be continued : for in either of thefe cafes, before we have pronounced the laft word, we find it neceffary to return pretty far back to fome of the preceding words, in order to give them fuch inflexions as are fuitable to thofe which the fenfe requires on the fucceeding words.   Thus, in pronouncing the fpeech of Portius in Cato, which is generally mifpointed, as in the following example :

> “ Remember what our father oft has told us,
> The ways of heav’n are dark and intricate,
> Puzzled in mazes and perplex’d in errors ;
> Our underftanding traces them in vain,
> Loft and bewilder’d in the fruitlefs fearch :
> Nor fees with how much art the windings turn,
> Nor where the regular confufion ends.”

‘ If, I fay, from not having confidered this paffage, we run the fecond line into the third, by fufpending the voice at *intricate*, and dropping it at *errors*, we find a very improper meaning conveyed ; and if in recovering ourfelves from this improper pronunciation, we take notice of the different manner in which we pronounce the fecond and third lines, we fhall find, that not only the laft word of thefe lines, but that every word alters its inflexion : for, when we perceive, that by miftaking the paufe, we have mifconceived the fenfe, we find it neceffary to begin the line again, and pronounce every word differently, in order to make it harmonious.

‘ But though thefe two inflexions of voice run through almoft every word of which a fentence is compofed, they are no where fo perceptible as at a long paufe, or where the fenfe of the words requires an emphafis : in this cafe, if we do but attend
                                                                    nicely

nicely to that turn of the voice, which finishes this emphatical word, or that member of a sentence where we pause, we shall soon perceive the different inflexion with which these words are pronounced.

' In order to make this different inflexion of voice more easily apprehended ; it may not, perhaps, be useless to attend to the following directions. Let us suppose we are to pronounce the following sentence :

' Does Cæsar deserve fame or blame ?

' This sentence, it is presumed, will, at first sight, be pronounced with the proper inflexions of voice, by every one that can barely read ; and if the reader will but narrowly watch the sounds of the words *fame* and *blame,* he will have an example of the two inflexions here spoken of : *fame* will have the rising, and *blame* the falling inflexion : but to make this distinction still clearer, if instead of pronouncing the word *fame* slightly, he does but give it a strong emphatic force, and let it drawl off the tongue for some time before the sound finishes, he will find it slide upwards and end in a rising tone ; if he makes the same experiment on the word *blame,* he will find the sound slide downwards, and end in a falling tone ; and this drawling pronunciation, though it lengthens the sounds beyond their proper duration, does not alter them essentially ; the same inflexions are preserved as in the common pronunciation ; and the distinction is as real in one mode of pronouncing as in the other, though not so perceptible.

' Every pause, of whatever kind, must necessarily adopt one of these two inflexions, or continue in a monotone : thus when we ask a question without the interrogative words, we naturally adopt the rising inflexion on the last word : as,

' Can Cæsar deserve blame ? Impossible !

Here *blame,* the last word of the question, has the rising inflexion, and *impossible,* with the note of admiration, the falling : the comma, or that suspension of voice generally annexed to it, which marks a continuation of the sense, is most frequently accompanied by the rising inflexion, as in the following sentence :

' If Cæsar deserves blame, he ought to have no fame.

Here we find the word *blame,* marked with the comma, has exactly the same inflexion of voice as the same word in the interrogative sentence immediately preceding ; the only difference is, that the rising inflexion slides higher at the interrogation than at the comma ; especially if it is pronounced with emphasis.

' The three other points, namely, the semicolon, colon, and period, adopt either the rising or falling inflexion as the sense or harmony requires, though in different degrees of elevation and depression.'

The

The author proceeds to illustrate thefe principles by a great variety of examples, fhewing, what flide or inflexion of the voice is fuited to exprefs the feveral paufes and diftinctions of punctuation, with clearnefs, ftrength, and propriety; and what pronunciation is required by emphafis, variety, harmony, and paffion.

This fubject leads him infenfibly into intricacies and diftinctions, whither perhaps few of his readers will be able to follow him; they who are able will undoubtedly profit by his ingenious fpeculations.

The following obfervation concerning the modulation of the voice in public fpeaking, is juft and important.

' The fafeft rule is to begin, as it were, with thofe of the affembly that are neareft to us; and if the voice be but articulate, however low the key may be, it will ftill be audible; and thofe who have a fufficient ftrength of voice for a public auditory, find it fo much more difficult to bring *down* than to raife the pitch, that they will not wonder I employ my chief care to guard againft an error by far the moft common, as well as the moft dangerous.

' Few fpeakers have a voice too weak for the public, if properly managed; as audibility depends much more on a proper pitch of voice, accompanied with diftinctnefs of articulation, than on a boifterous and fonorous loudnefs; this is evident from the diftinctnefs with which we hear a good actrefs in the eafy chit chat of genteel comedy; nay, even a fpeech afide, which is little more than a whifper, though uttered in a lower tone of voice, is fo articulated by a judicious actor, as to be equally audible with the loudeft burfts of paffion. A voice, therefore, is feldom inaudible from its want of force, fo much as from its want of modulation; and this modulation depends fo much on not fuffering the voice to begin above its natural pitch, that too much care cannot be taken to guard againft it.

' Much, undoubtedly, will depend on the fize and ftructure of the place we fpeak in: fome are fo immenfely large, as many of our churches and cathedrals, that the voice is nearly as much diffipated as in the open air; and often with the additional inconvenience of a thoufand confufed echos and re-echos. Here a loud and vociferous fpeaker will render himfelf unintelligible in proportion to his exertion of voice: as departing and commencing founds will encounter each other, and defeat every intention of diftinctnefs and harmony.

' Nothing but good articulation will make a fpeaker audible in this fituation; and a judicious attention to that tone of voice which is moft fuitable to the fize and imperfections of the place.'

As an effay towards reducing to practice the fyftem of inflexions, laid down in the prefent work, the author has attempted

tempted to mark them, as they occurred in Mrs. Yates's pronunciation of Mr. Sheridan's Monody in Memory of Mr. Garrick. The horizontal line expresses that monotone, or sameness of voice, which, he says, good pronouncers of verse often introduce to the greatest advantage. ' This monotone, he adds, generally falls into a lower key, and, as it is naturally expressive of awe, amazement, and admiration, is exceedingly suitable to solemn, grand, and magnificent subjects.'

' If dying' excellence' deserves' a tear',
If fond' remembrance' still' is cherished here',
Can' we persist to bid your sorrows flow'
For fabl'd' suff'rers, and delusive' woe ?
Or with quaint smiles dismiss the plaintive strain,
Point the quick jest, indulge' the comic' vein
Ere yet to buried Roscius' we assign'—
One kind' regret'—one' tributary' line' !
    His fame' requires we act a tenderer' part :'
His memory' claims' the tear' you gave his art' !
    The general voice,' the meed of mournful' verse',
The splendid sorrows' that adorned' his hearse',
The throng that mourn'd as their dead favourite pass'd',
The grac'd' respect that claim'd' him to the last',
While Shakspeare's' image' from its hallow'd' base',
Seem'd' to prescribe' the grave', and point' the place',—
Nor these,—nor all the sad regrets that flow
From fond fidelity's domestic' woe,—
So much are Garrick's' praise'—so much' his due'—
As on this' spot'—one' tear' bestow'd by you.'

It is impossible, as our author observes, to convey that justness of pause, that melody of voice, and that dignity of manner, which distinguish a good speaker. These are among the perishable beauties described in the Monody. But there are beauties of an inferior kind, which are not so incommunicable; and they, who attentively peruse what is said on the subject in this work, will not think *that* notation, which conveys to us a variety of just and pleasing inflexions, though unaccompanied with every other excellence, either an incurious or a useless discovery.

---

*Experiments and Observations relating to the various Branches of
Natural Philosophy; with a Continuation of the Observations
on Air. The Second Volume.* By Joseph Priestley, LL. D.
F. R. S. &c. 8vo. 6s. Johnson.

WE inform the public, with great pleasure, that this, though the fifth, is not likely to be the last volume, of Dr. Priestley's philosophical productions. In his preface he

feeds

feeds our expectation with the moſt flattering promiſes—He tells us, that in conſequence of ſome happy revolution in his circumſtances, he may be conſidered as entering upon a new period of life ; and that the volume before us is the reſult of an inclination to cloſe his philoſophical accounts, as they ſtand at preſent, and to open a *new one.* We feel warm in the hope that the ſucceſs of his ſingular toil and ingenuity may be in proportion to the advantageous change by which they are favoured. We ſhall, however, be amply ſatisfied if he proceeds with the rapidity and ſplendour which have hitherto crowned his exertions.

In the numerous catalogue of Dr. Prieſtley's diſcoveries there is not one more curious, or better ſupported by the evidence of experiments, than that which evinces the great uſe of vegetables, in purifying the atmoſphere after it has been corrupted by the reſpiration of animals, and other circumſtances which render it noxious. The firſt ſection of this volume confirms what he has before ſaid on this ſubject : his preceding volume informed the public of a ſingular property, by which the willow plant abſorbed air of different kinds, but inflammable air in the greateſt abundance : he has ſince made a variety of experiments, from which we learn the following particulars. 1. Inflammable air, after the abſorption of the willow plant, is diſcharged purified from its phlogiſton by the plant, which had retained this noxious principle for its own nouriſhment. 2. He confirms an hypotheſis which he had formerly ſupported, viz. that nitrous air is noxious as well to vegetable as to animal life. 3. It appears from this ſection that in ſome inſtances the willow plant may really abſorb a greater quantity of inflammable air than it can digeſt. In this caſe, the air, which it diſcharges after abſorption, is a mixture of pure and inflammable air; for, by applying a candle to this mixture, it goes off with a loud exploſion. 4. The Doctor very pertinently points out the wiſdom of nature, as it is evident from the growth of this willow plant in marſhy places, where a great quantity of inflammable air is continually diſcharged. Sect. II. may, we think, be conſidered as the moſt curious and entertaining part of this work. In an appendix to his laſt volume, Dr. Prieſtley announced his diſcovery of that great influence which light has upon water, or upon the air, which, in conſequence of being expoſed to the ſun, is produced from that water. Dr. Ingenhouſz purſued the enquiries which this diſcovery ſuggeſted, and wrote a whole volume, in which we are by no means convinced of his making proper acknowledgements to the ſource whence he derived his materials. Our readers may remember, that Dr. Prieſtley filled two jars with pump water, one of which was placed in the dark and the other exposed to the sun. In the former, after continuing for some time in the same circumstances, no air was produced. But in the latter, after standing a few days, a green matter was deposited, whence a quantity of air was emitted, which upon examination was found to be much purer than common air. The Doctor informs us, in this volume, that the green matter which appeared in this experiment, is discovered to be a vegetable, whose form and other peculiarities were most clearly seen through a microscope, by his friend Mr. Bewley.

An acquaintance with the nature of this green matter has led the Doctor to prove most clearly, that its operations resemble those of other vegetables in open air : that, by feeding on the noxious principle contained in the air, with which the water is impregnated, it purifies that air. His experiments produced in defence of this hypothesis are, in our opinion, decisive. By exposing water which contained no air to the light in a jar inverted in mercury, no effects were produced. By putting a quantity of the green matter, taken from water which had discharged all its air, into a jar of fresh water, pure air was produced as copiously as before. And, farther, by examining the air in any particular water, before and after the green matter was deposited from, or placed in it, he found that the green matter had always purified that air. Aquatics of different kinds were found, on being introduced into a jar of water and exposed to the sun, to produce effects similar to those already enumerated : a handful of these water-plants were put into a receiver containing eighty ounce measures of water, inverted in a bason of the same ; after standing three days, they had emitted eight ounce measures of air, which was found to be much purer than common air ; from which, as well as from other experiments, the Doctor infers, that in these experiments the air is generally in proportion to the capacity of the vessel ; and that during the whole process it seldom exceeds one-eighth of the quantity of water. The Doctor concludes this section with observing, that the experiments recited in it ' may help us to explain, why water, after issuing from the earth and employed in floating meadow land, becomes in time exhausted of its power of fertilizing it. When it issues from the earth, it contains air of an impure kind ; that is, air loaded with phlogiston. This principle the roots of the grass extract from it, so that it is then replete with dephlogisticated air, and consequently the plants it afterwards comes into contact with find nothing in it to feed upon.——I believe it is commonly imagined that the water deposits something in its course upon the earth

K 4

of

of its bed, and by that means becomes effete and incapable of nourishing plants.'—

Dr. Prieſtley, in his third ſection, gives the diſtinguiſhing properties of the plant which forms the green matter; its length proves it not to be the conſerva fontinalis; its ſeeds float inviſibly in the air; and will penetrate into water through the ſmalleſt apertures in the glaſs. It feeds upon phlogiſton, and grows in great abundance when putrid fleſh is put into a jar of water. But the air in the water may be ſo much loaded with the noxious principle as to prevent the air oozing out of the plant from being pure. The green matter will, moreover, appear in water impregnated with ſalt, or nitre; but it ſeems probable that water impregnated with fixed air, will not admit of its growth, till the fixed air has eſcaped. Dr. Prieſtley concludes this ſection with an experiment deſigned to prove in what part of the veſſel the ſeeds of this plant would firſt fall, and *we are aſtoniſhed* he ſhould not repeat the experiment, but leave a deciſion to conjecture, which might have been made with ſuch little trouble.

We cannot give a better general view of the contents of the fourth ſection than that which the Doctor himſelf has given.

' Having very ſoon obſerved that this green vegetable matter, or *water moſs*, was planted and propagated with more eaſe, and produced air more copiouſly, in ſome circumſtances than in others, and that various ſubſtances, animal or vegetable, were favourable to it, and others of both kinds unfavourable; I tried a great variety of them, and ſhall recite ſuch of the particulars as appear in any meaſure remarkable, and ſuch as may furniſh hints for the farther inveſtigation of what relates to this ſubject.

' The moſt remarkable circumſtance attending theſe experiments was, that ſome ſubſtances, concerning which I could have had no ſuch expectation a priori, inſtead of admitting the growth of this plant, when they began to putrify and diſſolve, which was the caſe with moſt vegetable and animal ſubſtances, yielded from themſelves a very great quantity of inflammable air; and it made no difference whether they were placed in the ſun or in the ſhade. Whereas other ſubſtances, which, if they had been confined by quickſilver, would have yielded, by putrefaction, inflammable air alſo, together with a portion of fixed air, only ſupplied the proper pabulum for this green matter, and the whole produce was pure dephlogiſticated air; the phlogiſton, which in other circumſtances would have been converted into inflammable air, now going to the nouriſhment of this plant, which, by the influence of light, yields ſuch pure air.'

It ſhould be attended to, that, in the numerous experiments following theſe obſervations, of all the materials employed,
onions

onions were thofe which admitted of the green matter with the greateft difficulty. In one part of this fection Dr. Prieftley informs us, that he found a piece of cabbage, which he had expofed in his jar for fome time, very foft but not at all offenfive. He fuppofes that the green matter had abforbed all the *phlogifton* of this fubftance, to which *alone* he afcribes the offenfivenefs of fmells.——What reafon is there for acceding to this theory? In that general decompofition which takes place, when a body begins to part with its phlogifton, many other component parts of the body fly off. And why fhould we afcribe to the phlogifton what may (as far as we know) with equal propriety be afcribed to any of the other ingredients which are let loofe at the fame time? We know of no experiment which gives a decifion in this cafe, but fhould rather wave acceding to the Doctor's hypothefis, till by the fame hypothefis he can account for the different fmells which proceed from different bodies in putrefaction. Ought not the putrid fmell of fifh to be the fame with the putrid fmell of flefh, if they depended on the operations of the fame fimple agent? It may be faid, that in thefe different cafes, the phlogifton is differently modified. We think this language, which has of late been too commonly ufed, is nothing more than a fpecious mode of concealing, under a mere name, the ignorance we cannot remove: it is, in other words, employing the occult quality of the ancients, and is equally trifling as to the conviction or fatisfaction which it gives an inquifitive mind. But, perhaps, the Doctor may have reafons for adopting this theory, to which we may be utter ftrangers; we have, therefore, only to wifh that he had referred us to them, or laid them before the public.

The next fection is nearly connected with thofe fections we have already reviewed; it contains a number of experiments relating to the effect of expofing animal fubftances in water to the light and in the dark. It appears that fifh have the property, in a fingular degree, of affording a nidus to the feeds of the green matter. It is the animal fubftance which of all others is moft likely to putrify in water, and probably it may derive its power of producing the green matter from a wife appointment of the Creator. Dr. Prieftley obferves, that the effect of light upon bodies putrefying in water may have a very falutary tendency in hot countries.——Undoubtedly, if the doctor could prove that in hot countries the fmalleft part of the putrified bodies were immerfed in water; and again, immerfed in fuch a manner (which is by no means probable) that the furfaces of thefe bodies were never expofed to the air; for in fuch circumftances it is well known, from an experiment recited in

this

this very section, that air, instead of being purified, is actually corrupted by the perishing body.

Though we are indeed most highly entertained by the instructive catalogue of experiments given in section sixth, we are yet by no means convinced of the truth they are designed to establish. The Doctor meant, in this section, to pave the way for determining the different degrees of nutrition in different bodies. With this view he collects the air emitted by them in a state of putrefaction, which he finds to be in general inflammable, mixed with a portion of fixed air. The substances which the Doctor employs in his experiments are onions, potatoes, carrots, parsnips, and other vegetables which we most commonly feed upon. But why not extend his trials to a much greater number of bodies? this was absolutely necessary to give the least plausibility to his theory; for, perhaps, *such bodies as are not nutritive* might yield the same kind of air, and in equal abundance. We cannot even suspect the contrary, till such experiments are first made; besides, what evidence have we to believe, that the nutritive quality in bodies is in proportion to the inflammable air they emit, or to the phlogiston they contain? we consider this as a step which should have been first established before the least dependence can be placed on another, which is wholly supported by it. From the testimony of universal experience it must be allowed, that animal are more nutritive than vegetable substances. And as we proceeded, we indulged the hope that the Doctor, in his next section, would have subjected animal substances to the same circumstances as those in which, agreeable to his preceding section, he had putrefied vegetable substances; but he unexpectedly, and for what reason we cannot guess, changes the mode of his experiments: we hence derive a very entertaining list of facts, shewing the result of putrefying flesh in jars inverted in quicksilver. And though the reader may not be altogether satisfied with the Doctor's theory of nutrition, he will yet find in this section many interesting observations. Amongst others the absolute necessity of water, and that in a considerable quantity, to the production of some airs, viz. nitrous, fixed, and inflammable air; but while this appears to be the consequence of several experiments, the Doctor fairly acknowleges, that when water has entered into the composition of air, he knows no method of discovering and restoring it. We know of no fact which militates against this theory excepting *one*, which, we dare say, the Doctor's experience will readily bring to his memory; the more concentrated the marine acid is, the greater abundance of inflammable air will it produce, if there is
dissolved

diſſolved in it any quantity of tin or iron. We cannot account for this phenomenon, on the ſuppoſition that water enters ſo abundantly into the compoſition of inflammable air.

There are few ſpeculations more curious than thoſe which have a tendency to ſhew the different degrees of phlogiſtication of which air is ſuſceptible, and through which it paſſes before it comes to its moſt putrid or noxious ſtate. Dr. Prieſtley has plainly ſhewn that the laſt, or that ſtate in which phlogiſton is united to air with the ſtrongeſt affinity, is the inflammable. He has pointed out ſome of the gradual purifications which reduce it from this ſtate into that of phlogiſticated air, or that in which a candle is extinguiſhed without any attendant exploſion. Section VIII. preſents us with ſome curious inſtances of this proceſs. Dr. Prieſtley had obſerved, that by introducing a mixture of iron-filings and ſulphur into a jar of nitrous air, a quantity of inflammable air was generally produced : he had formerly ſuppoſed that this change was owing to ſome revolution in the conſtitution of the nitrous air ; but with his uſual manlineſs and openneſs, he retracts this opinion, and gives a variety of experiments, ſhewing that the change muſt depend upon a generation of inflammable air, from the ſulphur and the iron-filings. But the ſame experiments, to uſe his own words, have led him alſo to the obſervation, ' that in this, and many other caſes of the diminution of common air by phlogiſtic proceſſes, a true inflammable air is firſt produced, and in its *naſcent* ſtate (as it may be called) is immediately decompoſed, previous to the phlogiſtication of the common air.' We ſhall repeat ſome of the leading facts which confirm theſe obſervations. A mixture of iron filings and ſulphur was introduced, while it was actually emitting inflammable air, into a quantity of common air ; and in the interval of a month, it diminiſhed the common air conſiderably : the mixture was then taken out of the common air, and upon trial was ſtill found to emit inflammable air. There can be no doubt that the common air in this experiment had been diminiſhed and phlogiſticated by an addition of inflammable air in its *naſcent* ſtate, or rather after it was *completely* though but *newly* formed. Dr. Prieſtley wiſhed to ſee whether a *ſtrong heat* would not produce this change in inflammable, when already made and mixed with common air : a very ſimple experiment decided the contrary. A mixture of common and inflammable air, however, after being kept a long time, diſcovered ſome little change, but ſtill there was always a reſidue of inflammable air : this change was produced much more completely, by admitting the inflammable by ſmall quantities into the common air.

Dr.

Dr. Priestley, in Section IX. examines and refutes two very important errors, which some of his philosophical friends had embraced and endeavoured to support. Dr. Ingenhousz asserts, that a quantity of air issues from the skin, and that perspiration, like respiration, phlogisticates air. Dr. Priestley proves to a demonstration, that this air does not issue from the skin, but from the water in which any part of the body subjected to trial is immersed. If you place a piece of glass or metal in water containing air, in an exhausted receiver, the phænomena, which Dr. Ingenhousz describes may be seen, in which case it is easily shewn that the air comes from the water itself; for if the water contain no air, and the surface of the glass or metal be wiped, the appearance, which Dr. Ingenhousz lays so much stress upon, cannot be produced. Dr. Ingenhousz's supposition, that water exhausted of its air is not proper for this experiment, because it absorbs all the air as readily as it issues from the skin, is very decisively refuted by Dr. Priestley. 1. If the experiment be made in water, this must be the only unexceptionable way of doing it. 2. Water by no means absorbs any air so fast as to give the least plausibility to Dr. Ingenhousz's supposition. And, 3. This air, agreeable to Dr. Ingenhousz's supposition, is phlogisticated, which we well know is of all others absorbed with the greatest difficulty. 4. 'Where are the air vessels necessary for the purpose pointed out by Dr. Ingenhousz, and what is their origin and connexion with other parts of the system; the present state of anatomy indicates nothing on the subject.' To place however the matter beyond all doubt, Dr. Priestley expelled all its air, by boiling it out of a portion of water, and plunged his arm into it; but though he continued his arm in this situation for half an hour, not a single bubble of air made its appearance. The Doctor observes, that he might have examined whether this water contained any air besides what it might have been supposed to have imbibed from the atmosphere in this interval, but that he neglected to do it, declaring *his confidence that it was unnecessary*. We are really astonished at the Doctor's carelessness in this particular instance. Why should he omit as a trifle, and leave to supposition, a fact which would have removed every shadow of an argument for the hypothesis he was endeavouring to overturn, especially as the toil it would have cost him must be so very inconsiderable? Another error which Dr. Priestley very ably corrects in this section is a very gross one espoused by Mr. Cruikshanks, who has declared, that perspiration actually phlogisticates air in some degree: he builds this opinion on a very slight foundation indeed, on a single experiment, in which water became turbid (after having kept his

his leg in it for fome time) when he mixed it with lime-water ; one fact related by Dr. Prieftley is fufficient to overturn this wild theory, which depends on the falfe principle, that fixed and phlogifticated are one and the fame air. Dr. Prieftley tied a bladder round his leg, with his leg in this confinement he flept a whole night, and the next morning examined the air in the bladder, which he found to be equally pure with common air.

[*To be continued.*]

The New Annual Regifter, or General Repofitory of Hiftory, Politics, and Literature, for the Year 1780. *To which is prefixed, A fhort Review of the principal Tranfactions of the prefent Reign.* 8vo. 5s. 3d. *in Boards.* Robinfon.

THE ufefulnefs of a Regifter, containing a particular account of the different tranfactions, and the multitude of mifcellaneous objects, worthy of notice, which occur in the year, is too obvious to require elucidation. In a work of fo extenfive a nature, next to fidelity of hiftorical detail, the qualities moft effentially requifite are judgement in the felection of the materials, and perfpicuity in the arrangement; without the former of which, the volume would become only a mafs of frivolous compilation ; and without the latter, a confufed and difgufting aggregate of mifplaced information, and mifconducted entertainment.

In the execution of the New Annual Regifter, we have the fatisfaction to find, that due regard has been paid to thofe important confiderations. The hiftorical part appears to be written with a freedom of fentiment, unbiaffed by political prejudices ; and the various articles, relative to biographical anecdotes and characters, manners of nations, philofophical papers, antiquities, literature, &c. are not only felected from the beft authorities, but digefted in a clear, methodical, and advantageous point of view.

A concife and general hiftory of the literature of the year is alfo given, accompanied with obfervations, which will ferve to afcertain the prefent ftate of learning in Britain ; and to fhew how far the genius, knowlege, and tafte of the nation, are in a declining, or a progreffive condition ; a circumftance not only interefting to curiofity, but which may, eventually, be productive of confequences much more important.

This being the firft volume of the work, it commences with a fhort review of the principal tranfactions of the prefent reign ; from which, as a fpecimen, we have taken the following extract.

' King

' King George the Second concluded his days on the twenty-fifth of October, 1760, with a glory not usual to princes, and especially to those who have reigned for many years, and died at a very advanced age. His abilities, if not of the first rate, were respectable, and his virtues rendered him the object of general esteem. There was a moderation in his political temper and conduct which suited him to the government of a free people; and during the whole of his reign, his subjects enjoyed as great, if not a greater portion of happiness than is common to nations.

' But it was not solely, or principally, owing to these things that he went out of the world with so much lustre. A considerable part of his reign had not a little been disturbed with political disputes: and events had happened, both foreign and domestic, which were sufficiently mortifying, and which, at times, affected his popularity. In the war that was concluded by the treaty of Aix-la-Chapelle, he had not been successful; and, during the course of that war, his throne had been shaken by a rebellion, which, however, served, in the end, to render it more firm, and to manifest to him the real affection of the great majority of his people. His natural attachment to Hanover, which was believed to have an undue influence upon his negotiations and engagements on the continent, had been a repeated subject of complaint: and the commencement of the war, in which the kingdom was involved at his decease, had been attended with several disagreeable events. The principal circumstances that spread such a glory around him at his death, were the victories with which his latter years had been crowned; and which were owing to a great minister, who had been forced upon him, much against his will, by the voice of the public; but to whom, when he had been obliged to receive him, he gave his full confidence and support. The spirit and abilities of this man, which bore down all opposition both at court and in parliament, which carried the nation along with him, and infused a noble emulation into our naval and military commanders, had raised the British name and empire to the highest degree of splendor, power, and political importance.

' In this state of the dignity and happiness of Great Britain, and in the midst of a successful war, king George the Third mounted the throne. To succeed to the crown in such a situation, was in itself a peculiar advantage; besides which there were many circumstances that concurred to recommend the young monarch to the universal affection of his subjects. The time of his life, having now attained the full age of manhood, being in his twenty-third year, naturally created a prejudice in his favour; and this prejudice was justly increased by the decency and regularity of his manners, and by the possession and the promise of many engaging virtues. There was, likewise, a disposition in all parties to unite in support of his government: for the attachment to the Stuart family was almost worn out; and those who retained the principles which had heretofore excluded them from the preferments

ments of the court, hoped that former distinctions would now be abolished. Even the circumstance of the king's being a native of this country, contributed not a little to his popularity. This, in itself, to a thinking mind, will appear a matter of no great moment; and especially when it is considered, that some of our best princes have been of foreign birth. However, in the enthusiasm naturally attendant on a new reign, it was likely to have its effect; and accordingly, it was artfully enough laid hold of, to captivate the minds of the people. The language, used by his majesty in his speech to his parliament, "born and educated in this country, I glory in the name of Briton," though it might almost seem to convey a reflection on our preceding monarchs, was repeated in rapture through the land; and was echoed back to the throne in many of the addresses which, according to custom, are presented from every quarter, on a fresh succession to the crown.

' The instant of the king's accession was distinguished by the earl of Bute's being sworn of the privy council, in conjunction with his royal highness the duke of York. This, perhaps, was no more than what might be expected, and, indeed, what ought to be done, from the station which his lordship had held, as groom of the stole, about his majesty's person, when prince of Wales. Nevertheless, speculative men would attend to it; and others would be looking up to a nobleman, who had been always understood to have great influence at Leicester-house, and who would probably arise to the plenitude of power.

' The first proceedings of the new reign did not indicate any great purposes of change in the measures of government. The king declared his resolution of prosecuting the war with vigour, and of supporting his allies; and public affairs continued apparently to be managed by Mr. Pitt, in connection with the duke of Newcastle and his party. The only considerable alterations that happened were the displacing of the earl of Holderneffe, in a few months, to make room for lord Bute's being introduced into the responsible office of secretary of state; and the removal of Mr. Legge, from the posts of under-treasurer and chancellor of the exchequer. The dismission of Mr. Legge, who was an excellent minister of finance, and in high esteem with the public, gave occasion to some speculation and dissatisfaction. It was imputed, at the time, though without any just ground, to some disputes having arisen between him and Mr. Pitt concerning the supplies necessary for the service of the year. The real cause of his removal was the disgust he had excited at Savile-house in the preceding reign, by refusing to resign his own pretensions to the representation of the county of Hants, in order to give way to sir Simeon Stuart. This sacrifice had been urged upon him by lord Bute, supported by the authority of the prince of Wales; and when the transaction came to be known, it was much insisted upon as an indication of a disposition not favourable to Whiggism.

I

' Not

' Not long after his majesty's accession, a bill was passed which was very popular, and honourable to government ; and that was, the act for extending the independence of the judges. The king himself went to the house, and in a speech to his parliament, recommended the consideration of this object. It had been enacted, in the reign of William the Third, that the judges should hold their commissions during their good behaviour ; a wise provision, which prevented their being removeable, as had heretofore been the case at the will of the sovereign. However it was still understood that their offices were determined at the demise of the crown, or at the expiration of six months afterwards. By the present bill, their commissions were rendered perpetual, during their good behaviour, notwithstanding any such demise. We have reason to believe that Sir Michael Foster, at that time one of the justices of the King's Bench, and a gentleman of eminent legal abilities, considered this act as unnecessary ; it being his opinion that the design of it was virtually included in the act of King William. But, upon the whole, it was thought better, and we imagine wisely, that the matter should be settled by express statute.

The many arrangements and regulations that necessarily take place on a new reign, and the public ceremonies to which it gives birth, serve to excite the attention, and even to increase the loyalty and affection of the people. Besides the common circumstances which contributed to the splendor of his majesty's accession to the crown, this splendor was not a little increased by his marriage. It was an event, likewise, in itself singularly happy. The invariably excellent character of the queen, whilst it hath secured the king's personal felicity, hath obtained for her the universal esteem of the nation ; and the numerous race of princes and princesses with which the royal nuptials have been blessed, will, we trust, add ornament and support to the throne, and afford farther stability to the general welfare.. The admirable pattern set by their majesties in private life cannot be too greatly applauded. Whatever may be thought of the administration of public affairs, every friend to his country must regret, that such an example of good order, fidelity, virtue, and domestic harmony, hath been so little followed by those who ought to have looked up to it with reverence and emulation.

' Whilst the attention of the court was so much employed by the marriage and coronation of the king and queen, and by other objects of ceremony and regulation, the great national concerns were not neglected. The war under the auspices of Mr. Pitt, was carried on with its usual vigour ; though the events of 1761, were not altogether so splendid as those which had taken place in the two preceding years. Belleisle, the largest of the islands belonging to the French king in Europe, was taken ; and the reduction of Pondicherry almost totally destroyed the power of that monarch in the East Indies. In the West Indies, Dominica was
added

added to the acquisitions we had already made in that part of the world.

'But, notwithstanding the success of our arms, the restoration of peace began to be a very desirable object. The large expences of the hostilities carried on by us in different quarters of the globe were felt by the public; though the amazing extent and prosperity of our commerce rendered them far less burthensome than they would otherwise have been. The drains of men and money occasioned by the German war and our continental connections, were particularly complained of; and by degrees excited much dissatisfaction. The inconsistency of Mr. Pitt's conduct, in this respect, with his former professions, became a frequent topic of declamation; and it was urged in so powerful a manner, as to make a deep impression on the minds of great numbers of persons. In 1761, the belligerent powers appeared sincerely desirous of coming to an accommodation. Accordingly, a negociation was opened between England and France; for which purpose Mr. Hans Stanley was sent to Paris, and Monsieur Bussy came to London. At first the prospect of terminating the war was very favourable; but, in the course of the negociation, fresh difficulties continually arose, which, at length, occasioned it to be entirely broken off. It is observable, that in the terms of peace prescribed by Mr. Pitt, he did not wholly exclude the French from North America. Louisiana was still to continue in their possession. Whether this was owing to that great man's superior sagacity, or to whatever cause, every friend to his country must regret that the treaty which was afterwards concluded, was not constructed on the same principles; as those calamitous events would in all probability have thereby been prevented, which have since shaken the British empire to its foundations.

'It appeared, in a little time, that the war, instead of being put an end to, was likely to become more extensive. During the late negociation, Spain had displayed an evident partiality in favour of France; and, indeed, had interfered in a manner which afforded just cause of offence to the English court. The famous family compact was now forming, which hath been attended with consequences so hostile to Great Britain. Mr. Pitt, who had the fullest conviction and intelligence of the designs of the Spanish crown against us, insisted upon an immediate declaration of war against that crown. But in this he was opposed by all the cabinet council, excepting his brother-in-law, Earl Temple. The measure was deemed too bold and precipitate; and it was understood that even the king himself, if his council had agreed to it, would have found it extremely difficult to consent to their resolution. Mr. Pitt, being thus counteracted in a matter of such great consequence, resigned his post of secretary of state, and was succeeded by Lord Egremont. At his resignation, he was prevailed upon to accept a pension of three thousand pounds a-year, and a peerage for his lady. Nothing was ever better merited than this penfion; and yet the acceptance of it was injurious to his popularity.'

From the various merit, and judicious plan of this work, we entertain the moſt favourable expectations of its being well received by the public.

MONTHLY CATALOGUE.

POETRY.

The American *War, a Poem; in Six Books.* 8vo. 4s. ſewed. Hooper.

AMongſt the many evils brought on this country by the American war, Reviewers have too much cauſe to lament the multiplicity of bad productions, both in verſe and proſe, which it has occaſioned. The poem before us conſiſts of no leſs than ſix tedious books, and makes one large octavo volume. Every tranſaction is here faithfully recorded, and every battle and ſkirmiſh minutely deſcribed; though there is not, at the ſame time, a page worth reading, or a line worth repeating, throughout the whole. We will give our readers a *ſhort* ſpecimen, which, we dare ſay, they will think *long* enough, of this performance.

' More than one hour a ſolemn ſilence reign'd;
Apparently Fort Sullivan was gain'd,
During the fight, the Britiſh ſoldiers ſtood
Inactive, and the hot engagement view'd!
Nor cou'd they now afford the leaſt relief,
Altho' each vex'd and diſappointed chief
Seem'd anxious for the fight, and all expreſt
A readineſs to come to cloſeſt teſt:
No boats they had to waft them ſafely o'er!
Nor cou'd they wade towards that hoſtile ſhore!
At leaſt, they had no cov'ring ſhips of war;
They ſtuck aground on Carolina's bar!
Thus, like the myrmidons of old they ſtood,
And the dread ſlaughter of the Britons view'd!
Lee join'd the coloniſts as they retir'd;
Shame! ſhame! he cry'd, with indignation fir'd:
We cannot ſtand, they ſaid, the cannonade,
The ſeamen 'gainſt Fort Sullivan have made;
Tho' the three frigates ſtill aground remain;
(From whence perhaps they ne'er will float again;)
Altho' like wrecks we can perceive moſt clear,
Th' Experiment and Briſtol both appear!
Tho' maſts and rigging overboard are thrown!
And but as one their batter'd port-holes yawn!

The'

Tho' from their scoppers to the briny tide,
We see the purple marks of slaughter glide!
Altho' we've swept the Briftol's quarter deck!
They seem to feel no cool difheart'ning check!
But with frefh fury, guns and mortars ply,
Which ftorm to fhun, we from our quarters fly!'

No part of this poem, (for we have toiled through it all) is better than the lines above quoted. Is it not aftonifhing that any man fo totally void of all poetical abilities as the author of the *American War*, could ever prevail on himfelf to publifh fuch intolerable jargon?

A Defcriptive Poem, written in the Weft Indies. *By* George Heriot. 4to. 2s. Dodfley.

If any of our readers be fond of that fpecies of writing,

' Where fmooth defcription holds the place of fenfe,

we recommend to them the perufal of this poem, in which all the peculiar phænomena, birds, plants, beafts, &c. of the Weftern world are accurately delineated. It may afford fome inftruction to the curious inveftigator of nature, but will not give much entertainment to a lover of the Mufes, as the following fpecimen will fufficiently convince the impartial critic.

' To thee, Flamingo, in defcriptive courfe,
I turn my verfe.—Straight, tall, majeftic bird!
With thy deep crimfon plumage, mixed with white,
Adorn'd in luftre gay; and thy long neck,
And ruddy legs, join'd to thy full-form'd breaft,
Approaching nearly to the height of man.
How fingular thy bill! thy tongue how ftrange!
Set with a double row of fharp hook'd teeth.
With legs and neck outftretch'd, thou wing'ft the air,
In flow and heavy flight, and when in crowds,
In order regular ye move.—Next of th' aquatic kind,
With flender, crooked necks, the Galdings view;
Some deck'd with fnow-white feathers, fome with grey,
And fome with fable blue, and red-caped crown.'

This may, for ought we know, be a very juft and exact defcription of thefe extraordinary birds; but the whole would perhaps found full as well in plain profe, efpecially as the lines have nothing in them very pleafing or poetical.—We have afterwards a minute account of the millepedes, tarantula, faw-fly, fire-fly, and twenty other wonderful infects.—Walk in, ladies and gentlemen, and fee them all for the fmall price of two fhillings; and if you are not fatisfied with our author's defcription, and wifh to view the originals, you have only to ftep into a veffel and crofs the Atlantic.

A familiar Epistle from a Cat at the Qu—n's P—l—ce, to Edmund Burke, Esq. on his Motion for the better Regulation of his Majesty's Civil Establishment, &c. 4to. 1s. 6d. Kearsly.

It is a common proverbial saying that, *a cat may look at a king,* which we by no means wish to dispute the truth of; but it does not follow that because she may *look at,* she has therefore a right to *abuse* him, which seems to be the design of this very indifferent performance, which has nothing to recommend it but a great quantity of virulence and scurrility in most intolerable metre, as the reader will see by the few following lines, where, speaking of the American war, puss purrs thus:

'———— it makes one quite frantic
To think how things go t'other side the Atlantic!
Where a war's carry'd on between friend and friend,
Which, whoever shall conquer, must fatally end.
Oh! curse on the authors! aloud exclaim'd he,
That they have their reward, heav'n grant I may see;
To their much injur'd country victims be led,
With B———— and the R-b-c-n lord, at their head.
Such victims alone the gods can appease,
Sweet peace can restore, and the people well please.
As he utter'd these words, a spontaneous sigh
Burst forth from my breast, and Amen did I cry.
That moment, my principles totally chang'd,
And all my ideas were newly arrang'd.
I now feel for my country; and when I compare
The past with the present, I cannot forbare
Sincerely to join in the wish of my friend
That signal dishonour and some fatal end,
The authors of this sad reverse may attend.
And whenever my r-y-l m-ster appears,
As I creep along by him, I always shed tears;
To think what a tract from his empire is rent,
Thro' his servants perverseness and mismanagement:
With the loss we've sustain'd in all branches of trade,
Ever since the impolitic breach has been made:
Then again I reflect on our numerous foes——
What will be the event of it God only knows.'

The remark in the last line is certainly a very true one, though neither sagacious nor poetical. The event of this poem may be much more easily foreseen; for, unlike the American war, it will do nobody any harm, will very soon be at an end, and, in a few days, be totally forgotten.

The Library. A Poem. 4to. 2s. Dodsley.

A vein of good sense and philosophical reflection runs through this little performance, which distinguishes it from most modern poems, though the subject is not sufficiently interesting to recommend

commend it to general attention.   The rhymes are correct, and the verfification fmooth and harmonious.   The author ranges his books fcientifically, and carries us through natural philofophy, phyfic, romance, hiftory, &c.—What he fays of phyfical writers is not lefs true than fevere; their aim, fays he, is glorious.

‘ But man, who knows no good unmix’d and pure,
Oft finds a poifon where he fought a cure;
For grave deceivers lodge their labours here,
And cloud the fcience they pretend to clear :
Scourges for fin the folemn tribe are fent ;
Like fire and ftorms, they call us to repent ;
But ftorms fubfide, and fires forget to rage ;
Thefe are eternal fcourges of the age :
’Tis not enough that each terrific hand
Spreads defolation round a guilty land ;
But, train’d to ill, and harden’d by its crimes,
Their pen relentlefs kills through future times.’

These lines are manly, nervous, and poetical.   We were ftill more pleafed with the following defcription of romance, which is full of fancy and fpirit.

‘ Hence, ye prophane ! I feel a former dread,
A thoufand vifions float around my head ;
Hark ! hollow blafts through empty courts refound,
And fhadowy forms with ftaring eyes ftalk round ;
See ! moats and bridges, walls and caftles rife,
Ghofts, fairies, dæmons, dance before our eyes ;
Lo ! magic verfe infcrib’d on golden gate,
And bloody hand that beckons on to fate :
“ And who art thou, thou little page, unfold ?
Say doth thy lord my Claribel with hold ?
Go tell him ftrait, fir knight, thou muft refign
Thy captive queen—for Claribel is mine.”
Away he flies ; and now for bloody deeds,
Black fuits of armour, mafks, and foaming fteeds ;
The giant falls—his recreant throat I feize,
And from his corflet take the maffy keys ;
Dukes, lords, and knights in long proceffion move,
Releas’d from bondage with my virgin love ; —
She comes, fhe comes in all the charms of youth,
Unequall’d love and unfufpected truth !
‘ Ah ! happy he who thus in magic themes,
O’er worlds bewitch’d, in early rapture dreams,
Where wild enchantment waves her potent wand,
And Fancy’s beauties fill her fairy land ;
Where doubtful objects ftrange defires excite,
And fear and ignorance afford delight.
‘ But loft, for ever loft, to me thefe joys,
Which Reafon fcatters, and which Time deftroys ;

L 3

Too

Too dearly bought, maturer Judgment calls
My bufy'd mind from tales and madrigals ;
My doughty giants all are flain or fled,
And all my knights, blue, green, and yellow, dead ;
No more the midnight fairy tribe I view
All in the merry moonfhine tipling dew ;
Ev'n the laft lingering fiction of the brain,
The church-yard ghoft, is now at reft again ;
And all thefe wayward wanderings of my youth,
Fly Reafon's power, and fhun the light of Truth.'

The reader will meet with many other paffages in this poem
that will give him pleafure in the perufal. It is obfervable, that
the author in his account of all the numerous volumes in every
fcience, has never characterifed or entered into the merits of any
particular writer in either of them, though he had fo fair an opportunity, from the nature of his fubject: this, however, for
reafons beft known to himfelf, he has ftudioufly avoided.

The Brothers, an Eclogue. By the Hon. Charles John Fielding.
4to. 1s. Walter.

At a time when the nobility of this kingdom feem not over
anxious of obtaining any character in the world of letters, and are
very feldom *guilty* of publication, we are glad, for the credit of
the nation, to fee a promifing young man of rank ftep forth as
a volunteer in the fervice, and make, confidering his youth
and inexperience, a figure fo refpectable. The little poem
before us, written by the honourable Mr. Charles John Fielding, younger fon to the earl of Denbigh, though not a firft
rate performance, is by no means deftitute of poetical merit. It
is infcribed to his elder brother, lord vifcount Fielding, and recites a converfation that paffed between them on their feveral de-
ftinations in life, the elder in the military line, the younger (our
author) deftined probably for the church, and fond of rural
amufements. They rally each other on their different tafte and
difpofitions : Damon is the contemplative youth, and Dorylas
the foldier, who thus laughs at the philofopher's tranquillity.

' Indulge thy dream ! in indolence reclin'd,
Wooe the foft waving of the weftern wind !
To moralizing brooks incline thine ear !
Pipe thy fweet lays to rocks that cannot hear !'—
— ' Dream on !—Be mine with martial rage to glow !
To hurl defiance on the trembling foe !
Be mine with this good faulchion to engage,
" Where the fight burns, and where the thickeft rage."
Be mine to force th' aftonifh'd troops to run
Before this look, like mifts before the fun !'

To this Damon replies :
' Hence to the war ! Indulge thy favage ear
With the wild fhrieks of comfortlefs Defpair !

With

With eager joy drink in the widow's cry!
Feast on the frantic mother's agony!
Hark! hark! "My son! my murder'd son!" she calls,
Then fainting o'er the bleeding body falls.
"My blooming hero shall not die," (she cries)
And strains him to her breast—her hero dies.
Enjoy her pangs! with rapture see her tear
The rev'rend honours of her silver hair!
Enjoy her pangs! and let each bursting groan,
That heaves her heart with madness, sooth thy own.'

These lines, though the sentiments are common and familiar, are smooth and harmonious. The expression *to run before a look*, and to *drink in* the widow's cry, with a few others to be met with in this poem, we could wish to see expunged. A first essay, however, should be always treated with indulgence; and to exercise the severity of criticism on the efforts of so young a muse as Mr. Fielding's, would be inhumanity. From this specimen of our honourable writer's genius and abilities, we have reason to hope that he will hereafter produce something well deserving of the public approbation. It would be injustice not to add, that the tenderness and fraternal affection running through this poem, the indisputable marks of a good and well-disposed mind, must palliate its defects, and give a lustre to its beauties, in the opinion of every feeling and intelligent reader.

Poems for the Vase at Bath Easton, &c. By a Derbyshire Highlander. 4to. 2s. 6d. Rivington.

These poems were written, as we are informed in the title-page, for the *vase at lady Miller's.* The production, we suppose, of some unsuccessful candidate for the myrtle wreath, who has taken this method of arraigning the taste of the Bath Easton judges, and made his appeal to the public, who, we are afraid, will confirm their decree, and once more consign his verses to oblivion. They seem to be the hasty effusion of a cold and incorrect writer, who throws out his undigested thoughts on any subject, without judgment or selection, and clothes them in very slovenly and prosaic numbers. In the verses on *speculation*, the theme given out at Bath Easton, in 1779, and which our author absurdly calls an *epigram* (of ten pages), he gives his readers this agreeable promise:

'Hail speculation! hail thou theme sublime,
Thou best of parents to the sons of rhime!
Descend to earth, and visit my poor cell,
Where flow-placed hebetude and dullness dwell.'

From these habitations of *hebetude* and *dullness* we cannot expect much entertainment, and are not therefore surprised to meet, a little farther on, with the following specimen of our author's wit and humour:

Make

Make way—the lawyer comes with formal face!
Screw'd up and wrinkled like his knotted cafe;
With tainted bag, that holds volcanic flame
To burn our happinefs, and raife our fhame;
To fright mankind, and aggravate their fears,
And fet the world together by the ears:
Full on his head, his patch as black as fin,
Shews the dark grumous ftate his brain is in;
Or perhaps denotes, his pleading by command,
That there the devil lays his ebon hand!
This harpy's plan is only to embroil,
And nurture ftrife, and fpeculate for fpoil.

This is equalled, if not excelled, by his defcription of the
doctor:

Look here again! the doctor now appears,
His pompous wig envelopes both his ears;
Seize his fine cane to gaurantee my pate,
And I will all his mummery relate.
Burn firft his wig—this robs him of his ftrength;
Then make him write his nonfenfe at full length:
As Dalilah poor Samfon erft did fhave,
Shave clofe this puffing, peruke-pated knave;
Condemn laud. liq. merc. dulc. and cort. peru.
Bid him prefcribe a phyfic that is new:
If he refufe, then recipe the tote,
And, to a fcruple, pour them down his throat.

The reft of the poems are of a piece with this: the author talks
of *yefty* tides, *abluent* waves, *daify-dappled* ground, *dædal* fcenes,
fugared notes, *rubified* blood, &c. &c. &c. We will not therefore
trouble our readers with any more quotations; but will conclude
with our author's own opinion of this work, in a letter to his
bookfeller, *Mr. Roome* of *Derby*, prefixed to the poems:—' I
blufh exceedingly (fays he) at the very thought of your ufher-
ing into a world, that has now acquired the moft correct and juft
rafte for every thing that is elegant in the arts and fciences, *a
parcel of rhimes which are very much below mediocrity.*' With
this opinion of E. B. L. the Derbyfhire Highlander, who muft
certainly beft know the merit of his own works, we entirely coincide, and hope that no future *vafes* at Bath, or elfewhere, may
lead him into the like temptation, or induce him to fend any
more works to Mr. Roome, ' † either as a fubftratum for apple-
pies, or for a facrifice to Sterquilinus, or Cloacina.',

An Effay on Prejudice; a Poetical Epiftle to the Hon. C. J. Fox.
4to.   1s.   Faulder.

Prejudice, in the proper fignification of the word, undoubtedly
means a hafty determination in any point, without previous ex-

---

† See the prefatory letter to Mr. Roome.

amination,

1

amination, as the etymology and derivation fufficiently indicate,
and confequently muft be mifunderftood (as it frequently is)
when applied to general and received opinions, which are ufually
founded on mature judgment and deliberate attention.   The author of this epiftle has, amongft many others, adopted this mif-
conception of the term, as our readers will be convinced of, when
we inform them that the *prejudices* which this gentleman means
to guard his friend againft, are nothing lefs than the immortality of
the foul, and the certainty of a future ftate ; *prejudices* which our
author, in the metre of Sternhold and Hopkins, endeavours moft
warmly, though not very poetically, to extirpate.   That his arguments are neither very new nor very cogent, will appear from
the following lines.

> " T' anatomife the foul is vain ;
>   Vain too all human art,
> To trace it reafoning with the brain,
>   Or throbbing with the heart.
>
> " Had it an effence of its own,
>   Nor part of body grew,
> Why do the pangs that wound the one,
>   Affect the other too ?"
>
> ' What is it then ? 'tis action, thought,
>   Senfation, paffion, breath——
> With us alike to reafon brought,
>   It with us finks to death.'

Such is our author's religion ? let us hear his philofophy.

> ' Though modified in various fhapes,
>   Matter remains the fame :
> Trees, foffils, minerals—— men or apes——
>   It differs but in name.
>
> 'Tis the fame animating feed,
>   The fame prolific fire,
> Gives dogs their inftinct, horfes fpeed,
>   Or warms Achilles' ire.'

Such religion and fuch philofophy naturally take fhelter in
the Epicurean fyftem.

> Dona præfentis cape lætus horæ.
> *Let us eat and drink, for to-morrow we die.*

A refolution to which his political Pylades, to whom it is addreffed,
will probably have no objection.   We are not therefore furprifed that the poem fhould thus conclude.

> ' The prefent's thine—fate rules the reft——
>   No future terrors fear ;
> Enjoy the fleeting hour ; be bleft——
>   And make thy heaven here.'

We

We cannot but be of opinion that the meafure made ufe of in this little piece is ill adapted to a fubject fo ferious and important, and the poetry too indifferent to do any mifchief; from fuch antagonifts, therefore, religion has little to fear; Chriftianity may fay in the words of Terence:

Utinam fic fient, male qui mihi volunt!

Poems by Ab. Portal. 8*vo* 5*s. fewed.* Kearfly.

The poetical character of this writer is fufficiently known to the generality of our readers by his former publications, Olindo and Sophronia, a tragedy; War, an ode; Innocence, a poetical effay; and four Nuptial Elegies. Thefe, and about twenty other pieces on various fubjects, compofe the prefent collection. Among thofe that might be mentioned with applaufe, is an elegy, entitled Cynthia, the production of an ingenious lady, whofe name, we are told, is Mrs. H—lt–n. The author has dedicated his Poems to R. B. Sheridan, efq. in fome complimentary verfes, which have a confiderable fhare of the poetic fpirit.

An Enquiry into the Authenticity of the Poems afcribed to Offian. *By* W. Shaw. 8*vo.* 1*s.* 6*d.* Murray.

Soon after thofe poems were firft publifhed, doubts of their authenticity were entertained by feveral perfons, particularly by Dr. Johnfon; who, in his Tour into the Hebrides, has endeavoured to fupport his opinion with a variety of arguments. Since that time, the authenticity of thofe poems has been no lefs zealoufly afferted by Mr. Smith and Mr. M'Nicol; the latter of whom even affirmed, that the original, written in the Galic language and character, might be feen by any perfon who fhould apply to John Mackenzie, efq. of the Temple, Secretary to the Highland Society. The author of this Enquiry labours to confirm the opinion entertained by Dr. Johnfon; in fupport of which he fpecifies a number of circumftances, relative to the internal and external evidence of the authenticity of the poems. He informs us, that in fpring 1778, he fet out for the Highlands and Hebrides, to collect vocables for a Galic Dictionary; refolved alfo to make enquiry, in this excurfion, concerning the Poems of Offian: that, after the moft induftrious fearch, he could not obtain from the inhabitants any oral fpecimen of Offian's Poems; nor had he greater fuccefs in all his enquiries after manufcripts: that fuch as he had heard of the former, or feen of the latter, were only the compofitions of the fifteenth century. He adds, that, on his return to London, he waited on Mr. Mackenzie in the Temple; when looking over the volumes in manufcript, which, he fays, are written in the Irifh dialect and character, on the fubject of Irifh and Highland genealogy, he could find in them no compofitions of Offian.

Such

Such is the evidence produced by this writer againſt the authenticity of Oſſian's Poems. His arguments are drawn up with a conſiderable degree of plauſibility : but, in reſpect to facts, he has given us no other teſtimony than his own unſupported aſſertion. This circumſtance merits the greater regard, as one anecdote which he mentions relative to Dr. Ferguſon, has been poſitively contradicted by that gentleman, in the public papers.

✓ N O V E L S.

The Hiſtory of the Hon. Mrs. Roſemont, *and Sir* Henry Cardigan. *2 vols. ſmall 8vo. 5s. ſewed.* Hookham.

Though this novel be founded on ſome improbable circumſtances, and the narrative be, in ſeveral places, deſtitute of natural connection, it diſcovers many traces of a lively fancy ; the characters are not only well ſupported, but happily contraſted with each other ; and the whole, if we except ſome grammatical inaccuracies, is written in an eaſy and agreeable manner.

Maſquerades ; or What you will. 4 vols. Small 8vo. 12s. Bew.

This novel, the production of the author of Eliza Warwick, may juſtly lay claim to entertainment, which is, however ſometimes precluded by an unpleaſing prolixity. But its principal blemiſhes are a levity of ſentiment that occaſionally breaks forth in oppoſition to moral reſtraint.

Diſtreſſed Virtue, or the Hiſtory of Miſs Harriet Nelſon. *3 vols. 12mo. 9s.* Noble.

Virtue in diſtreſs in an intereſting object ; but its effects are totally fruſtrated by the incapacity of this writer.

✓ D I V I N I T Y.

Sermons preached before the Univerſity of Cambridge. *By* Peter Stephen Goddard, *D. D. 8vo. 4s. boards.* Rivington.

In an academical pulpit, it is expected that a preacher ſhould rather diſplay his ingenuity than his piety. When we therefore ſee a volume of ſermons, lately preached before one of our univerſities, we are led to expect, not a collection of merely practical diſcourſes, arguments in ſupport of ſelf-evident propoſitions, and inſtructions adapted to the capacities of old women ; but ſome learned and judicious illuſtrations of ſcripture, ſome important doctrines of Chriſtianity rationally explained and defended, ſome new enquiries, ſome curious diſquiſitions, or, if the ſubjects ſhould be trite and exhauſted, ſome ſpecimens of genuine oratory.

Dr. Goddard has given us fourteen ſermons on the following ſubjects : A true and zealous Chriſtian the greateſt and beſt of Characters ; Eternal Life clearly and fully revealed by the Goſpel only ;

only; Ridicule the Teſt of Truth; the Freedom of Man's Will conſiſtent with the Grace of God; our Lord's Treatment of the Woman of Canaan explained and juſtified; Needleſs Curioſity; a Day of Grace and a Day of Wrath; Sins of Infirmity and Sins of Preſumption; Covetouſneſs Idolatry; Criminal Compliances with prevailing Cuſtoms; Hezekiah's Behaviour on receiving the Meſſage from God by Iſaiah; Duty of Prayer; Duty of the Preacher and his Hearers; Adoratio Dei, Concio ad Clerum.

In theſe diſcourſes the learned and ſpeculative reader will find but a moderate entertainment. The author's manner of writing is plain, ſimple, and unaffected. But the generality of his obſervations are trite and obvious; and his ſtyle not always correct. The following are ſome of thoſe verbal inaccuracies, which we have obſerved in this volume: 'The beſt rules, though *never* [ever] ſo well applied,' p. 242.—' Our hearts deſire is that our people *might* [may] be ſaved,' p. 243.—' What is *ſpoke* [ſpoken] to them,' p. 236.—' The advantages he *lays* under' [lies under] p. 248.

It may be ſaid, that theſe are ſmall and inconſiderable defects; but we ſee no reaſon, why ungrammatical expreſſions ſhould be leſs exceptionable in the Engliſh language than in Latin or Greek.

The Neceſſity of Religion to National Proſperity. A Sermon preached at the Aſſizes, holden at Hertford, *on* Monday, 30*th of* July, 1781. *By the Rev.* Ludlow Holt, *LL. D.* 4*to.* 1*s.* Rivington.

The author of this diſcourſe, with great propriety and energy, repreſents the neceſſity of religion to national proſperity.

A new Tranſlation with a Paraphraſe of ſome Parts of Eccleſiaſtes. 8*vo.* 1*d.* Lowndes.

Whether this is only a ſpecimen, or all the tranſlator means to publiſh, we are not informed. The tranſlation differs very conſiderably from the common verſion; but the author enters into no critical enquiries. His performance appears to diſadvantage in its preſent form, which is, with reſpect to paper and type, no better than the Hiſtory of Robin Hood, or Tom Thumb.

Hymns in Proſe for Children. 12*mo.* 1*s.* Johnſon.

Two ſmall volumes were publiſhed in 1778; the firſt intitled, Leſſons for Children from two to three years old; the ſecond, Leſſons for Children of three years old. In 1779, two other volumes were publiſhed on the ſame plan; viz. Leſſons for Children of three years old, part II. Leſſons for Children from three to four years old *.

---

* Two ſimilar productions were publiſhed about the beginning of the preſent year, by other hands. See Crit. Rev. Jan. 1781.

This

This volume is a continuation of the former, and is intended to give the young reader a proper idea of the Creator and his works. It is the production of Mrs. Barbauld, and is written with that delicacy of style and sentiment which appears in all the compositions of that ingenious lady.

✓CONTROVERSIAL.

The General Doctrine of Toleration applied to the particular Case of Free Communion. By Robert Robinson. *8vo. 1s.* Buckland.

The purport of this tract is to shew, that it is just and right, and agreeable to the revealed will of Christ, that baptist churches should admit into their fellowship such persons as desire admission on profession of faith and repentance; though they refuse to be baptized by immersion, because they sincerely believe they have been rightly baptized by sprinkling in their infancy.

We should consider this writer as a rational advocate for religious toleration, did not his invectives against infant baptism, by sprinkling, induce us to believe, that he is tinctured with a little of the old leaven; and not entirely free from a superstitious attachment to the mere forms and ceremonies of religion.

Remarks on Mr. Lindsey's *Dissertation upon praying to* Christ. *Also a Second Letter to the rev. Mr.* Jebb, *(now Dr.* Jebb.*) 8vo. 2s.* Crowder.

In the Dissertation, which has given occasion to these Remarks, Mr. Lindsey endeavours to shew the unlawfulness of all religious addresses to Jesus Christ. He therefore asserts, that Christ never taught men to worship or pray to himself. The author of this tract allows the truth of this assertion; but contends, that our Saviour has declared, 'there would be honour due to him by his Father's grant, in such language, as may comprehend supplication to him, as well as any other instance of respect.'—Mr. Lindsey maintains, that the religious worship of Christ, in the offering up of prayer to him, is not deducible from his character, office, or any divine power ascribed to him. This writer, on the other hand, alleges, that it is deducible from what the scripture says of his exaltation as a prince and a saviour, to give repentance and remission of sins, of his being the head over all things to the church, of his having the keys of hades, &c.—Mr. Lindsey observes, that Christ has entirely precluded the offering of religious worship to himself, or any other person whatever, by always praying to his heavenly Father, and uniformly directing others to pray to him alone. Our author insists, that it is false reasoning to say, because Christ gave his disciples a model for their supplications to the Father, that he himself is never to be invoked; that he has given his approbation to this divine precept, 'Thou shalt worship the Lord thy God, and him only shalt thou serve;' and yet he says to his disciples, Joh. xii. 26. 'If any man serve me, me, him will my Father honour:' so that it does not follow, because Jehovah is only to be served, that no service is to be paid to Jesus Christ.—Mr. Lindsey remarks, that the apostles never teach, that prayer was to be offered to Christ. This writer replies, that the apostles have given us an example of calling upon Christ in their own conduct, and have spoken of it in such a manner, as sufficiently to discover, that they looked upon it as a thing fit and laudable in their converts. He produces a variety of texts in proof of this assertion, and concludes, ' that it becomes us to acquiesce in, and behave suitably to such direction, as is offered by God concerning our duty, though it may not be so full and copious, as we might have expected, or delivered in so express and formal a manner, as we might have looked for.'

This writer appears to be a man of learning, actuated by a sincere desire, that the point in controversy may be fully and fairly discussed.

An Examination of Thelyphthora, on the Subject of Marriage. By John Palmer. 8vo. 1s. 6d. Johnson.

The author of Thelyphthora has laid it down as a principle, in his system of polygamy, that ' the personal union of the man and woman is the only marriage ordinance appointed by God. This notion the writer of the present treatise endeavours to refute, by shewing, that the first pair were united in a solemn manner by the Creator, who brought the woman to the man, presented her to him, and gave them a blessing, before any personal union commenced ; that our Saviour plainly alludes to a marriage ceremony among the antediluvians, when he says, ' they married wives, and were given in marriage ;' that a marriage-ceremony was required in the patriarchal times, as appears from the case of Shechem, who entreated his father to procure him Dinah to be his wife, after her violation : that, under the Mosaic dispensation, the same form was continued ; and that, according to Mr. M.'s own acknowlegement, betrothed persons were considered as husband and wife before any other connection took place.

This writer takes notice of some absurd consequences attending the Madanean system ; such as these : that, upon the principles therein advanced, there can be no such crime as fornication ; that an unbetrothed maiden cannot be debauched ; that a personal connection with her is an act of marriage ; that a rape is a religious rite ; and that a man may seduce as many women, provided they are disengaged, as he chooses, &c.

If this publication meets with a favourable reception, the author designs to pursue the subject.

M I S—

MISCELLANEOUS.

√ *The Adventures of a Hackney Coach, vol. II. 8vo. 2s. 6d. sewed.* Kearsly.

This is as execrable a hack as any private gentleman would wish to be drove in ; being nothing but a heap of uninteresting ill-written adventures, in a pompous and turgid style. The author aukwardly affects the pathetic and sentimental manner of the celebrated Tristram Shandy, and endeavours to imitate what is inimitable.

√ Otho *and* Rutha : *a Dramatic Tale. By a Lady. Small 8vo. 3s.* Bew.

The author's design in this Tale is to inculcate such truths as are of eternal and essential importance to human life : 1. that its whole economy is superintended and regulated by a wise and beneficent Providence, which renders its most gloomy vicissitudes and adverse occurrences, ultimately productive of the highest felicity, not only to communities, but even to individuals ; 2. that every external advantage, which man can either acquire or possess, is laborious in its attainment, faithless in its pretences, and unsatisfactory in its enjoyment ; 3. that piety and virtue, improved and cultivated, constitute the supreme happiness of an intelligent creature.

This Tale is written in a style, which resembles blank verse. The lessons of morality, which it suggests, are edifying and important.—We shall place it on the same shelf with the ' Death of Abel.'

√ *The Unfortunate* Caledonian *in* England ; *or, Genuine Memoirs of an impressed young Gentleman, in the Year* 1779. *8vo. 2s. 6d. sewed.* Wade.

Whether these Memoirs of an Impressed young Gentleman be genuine or fictitious, they certainly afford entertainment. The incidents are interesting ; the characters well delineated ; and several places accurately described. The narrative is also frequently enlivened with agreeable pieces of poetry. From the ingenuity which the author discovers, we regret the disaster he has experienced ; and are glad to find, that, after a variety of fortune, he has at last attained the accomplishment of his wishes.

√ *An Introduction to* English *Grammar ; to which is annexed a Treatise on Rhetorick. By* Joshua Story. *The Second Edition with Additions.* 12mo. 1s. 6d. Evans.

We have given a favourable account of this Grammar in our Review for January 1779.—The present edition is improved in several places, and enlarged by a Treatise on Rhetoric, collected from the most eminent authors on that subject.

I   *Con-*

Considerations on the Propriety and Expediency of the Clergy acting in the Commission of the Peace. 8vo. 6d. Johnson.

The author of these Considerations acknowleges himself to be both a clergyman and a magistrate; and he endeavours to procure the same distinction for his reverend brethren, whom he represents as particularly qualified, on various accounts, for acting in the commission of the peace. We know not what peculiar circumstances may concur to render this gentleman highly useful in his double capacity; but should be of opinion, that the clerical duties alone are, in general, sufficient to employ the attention of a faithful and diligent pastor. To invest the clergy, therefore, with a judicial office, would seem to be a measure incompatible with the right discharge of their original function; and we may add, that the union of civil and ecclesiastical authority is far from being an alliance favourable to the meek and humble spirit which is the essential ornament of a Christian teacher.

A Letter to the Jury who convicted Mr. Shelly, the Silversmith. By Robert Holloway. 8vo. 1s. Brewman.

Prefixed to this letter is a dedication to the lord mayor, in which it must be acknowleged that the author, who, it seems, is an attorney, is far from rendering his meaning perfectly intelligible. The purpose of the letter is to evince, that Mr. Shelly experienced rigorous treatment in being convicted of the criminal charge for which he was indicted.

The Southampton Guide: Or, an Account of the present State of that Town. Its Trade, Public Buildings, Charitable Foundations, Churches, Fairs, Markets, Play-houses, Assembly Rooms, Baths, &c. together with a Description of the Isle of Wight, Netley Abbey, Lymington, Lyndhurst, Redbridge, New Forest, Romsey, Broadlands, Bellevue, Bevis Mount, St. Dennis, Tichfield, &c. Interspersed with many curious and useful Particulars. A new Edition, 12mo. 1s. Law.

The editor of this little Directory has improved the present edition, so as to render it a proper pocket-companion for the visitants of Southampton.

The Question-book: Or, a Practical Introduction to Arithmetic, Containing a great Variety of Examples in all the Fundamental Rules. By Thomas Molineux. 12mo. 1s. 6d. Bathurst.

To this short introduction to arithmetic the author has added a Key, containing the answers to the Questions. The answers to the questions will certainly lessen the labour of the teacher; as the author tells us he hath experienced in his own school.

THE

CRITICAL REVIEW.

For the Month of *September*, 1781.

Memoirs of Thomas Hollis, *Efq. F. R. and A. S. S.* 2 *vols.*
4*to.* 4*l.* 4*s. in boards.* Cadell.

THERE is no fpecies of literature more ufeful than biography. The memoirs of thofe perfons, who have
diftinguifhed themfelves by their learning, their ingenuity,
their patriotic virtues, or their military exploits, are calculated to gratify a laudable curiofity, and excite a noble emulation. Yet it is not neceffary, that the biographer fhould
confine his enquiries to the lives of thofe, who have been
the objects of public admiration and applaufe. True greatnefs, like true happinefs, does not confift in outward pomp and
oftentation, but is feated in the mind; and is frequently found
in retirement and obfcurity. The life of Ariftides or Atticus
may afford more ufeful inftruction, than that of Alexander
or Julius Cæfar: the private virtues of the former may
ferve as examples to thoufands; while the heroifm of the
latter can only be imitated by princes or warriors.

The Memoirs now before us prefent to our view one of the
moft refpectable and exemplary characters, which the prefent
age has produced. This character, we confefs, is attended
with fome remarkable fingularities; but, at the fame time,
it is diftinguifhed by many extraordinary virtues, by an ingenuous fimplicity, an inviolable integrity, and an unlimited
benevolence.

Thomas Hollis, efq. of Corfcombe in the county of Dorfet,
was born in London, April 14, 1720.

Thomas, his great-grandfather, was of Rotheram in the county of York, a whitesmith by trade, and the founder of the hospital at Sheffield, for the maintenance of sixteen poor cutlers' widows.—He was of the Baptist persuasion.

In the time of the Civil Wars he left Yorkshire, and settled, with his family, in London; and, in 1679, took a lease for ninety-nine years of Pinner's-Hall, formerly the place of meeting of the principal independents, Oliver Cromwell, and others. This gentleman died in 1718, at the age of eighty-four, and left three sons, Thomas, Nathaniel, and John; and one daughter, Mary.

Thomas, his eldest son, an eminent merchant in London, augmented the Sheffield charity, and the trust for Pinner's-Hall; but more particularly distinguished himself by his benefactions to New England, especially to Harvard College, in Cambridge, where he founded a professorship for the mathematics and natural philosophy, and ten scholarships for students in those and other sciences; which, with other endowments, amounted to nearly 5000l.

His brothers, Nathaniel and John, were joint contributors in many of his gifts. The latter, in particular, was a considerable benefactor to the Sheffield trust, and to the Baptist and Independent Societies.

Nathaniel had one son, Thomas, who died in 1735, three years before his father, leaving only one son, Thomas, the subject of these Memoirs, who inherited the fortune of his father, and of his great uncle Thomas, the latter dying in 1730, without issue.

His mother was the daughter of Mr. Scott of Woolverhampton, in whose family he was placed, till he was four or five years of age. From Woolverhampton he was brought to London, and not long afterwards sent to the great free-school of Newport, in Shropshire, where he staid till he was eight or nine years old. From hence he was removed to St. Albans, and put under the care of Mr. Wood. In his thirteenth, or fourteenth year he was sent to Amsterdam, to learn the Dutch and French languages, writing, arithmetic, and accounts. After a stay of about fifteen months he returned to London to his father, with whom he remained till his death, in 1735. After this he passed some years in the house of his cousin, Timothy Hollis, esq.

It was now determined by his friends, that he should have a liberal education, suitable to the ample fortune he was to inherit; he was therefore placed under the tuition of the learned Dr. John Ward, Professor of Rhetoric in Gresham College, where he studied the languages, particularly Latin, and went

through

through a courfe of logic, rhetoric, hiftory, and other branches of learning.

In February, 1739-40, he took chambers, and was admitted as a law-ftudent in Lincoln's Inn. Here he remained till the year 1748; but it does not appear, that he applied himfelf profeffedly to the ftudy of the law; nor, on the other hand, did he wafte this interval in idle amufements or diffipation. He appears to have formed his conduct, very early, on the benevolent and public fpirited model of his worthy predeceffors, improved by his own good fenfe and obfervations.

On July 19, 1748, he fet out on his travels for the firft time; and paffed through Holland, the Auftrian and French Flanders, part of France, Switzerland, Savoy, and Italy; returning through Provence, Britany, &c. to Paris, accompanied by his friend Thomas Brand, efq.

Of this tour he has left a curious and copious journal; from which it appears, that very little efcaped his notice, where he could have proper information, relating to arts and fciences, public roads, manufactures, trade, antiquities, and what is called virtù, of which he became an able connoiffeur, and a generous encourager.

His fecond excurfion commenced July 16, 1750, when he travelled through Holland and the northern and eaftern parts of Germany to Italy, Sicily, Malta, Lorrain, &c.

While he was abroad he commenced many valuable friendfhips with men of learning and eminence, favourers and promoters of ufeful arts and fciences.

Upon his return to England in 1753, he began his collections of books and medals ' for the purpofe, as he expreffes himfelf, of illuftrating and upholding liberty, and preferving the memory of its champions, to render tyranny and its abettors odious, to extend fcience and art, to keep alive the honour and eftimation of their patrons and protectors, to make the whole as ufeful as poffible, abhorring all monopoly; and to recommend the fame benevolent fpirit to pofterity.'

In purfuance of this generous plan he employed his thoughts, his time, and his fortune; and, with an uncommon liberality of fentiment, extended his munificence to perfons of different perfuafions, and to foreigners, without diftinction.

He prefented two large and valuable collections of books to the public library at Berne, with an intimation only, that they were fent by ' an Englifhman, a lover of liberty, and a citizen of the world, as a fmall token of his unfeigned refpect for that Canton, and the brave, worthy, and free people of Switzerland.'

M 2

He

He was a conſtant and liberal benefactor to Harvard College in New England, from the year 1758 to the year 1773; and tranſmitted many munificent donations, eſpecially of books, to Leipſic, Hamburgh, Gottingen, Leyden, Geneva, Venice, Rome, Sicily, Sweden, and other foreign countries.

To enumerate his preſents to private individuals would greatly exceed the limits of this article. A multitude of theſe remain, moſt probably, a ſecret even to the perſons, who received them. It was an amiable and ſtriking feature in his character to

' Do good by ſtealth, and bluſh to have it known.'

We ſhall therefore content ourſelves with extracting a few of thoſe paſſages, which relate to his literary tranſactions, or contain any memorable circumſtance ; omitting every thing of a political nature.

From the time of his return from his travels he paid great attention to the public ſocieties in this country, inſtituted for the promotion of learning and ſcience, and was a member of moſt, if not all of them ; but took an early reſolution of avoiding all public ' diſtinctive offices' among them.

The Britiſh Muſeum was an object of his particular regard and benevolence. He conſidered it as a literary foundation, calculated to do the higheſt honour to the Britiſh name ; and in that view he contributed many things to its valuable ſtores, from his own collections.

In 1760, he applied to Mr. Millar, to reprint Dr. Wallis's Latin Grammar of the Engliſh tongue, ' for the benefit of foreigners, and the ſpreading of the principles of truth and liberty,' which, in his opinion, were moſt ably and effectually diſcuſſed by Engliſh writers, and little underſtood by the ſubjects of deſpotic governments abroad. Mr. Saville, according to the Independent Whig, is ſaid to have replied to a Frenchman, who exulted upon the fine writings of his countrymen, ' That there were but two ſubjects in nature worth a wiſe man's thoughts, and they durſt ſpeak of neither.' This anecdote Mr. Hollis has quoted in his Notes on Sydney's Life, p. 34, and a paſſage from Voltaire, wherein the Engliſh are called, ' les precepteurs des nations.' But the proficiency of the nations muſt be very ſmall, if they are unacquainted with the language of their preceptors. Dr. Wallis's Grammar was intended to obviate this defect ; and to that end his inſtructions are conveyed in a tongue, which ſcholars in all countries and of all degrees, underſtand in ſome meaſure at leaſt, and was therefore the fitteſt to open the way for foreigners

reigners to the treasures of English learning. To revive this noble and benevolent purpose of the author, was Mr. Hollis's view in republishing this excellent work, which appeared in the year 1765, with a preface by the late Mr. Bowyer.

Mr. Hollis, it is certain, did not think with, or conform to the church of England; but the following letter is an instance, among many others, which might be produced, that he acted for the real interests of that church with as much propriety as the most zealous of her members could have done.

July 29, 1760. ' Being informed, that Mr. S. is very ill, and not likely to recover, I think it my duty, as patron of the living of L. to look about me in time, in order to find out, if possible, an able and worthy clergyman to succeed him, in benefit to that parish and neighbourhood, and so in some sort to the public.

' At present I have no person in view for it. But it is my intention, my fixed intention, to bestow the living on that clergyman, who shall answer nearest to the following description :

—' A clergyman forty-five to fifty-five years of age, of a sound constitution, and without remarkable defect in person or voice; one who has had a regular education, and no changeling, is truly, in civil principles, a Whig, has officiated always as a curate, is active in disposition, yet mild in manners; is beloved by his neighbours, and has a clear and undoubted character; one who will content himself with this living, without [an additional] curacy, and reside upon and serve it; or will engage, upon his honour, to resign it instantly, in case of future preferment. And it is my farther request, that you conduct it with all the stillness and privacy that is possible, not only at present, but even when Mr. S. shall be no more.'

In December following, a proposal was made to Mr. Hollis to become a candidate for a borough in the ensuing election of a new parliament; his answer was, that though he would give almost his right hand to be chosen into parliament, yet he could not give a single crown for it by way of bribe.

Writing to a friend about the same time, he says : ' We are already beginning to prepare for the grand septennial riot. Let those play the game who choose it. For my own part, though I had rather possess a seat in a certain place, than any other temporal advantage whatever, yet I remember too well the saying of an ancient to think of it. " I can live contented without glory, but cannot suffer shame." Honest Plutarch records it, I think, but I am not certain.'

M 3

In

In January 1761, was publifhed, under the care and direction of Mr. Hollis, a new edition of Toland's Life of Milton, together with his Amyntor, in a handfome octavo volume. This, and Milton's profe works, he fent as prefents to many private perfons, both at home and abroad, and to a confiderable number of public libraries in foreign countries.

It may be obferved, that, at this time, there were feveral editions of Milton's profe-works. Toland's edition, printed in 3 vols. folio, in 1698 ; Dr. Birch's, in 2 vols. folio, in 1738 ; and Mr. Baron's, in 2 vols. quarto, in 1753, before the editor was acquainted with Mr. Hollis *.

Mr. Hollis's veneration for Milton made him particularly inquifitive after every thing, that in any refpect related, or formerly belonged to this great man, as portraits, &c. The following anecdote may ferve to fhew, how far he extended this laudable enthufiafm : June 12, 1761, he bought a bed, which once belonged to John Milton, and on which he died. This bed he fent as a prefent to Dr. Akenfide, with the following card : ' An Englifh gentleman is defirous of having the honour to prefent a bed, which once belonged to John Milton, and on which he died, to Dr. Akenfide ; and if the doctor's genius, believing himfelf obliged, and having flept in that bed, fhould prompt him to write an ode to the memory of John Milton, and the affertors of Britifh liberty, that gentleman would think himfelf abundantly recompenced.'— His biographer adds : ' the doctor feemed wonderfully delighted with this bed, and had it put up in his houfe. But more we do not know of the *delight* the doctor took in his prefent, not the leaft memorandum of an acknowledgment to Mr. Hollis for it appearing. And as to the ode, the doctor might learn from his friend Dyfon, that an encomium on Milton, as an affertor of Britifh liberty, at that time of the day, was not the thing.'

Mr. Hollis's connections with the colonies, and his zeal for their improvement, and particularly his correfpondence with Dr. Mayhew, who it feems became obnoxious to the governors of Maffachufets, on account of his writings in favour of civil liberty, have been alleged as evidence of his fomenting that factious fpirit among the Americans, which has ended in their declaring themfelves independent on the mother country. ' But fuch an idea, fays his biographer, appears from undoubted teftimony to have been the moft remote from Mr. Hollis's wifhes and endeavours. On the contrary, he endeavoured to inculcate loyalty to the king and his go-

* Mr. Baron died in 1768.

vernment,

vernment, and to create a good opinion of his majefty among his provincial fubjects.

'Let you and I, dear fir, fays he, writing to Dr. Mayhew, continue to wifh well to our country, our king, and their approved faithful fervant William Pitt.' And in the fame letter he fays : 'I think I am well informed, that our honeft excellent young king has ordered, that fuch of the French prifoners of war as will be in want of cloathing the enfuing winter (1761) fhall be clothed at his expence.'

And to mention no more inftances, Auguft 12, 1762, in Mr. Hollis's Diary is this article on the birth of his royal highnefs the prince of Wales : 'This morning the queen was delivered happily of a prince. Pray God blefs him, and endow him with all thofe noble qualities, which are fuitable to a chief ruler of a free and magnanimous people.'—This is the language of benevolence and fincerity.

In 1762, was publifhed at Rome, a Differtation, De Deâ Libertate, ejufque cultu apud Romanos, & de Libertinorum Pileo, written by Rodulphini Venuti, at the requeft of Mr. Hollis.—The Pileus Libertatis, or cap of liberty, was a favourite emblem with Mr. Hollis, and diftinguifhes the prints, and books, which have been publifhed by his direction.

About this period, Mr. Hollis employed Mr. Elmfly, the bookfeller, to collect every thing he could meet with written againft the Jefuits ; which commiffion Mr. Elmfly executed with great fuccefs. The collection was a noble one, and was fent to the public library of Zurich ; concerning which Mr. Hollis writes thus to a friend.

'The collection of books and papers, relating to the Jefuits, was fhipped laft week for a proteftant univerfity abroad, diftant fome hundred miles from this happy country. It was my defire and intention to have lodged this fingular collection in the Britifh Mufeum. But the behaviour of a committee of the truftees was fo ftrange towards me, on a particular occafion, that I could not refolve any longer, with any degree of magnanimity, to fend it to that place : in any other in this nation, fuch a fort of collection would have been almoft loft.'—It muft however be obferved, to the honour of Mr. Hollis, that he was afterwards a conftant benefactor to the Britifh Mufeum.

March 31, 1763, Mr. Hollis finifhed his new edition of Sydney's works, which he fays, 'he completed, after great and continued labour, and at a confiderable expence on his own part ; having undertaken it without a fingle bye view, and alone, from the love he bore to liberty and the author's memory.'

M 4   This

This publication gives our excellent biographer occasion to make the following remarks on a scandalous reflection, which not long since was thrown on the character of Sydney.

' When a certain writer pretended to fix upon Algernon Sydney, by authentic memorials, an intrigue with Barillon the French ambassador, in favour of the projects of Lewis XIV. and Charles II. all the world were in amazement, never once recollecting, that this astonishing phenomenon had been accounted for by bishop Burnet, from most undoubted authority. Let us hear him once more :

" Sydney was ambassador in Denmark at the time of the Restoration, but did not come back till the year seventy-eight, when the parliament was pressing the king into a war. The court of France obtained leave for him to return. He did all he could to divert people from that war ; so that some took him for a pensioner of France ; but to those to whom he durst speak freely, he said he knew it was all a juggle ; that our court was in an intire confidence with France, and had no other design in this shew of war, but to raise an army, and keep it beyond sea, till it was trained and modelled." Hist. O. Tim. vol. i. p. 538.

' Burnet's authority must, in this instance, be beyond dispute. There is no doubt, but he had this intelligence from the Russel family, and that of lord Essex. And in this account is included the defence of lord Russel, as well as of Sydney, against the malevolent colours put upon their transactions with Barillon, by the Scotch historian, if any such there were ; which indeed would only prove, that these two worthy patriots outwitted both Barillon and his master.

' But the best account that can be given of all these defamatory letters, produced or referred to, either by Dalrymple or Macpherson, is to rank them among such *impostures* as have lately amused the world, under the name of Ganganelli ; undoubtedly the Jesuit was very ingenious, who forged them ; and, notwithstanding all that Voltaire has said to expose his roguery, was full as worthy of credit as our two doughty North Britons.'

In September this year, Mr. Hollis employed himself in sorting his tracts, of which he had a large and curious collection ; and found he had as many modern ones as would make forty-four octavo volumes, exclusive of the tracts published in the time of the civil wars, the quartos, and some few others.

We take notice of this unimportant circumstance, for the sake of the following useful remark :

' Per-

' Perhaps, it would be hard to find (in all Europe) a collection chofen with more judgment, or of a more beneficial tendency to public good, than that of Mr. Hollis. Other collections may contain more tracts of the fort, which are called curious, or which may make a fuperior figure in their arrangement, by the uniformity and fplendor of binding and decoration : but there they too often 'ftand to be looked at, and kept *in excellent prefervation*, unfoiled by the dirty hands of thofe, who would wifh to be made wifer by their contents.

' No man knew the value, the fcarcity, or the ufe, of a mafter-tract, as he ufed to call an excellent performance, better than Mr. Hollis ; and yet he had fo little notion of appropriating fuch tracts to his own particular ufe, that where he knew a particular book or pamphlet fell in with the defigns of a man of learning and worth, and would be fubfervient to any laudable work he was carrying on, he made no fcruple to prefent him with the only copy he had, and perhaps the only one that could poffibly be procured.'

The fatire in this paffage is far from being too fevere. All that can be faid in favour of fome collectors of books, who have neither inclination nor abilities to improve the world by their own productions, is, that they preferve thofe books for the ufe of pofterity.

April the 20th, Mr. Hollis prefented to Chrift's College, Cambridge, a printed uncut copy of Mr. Locke's two Treatifes of Government, 1698, with many manufcript corrections, alterations, and additions in it, in the hand-writing of Mr. Locke and Mr. Cofte, from which copy the edition of thofe treatifes, publifhed this year (1764) and procured by Mr. Hollis, was printed.

Jan. 1, 1765, were publifhed Locke's Letters on Toleration, from the firft editions of them, which Mr. Hollis collated himfelf. The firft Letter was printed in 12mo, in Latin, at Gouda, 1689, and tranflated into Englifh by Mr. Popple, author of the Rational Catechifm. The fecond and third, in the years 1690, and 1692.

March 22, he purchafed, out of the library of Dr. Leatherland, one hundred and forty-five volumes and tracts, relating to the Hiftory of England, chiefly during the civil wars ; and prefented them to Mrs. Macaulay, in return for the fecond volume of her hiftory.

The learned Mr. Spence had been the occafion of Mr. Dodfley's reprinting Henry Neville's book, intitled, Plato Redivivus ; and Mr. Hollis finding, that 300 copies of that edition were left upon Mr. Dodfley's hands, commiffioned Mr.

Millar

Millar to purchafe them ; which he did, for fifteen pounds ; and caufed Mr. Millar to republifh the book, with a new title page, and paid him twenty pounds for the purchafe-money, and for the new title, and advertifing the book.   Mr. Spence had written a fhort account of the work and the author, for the ufe of Dodfley's edition : inftead of which was prefixed to this republication a larger account of Mr. Neville.

Sept. 7, he fent to the London Chronicle a piece of drollery, as he calls it, by Henry Neville, intitled, The Ifle of Pines, with a fhort Preface, figned Harpocrates, of which he alfo procured an elegant edition, 12mo, in 1768, printed for Cadell, to which was prefixed, a fatirical and not over-delicate piece, intitled, The Parliament of Ladies ; firft printed in 1647.

The firft edition of the Ifle of Pines was printed at London, in 4to, 1668.   The title is as follows :

' The Ifle of Pines, or a late Difcovery of a fourth Ifland near Terra Auftralis Incognita, by Henry Cornelius Van Sloettan ; wherein is contained, a true Relation of certain Englifh perfons, who, in Queen Elizabeth's Time, making a Voyage to the Eaft-Indies were caft away, and wrecked near the Coaft of Terra Auftralis Incognita, and all drowned, except one Man and four Women.   And now lately, A. D. 1667, a Dutch Ship making a Voyage to the Eaft-Indies, driven by foul Weather there, by Chance have found their Pofterity fpeaking good Englifh, to amount, as they fuppofe, to ten or twelve thoufand Perfons.   The whole Relation, written and left by the Man himfelf a little before his Death, and delivered to the Dutch by his Grandchild, is here an-nexed, &c.'

Mr. Hollis's edition of the Ifle of Pines, does not contain the whole of what is to be found in the old quarto.   For what reafon he omitted fo much of it (having publifhed only about nine pages out of thirty-one, of which the quarto pamphlet confifts), does not appear, particularly the laws enacted by Henry Pine, for the goverment of the inhabitants.

Mr. Hollis called it a piece of drollery, but it feems to have been intended by Neville for a ferious reprefentation of the happinefs that might accrue to fociety by following the dictates of nature, according to the circumftances in which the founder of a community might be placed, in a defert, fupplied with a few accommodations moft neceffary for the prefervation of the fpecies.

Neville indeed furnifhes Pine with a Bible ; from whence Pine forms his rules of government ; which, probably, might be intended to fhew, how well the couduct of mankind might
be

be regulated by the simple documents of the word of God, without that load of human forms and ceremonies, with which it has been defaced and corrupted.

In the spring of the year 1766, was published the Confessional : a work which will be held in veneration, when the church of England has the magnanimity to think freely, and explode—what ought to be exploded. This book, as the editor infinuates, owed its public appearance to Mr. Hollis.

In 1767, he prevailed with Mr. Baron to revise, and with Mr. Millar to reprint, Marchamont Nedham's Excellence of a Free State, in octavo.

This tract, says our author, is well written, and upon sound principles ; but was attended with the common fate of the works of all such writers as Nedham, who had been a sort of periodical hackney to different parties ; and when a man has lost his reputation for steadiness and consistency, let him write and speak like an angel, he reaps no other reputation from his abilities, but that of being a graceful actor on the political stage : a useful admonition to some of our modern renegado patriots, and others, who have changed their party through disgust and disappointment.

The same year Mr. Hollis formed a plan for publishing a new edition of Milton's prose works. With this view, he had collected a number of curious and valuable notes ; and one sheet was actually printed, when the whole design was totally frustrated by an unexpected refusal, on the part of Mr. Millar, the bookseller, to perform his agreement.

In 1768, Mr. Locke's Works were published in four vols. 4to. As Mr. Hollis had for some time been meditating a new edition of them, he was consulted on this occasion. But the only concern he had in this republication, was that of recommending the insertion of the Latin Letter on Toleration, with Proast's Pieces, written against that Letter ; supplying Mr. Basire, who engraved the effigies of the author, with a fine original drawing by signor Cipriani, and correcting Le Clerc's Life of Locke, which was prefixed.

Our biographer, in his Observations on the Edition of Mr. Locke's Works, published in 1777, has this remark :

' In the Life of Mr. Locke, prefixed to the last edition in quarto, we find a note at the bottom of the first page, in which it is thus written : ' Frequent notice is likewise taken of Mr. Locke's wife, in his letters to Mr. Clarke, (for the use of whose son Mr. Locke drew up most of the thoughts on education) between 1692 and 1702.'

As

' As there is no record, that we know of, which exhibits the marriage of Mr. Locke the philosopher, we imagine the lady here noticed must have been the *wife* of his father, though the expression refers to letters written between the years 1692 and 1702, and points out the *wife* of Mr. Locke, who wrote the letters, which could not be John Locke the father. There is, therefore, here mentioned a fact hitherto unknown, or certainly an inaccuracy of diction which wants correction.'— So far the present biographer.

As the author of the foregoing anecdote refers the reader to Locke's Letters to Mr. Clarke, we have had recourse to those Letters, which are still preserved in the British Museum. And we shall subjoin some of those passages, which, we apprehend, gave occasion to the note in question.

' Bishop-Stortford, 13 May, 1692.

'——Present my service to madam, my wife, and the rest of your family.   J. Locke.

' To Edward Clarke, esq. member of parliament, at Mrs. Henman's, over-against Little Turnstile, Holborn.'

' Oates, 28 Oct. —92.

——' Present my humble service to madam, to whom I heartily wish a short and safe hour.   I shall take care to have the coach sent for my wife to-morrow, and shall make all your compliments to Sir Francis and my lady.'

' Oates, 31 Oct. —92.

——' My wife came safe and well hither on Saturday, and you had completed your kindness, if you yourself had come with her. . . . My wife I shall take care of as her mother desires, and I think she need be in no pain about her, whilst she is here, where every body is so disposed to take care, and make much of her, as she very well deserves.   But my lady intending to write to Mrs. Clarke herself, I shall say no more on that subject.

' To Edw. Clarke, esq. member of parliament, at Richard's Coffee-house, near Temple-Bar.'

' Oates, 2 Nov. —92.

——' My wife, and I, and all here (except Mrs. Cudworth, who also is much mended) are well, and according to our respective duties, salute you.'

' Oates, 28 Nov. —92.

——' My lady, my wife, and all here are well, give their service to madam, and wish you joy of your lusty boy.'

' Oates, 23 Dec. —92.

——' My wife is very well, and sends her duty.   My lady and Mrs. Cudworth, &c. present their services to you and Mrs. Clarke.'

' Oates,

'Oates, 15 Oct. —94.

—' My love to my wife, and the rest of the good company with her at Chipley.'

'London, 9 Sept. —97.

—' Pray give my service to your wife, and my wife, and to your son.'

'Oates, 7 May, —98.

—' My lady Masham has said something to me concerning my wife. Since she has been here, she has been very reserved. If it be her usual temper, it is well. If it be present thoughtfulness, it is worth your consideration. How I shall carry myself to her, you must instruct me, for I love her, and you know I am at your disposal to serve you.—She tells me, she thinks Mrs. Clarke mends.'

'Oates, 30 Nov. 1702.

—' I was glad to see your hand some time since upon a cover, which brought me a letter from my wife.'

In this manner Mr. Locke speaks of his *wife*, in twenty or thirty letters to Mr. Clarke, during a correspondence of ten years, without ever intimating, in any plainer terms, who the lady was, whom he distinguishes by this appellation. His biographer has only mentioned the fact, and left the reader to determine, in what sense we are to understand the philosopher. For our part, we are persuaded, that the lady above mentioned, was a daughter of Mr. Clarke's ; and that Mr. Locke, being an old bachelor of sixty at the commencement of this series of letters, only amused himself with the idea of a *nominal wife*.

In 1769, Mr. Hollis procured the republication of a book, intitled, The Romish Horseleech *, or an impartial Account of the intolerable Charge of Popery to this Nation, &c. by Th. Staveley, esq. first published in 1674.

In August, 1770, Mr. Hollis went to his estate in Dorsetshire, with a design to regulate his affairs at Corscombe, and return to London about Christmas, and afterwards to take his leave of the town, and retire. He did not however entirely drop his intercourse with such of his former correspondents, as were proper either to give or receive intelligence of such matters, as employed his care and concern for the public.

We have given an account above of Mr. Hollis's edition of Algernon Sidney's Works in the year 1763. ' That edition being nearly sold off, it was determined by the proprietors to reprint it ; but Mr. Hollis being apprised of some errors in

---

* See Crit. Rev. vol. xxix. p. 6.

the

the text of the Difcourfes on Government, prevailed with the learned and ingenious Mr. J. Robertfon, to revife the whole impreffion ; which that gentleman undertook, and performed greatly to the advantage of that important work.' In this edition are added, Letters of Algernon Sydney, taken from Thurloe's State-Papers, which were not publifhed in 1763 ; and many hiftorical Notes, illuftrating the text. Mr. Hollis, in fome of his letters, fpeaks of this edition with the higheft encomiums. It was publifhed in 1772.

This was the laft publication in which Mr. Hollis was any ways interefted or concerned, the fhort remaining period of his life being chiefly fpent in building and repairs at his farm.

Jan. 1, 1774, as he was walking in the fields at Corfcombe, and giving directions to his workmen, he fuddenly dropped down in a fit, and expired. He had written feveral notes that morning upon bufinefs : the conclufion of one to his fervants at his houfe in Pall-Mall, to prepare for his coming to town (and probably the laft) was, 'I have to thank God for continuing me in health, of his bounty ; and I wifh you all well. T. H.'

In order to preferve the memory of thofe heroes and patriots, for whom he had a veneration, as the affertors of liberty, and the defenders of his country, he called many of the farms and fields in his eftate at Corfcombe by their names, and by thefe names they are ftill diftinguifhed.

In the middle of one of thefe fields, not far from his houfe, he ordered his corpfe to be depofited in a grave ten feet deep, and the field to be immediately plowed over, that no trace of his burial-place might remain.

There are feveral fketches of his character at the conclufion of thefe Memoirs. We fhall give our readers the firft, as it is the fhorteft.

'Thomas Hollis, efq. of Corfcombe, in Dorfetfhire, was a man formed on the fevere and exalted plan of ancient Greece, in whom was united the humane and difinterefted virtue of Brutus, with the active and determined fpirit of Sydney ; illuftrious in his manner of ufing his ample fortune, not by fpending it in the parade of life, which he defpifed ; but by affifting the deferving, and encouraging the arts and fciences, which he promoted with zeal and affection ; knowing the love of them leads to moral and intellectual beauty ; was a warm and ftrenuous advocate in the caufe of public liberty and virtue, and for the rights of human nature and private confcience. His humanity and generofity were not confined to the fmall fpot of his own country ; he fought for merit in every part of the globe, confidering himfelf as a citizen of the world, but

con-

concealed his acts of munificence, being contented with the confcioufnefs of having done well. Pofterity will look up with admiration to this great man, who, like Milton, is not fufficiently known by this degenerate age, in which he lived, though it will have caufe to lament the lofs of him.'

The Appendix, forming a fecond volume to thefe Memoirs, contains, Obfervations on the Character and Writings of Milton, with Remarks on Dr. Johnfon's Life of Milton, in the Second Volume of his Biographical Prefaces. An Account of Algernon Sydney; Hubert Languet, the Author of Vindiciæ contra Tyrannos; George Buchanan; John Poynet, Bifhop of Rochefter, and Winchefter; Edmund Ludlow; John Trenchard; Richard Baron; Francis Hutchefon; and Sir Samuel Morland.

It contains, likewife, a Lift of all the Benefactions of Mr. Hollis and his Family, to Harvard College, in New-England; the Correfpondence of the Prefident of the College, and others, with Mr. Hollis on thefe Donations; An Account of the Fire which deftroyed that College in 1764; The Character of Dr. Mayhew of Bofton; Scaliger's Opinion of the original Manner of Printing; Two Proclamations of Charles II. A Proteftation of Charles I. A Decree of the Star-Chamber in 1637, concerning Printing; Mifcellaneous Effays, written by Mr. Hollis, and inferted in the public Papers; Letters to Mr. Hollis from feveral Correfpondents; A Plan for preventing the Growth of Popery in England; Advice to a young Painter at Rome; Verfes on Sydney and Hambden; Bradfhaw's Epitaph, engraved on a Cannon at the Summit of a fteep hill, near Martha Bray, in Jamaica; Infcriptions; A Lift of the Coins, Medals, Gems, Pictures, and Sculptures, in the Collection of Mr. Hollis, &c.

This work appears to have been drawn up by a very able hand. The obfervations on men and things, which are occafionally introduced, are acute, manly, and judicious. The defence of Milton, againft the Author of his Life, lately publifhed, is written with poignancy and fpirit. In a word, neither Mr. Hollis, nor any of his favourite heroes, could have found in the prefent age a more mafterly advocate. The only exception, perhaps, which an impartial and difcerning reader can make to this performance, is the warmth and prolixity with which our biographer frequently expatiates on the political affairs of this country and her colonies, and his violent prepoffeffion in favour of our American patriots.

This work is elegantly printed; is adorned with many beautiful engravings, and will do equal honour to the author, to Mr. Hollis, and his friend the executor, under whofe patronage it was publifhed.

Expe-

Experiments and Observations relating to various Branches of Natural Philosophy, with a Continuation of the Observations on Air. Vol. II. By Joseph Priestley, *LL. D. (Concluded from page 141.)*

DR. Priestley with great justice complains, in the beginning of his tenth section, that, notwithstanding the pains he has taken to deny it, the opinion has still been ascribed to him, that common air, by the addition of phlogiston, becomes fixed air. The numerous facts scattered through his preceding volumes, and the clear and decisive experiments of his friend Mr. Bewly, in his appendix to the second volume, proving that fixed air is an acid sui generis, seem to have been forgotten, or not to have been duly regarded. Mr. Cruickshank thinks that some experiments of his are decisive in favour of this opinion ; Dr. Priestley observes, that his friend Mr. Kirwan is inclined to support it ; and, we presume, will not easily give up a notion on which is founded a theory he is so apparently fond of as that of Dr. Crawford's system of heat.

A great part of this section is already published, in a letter to Mr. Kirwan, annexed to the translation of Scheele's Treatise on Air and Fire; and, in our opinion, the arguments and facts it contains are so striking, that we felt some astonishment at finding no reply by Mr. Kirwan in the work we have referred to, on the supposition that he still retains his opinion ; and no acknowledgement, on the other hand, in case he had resigned it. 1. Dr. Priestley, on the supposition that the addition of phlogiston does convert common into fixed air, begs to know why the addition of more phlogiston does not change the whole of any portion of common into fixed air, which we know never to be the case. 2. The whole fallacy results from the effect of breathing through lime water, which, by this operation, is generally rendered turbid. But Dr. Priestley observes, that the quantity of fixed air commonly incorporated with the atmosphere is sufficient to account for this appearance, especially if, as we may readily suppose, the addition of phlogiston to any portion of common air lessens its affinity to the fixed air it contains. Besides, to use the Doctor's own words, ' considering the great diminution of common air by phlogistic processes, there is no greater appearance of fixed air produced by respiration than has been supposed to be contained in common air, and to be precipitated from it, even admitting, as I do, that the whole of the diminution is not owing to the precipitation of fixed air. Breathing into lime water seems to have been the principal circumstance that has
led

led to the miſtake I am now animadverting upon. But few perſons are aware how ſmall a proportion of fixed air is neceſſary to make a very turbid appearance in a great quantity of lime-water.'

The experiments which the remainder of this ſection contains are naturally ſuggeſted by the opinion which he has thus ſo fairly examined, and ſo ably refuted. ' It muſt be allowed, he ſays, to be a curious ſubject of enquiry, to aſcertain the quantity of fixed air naturally contained in a given quantity of common air, or to trace the ſource of the fixed air which appears in ſome proceſſes for phlogiſticating common air.' Now, in ſome of theſe proceſſes, it ſeems to be more conſiderable than in others, and in ſome the Doctor finds no fixed air at all. This remarkable difference he is not able to account for at preſent; but he lays down a ſeries of facts, which he leaves to ſpeak for themſelves. One curious concluſion ſeems to flow from the contents of this ſection; that the diminution of air by breathing ſeems to be leſs than by putrefaction and ſeveral other proceſſes; and though air be not completely phlogiſticated by this means (' as the animal dies before the air arrives at that term,') yet the diminution ſeems to be leſs even in proportion to the degree of phlogiſtication.

Sect. XI. gives us ſome proceſſes in which phlogiſton produces a great decompoſition of fixed air; and others, in which the phlogiſtication does not ſeparate from the corrupted air, enough to make lime water turbid.

Sect. XII. preſents us with ſome very remarkable changes produced in different kinds of air, by placing them in circumſtances in which common air would be phlogiſticated. Inflammable air in one inſtance was diminiſhed one eighth of its bulk, nitrous air one half, but phlogiſticated air diſcovered the leaſt change of any, which led the Doctor to ſuppoſe, in oppoſition to ſome previous concluſions of his own, as well as of others who have purſued the ſame tract with himſelf, that in phlogiſticated air the phlogiſton is more ſtrongly united to its baſis than in any other.

Sect. XIII. contains the curious diſcovery, that air is neceſſary as well to the life of fiſhes as to that of men and other animals. Dr. Prieſtley found that fiſhes phlogiſticate the air contained in the water in which they live. That ſome fiſhes, which he placed in water deprived of its air by boiling, lived no longer in it than three hours and a half. And that water impregnated with phlogiſticated air killed them within the ſpace of an hour. Nitrous air mixed with the water in which he placed some fishes, killed them in less than a minute's time.

Sect. XIV. must to those who are in the least versed in aerial experiments contain information of the most interesting nature; it teaches us how to procure dephlogisticated air with very little toil and expence. ' For this purpose nothing more is necessary than an earthen retort and a reverberatory furnace;' (for which, however, one black pot or Hessian crucible inverted over another answers very well.) ' Every ounce of nitre, by the help of this apparatus, will yield a hundred ounces of very pure air, and the fire may be so regulated, that the production of air shall be more equable, and the process more manageable than in any other method hitherto employed.' The Doctor supposes, that those who cannot furnish themselves with a reverberatory, may succeed very well in the same process, by covering the retort with coals in a common fire. This method is that in which the Doctor first procured pure air, without knowing what he had gotten. Mr. Scheele, however, is the person to whom we must give the credit of reducing it to practice. One ounce of alum, by this method of operating, may be made to yield sixty ounces at least of pure, mixed with a small portion of fixed air.—— This experiment, as well as a variety of other facts, in which the vitriolic acid alone is concerned in the production of pure air, led the Doctor to correct his theory of the constituent principles of air: he had formerly supposed these to be an earth, the nitrous acid and a quantity of phlogiston; but he now wishes not to specify the particular acid, but more generally to say, that some acid principle is necessary to the constitution of air: his reasonings on this subject, he observes, lead us to a method of obtaining a truly primitive earth, or an earthy principle common to all earths and metallic calces whatsoever.

In the course of this section it appears that all that mercury wants to make it capable of yielding pure air, is the loss of its phlogiston, and the acquisition of some acid principle. ' But since (according to Dr. Crawford's theory, which Dr. Priestley does not pretend to have properly considered) air, in parting with its phlogiston, acquires the principle of heat, are not these two things the same, heat and pure acid, which is nearly the idea of Mr. Scheele?—But as this principle of heat does not, in any other case, appear to assume the form of air, and has not been found to have weight, which all acids, and dephlogisticated air also, have; it seems to be more probable, that the calx in parting with this phlogiston,

giston, takes from the air two distinct principles at the same time, viz. That of heat, (*if Dr. Crawford's theory be true,*) and this acid.'—We think Dr. Priestley has, in this passage, bestowed much fruitless pains upon two most absurd and extravagant systems; his objection to Scheele's theory is indeed decisive, but it is one only of a multitude which might be produced to the same effect. He wisely expresses his doubts about Dr. Crawford's system; but probably he feels himself no longer a sceptic. The silence with which Dr. Crawford has regarded a most reputable adversary, who has charged him in the most pointed manner, of blunders, and of absurdities, is to us an evidence more than presumptive, either that he has nothing to say in defence of himself, or a great deal to unsay concerning his theory. We have expected some answer for a long time, and we hope our expectations will not at last be disappointed.—This section concludes with a decisive fact, proving that mercury calcines much more easily in dephlogisticated than in common air. The Doctor intimates that, by an attention to this fact, ' the precipitate per se may be made with much less time and expence than it now is.'

Several of Dr. Priestley's friends had expressed some little doubt to him, of the accuracy of nitrous air, as a test of the purity of other airs. This scepticism, relating to one of his most important discoveries, has called forth a great part of the fifteenth section: Dr. Priestley really finds that an animal will live much longer in dephlogisticated air, than the nitrous test of its purity would lead him to expect. The air in which a mouse lived three hours, and which, when the mouse was taken out, was found to be very little phlogisticated, by the nitrous test was discovered to be only four times purer than the common air in which a mouse would have lived half an hour only. This striking difference between the two tests Dr. Priestly ascribes to the confinement of the animal, *which prevented it from phlogisticating the air so fast as it would have done in case it had been more vigorous.* This is conjecture only, and, we think, to give it *as such* the least weight, the Doctor has first of all a great deal to do; he should certainly have afforded us *some* reason to believe from experiment, that animals in a weak state do really phlogisticate air less than when in full strength. An enquiry which would inform and convince us in this particular, would, independent of its connexions with the difficulty advanced in this section, be so interesting and curious, that we much regret the Doctor's inattention to it. The offensiveness of breath, which is the usual attendant of the human constitution in its last state of weakness, if it depend on the phlogiston of the respired air,

ought

ought moft certainly to be attended to in this cafe.   Befides, if, as may be fairly concluded from fome other parts of his works, it be the Doctor's opinion that the nutrition of the human frame is in proportion to the phlogifton *it imbibes* from the food employed for its nourifhment, how are we to reconcile this with the idea, that the moft healthy and vigorous conftitutions difcharge the greateft quantity of *fuperabundant* phlogifton; or that their blood is leaft able to retain that principle which conftitutes the nutritious quality of our aliment?   It cannot be alledged here, that this is owing to the greater quantity of aliment which they take; for we very well know, that fome of the moft healthy, vigorous, and fucculent perfons, are thofe who have very fmall appetites. In our opinion, the difficulty of reconciling the two tefts ftill operates with full force; and we are much furprifed that the Doctor, who is generally fo copious on moft fubjects, fhould be contented with one experiment only, in a cafe which combats his moft ufeful, if not his moft brilliant difcovery.—The remainder of this fection is employed in correcting a moft egregious blunder committed by Dr. Ingenhoufz.   This is an office which we find him difcharging more than once in the courfe of this volume; and we are apt to think, from our own experience, that if the delicacy of friendfhip had not reftrained him, he might have informed the public of many other errors in that gentleman's work, which are too glaring to be overlooked by the moft common experimentalift; in the prefent inftance, however, it is fhewn, that Dr. Ingenhoufz is wrong, in what the Doctor flattered himfelf was a moft important difcovery, viz. that of making dephlogifticated air ferve thirty times longer than when it is ufed in the common way.   It is evident, at firft fight, that Dr. Ingenhoufz falls here into Meffrs. Kirwan and Cruickfhank's error, viz. that phlogiftication changes common into fixed air; and that by paffing air after it is breathed through lime-water, you deprive it of its noxious ingredients.—The Doctor is not contented with the decifive facts he has enumerated in other cafes, in oppofition to this opinion, but he makes an experiment, in which two mice are thrown into convulfions by the frequent refpiration of pure air, notwithftanding the precautions prefcribed by Dr. Ingenhoufz.

Sect. XVI. contains fome obfervations on fixed air.— Sect. XVII. treats of the ftate of air in water, by which it appears, that the air you expel from water in general contains a portion of fixed air; that the air you get from lime-water is much purer than common air; and that the air you expel from water in which vegetables have grown, is dephlogiftigifticated.—Sect. XVIII. prefents us with a variety of obfer-vations on the nature of fixed air. 1. From fome facts re-cited by Dr. Prieftley we are left in fome doubt, whether or not there be any water in the conftitution of nitrous air. 2. He finds no difference in the ftrength of nitrous air procured by a flow produce, and that which was produced with great rapidity. 3. Dr. Prieftley points out the changes in nitrous air, when produced from iron. 4. He defcribes the changes in the colour of liquids by which air is confined. 5. The Doctor proves that nitrous air is not changed by expofure to water in a fand-heat. 6. He treats of a fingular change pro-duced in nitrous air, after being long kept in water.—Sect. XX. is employed in refuting another blunder of which the Abbé Fontana is the author, and Dr. Ingenhoufz the publifh-er. Dr. Prieftley begins this fection with fhewing the ftrik-ing diminution produced in a quantity of nitrous air, merely by throwing it up into a long tube filled with water. Hence, he obferves, how important it is in meafuring the purity of air by this teft, to bring the two airs into contact through as fhort a paffage of water as poffible.

Dr. Ingenhoufz, in his book, fays that the Abbé Fontana had difcovered a method of employing nitrous air as a teft, in the ufe of which the ftrength of the nitrous air was of little or no confequence ; inftead of throwing equal meafures of nitrous and common air into the eudiometer, he would throw feveral meafures of nitrous air, fo that however weak, the abundance of the air ufed agreeably to this mode might fupply phlogifton enough to the common air, and at the end of the operation, the diminution would be juft the fame, as if one meafure only were ufed. In this inftance Dr. Ingen-houfz and the Abbé Fontana muft have proceeded folely from conjecture ; they could never have examined the accuracy of this mode by experiment, or they muft have obferved the difference which Dr. Prieftley difcovered. This, however, is not the only cafe in which we have lately detected philofophers, in the recommendation of inftruments and other modes of ope-ration, of the ufe, or the accuracy of which they could have no other evidence than fuch as their own fpeculative and unexperi-enced imaginations afforded them. With refpect to eudiometers, machines for determining the conducting powers of heated bodies, we could produce feveral inftances in which it was ab-folutely impoffible for the authors either to try or to con-ftruct what they propofed : they would otherwife have dif-covered how much they infulted the credulity of others, and expofed their own prefumption and ignorance. Dr. Prieftley is not contented with facts alone, on the prefent occafion, but

pro-

produces some striking arguments to complete the refutation of this error; and we are not a little surprised to find him praise, at the conclusion of this section, as a display of ingenuity, what he has previously exposed, as contrary to fact and the most obvious arguments.

We are very sorry that the limits within which we are necessarily confined will not allow us to follow the author through those curious sections in which he treats of dephlogisticated nitrous air, or that species of nitrous air in which a candle will burn with an enlarged flame. We pass on to the twenty-second section, which presents us with a most wonderful and unaccountable phænomenon: in his second volume Dr. Priestley informed us, that a portion of alkaline air, in consequence of passing the electric shock or spark through it, would be considerably increased; that the additional air produced by this operation was inflammable; and that, in consequence of the admission of water to the increased portion of air, all that was alkaline would be absorbed. In this volume Dr. Priestley supposes that he found the limit of the increase; and that the whole air, after the process, was nearly as possible three times as much as that which the alkaline air alone had occupied.

From the authority of a very accurate correspondent, we must beg leave to inform the Doctor, that he is certainly mistaken in this particular.—For, 1. By discharging two hundred explosions of a two-gallon jar through half a cubic inch of this air, it was actually increased to above seven times its bulk. 2. A great variety was found in consequence of sending the explosion through different *specimens* of this air. 3. By the admission of water into the tube employed in the experiment, all, or by far the greatest part of the alkaline air, was absorbed. From this strange fact, we feel a host of doubts arising in most formidable array in our minds against the Doctor's whole theory of the constitution of atmospheric air. 1. Where is the constituent earth in this experiment necessary for the production of so much air? 2. Where the acid? It cannot be urged that these are derived from the alkaline air; that continues apparently unaltered, for on being mixed with water, the water discovers all the properties which it possesses when impregnated with alkaline air, without undergoing the process in this experiment. We might have asked farther, whence comes the phlogiston also? But Mr. Bewly answers, in the Appendix, that it probably comes from the alkali, which abounds with it; and that the electric fluid may possibly add to the quantity of inflammable air contained in the alkaline air, by carrying phlogiston with it from the

bodies

bodies which conduct it. This ingenious conjecture, however, ought to derive some support from facts; we wish to learn, that some trials have been made, proving that the alkaline air in this experiment is dephlogisticated; and, farther, that the increase is not so great, when the shock is conveyed through conductors, which cannot be supposed to lose their phlogiston: when we are satisfied in these particulars, we shall eagerly wish to know the latent sources of the earth and the ——d, requisite, agreeable to the Doctor's theory, for this a———rance.

Sect. XXIII. treats of the volatility of the mercury, which is in contact with the vitriolic acid air, when the electric explosion is conveyed through it. This, like the former section, is calculated to surprise as well as to entertain us.

The remainder of this volume contains a variety of interesting novelties, but they are of that miscellaneous nature which will not allow us to give any general view of them. In his miscellaneous experiments in electricity, Dr. Priestley informs us, from his own experience, that in *all* instances, in which jars are over-charged, after they have been once cracked and then mended with cement, that the second rupture takes place close to the cement, excepting where the glass is very thick. His sad experience, we acknowledge, as he describes it in this section, is very great; but a single fact, in which we have known a thin green glass phial, after undergoing the process he describes, break at a great distance from the cement, is sufficient to convince us that the Doctor is wrong in making the position so general.——Towards the conclusion of this volume we find a very valuable recapitulation of the principal facts contained in the preceding volumes. We think it might have been greatly improved, if the Doctor had subjoined to each general position, a few of the leading experiments which evince and confirm it. We have heard many persons complain, that when they wish to repeat his experiments they know not where to begin, or where to find, some of the most instructive and entertaining; we apprehend, the mode he has observed in part seventh, vol. ii. of his History of Electricity, would be of great use in such cases.

Dr. Priestley, we hope, will ascribe the freedom of our strictures on several parts of the excellent work before us, to a vanity, which is flattered by discovering a few trifling errors amidst that crowd of excellencies, by which he commands our praise and admiration. If the encouragement he received were adequate to our wishes, he would indeed be most amply rewarded: he would proceed, in the new philosophical world which he has discovered, without meeting any obstructions,

but

but ſuch as muſt neceſſarily reſult from the novelty and variety of his enquiries.　　　　　　　　　　　　　　　　　**C.**

---

*Phyſiological Diſquiſitions ; or, Diſcourſes on the Natural Philo-
ſophy of the Elements.* 1. *On Matter.* 2. *On Motion.* 3.
On the Elements. 4. *On Fire.* 5. *On Air.* 6. *On Sound and
Muſic.* 7. *On Foſſil Bodies.* 8. *On Phyſical Geography, or the
Natural Hiſtory of the Earth.* 9. *On the Weather.* By W.
Jones, *F. R. S. Rector of* Paſton *in* Northamptonſhire, *and
Author of an Eſſay on the firſt Principles of Natural Philoſophy.*
4to. 1l. 1s. *in boards.* Robinſon.

TO this work the author has prefixed a handſome dedication, but rather too long for the faſhion, to the ſecretary
at war ; and the convenience of the reader is happily conſulted in a new ſort of index to all the figures in the copper-
plates, explaining briefly the ſubject and meaning of each.
In an introduction he explains, at large, the nature and deſign of his undertaking, and gives a particular account of a
former publication on the ſame ſubject, which was preparatory
to the preſent work. The grand principle which he has in view
is to exemplify and prove *the action of the elements on one another,* that all natural philoſophy may be reduced to one ſimple
and univerſal law ; and we muſt acknowledge that this principle, as the author has purſued it, leads us to a new proſp-
pect of the œconomy of nature. There is ſuch a variety of
matter in this work, that we cannot enter far into particulars, otherwiſe we would ſet down the author's arguments,
which are adduced to ſhew the inſufficiency of the eſtabliſhed
demonſtration of a vacuum, in pages vi. and vii. of the Introduction. He obſerves, that there are four diſtinct forms of
philoſophy, which muſt be applied to by thoſe who would underſtand natural philoſophy in its proper extent ; viz. the
mythological, ſyſtematical, experimental, and ſacred ; of all
which, with their excellencies and their defects, he has given
a particular account, and has made his uſe of them in the
courſe of the work. Speaking of the improved ſtate of experimental philoſophy, he has the following reflection, ' I
have often indulged a wiſh that I could exhibit to the wiſe
men and heroes of ancient times ſome of thoſe wonderful
improvements, which are now ſo familiar to us, but were totally unknown to them. I would give to Ariſtotle the electrical
ſhock ; I would carry Alexander to ſee the experiments upon
the Warren at Woolwich, together with all the evolutions and
firings of a modern battalion ; I would ſhew to Julius Cæſar,
　　　　　　　　　　　　　　　　　　　　　　　the

the invader of Britain, an Engliſh man of war; and to Archimedes, a fire engine, and a reflecting teleſcope.'

In deſcribing the qualifications which he expects in his readers, he obſerves, that his work is properly *phyſiological,* and its demonſtrations rather from plain facts, accommodated to all capacities, than from abſtruſe reaſonings; whence all perſons of a liberal education may think themſelves equal to the ſubject as he has treated it. An apology is made for deferring the publication of a diſcourſe on electricity, intended as a part of this volume; which would have been too bulky with that addition; and the author's partiality to the philoſophy of muſic, has tempted him to tranſgreſs the bounds he had at firſt allotted to that branch. Muſical philoſophers are ſcarce; of electrical philoſophers there is great plenty; and therefore, it is probable, the author has diſappointed more than he has gratified by the ſubſtitution of muſic for electricity; but we hope it will not be long before his original deſign will be accompliſhed; as many will wiſh to ſee how electricity will confirm his principle. In this introduction many things are advanced concerning the alliance between philoſophy and divinity, and ſome celebrated writings are cited as authorities; amongſt the reſt an extraordinary character is given of our ancient Engliſh philoſopher, commonly known by the name of Friar Bacon. Some ſtrictures are alſo added on the abuſe of natural philoſophy, by Voltaire and others.

As a ſpecimen of the author's ſtyle and manner, we ſhall preſent the reader with the laſt paragraph of his introduction, in the whole of which the learned reader will find many intereſting obſervations.——' I have now, as I hope, fully explained the conſiderations which prevailed with me to write on natural philoſophy; and I can ſincerely affirm, that the work is rather a work of duty than of oſtentation; to which, if the reader is inclined to do juſtice, I muſt deſire him to remember, that my whole ſcheme ſhould be taken together, and that this book is but a part of it. When I firſt looked forward upon the plan, I had a very different idea from that which preſents itſelf to me, now I look back upon it. Had it appeared then as it does now, I ſhould have left it for ſome better hand to execute; and were I to detain a work of ſo much difficulty, and comprehending ſuch a variety of ſubjects as will be found in it, till I could approve it, and be ſatisfied that I had done what I might and ought to have done, it would never come abroad. I muſt therefore hope to correct ſome things by farther examination; and I ſhall never be aſhamed to improve what I publiſh, by means of ſuch hints as friendly information, or even hoſtile criticiſm itſelf, ſhall

hereafter throw in my way. If ſome ſhould neglect my philoſophical writings, either on the juſt ground of their own ſuperior knowledge, or from lower motives of vanity, envy, or
intereſt ; I know that every author muſt commit his works to
the times in which he writes, whether they are favourable or
adverſe to his undertaking; and when he has launched his
veſſel, he muſt leave it to the chance of the wind and the weather. My mind, however, ſuggeſts to me that this book will
not be totally thrown aſide and forgotten. The natural agency of the elements, for which I have pleaded, and, which I
hope to carry farther, (however imperfectly) is ſo reaſonable,
ſo ſtriking, ſo intimately interwoven with the moſt agreeable
and intereſting parts of literature, that it muſt, when it comes
to be better underſtood, find friends and favourers, either in
this country, or ſome other ; with abilities to defend what
ſhall have been rightly done in this great ſubject, and to improve it by their own more ſucceſsful labours.'

In the diſcourſe *on Matter*, he conſiders the different forms
in which the elementary parts of bodies appear, and how the
properties of bodies may ariſe from the configuration of their
parts. Diviſibility of matter is ſhewn to be not infinite, but
only indefinite ; inaſmuch as matter muſt be ſuppoſed to con-
ſiſt of *units* as the rudiments of bodies. All the primary properties of matter are reduced to *hardneſs* and *mobility* ; and
many facts are introduced to illuſtrate the ſecondary properties of bodies from their compoſitions and decompoſitions.
The continuity of matter is ſhewn to be neceſſary to many of
its effects ; and diſcontinuous matter is ſaid to act by means of
other matter co-operating with it. It is alſo ſhewn how bodies may increaſe in bulk, and yet preſerve their continuity.
Atoms, in a ſtate of ſeparation, do not gravitate ſpecifically,
as when in maſſes, and as all matter has not a tendency to-
ward a centre, gravity is not eſſential to matter. The polarity of atoms is explained and exemplified, and the viſibility
of matter ſuppoſed to be a conſequence of its concreting into
maſſes. To theſe phyſical obſervations on matter the author
has ſubjoined its mythological hiſtory, in the fabulous characters of *Saturn* and *Proteus*, and the *Satyrs*, together with
the Pythagorean philoſophy, founded on the transformations
of matter, and the phænomena of generation and corruption
in the œconomy of nature.

The diſcourſe *on Motion* is chiefly employed in the inveſtigation of its cauſes. As matter has no active properties of its
own, but by its nature indifferent to motion, its motion muſt
originate from, and be preſerved by the influence of inviſible
power : but this power does not act without the intervention
of ſecond cauſes, of which there is a chain, each depending
on

on the other, and all fubordinate to the Creator. Nature is to be confidered as a connected fyftem, becaufe nothing can be learned of matter by confidering it abftractedly. This reafoning is illuftrated from the relation between the limbs and the body in an animal. Bodies do not continue to move without the continuation of a moving force. Life is kept up conftantly by the caufes of life; fo motion by the caufes of motion. To fay that the body lives to-day, becaufe it lived yefterday, is to give as good a reafon for the continuance of life, as Defcartes gives for the continuance of motion. The cafe of a moving pendulum is very fubtile, yet fuppofed to be reducible to the general rule. Some caufes are known to the bodily fenfes; others are inferred by rational deduction from the laws of nature. In reviewing the different kinds of motion, he finds there is fuch a thing in nature as uniform motion in a right line; and that the motion of fluids is both progreffive and vibratory, admitting of great variety in the fame fluid, without interruption to itfelf. All motion muft be in the direction of its caufe; whence all attraction, commonly fo called, muft refolve itfelf into impulfe. We fay of a plafter that it draws; but it cannot act in the direction of the effect; the force is from the *vis vitæ* propelling the fluids towards the plafter. When a body retains its motion without diminution, it is moved by a caufe which would renew the motion if it were ftopt: hence projection cannot be admitted as a principle of motion in nature; it is a principle only of that motion which is violent and artificial. A parallel is here introduced, to fhew that the planetary motions may be effected by very gentle forces, acting infenfibly. All motions are to be referred to corporeal caufes; philofophy cannot proceed without them: all experiments on the elements tend to fhew how fome matter produces changes in other matter: nothing elfe is intelligible. The principle of a circulation in nature is purfued at large, and contended for as a folution of many difficulties in nature, not otherwife to be accounted for. Motion in a plenum is poffible or impoffible under different circumftances which fhould be diftinguifhed. Refiftance is no argument againft the admiffion of impelling forces, for the caufe of motion, whatever it may be, rare or denfe, can never be faid to refift the motion which it caufes.

The matter of this difquifition, which, however abftrufe, is neceffary to be introduced into philofophy, is made more plain in what the author calls a recapitulation, from which a reader may foon fee what it contains, and judge of its merits.

[*To be continued.*]

A Ge-

A General View of the Writings of Linnæus. *By* Richard Pulteney; *M. D. F. R. S.* 8*vo.* 7*s.* Payne.

THE great genius and comprehensive talents of the cele-brated philosopher, whose writings form the subject of this work, must render an account of whatever concerns him highly interesting to all the lovers of natural science. We are, therefore, glad to find that the author of the present vo-lume has intermixed with the General View some memoirs of this illustrious professor. Dr. Pulteney's principal design, however, is to exhibit a detail of Linnæus's writings, in the order in which they were published ; and the biographical anecdotes are introduced only for the sake of connexion, or to relieve the tediousness which would arise from an uninter-rupted recital of the author's various publications. For the satisfaction of those who are unacquainted with the history of this immortal Swede, the father of modern botany, we shall present them with a few particulars of his life.

'Charles Von Linnè, the son of a Swedish divine, was born May 24, 1707, at Roeshult, in the province of Smaland, in Sweden ; of which place his father had the cure, when this son was born, but was soon after preferred to the living of Stenbri-hult, in the same province, where dying in 1748, at the age of 70, he was succeeded in his cure by another son. We are told, in the commemoration-speech on this celebrated man, delivered in his Swedish majesty's presence, before the Royal Academy of Sciences at Stockholm, that the ancestors of this family took their firnames of Linnæus, Lindelius, and Tiliander, from a, large lime-tree, or linden-tree, yet standing on the farm where Lin-næus was born ; and that this origin of firnames, taken from na-tural objects, is not very uncommon in Sweden.

'This eminent man, whose talents enabled him to reform the whole science of natural history, accumulated, very early in life, some of the highest honours that await the most successful pro-ficients in medical science ; since we find that he was made pro-fessor of physic and botany, in the university of Upsal, at the age of thirty-four ; and six years afterwards, physician to his sovereign, the late king Adolphus ; who, in the year 1753, honoured him still farther, by creating him knight of the order of the Polar Star. His honours did not terminate here, for in 1757, he was ennobled ; and in 1776, the present king of Sweden accepted the resignation of his office, and rewarded his declining years by doubling his pension, and by a liberal donation of landed property, settled on him and his family.

'It seems probable, that his father's example first gave Lin-næus a taste for the study of nature ; who, as he has himself in-formed us, cultivated, as his first amusement, a garden plenti-fully stored with plants. Young Linnæus soon became ac-

quainted

quainted with thefe, as well as the indigenous ones of his neighbourhood. Yet, from the ftraightnefs of his father's income, our young naturalift was on the point of being deftined to a mechanical employment : fortunately, however, this defign was over-ruled. In 1717, he was fent to fchool at Wexfio, where, as his opportunities were enlarged, his progrefs in all his favourite purfuits was proportionably extended. At this early period he paid attention to other branches of natural hiftory ; particularly to the knowlege of infects : in which, as is manifeft from his oration on the fubject, he muft very early have made a great proficiency, fince we find that he was not lefs fuccefsful herein, than in that of plants, having given them an arrangement, and eftablifhed fuch characters of diftinction, as have been univerfally followed by fucceeding entomologifts.

‘ The firft part of his academical education, Linnæus received under profeffor Stobæus, at Lund, in Scania, who favoured his inclinations to the ftudy of natural hiftory. After a refidence of about a year, he removed, in 1728, to Upfal. Here he foon contracted a clofe friendfhip with Artedi, a native of the province of Angermannia, who had already been four years a ftudent in that univerfity, and, like himfelf, had a ftrong bent to the ftudy of natural hiftory in general, but particularly to ichthyology. He was moreover well fkilled in chemiftry, and not unacquainted with botany, having been the inventor of that diftinction in umbelliferous plants, arifing from the differences of the involucrum. Emulation is the foul of improvement, and, heightened as it was in this inftance by friendfhip, proved a moft powerful incentive. Thefe young men profecuted their ftudies together with uncommon vigor, mutually communicating their obfervations, and laying their plans, fo as to affift each other in every branch of natural hiftory and phyfic.

‘ Soon after his refidence at Upfal, our author was alfo happy enough to obtain the favour of feveral gentlemen of eftablifhed character in literature. He was in a particular manner encouraged in the purfuit of his ftudies by the patronage of Dr. Olaus Celfius, at that time profeffor of divinity, and the reftorer of natural hiftory in Sweden ; fince fo diftinguifhed for oriental learning, and more particularly for his Hierobotanicon, or Critical Differtations on the Plants mentioned in Scripture. This gentleman is faid to have given Linnæus a large fhare of his efteem, and he was fortunate enough to obtain it very early after his removal to Upfal. He was at that time meditating his Hierobotanicon, and being ftruck with the diligence of Linnæus, in defcribing the plants of the Upfal garden, and his extenfive knowlege of their names, fortunately for him, at that time involved in difficulties, from the narrow circumftances of his parents, Celfius not only patronized him in a general way, but admitted him to his houfe, his table, and his library. Under fuch encouragement, it is not ftrange that our author made a rapid progrefs, both in his ftudies, and the efteem of the profeffors ;

feffors : in fact, we have a very ftriking proof of his merit and attainments, inafmuch as we find, that after only two years refidence, he was thought fufficiently qualified to give lectures occafionally from the botanic chair, in the room of profeffor Rudbeck.'

Linnæus was foon afterwards appointed by the Royal Academy of Sciences at Upfal, to make the tour of Lapland, with the view of exploring the natural hiftory of that arctic region. This tour had been made for the firft time, by the elder Rudbeck, in 1695, at the command of Charles XI. but unfortunately, almoft all the obfervations which that traveller had made, perifhed in the terrible fire at Upfal, in 1702. Linnæus fet out from Upfal, on this journey, about the middle of May, 1732 ; equally a ftranger to the language and to the manners of the Laplanders, and without any affociate. He even traverfed what is called the Lapland Defert ; a tract of territory deftitute of villages, cultivation, or any conveniences, and inhabited only by a few ftraggling people.

'In this diftrict, fays the biographer, he afcended a noted mountain called Wallevari, in fpeaking of which he has given us a pleafant relation of his finding a fingular and beautiful new plant (Andromeda tetragona) when travelling within the arctic circle, with the fun in his view at midnight, in fearch of a Lapland hut. From hence he croffed the Lapland Alps into Finmark, and traverfed the fhores of the North fea as far as Sallero.

'Thefe journies from Lula and Pitha, on the Bothnian gulph, to the north fhore, were made on foot, and our traveller was attended by two Laplanders ; one his interpreter, and the other his guide. He tells us that the vigour and ftrength of thefe two men, both old, and fufficiently loaded with his baggage, excited his admiration, fince they appeared quite unhurt by their labour, while he himfelf, although young and robuft, was frequently quite exhaufted. In this journey he was wont to fleep under the boat with which they forded the rivers, as a defence againft rain, and the gnats, which in the Lapland fummer are not lefs teazing than in the torrid zones. In defcending one of thefe rivers, he narrowly efcaped perifhing by the overfetting of the boat, and loft many of the natural productions which he had collected.

'Linnæus thus fpent the greater part of the fummer in examining this arctic region, and thofe mountains, on which, four years afterwards, the French philofophers fecured immortal fame to fir Ifaac Newton. At length, after having fuffered incredible fatigues and hardfhips, in climbing precipices, paffing rivers in miferable boats, fuffering repeated viciffitudes of extreme heat and cold, and not unfrequently hunger and thirft ; he returned to Tornea in September.'

He

He arrived at Upsal in November, after having performed, and that mostly on foot, a journey of ten degrees of latitude in extent, exclusive of the many deviations which the accomplishment of his design rendered necessary. The result of this journey was not published till several years afterwards; but he lost no time in presenting the Academy with a catalogue of the plants which he had discovered; which, even so early as that period, he arranged according to the system since denominated the sexual.

In 1733, we find his great naturalist visiting and examining the several mines in Sweden; where he formed his first sketch of his System on Mineralogy, which appeared in the early editions of the *Systema Naturæ,* but was not exemplified until the year 1768.

The next incident in the history of this celebrated person, was his being sent, with several other naturalists, by the governor of Dalekarlia, into that province, to investigate its natural productions. After accomplishing the purpose of this expedition, he resided some time in the capital of Dalekarlia, where he taught mineralogy, and the docimastic art, and practised physic. In 1735, he travelled over many other parts of Denmark and Germany, and fixed in Holland, where he chiefly resided until his return to Stockholm, about the year 1739. Soon after he had fixed his residence at this place, he married one of the daughters of Dr. More, a physician at Fahlun, in Dalekarlia, with whom he became acquainted during his stay in that town.

In 1735, the year in which he took the degree of doctor in physic, he published the first sketch of his *Systema Naturæ,* in the form of tables only. It thence appears, as the biographer observes, that, before he was twenty four years old, he laid the basis of that great structure which he afterwards raised, and which will perpetuate his fame to the latest ages of botanical science.

In 1736, Linnæus visited England, where he formed many friendships with men at that time distinguished for their knowledge in natural history: but though Boerhaave had furnished him with letters of recommendation to sir Hans Sloane, we are told, that he met not with that reception which he had reason to expect. For this treatment, Dr. Pulteney, with great probability, assigns the following cause.

' Dr. Boerhaave's letter to sir Hans Sloane, on this occasion, is preserved in the British Museum, and runs thus—" Linnæus qui has tibi dabit literas, est unice dignus te videre, unice dignus a te videri; qui vos videbit simul, videbit hominum par, cui simile vix dabit orbis."—This encomium, howsoever quaintly ex-

expreffed, yet was in fome meafure prophetic of Linnæus's future fame and greatnefs, and proves how intimately Boerhaave
had penetrated into the genius and abilities of our author ; and,
ftrained as this parallel might be thought, it is likely however
that the opening of the fexual fyftem, fo different from Ray's,
by which fir Hans Sloane had always known plants, and particularly the innovations, as they were then called, which Linnæus had made in altering the names of fo many genera, were
rather the caufe of that coolnefs with which he was received by
our excellent naturalift.   Probably we have. reafon to regret this
circumftance ; for otherwife Linnæus might have obtained an
eftablifhment in England, as it has been thought he wifhed to
have done ; and doubtlefs his opportunities in this kingdom
would have been much more favourable to his defigns, than in
thofe arctic regions where he fpent the remainder of his days.
In the mean time, we may juftly infer the exalted idea that Linnæus had of England, as a land eminently favourable to the
improvement of fcience, from that compliment which, in a letter to a friend, he afterwards paid to London, when, fpeaking
of that city, he called it, " Punctum faliens in vitello orbis."

   In 1738, this great naturalift made an excurfion to Paris,
where he had the infpecting the Herbaria of the Juffieus, at
that time the firft botanifts in France ; and alfo the botanical
collections of Surian and Tournefort.   He intended going
thence to Germany, to vifit Ludwig, and the celebrated Haller, with whom he maintained a clofe correfpondence ; but he
was obliged to return to Holland without enjoying this pleafure.

   Dr. Pulteney then proceeds to give an account of the feveral fcientific productions which Linnæus publifhed previous to
this time.   Thefe are, the *Syftema Naturæ, Fundamenta Botanica, Bibliotheca Botanica,* and *Genera Plantarum.*   The laft
of thofe is juftly confidered as the moft valuable of all the
works of this celebrated author.   What immenfe application
had been beftowed upon it, the reader may eafily conceive, on
being informed, that, before the publication of the firft edition, the author had examined the characters of eight thoufand
flowers.   The laft book of Linnæus's compofition, publifhed
during his ftay in Holland, was. the *Claffes Plantarum ;* which
is a copious illuftration of the fecond part of the *Fundamenta.*

   About the latter end of 1738, or the beginning of the fubfequent year, Linnæus returned to his native country where
he fettled as a phyfician, at Stockholm.   It is faid, that at firft
he met with confiderable oppofition, and. was oppreffed with
many difficulties ; but at length he furmounted all, and acquired extenfive practice.   The intereft of count Teffin, who
became his zealous patron, procured him the rank of phyfician

   3   to

to the fleet, and a ſtipend from the citizens for giving lectures in botany. The biographer obſerves, that the eſtabliſhment of the Royal Academy of Sciences at Stockholm, of which Linnæus was appointed the firſt preſident, ſerved not a little to favour the advancement of his fame, by the opportunity which it afforded of diſplaying his abilities. In 1741, upon the reſignation of Roberg, he was conſtituted joint profeſſor of phyſic, and phyſician to the king, with Roſen, who had been appointed the preceding year.

Dr. Pulteney afterwards gives an account of the *Iter Oelandicum & Gotlandicum, Iter Scanicum, Flora Suecica, Fauna Suecica, Materia Medica*, and *Philoſophia Botanica* ; the hiſtory and nature of which works he briefly explains.

In 1755, Linnæus was honoured with a gold medal by the Royal Academy of Sciences of Stockholm, for a paper on the ſubject of promoting agriculture, and all · branches of rural oeconomy ; and in 1760, he obtained a premium from the Imperial Academy of Sciences at Peterſburg, for a paper relative to the doctrine of the ſexes of plants.

The author of the General View, afterwards gives a large analyſis of the *Syſtema Naturæ*, and of the *Genera Morborum* ; with a ſhort account of the papers written by Linnæus, in the *Acta Upſalienſia*. The laſt of this great man's treatiſes was the *Mantiſſa Altera*, publiſhed in 1771.

We are told that Linnæus, upon the whole, enjoyed a good conſtitution ; but that he was ſometimes ſeverely afflicted with a *hemicrania*, and was not exempted from the gout. About the cloſe of 1776, he was ſeized with an apoplexy, which left him paralytic ; and at the beginning of the year, 1777, he ſuffered another ſtroke, which very much impaired his mental powers. But the diſeaſe ſuppoſed to have been the more immediate cauſe of his death, was an ulceration of the urinary bladder ; of which, after a tedious indiſpoſition, he died on the 11th of January, 1778, in the 71ſt year of his age.

‡ In the commemoration · ſpeech, delivered by Dr. Bæck, phyſician to the king of Sweden, Linnæus's ſtature is deſcribed as being " diminutive ; his head large ; his look ardent, piercing, and apt to daunt the beholder. His ear not ſenſible to muſic ; his temper quick ; his memory good, though in the latter period of his life liable to fail him ſometimes ; his knowlege of languages confined, yet no intereſting diſcovery eſcaped him. In ſummer he uſed to ſleep from ten to three o'clock, in winter from nine to ſix, and inſtantly to ceaſe from his labours when he found himſelf not well diſpoſed for them. He was an agreeable companion, of quick ſenſibility, but eaſily appeaſed."

The remaining part of the volume contains an account of the *Amænitates Academicæ* ; with obfervations, tending to fhew the utility of botanical knowledge in relation to agriculture, and the feeding of cattle : accompanied with a tranflation of Linnæus's Pan Suecus, accommodated to the Englifh plants, with references to authors, and to figures of the plants.

In this volume, Dr. Pulteney has given fuch a detail of the various works of the celebrated naturalift, as muft not only render them more generally known, but afford the fatisfaction of tracing the progrefs of that illuftrious philofopher through his different refearches and improvements, in the fciences which he cultivated. Judicious obfervations are likewife frequently interfperfed in the work ; and the whole, we doubt not, will prove both acceptable and ufeful to thofe who take delight in the pleafant purfuits of natural hiftory.

A Tour through Monmouthshire *and* Wales.   *By* Henry Penruddocke Wyndham. *The Second Edition.* 4*to.* 1*l. in boards.* Wilkie.

FROM a very fmall fize, this Tour is now enlarged to a quarto volume ; not by means of dull and frivolous narrative, as is too frequently the cafe in the recital of travels, but by defcriptions of what are curious, and remarks of what are interefting to a reader defirous of information.

The author gives the following account of coracles, a fingular fort of boats ufed in fome parts of Caermarthenfhire.

' They are generally 5½ feet long, and 4 broad ; their bottom is a little rounded, and their fhape nearly oval. Thefe boats are ribbed with light laths or fplit twigs, in the manner of bafket work, and are covered with a raw hide, or ftrong canvas, pitched in fuch a mode as to prevent their leaking. A feat croffes juft above the centre, towards the broader end. They feldom weigh more than between 20 and 30 pounds. The men paddle them with one hand, while they fifh with the other ; and when their work is completed, they throw the coracles over their fhoulders, and, without difficulty, return with them home.'

We are told that the neighbourhood of Haverfordweft claims the merit of having practifed inoculation of the fmall-pox before it was even known to the other counties of Britain ; for while the London phyficians, on the recommendation of Lady Mary Wortley Montague, were cautioufly trying the experiment on fome condemned criminals, the more hardy native of Pembrokefhire dared to inoculate himfelf, without the affiftance of either phyfician or preparation. In order to procure the diftemper, they either rubbed the variolous matter, taken from ripe puftules, on feveral parts of the fkin ; or pricked the fkin with

needles,

needles, previoufly infected. They called this buying the fmall-pox, as it was the cuftom to purchafe the matter from each other.

We fhall prefent our readers with the fubfequent account of the Welch horfes.

' The little horfes, which we employed in this expedition, were exceedingly hardy, and poffeffed a ftrength much fuperior to their appearances.   They would conftantly travel with heavy burdens forty miles a day, even without the affiftance or refrefhment of a fingle feed of corn.   A horfe, that did not appear equal to more than eight or nine ftone, fometimes carried all our baggage in a fort of panniers, with our poftman riding between them ; and though his flefh lay like furrows between his ribs, and his back was as fharp as a wedge, yet he purfued his ftages, with the weight of at leaft thirty ftone, without ftop or fatigue. Thefe horfes are no fooner difengaged from their faddles, than they are turned into a common pafture for the night ; no confideration being had, either to the weather, or to their journey, or to their heat, which might have arifen from it.

' Every inn in the country is provided with a paddock for this purpofe ; and left any accident fhould happen to the mares in this common field, where horfes, as well as geldings, are promifcuoufly admitted : the people have a cuftom to *modrwy y caffeg*, that is, to ring the mares, which they perform with a fmall leather thong, and which, preventing all mifchievous intercourfe, intimates a fimilar prohibition to that of the padlock among the jealous Spaniards.'

The condition of the inhabitants about Conway is reprefented as extremely deplorable.

' Their habitations, fays the traveller, are low, mud-built hovels, raifed over the natural earth, which is as deficient in point of level within, as without.   Notwithftanding the feverity of the climate, the windows are frequently deftitute of a fingle piece of glazing.   If the inhabitants wifh to enjoy the light, they muft at the fame time fuffer the cold : they wear neither fhoes nor ftockings, and chiefly fubfift upon the coarfe diet of rank cheefe, oat bread, and milk.   Such penury anticipates old age, and I have feen perfons of forty, from their decrepid and wrinkled features, appear, as if they had paffed their grand climacteric.   A melancholy dejection is fpread over their countenances, which are ftrangers to the fmiles of chearfulnefs and pleafure.

' If we carry our obfervations to the mountains, we fhall find, among thofe dreary waftes, a poverty ftill more extreme than below ; in many of thofe parifhes a grain of wheat has never been feen ; even the cheap luxury of garden greens is unknown ; and according to the ftrong expreffion of a lowland Welfhman, there are hundreds of families, who have never tafted a leek.   They continue in the fame unimproved ftate, as in the time of Giraldus, who thus defcribes them ; " They neither live in towns, in ftreets, nor in camps.   It is not their cuftom to erect grand palaces, nor large and fuperfluous buildings of ftone and mortar. They are otherwife content with roofs of thatch, fufficient from year to year, and

which

which will anſwer all their purpoſes, with as little labour as expence.   They are ignorant of the luxuries of either orchards or
gardens."

'Notwithſtanding this apparent miſery, we cannot pronounce
theſe mountaineers miſerable ; if content be happineſs, they are
certainly happy : they are all equally poor, and while poverty is
not particular, it cannot be conſidered as a misfortune.   They are
robuſt, healthy, and live to a great age, and as they are ignorant of thoſe many refinements, which civilized luxury has
taught us to conſider as neceſſaries of life, they have therefore no
want of them, there is

"No craving void left aching in their breaſt."

For this reaſon, we ſee mirth and chearfulneſs, united with poverty, in the moſt humble cot upon the highlands, when a ſmaller
degree of poverty has ſpread a diſcontented gloom, over the
whole face of the lowlands.   All happineſs is by compariſon ; ſo
theſe lower people are comparatively miſerable : for they are tan-
talized with appetites which they cannot gratify, while they behold with envy, many pleaſures enjoyed by others, which partial
nature has forbidden them even to hope for.

'But how happens it, that they ſhould not attempt to relieve
their wants by aſking charity ? for, I believe this is the only
country in Europe, in which the traveller can eſcape the ſolicitations of ſuch abject wretches.   If there was any neglect in the execution of the poor laws, beggary muſt be the conſequence : or,
if it was common, (as, however incredible it may appear, I was
well informed) for theſe miſerable beings to hoard up from the
ſcanty profits of their daily labour, and ſtarve themſelves to indulge their avarice ; we ſhould think, they would then naturally
apply to charity in order to gratify that paſſion.   We muſt have
recourſe to the firſt principle of this country to reſolve the queſtion ; it has been obſerved, that this barbarous mode of life has
continued for a long ſucceſſion of generations, and, probably, the
preſent may find ſome comfort in the reflection, of living as well as
their anceſtors ; and perhaps, it is as difficult to make a nation, ſo
bigotted to opinion as the Welſh is, change the ſmalleſt article in
their manners, (however beneficial it might be to them,) as it
would be to force them to aboliſh their dreſs, or their language.'

This volume is ornamented with a number of plates well engraved.

---

*Remarks on the Influence of Climate, &c. on the Diſpoſition and
Temper, &c. of Mankind.*   [*Concluded from p.* 107.]

IN the eleventh chapter, the author conſiders the effects of a
warm climate upon manners and behaviour.   He remarks,
that warm climates have been long ago obſerved to be earlier,
and more completely civilized, than cold ones ; but he is of
opinion that this politeneſs has always conſiſted in the obſervance of certain fixed and ſtated ceremonials, adapted to
the

the situation and character of the people. A circumstance no less observable, respecting the manners of the people of hot climates, is their immutability. Montesquieu, who has attempted to account for this principle, assigns, as one reason for it, the high degree of sensibility which a hot climate naturally inspires, and which is almost constantly joined to an indolence of mind, connected with that of the body. Another reason is derived from the nature of the government, which in such countries is generally despotic. But perhaps the most powerful cause of this immutability, as the author observes, is the confinement of the women. Whatever cause we admit, it is highly probable, that the uniformity of manners contributes not a little to preserve the mode of government unchanged.

The next chapter treats of the influence of a cold climate on the manners. The author observes, that the manners of the northern nations, compared with those of warm climates, appear rough and austere. Their address is usually blunt and unpolished; and they have few ceremonials to regulate their behaviour. This character results from the temper of the people, who are endowed with little sensibility, are of a bold and resolute spirit, and accustomed to strong bodily exertions. It is also observed, that the manners of cold climates are much less permanent and uniform than those of the opposite temperature.

In the succeeding chapter, the author takes a view of the effect of temperate climates upon the manners. For what the author advances on this subject, we shall have recourse to the work.

' Politeness and elegance of behaviour have always attained to the greatest perfection in temperate climates: this has been owing in some measure to the greater perfection of arts in general. But I apprehend, that the disposition of the people to activity, joined with a degree of sensibility; and a government with some share of liberty, and which consequently admits of a free communication of sentiment, are the principal reasons.

' The last of these, as far as relates to a free intercourse of company and conversation between the sexes, is perhaps the most active cause of any, and subsists only in moderate climates; the female sex, in cold ones, being disregarded, and in hot ones, being in a state of confinement. While in Asia the fair sex are considered only as a possession, in Europe they are objects of tenderness, esteem, and rational attachment. This inspires a habit of attentive and respectful behaviour; their beauty excites admiration and love; and even their very weakness adds force to their influence, under the idea of delicacy. Generosity prevents oppression, where there can be no resistance; and rouses valour and gallantry in their defence. Whatever they say is heard with peculiar attention; and even their foibles are construed into perfections.

fections.   Besides, by their being at liberty, they are enabled to take a part in the bufinefs of the world; to manage domeftic affairs, which are there regarded as their peculiar province; and to bear an almoft equal part in the adventures of life; and thus to render themfelves objects of efteem, when their perfonal attractions are no more.

'Another circumftance highly favourable to the influence of the fair fex, in moderate climates, is, that in them their beauty and underftanding accompany each other; fo that a woman is at the fame time an object of paffion and of refpect.   This circumftance, joined to that of their being but one object, (polygamy not being practifed) and of confequence the hopes of offspring depending on her only, inhances much their confequence in fociety: and of courfe tends to render the manners of the other fex fuch as are agreeable to them; that is, attentive, polifhed, and elegant.

'In Afia, the cafe is directly the reverfe; the women are there fecluded from converfation with the other fex, and are regarded chiefly in the light of an object for the gratification of paffion; and even this regard is divided among a number.   Their beauty is tranfient, their manners difpofed to be profligate, and their minds uncultivated; they bear no part in the affairs of life, and are efteemed to be in an inferior ftation in point of rank; confequently, they can neither be objects of refpect, efteem, or rational attachment.   No wonder then, that the other fex fhould be little difpofed to cultivate a mode of behaviour adapted to their inclinations.   In very cold countries, the fair fex, though under no reftraint in point of perfonal confinement, are, as I have before remarked, but little refpected; and of confequence their intercourfe with the other fex has but little effect upon the manners.   In Ruffia, until of late years, they were held to be fcarcely fuperior to domeftic fervants; were accuftomed to be beaten, at the pleafure of their hufbands; and even the fign of efpoufal itfelf, was an inftrument of chaftifement.   By communication with other nations, this brutality is in a great meafure worn off; and Ruffia, in confequence, rifes in the efteem and refpect of Europe: enough, however, is yet left to fhew the natural difpofition of the people.

'Some refpectable writers have attributed this fituation of the female fex in cold climates, to the rude ftate of the people, but without reafon.   Our anceftors, the ancient Germans, whofe country, though cold, was not extreme in degree, held the fair fex in the higheft eftimation, and even veneration; and the fame is the cafe with the favage nations in fome of the more temperate climates of America.'

Dr. Falconer afterwards confiders the influence of climate upon the intellectual faculties; and treats firft of a hot climate; beginning with obfervations on literature.   He obferves, that the fame caufes which influence the difpofition and manners, have alfo a proportionable effect upon the intellects.

lects. The great characteristic of the inhabitants of hot climates is sensibility; the influence of which extends to the mental powers. Hence, our author observes, the fruits of fancy and imagination have always abounded most in the South; in support of which remark, he produces several authorities: but that the severer studies, and such as require diligence and perseverance, as well as genius and sensibility, have been less successful in hot climates.

The author next examines the effects of a hot climate on the intellectual faculties, with respect to inventions and arts. The sensibility and vivid imagination of hot climates, he remarks, have been favourable to suggesting discoveries; and this he endeavours to evince by a variety of examples.

In the subsequent chapter, Dr. Falconer traces the effect of a cold climate on the intellectual faculties, in regard to literature and the arts; and in the sixteenth, he pursues the same enquiry, relative to a temperate climate. He observes, that the inhabitants of temperate climates, of Europe especially, have far excelled the rest of the world in almost every article of literature; and that, though we allow to hot climates the priority in most inventions, yet, that the application and improvement of discoveries is due in a much superior degree to temperate climates.

In the six chapters immediately succeeding, Dr. Falconer considers the influence of climate upon laws, customs, the form of government, and religion; in accounting for the various modifications of all which, he has recourse to the different degrees of sensibility, that distinguish the inhabitants of hot, of cold, and of temperate climates.

After treating of those subjects, the author mentions the influence of the properties and qualities of the air, which he had hitherto only considered in respect of its temperature. But he observes that the air may affect us by other means, viz. by its weight, and peculiar impregnations. Of the latter, however, our knowlege is too imperfect to admit of much observation.

In the second book, consisting of four chapters, the author treats of the influence of situation and extent of a country; which, as well as its climate, is supposed to have some effect in several of the respects above mentioned. The third book, containing five chapters, is employed in explaining the influence of the nature of the country itself; and the fourth book, comprehending two chapters, is devoted to the influence of population. The author endeavours to shew, that the greater or smaller number of inhabitants in a country, in proportion to its extent, is an active cause in influencing

the

the people.   But not being guided in this enquiry by such fixed and determinate principles, as admit of a clear and systematic elucidation, we must refer our readers, for what the author advances on this subject, to the work itself.   The fifth book, containing likewise two chapters, is employed on the influence of diet.   From this book, we shall select what the author advances relative to the use of tea.

' Tea appears, from the best experiments, to produce sedative effects upon the nerves, diminishing their energy, and the tone of the muscular fibres, and inducing a considerable degree, both of sensibility and irritability, upon the whole system.   It also promotes the thinner evacuations very powerfully, and diminishes the flesh and bulk of those who use it.   These effects tend to impair the strength, and promote the other consequences of it upon the nervous system above described.   Hence the use of tea has been found very agreeable to the studious, especially those engaged in the composition of works of genius and imagination, and hence is emphatically styled the poet's friend.   But, on the other hand, I believe that, at least with us, it has had the effect of enfeebling and enervating the bodies of our people, and of introducing several disorders that arise from laxity and debility ; and has been of still more consequence in making way for the use of spirituous liquors, which are often taken to relieve that depression which tea occasions.

' From these effects of tea, I cannot but think that its consequences, on the whole, have been highly prejudicial.   It evidently injures the health, and, by the consequences last mentioned, tends to corrupt the morals of the people : and, in my opinion, by the effects it produces upon the nerves, contributes to abate courage, vigour, and steadiness of mind : circumstances surely of themselves sufficient to discredit its use, with those who are engaged in any situation of life that requires exertion and resolution.   Perhaps, however, in the hot climates of China and India, the use of this liquor may not be so prejudicial as in the colder ones ; it may there tend to abate the weariness occasioned by heat, and, as a grateful diluent, promote the thinner evacuations ; which possibly may, by causing it to pass off quickly, counteract, in some measure, its bad effects.   But the noxious qualities of this plant are not unknown even in its native countries.   The Japanese are subject to the diabetes, and to consumptive disorders resembling the atrophy, from its use ; and the Chinese, it is said, are so sensible of these consequences, that they rarely drink green tea at all, which is the most remarkable for these effects.   Perhaps the diminutive stature, and cowardly, and at the same time acute and tricking disposition of the Chinese, may be owing, in no small degree, to the use of this vegetable.'

The subject of the sixth book, which occupies almost the half of the volume, is the influence of way of life.   In treating

ing of this subject, the author confines himself, in general, to the various degrees of civilisation among mankind ; adding, however, some remarks on the different occupations and modes of living, that usually occur in the progress of improvement. The first chapter treats of the influence of a savage state ; the second, of the influence of a barbarous state, or way of life, upon mankind. The latter state the author distinguishes from the former by some particular circumstances, which it is unnecessary for us to mention. The third chapter delineates the effects of a life of agriculture upon mankind ; the fourth, the effects of a commercial life ; the fifth, the effects of literature and science ; and the sixth, the effects of luxury and refinement.

On a theory so extensive as that which Dr. Falconer has attempted to elucidate, many are the arguments supported by satisfactory observations ; but numerous, likewise, must be those which are entirely conjectural, and are indebted for their origin only to the ingenuity of the writer. He has, however, treated this curious subject, of the influence of climate, with great plausibility ; and, though we cannot always agree with him in opinion, in respect to the efficacy of the causes which he assigns, we acknowlege that he, in general, applies with judgment the various facts collected for the establishment of his doctrines ; and he discovers an extent of enquiry, which must place his industry in the most favourable point of view.

The Beauties of Spring. A Poem. 4to. 3s. Nicoll.

WE do not know a more unfortunate circumstance for a young author, especially an anonymous one, than an injudicious *title* to his performance. If the greatest genius of the present age should produce a very excellent epic poem, and name it Paradise Lost, he would not perhaps receive more for the copy than Milton did for his immortal work on the same subject ; and the dramatist who should write a good tragedy on the story of Lear, or Macbeth, would hardly obtain a third night.—We are much afraid that the author of the Poem before us has taken a great deal of pains to very little purpose. The *beauties of spring* have already been so amply described, and so nobly treated by Thomson, that few readers will bring themselves to imagine that any other writer can treat this subject with equal force, elegance, and propriety.—The poem, notwithstanding, though it is too long, has many fine passages, and is, undoubtedly, the work of a very able writer. The language throughout is pure, the sentiments

ments

A

ments natural, and the numbers harmonious. The following defcription, from the ancient and well-known monarchy of the bees, is full of fine imagery, and is written fo much in the ftyle and manner of the author of the Seafons, that it might, perhaps, without injuftice, be afcribed to him.

Thrice noble race! who in fmall room poffefs
A wond'rous portion of ætherial fire,
Heaven's own inftinctive fpirit! fure, from man,
Who to his rav'nous appetite devotes
Your lives and treafures, you may juftly claim
The flight return of unfubftantial praife.
At Spring's approach, before the Pleiads fhine
On Taurus' brawny fhoulder, when the clouds
Difpart awhile, and o'er the vale emit
The fun's effulgence; on the fuburb plank,
Before the portal of the ftraw-built town,
Cluft'ring they fwarm, and in the tepid gleam
Delighted bafk. Meantime their youth expand
The filmy wing in many a fhort effay.
But foon their labour fervid glows. At once
All join their aid. Without, and deep within
The fecret conclave of the hive, 'tis nought
But ceafelefs hurry. Hark, the buzzing found
Increafes every moment! Thofe who pafs
In fearch of honey to the diftant field,
Beneath the crouded entrance ever meet
Returning fwarms, whofe loaded thighs difpenfe
A rich ambrofial fmell. Tho' fcarce a leaf
Or bloffom decks the foreft, fcarce a flower
Adorns the mead or riv'let's fide, but yields
A lufcious banquet, moft they love to haunt
The garden's fcented product; from the cups
Of hyacinth to fip the morning dew;
To feaft conceal'd within the tulip's cell,
Or pant enamour'd on the lily's breaft.
Nor range they feldom o'er the defert brake,
Where, far from public view, in modeft pride,
The fweetly-blufhing cynorrhodon blows,
And honeyfuckle fondly intertwines
Its branches with the hawthorn. Each purfues
The tafk affign'd him. Some of fwifteft wing
The fragrant dews and effences collect.
Undaunted centry, fome before the gate
Stand marfhall'd. Others, bleft employ, receive
The fpicy load, and fill their waxen cells
Of curious texture. Part more wife thro' age,
O'er whom their gracious monarch ftill prefides,
In clofe debate attend their ftate affairs;
As beft conduces to the gen'ral good,

En-

Enacting laws, advifing horrid war,
Or planning fchemes of amity and peace.'

Our author's view of the feafon beyond the polar circle and within the tropics, is not only new, but extremely amufive and poetical. In the fecond book, the profpect from the top of Ætna, and the wood-fcene, are finely painted. The author here takes an opportunity of paying the deferved tribute of applaufe to his great exemplar, whom he has fo happily imitated, in thefe beautiful lines:

‘ Nor, gentle fon of Tweed, be thou unfung,
Thou who, reclining on thy parent's bank,
In childhood bad'ſt the neighb'ring woods refound
To fweeteſt ſtrains of Arcady. Of all
Thou beſt can'ſt find a paſſage to the heart,
And fway the rifing bofom at command.
With Nature's charms delighted, I adore
Thy lofty flights ; but, of an humbler wing,
Endeavour not to foar fublime with thee.
Content to revel in the vernal gale,
I ride not on the thunder-ſtorm, nor fweep
O'er earth in Autumn with the fhadowy clouds,
Nor mount on Winter's tempeſts. Thefe are heights,
Amazing heights, by thee alone attain'd !'

We recommend the whole Poem to our readers, as well worthy of their attention.—If the two books were divided into three or four, and fupplied with another title, we doubt not but it would meet with general approbation.

Biographical Anecdotes of William Hogarth ; *and a Catalogue of his Works chronologically arranged ; with occafional Remarks.* 8-vo. 3s. Nichols.

THIS may be confidered as an agreeable enlargement of Mr. Walpole's life of Hogarth : the author, who figns only the initials of his name (J. N.) feems to have been well acquainted with many of that painter's intimate friends, from whom he has occafionally collected a number of little incidents, and entertaining anecdotes, of Hogarth's private life and manners ; he has likewife been able to draw, from the fame fource, a difcovery of feveral prints and drawings, not taken notice of in Mr. Walpole's, or any other catalogue of this artiſt's ingenious performances, to arrange them in chronological order, and to trace the rife and progrefs of a genius fo ftrikingly original.

The

The following anecdote of Hogarth's marriage is not unentertaining.

' In 1730, (says our author) Mr. Hogarth married the only daughter of Sir James Thornhill, by whom he had no child. This union, indeed, was a stolen one, and consequently without the approbation of Sir James and his lady, who, considering the extreme youth of their daughter, then barely eighteen, and the slender finances of her husband, as yet an obscure artist, were not easily reconciled to the match. Soon after this period, however, he began his Harlot's Progress ; and was advised to have some of his pictures placed in the way of his father-in-law. Accordingly, one morning early, Mrs. Hogarth undertook to convey several of them into his dining-room. When he arose, he enquired from whence they came ; and being told by whom they were introduced, he cried out, " Very well ; the man who can produce representations like these, can also maintain a wife without a portion." He designed this remark as an excuse for keeping his purse-strings close ; but soon after became both reconciled and generous to the young couple. Lady Thornhill's forgiveness was but slowly obtained, though it followed at last.'

Our author has acquainted us with a project of Hogarth's, which we believe is not generally known; and which we shall therefore lay before our readers.

' Hogarth had projected a Happy Marriage, by way of counterpart to his Marriage à la Mode. A design for the first of his intended six plates he had sketched out in colours ; and the following is as accurate an account of it as could be furnished by a gentleman who, long ago, enjoyed only a few minutes sight of so imperfect a curiosity.

' The time supposed was immediately after the return of the parties from church. The scene lay in the hall of an antiquated country mansion. On one side, the married couple were represented fitting. Behind them was a group of their young friends of both sexes, in the act of breaking bride-cake over their heads. In front appeared the father of the young lady, grasping a bumper, and drinking, with a seeming roar of exultation, to the future happiness of her and her husband. By his side was a table covered with refreshments. Jollity rather than politeness was the designation of his character. Under the screen of the hall, several rustic musicians in grotesque attitudes, together with servants, tenants, &c. were arranged. Through the arch by which the room is entered, the eye was led along a passage into the kitchen, which afforded a glimpse of sacerdotal luxury. Before the dripping-pan stood a well-fed divine, in his gown and cassock, with his watch in his hand, giving directions to a cook, drest all in white, who was employed in basting a haunch of venison.

' Among

' Among the faces of the principal figures, none but that of the young lady was completely finished. Hogarth had been often reproached for his inability to impart grace and dignity to his heroines. The bride was therefore meant to vindicate his pencil from so degrading an imputation. The effort, however, was unsuccessful. The girl was certainly pretty; but her features, if I may use the term, were uneducated. She might have attracted notice as a chambermaid, but would have failed to extort applause as a woman of fashion. The parson, and his culinary associate, were more laboured than any other parts of the picture. It is natural for us to dwell longest on that division of a subject which is most congenial to our private feelings. The painter sat down with a resolution to delineate beauty improved by art; but seems, as usual, to have deviated into meanness; or could not help neglecting his original purpose, to luxuriate in such ideas as his situation in early life had fitted him to express. He found himself, in short, out of his element in the parlour, and therefore hastened, in quest of ease and amusement, to the kitchen fire. It must be allowed, that such a painter, however excellent in his walk, was better qualified to represent the vicious parent, than the royal preserver of a foundling.

' The sketch already described was made after the appearance of Marriage à la Mode, and many years before the artist's death. Why he did not persevere in his plan, during such an interval of time, we can only guess. It is probable that his undertaking required a longer succession of images relative to domestic happiness, than had fallen within his notice, or courted his participation. Hogarth had no children; and though the nuptial union may be happy without them, yet such happiness will have nothing picturesque in it; and we may observe of this truly natural and faithful painter, that he rarely ventured to exhibit scenes with which he was not perfectly well acquainted.'

In the course of this work we meet with some verses written by Garrick, prefixed to two or three of the prints; some elegant Latin poetry by Loveling; together with some sensible remarks, by the author, on Hogarth's performances: which form all together an agreeable farrago, and may afford entertainment to the admirers of Hogarth, and the lovers of virtù.

Scottish *Tragic Ballads.* Small 8vo. 2s. 6d. sewed. Nichols.

TO the admirers of ancient Scottish poesy, this little volume will afford considerable entertainment. It contains Hardyknute; Child Maurice; Adam o Gordon; Sir Hugh, or the Jew's Daughter; Flodden Field; Edward; Sir Patrick Spence;

Spence; Lady Bothwell's Lament; Earl of Murray; Sir James the Rofe; Laird of Woodhoufelie; Lord Livingfton; Binnorie; Death of Menteith; Lord Airth's Complaint; and I wifh I were where Helen lyes; with two or three fragments of old tragic ballads. Moſt of thefe compofitions, as the editor acknowleges in his preface, have appeared already; but in this edition, we are told, they are given much more correct, &c. Hardyknute, publifhed, as fome of our readers may remember, fome years ago in a fmall volume, entitled the Union, a collection of Scotch and Englifh poems, now appears in its original perfection, *with alterations and additions*; for which the editor, as he informs us, was indebted to the memory of a lady in Lancafhire, who, we fuppofe, had it by tradition; to whom we are alfo obliged for feveral pieces exhibited in this collection. To thefe, the editor has added two prefatory diſſertations, one on the oral tradition of poetry, and the other on the old tragic ballad: in the latter of thefe, our editor, fpeaking of the caufe of our pleafure in feeing a mournful event reprefented to us, or hearing it defcribed, judicioufly obferves that ' it feems to arife from the mingled paffions—of the art of the author—curiofity to attend the termination—delight arifing from reflection on our own fecurity, and—the fympathetic fpirit.'—This is, we think, one of the fulleſt and beſt explanations of the pleafure above mentioned, that we have hitherto met with. What follows is equally juſt and fenfible.

' It is amufing, fays he, to obferve how expreffive the poetry of every country is of its real manners. That of the Northern nations is ferocious to the higheſt degree. Nor need we wonder that thofe, whofe laws obliged them to decide the moſt trifling debate with the fword, delighted in a vein of poetry, which only painted deeds of blood, and objects horrible to the imagination. The ballad poetry of the Spaniards is tinged with the romantic gallantry of that nation. The hero is all complaifance; and takes off his helmet in the heat of combat, when he thinks on his miſtiefs. That of the Englifh is generous and brave. In their moſt noble ballad, Percy laments over the death of his mortal foe. That of the Scots is perhaps, like the face of their country, more various than the reſt. We find in it the bravery of the Englifh, the gallantry of the Spanifh, and I am afraid in fome inſtances the ferocity of the Northern.'

Of the few new ballads here prefented to the public, the following is the beſt, with which we ſhall therefore treat our readers.

T H E

THE DEATH of MENTEITH.

From TRADITION.

' Shrilly fhriek'd the raging wind,
　And rudelie blew the blaft ;
Wi awfum blink, throuch the dark ha,
　The fpeidy lichtning paft.

" O hear ye nae, frae mid the loch,
　Arife a deidly grane ?
Sae evir does the fpirit warn,
　Whan we fum dethe maun mane.

" I feir, I feir me, gude fir John,
　Ye are nae fafe wi me :
What wae wald fill my hairt gin ye
　Sold in my caftle drie !"

" Ye neid nae feir, my leman deir,
　I'm ay fafe whan wi thee ;
And gin I maun nae wi thee live,
　I here wad wifh to die."

' His man cam rinning to the ha
　Wi wallow cheik belyve :
" Sir John Menzeith, your faes are neir,
　And ye maun flie or ftrive."

" What count fyne leids the cruel knicht ?"
　" Thrie fpeirmen to your ane :
I red ye flie, my mafter deir,
　Wi fpeid, or ye'l be flain."

" Tak ye this gown, my deir fir John,
　To hide your fhyning mail :
A boat waits at the hinder port
　Owr the braid loch to fail."

" O whatten a piteous fhriek was yon
　That fough'd upon my eir ?"
" Nae piteous fhriek I trow, ladie,
　But the rouch blaft ye heir."

' They focht the caftle, till the morn,
　Whan they were bown'd to gae,
They faw the boat turn'd on the loch,
　Sir John's corfe on the brae.'

　To the Ballads the editor has fubjoined fome ufeful notes
and a gloffary ; an article which, though of little fervice to
a Scotchman, will be found extremely neceffary to the mere
Englifh reader.

　We cannot conclude this article, without remarking, that
the tragic ballad called Lady Bothwell's Lament, which is re-

printed

printed in this collection, appears to great advantage, from the judicious amendment which our editor has beſtowed upon it. In his note he ſays:

' Theſe four ſtanzas appeared to the editor to be all that are genuine of this elegy. Many additional ones are to be found in the common copies, which are rejected as of meaner execution.'

Lady Bothwell's Lament, as it now ſtands, is perhaps one of the prettieſt elegiac poems in our language, as it excels every thing of the kind in nature, pathos, and ſimplicity. It may be read over and over, with the greateſt pleaſure;

decies repetita placebit.

We ſhall therefore inſert this elegant *morceau*, for the entertainment of our readers.

It may be neceſſary to premiſe, that the old Scottiſh word *balow*, in the firſt line, ſignifies *huſh*. The afflicted and deſerted mother is ſuppoſed thus to addreſs the infant in her lap.

' LADY BOTHWELL'S LAMENT.

' Balow, my babe, lye ſtill and ſleip,
It grieves me ſair to ſee thee weip;
If thou'lt be ſilent I'll be glad,
Thy maining maks my heart full ſad;
Balow my boy, thy mither's joy;
Thy father breids me great annoy.

' Whan he began to ſeik my luve,
And wi his ſucred words to muve;
His feining fauſe, and flattering cheir,
To me that time did nocht appeir;
But now I ſee that cruel he
Cares neither for my babe nor me.

' Lye ſtill, my darling, ſleip a while,
And whan thou wakeſt ſweitly ſmile:
But ſmile nae as thy father did
To cozen maids: nay, God forbid,
What yet I feir, that thou ſold leir
Thy father's heart and face to beir!

' Be ſtill, my ſad one: ſpare thoſe teirs,
To weip whan thou haſt wit and yeirs;
Thy griefs are gathering to a ſum,
God grant thee patience when they cum
Born to ſuſtain a mother's ſhame,
A father's fall, a baſtard's name.
Balow, &c.'

Two Discourses; on Sovereign Power, and Liberty of Conscience; Translated from the Latin *of* G. Noodt, *formerly Professor of Law in the University of* Leyden, *by* A. Macaulay, *A. M.* 8vo. 5s. Dilly.

THE design of this work is to enquire into the nature and extent of sovereign power; and into the true principles of toleration in matters of religion. The judicious manner in which the author treats those subjects, soon recommended both the Discourses to the attention of the public; and they have since been translated into different languages.

In the former of those discourses, the author sets out with delineating the difference between a prince and a tyrant.

‘ I have often been astonished, says he, gentlemen, that some men of great and eminent abilities, who have professed to treat of sovereign power, should ascribe the same rights to a prince and to a tyrant; than which no two characters can be conceived more widely opposite. The one governs his subjects by their own consent; the other against their consent: the one has the public good solely in view; the other only consults his own advantage: the one observes the laws; the other tramples them under foot: the one regards the life, liberty, and property of every individual as sacred things, and from which he with-holds his hands, his looks, nay his very desires; the other imagines that he possesses an absolute right to all those, and that he may dispose of them according to his own pleasure. In short, the one resembling the Supreme Being; and, according to his example, desirous of promoting the happiness of mankind; is beloved, respected, and adored both at home and abroad; all flock to him, as to the source of their felicity, with a determined resolution to devote themselves to the service of a prince, whose soul, they perceive, animates, unites, and governs them, by whom they are rendered flourishing and happy: the other, born for a public plague, never promotes the happiness of any worthy citizen, but rather does all the mischief he can to the whole world; therefore becomes an object of universal disgust, abhorrence, and execration; and wherever he goes, like a beast of prey moving from his den, he spreads fear, terror, and desolation all around him. But it is an evident dictate of reason, that a prince should not be confounded with a tyrant; and also, that the power of the former should not be allowed to operate according to his own caprice, but be confined within the limits of justice and the laws: yet, notwithstanding, it happens, by I know not what fatality, to be a generally-received maxim, that it is essential to the nature of sovereignty, that the prince should be raised above the laws; insomuch, that if he regard nothing but his own interest, to the entire neglect of his subjects, they have no other remedy than the glory to obey, and to suffer patiently; and, that he is responsible for his conduct to God alone, from whom, according to them, all supreme authority is originally derived. Few there are who in this question take the part of the people. The cause of the tyrant is generally maintained under the specious appellation of prince; and, if the interests of the prince and people should happen to clash, so as to render necessary the diminution, or even entire destruction of one party; in such a case, those people would fain persuade themselves and others, that to allow the prince a full liberty of oppressing his subjects by acts of injustice and enormous cruelty, would be more just and advantageous, than to permit the subjects to repress the violence of a prince bent upon their ruin: as if they who have been allotted to live under the authority of others, were not of the same species with those who exercise that authority; or, as if those alone were to be regarded upon the footing of men, to whom the consent of other men has delegated an authority over themselves! For my own part, when I enquire into the reasons of a sentiment so illiberal and inhuman, I am at a loss to reconcile them in any point of view to the law of nature. Whoever you be that entertain such sentiments, whether princes or courtiers, give me leave to say, that you pervert what is in itself excellent and sacred; and that by means of your ambition or mean adulation, civil government, which was established to secure the peaceful enjoyment of the conveniences and pleasures of life, is turned to the destruction of mankind: that you reject truth, justice, and public utility, and adopt maxims that are destructive, unjust, and precarious; for an unlimited power can never be secure nor durable.'

The author next proceeds to shew, that unlimited power is no necessary consequence of greatness; that though God himself were the author of sovereignty, yet would that give princes no right to claim an unlimited power; that all men are by nature equal; but that this natural liberty does not authorize licentiousness. He shews that men have been led by nature to live in society; and proves from the nature and design of civil society, that sovereign power should not extend beyond what is necessary for the public good. He contends, that it matters not, whether a prince have solemnly engaged to follow certain laws or not; and that a people who submit to the discretionary authority of a prince, do not therefore invest him with unlimited power.

The second part of the first discourse is chiefly an illustration of the Lex Regia of the Romans, or that law upon which the

su-

supreme authority of the emperors was founded. In treating of this subject, the author makes several just observations, tending to elucidate and ascertain the meaning of Ulpian, in regard to the extent of the sovereign power. He maintains that the Roman emperors were not exempted from the observance of all the civil laws ; and for this opinion, he produces strong arguments in opposition even to the authority of Dio Cassius.

' It will be replied, however " that the authority of Ulpian is no less express, who in general terms asserts, that the prince is discharged from all obligation to observe the laws." Granted : but when, I pray, and by what law, was he exempted ? " By the Lex Regia, it will be said, which was enacted under Augustus, and by which the Roman people are said to have transferred to that prince, in his own person, all their empire and all their power." I must beg leave to inform those who build their opinions upon this point, that most of the emperors who succeeded Augustus, received their government by a single decree of the senate, or by a single law, to which the ancient civilians afterwards gave the name of the royal or imperial law ; that Augustus never received the empire under any such name, but by a variety of laws, and ordinances of the senate, passed at different times. Should you be surprized at this, I would have you attentively examine the whole course of Augustus's life, trace all his consulships in the order that Dio Cassius hath related them, and you will be convinced of the truth of the above assertion : I could adduce a variety of arguments in proof of it, had I not been anticipated by a writer of distinguished eminence, one of the greatest ornaments not only of this university, but of the republic of letters ; I mean Gronovius. I will only add one remark, which seems not to have occurred to that illustrious writer, nor to any other author, so far as I recollect, and it is this : that by whatever ordinance of the senate Augustus might have been exempted from the laws, it was not the same by which the supreme government of the empire was conveyed to him ; for this (if we believe Dio Cassius) took place in the seventh consulship of Augustus. But it was in his tenth consulship, according to the same author, that the senate passed a decree by which he was exempted from the observance of the laws : and even in that decree to which our author refers, the emperor was not set above all the laws, but only above one, and that was the Cincian law ; although Dio in this place expresses himself in terms too general. And this I ground upon the narration of our historian himself ; for, speaking of the reasons which induced the senate to exempt

empt

empt Auguſtus from the laws, he informs us, that the emperor having promiſed to diſtribute a certain ſum of money among the people, pretended afterwards that the, laws would not permit him to perform his promiſe, without the conſent of the ſenate ; in conſequence of which, that this emperor might be enabled to extend his liberality beyond the limitation of the Cincian law, Dio ſays " that the ſenate diſcharged him from the obligation of the laws."   This form of expreſſion, according to the uſual modes of ſpeech among the Romans, ought to be confined to the Cincian law ; but Dio, who was a Greek, extends it to all laws in general, whether from ignorance or flattery I cannot ſay, but he certainly had no right nor reaſon to take ſuch liberties.'

The learned profeſſor ſeems clearly to evince, that Auguſtus was not freed from the obſervance of all the laws, but of thoſe only which the ſenate had nominally diſpenſed ; and that he was under equal obligations to obſerve the reſt as any other private citizen.

In the difcourſe on Liberty of Conſcience, the author ſhews, that by the law of nature and nations, religion is not ſubjected to human authority ; that by the law of nature, every man is at liberty to conduct himſelf according to his own judgment, in matters which relate only to himſelf; that the nature of religion requires, that every one be free to follow his own judgment ; and that this freedom is abſolutely neceſſary, on account of the unavoidable diverſity and infinite variety of ſentiments among men.   He remarks, that to refuſe liberty of conſcience, is, to encroach on the rights of God, and to counteract his intention ; and that intolerance cannot be vindicated by any reaſonable motive.   He contends, however, that every man ought to ſubmit to the eccleſiaſtical diſcipline of that ſociety of which he is a member ; and he afterwards defines, with preciſion, the extent of eccleſiaſtical authority.

The ſecond part of this diſcourſe contains anſwers to the objections againſt toleration.   The whole of the author's obſervations and arguments, in both diſcourſes, evinces a clear uuderſtanding, an attentive examination of the ſubjects, and a ſtrong attachment to the principles of civil and religious liberty.

Eight Sermons preached before the Univerſity of Oxford.   *By* James Bandinel, *D. D. of* Jeſus *College, and Public Orator of the Univerſity.* 8vo.   4s.   Cadell.

THESE difcourſes were preached before the Univerſity in the year 1780, in purſuance of the will of the late rev. and pious John Bampton, M. A. canon of Saliſbury ; who left

left an estate of 120l. a year, for the establishment of a lecture, to be preached at St. Mary's, by a lecturer chosen annually, on the following subjects : ' To confirm and establish the Christian faith, and to confute all heretics and schismatics ; upon the divine authority of the holy scriptures ; upon the authority of the writings of the primitive fathers, as to the faith and practice of the primitive church ; upon the divinity of our Lord and Saviour Jesus Christ ; upon the divinity of the Holy Ghost ; upon the articles of the Christian faith, as comprehended in the Apostles and Nicene creeds.' These lectures are to consist of eight sermons, to be continued every year by a different lecturer, and to be printed within two months after they are preached.

As the Kislingbury estate is a nursery for poets at Cambridge, this Lecture will be a nursery for orthodox divines at Oxford. It will call forth their abilities, and produce many elaborate volumes in confutation of heretics, in defence of the fathers *, &c. The articles of faith, which the lecturer is to maintain, are already prescribed. He can be no Socinian, Pelagian, Arian, Semi-arian, or heretic of any other denomination. And he will certainly produce innumerable arguments in support of his thesis : for, as Hudibras says,

> What makes all doctrines plain and clear ? —
> About two hundred pounds a year †.

There is however one circumstance in the will, which is much to be regretted ; and that is, the time limited for the publication of the lectures. When the pious John Bampton fixed upon two months, alas ! he had totally forgotten the wise and prudent advice of the poet, ' Nonum prematur in annum.'

In this course of lectures the author sets out with a general vindication of the claim, which the gospel makes to the title of truth, by arguments deduced from the nature and intrinsic excellence of its doctrines.

In this discourse there are certainly many just observations ; but the following passages seem to be either obscure, or controvertible.

' It is more than probable, that God did not leave our first parent in a state of darkness and uncertainty, exposed to all the miseries, which spring from ignorance and error ; but originally gave him some rule of life, discovered to him by immediate re-

---

* An arduous task   See Taylor's Observations on Mr. Gibbon's Hist. p. 83—98. Dail, James, &c.
† Hud. part iii. canto 1.

relation

velation all the neceffary truths of what is called natural religion.'

Does not our author here confound natural and revealed
religion ? By natural religion is meant, that knowlege, veneration, and love of God, and the practice of thofe duties
to him, our fellow-creatures, and ourfelves, which are dif-
coverable by the right exercife of our faculties, on confidering
the nature and perfections of God, and our relation to him,
and to one another. By revealed religion is meant, natural
religion explained, enlarged, and enforced, by the exprefs de-
clarations of God himfelf, communicated to mankind by his
prophets, or infpired teachers. According to our author's reprefentation, Adam had no notion of natural religion ; ' *all*
the neceffary truths' of what is called by that name, being,
he fays, ' difcovered to him by *immediate revelation.*' If this
was the cafe, what idea can we form of that ftate of perfection in which, divines tell us, our firft parent was created ?
and what fhall we fay of St. Paul, who afferts, Rom. i. 19, 20,
ii. 14, 15. that the light of nature is fufficient to teach men
the moft important part of their duty ?

' That the divine interpofition, fays our author, is not contrary to our natural notions, is evident from a common opinion,
which prevailed in all ages and countries, that their founders and
legiflators had conferences with, and received inftructions from,
fome fuperior being.'

An attempt to prove, that a divine interpofition is agreeable to our natural notions, from the prevalence of lies and
impoftures, cannot, we apprehend, do any fervice to Chriftianity.

Our author is a ftrenuous advocate for the doctrine of types,
in a very extenfive fenfe.

' *Every part,* he fays, of the ritual worfhip, bore an emblematical relation to the fpiritual one, which was to fucceed
it.'—

It has been obferved by a writer, whofe name we forget,
that every nail in the temple was typical. An excellent rea-
foner fpeaks of this notion in the following terms :

' Thus much concerning types and typical reafonings. I
concern not myfelf with what the ancients have in fact faid,
nor with their methods of arguing. Had they defigned to have
expofed Chriftianity to the common fcorn of all its adverfaries,
I know not how they could more effectually have done it, than
by making types and prophecies of every thing. If Chriftians
will perfift in fuch methods of reafoning, and will defend fuch
wild arguings as the word of God, I fhall not wonder, if
Atheifts

Atheifts and Deifts, fcoff at their credulity, and reject that which is fupported by manifeft folly and abfurdity.' Sykes on the Chriftian Religion, chap. 12.

In the fecond lecture the author endeavours to eftablifh the truth and authority of the fcriptures from external evidence, viz. their antiquity, the teftimony of heretics, the fuffrages of profeffed enemies, the harmony and correfpondence of the fcriptures, their wonderful prefervation, the miracles performed by the firft preachers of Chriftianity, the accomplifhment of prophecies, &c.

In the third, he purfues the argument from prophecy, and lays a particular ftrefs on types and fymbols. Thus he fays, ' Noah being typical of our Saviour, and the deluge of baptifm, the bleffings contained in the covenant made with him, in confequence of the flood, are likewife typical of the bleffings promifed by the evangelical covenant, in confequence of our fpiritual regeneration by the waters of baptifm. . . The analogy between the remiffion of debts in the Jubilee, and the remiffion of fins under the gofpel covenant, is obvious to every underftanding ; and the releafe of all flaves, the total ceffation of the toil and labour of agriculture, and the reftoration of every man to his poffeffions, tribe, and family, were plainly fymbolical of that acceptable year of the Lord, wherein man was to be delivered from the fervitude he was held under by fin and fatan, and reftored to all the bleffings which had been loft by the fall.'

In the fourth fermon, purfuing the fame train of reafoning, he tells us, that the firft emblematical notice given of a future redemption, was undoubtedly by the inftitution of facrifices ; that God's acceptance of them was a facramental fign and pledge of his reconciliation to man through faith in Him, the anticipating and retroactive virtue of whofe blood would extend the benefits of falvation through all ages ; that the form of impofition of hands and confeffion of fins, as ufed in all facrifices, was very expreffive of transferring the fins confeffed upon the victim, and devoting it to bear the punifhment of them ; that the incenfe offered and the blood fprinkled were fymbols of Chrift's prefenting himfelf with his blood in the heavens ; exhibiting, in the prefence of God, the merits of his fufferings ; that his fufferings were vicarious, and his blood piacular, &c.

The union of the divine and human nature in the perfon of Chrift is the fubject of the fifth lecture. In order to afcertain the divinity of our Saviour, he endeavours to prove his temporal and eternal pre-exiftence.—His firft argument, in proof of this point, is perfectly new ; ' I fhall content myfelf, he fays, with quoting a few plain paffages, which have a general reference to this doctrine.   Thus, from Chrift's faying to his difciples, " as my father hath fent me, fo fend I you," we may *fairly infer*, that he, as well as the apoftles, had a being before he had his miffion.'

If by this text the author means to prove our Saviour's exiftence before his incarnation, he has miffed his aim moft egregioufly! The expreffion can only prove, that our Saviour exifted before the commencement of his public miniftry.

The fixth difcourfe is an illuftration of this text: ' There muft be herefies among you,'   1 Cor. xi.   19.

Some of the primitive fathers. and ecclefiaftical writers, in the warmth of their zeal, afcribed all herefies and fchifms to the artifices of the devil.   Our author loudly joins in the cry.

‘ To effect his purpofe, fays he, the enemy of mankind has never failed finding proper inftruments among the ignorant, the vain, the ambitious, and the contentious.   When churches indeed are guilty of fuperftition and idolatry, or any other corruption either in faith or practice ; fo far from endeavouring or willing to difunite them by diverfities of opinions, he will by all poffible means ftrengthen the bands of their union in his intereft, keep them firmly and fteadily attached to their corruptions.   On the contrary, the nearer a church approaches in its doctrine and worfhip to ancient and primitive purity, the more he exerts every nerve, and employs all his fubtilty and malignity to weaken and difgrace it by contentions and divifions, if not againft faith yet againft charity.'

Upon reading the former part of this quotation, where we are told, that when a church is corrupt, the devil will ‘ ftrengthen the bands of its union,' who would imagine, that our author would acknowlege the exiftence of any of thefe diabolical operations, herefies and fchifms, in the church of Rome ? Yet fo it is, in the fame difcourfe he fpeaks of its internal divifions in thefe terms : ‘ Let this pretended patron of union and concord recollect the bitter and fierce contentions, that have been among its members, about the depofing power, the perfonal infallibility of the pope, the authority of general councils, the immaculate conception, and various other doctrines ; Thomifts, Scotifts, Occamifts ; Dominicans, Francifcans, Janfenifts, Molinifts, and Jefuits, all againft each other, nay council againft council, and pope againft pope.'

Here the devil, we find, has been as active in fomenting difcord, as in any reformed church whatever : ‘ he has,' to ufe our orator's emphatical words, ‘ exerted every nerve, and employed all his fubtilty and malignity, to weaken and difgrace
that

that church by contentions and divisions.' Either therefore the church of Rome ' approaches in its doctrine and worship to ancient and primitive purity,' or our author's representation of the craft and malignity of the devil is chimerical and erroneous. Which is the case, we leave the author to determine.

The design of the seventh lecture is to shew, that the scriptures are the only rule of faith, the sole and infallible judge in all doubts and controversies ; and that it is absurd to have recourse to miracles of a later date, to traditions, and pretended infallible guides.

In the foregoing discourses our author having treated of what he apprehends to be the chief fundamental points, contained in the speculative part of our religion, in his concluding sermon considers that evangelical righteousness, to which alone our Saviour has annexed the reward of eternal happiness.

Here, we apprehend, he misrepresents some points of doctrine. For instance :

' When salvation, he says, is ascribed to God's *free grace,* we ought to conclude, that our own endeavours are supposed to co-operate with it.'—

Salvation by grace, in St. Paul's Epistles, means that salvation, which was proposed to mankind through the gospel, by the free bounty and benevolence of the Deity, without regard to *any prior* obedience. Our author's notion of free grace is contradictory ; at least, it is not the doctrine of St. Paul.

' When we are said to be justified through faith, he tells us, we should understand such a faith, as is productive of good works.' —This is not always true. Justification by faith in the Epistles of St. Paul, generally means an admission into a state of pardon, favour, and acceptance under the gospel, through a belief in the Messiah, without including the idea of works.— St. James, when he speaks of our *final* justification, uses a different language, and says, ' By works a man is justified, and not by faith only.' Our author does not seem to enter into the notion of this two-fold salvation and justification, which alone can render many passages in the apostolical epistles intelligible and consistent.

To this course of lectures is added a discourse on the following passage in St. Paul's Epistle to the Romans, ' I have great heaviness and continual sorrow in my heart For I could wish that myself were accursed from Christ for my brethren,' ch. ix. 2, 3.

The author throws these words, ηυχομην γαρ αυτος εγω ειναι αναθεμα απο τε Χριςε, into a parenthesis, in this manner : ' I have

have great heavineſs and continual ſorrow in my heart (for I myſelf likewiſe once was an excommunicate outcaſt from Chriſt) on account of my brethren, my kinſmen according to the fleſh.'——The word *ηυχομην,* he thinks, is not potential, that is, has not the leaſt idea of a wiſh annexed to it, but barely denotes ſomething, which the apoſtle had formerly done. Thus Homer, he obſerves, frequently uſes the word : *διος παις ηυχετο ειναι* : ' He gloried in being,' or ' he profeſſed that he was,' or ſimply, ' he was the ſon of Jupiter.'

This explication would have been ſomething more ſatisfactory, if *ευχομαι* had ever been uſed *pleonaſtically* by St. Paul. We have the word in ſeveral parts of his Epiſtles : *Ευξαιμην,* tr. *I would* to God, Acts xxvi. 29. *Ηυχοντο, they wiſhed* for the day, Acts xxvii. 29. *Ευχομεθα, we wiſh,* 2 Cor. xiii. 9. *Ευχομαι, I pray* to God, v. 7, &c. This objection, we confeſs, is of no great force : we therefore lay no ſtreſs upon it.

Mr. Keeling, in a ſermon printed in the year 1766 *, endeavours to explain this paſſage by a different mode of interpretation, thus : ' I myſelf could wiſh to be accurſed or ſeparated from Chriſt ; or, according to the ſcripture expreſſion a little before, to be delivered up, in the ſame manner, or degree, that Chriſt was accurſed from God for a time, if this could be effectual to the ſalvation of my brethren.'

In favour of Mr. Keeling's interpretation it may be obſerved, that the following expreſſions of our Saviour might poſſibly ſuggeſt this hyperbolical declaration of St. Paul : ' The good ſhepherd giveth his life for the ſheep. Greater love hath no man than this, that a man lay down his life for his friends.' Joh. x. 11. xv. 13.—Dr. Bandinel's however is certainly an ingenious and a happy conjecture.

Thoughts on the Nature of the Grand Apostacy. With Reflections and Obſervations on the Fifteenth Chapter of Mr. Gibbon's Hiſtory, &c. By Henry Taylor, *Rector of* Crawley, *and Vicar of* Portſmouth *in* Hants. 8vo. 3s. 6d. Johnſon.

MANY eccleſiaſtical writers, from the firſt to the eighteenth century, have recorded a multitude of impudent forgeries, and abominable lies, under the name of viſions and miracles ; and have given us their own errors and groundleſs conceits, as the doctrines of the goſpel. Writers of a later date, who have not been much acquainted with the ſcriptures, have

---

* See Crit. Rev. vol. xxii. p. 158.

taken

taken their ideas of our religion, from thefe mifreprefentations. For example : they have adopted the notions of Calvin, concerning original fin, irrefiftible grace, and predeftination, and confidered them as the documents of St. Paul. Under this deception, they have abufed and inulted the facred writers, and defpifed Chriftianity itfelf, for abfurdities, which have no exiftence in the fcriptures. Probably indeed, in a lucid interval of good humour, they have perceived and acknowleged fomething great and wonderful in the Chriftian religion ; but having no juft idea of its genuine doctrines, and fixing their attention upon fome paffages which have been grofsly perverted, they have, with an unpardonable duplicity, employed their wit, when they fhould have ufed their underftanding, and told us, that the apoftles nod, when it is only they themfelves that dream.

The excellent author of this tract, in his preface, thus humoroufly apologizes for thofe writers, who treat any of the doctrines of Chriftianity with an air of ridicule.

Whatever fome people may think, a fneer, he fays, has many ufes.

‘ I fhall mention a few of them for general information.
‘ 1. A fneer will entertain the reader, put him in a good humour, and conciliate him to the fide of the fneerer.
‘ 2. It is better adapted to the apprehenfion of the generality of writers, as well as readers, than more folid reafoning.
‘ 3. It is of admirable ufe in evading the force of an argument, which the fneerer is unable to anfwer ; by leading the reader away from the precife ftate of the queftion ; and, in fhort, it ferves not only to conceal a thoufand imperfections, but, as Sancho Panfa fays of fleep, it covers the fneerer all over, like a cloak – thoughts and all ; by which means he lies as fecure and fnug from all poffibility of an attack, as a fcuttle fifh under a cloud of its own making.’

It has been obferved, that fneers can have no place in an hiftorical narration.

‘ But, fays our author, can the judicious Dr. John Moore, or any other fenfible proteftant, avoid fneering at the hiftorical narration of the wonderful travels of the houfe of Loretto, or many other parts of hiftory he meets with in the Roman legends, though ever fo gravely related ? Or can any man be convinced of their abfurdity by reafon and argument ? No certainly ; nothing but a fneer can avail on fuch fubjects. A papift may tell us with a grave face, that he faw the devil upon a cow’s back ; and that Eutychius fet a bear to bring home the fheep of the monaftery. But what proteftant can help fneering at the FIRM
CON-

CONSISTENCY of their faith, who are expected to believe such stories, and the impudence of those saints, who invented them ?'...

——' I would farther observe, that we frequently give the sneerer too much credit ; for that many things which we look upon as sneers, are nothing better than mistakes and errors of judgment. Witness the three Creeds, that are held by Mr. Jenyns, Tertullian, and Mr. Gibbon. First, the ingenious Mr. Soame Jenyns argues, that a seeming impossibility may be a mark of truth ; and he believes, because it seems to be impossible. Then comes the great Tertullian, who leaves Mr. Jenyns a little way behind, and he believes, not because it seems to be impossible, but because it actually is so.

' The third extraordinary believer is Mr. Gibbon ; and he informs us, that the revolution of seventeen centuries hath shewn us, that an event foretold by the apostles is contrary to experience, and an error ; and we must not press too closely the mysterious language of prophecy and revelation : and yet he declares Christianity to be a divine revelation, and a genuine revelation, fitted to inspire the most rational conviction.

' Now who would not imagine all this to be a sneer and a bam ? Can a man possibly believe a religion because it seems to be impossible, or because it really is so ? or that a lying prophecy can be a divine revelation, and fitly adapted to inspire a rational conviction ?——And yet in truth there is neither sneer nor design in all this. It is the honest truth, the true history, the exact description of what these philosophers say they feel in their own minds. Mr. Jenyns manifestly understands Tertullian to be in earnest ; and he certainly is so himself, and very sanguine upon the subject, or he would not have been so piqued at the superiority of Tertullian's faith in comparison with his own, as to forget his usual politeness, and be guilty of such a solecism in good breeding against so great a man, as to call him a mad enthusiast. This is the very style of bigotry, and deserves no other answer than, Bona verba quæso !

' Indeed there is not the least appearance, in either of these three confessions, of any thing that discovers levity or sneer ; or transgresses the boundary of what is solemn, grave, and dull. Mr. Gibbon seems as serious as Mr. Jenyns, though not so warm : he considers the faith of Tertullian with a temper devoid of jealousy, and endeavours to defend him, and all the ancients with him, in a candid manner ; for he lays it down as a fact to argue from, that the faith of the ancients was of a more FIRM CONSISTENCE than the doubtful and imperfect faith of the moderns. It is an ingenious conjecture, and would do wonders, if it could stand a fair examination ; but Mr. Gibbon has unfortunately mistaken the nature of the Christian faith, the perfection of which does not consist, as he here supposes, in delivering over, without hesitation, to eternal torments the far greater part of the human species, nor in believing every thing that is offered to

our

our acceptance; but in believing the truth, and rejecting the falshood: for when Tertullian tells us the story of a vestal virgin carrying water in a sieve, and that the statues of Castor and Pollux brought the first news to Rome of the victory over Perseus; it is so far from exhibiting a meritorious faith, that it discovers a weak and culpable credulity. The true genuine faith of a Christian is founded upon rational evidence, and will reach no farther than such evidence will justify. Contradictions, absurdities, and impossibilities, are not its objects.' —

—' As, in the case of these creeds, we are apt to imagine a sneer was intended, when upon examination we find nothing more than an innocent confusion of ideas, and error of judgment, arising from the chaos of a heated imagination, or perhaps too much learning; so, at other times we deceive ourselves with the apprehension of a sneer, when upon examination we find only a defect of memory, to which the best of men are sometimes liable. In both these cases the suspicion of a sneer is groundless, and arises from our own inattention, in not considering how very defective in judgment or memory men may sometimes be; which defect, when we meet with to any great degree, in those who generally speak the words of truth and soberness, we rashly conclude that they are not in earnest, and mistake their imperfections for sneer and wit. But in this we are guilty of a very great injustice: for as mankind is undeniably the most nonsensical of all God Almighty's creatures, no man can have a right to set bounds to another man's nonsense.—Every one should be contented with his own share; and if Providence has vouchsafed to our neighbour such an abundance of it, that he can digest contradictions better than we can, it should not be the object of our envy, but of our admiration.

' When bishop Bull is speaking of Tertullian, he tells us, that he did not care what he said of God, if he did but answer his adversary.—This to be sure was extremely wrong, and highly to be blamed. But it is a very different thing when philosophers, in the heat of their metal, in the pursuit of truth, or fame, shall happen to forget, and by that means contradict, what they have just before said. And this is still more excusable, when it is the effect of zeal in such young converts as have just taken up a new religion, and discarded an old one: for here it may be in a manner expected, that some spice of the old leaven may be as difficult to shake off as was the poisoned shirt of Hercules; and this observation is confirmed by Ovid, who informs us, that the heart of Daphne continued to beat as usual, even when she was changed in all outward appearance: Sentit adhuc trepidare novo sub cortice pectus. And as this is the case, we ought in justice to excuse Dr. Maclaine, in having read two-thirds of Mr. Jenyns, before he found, what he calls, the strange things in it, to be meant in earnest. And I must confess, I did not see the trim of Mr. Gibbon, till I had read him more than once: and at length I found, or seemed to find, sufficient reason to acquit him of any evil defign againft the truth, and rather to confider him as being in a ftate of doubt and uncertainty, upon meeting with difficulties which he could not explain, and wavering in his opinions, like a wave in the fea, driven with the wind, and toffed, James i. 6. Or 'perhaps he may be more properly compared, in the words of the Pfalmift, to the mariners themfelves in a tempeft; 'they reel to and fro, and ftagger like a drunken man, and are at their wit's end.'——

— ' Away then with the idle notion of infidelity and fneers. If thefe philofophers believe Chriftianity, as they declare they do, they are Chriftians, by whatever accident it has happened, and whatever degree they may occupy in the fcale of faith, from the burning to the freezing point. And if they have actually found it neceffary to difcard their reafon, in order to make room for their faith; is it not moft unreafonable and unjuft in their adverfaries, merely upon that account, to call in queftion their title to the name of Chriftian, which they have purchafed at fo dear a price? And upon what pretence? Have they not for fome time figured in the world as the defenders of our faith? and with as great an eclat as any of the moft Chriftian, moft Faithful, or moft Catholic princes in Europe?——Have they not confcientioufly followed the example of the Roman church, both in the rafhnefs and fuddennefs of their judgment, as well as in the uncertainty of their determinations? If any of their adverfaries are fo bold as to deny this, we appeal to fact: let them be confounded and put to fhame, by the following undeniable teftimony of Melchior Canus, the learned bifhop of the Canaries. " It is ufual, believe me, fays he, for all the judges of the church, when they publifh their decrees, to be driven on by a certain rafhnefs and fuddennefs of judgment, as by a wind; fo that nothing can be looked upon as folid, grave, or certain."

' I pretend not to judge whether this be the haven where thefe defenders of the faith would be; but (to fpeak without the figure) it is the ftate to which their arguments tend to reduce revelation: and it muft be owned, even by their adverfaries, that they have not only diligently followed the example of all the judges of the church; but been driven on like them as by a fquall of wind, and anchored at laft in the very fame port; in the fairy-land of legendary romance, confufion, and uncertainty. And what modeft man will dare to oppofe himfelf to fuch a refpectable authority as that of Melchior Canus, bifhop of the Canaries, and all the judges of the Roman church?'

Mr. Gibbon having fpecified five caufes, as favouring the rapid progrefs of Chriftianity, our author confiders thefe caufes; and obferves, that the learned hiftorian has not once attempted to prove, that any of them affifted the *truth* of the Chriftian religion; but merely, that they favoured the rapid progrefs of the church, as a fociety or party, without any examination into the truth of the principles they profeffed to be.

believe ; or whether they believed them, or not : whereas th progress of the *truth*, or the means, whereby the Christian *faith* obtained so remarkable a victory over the established religions of the earth, had been. before accounted for by Mr. Gibbon'satisfactorily, ' from the convincing evidence of the doctrine itself, and the ruling providence of its author,' without any of these secondary causes.

The first cause, which he specifies, is the inflexible, or, as he afterwards calls it, the exclusive, zeal of the Christians. But how, says this writer, an exclusive or inflexible zeal could serve the cause of truth more than that of faishood, and bring men into the Christian church, rather than keep them out of it, is not easy to conceive.

The second cause, alleged by Mr. Gibbon, is the immediate expectation of another world, or a future state.

But how, replies Mr. Taylor, can this principle assist the *truth* of Christianity, when it is itself the consequence of our believing the truth of Christianity ? Can it be both the cause and effect ? as in the old monkish riddle, Mater me peperit ; pario mox filia matrem !

The third cause is the miraculous powers ascribed to the Christian church.

This, says our author, is so far from proving the truth of Christianity, that the very doctrines, which the fathers endeavour to establish by their pretended miracles, such as the worship of the saints and reliques, recoil upon the monkish fathers themselves, and prove, that their testimony is not to be credited, and that their pretended miracles cannot be authenticated by any evidence, that can be depended upon.

The fourth cause is the practice of Christian virtues.

But, as our author observes, when Mr. Gibbon comes. to this subject, we find not a single virtue mentioned, nor any thing specified, but instances of weakness and superstition, tending to corrupt the true principles of Christianity.

The fifth cause is the union and discipline of the Christian republic.

But, says this writer, when we confider, how the power arising from the union of the churches, or the constitution of the primitive church, was used in Asia by the councils, in establishing idolatry, and persecuting both orthodox and heretics, and driving the members of the church into Arabia and other countries for safety ; and afterwards, how it was used in Europe, in defending the idolatry established by the Afiatics, and wading through seas of blood to establish the same errors, it must be confessed, that instead of assisting the *truth*, or even the rapid progress of Christianity, considered merely

as

as a fociety, it has been the great hinderance to both; and the whole proteftant church has been obliged to feparate from the church of Rome, merely upon account of the many errors fhe received from Afia, and to break that union, rather than to continue to join in the fame abominations.

In this manner our author fhews, that the caufes, fpecified by Mr. Gibbon, fo far from anfwering the purpofe he has affigned, prevented, either jointly or feparately, not only the purity of the Chriftian faith, but its univerfality; and that the kingdom of God and his church will not prevail over all, till the very exiftence of thofe caufes fhall ceafe, which firft produced the apoftacy.

To thefe obfervations the author has annexed three differtations. The firft on the paroufias of Chrift.

Dr. Hammond and fome other writers fuppofe a threefold coming of Chrift, one at his birth, another at the deftruction of the Jewifh polity, and a third at the day of judgement.

Our author, on the other hand, maintains, that the fecond, or middle, paroufia is no fcripture doctrine.

The prophet Daniel, he obferves, fpeaks of no more than two paroufias of Chrift: the one in the prophecy of the feventy weeks, ch. ix. 26. when the Meffiah fhall come, and be cut off; and the other when he fhall come in the clouds of heaven, ch. vii. 14.

Neither Chrift himfelf, he fays, nor any of his apoftles, fpeak of the deftruction of Jerufalem as a paroufia of Chrift. On the contrary, he repeatedly declared, that he was not to be expected at that time; and that when he fhould come, his prefence would not be a fecret, but known to all the world.

He adds:

‘ Allowing that fuch words as εγγυς near, ηγδικε is come near, &c. are often ufed by the apoftles, when fpeaking of Chrift's paroufia, yet it muft be confeffed, that they are alfo ufed concerning things at a great diftance, efpecially in prophecy: as in this paffage in the Revelation of St. John: " The Revelation of Jefus Chrift, which God gave unto him, to fhew unto his fervants things which muft fhortly (εν ταχει) come to pafs;" yet fome of thefe things, we are affured by the prophet himfelf, were at more than a thoufand years diftance.’

From this, and feveral other texts of fcripture, which he produces, it is reafonable, he thinks, to conclude, that the facred writers meant nothing more by fuch expreffions, than our divines do, when they remind men of the near approach of that time, when they fhall appear before the judgement

feat

feat of Chrift ; by which every one underftands them to mean the fhort duration of human life.

When our Saviour fays, ' There be fome ftanding here, who fhall not tafte of death, till they fee the fon of man coming in his kingdom,' it may be faid, that he alludes to the deftruction of Jerufalem. But our author fuppofes, that he refers to his transfiguration. And to corroborate this opinion, he remarks, that both Matthew and Luke have the fame various reading, εν τη δοξη, in his glory, that is, in the Shechinah, as he appeared in the Old Teftament. That this is the true reading feems, he thinks, to be confirmed by his actual appearance in Schechinah a few days after to Peter, James, and John, the hiftory of which immediately follows in all the three evangelifts.

The fubject of the fecond differtation is the Millennium ; or a thoufand years reign of Chrift upon earth, preceded by the converfion of the Jews ; when the fubjects of his kingdom fhall live according to the precepts of the gofpel, and the will of God be done on earth, as it is in heaven.'

The third differtation confifts of fome ingenious obfervations and inferences, in favour of divine revelation, from the prefent exiftence of the Jews, and the propagation of the knowlege of the true God over a great part of the globe, which were both foretold before thefe events, and are at prefent inconteftible facts.

This piece is the production of the late Mr. Wavell, rector of St. Maurice, in Winchefter.

FOREIGN ARTICLES.

Mémoire fur les Enfans Trouvés ; préfenté à MM. les Procureurs du Pays de Provence, par les Recteurs de l'Hôpital Général de S. Jaques d'Aix. 4to. Aix.

AS this excellent memoir was extorted by neceffity, and dictated by humanity to good fenfe, and as it treats of a fubject highly interefting to every nation in a certain ftage of refinement, luxury, and corruption, we fhall give a longer extract of it, than we fhould chufe to give of more bulky and lefs ufeful publications.

The gentlemen entrufted with the adminiftration of the General Hofpital of Aix, had obferved with concern, the horrible degree to which the mortality of foundlings in Provence, and particularly at Aix, had rifen ; efpecially in the year 1776, when, out of *one hundred and fifteen* foundlings carried to their Hofpital, not lefs than *one hundred and three* had died within one year.

By this fhocking obfervation they were induced to trace the caufes, and to propofe the remedies of that evil publicly ; to ftate the cafe to the public, and to requeft its charitable affiftance.

They impute the misfortune to three main causes; to the diseases by which such children are liable to be attacked from their births; to the unhealthiness and bad diet of the place where they are kept till proper nurses can be procured for them; and to the scarcity of such nurses.

Of these three causes, the first operates on the unhealthiness and mortality of foundlings in all countries, in general; the two latter cannot but increase that mortality, likewise, wherever they take place; but it is chiefly to them, that the excessive mortality of the unfortunate foundlings carried to the Hospital of Aix is to be attributed.

From continual experience it appears indeed, that whatever care may be taken of new-born children, most of them must inevitably perish, whenever a great number are crouded together in the same place; so hurtful are their emanations, and that uncleanliness which is natural and inevitable in infancy.

The want of proper nurses in the Hospital of Aix arises from their inadequate wages, and from their well-grounded fears of being infected with some venereal disease by the nurselings.

The remedies proposed by the author of this memoir are: to procure to foundlings, dry nurses only; to rear them by hand, by substituting to woman's milk some other milk or proper aliment; an expedient very generally and successfully used in Russia, Denmark, Great Britain, Ireland, Germany, and especially in Swabia, and Franconia, and in Swisserland; and not to keep numbers of children crowded in hospitals, but to disperse them in country villages, where sufficient numbers of fit dry nurses might always be found.

But in order to preserve foundlings, and to render them useful members of the state, proper care must be taken to initiate and habituate them early to industry and good morals. Now, though there are country people in easy circumstances, industrious, and humane enough to give to foundlings, entrusted to their care, the same education as to their own children; and though there are also virtuous curates, charitable enough to watch over those that are reared in their respective parishes; yet there are also many crying abuses: children absolutely starving, disputing their food with hogs; forced not only to subsist themselves, but their cruel and lazy nurses too, by begging in the villages and roads, and severely abused when they happen not to receive alms for their use. Some of these nurses procure as many children as they can, and then sell them; one, among others of Noyers, found means to procure thirteen children from different hospitals; who shut them up at night in a stable, and sold such as were above seven years of age, at the rate of fifteen to eighteen livres a head!

The only means for preventing such execrable excesses, are incessant cares, visits, enquiries, and even encouragements on the side of the administrators; who, however humane or zealous in the cause of humanity, can, on account of their own circumstances, seldom afford to bear all the expence and trouble at their own charge.

Such were the circumstances and motives which induced the administrators of the Hospital of Aix to apply to the faculty of physic at Paris, to the nobility and clergy of Provence, and even to the government of France. The former immediately favoured them with the most ample and best informations for the preservation of the health of the poor children: it is to be hoped that the latter

will

will likewife act up to their duty and interefts; and that the calamities fuffered by the objects of one charitable inftitution, will raife
a fpirit and zeal for preventing the recurrence of the like fufferings
in many others.

Defcription de la Lorraine *et du* Barrois, &c. *par M.* Durival, &c.
2 *Vols.* Nancy.

THE preface of this valuable work contains a concife and critical
account of ancient and modern maps, and geographical and
political defcriptions of Lorrain; thefe are fucceeded by a fhort
hiftory of that country and its fovereigns; and its general mathematical, phyfical, œconomical, and political defcription : the fecond
volume exhibits the particular geographical account of each bailli-
wick. The firft volume has been illuftrated by Mr. Arrivel with a
neat fmall map; and the fecond, adorned by Mr. Eifen with a
view of *Bitfch*. The firft tolerable map of Lorrain was drawn up
by Gerard Mercator, in 1568; and the lateft minute defcription of
that country, is the Notice de la Lorraine, compiled by Abbé Calmet, and publifhed by his nephew and fucceffor, Dom Fangé, in
two volumes, in folio.

Mr. Durival himfelf publifhed, in 1748, an Alphabetical Table of
all the Places in Lorrain and Bar; this table he improved in 1753,
with the addition of a Memoir on the State of thefe Duchies; the
work was afterwards improved by farther addition, in the fucceffive
editions in 1766, 1769, and 1770; and in 1774, by an Effai d'Introduction hiftorique. But when all thefe fucceffive labours became
defective, by the lateft royal regulations and the foundations of the
bifhopricks of Nancy and St. Diez, he refolved on collecting his feveral former publications into the prefent work, in which both the
political and the geographical ftate is exhibited, fuch as it was in
1779.

The ancient hiftory of thefe conntries are given, is fhort, but
fufficient; the events which were moft interefting for them, are
judicioufly felected, and drawn up from authentic authorities. Accounts of the fmaller, but fovereign branches of the reigning family; of remarkable heroes, learned men, and eminent artifts; and
of particular laws compiifed in the fifteen volumes of the Statutes of
Lorrain and Bar, are likewife interwoven.

But at the year 1691, this hiftory becomes fo minute as to enter
into feveral interefting details, not to be found in the laft volume of
the lateft edition of Dom. Calmet's Hiftory of Lorrain; and the
details of king Stanillaus's reign in Lorrain are ftill more full and
minute.

The phyfical geography, on the contrary, is too fhort, and unfa-
tisfactory. Pont à Mouffon, and Nancy have botanical gardens, and
fome men of learning and collectors of natural and artificial curiofi-
ties. The corn produced by the country is fufficient to fubfift its
inhabitants; and very good harvefts fupply an exportation of about
400,000 facks. The nobility have been ftripped of the fuperior
courts of juftice, on their lands; and, in return for the lofs of real
authority, been flattered with higher titles, of barons, counts, and
marquifes.

The number of births in Lorrain and Bar, amounted in 1776, to
32,171 : thefe are by the author multiplied by 25, and the total
number of the inhabitants of thofe countries eftimated at 804,273
perfons. A national antipathy, between the two nations inhabiting

Lorrain and Bar, is even now subsisting, though the hostilities of their former respective sovereigns have ceased almost three hundred years since. Their chief dialects and idioms are French, Messin or that of the district of Metz, Vogien, and corrupt German. The inhabitants are divided among a great number of bishopricks, viz. Treves or Trier, Metz, Tull, Verdun, Nancy, St. Diez, Maynz, Chalons, Langres, Strasburgh, and Besançon; and a few places, such as the ladies-abbey of Remiremont, depend immediately on the pope. The bishopricks of Nancy and St. Diez, were established on the 19th of November, 1777, and the former endowed from the revenues of the primatical chapter of Nancy, and the latter from these of the earldom of St. Diez, granted for this purpose by king Stanislaus, those of the convents of Etival and Autrey, and part of these of the abbot of Moyen Moutier. The ecclesiastical code which gave rise to famous disputes with the pope, is still in force. The civil law is exceedingly various, and there are bailliwics in these countries, in which five or even more, different statutes prevail, besides the Roman law. The supreme court of justice is at Nancy, and has, since 1775, been styled a parliament.

The coin of Lorrain is different from that of Bar, and both from that of France. In 1766, the whole of the revenues of Lorrain and Bar, amounted to 9,282,623 livres of Lorrain, equal to 7,186,553 livres of France; and the expenditure to 1,647.705 livres of France.

The university was, in 1768, transferred from Pont à Mousson to Nancy, the capital, which has besides a royal academy of sciences, a college of physicians, and a college or company of surgeons. Both the duchies have produced many eminent painters, sculptors, and other artists. The first painter, Peter Jacobi, lived in 1508.

The first volume concludes with a list of fairs.

The second contains the geographical description; with a short account of the history of the chief places, and the number of their houses. Nancy contained, in 1777, 29,468 persons; and among those, not less than 358 monks, and 631 nuns.

Questions Politiques. 122 _Pages in Octavo._

THE anonymous author treats of the following questions: 1. _Means for improving public education?_—Here he affirms that in the schools of protestant countries, youth are taught mere words and phrases from the classics; and that the schools of catholic countries are beneath notice and criticism.

But these assertions appear to us to be exaggerations. In most countries of Europe a spirit of improvement has arisen for these several years past, and already produced several essential and practical advantages. Both in the catholic and protestant countries of Germany, in particular, not only a very great number of writers and teachers, but most governments also, have been assiduously, zealously, and successfully intent on the improvement of public and private education.

The author proposes a more general study of the French language, and to have every object of knowledge taught in that as well as in the respective native tongues, in order to render the French the universal language, as it is already that of courts and of the beau monde.

2. _Means for allowing liberty, to nations habituated to despotic government, without any risk for the sovereign._—An interesting problem this, for several countries of Europe, and especially for Russia. The

The author advises, not to declare a nation under such delicate circumstances, directly, and publicly, free, but silently to indulge and habituate her by successive degrees, to the enjoyment of the advantages of liberty.

3. *On the best means for securing the succession to sovereignty, against lawless and unconstitutional usurpations.*—The civil power must be sufficiently ballanced against the military power, and especially no military officers assumed into the privy council.

4. *How far a talent for imitation, may supply the want of inventive genius in the administration of government?*—This must depend on the quantum of the genius for the observing and distinguishing, by which that talent for imitation may happen to be attended.

5. *Whether it is expedient to exclude foreigners from all places of trust and power in the state, the church, and the army?*—Denied, for many reasons.

6. *The best method for promoting the prosperity of a nation, subject to the power of an arbitrary prince.*—First of all, a good education of her future sovereign; for which our author thinks it necessary to entrust the presumptive heir with the establishment and government of some township, to be settled by him, with the assistance of his tutor, by way of forming and improving his judgment and heart; then, some excellent practical maxims for his future government; where, however, the main question always is, Whether the absolute prince will chuse to adopt and follow them?

7. *Whether a great part of the now overgrown and oppressive armies might not be spared, by the construction of good fortresses on the frontiers and the main passages into a country, supposing even that its neighbours would not reduce their standing armies in the same proportion?*—Affirmed by the author: but he seems to think that the standing armies of most princes are solely intended for defence. If that were the case, Spain, France, and several other powerful states, might surely avail themselves of the fortunate situation, and the solid compact strength of their countries, for reducing the number of their standing armies, to the evident annual saving of many millions of money and for an immense improvement of population, agriculture, &c. On the other hand, we are apt to consider the keeping up some other disproportionate armies, as a measure not of choice, but of desperate necessity.—*To be or not to be, is* THERE *the question.*

8. *Which are the true principles, by which the engagements and negotiations of the powers of Europe ought to be governed?*—Answered by elementary propositions; of which those concerning trade and commerce would, however, not be entirely relished by the sect of oeconomists.

Monumenta Matthæiana ;—*Vetera Monumenta, quæ in Hortis* Cælimontanis *et in Ædibus* Mathæiorum *asservantur, nunc primum in unum collecta et Adnotationibus illustrata a* Rodolphino Venuti, *et a* Jo. Christoph. Amaduzio. 3 *Volumes in folio, with Plates.* Romæ, *sumptibus* Venantis Monaldini, *Bibliopolæ.*

THE villa, gardens, and palaces, in which the celebrated antiques described and delineated in these volumes, were collected and preserved, belong to the noble family of Mattei. The villa and gardens were raised by Cyriacus Mattei, between 1581, and 1586; the palace, by his brother, Asdrubal, in 1616, on the scite of the

Q 3

ancient

ancient Circus Flaminius. Both brothers were affiduous collectors of all forts of antiques; and both the villa and palace have been celebrated in all the accounts of Rome, for the rich collections contained in them; though but a few drawings and plates of thefe hoarded treafures were publifhed in the *Raccolta*, by Spon, Montfaucon, Winkelmann, and others. The news of a complete account and difplay of the particulars of thefe collections, could not therefore but prove very acceptable to antiquaries and dilettanti.

The illuftrations of the figures were undertaken by Rodolfino Venuti, who died in 1763, when he had fcarce finifhed his firft volume; and was fucceeded in this tafk by Signor Amaduzzi, profeffor of the Greek Language in the Archigymnafium Sapientiæ, at Rome.

The firft volume contains the ftatues; the fecond, bufts, hermæ, and relievos; and the third other relievos and infcriptions. All thefe works of art are in ftone or marble; none in metal. Few of the plates are well drawn, or elegantly engraved.

In a preface of 64 pages, prefixed to the firft volume, Signor Amaduzzi gives a minute account of the family of the Mattei, of their buildings, and of the defign of his work: this account is interfperfed with many digreffions on the buildings that had formerly occupied the fame fpot; on thefe in the environs; on famous villas and gardens in general; and on the new Mufeum Vaticanum Clementinum.

Both the villa and the gardens of the Mattei are now greatly decayed: a great part of the antiques formerly contained in them have been transferred to other proprietors or collections; efpecially twelve of the fineft ftatues, and feveral bufts and relievos to the new Mufeum Vaticanum. All thofe have, however, been exhibited or at leaft enumerated in this work.

The engravings are indifferent; and the illuftrations liable to many doubts, objections, and cenfures. The firft volume contains 106 copper plates, exhibiting the fame number of ftatues; and 116 pages of letter prefs; the fecond volume, 90 copper plates, and 109 pages of letter prefs; and the third, 74 copper plates, and 193 pages of letter prefs: to this third volume, an Index of the infcriptions, and an Index Rerum on the whole work, are fubjoined. The three volumes fell at Rome for 360 paoli.

FOREIGN LITERARY INTELLIGENCE.

Entwurf einer Anweifung zur Landbaukunft, nach œkonomifchen Grundfætzen; or, A Sketch of an Introduction to rural Architecture on œconomical Principles; by George Henry Borbeck. *Part. I. with 6 Cuts,* 8vo. Goettingen (German).

IF the fubject of this valuable treatife is lefs brilliant than thofe generally treated by moft writers on architecture, it is however more generally interefting and ufeful to the bulk of a nation; as it regards. in fome degree, the wants and conveniencies of all its members. It is here treated with folidity of thought, clearnefs of method, and in a good ftyle.

De i Camerti Umbri, Differtazione Apologetica Iftorico-critica. 8vo. Camerino.

When Signor Pallota. a native of Camerino, an epifcopal city in the ecclefiaftical ftate, was raifed to the purple, his native place, **perhaps**

perhaps a little too proud on this great event, caused a cantata to be printed, in which, among other displays of her past and present glories, she asserted, that Macerata, another episcopal city of the same state, and of almost equal importance, had formerly been subject to the dukes of Camerino. This effusion, either of truth or of vanity, was warmly resented by the city of Macerata, which published a reply, or Risposta d'un Cavalier Maceratise ad un suo Amico in Camerino: this reply was answered by the present very learned and very warm apological historico-critical dissertation on the city of Camerino; said to have been written by a certain famous lawyer of that place, Signor Pietro Antonio Frasca.

This champion of Camerino demonstrates, by a number of passages from Livy, Cicero, Cato, Frontinus, &c. &c. that Camerinum was, so early as the fifth century from the foundation of Rome, a very flourishing place; that Macerata, on the contrary, did not begin to emerge into notice till the tenth century of the Christian æra. He confutes the assertions of his antagonist against the antiquity of Camerino, and gives the history of that place, drawn up from inscriptions, ancient monuments, and contemporary writers; enlarges on the extent of the empire of her ancient counts and marquisses, and on her various revolutions and fates under the Cæsars, the Goths, the Lombard kings and dukes, and under her own dukes; and at last evinces by seemingly irrefragable arguments, that not only Macerata has never had any jurisdiction over Camerino, but that the same Macerata has, on the contrary, been subject to the ancient sovereigns, and especially to the dukes of Camerino of the family of Verano.

To readers, not fired by patriotism either for Camerino or for Macerata, so zealous a discussion of so useless a question, may indeed appear somewhat ridiculous: but there is perhaps no nation that has not appeared sometimes to others guilty of the same or much greater mistakes. 'To proportion the eagerness of contest to its importance, seems too hard a task for human wisdom.' Happy those whose warfare begins and ends in the waste of only ink and paper, and some idle hours.

Lettre de M. Oberlin, *Prof. en l'Université de* Strasbourg, à M. *le Comte de* Stawronski, *Chambellan de S. M. Imp. de toutes les* Russies, *sur un* Bijou, *dont ce Seigneur a fait l'Acquisition à* Rome, *et qui se trouve Presentement au Cabinet de sa dite Majesté.* One sheet in 8vo. *with a Cut.* Strasburgh.

The jewel in question is a golden plate with a small gold chain reaching round the back part of the head, and serving to fasten the plate over the forehead, and behind the toupee. Such plates were frequently worn by the ladies of the ancient Romans, and are represented on many ancient figures. A golden plate of this kind was found in an urn, not far from Civita Lavinia, or the ancient Lanuvium; it came into the museum Vettori, from hence through several hands into those of Count Stawronsky, and from his into the cabinet of the empress of Russia. As Antoninus Pius had a villa in the environs of Lanuvium, Messrs. Oberlin and Reiffenstein suppose that the plate in question has once been worn by one of his princesses.

Les Helviennes, *ou Lettres provinciales Philosophiques.* 12mo. Paris.

These new Provençal letters are not indeed written by a Pascal, but with a view similar to his, and not destitute of merit. The
author

author introduces a country lady, ambitious of acquiring the title or a philosophical baroness, and applying for instruction to a chevalier ——, her countryman, a zealous disciple of the modern philosopher of Paris, and eager to enlighten his country, le Vivarais, the district of the ancient Helvii. Hence a very familiar and very curious correspondence between him and the lady, to whom he faithfully develops all the modern philosophical systems, without ever startling at the contradictions, physical errors, absurdities, and ridiculous consequences, found afterwards by a serious and knowing country gentleman, in the works of Messrs. Buffon, Telliamed, Diderot, Robinet, La Mettrie, d'Alembert, Voltaire, &c. &c. After having thus exposed the physical errors of his modern philosophy, the author proposes to proceed to their metaphysical, moral, political, historical, and theological notions, which will probably furnish him with abundant materials for several future volumes.

Essais des Sermons prêchés à l'Hotel Dieu de Paris ; *par M.* *** *D. D. de la Faculté de Paris. C. R. et B de S. V.* 12mo. Paris.

Three sermons preached on very solemn and awful occasions; at the professions and consecration of nuns, who devote themselves to the service and nursing of the sick, in the Hotel Dieu, or great hospital of Paris; a sacrifice infinitely disgusting and dangerous, but truly meritorious and heroical, made for giving to every patient of whatever rank or religion, all the assistance that can be derived from the most active and most industrious charity. This noble establishment has subsisted for many centuries; and afforded numberless instances of truly Christian charity and perseverance on the part of the nuns : and it is impossible to read the account of the epidemic disease of 1348, (the most horrible with which France has ever been afflicted) without a mixture of terror and admiration. Paris was almost entirely depopulated : above five hundred persons died every day, only at the Hotel Dieu : but the most painful, dangerous, and unceasing services, and death itself, served only to kindle the zeal of the nuns, who devoted themselves to the service of the unfortunate victims of the disorder; the whole number of those nuns perished twice over, yet the places of those who had just died were immediately filled up again.

Essai sur l'Art de cultiver la Canne de Sucre, et d'en extraire la Sucre. Par M. Cazeaux, *de la Société Royal de* Londres. *One vol. in* 8vo. Paris.

An accurate and instructive work on a subject interesting to all nations who have sugar plantations. The judicious author intends to analise the mucous and sweet body of sugar, for the improvement of the wines of Europe, according to the principles laid down in M. Beguillet's OEnology; by which means the use of sugar, already so valuable in itself, will be still farther increased.

He gives a table of the rain that fell in the island of Grenada in 1773; and indicates the use of such tables, which ought to be kept by public appointment, for the improvement of agriculture. He shows that such a table will exactly answer to that of the crop, for those who know how to manage sugar plantations : and he forms a system of that culture, founded both on theory and practice.

He proves that all sorts of sugar canes, if skilfully managed, will yield nearly the same sort of sugar : and he explains also the methods of verifying the boilings of sugars, and the difference between the proceedings of the European and American sugar houses.

L' Art

L' Art des Accouchemens; par M. Baudeloque, Membre du Collège et Adjoint au Comité perpétuel de l' Académie Royale de Chirurgie. 2 Vols. 8vo. Paris.

The refult of obfervation and application, warmly approved by the royal academy of furgery, and illuftrated with a fett of elegant and accurate plates, engraved under the author's own infpection.

Effai fur les Alimens, pour fervir de Commentaire aux Livres diététiques d' Hippocrtae. Nouv. Ed. corrigée & augmentée. 2 Vols. 12mo. Paris.

By the celebrated Dr. Lorry, one of the warmeft admirers of Hippocrates, Sanctorius, and Boerhaave; whom he has taken for the fafeft guides, in collecting all the certain knowlege on the nature of aliments, into a regular and practical fyftem.

Ephemerides Aftronomicae, anni 1781, ad Meridianum Vindebonenfem Juffu Auguftorum calculatae a Maximiliano Hell, Aftronomo Cafareo Regio. Cum Appendice Obfervationum. Viennae.

The twenty-fifth volume of this ufeful annual publication of Abbé Hell's: it contains the heights of the thermometer and barometer obferved at Vienna, three times each day, in 1779; aftronomical obfervations made at Buda or Ofen, in Hungary, by M. Weifs; others made at Prague by M. Zeno; at Manheim, by M. Mayer; at Crémfmünfter, by M. Fixmin; at Tyrnaw, by M. Taucher; at Warfaw, by M. Byferzycky; thofe of Erlaw, in Hungary, made in a new and very fumptuous obfervatory, conftructed and furnifhed at the expence of prince Efterhazy, bifhop of that place, by Abbé Madaraffy, whofe meteorological and aftronomical obfervations are here included: the latitude of this new obfervatory is 47° 53′ 54″, and its longitude, 1 h. 12′ 54″ eaft of Paris. M. Hell concludes his appendix with a critical examen of a new map of Hungary, by Mr. Krieger, pretended to have been drawn up from aftronomical obfervations.

MONTHLY CATALOGUE.

POETRY.

The Beuty of Beauties. A Collection of Sonnets. 4to. 2s. Baldwin.

PORTRAITS of the moft celebrated beauties now living in England, drawn by a very bad poetical painter, who has paid fo little regard to difcrimination, that any one of the characters will fuit the whole groupe.

' O thou, in whom nature's perfections are join'd,
A figure enchanting, an elegant mind!
In whom ev'ry winning attraction is found,
Whofe voice to the foul, is a zephyr of found;
Forgive each allufion, by rapture exprefs'd,
Nor the feelings misjudge which arife in the breaft:
For fince, by each virtue adorn'd, you appear,
'Tis the charter of nature to love, and revere!'

What

What our author means by a *zephyr of found*, we cannot poffibly tell ; nor why it fhould be the *charter* of nature to *love*, any more than to *eat*, *drink*, or *fleep*. In the verfes on Mifs Thynne we are told that *love*

    ' When dufky fhades add horror to the fcene,
       He'll footh, with gentleft note, her cares to fleep ;
    Then wander forth, 'midft tempefts bleak and keen,
       And lend the *brow* of night, an *eye* to weep !'

The idea of *lending* an *eye* to the *brow* of night, is too fublime to be underftood. To the countefs of Jerfey he fays :

    ' Yes,—and thofe fprightly eyes can weep,
    And to the tale of mis'ry, *progrefs keep.*—
    Praife to her heart !—the tears which forrow move,
    Are brilliant *jewels* on the *check* of love !'

Keeping progrefs to any thing, is certainly a new, but not a very elegant phrafe ; and *jewels* on the *cheek*, are ornaments which we very feldom meet with. Mrs. Harcourt, this gentleman affures us, looks as lovely

    ' —— as *conqueft*, to the fight !'

A very ftrange fimilitude ; and in his Serenade, as he calls it, to Lady Townfhend, he carries us,

    ' Thro' blooming vales, and ever-*fadelefs* groves,'

Fadelefs is, we believe, a word of this poet's own *coining*, we hope it will never be *current*.

If after this glimpfe of the *BeWy*, any of our readers defire to purfue the game, we can only think them very eager fportfmen, and wifh them much diverfion.

Ode to the Genius of the Lakes in the North of England. 4to. 2s.
      Richardfon *and* Urquhart.

The author of this Ode informs us, in the advertifement prefixed, that he difclaims the idea of offering it to the public as a literary production, and throws the piece only into the way of *actual tourifts*. The word *tourift* is, we believe, not to be met with in Johnfon's, or any other Englifh Dictionary, though the meaning of it is fufficiently obvious ; but as we are not *actual tourifts*, unlefs wandering through the regions of literature may entitle us to that diftinction, it cannot be expected that we fhould receive much entertainment from this poem. Even the beft poetical defcription of places gives us, indeed, but imperfect notions of the object reprefented, and not a twentieth part of the pleafure which we receive from the

      oculis fubjecta fidelibus.

Let the reader take, for inftance, the following ftanza of the Ode before us.

                            Lo !

Lo ! thy wand'ring eye to pleafe,
   O'er Thurfton's fmooth expanfe,
Verg'd with lawns of tufted trees,
   The lightfome fun-beams dance.
On Windermere's long-fcatter'd ifles
Though Kirkfton frown, fair Orreft fmiles.
Chearful Whythop waves his woods:
And round Derwent's glaffy floods,
With many a fringed glade between,
Falcon's cliffs fublime are feen.
And hark ! to greet thy ear, remote
(While nearer flows the ftock-dove's note)
Down Harter-hills, and Swarth-fell fteep,
A thoufand humming cataracts fweep ;
  The eagles fcream on Glaramara high,
And Ulls' grand echoing founds reverb'rate through the fky.'

In thefe lines, which run fmooth and eafy, mention is made of a number of very fine places. But what idea can we form of them from a fketch fo loofe and indifcriminate? Plain profe feems a better vehicle for all information of this kind, as it can not only defcend to the moft minute particulars, and muft, therefore, better anfwer the purpofe of exciting curiofity ; but will, at the fame time, prove more entertaining, efpecially where the verfification, as is the cafe with regard to this Ode, does not rife above mediocrity.

A Poetical Epiftle; attempted in the Style of Churchill's *Epiftle to* Hogarth. 4to. 1s. Fielding.

The weak effufion of querulous malevolence, venting itfelf in very bad rhimes againft fome private characters, heavens knows where. The whole is *tellum imbelle fine ictu* : the defign is invidious, and the verfes contemptible.

The Royal Naval Review, or a late Trip to the Nore. 4to. 1s. 6d. Kearfly.

As a fpecimen of this production, a few lines from the beginning will be fufficient :
   How fhall I tell where I have been,
   Where I the rareft things have feen ?
     O Dick ! beyond a doubt,
   Such fights again cannot be found,
   Such tricks ne'er play'd on Englifh ground,
     But by the felf-fame rout.
   At a Great Houfe, hard by the way
   Where we do fometimes fell our hay ;
     My memory here but lame is ;
   Pfhaw, where folks fay what they don't mean ;
   Plague ! rat it now, what is its name ?
     Oh ! aye—'tis call'd St. James's.

We

We know not whether, to read the whole of this rhapsody, might not, on some constitutions, have an effect similar to that which is sometimes produced by a real *Naval Trip to the Nore.*

The Cow-Chace; an Heroic Poem, in Three Cantos. 4to. 1s. Fielding.

This poem was written, as we are informed in an advertisement prefixed to it, by the gallant and unfortunate Major André—He was a brave officer, and much to be lamented ; we shall therefore say nothing of his poem.

✓ DRAMATIC.

The Baron Kinkvervankotsdorsprakingatchdern. *A new Musical Comedy. As performed at the Theatre-Royal in the* Hay-Market. *By* Miles Peter Andrews, *Esq.* 8vo. 1s. 6d. Cadell.

This piece would afford ample matter for the severity of criticism, but

  '' We war not with the dead.'

It has been tried, condemned, and executed ; and peace be to its manes!

Nathan the Wife. A Philosophical Drama. 8vo. 1s. 6d. Fielding.

A heap of unintelligible jargon, very badly translated from the German original, written it seems by G. E. Lessing. The translator informs us, in his preface, that the author of this drama *stands* very high in the opinion of his countrymen, *because* he *stands* foremost amongst the late reformers, to whom Germany is indebted for its present *golden* age of literature. The reader will here please to observe, that this German author, in the elegant language of his translator Mr. Raspe, *stands* because he *stands* ; we wish he may not *fall, because* he *falls* infinitely beneath all criticism ; and can only say that if this is the golden age of German literature, it appears, at least by this specimen, to put on a very *leaden* appearance.

✓ POLITICAL.

A Review of the Conduct of his Excellency John, *Earl of* Buckinghamshire, *Lord-Lieutenant and Governor-General of* Ireland, *during his Administration in that Kingdom.* 8vo. 1s. Robinson.

This pamphlet, written with more than common correctness, contains a high panegyric on the earl of Buckinghamshire ; whom the author paints in an amiable light, as a man ; and in a respectable view, as a minister, and the friend of Ireland. Indeed, the important concessions, made to the sister kingdom, during his administration, must ever throw a lustre on the domestic government of that period.

Re-

Remarks on Commodore Johnstone's *Account of his Engagement with a* French *Squadron,* April 16, 1780, *in* Port Praya *Road, in the Island of* St. Jago. 8*vo.* 6*d.* Debrett.

The defign of thefe Remarks, which feem to be re-printed from news-papers, is to impeach the commodore with mifconduct during the action, and with perplexity in his narrative. The whole, however, appears to be nothing more than a groundlefs and invidious effort of detraction.

MEDICAL.

Cafes in Midwifery; with References and Remarks. By William Perfect, *Surgeon. Vol. I.* 8*vo.* 6*s. fewed.* Dodfley.

The cafes related in this volume prefent us with a variety of obfervations, made in the courfe of the obftetrical employment ; and, confidered as a collection of facts, muft prove ufeful to practitioners in that art.

Cafe I. The delivery of a dead fœtus, from the mother's being afflicted with a lues venerea, which proved fatal.—Cafe II. Labour retarded by the circumvolutions of the funis about the neck of the child.—Cafe III. The funis uncommonly fhort, and impeding the birth, by being twifted round the child's neck.—Cafe IV. A lingering labour, occafioned by the extraordinary fhortnefs of the funis. —Cafe V. A retention of the placenta, and a fingular infertion of the funis into its central part.—Cafe VI. A prefentation of the funis and belly ; the child turned and delivered.—Cafe VII. A woman was pregnant with twins ; one of which was born breech foremoft, and the other delivered with the forceps.—VIII. A flooding, and the labour protracted by the rigidity of the membranes. The two cafes laft mentioned are related in a letter to the late Dr. Colin Mackenzie, and accompanied with the doctor's anfwer.—Cafe IX. Twins, with an intervention of fix days between their births.—Cafe X. A breech prefentation, in a letter to Dr. Mackenzie, with his anfwer.—Cafe XI. A gonorrhœa virulenta in the fourth month of pregnancy —Cafe XII. A large head ; the pelvis diftorted ; and delivery effected by the crotchets ; in a letter to Dr. Mackenzie, with his anfwer.

We fhall proceed no farther in fpecifying the various cafes recited by Mr. Perfect, but fhall refer our readers to the work ; obferving only that the author generally illuftrates them by fimilar cafes from other writers on midwifery ; and that the volume derives confiderable merit from the correfpondence of Dr. Mackenzie.

The New Britifh Difpenfatory. 12*mo.* 3*s.* Newbery.

This production contains the preparations and compofitions of the new London and Edinburgh Pharmacopœias ; the prefcriptions of the latter not being given at full length ; but only the occafional difference remarked between them and thofe ordered by the college of London. The compiler has added notes, pointing out, concisely, the methods of distinguishing the goodness of most articles in the materia medica ; and has subjoined the recipes of several nostrums, said to have been analysed by the late Robert Dossie, Esq.

A Dissertation upon the Nervous System. 8vo. 1s. 6d.

A complicated and incoherent production, abstruse without investigation, and laboured without apparent design.

✓ CONTROVERSIAL.

A Reply to a second Letter on the Duration of our Lord's Ministry, from the Rev. Joseph Priestley, LL. D. F. R. S. *By* W. Newcome, *D. D. bishop of* Waterford, 12mo. 2s. Robinson.

In this letter his lordship suggests some very material considerations in favour of his hypothesis*, and evidently shews, that he has studied the subject with great accuracy and discernment. As many of the points in the debate seem to be ambiguous, Dr. Priestley will probably reply ; and if his lordship should follow his example, the controversy may be continued without end. In the mean time, it is in excellent hands, is conducted with liberality, politeness, and learning, and cannot but afford some agreeable information to the lovers of biblical criticism.

We shall give our readers the conclusion of this letter :

' Many considerable writers have assigned a duration to our Lord's ministry differing from that which we suppose in our respective harmonies. Scaliger, Sir Isaac Newton, Whiston, Stillingfleet, Allix, Wells, &c. compute five passovers between our Lord's baptism and crucifixion. I formerly quoted Whitby as opposing this opinion : but I find that he afterwards acceded to it. For my own part, I do not see that it has any foundation in the gospels. We cannot infer a distinct feast from that recorded John v. 1, because Jesus's disciples are said to have plucked and eaten ears of corn. And other passovers, suggested by some, are still more weakly founded : Macknight for instance, introduces one soon after the payment of the tribute-money ; because the Talmud says that the tribute was demanded in the last month of the Jewish year.

' I will next very briefly state the conveniencies and inconveniencies of comprehending our Lord's ministry within the space of two years and about six months : of which opinion G. J. Vossius says that, if he could recede from that in which Mr. Mann has closely followed him, 'ad nullam potius dilaberetur quam illam, biennium et paucos menses durasse πολλίας Christi : quod a

---

* See Crit. Rev. vol. l. p.131. vol. lii. p. 115.

veritate

veritate proxime recedit, et veterum multorum nititur auctoritate. And again : facile huic subscribent sententiæ, quibus durius videtur, quod de ἱερέων προτέρων in c. vi. 4. admisso superius dicebamus.

'Let it be supposed that John v. 1. was the feast of pentecost immediately after the first passover.

'The advantages of this system are: 1. Jesus attended the feast which directly followed the first passover; and, because the Jews sought his life at that time, he intermitted his attendance on the four succeeding feasts of tabernacles, the dedication, the passover, and pentecost. But, when his ministry drew towards a conclusion, he attended the feasts of tabernacles, of the dedication, and of the passover at which he suffered. There seems to be a remarkable fitness in this conduct : whereas, on the plan of my Harmony, three feasts between John ii. 13. and v. 1. remain unattended for general reasons only.

'2. Thus too Herod heard of Jesus's fame a year sooner than I have supposed : yet not till Jesus had preached and wrought miracles in Galilee for near twelve months.

'If any should think that, John v. 1. some other feast is meant besides the pentecost subsequent to the first passover, for example the feast of tabernacles in the same year, let him observe how difficult it will be to find a place for it between the season of ripe corn referred to Luke vi. 1. and the raising of the widow of Nain's son, Luke vii. 11.

'The only inconvenience of supposing John v. 1. to be the first pentecost in our Lord's ministry is that there seems to be less time allowed for our Lord's important instructions and actions during the fifty days between John ii. 13. and v. 1. than the decorum and full effect of them require. I have so little attachment to my own plan, that, if I could obtain satisfaction on this point, on which I would gladly know the opinion of able critics, I would readily relinquish it : and I will propose to my readers a distribution of this time, which may recommend itself to them, though I cannot acquiesce in it myself.

		Days
'Suppose then that		
'Jesus was at Jerusalem some days before the passover, John ii. 13 : and after it	——	3
'That he passed in Judea	——	10
'In the journey to Samaria and stay at Sichar	——	3
'In the journey to Cana and stay	——	5
'In the journey to Nazareth, and stay	——	5
'[These two last articles may be supposed to comprehend his preaching in the synagogues of Galilee.]		
'In his stay at Capernaum	——	4
'In his tour about all Galilee	——	16
'In his journey to Jerusalem	——	4
		50

'My

'My readers will likewise obferve, and calculate as they think fit, what numbers of miles our Lord travelled in this fpace of time.

'Thus have I freely given you my fentiments on the fubject of our amicable debate: I have endeavoured to deliver them with the refpect due to your eminence as a fcholar, and with the good manners and good will which we owe to each other as gentlemen and as Chriftians. I am, &c.'

In the foregoing extract his lordfhip fhews that moderation, which is always amiable, particularly in points of doubtful difputation.

Gibbon's Account of Chriftianity confidered: together with fome *Strictures on* Hume's *Dialogues concerning Natural Religion. By* Joſeph Milner, *A. M.* 8vo. 3s. Robinfon.

This writer divides his work into three parts. In the firft, he examines fome facts and characters, which, he thinks, are mifreprefented by Mr. Gibbon; in the fecond he gives an account of what he calls evangelical truth, or the vital parts of Chriftianity; and, in the third, he defends what he ftyles Chriftian principles.

From the general tenor of this work, we are inclined to form a favourable opinion of the author's piety and learning. But when we read his account of original fin and imputed righteoufnefs; his invectives againft human reafon, and his frequent allufions to myfterious feelings and experimental illuminations, we are induced to believe, that his theological abilities would have been more properly employed in writing comments on the works of Jacob Behmen or William Law, than in maintaining a controverfy with fuch a formidable adverfary as Mr. Gibbon.

MISCELLANEOUS.

The Theory of the Syphon, plainly and methodically illuftrated. 8vo. 1s. 6d. Richardfon *and* Urquhart.

The manner in which a fyphon acts is explained in this pamphlet with great perfpicuity, upon the principles of hydroftatics; and the philofophical author has likewife fhewn, by mathematical reafoning, the ufe of this inftrument in accounting for reciprocating fprings.

The Neptune of Europe. 2s. Bell.

This pamphlet contains a lift of the naval force of Great Britain, and the other maritime powers of Europe, with the names of the commanders, and a variety of particulars relative to the marine eftablifhments of each nation. The whole is digefted in a methodical manner, and may be ufeful, fo far as the fluctuating ftate of temporary appointments will permit.

THE
CRITICAL REVIEW.

For the Month of *October*, 1781.

Eight Sermons preached before the University of Oxford. *By* Timothy Neve, *D. D. Chaplain of* Merton College. 8*vo.* 3*s.* 6*d.* Cadell.

THIS is the second volume, which we owe to the benefaction of the pious Mr. John Bampton ; containing a general defence of Christianity, of the orthodox opinion concerning the divinity of our Saviour, &c.

The design of the first discourse is to prove, that Jesus Christ is the predicted Messiah. Here the author, before he proceeds to the prophecies of the Old Testament, on this subject, makes the following observation : ‘ Without the agency of a superintending Providence it would have been an utter impossibility to imagine, that a regular, well-arranged, and consistent plan, could be carried on for upwards of four thousand years ; and under the administration of different persons of various countries, callings, and interests, who, in their several successive generations, should have the same point perpetually in view ; to which, as to a common center, they should all uniformly tend, without any, the least, variation or contradiction. Such a continued harmony and union, both of scheme and sentiment must owe its progress, as well as its rise, to that God who is great in counsel, and mighty in work, who giveth wisdom, and knowlege, and understanding.’

This remark is perfectly just. But if the author had confined himself to that astonishing series of prophecies, which *gradually* unfold almost every circumstance relative to the

Meſſiah, and exactly *coincide* and *centre* in the perſon of Jeſus Chriſt, his argument would have been as ſtrong and concluſive, as it is now, by the addition of the following types and ſhadows : ' The command to Abraham ·to offer his ſon Iſaac ; the bleſſing imparted to Judah ; the ſufferings, exaltation, and perſon of Joſeph ; the prieſthood of Melchiſedeck and Aaron ; the call, election, and government of Moſes ; the triumphs of Joſhua ; the reign of David ; the redemption of the firſt born ; the brazen ſerpent ; the killing of ſacrifices, more eſpecially of the paſcal lamb, the actions and ceremonies upon the great day of expiation, attending both the ſcape-goat, and the goat appointed for the ſin offering, whoſe blood was to make atonement : all theſe various myſtical emblems, whether perſonal, occaſional, or perpetual, look to one and the ſame grand character, which gave them their importance.'

Nothing can be more eaſy than to find a thouſand circumſtances, like theſe, in the hiſtory of the Bible. But what authority have we to call all theſe things ' prefigurative types' of the Meſſiah ! An inventive genius may probably find a *reſemblance* between the hiſtory of Joſeph (even perhaps in the affair of Potiphar's wife *) and that of Jeſus Chriſt ; but no prudent writer would attempt to reſt the cauſe of Chriſtianity on any of theſe arbitrary ſuppoſitions.

The ſubject of the ſecond lecture is ' the true knowlege of God and Chriſt.'

In the firſt paragraph the author gives us this obſervation : ' To know or believe in general, that there is a God, ſome ſupreme ſelf-exiſtent being, who is the author of nature, who hath given life and being unto us, and to every other creature, muſt undoubtedly yield us no ſmall pleaſure in the diſcovery, from the exerciſe and improvement of our intellectual faculties ; but can ſuggeſt to us no *nearer* a relation to him, than that of *creator* and governor of the univerſe ?'

Is it poſſible to conceive a *nearer* relation, than that of a creature to his Creator ?

In commenting on theſe words, Ἀυτη εςιν ἡ αιωνιος ζωη ἱνα γινωσκωσι σε τον μονον αληθινον Θεον, και ὁν απεςειλας Ιησουν Χριςον. John xvii. 3. Our author ſays : ' By a ſmall alteration in the punctuation, they may be thus rendered : " This is life eternal to know thee, and Jeſus Chriſt, whom thou haſt ſent, to be the only true God." Thus making them bear their teſ-

---

* Her ſolicitations may poſſibly be ſuppoſed by theſe ingenious writers to typify this propoſal of Satan : ' If thou wilt worſhip me, all ſhall be thine.'

timony

timony to the essential inherent divinity of the blessed Jesus, and his consubstantiality and co-equality with the Father. Thus was this verse understood and interpreted by some of the ancient writers of the church.'

All the writers of the three first centuries understand the text in the usual sense ; and the learned and orthodox bishops, Pearson and Bull, expressly acknowlege these words, 'the only true God,' to be meant of the Father only, by way of supreme eminence, in contradistinction to the Son, who was sent by him *.—But the point will scarcely admit any debate ; and we are surprised, that our learned author should introduce this forced and unnatural interpretation into his discourse. The reason why we ought to know Jesus Christ, is, what he himself plainly signifies, his being *sent* to make known unto us all things, which he *heard* of his Father, ch. xv. 15.

'The gospel covenant, says the author, was attended with such prodigious and astonishing operations, as fully attested its author and finisher to be God. In his own person he is described to be God, manifest in the flesh. . .What less than the Son of God manifested could so effectually destroy the works of the devil ?'

No inference in favour of our Saviour's consubstantiality and coequality with the Father, can be derived from these premises: The superintending providence of God, which is mentioned above, is able to produce the greatest effects. The learned reader will observe, that our author has here implicitly adopted that very questionable text, ' God manifested in the flesh.'

The third discourse exhibits the comparative excellency of the Christian morality.

Here we have many observations calculated to shew, how far Christianity is superior to all the discoveries of natural religion ; a point which, in general, will be readily granted. But we are sorry to see this learned writer injuring nature, for the purpose of magnifying the riches of divine grace ; and depreciating the labours of those, who have attempted to investigate the principles of natural religion. ' Many ingenious *romances*, he says, have been published in support of what the writers have been pleased to style the Religion of Nature.'

This stroke of satire is, we suppose, chiefly aimed at Wollaston : a writer, who has done honour to humanity, and an essential service to the cause of Christianity, by shewing us,

---

* Pearson on the Creed, p. 40. Bull. Def. sect. 4. cap. 1. § 2. See Clarke's Reply, p. 59.

that

that revelation and nature unite in proclaiming the fame great and effential truths of morality.

Our author himfelf acknowleges fomething to this effect, in the prefent difcourfe, when he fpeaks of the heathen philofophers : ‘ They have, he fays, defcanted nobly on thefe virtues [juftice and fortitude], and have given fuch rules concerning them, as have done honour to themfelves and to human nature. But fo far is this from detracting from the fuperior excellency of Chriftianity, that it is a confirmation of its merit. It fhews, that what our bleffed Saviour taught, is agreeable to the more exalted, rectified underftandings of men of the moft enlightened capacities; that it falls in with the powers of natural confcience, and adds new life and vigour to it.’

This, if we miftake not, is a material conceffion in favour of human reafon, but not confiftent with other paffages, where the impotency of nature is ftrongly afferted and maintained.

In the fame difcourfe, our author throws the following fevere reflection on Cicero :

‘ The firft duty, fays this great reafoner, of juftice, is, that no man hurt another, except he be provoked by an injury.—Is this a doctrine fit to be named with the Chriftian law ? Shall *he* prefume to direct us in our duty to one another, who allows us the liberty of *revenge*, when *irritated* by an injury ?

The words of Cicero are thefe : ‘ Juftitiæ primum manus eft, ut ne cui quis noceat, nifi laceffitus injuriâ.’ De Offic. lib. i. cap. 7. To juftify the foregoing reflection, our author gives an unfavourable turn to his tranflation. But the objection will difappear, if we only tranflate the paffage, more agreeably to the original, in this manner : ‘ that no man hurt another, unlefs he be injurioufly attacked ’ There is nothing in this, but what felf-defence, and the laws of every Chriftian country allow in all cafes, wherein it may be expedient to reftrain violence and outrage, to maintain private right and property, and to fecure to the honeft and peaceable the advantages of civil life. It is plain from what follows, that Cicero did not allow revenge, or any other private paffion, to take place. For, treating of injuftice, he fays : ‘ Qui injufte impetum in quempiam facit, aut irâ, aut aliquâ perturbatione incitatus, is quafi manus adferre videtur focio.’ And he adds with a noble fpirit of benevolence : ‘ Qui non defendit, nec obftitit, fi poteft, injuriæ, tam eft in vitio, quàm fi parentes, aut amicos, aut patriam deferat ’— ‘ He that injurioufly falls upon another, whether prompted

by

by rage, or other violent paffion, does, as it were, leap at the throat of his companion ; and he that refufes to help him when injured, and to ward off the wrong, if it lies in his power, is as plainly guilty of bafenefs and injuftice, as if he had deferted his father, his friends, or his native country.' Cockman's Tranfl.

If our author were to be attacked by a highwayman, and in danger of lofing his moiety of the Bampton eftate, he would think it no breach of Chriftianity to comply with Cicero's maxim, and ufe his piftol, ' ut *noceat* latroni,' in order to deter the ruffian from his purpofe, or to fhoot him.

The fourth difcourfe points out the pre-eminence of the Chriftian over the Mofaical law. The fifth contains obfervations on the time and place of Chrift's nativity, and the dignity and excellency of his perfon. The fixth is calculated to fhew, ' that difhonouring Chrift is difhonouring God.' John v. 23.

' Chrift, he fays, may be difhonoured, if his divinity be denied. This fort of difhonour is what we may prefume the apoftle chiefly aimed at in the text.'

The text has not the leaft tendency to prove the doctrine, which the author endeavours to maintain in this difcourfe, viz. our Saviour's ' unity of effence, and equality in power, glory, and dignity with the Father.' The following words, in point of argument, would have been as much to the purpofe : ' He that receiveth *you*, receiveth *me* ; and he that receiveth *me*, receiveth *him* that fent *me*.' In this paffage no unity of effence either is or can be implied ; why therefore fhould it be implied in the other ?—The lecturer however grounds the doctrine itfelf on other proofs ; among which are the following :

' Can we allow ourfelves to fuppofe, that the Saviour of mankind, who came into the world, as well to promote the honour of God, as the happinefs of men, would upon any account, and without any refervation, have " made himfelf equal with God," and pronounced, that " he and his Father are one," if he was abfolutely nothing more than a finite creature, exifting in time, and had no fuch equality with the Father, and no communication or participation of the deity with him ?'

In the fame ftrain of reafoning a papift may afk, why did our Saviour exprefsly fay, ' this is my body,' if he did not intend to affert the doctrine of tranfubftantiation ? One anfwer will ferve for both thefe queftions : men pervert the fcriptures by their falfe interpretations.

R 3   With

With refpect to the former of thefe texts, ' he made him-felf equal with God,' our author takes a calumny of the Jews for an affertion of our Lord himfelf. To their accufation of his making himfelf equal with God, our Saviour replies, not by reprefenting himfelf as coeffential with the Father, but by referring all his works to Him, and fhewing, that he really was, what he pretended to be, the promifed Meffiah, the Son of God, fent forth by him, and invefted with his power and authority : ' The fon, fays he, can do nothing of himfelf, but what he feeth the father do.' v. 19.

As to the fecond text, for which he refers us to John xvii. 22. if he had confidered the verfe with any degree of im-partiality and attention, he would have perceived, that it is no proof of the doctrine he maintains. Let the reader judge. ' The glory which thou gaveft me, I have given them, that *they* may be ἐν *one*, even as *we* are ἐν *one*.' This indifputably fhews, that the Father and the Son are one in the fame fenfe as Chriftians are one with Chrift, and with one another ; not by a union or famenefs of effence, but of affection, agreement, and defign.

The fubject of the feventh lecture is the neceffity of inward faith and outward confeffion.

Treating of herefy and fchifm he fays : ' If different fects are formed and encouraged upon principles of fpeculation and abfolute indifference, we are authorized by St. Paul to give fuch diffenfions the appellation of fchifms and herefies.'

The words heretic and fchifmatic are opprobrious appellations. Infpired apoftles, who could not be deceived in any article of the Chriftian religion, would undoubtedly apply thefe terms with ftrict propriety. But for us, who can pretend to no fuperna-tural light, nor any degree of reafon, but what our author and others have treated with *contempt*, it muft be abfolute pre-fumption to call thofe heretics, who receive the fcriptures with all poffible veneration, and only peaceably and quietly, to the beft of their judgment, explain them in a fenfe dif-ferent from ours. This is not, what fome infolently call it, ' being wife above what is written,' or denying the words of revelation ; but only a difference of fentiment, with refpect to the meaning of the facred writers, in points, wherein the greateft men have formed a variety of opinions.

In the laft fermon our author enquires into the caufes of the inefficacy of the word and faith.

The remarks, which we have here made on thefe difcourfes, have not been fuggefted by heretical pravity, or any fpirit of oppefition ; but with a fincere defire to promote the facred caufe of Chriftianity, and recommend a defence of our holy faith by arguments, which are not infignificant, and foreign from the purpofe, but pertinent and conclufive. This writer, throughout the whole feries of his lectures, appears to be a perfon of unqueftionable abilities; and has undoubtedly made a number of ufeful obfervations. But he fhould have been more cautious and critical in the felection of his arguments. He fhould have imitated the fifhermen, mentioned in the gofpel, ' who fat down, and gathered the good into veffels; but caft the bad away.'

Bibliotheca Topographica Britannica. *No II. Part I. Containing Reliquiæ* Galeanæ, *or, Mifcellaneous Pieces by the late learned Brothers* Roger *and* Samuel Gale. *4to. 2s. 6d. fewed.* Nichols.

THERE are few writers of eminence, who do not leave at their death, fome fketches of projected works, fome curious tracts, or fragments, which have never been publifhed. Thefe pieces frequently fall into the hands of carelefs or ignorant perfons, and in a fhort time perhaps are either mutilated or deftroyed. With a defign to prevent in fome degree fuch loffes as thefe, in one department of literature, British Topography, the editors of the Bibliotheca Topographica have undertaken to publifh fome valuable pieces on that fubject, now in their poffeffion; and fuch others as fhall hereafter be communicated to them, and found to contain any ufeful information.

The firft publication, which has appeared on this plan, is the Hiftory and Antiquities of Tunftal in Kent, by the late Mr. Mores; the Reliquiæ Galeanæ now before us is the fecond.

Thefe Reliques are accompanied with Memoirs of the family of Gale.

The moft celebrated perfon of this family was Dr. Thomas Gale, born at Scruton, in Yorkfhire, in 1636, mafter of St. Paul's fchool from 1672 to 1697, and afterwards dean of York, till his death, which happened at his deanery houfe, in 1702, in the 67th year of his age.

The following books, which he publifhed, are illuftrious teftimonies of his induftry and learning.

1. Opufcula Mythologica, Ethica, & Phyfica, Gr. & Lat. Cantab. 1671. 8vo.—This collection contains Palæphatus, Heraclitus, & Anonymus, de Incredibilibus; Phurnutus de Naturâ Deorum; Salluftius Phil. de Diis & Mundo; Ocellus Lucanus; Timæus Locrus de Animâ Mundi; Demophili,

R 4   De-

Democratis, & Secundi Sententiæ Morales ; Joh. Pediasimus de Muliere ; Sexti Pythagorei Sententiæ ; Theophraftus ; Pythagoreorum Fragmenta ; Heliodori Optica, This volume was reprinted at Amfterdam, in 1688. 8vo. with the addition of Eratofthenis Catafterifmi, Homeri Vita, [Heraclidis Pontici] Allegoriæ Homeri, &c.

2. Hiftoriæ Poeticæ Scriptores antiqui, Gr. & Lat. Par, 1675. 8vo. Thefe are, Apollodorus, Conon, Ptolomæus Hephæftion, Parthenius, & Antoninus Liberalis.

3. Rhetores Selecti, Demet. Phalereus, Tiberius Rhetor, Anonymus, & Severus Alexandrinus, Gr. & Lat. Oxon. 1676. 8vo.

4. Jamblichus de Myfteriis, Gr. & Lat. Oxon. 1678. 8vo.

5. Pfalterium juxta exemplar Alexandrinum, Oxon. 1678. 8vo.

6. Herodoti Opera, Lond. 1679. fol.

7. ' An edition of Cicero's works was revifed by him, Lond. 1681. 1684. 2 vol. fol.'

We are not informed upon what authority this is faid ; nor what fhare Dr. Gale took in the revifal. The preface to the edition of 1681 was written by Adam Littleton ; but Gale's name is not mentioned in it. It is included, we fuppofe, in the word *correctoribus : ' exactiffima cura in correctoribus* non defuit.' Littleton's preface is a piece of pedantic Latin.—We know of no edition in 1684.

8. Hiftoriæ Anglicanæ Scriptores quinque, Oxon. 1687. folio.

This volume contains Annales Marganenfes, Chronicon Th. Wikes, Annales Waverleienfes Hiftoria Galf. Vinefalvi, & Hiftoria Walteri de Hemingford.

9. Hiftoriæ Britannicæ Saxonicæ, Anglo-Danicæ, Scriptores quindecim. Oxon. 1691. fol.—Thefe fifteen writers are, Gildas, Eddius, Nennius, Afferius. Ran. Higden, Gul. Malmefburienfis, Anonymus Malmefb. Anonymus Ramefienfis, Anonymus Elienfis, Thomas Elyenfis, Joan. Wallingford. Rad. de Diceto, Anonymus, Joan. Fordun, and Alcwinus. To this volume is added an Appendix, containing extracts from Ptolemy's Geography, &c.

This is called by Gale the *firft* volume ; and that which contains the Quinque Scriptores, though publifhed four years before the prefent, is called the *fecond*, as the authors are of a more modern date. It has no connection, as M. Frefnoy and others have imagined, with the volume of Englifh writers compiled by Mr. William Fulman, under the patronage of bifhop Fell, in 1684.

Dr.

Dr. Gale was the author of the inscriptions on the monument, in memory of the dreadful conflagration of London, in 1666; a discourse concerning the Origin of human Literature with Philology and Philosophy, in the Phil. Transf. vol. VI. p. 2231; and a Letter concerning two Roman Altars found in Northumberland, N° 231.

He left in MS. Originis Philocalia, variis MSS. collata, emendata, & novâ versione donata; Jamblichus de vitâ Pythagoræ; Antonini Itinerarium Britanniæ; Sermons on several occasions, published by his son in 1704, and other MSS. specified in the Catalogus Manuscriptorum Angliæ & Hiberniæ, iii. p. 185.

Fabricius, in his Bibliotheca Græca, xiii. 640. has very properly distinguished this learned writer from Theophilus Gale, author of the Court of the Gentiles; but with this inaccuracy, that Theophilus is said to be the father of Thomas: whereas the former was the son of Theophilus, prebendary of Exeter, and of a different family. [Theophilus was educated at Magdalen College, Oxford; but had his inclinations biassed towards the Presbyterians and Independents; and after the Restoration was a professed dissenter, and lost his fellowship for non-conformity.]

Roger Gale, esq. the eldest son of the dean, was fellow of the Royal and Antiquarian Societies, Commissioner of Excise, &c. Though he was considered as one of the most learned men of his age, he only published the following books and tracts:

1. Antonini Iter Britanniarum, commentariis illustratum Thomæ Gale, S. T. P. &c. Lond. 1709. 4to. This work was much improved by the editor, who, in the preface, has very properly pointed out, what parts of it were his father's, and what his own.—Mr. Gough has three copies of this edition, enriched with many valuable MS. notes by Mr. Roger Gale, Nicholas Man, esq. and Dr. Ab. Francke, fellow of Trinity College, Cambridge, and rector of West Dene in Wiltshire, 1728; and a fourth with MS. various readings from the two MSS. whence H. Stephens first printed this Itinerary.

2. The Knowlege of Medals, translated from the French of M. Jobert, 1697, 1715, 8vo.

3. Registrum Honoris de Richmond, Lond. 1722. fol.

4. A Discourse on the four Roman Ways in Britain. Leland's Itin. Vol. VI.

Some other pieces of his are printed in the Philosophical Transactions, vol. xxx. xliii. Horsley's Britannia Romana, p. 332. Archæologia, vol. ii. Gent. Mag. vol. xii. p. 135. &c. He died at Scruton, in 1744, in the 72d year of his age.

age.   His MSS. and Roman coins he left by will to Trinity College, Cambridge, of which he was once fellow.

Charles Gale, the dean's second son, was rector of Scruton, [a living in the gift of the family] and died in 1738.

Samuel, the youngest of the dean's sons, was land-surveyor of the customs, and one of the revivers of the Society of Antiquaries in 1717; a man of great learning, and well versed in the antiquities of England, for which he left many valuable collections behind him; but printed nothing in his life-time, except a History of Winchester Cathedral, Lond. 1715, begun by Henry, earl of Clarendon, and continued to that year, with cuts.   His Essay on Ulphus's Horn at York is in the Archæologia, vol. i. and another on Cæsar's Passage over the Thames, in the same volume; criticised in vol. ii. p. 145.—He died in 1754, at the age of 72.

As he was a bachelor, and died intestate, administration of his effects was granted to his only sister Elizabeth; who, in 1739, became the second wife of Dr. Stukeley, and died before her husband, leaving no children.   By this incident all her brother's MSS. fell into the doctor's hands.   Since his decease, Dr. Ducarel has (by the generosity of Mrs. Fleming, Dr. Stukely's daughter by his first wife) been favoured with several of Mr. Samuel Gale's MSS. which are now, 1781, in his possession.   Among these are, Mr. Gale's History of York Cathedral in folio, often mentioned by Mr. Drake in his Eboracum, who also cites a MS. drawn up by Mr. Gale, on the city of York; a Tour through many parts of England, 1705; an Account of some Antiquities at Glastonbury, and in the Cathedrals of Salisbury, Wells, and Winton, 1711; of Sheperton, Cowey-Stakes, &c. 1748; Observations upon Kingsbury, in Middlesex, 1751; an Account of Barden, Tunbridge-Wells, &c. with a List of the Pictures at Penshurst; an Account of a Journey into Hertfordshire, Bucks, and Warwickshire, 1720; and Mr. Roger Gale's Tour into Scotland, in 1739.

These are some of the most material circumstances of the literary kind, mentioned in the memoirs now before us.

The remaining part of this publication consists of Mr. Samuel Gale's Tour above mentioned, through Oxford, Gloucester, Bristol, Bath; Salisbury, Portsmouth, the Isle of Wight, Petworth, Hampton Court, &c. which was revised by the author in 1730.

From the observations of this learned antiquary, which indeed are in general rather cursory and superficial, we shall only extract his opinion concerning the origin of Stone-henge.

‘ Some

'Some writers, he says, will have Stone-henge to be a Roman work; Inigo Jones endeavours, in his book called Stone-henge Reftored, to prove it a temple dedicated by them to the god Cælum [Cælus]; for which he alledges the order and fcheme of the building, confifting of four equilateral triangles, infcribed in a circle, with a double portico : a fcheme much ufed by the Romans. But this has been refuted.

'Mr. Aubrey is of opinion, that it was a temple of the druids, before the Romans entered Britain; that it was a monument built by the old inhabitants of the ifle; fome, that it was a monument built by the Britons in memory of their queen Boadicea; others, that it was the fepulchre of Uther Pendragon, Conftantine, Aurelius Ambrofius, and other Britifh kings; others, that it was a monument erected by Ambrofius in memory of the Britons here treacheroufly flain by the Saxons at a treaty. To this laft opinion I fhould rather adhere, being induced thereto from the name of Ambrofius ftill retained in the neighbouring town of Ambrefbury, once celebrated for its famous monaftery of 300 monks, founded here by this very Ambrofius, on condition, that they fhould pray for the fouls of thofe, that were flain by the treachery of Hengift the Saxon. I think, we have reafon to believe him the founder of the one, as well as the other; and from the rudenefs and barbarity of the ftructure, I conclude it to be a Britifh monument, the Romans always leaving indifputable marks of their grandeur, elegance, and particular genius; of any of which our Stone-henge has not the leaft refemblance : nor was ever any infcription found hereabouts, to give it a relation to thofe auguft conquerors; nor indeed could I ever find, that any of their coins were ever dug up in or near this ftructure.'

This account of the origin of Stone-henge is the fame as that which is given us by Geoffrey of Monmouth, anno 1150, who tells us, that 460 Britifh nobles, treacheroufly murdered by Hengift, when they were affembled for the purpofe of entering into a treaty with the Saxons, were buried there; and that it was alfo the fepulchre of Ambrofius himfelf[*]; but that fabulous hiftorian has added many circumftances to it, which are abfurd and ridiculous. He relates, that the ftones were originally brought from the fartheft part of Africa, and placed in Ireland by giants, who inhabited that country, forming a ftructure, which was called Chorea Gigantum, or the Giant's Dance; that they poffeffed a myftical or medicinal virtue; and were removed from Ireland to the place where they now ftand, by the art of Merlin the conjurer. Geoffrey adds, contrary to our author's opinion, that when Ambrofius vifited the place, he found ' a monaftery, which maintained

---

[*] Galf. Monumet. Hift. Brit. lib. vi. 15. lib. viii. 9—12. 16.

300 friars, situated on the mountain of Ambrius, an abbot, who is reported to have been the founder of it, long before that time: qui *olim* fundator ipsius extiterat *.' Giraldus Cambrensis, an. 1180, and Matthew of Westminster, an. 1360, gravely relate this incredible story †. Giraldus expresses himself in different words; but, as he says, ' juxta Britannicam historiam.' Matthew evidently transcribes his account from Geoffrey, placing the massacre in the year 461, and the erecting of the monument in 490. Walter of Coventry, an. 1217, likewise sets it down as authentic history. Nennius, an. 620, relates the story of the massacre; but says nothing of the monument ‡. William of Malmesbury, an. 1141, mentions the massacre §. Ranulphus Higden, an. 1350, records the story of the massacre, and the removal of the stones from Ireland to Salisbury Plain, on the faith of British history : ' secundum traditionem historiæ Britannicæ ||.' Fordun, the Scotch historian, an. 1360, takes notice of the massacre ¶. John of Tinmouth, an. 1366, calls the place Mons Ambrosii : ' Mons Ambrosii, qui nunc vulgò Stanhenges dicitur **.' Polydore Virgil, an. 1533, asserts, that it was erected, not to the memory of the British nobles, but to the honour of Ambrosius, who, according to his account, was buried there ††. John Twine (1550), a diligent and respectable antiquary, speaks of Stonehenge, as the sepulchre both of the British nobles and Ambrosius : ' In editiore loco, ex ejus nomine Mons Ambrosii dictus, sepultus est Aurelianus Ambrosius ; ubi ipse prius, Ambrosii Merlini mathematici, scientiâ fretus, ut fertur, gigantum choream, vel immensæ magnitudinis saxa, in memoriam occisorum & sepultorum ibi Britannorum procerum, erexerat ‡‡.

Camden only gives the sentiments of others, and laments, that we have no records now remaining, which might ascertain the origin of this stupendous work : ' De his non mihi subtiliùs disputandum, sed dolentiùs deplorandum, obliteratos esse tanti monumenti authores §§.'

We have here cited some of the earliest writers now extant, on the subject. Most of them, we confess, may have taken their accounts from Geoffrey of Monmouth ; and consequently their reports depend on the credit of *one* fabulous historian. Dr. Brady, in his History of England, has ob-

<hr/>

* Ibid. vi. 15. † Giraldi Topog. Hib. dist. ii. cap. 18. Matt. West. sub. an. 461, 490. ‡ Nennii Hist. Brit. cap. 48. § W. Malmesb. lib. i. cap. 1. || Ran. Higd. Polychr. lib. v. ¶ Forduni Scot. Hist. lib. iii. cap. 15. ** In Vitâ Dubricii. †† Polyd. Verg. Angl. Hist. lib. iii. ‡‡ Twinus de Reb. Alb. lib. ii. p. 117. §§ Camd. Brit. p. 220. ed. 1600.

ferved, that the story of the maffacre ' feems to have been taken out of Witichindus, and applied to the Britons, where the fame things are fpoken verbatim of the Saxons and Thuringians.' But this is an unreafonable cenfure. The fame piece of hiftory is in Nennius : and therefore Witichindus † was not the original author ; nor Geoffrey the perverter of it. For Nennius wrote about the year 620 ; and the monk of Corbey, above three hundred years afterwards, an. 950.

Though Geoffrey of Monmouth and Giraldus Cambrenfis have related the ftory with the fame ridiculous circumftances, yet it does not appear, that the latter has copied the former. Their expreffions on this occafion are very different. We may therefore confider Giraldus as a collateral evidence in favour of Geoffrey : more efpecially as he was his contemporary, and not in the leaft inclined to adopt his affertion ‡.

Every reader, without doubt, muft at once explode the fable of the giants ; but from the concurrent teftimonies of fo many early writers, and others which might be added, we may reafonably conclude, that the ftory of the maffacre is not without fome foundation. Nennius relates it circumftantially ; telling us, that three hundred Britons were put to death : ' Omnes feniores ccc. Guortigerni regis funt jugulati.' This is the beft authority we have ; as Nennius is fuppofed to have lived within a hundred and twenty years after the faét. There is nothing this kind, for obvious reafons, in the Saxon annals.

As to the ftruéture being the fepulchre of the Britifh nobles, Ambrofius, and others, we can only fay, that it is not improbable ; and that the teftimony of the Britifh hiftory is, in *fome* degree, corroborated by the name of Ambrefbury : quafi Ambrofii vicus. We may add, that the probability is increafed by the agreement of Geofrey of Monmouth, Giraldus, and others, and by our not having the leaft authority, on the other hand, for fuppofing it to have been a druidical temple, much lefs a Roman fabric.

Camden fays, ' Certè offa humana hic fæpiùs effoffa fuerunt.' · Perhaps fome opulent antiquary may hereafter undertake to examine the ground more effeétually ; and we can only wifh, that the mattock and the fpade may procure him that fatisfaétion, which the Britifh hiftorians cannot give.

---

† Witichindi Annales, lib. i. p. 2. Inter Rer. Germ. Script. à Meibomio editos. tom. iii. p. 158.
‡ Vid. Giraldi Camb. Defc. cap. 7.

The

The Constitution of England, *or an Account of the* English *Government ; in which it is compared with the Republican Form of Government, and occasionally with the other Monarchies in* Europe. *By* J. L. de Lolme, *Advocate, Citizen of* Geneva. *The Third Edition.* 8vo. 6s. *boards.* Robinson.

THE merit of this work is already so well known to the public, that we shall decline any farther recommendation of it in our Review ; where it has, on former occasions, been twice the subject of our approbation. The work is now enlarged by the addition of four chapters ; two of which relate to the law in respect of civil matters, and to the courts of equity ; one contains thoughts on the attempts that may at particular times be made to abridge the power of the crown, and on some of the dangers by which such attempts may be attended. The fourth additional chapter comprises farther thoughts on the right of taxation, lodged in the hands of the representatives of the people ; with an account of the danger to which this right may be exposed.

Mr. De Lolme gives, we think, a more just and precise account of the nature of the courts of equity than is to be found in any other writer on the English constitution.

' The generality of people, says he, misled by this word *equity,* have conceived false notions of the office of the courts we mention ; and it seems to be generally thought that the judges who sit in them, are only to follow the rules of natural equity ; by which people appear to understand, that in a court of equity, the judge may follow the dictates of his private feelings, and ground his decisions on the peculiar circumstances and situation of those persons who make their appearance before him. Nay, Dr. Johnson, in his abridged Dictionary, gives the following definition of the power of the Court of Chancery considered as a court of equity : " The chancellor hath power to moderate and temper the written law, and subjecteth himself only to the law of nature and conscience :" for which definition dean Swift, and Cowell, who was a lawyer, are quoted as authorities. Other instances might be produced of lawyers who have been inaccurate in their definitions of the true office of the judges of equity. And the above named doctor himself is on no subject a despicable authority.

' Certainly the power of the judges of equity cannot be to alter, by their own private power, the written law, that is, acts of parliament, and thus to control the legislature. Their office only consists, as will be proved in the sequel, in providing remedies for those cases, for which the public good requires that remedies should be provided, and in regard to which the courts of common law, shackled by their original forms and institutions,

tions, cannot procure any;—or in other words—the courts of equity have a power to administer justice to individuals, unrestrained, not by the law, but by the professional law difficulties which lawyers have from time to time contrived in the courts of common law, and to which the judges of those courts have given their sanction.'

Mr. De Lolme has formerly shewn, it is to the indivisibility of the governing authority in England, that the community of interest which takes place among all orders of men, and consequently the superior liberty the people enjoy, are owing; and respecting the truth of this observation, he produces many convincing arguments, in the chapter on the attempts towards abridging the power of the crown.

We shall present our readers with the following passage from the chapter on taxation.

' But here a most important observation is to be made; and I entreat the reader's attention to the subject. This right of granting subsidies to the crown, can only be effectual when it is exercised by one assembly alone. When several distinct assemblies have it equally in their power to supply the wants of the prince, the case becomes totally altered. The competition which so easily takes place between those different bodies, and even the bare consciousness which each entertains of its inability to hinder the measures of the sovereign, render it impossible for them to make any effectual constitutional use of their privilege. " Those different parliaments or estates (to repeat the observation introduced in the former part of this work) having no means of recommending themselves to their sovereign, but their superior readiness in complying with his demands, vie with each other in granting what it would not only be fruitless, but even dangerous to refuse. And the king, on the other hand, soon comes to demand as a tribute, a gift which he is confident to obtain." In short, it may be laid down as a maxim, that when a sovereign is made to depend, in regard to his supplies, on more assemblies than one, he, in fact, depends upon none. And indeed the king of France is not independent on his people for his necessary supplies, any otherwise than by drawing the same from several different assemblies of their representatives; the latter have in appearance a right to refuse all his demands; and as the English call the grants they make to their kings, aids or subsidies, so do the estates of the French provinces call their's, *dons gratuits*, or free gifts.

' What is it, therefore, that constitutes the difference between the political situation of the French and English nations, since their rights thus seem to be the same? The difference lies in this, that there has never been in England more than one assembly that could supply the wants of the sovereign. This has always
kept

kept him in a state, not of a seeming, but of a real dependence on the representatives of the people for his necessary supplies; and how low soever the liberty of the subject may, at particular times, have sunk, they have always found themselves possessed of a most effectual means of restoring it, whenever they have thought proper so to do. Under Henry the Eighth, for instance, we find the despotism of the crown to have been carried to an astonishing height; it was even enacted that the proclamations of the king should have the force of law; a thing which even in France, never was so expressly declared: yet no sooner did the nation recover from its long state of supineness, than the exorbitant power of the crown was reduced within its constitutional bounds.

' To no other cause than the disadvantage of their situation, are we to ascribe the low condition in which the deputies of the people in the assembly called the general estates of France, were always forced to remain.

' Surrounded as they were by the particular estates of those provinces into which the kingdom had been formerly divided, they never were able to stipulate conditions with their sovereign; and instead of making their right of granting subsidies to the crown serve to gain them in the end a share in legislation, they ever remained confined to the naked privilege of " humble supplication and remonstrance."

' Those estates, however, as all the great lords in France were admitted into them, began at length to appear dangerous; and as the king could in the mean time do without their assistance, they were set aside. But several of the particular estates of the provinces are preserved to this day: some, which for temporary reasons had been abolished, have been restored: nay, so manageable have popular assemblies been found by the crown, when it has to do with many, that the kind of government we mention is that which it has been found most convenient to assign to Corsica; and Corsica has been made un pays d'etats.

' That the crown in England should, on a sudden, render itself independent on the commons for its supplies, that is, should on a sudden successfully assume to itself a right to lay taxes on the subjects, by its own authority, is not certainly an event in any degree likely to take place, nor indeed that should raise any kind of political fear. But it is not equally impracticable, that the right of the representatives of the people might become invalidated, by being divided in the manner that has just been described.

' Such a division of the right of the people might be effected several different ways. National calamities for instance, unfortunate foreign wars, attended with loss of public credit, might suggest methods for raising the necessary supplies, different from those which have hitherto been used. Dividing the kingdom into a certain number of parts, which should severally vote subsidies to the crown, or even distinct assessments made by the dif-

4

ferent

ferent counties into which England is now divided, might, in the circumftances we fuppofe, be looked upon as adviteable expedients; and thefe, being once introduced, might be continued afterwards.

' Another divifion of the right of the people, much more likely to take place than thofe juft mentioned, might be fuch as might arife from acquifitions of foreign dominions, the inhabitants of which fhould in time claim and obtain a right to treat directly with the crown, and grant fupplies to it, without the interference of the Britifh legiflature.

' Should any colonies acquire the right we mention—fhould, for inftance, the American colonies have acquired it, as they claimed it, it is not to be doubted that the confequences that have refulted from a divifion like that we mention in moft of the king-doms of Europe, would alfo have taken place in the Britifh dominions, and that that fpirit of competition which has been above defcribed, would in time have manifefted itfelf between the different colonies. This defire of ingratiating themfelves with the crown, by means of the privilege of granting fupplies to it, has even been openly confeffed by an agent of the American colonies, when, on his being examined by the houfe of commons, in the year 1766, he faid, "the granting aids to the crown, is the only means the Americans have of recommending themfelves to their fovereign." And the events that have of late years taken place in America, render it evident that the colonies would not have fcrupled going any lengths to obtain favourable conditions at the expence of Britain and the Britifh legiflature.

' That a fimilar fpirit of competition might be raifed in Ireland, is alfo fufficiently plain from certain late events. And fhould the American colonies have obtained their demands, and at the fame time fhould Ireland and America have increafed in wealth to a certain degree, the time might have come, at which the crown might have governed England with the fupplies of Ireland and America—Ireland with the fupplies of England and of the American colonies—and the American colonies with the money of each other, and of England and Ireland.'

It may be obferved, in general, of this fenfible writer, that he has inveftigated the Englifh conftitution with great difcernment; that his obfervations are drawn from a knowlege of human nature, confirmed by the evidence of hiftory; and that his political fpeculations, at the fame time that they are ingenious, are intimately connected with the fundamental principles of government.

Illuf-

Illustrations of Euripides, *on the* Ion *and the* Bacchæ. *By* Richard Paul Jodrell, *Esq.* F. R. S. 2 *Vols.* 8*vo.* 10*s.* 6*d.* *boards.* Dodsley.

CRITICAL knowlege, particularly that portion of it which is exerted on the illustration of ancient authors, has been of late years much out of fashion : what is useful has been laid aside, by modern readers, for what is agreeable ; and instruction neglected to make room for entertainment. We are happy to find, that there is a probability of its being revived ; and that there are yet, in the decline of British literature, men of taste, genius, and learning, who think their time well employed in the study and elucidation of the best classic writers of antiquity. Mr. Jodrell, the author of the work now before us, seems, if we may judge from this specimen of his abilities, to be a gentleman of profound erudition and extensive reading, a cool and penetrating judgment, with a sufficient degree of acumen and sagacity, to make his opinions respectable. What the reader may expect from this performance, will best appear from the author's own words, in his preface, where he informs us that,

' The contemplation of a Grecian drama under every point of view constitutes the design of these Illustrations. The preliminary essay discusses the history, mythology, laws, and customs, on which the fable is founded, and is intended to prepare the mind of the reader by connecting several observations, which would obtrude on his attention with more inconvenience, if they were separately dispersed The intermediate notes arise from the passage, to which they refer in the original and English translation by substituting the different texts, and are consequently very miscellaneous in the several objects of their critical enquiry. As the author was not limited in the narrow boundary of an editor's or translator's page, he has often indulged himself with the full investigation of the subject, when the nature of it has been interesting enough, or the materials sufficiently copious to require it. The final essay contains an analysis of the several beauties and defects of the drama, considered under the constituent parts of its plot, characters, sentiments, and language : it traces the delicate connexion of the choral odes, that important and beautiful part of an ancient tragedy, and illustrates the history of the Grecian theatre in a new and comprehensive mode of criticism : it also extends its inquiry to the more modern plays on the same subject, which have been represented on the Roman, Italian, French, and English stages. The few annotations, which follow this final essay, are only calculated for the attentive reader of the original, as they chiefly relate to the Greek text, and therefore

therefore the tranflation of the lines, to which they refer, has been omitted.'

The promife here given of what he meant to do, Mr. Jodrell has, in the fubfequent work, moft faithfully and diligently performed. In his elucidation of obfcure paffages, he has taken infinite pains in collecting and laying before his readers the opinions and conjectures of all the commentators, ranfacked the old fcholiafts, and produced fimilar expreffions from a variety of ancient writers; nothing indeed efcapes him, that can tend to the illuftration of his favourite author.——From the following note on a fingle word, our readers will be able to form fome idea of Mr. Jodrell's critical judgment, and extenfive reading, which is taken from the 35th page of his annotations on the Ion.

‘ Verfe 82. Τ.θρίππων
      96. Chariot of the fun.

‘ The original expreffion here implies the quadriga, or chariot of the fun, drawn by four horfes: and all the poets, painters, and fculprors, both ancient and modern, have almoft univerfally beftowed this compliment on Apollo. The Scholiaft on our author's Phoeniffæ has given the Greek names of thefe four fteeds, which tranflated into Englifh imply, Time, Splendour, Lightning, Thunder; but Ovid in his ftory of Phaeton, though he derives the etymology of them from the Greek language, correfponds in one inftance only of thefe four names with this Scholiaft,

     “ Intereà volucres Pyroeis, et Eous et Æthon,
       Solis equi, quartufque Phlegon.”

                         (Met. l. II. v. 154.)

‘ There are other names affigned to thefe horfes of the fun by Fulgentius, who thus explains the propriety of them; Erythræus, or red, becaufe the fun rifes with red ftreaks at the morning dawn; Actæon, or fplendent, becaufe about the third hour he fhines with a greater degree of refulgence; Lampos, or glowing, becaufe at the meridian he has afcended the central circle; and Philogeus, or the lover of the earth, becaufe about the ninth hour, verging towards the weft, he leans on the declivity: and the reafon of the fun's quadriga is thus explained by him, either becaufe he performs the annual revolution by the divifion of the four feafons, or becaufe he meafures the fpace of the day in a path, which may be divided into four parts quadrifido limite: the only inftance in any record of antiquity, which I ever met to the contrary, is an affertion of the Scholiaft of Sophocles on the Ajax on the word λευκοπωλω; who there remarks, that the fun has two white horfes for his car, Lampos and Phaeton: but the paffage to which the Scholiaft there alludes (though he does not

mention

mention it) will ferve to correct his error. For Homer in his 23d Odyffey mentions the chariot of Ἦως, or Aurora, as drawn by two horfes, correfponding to thefe names of Lampos and Phaeton : thefe by miftake he has transferred to the Sun, who in poetical mythology is a diftinct perfonage from Aurora ; and though this goddefs is fometimes honoured with the chariot of the god Apollo, as in Virgil,

> " Auroram Phaetontis equi jam luce vehebant."
>   (Æn. 5. v. 105.)

And fometimes has a quadriga of her own, as in the fame Roman poet,

> " Rofeis Aurora quadrigis,"   (Æn. 6. v. 353.)

Yet fhe has oftener perhaps the humbler biga, or the car, drawn by two horfes, as in Homer. Thus to give an inftance from the fame refpectable authority,

> " Aurora in rofeis fulgebat lutea bigis."   (Æn. 7. v. 26.)

And Tzetzes, in his commentary upon Lycophron, citing Homer, exprefsly calls Lampos and Phaeton the horfes of the day, Ἡμέρας. The biga was alfo the lefs afpiring equipage of fober Night, as I fhall fhew in a fubfequent note of this play. Befides this miftake of the Scholiaft of Sophocles, there is a remarkable exception to the eftablifhed opinion of the fun's quadriga, which Montfaucon has inferted in his Antiquité Expliquée from Maffei, where the chariot of this god, from which Phaeton has juft tumbled, has only two horfes ; quoique tous les anciens (as the author juftly obferves) en affignent quatre au Soleil, & deux feulement à la Lune, comme dit Tertullien dans fon livre des fpectacles. The moderns, as well as the ancients, have in general been attentive to this circumftance : thus Apollo in the celebrated picture by Guido Rheni, in the Palazzo di Rofpigliofi at Rome, has his chariot drawn by four horfes, and is improperly called the Aurora. But the author of the Polymetis, obferving the defects of Rubens in mifreprefenting the allegorical perfons of the ancients, very judicioufly remarks, " Such I fhould take the mean ftaring Apollo to be in a chariot drawn by two horfes." (Dial. 18. p. 296.)'

From this quotation it appears, that Mr. Jodrell is indefatigable in his refearches ; and that he has carefully confulted every book and manufcript that could give him the leaft hint concerning his fubject.—In the note immediately fubfequent to the above, the reader, whofe curiofity may lead him to the inveftigation of that long-contefted point, the finging of fwans, fo frequently mentioned by the ancient writers, will find a full difcuffion of it, with all the arguments and proofs on both fides of the queftion. The beft, however, and moft entertaining parts of this performance,

ance, are the *preliminary* and *final* essays; the former giving a distinct and accurate account of the fable on which each tragedy is founded, and a complete history of all the persons concerned, together with a description of the scene of action, and the mythology, laws, and customs occasionally alluded to; the latter, containing a regular criticism on the tragedy, the plot, characters, sentiments, &c. Both of these are extremely useful and necessary to all who are desirous of being intimately acquainted with the ancient drama. The *final essays* are the most amusing; from one of which we shall therefore extract a few pages, for the entertainment of our readers, sufficient to convince them, that this author's taste and judgment, with regard to the beauties and faults of the Grecian tragedies, are not less to be admired than his knowlege and learning. Instead of blindly idolizing his darling poet, as modern translators and commentators are apt to do, he makes such judicious objections to the defective plots of his author as reason and good sense naturally suggest; and censures Euripides for his absurd conduct, in the following remarks on some parts of the Ion.

'Euripides, says he, has introduced an innovation, and opened the prologus of his plays with a dramatic character who informed the theatre of the history of the plot,'—'who, not contented with conveying the previous intelligence of the facts prior to the supposed commencement of the play, anticipates also the important events contrived within it; such as the design of Apollo to impose his own son on Xuthus; and Creusa's discovery of Ion, as her illegitimate offspring from the embrace of the god; nor is there a single circumstance related by him, which is not in the sequel of the drama revealed with greater propriety: this innovation therefore of Euripides must be confessed to be so far from an improvement, that in reality it becomes a very essential disadvantage: the curiosity of the spectator from this immediate information naturally relaxes its animating vigour: and the passions, which the duty and interest of every dramatic author require him to suspend, lose a considerable portion of their invigorating influence: hence instead of the sudden pleasure, bursting from the incidents gradually unfolded, the mind feels an effort of a less active nature:

" Primus at ille labor versu tenuisse legentem
  Suspensum, incertumque diu, qui denique rerum
  Eventus maneant." (Vida de Arte Poetica, l. 2. v. 100.)

" As yet unfold the event on no pretence,
"'Tis your chief task to keep us in suspence."
                                Pitt's Vida's Art of Poetry. B. 2.

S 3

' The

' The next objection to the plot is of a nature more important : this is the anticipation by Creufa of the difcovery of her fecret connexion with Apollo in the middle of the play to the Chorus and the Tutor ; which occafions a repetition of it in the cataftrophe, to which it ought to have been referved, when her fituation would naturally have extorted the delicate confeffion in the moment of parental tranfport for the fortunate recovery of her loft infant : neceffity would then have obliged her to reveal, what inclination alone does now ; and fhe might have been excited without this difcovery to poifon Ion, whom fhe then imagined to be the fpurious fon of her hufband Xuthus, either from a principle of difappointed private revenge, or of barbarous policy, to prevent the ufurpation of her hereditary throne by a ftranger : the management therefore of the poet appears to me in this refpect inartificial ; and, if we confider it philofophically, perhaps unnatural : the decorum of female modefty is violated ; for would any woman in the fituation of Creufa thus voluntarily proclaim her own difgrace ? Would fhe, in defiance of the moft delicate fentiment of the female mind, facrifice her own reputation, becaufe fhe apprehended the ingratitude of her lover and her hufband ? What remains after this, but to exclaim in the words of Medea in Apollonius,

   " 'Ερρέτω αἰδώς,
'Ερρέτω ἀγλαΐη." (Argon. l. 3. v. 785.)
   Now farewell fhame,
 Farewell renown.

How charmingly, on the contrary, has Ovid painted the exceffive reluctance of the chafte and dying Lucretia to reveal even to her father and to her hufband the audacious act of Tarquin ; as it revolted fo violently againft the innate modefty of her fex :

  " Ter conata loqui, ter deftitit ; aufaque quartò
   Non oculos adeò fuftulit illa fuos ;
  Hoc quoque Tarquinio debebimus ? eloquar, inquit,
   Eloquar infelix dedecus ipfa meum :
  Quàque poteft, narrat ; reftabant ultima ; flevit,
   Et matronales erubuere genæ." (Faft. l. 2. v. 824.)

' The next defect in the plot, which I fhall mention, is the prolix narrative of the domeftic of Creufa to the Chorus in the interefting moment, when he informs them of the difcovery of the poifon at the banquet : as accomplices in the crime of their royal miftrefs, they naturally expect to be involved in the fame punifhment, which threatens to be of the moft formidable nature : the account therefore, inftead of containing no lefs than 106 lines, ought to have been concife, and adapted to the anxiety of the hearers in this alarming interval of horror : how extremely unnatural is it to torture the Chorus with an impertinent defcription of the tent, the figures of the Delphic tapeftry, and the ceremonies of the banquet, while their minds muft have been
              agitated

agitated in this state of uncertainty! The poet has here suffered his imagination to wanton in luxuriance at the expence of dramatic propriety; and the whole passage may be confidered as a fair illustration of the beautiful cypress of Horace, elegantly designed, when the real object to be painted is a shipwreck:

    " Sed nunc non erat his locus, et fortasse cupressum
    Scis simulare; quid hoc, si fractis enatat exspes
    Navibus, ære dato qui pingitur?" (De Art. Poet. v. 21.)

' This purple shred therefore must be condemned, as a rich but affected ornament misplaced, and though it dazzles the eye, it revolts against the judgment. The last objection to the plot, which I shall mention, is that of the machinery of Minerva in the catastrophe of the piece: it is evident, says Aristotle, " that the unravelling of the fable ought to happen from the subject itself, and not by the use of machinery, as in the Medea: but the machinery, if used, should relate to things out of the drama itself, either to such past events, which it is impossible for man to know, or to those in future, which require prediction and explanation; for we admit, that the gods can difcern all things:" Hence we may collect, that Aristotle disapproved in general of machinery in the drama; but, if there introduced, he limits it to particular objects and circumstances: if the introduction of Mercury in the Prologus be measured by this standard of criticism, it must immediately be condemned, as defenceless; but this of Minerva in the catastrophe will be found to contain all those circumstances prescribed by Aristotle and Horace;

    " Nec deus interfit, nisi dignus vindice nodus
    Inciderit."   (De Art. Poet. v. 192.)

For the goddess reveals to Ion the connexion of Apollo with Creusa, palliates the reponse of the oracle, declares the resolution of the god to disclose the truth hereafter at Athens, and foretells the future glory of Ion and his descendents in Asia and Europe. " There are but four pieces in Euripides, says Dacier, where the presence of gods is conducted with any regard to this rule of Aristotle: those are the Iphigenia in Tauris, the Helena, the Ion, and the Electra: and yet I am persuaded that in those very pieces Euripides could have discovered in his art other means of dispensing with these machines." These are the principal defects, which appear to me in the conduct of the plot; but with all its imperfections it has many beauties to counterbalance them.'

Mr. Jodrell then enters into a description of the several characters of the play, and executes it with an equal degree of taste and judgment. He considers the songs of the chorus, and determines impartially on the propriety and impropriety of them.—The style of these volumes is, in general, agreeable and perspicuous. When a writer is complete master of

his

his subject, he will always deliver himself with ease and propriety.

—— et vox et verba sequuntur.

It is observable of this work, that two volumes of illustrations are employed on two plays only of Euripides; if the author proceed, and as much criticism be exhausted on every tragedy, it will become very voluminous. This ingenious critic, notwithstanding, has promised, in his preface, to pursue his plan of dramatic enquiry on the other plays, if he should be flattered by any success in the present publication. We can, on our part, assure him, that if he continue his observations with the same spirit and assiduity, we shall be happy to peruse them; in the mean time, these volumes will, we doubt not, be considered as a valuable acquisition to the world of literature, and more especially in the two universities, where classical knowlege is still, we hope, held in some esteem, and to whom our warmest recommendation will be totally unnecessary.

Select Odes of Pindar *and* Horace *translated; and other Original*
Poems: together with Notes, critical, historical, and expla-
natory. By the Rev. William Tasker, *A. B. Vol. I. 8vo.*
7s. 6d Dodsley.

AS this work has been long since published, and no notice of it taken by us, it may be necessary to make some apology for our neglect, which we can, with great truth, assure the ingenuous author, did not arise from any contempt of his performance. The true and only cause was, that we have been in constant expectation of the succeeding volumes promised in the title-page; as we would always wish rather to review the whole of any work at once, than to give our opinion, at different times, of detached parts. Mr. Tasker, however, having probably, for reasons best known to himself, laid aside his intention of publishing the other volumes, we shall proceed to the consideration of this, which is not without a considerable share of poetical merit. A translation of Pindar and Horace's Odes, especially of those which this author has selected, was an arduous task; the best of Pindar's, as he very properly observes in his prefatory essay, had already been *picked out* by Mr. West. Mr. Tasker has, consequently, been confined to the most inconsiderable and inferior compositions of a most unequal poet; add to this that, as he farther remarks:

4

• One

' One part even of the literati are prejudiced against Pindar's odes, as flighty and incoherent compositions ; and that the other part are such enthusiastic admirers of them, that they look upon these poems as something more than human ; and consequently will be disappointed in any translation ; besides, that the Olympic and other sacred games, which were held in such high veneration throughout all Greece, lose their dignity with the English reader.'

With all these and many other disadvantages, Mr. Tasker, has contested ; and, with a spirit that does him honour, given us an harmonious and animated version of several odes, which we do not recollect were ever before so well translated.—From these, we shall select part of the 8th Nemean, inscribed to Deinias, on his victory in the foot-race.

'S T R O P H E I.

' O beauty ! herald of the queen of love,
(Whose sweets ambrosial, mortals prove)
    Thron'd on the youth's or virgin's eye,
'Tis you announce th' approaching extasy ;
    Your influence ruleth unconfin'd,
        While your capricious mind
Is now to one, now to another kind.
    O goddess of the human heart !
    To merit's claim thy power impart,
    And grant throughout thy wide domain,
That virtuous youths who love, may never love in vain.

'A N T I S T R O P H E I.

' When thundering Jove Ægina wed,
The loves thus crown'd the nuptial bed ;
From whose celestial warm embrace
Budded the honour of his race
Ænone's king, renown'd in fight,
The rising glory of his age,
In action bold, in council sage,
And of desiring eyes all lovely to the sight.
'Each neighbouring hero, honour's flower,
Uniting own'd the monarch's power,
    The various chieftains glad obey,
And court the scepter of his righteous sway ;

E P O D E I.

The kings, who led their peaceful flocks
O'er Athens, and her craggy rocks,
Or where old Pelops' sons maintain
O'er hardy Sparta their extensive reign.

O righteous

O righteous judge ! great Æacus ! attend,
  To thee the humble knee I bend,
  The Lydian mitre in my hand,
  Whose sacred borders all around,
Embroider'd are with music's variegated sound ;
  Regard thy native land,
  For thy Ægina, city fair,
And her great citizens, I offer up the prayer ;
  And ample thanks prefer to thee
  For Deinias' late victory ;
When rivalling his sire, the vigorous son
In Nemea's double course, the prize of swiftness won.

STROPHE II.

  The happiness the gods implant,
  A lasting root shall never want :
  Such as old Cinyras possest,
  In Cyprus' isle, with riches blest.
I stop my rapid foot in glory's dubious course
  And draw new breath, to gain fresh force.
  O Cinyras ! a doubtful name
  Nor yet establish'd in the list of fame ;
  In various strains bards sing of thee,
  What worth from envy e'er was free ?
  Consistent with the wiser few
  For me to sing thy praise anew,
And try thy virtues by the test of truth,
Were but to lay up food for envy's carping tooth :
  Envy which spares th'ignoble croud,
While at transcendent worth she ever rails aloud.

ANTISTROPHE II.

  The master of the seven-fold shield,
  Great Ajax self, was forc'd to yield
  To envy's power ; by her oppress'd
He plung'd his conquering sword in his heroic breast ;
  (Such is th' oblivious fate decreed
  To warrior-chiefs, who cannot plead !)
  What time Laertes' wily son
  The Græcian votes clandestine won,
  The hero of unconquer'd hand and heart
  A victim fell to Ulyssean art ;
Robb'd of Achilles' golden arms resign'd his breath,
And quench'd his mighty rage, wrestling with mightier death.

'EPODE II.

  But far more potent in th' imbattled field
  The Telamonian spear and shield
  Mingled the living with the dead,
  While orator Ulysses fled ;

Or when they fought upon the plain,
Round great Achilles newly-slain,
Or in what other martial strife
The heroes hazarded their life :
But subtle rhet'ric's specious flowers,
Artfully strew'd in ancient hours,
Bore down and swallow'd sober sense
In the full vortex of strong eloquence :
Such power the gods to eloquence decreed,
To sink the glorious act, and raise th' ignoble deed !

S T R O P H E   III.

A different custom far be mine,
Confirm my wish, O Jove divine !
Do thou approve my flowing lays,
While they ne'er sink to venal praise :
Grant me an humble life to lead,
In virtue's simple path to tread ;
When Pindar's bones are laid in earth,
Let no son blush to own his birth,
From him deriv'd—nor pine that others hold
Vast tracts of land, and mines of richest gold ;
Some distant offspring may inherit
Pindar's sole heritage, poetic spirit,
Who, warm with Phœbus' heavenly fire
In honour's cause attun'd his lyre,
Pursu'd th' example of the candid few,
To praise, where praise ; and blame, where blame was due.'

This, as our readers will easily perceive, is a faithful and not inelegant translation ; neither servilely close, nor too loosely paraphrased. One line of it is, however, for want of proper explanation, almost unintelligible to the mere English reader, though it adheres strictly to the original ; that we mean, where Mr. Tasker has rendered the words μιτραν καναχηδα πε-ποικελμεναν mitram sonore variatam by *the mitre embroidered with music's variated sound*; the *embroidery* of *sound* is certainly an unwarrantable expression, which even the *licentia Pindarica* can hardly excuse.

To the translation of Pindar, Mr. Tasker has subjoined some explanatory notes, which illustrate the original, and which shew him to be a man of learning and taste.——We are sorry to hear that, as he informs us in his preface, he is a *sequestrated* rector ; and that this work was executed under complicated distress, embarrassment, and perplexity. When men of genius and abilities languish in penury, and are perpetually struggling with misfortunes, it is a reproach to the rich and great. We sincerely wish it were in our power, by any thing which we could say in his favour, to be the means of removing every obstruction to his happiness, or to the free exertion of his talents.

A complete Collection of the Medical and Philosophical Works of John Fothergill, *M. D. F. R. S. and S. A. With an Account of his Life ; and Occasional Notes ; by* John Elliot, *M. D.* 8vo. 7s. 6d. boards. Walker.

DR. Fothergill being so well known as a judicious and experienced physician, a collection of his medical works, which lay scattered in numerous publications, cannot fail of proving highly acceptable to all who are more immediately interested in the improvements of that science. The ingenious editor of this volume, therefore, for the pains he has taken in searching for so many useful but detached materials, merits the thanks of every gentleman of the profession ; and he is farther entitled to their acknowledgments, for the account which he has so distinctly delivered of Dr. Fothergill's life.

From those biographical memoirs, we find that Dr. Fothergill was born in 1712, in the neighbourhood of Richmond, in Yorkshire. Having served an apprenticeship to an apothecary named Barclay, who then resided at Bradford, he went to the university of Edinburgh, where he took the degree of Doctor of Physic, in 1736. Passing thence to the continent, he made a short stay at Leyden ; and after visiting Aix-la-Chapelle, and Spa, returned to England, and, about the year 1740, fixed his residence at London.

The following anecdote mentioned by the biographer, is worthy of being kept in remembrance.

‘ A friend of his, a man of a worthy character, who has at this time an income of about one hundred pounds a-year church preferment, was, in the earlier part of his life, seated in London upon a curacy of fifty pounds per annum, with a wife and a numerous family. An epidemical disease, which was at that time prevalent, seized upon his wife and five of his children : in this scene of distress he looked up to the doctor for his assistance, but dared not apply to him, from a consciousness of his being unable to reward him for his attendance. A friend, who knew his situation, kindly offered to accompany him to the doctor, and give him his fee. They took the advantage of his hour of audience, and after a description of the several cases, the fee was offered, and rejected ; but a note was taken of his place of residence. The doctor called assiduously the next and every succeeding day, till his attendance was no longer necessary. The curate, anxious to return some grateful mark of the sense he entertained of his services, strained every nerve to accomplish it ; but his astonishment was not to be described, when, instead of receiving the money he offered, with apologies for his situation, the doctor put ten guineas into his hand, desiring him to apply to him without diffidence in future difficulties.’

Dr.

Dr. Fothergill's liberality is farther evinced by his behaviour in the contest between the Fellows and Licentiates of the College of Physicians; during which he is said to have subscribed five hundred pounds towards bringing it to a legal decision. He also greatly contributed to the establishment of a charitable institution at Ackworth in Yorkshire.

Of the cause of his death, his legacies, person, and character, Dr. Elliot gives the following account.

'Those who have been most successful in imparting health to others, are not always equally fortunate in their applications to themselves. The temperance and regularity of Dr. Fothergill might seem to promise a long life, free from the miseries of disease. He had not, however, that happiness. About two years before his death, he had been afflicted with a disorder which he apprehended, though without foundation, to be an irregular gout. It terminated in a suppression of urine, from which he obtained a temporary relief; but it returned again with greater violence, and, notwithstanding every effort of the medical gentleman who attended him, put a period to his existence on the 26th day of December 1780, in the 69th year of his age. On dissection, the disease appeared to have been occasioned by a schirrous enlargement of the prostate, which compressed the neck of the bladder so as to prevent the introduction of a catheter. His remains were, on the 5th of January following, deposited in the burial-ground at Winchmore-Hill, being attended by more than seventy coaches and post-chaises filled with Friends, who seized this last occasion to pay a tribute of respect to the memory of the deceased.

' Dying a batchelor, he devised the bulk of his fortune to a maiden sister, who resided with him for many years before his death. He likewise bequeathed handsome legacies to his other relations and friends. His library, which consisted of an excellent collection of books in physic and natural history, particularly the latter, has lately been sold by auction; and Dr. Hunter has purchased his collection of shells and corals of his executors for 1200l. our author, by his will, having given directions that it should be appraised after his death, and that Dr. Hunter should have the refusal of it at five hundred pounds under the valuation.

' The person of Dr. Fothergill (says Dr. Hird) was of a delicate, rather of an extenuated make. His features were all character. His eye had a peculiar brilliancy of expression; yet it was not easy so to mark the leading trait, as to disengage it from the united whole. He was remarkably active and alert, and, with a few exceptions, enjoyed a general good state of health.

' His dress was remarkably neat, plain, and decent, peculiarly becoming himself; a perfect transcript of the order, and, I may add, of the neatness of his mind. He thought it un-

worthy

worthy a man of fenfe, and inconfiftent with his character, to fuffer himfelf to be led by the whim of fafhion, and become the flave of its caprices.

' At his meals he was remarkably temperate ; in the opinion of fome, rather too abftemious, eating fparingly, but with a good relifh, and rarely exceeding two glaffes of wine at dinner or fupper ; yet, by this uniform and fteady temperance, he preferved his mind vigorous and active, and his conftitution equal to all his engagements.

' The character of Dr. Fothergill will receive no injury, confidered either as a profeffional man or a member of fociety, if compared with any perfon of the prefent age. In the former capacity, he was learned, careful, and affiduous ; in the latter, humane, benevolent, and attentive to the wants and miferies of mankind. In the exercife of the duties of his calling, he fpent almoft the whole of his life ; and had very little time to devote to pleafure or amufements, had he poffeffed any inclination for fuch relaxations. He had, however, a confiderable propenfity to natural hiftory, and fpared no expence to obtain whatever was fcarce, curious, or valuable in thofe purfuits to which he had turned his attention. But, though devoted to bufinefs, to fcience, and to literature, he was not negligent to the political fyftem of his country, and entertained fentiments of liberty and the Britifh conftitution which did honour to him as an Englifhman. He fincerely felt for the diftreffes of thofe who were involved in the calamities arifing from the prefent unnatural war ; and is faid to have contributed very liberally to the relief of many of the unfortunate fufferers. Where fo many good qualities refided, it would be invidious to point out trifling, inoffenfive foibles. Some fuch fell to the fhare of our author. They were, however, more than compenfated by his virtues ; and the public, as well as his friends, hath fuftained, by his death, an irreparable lofs.'

The following is a catalogue of the medical treatifes in this volume.

' I. Differtatio Medica Inauguralis de Emeticorum Ufu in variis Morbis Tractandis.—II. Remarks on the Neutral Salts of Plants, and on Terra Foliata Tartari.—III. Effay upon the Origin of Amber.—IV. Obfervations on the Manna Perficum.—* IV. Obfervations on a Cafe publifhed in the laft Volume of the Medical Effays, &c. of recovering a Man dead in Appearance, by diftending the Lungs with Air. Printed at Edinburgh, 1744. —V. De Diaphragmate Fiffo, & mutatis quorundam Vifcerum Sedibus, in Cadavere Puellæ decem Menfium obfervatis, Epiftola. —VI. An Account of fome Obfervations and Experiments made in Sibiria, extracted from the Preface to the Flora Sibirica, five Hiftoria Plantarum Sibiriæ, cum Tabulis Æri incifis. Auct. D. Gmelin. Chem. & Hift. Nat. Prof. Petropoli, 1747. 4to. Vol. I.—VII. An Account of the Putrid Sore Throat. Part I. Of the

the Sore Throat attended with Ulcers, as it appeared in Spain, Italy, Sicily, &c. Part II. Of the Sore Throat attended with Ulcers, as it has appeared in London, and Parts adjacent.—VIII. Of the Use of the Cortex Peruvianus, in Scrophulous Diforders.—IX. A Letter to the Medical Society, concerning an Aftringent Gum brought from Africa.—X. Experiments on mixing Oils, refinous and pinguious Subftances with Water, by Means of a Vegetable Mucilage: in a Letter from Mr. James Bogle French, Apothecary in London, to Dr. John Fothergill. With Remarks by the fame. Experiments on mixing Oil and Water by means of a Mucilage. Experiments on mixing Oils, &c. by Attrition. Remarks on the preceding Experiments, by J. Fothergill, M. D.—XI. A Letter relative to the Cure of the Chin-Cough.—XII. Obfervations on the Ufe of Hemlock.—XIII. Remarks on the Hydrocephalus Internus.—XIV. Of the Cure of the Sciatica.—XV. Of the Ufe of Tapping early in Dropfies.—XVI. Remarks on the Ufe of Balfams in the Cure of Confumptions.—XVII. Remarks on the Cure of Confumptions.—XVIII. Some Account of the Cortex Winteranus, or Magellanicus, by John Fothergill, M. D. F. R. S. with a Botanical Defcription by Dr. Solander, F. R. S. and fome Experiments by M. Morris, M. D. F. R. S. Experiments on the Cortex Winteranus, or Magellanicus, by Dr. Morris. XIX. Of a painful Affection of the Face.—XX. Of the Management proper at the Ceffation of the Menfes.—XXI. The Cafe of a Hydrophobia. Additional Directions for the Treatment of Perfons bit by Mad Animals.—XXII. Cafe of an Angina Pectoris: with Remarks.—XXIII. Farther Account of the Angina Pectoris.—XXIV. Farther Remarks on the Treatment of Confumptions, &c.—XXV. Obfervations on Diforders to which Paints in Water-Colours are expofed.'

To thefe are fubjoined, an Account, by Dr. Fothergill, of the late Peter Collinfon, Efq. F. R. S. in a letter to a friend; and an effay on the character of the late Alex. Ruffell, M. D. read before the Society of Phyficians the fecond of October 1769. From the two laft mentioned articles, Dr. Fothergill appears to have been a man of tender feeling, warm in his attachments, and far from being ill qualified for defcribing an amiable character.

The Mirror. A Periodical Paper, publifhed at Edinburgh in the Years 1779, and 1780. 3 vols. 12mo. 9s. boards. Cadell.

THE idea of this publication, we are informed, took its rife in a company of gentlemen, whom particular circumftances of occafion brought frequently together, and whofe converfation often turned upon literary and moral fubjects.

jects. Of the members who composed this rational and elegant society, no hint, which can lead to a discovery, is given in the course of those volumes. It is evident, however, that they have been men of taste, sentiment, and learning; and, considering the narrow sphere of the capital in which they lived, with the circumscribed field of observation which they consequently enjoyed, they have furnished such a variety of entertainment as was hardly to be expected in a work of this kind.—Of the many disadvantages they laboured under, we shall give their own account.

' The situation of the authors of the Mirror was such as neither to prompt much ambition of literary success, nor to create much dependence on it. Without this advantage, they had scarcely ventured to send abroad into the world a performance, the reception of which was liable to so much uncertainty. They foresaw many difficulties, which a publication like the Mirror, even in hands much abler than theirs, must necessarily encounter.

' The state of the times, they were sensible, was very unpropitious to a work of this sort. In a conjuncture so critical as the present, at a period so big with national danger and public solicitude, it was not to be expected that much attention should be paid to speculation or to sentiment, to minute investigations of character, or pictures of private manners. A volume which we can lay aside and resume at pleasure, may suffer less materially from the interruption of national concerns; but a single sheet, that measures its daily importance with the vehicles of public intelligence and political disquisition, can hardly fail to be neglected.

' But, exclusive of this general disadvantage, here were particular circumstances which its authors knew must be unfavourable to the Mirror. That secrecy which they thought it necessary to keep, prevented all the aids of patronage and friendship; it even damped those common exertions to which other works are indebted, if not for fame, at least for introduction to the world. We cannot expect to create an interest in those whom we have not ventured to trust; and the claims even of merit are often little regarded, if that merit be anonymous and unknown.

' The place of its publication was, in several respects, disadvantageous. There is a certain distance at which writings, as well as men, should be placed, in order to command our attention and respect. We do not easily allow a title to instruct or to amuse the public in our neighbour, with whom we have been accustomed to compare our own abilities. Hence the fastidiousness with which, in a place so narrow as Edinburgh, home productions are commonly received; which, if they are grave, are pronounced dull; if pathetic, are called unnatural; if ludicrous, are termed low. In the circle around him, the man of business

sees

fees few who fhould be willing, and the man of genius, few who
are able, to be authors; and a work that comes out unfupported
by eftablifhed names, is liable alike to the cenfure of the grave,
and the fneer of the witty. Even folly herfelf acquires fome merit
by being difpleafed, when name or fafhion has not fanctified a
work from her difpleafure.

'This defire of levelling the pride of authorfhip is in none
more prevalent than in thofe who themfelves have written. Of
thefe the unfuccefsful have a prefcriptive title to criticifm;
and, though eftablifhed literary reputation commonly fets men
above the neceffity of detracting from the merit of other candi-
dates for fame, yet there are not wanting inftances of monopo-
lifts of public favour, who wifh not only to enjoy, but to guide
it, and are willing to confine its influence within the pale of their
own circle, on their own patronage. General cenfure is of all
things the eafieft; from fuch men it paffes unexamined, and its
fentence is decifive; nay, even a ftudied filence will go far to
fmother a production, which, if they have not the meannefs to
envy, they want the candour to appreciate with juftice.

'In point of fubject, as well as of reception, the place where
it appeared was unfavourable to the Mirror. Whoever will examine the works of a fimilar kind that have preceded it, will eafily
perceive for how many topics they were indebted to local characters and temporary follies, to places of public amufement, and
circumftances of reigning fafhion. But, with us, befides the
danger of perfonal application, thefe are hardly various enough
for the fubject, or important enough for the dignity of writing.
There is a fort of claffic privilege in the very names of places
in London, which does not extend to thofe of Edinburgh. The
Canongate is almoft as long as the Strand, but it will not bear
the comparifon upon paper; and Blackfriars-wynd can never
vie with Drury-lane in point of found, however they may rank
in the article of chaftity. In the department of humour, thefe
circumftances muft neceffarily have great weight; and, for papers of humour, the bulk of readers will generally call, becaufe
the number is much greater of thofe who can laugh than of thofe
who can think. To add to the difficulty, people are too proud
to laugh upon eafy terms with one, of whofe title to make them
laugh they are not apprifed. A joke in writing is like a joke
in converfation; much of its wit depends upon the rank of its
author.

'How far the authors of this paper have been able to overcome thefe difficulties, it is not for them to determine. Of its
merits with the public the public will judge; as to themfelves,
they may be allowed to fay, that they have found it an amufement of an elegant, and, they are inclined to believe, of a ufeful kind. They imagine, that, by tracing the manners and fentiments of others, they have performed a fort of exercife, which
may have fome tendency to cultivate and refine their own; and
in that fociety which was formed by this publication, they have

drawn somewhat closer the ties of a friendship, which they flatter themselves they may long enjoy, with a recollection, not unpleasing, of the literary adventure by which it was strengthened and improved.

'The disadvantages attending their publication they have not enumerated, by way of plea for favour, or apology for faults. They will give their volumes as they give their papers, to the world, not meanly dependent on its favour, nor coldly indifferent to it. There is no idea, perhaps, more pleasing to an ingenuous mind, than that the sentences which it dictates in silence and obscurity, may give pleasure and entertainment to those by whom the writer has never been seen, to whom even his name is unknown. There is something peculiarly interesting in the hope of this intercourse of sentiment, this invisible sort of friendship, with the virtuous and the good; and the visionary warmth of an author may be allowed to extend it to distant places, and to future times. If, in this hope, the authors of the Mirror may indulge, they trust, that, whatever may be thought of the execution, the motive of their publication will do them no dishonour; that, if they have failed in wit, they have been faultless in sentiment; and that, if they shall not be allowed the praise of genius, they have, at least, not forfeited the commendation of virtue.'

The professed design of this work, and to which it is indebted for its name, is, ' to hold, as it were, the mirror up to nature, to shew virtue her own features, vice her own image, and the very age and body of the time his form and pressure.' In general, this design is invariably pursued; and we meet with few papers, in which entertainment only appears to have been the scope of the authors.

The scarcity of humorous writers in Scotland having often been remarked, we shall lay before our readers the following paper on that subject.

' In a paper published at Edinburgh, it would be improper to enter into any comparison of the writers of this country with those on the other side of the Tweed: but, whatever be the comparative rank of Scottish and English authors, it must surely be allowed, that, of late, there have been writers in this country, upon different subjects, who are possessed of very considerable merit. In one species of writing, however, in works and compositions of humour, there can be no sort of doubt that the English stand perfectly unrivalled by their northern neighbours. The English excel in comedy; several of their romances are replete with the most humourous representations of life and character, and many of their other works are full of excellent ridicule. But, in Scotland, we have hardly any book which aims at humour, and, of the very few which do, still fewer have any degree of merit. Though we have tragedies written by Scots au-

authors, we have no comedy, excepting Ramfay's Gentle Shepherd ; and though we have tender novels, we have none of humour, excepting thofe of Smollett, who, from his long refidence in England, can hardly be faid to have acquired in this country his talent for writing : nor can we, for the fame reafon, lay a perfect claim to Arbuthnot, who is a ftill more illuftrious exception to my general remark. There muft be fomething in the national genius of the two people which makes this remarkable difference in their writings, though it may be difficult to difcover from what caufe it arifes.

' I am inclined to fufpect, that there is fomething in the fituation and prefent government of Scotland, which may, in part, account for this difference in the genius of the two countries. Scotland, before the union of the two kingdoms, was a feparate ftate, with a parliament and conftitution of its own. Now the feat of government is removed, and its conftitution is involved in that of England. At the time the two nations came to be fo intimately connected, its great men were lefs affluent than thofe of England, its agriculture was little advanced, and its manufactures were in their infancy. A Scotfman was, therefore, in this fituation, obliged to exert every nerve, that he might be able to hold his place.

' If preferment, or offices in public life, were his object, he was obliged to remove from home to a city, which, though now the metropolis of the united kingdoms, had formerly been to him a fort of foreign capital. If wealth was the object of his purfuit, he could only acquire it at home by great induftry and perfeverance ; and if he found he could not eafily fucceed in his own country, he repaired to other countries, where he expected to be able to amafs a fortune. Hence it has been remarked, that there are more natives of Scotland to be found abroad than of any other country.

' People in this fituation are not apt to indulge themfelves in humour ; and few humourous characters will appear. It is only in countries where men wanton in the extravagancies of wealth, that fome are led to indulge a particular vein of character, and that others are induced to delineate and exprefs it in writing. Befides, where men are in a fituation which makes it neceffary for them to pufh their way in the world, more particularly if they are obliged to do fo among ftrangers, though this may give them a firmnefs and a refolutenefs in their conduct, it will naturally produce a modeft caution and referve in their deportment, which muft chill every approach to humour. Hence, though the Scots are allowed to be brave and undaunted in dangerous fituations, yet bafhfulnefs, referve, and even timidity of manner, unlefs when they are called forth to action, are juftly confidered as making part of their character. Men of this difpofition are not apt to have humour ; it is the open, the carelefs, the indifferent, and the forward, who indulge in it ; it is the man who does not think of intereft, and who fets himfelf above

at-

attending to the proprieties of conduct. But he who has objects of interest in view, who attends with circumspection to his conduct, and finds it necessary to do so, is generally grave and silent, and seldom makes any attempt at humour.

' These circumstances may have had a considerable influence upon the genius and temper of the people in Scotland ; and if they have given a particular formation to the genius of the people in general, they would naturally have a similar effect upon its authors : the genius of an author commonly takes its direction from that of his countrymen.

' To these causes, arising from the present situation and government of our country, may be added another circumstance, that of there being no court or seat of the monarch in Scotland. It is only where the court is, that the standard of manners can be fixed ; and, of consequence, it is only in the neighbourhood of the court that a deviation from that standard can be exactly ascertained, or a departure from it be easily made the object of ridicule. Where there is no court, it becomes of little importance what dress the people wear, what hours they observe, what language they express themselves in, or what is their general deportment. Men living at a distance from the court become also unacquainted with the rules of fashion which it establishes, and are unable to mark or point them out. But the great subject for wit and ludicrous representation arises from men's having a thorough knowlege of what is the fashionable standard of manners, and being able to seize upon, and hold out a departure from it, in an humourous point of view. In Scotland, therefore, which, since the removal of the court, has become, in a certain degree, a provincial country, there being no fixed standard of manners within the country itself, one great source of ridicule is cut off, and an author, by that means, is not led to attempt humourous composition, or, if he does, has little chance of succeeding.

' There is another particular which may have had a very considerable effect upon the genius of the Scots writers, and that is, the nature of the language in which they write. The old Scottish dialect is now banished from our books, and the English is substituted in its place. But though our books be written in English, our conversation is in Scotch. Of our language it may be said, as we are told of the wit of sir Hudibras, that we have a suit for holidays and another for working-days. The Scottish dialect is our ordinary suit ; the English is used only on solemn occasions. By this means, when a Scotsman comes to write, he does it generally in trammels. His own native original language, which he hears spoken around him, he does not make use of ; but he expresses himself in a language in some respects foreign to him, and which he has acquired by study and observation. When a celebrated Scottish writer, after the publication of his History of Scotland, was first introduced to lord Chesterfield, his lordship, with that happy talent of compliment for which he was so remarkable,

markable, addreſſed him, at parting, in theſe words : " I am happy, ſir, to have met with you,—happy to have paſſed a day with you,—and extremely happy to find that you ſpeak Scotch.— It would be too much, were you to ſpeak, as well as to write our language, better than we do ourſelves."

' This circumſtance of a Scottiſh author not writing his own natural dialect, muſt have a conſiderable influence upon the nature of his literary productions. When he is employed in any grave dignified compoſition, when he writes hiſtory, politics, or poetry, the pains he muſt take to write in a manner different from that in which he ſpeaks, will not much affect his productions ; the language of ſuch compoſitions is, in every caſe, raiſed above that of common life ; and, therefore, the deviation which a Scottiſh author is obliged to make from the common language of the country, can be of little prejudice to him. But if a writer is to deſcend to common and ludicrous pictures of life ; if, in ſhort, he is to deal in humourous compoſition, his language muſt be, as nearly as poſſible, that of common life, that of the bulk of the people : but a Scotſman who wiſhes to write Engliſh cannot eaſily do this. He neither ſpeaks the Engliſh dialect, nor is it ſpoken by thoſe around him : any knowlege he has acquired of the language is got from books, nor from converſation. Hence Scottiſh authors may have been prevented from attempting to write books of humour ; and, when they have tried it, we may be able, in ſome meaſure, to account for their failure.

' In confirmation of theſe remarks, it may be obſerved, that almoſt the only works of humour which we have in this country, are in the Scottiſh dialect, and moſt of them were written before the union of the kingdoms, when the Scotch was the written, as well as the ſpoken language of the country. The Gentle Shepherd, which is full of natural and ludicrous repreſentations of low life, is written in broad Scotch. Many of our ancient Scottiſh ballads are full of humour. If there have been lately any publications of humour in this country, written in good Engliſh, they have been moſtly of that graver ſort, called irony. In this ſpecies of writing, where the author himſelf never appears to laugh, a more dignified compoſition is admiſſible ; and, in that caſe, the diſadvantage of writing in a language different from that in which the author ſpeaks, or thoſe around him converſe, is not ſo ſenſibly felt.'

If, in this work, an Engliſh reader may ſometimes perceive Scotticiſms, ſuch ſlight blemiſhes will readily be forgiven, amidſt obſervations which are diſtinguiſhed by their juſtneſs, and ſentiments which are ſo ſtrongly marked with the impreſſions of ingenuity.

Phy-

✓ *Phyfiological Difquifitions ; or, Difcourfes on the Natural Philo-*
fophy of the Elements. By W. Jones, *F. R. S.* [*Continued*
from p. 187.]

WE have already given an account of the two firft difcourfes of this work. In the next difcourfe, *on the Ele-*
ments, the author has brought together many obfervations and
experiments, fome of which fhew how difficult it is to exhibit the elements in their fimple form. It is curious to fee
how earth is metamorphofed and difguifed in gems, metals,
&c. He is certainly right in his obfervation, that ' nature
does not prefent us with a multitude of principles, but with
an endlefs variety arifing from the different combinations of
a few.—Chemiftry, he adds, is a dangerous field for fpeculation ; it is a fcience where art runs fo many divifions upon
nature, and the active elements do fo interfere with and difguife the others, that the chemift, who refolves to be a philofopher upon his own ground, is very foon bewildered, and
becomes vifionary in his reafonings and principles.' From a
confideration of this fubject the author concludes, that the
ancient doctrine of the *four elements* is as good as any, and
generally confirmed by the decompofition of animals, plants,
and foffils ; efpecially by the firft. The ancients diftinguifhed
the elements into *active* and *paffive* : if they were right in this,
the doctrine muft have its ufe in philofophy, and merits to be
confidered. The comparative dignity of the elements, the
arguments for which are here difplayed, is rather a matter of
curiofity than utility.

In the difcourfe *on Fire*, which contains 137 pages, the author has taken a large compafs, and feems to have beftowed
much time and labour upon this fruitful fubject, which was
too much neglected in the laft age. He divides fire into *folar-*
culinary, and *elementary :* fhews, by a feries of experiments,
that it is an extended fubftance or body ; and that it is actually transfufed from one portion of matter to another. In
confidering the *penetrating* power of fire, its moft remarkable
property, he found that the penetration of cold, compared
with that of heat, under like circumftances, was only as 5 to
14 ; from which it appears, that fluids acquire heat much
fooner than they lofe it. Some of the experiments, p. 92,
which fhew how light is disturbed by fire, are new ; and the
reafon given for it feems to be the true one ; namely, that
light is progreffive, and fire vibratory. Next to the penetrating is the *expanding* power of fire. When fire is agitated
with that motion which occafions heat, it always acts as if
it *wanted more room*, or, as if every particle of fpace were
a ra-

a radiant point of fire. Here the author confiders the expanfive force of gunpowder, and explains it nearly in the fame terms as before, in his introduction. The expanfive power of fteam is defcribed next, and two remarkable accidents are mentioned, to fhew the aftonifhing effects of it. A pyroftatical machine is introduced, to meafure the force of fire in expanding bodies when heated by it; and the flame of a fmall taper is found capable of raifing a weight of 500 pounds. The flame is not applied to the place of the *power,* but of the *weight;* fo that the whole force of the machine acts againft it. The different forts of thermometers are treated of, and other effects of fire are defcribed at large, under the heads of *ebullition, folution, liquefaction, evaporation, clarification,* and *induration.* The different methods of *exciting* fire lead the author to fome ftriking reflexions on the difcovery and application of that neceffary element; which are fucceeded by an inquiry into the heat of bodies fwiftly projected. From page 136 to 154, he inveftigates the principles on which fire is fupported in burning fuel; and concludes, that air and fire are one homogeneous fubftance. He fays he difcovered, twenty years ago, that burning charcoal confumes more air than any other fort of fuel. The experiments in this part of the work are too many to be mentioned particularly; nor fhall we pronounce any opinion relative to their purport, but leave them to the confideration of our philofophical readers, who confult the work itfelf. For the conftructing of a new and more general *fcale of heat,* which he has given in the work, from the freezing of mercury to the white heat of a furnace, he invented a way of difcovering *original* heat from heat *communicated;* by the ufe of which theorem he carries the degrees of Fahrenheit's fcale fo high as 3000; which we believe has never been done before. The adhefion of quickfilver to iron, occurred as a fingular fact in thefe experiments; whence the practical mechanic may hereafter derive fome advantage. From his fcale of heat he makes a tranfition to the heat of climates, and places the mean temperature of the earth's body at 48 degrees. In confidering the origin of cold, and the many ways of producing it, he fuppofes heat and cold to be properties or effects of the fame element; as the air is the fame thing, whether it blows a ftorm, or finks into a calm: heat and cold are nothing but the higher and lower degrees of fire. The effects of freezing, and the force of it, give occafion to fome new experiments. This difcourfe is concluded with fuch mifcellaneous obfervations as could not properly be introduced under the former heads; fuch as, the retention of vifible fire

T 4

in

in bodies feemingly opaque ; the relation of heat to the prifmatic colours ; the lachrymæ Batavicæ ; the retention of heat ; the heat of bodies from the fun ; the effects of burning mirrors, &c. The philofophical part of this treatife on fire is followed by a philological hiftory of it, profane and facred ; wherein the worfhip of fire and its antiquity are confidered. Here the author attempts to elucidate many particulars in the Grecian mythology. Its metaphorical or fymbolical ufes give occafion to other remarks, which are applied to fome paffages of Scripture, to fhew the relation between philofophy and theology. Lactantius's obfervation at the end is very curious, yet fo obvious, that every perfon who reads it will wonder he did not think of it before. The heathens fuppofed that the gods envied man the ufe of fire ; that it was therefore obtained by ftealth ; and that this theft was the original crime which brought all evil into the world. If we do juftice to this difcourfe on fire, we muft allow it to be the moft comprehenfive we have ever yet feen upon this interefting part of philofophy. The analyfis we exhibit is intended only to give a view of the author's matter : to fhew his manner of treating the fubject, we muft have given many paffages more at large than our plan will admit.

The difcourfe *on Air,* though not fo particular as that on fire, comprehends much ufeful knowlege, with many new obfervations. The author treats firft of its nature and fubftance ; fhews that it contains fire as its active principle ; examines the conftitution of the atmofphere, with the force of the wind, its velocity, and ferpentine motion. Thence he proceeds to the confideration of the barometer, and its ufe in meafuring elevations. In this part of the work he enquires minutely into the phænomenon of the fufpenfion of mercury in a glafs tube to the height of 70 or 80 inches, and lays great ftrefs upon it, as demonftrating the preffure of another fluid more fubtle than air ; and he has brought fome great authorities to confirm the notion from Mr. Huygens, Dr. Wallis, and Dr. Jurin. A confiderable part of this difcourfe is employed on the modern difcoveries relating to fixed air and elaftic vapours, particularly on that elegant difcovery of Dr. Prieftley, that air is purified by the growth of vegetables ; which has been carried farther by Dr. Ingenhoufz. This leads the author to what he regards as additional evidence in proof of his favourite doctrine, the tranfmutability of air and fire ; which, whether it be true or not, time muft difcover.

This difcourfe, like the former, comprehends the philological confideration of air, and its fignification in the heathen

my-

mythology. Mr. Jones endeavours to shew, in opposition to Mr. Bryant, that the eagle was not a symbol of the solar fire, but of the element of air. Here the mythology of the air leads him to consider the notion of *inspiration*, sacred and profane, among prophets, sybils, and ventriloquists : and he concludes with supposing that the serpent, so universally worshipped by the ancient heathens, was a symbol of the air.

The sixth discourse of this work treats of the philosophy of sounds in general, and very largely of musical sounds ; the theory of which is but little known to many eminent musicians. It may readily be perceived that the author, as a practical musician, has a particular interest in the matter of this subject, and has bestowed much attention upon it. Readers who are musically disposed, may find the same pleasure from this enquiry ; we can only shew what the discourse comprehends. The author first explains the nature of sonorous bodies, and teaches how sound is generated. Some experiments incline him to think, that air alone is not an adequate vehicle of sound. The distance to which sound flies, and its velocity, have often been considered before by others. In explaining the nature of musical consonance, he compares strings to pendulums, as Galilæo did first, and from him Dr. Holder and other writers. He derives the scale of music from the systematical divisions of a musical string, and goes through the composition and resolution of the diatonic intervals. Having pointed out some difficulties in the doctrine of *coincident pulses*, he proceeds to the monochord and its divisions, with the imperfection of the systematical scale, and the ways of tempering or correcting it, according to different authors, and a manuscript treatise of the late Mr. Davis, of Harwich. The sympathy observable in musical sounds, and the generation of harmonics, direct and reverted, are particularly treated of, with their application to the organ. A new theory of the Eolian harp is proposed, with a harp of a new construction, which will sound in the open air. To the philosophical part, critical remarks are added, on the ancient and modern style of music, which shew how much the author has meditated on this science. Should they meet with the attention of learned masters, the present corrupt style of music, condemned by many judges, as too nearly related to *bombast* in writing, which affects pomp of sound with little sense, might in time be reformed.

[*To be continued.*]

A Ge-

A General History of Connecticut, *from its first Settlement under* George Fenwick, *Esq. to its latest Period of Amity with* Great Britain ; *including a Description of the Country, and many curious and interesting Anecdotes.* 8vo. 5s. 3d. *boards.* Bew.

COnnecticut is the moft flourifhing, and proportionably the moft populous province in North America ; deriving its name from the great Indian fachem, or king, who occupied a large tract of this country when it was firft invaded by the Englifh, in 1634. The author of this hiftory, after giving an account of the charters granted to this province, relates the proceedings of the firft fettlers, in refpect of their religious and civil eftablifhments. They were, from the beginning, violent puritans, and exercifed the moft fevere perfecution againft all who differed from them in matters of religion For fome time, the province was not under the government of any one general executive power ; but the feveral towns claimed each a diftinct legiflative authority. Of the laws made by thofe little democracies, and denominated *blue laws* by the neighbouring colonies, we meet with the following curious fpecimen.

' The governor and magiftrates, convened in general affembly, are the fupreme power under God of this independent dominion.

' From the determination of the affembly no appeal fhall be made.

' The governor is amenable to the voice of the people.

' The governor fhall have only a fingle vote in determining any queftion ; except a cafting vote, when the affembly may be equally divided.

' The affembly of the people fhall not be difmiffed by the governor, but fhall difmifs itfelf.

' Confpiracy againft this dominion fhall be punifhed with death.

' Whoever fays there is a power and jurifdiction above and over this dominion, fhall fuffer death and lofs of property.

' Whoever attempts to change or overturn this dominion fhall fuffer death.

' The judges fhall determine controverfies without a jury.

' No one fhall be a freeman, or give a vote, unlefs he be converted, and a member in full communion of one of the churches allowed in this dominion.

' No man fhall hold any office, who is not found in the faith, and faithful to this dominion ; and whoever gives a vote to fuch a perfon, fhall pay a fine of 1l. for a fecond offence, he fhall be disfranchifed.

' Each

' Each freeman shall swear by the blessed God to bear true allegiance to this dominion, and that Jesus is the only King.

' No Quaker or Dissenter from the established worship of this dominion shall be allowed to give a vote for the election of magistrates, or any officer.

' No food or lodging shall be afforded to a Quaker, Adamite, or other Heretic.

' If any person turns Quaker, he shall be banished, and not suffered to return but upon pain of death.

' No priest shall abide in the dominion : he shall be banished, and suffer death on his return. Priests may be seized by any one without a warrant.

' No one to cross a river, but with an authorized ferryman.

' No one shall run on the Sabbath-day, or walk in his garden or elsewhere, except reverently to and from meeting.

' No one shall travel, cook victuals, make beds, sweep house, cut hair, or shave, on the Sabbath-day.

' No woman shall kiss her child on the Sabbath or fasting-day.

' The Sabbath shall begin at sunset on Saturday.

' To pick an ear of corn growing in a neighbour's garden, shall be deemed theft.

' A person accused of trespass in the night shall be judged guilty, unless he clear himself by his oath.

' When it appears that an accused has confederates, and he refuses to discover them, he may be racked.

' No one shall buy or sell lands without permission of the selectmen.

' A drunkard shall have a master appointed by the selectmen, who are to debar him from the liberty of buying and selling.

' Whoever publishes a lye to the prejudice of his neighbour, shall sit in the stocks, or be whipped fifteen stripes.

' No minister shall keep a school.

' Every rateable person, who refuses to pay his proportion to the support of the minister of the town or parish, shall be fined by the court 2l. and 4l. every quarter, until he or she pay the rate to the minister.

' Men stealers shall suffer death.

' Whoever wears cloaths trimmed with gold, silver, or bone lace, above two shillings by the yard, shall be presented by the grand jurors, and the selectmen shall tax the offender at 3col. estate

' A debtor in prison, swearing he has no estate, shall be let out, and sold, to make satisfaction.

' Whoever sets a fire in the woods, and it burns a house, shall suffer death ; and persons suspected of this crime shall be imprisoned, without benefit of bail.

' Whoever brings cards or dice into this dominion shall pay a fine of 5l.

' No one shall read Common-Prayer, keep Christmas or saints-days, make minced pies, dance, play cards, or play on any

i

inftrument of mufic, except the drum, trumpet, and Jews-harp.

' No gofpel minifter fhall join people in marriage ; the magif-trates only fhall join in marriage, as they may do it with lefs fcan-dal to Chrift's church.

' When parents refufe their children convenient marriages, the magiftrates fhall determine the point.

' 1 he felectmen, on finding children ignorant, may take them away from their parents, and put them into better hands, at the expence of their parents.

' Fornication fhall be punifhed by compelling marriage, or as the court may think proper.

' Adultery fhall be punifhed with death.

' A man that ftrikes his wife fhall pay a fine of 10l. a woman that ftrikes her hufband fhall be punifhed as the court directs.

' A wife fhall be deemed good evidence againft her hufband.

' No man fhall court a maid in perfon, or by letter, without firft obtaining confent of her parents : 5l. penalty for the firft of-fence ; 10l. for the fecond ; and, for the third, imprifonment during the pleafure of the court.

' Married perfons muft live together, or be imprifoned.

' Every male fhall have his hair cut round according to a cap.'

The colonial laws, which have been enacted by the autho-rity of the charter, are decent in comparifon of the blue laws, but not unexceptionable. Of this the following law is an ex-ample : when a trefpafs is committed in the night, the in-jured perfon may recover damages of any whom he may think proper to accufe, unlefs the accufed can prove an alibi, or will clear himfelf by an oath ; which oath, however, it is in the option of the juftice either to adminifter or refufe. It is an inviolable maxim with them, that no Englifh law be in force in the province, till it has formally received the fanction of the General Affembly, and been recorded by the fecretary. We are prefented with an anecdote which evinces their remark-able fcrupulofity on this fubject.

' Above thirty years ago, a negro caftrated his mafter's fon, and was brought to trial for it before the fuperior court at Hert-ford. The court could find no law to punifh the negro. The lawyers quoted the Englifh ftatute againft maiming ; the court were of opinion that ftatute did not reach this colony, becaufe it had not been paffed in the general affembly ; and therefore were about to remand the negro to prifon till the general affembly fhould meet. But an ex-poft-facto law was objected to as an in-fringement upon civil liberty. At length, however, the court were releafed from their difficulty, by having recourfe to the vote of the firft fettlers at Newhaven, viz. That the Bible fhould be their law, till they could make others more fuitable to their cir-cumftances. The court were of opinion that vote was in full force,

force, as it had not been revoked; and thereupon tried the negro upon the Jewish law, viz. eye for eye, and tooth for tooth. He suffered accordingly.'

The author, having recited the political transactions of the province, afterwards describes the country, with the manners, commerce, and other circumstances relative to the inhabitants; sometimes interspersing historical and biographical anecdotes connected with the subject.

Except the Mississippi and St. Laurence, the Connecticut is the largest river belonging to the English plantations in America. It is five hundred miles long, and four miles wide at its mouth. Above five hundred streams, which issue from lakes, ponds, and flooded lands, fall into it; many of them larger than the Thames at London.

The inhabitants of New London, we are told, have the credit of inventing tar and feathers as a punishment for heresy. They first inflicted it on Quakers and Anabaptists.

' Was I, says the author, to give a character of the people of Norwich, I would do it in the words of the famous Mr. George Whitefield, (who was a good judge of mankind,) in his farewel-sermon to them a short time before his death; viz. " When I first preached in this magnificent house, above twenty years ago, I told you, that you were part beast, part man, and part devil; at which you were offended. I have since thought much about that expression, and confess that for once I was mistaken. I therefore take this last opportunity to correct my error. Behold! I now tell you, that you are not part man and part beast, but wholly of the devil."

Of an inhabitant of Pomfret we cannot omit inserting the following anecdote, on the authority of the author.

' In Pomfret lives colonel Israel Putnam, who slew a she-bear and her two cubs with a billet of wood. The bravery of this action brought him into public notice: and, it seems, he is one of fortune's favourites. The story is as follows:—In 1754, a large she-bear came in the night from her den, which was three miles from Mr. Putnam's house, and took a sow out of a pen of his. The sow, by her squeaking, awoke Mr. Putnam, who hastily ran in his shirt to the poor creature's relief; but before he could reach the pen, the bear had left it, and was trotting away with the sow in her mouth. Mr. Putnam took up a billet of wood, and followed the screamings of the sow, till he came to the foot of a mountain, where the den was. Dauntless he entered the horrid cavern; and, after walking and crawling upon his hands and knees for fifty yards, came to a roomy cell, where the bear met him with great fury. He saw nothing but the fire of her eyes; but that was sufficient for our hero: he accordingly directed his blow, which at once proved fatal to the bear, and saved his own

4   life

life at a moſt critical moment. Putnam then diſcovered and killed two cubs; and having, though in Egyptian darkneſs, dragged them and the dead ſow, one by one, out of the cave, he went home, and calmly reported to his family what had happened. The neighbours declared, on viewing the place by torch-light, that his exploit exceeded thoſe of Sampſon or David.'

It appears from the account given by this writer, that a ſpirit of litigation greatly prevails in Connecticut.

' The ſingular nature of ſome of the ſuits, ſays he, entitle them to particular notice. When the ice and floods prevail in the great river Connecticut, they frequently cut off large pieces of ground on one ſide, and carry them over to the oppoſite. By this means, the river is every year changing its bed, to the advantage of ſome perſons, and the diſadvantage of others. This has proved the ſource of perplexing law-ſuits, and will moſt likely continue to produce the ſame effects ſo long as the demi-annual aſſemblies remain in the colony; for the judgment of the aſſembly in May is reſcinded by that in October, and ſo vice verſa. Thus a law-ſuit in Connecticut is endleſs, to the ruin of both plaintiff and defendant. The county and the ſuperior courts, alſo, in different years, give different judgments: and the reaſon is the popular conſtitution of the colony, whereby different parties prevail at different times, each of whom carefully undoes what the others have done. Thus the glorious uncertainty of law renders the poſſeſſion of property in Connecticut extremely precarious. The queſtion, however, touching the lands removed from place to place by the floods and ice, requires the ſkill of both juriſts and caſuiſts. The moſt ſimple caſe of the kind that has been communicated to me, is the following: a piece of land belonging to A. in Springfield, with a houſe, &c. ſtanding upon it, was removed by the flood to another town, and ſettled on land belonging to W. A. claimed his houſe and land, and took poſſeſſion of them; whereupon W. ſued A. for a treſpaſs, and the court ejected A. But A. afterwards obtained a reverſion of the judgment; when W. again ſued A. and got a decree that A. ſhould remove his own land off from the land of W. or pay W. for his land. Further litigation enſued, and both parties pleaded that the act of God injured no man according to the Engliſh law. The judges ſaid, the act of God in this caſe equally fell upon A. and W. The diſpute reſts in ſtatu quo, the juriſ-prudence of Connecticut not having yet taught mankind what is juſt and legal in this important controverſy.

' Suppoſing the flood had carried A's ſhip or raft on W's land, the ſhip or raft would ſtill belong to A. and W. could recover no damage; but then A. muſt take away his ſhip or raft in a reaſonable time. Yet in the caſe where an iſland or point of land is removed by the waters, or an earthquake, upon a neighbouring ſhore, Q. Ought not the iſlanders to keep poſſeſſion of the ſuperficies?—This may be a new caſe in Europe.'

The

The manner of visiting the sick in this province is also remarkable.

' The minister demands of the sick if he be converted, when, and where? If the answers are conformable to the system of the minister, it is very well; if not, the sick is given over as a non-elect, and no object of prayer. Another minister is then sent for, who asks if the sick be willing to die—if he hates God—if he be willing to be damned, if it please God to damn him? Should he answer No, this minister quits him as did the former. Finally, the sick man dies, and so falls out of their hands into better.'

The author informs us, that the women of Connecticut are strictly virtuous, and resemble more the prude than the European polite lady. They are not permitted to read plays; cannot converse about cards or operas; but will speak intelligently on history, geography, and mathematics. They are great casuists, and many of them remarkably well skilled in Greek and Latin.

This history is written in a lively, and sometimes sarcastic, rather than historical manner. It contains a full account of the province; and the writer has added an Appendix, comprising a summary detail of the proceedings of the people of Connecticut, immediately leading to their commencement of hostilities against the mother-country. The author acquaints us, that, on this subject, some events have been erroneously represented in Great Britain; but for those particulars, not generally interesting, we shall refer our readers to the work.

Tracts on Inoculation, written and published at St. Petersburg *in the Year* 1768, *by Command of her* Imperial *Majesty, the Empress of all the* Russias : *with Additional Observations. By the Hon. Baron* T. Dimsdale, *Physician and actual Counsellor of State to her* Imperial *Majesty, the Empress of all the* Russias, *and F. R. S.* 8vo. 3s. *boards.* Owen.

IN this production Baron Dimsdale presents the public with an account of his journey to Russia, in the year 1768, with five small tracts written by the command of the empress, while he was at St. Petersburg. They were, by her majesty's order, originally published in the Russian language, from which they are now translated.

The first chapter contains an account of the baron's journey to Russia, and of the introduction of inoculation into that country. On this expedition, the baron was accompanied by one of his sons, who was bred to the profession of physic.

The

The day after their arrival at St. Peterſburg, they had the honour to dine with the grand duke, who received them with the utmoſt politeneſs and affability ; and after dinner, upon taking leave, his imperial highneſs gave them a general invitation to his court and table, as often as it was convenient to them. The empreſs arrived in the city the ſame evening ; and the next day they received orders to attend her majeſty at ten o'clock, on the day following, at her ſummer palace. The baron informs us, that, though he was prepared to expect very much from the excellent underſtanding and politeneſs of her majeſty, yet her extreme penetration, and the propriety of the queſtions ſhe aſked, relative to the practice and ſucceſs of inoculation, greatly ſurpriſed him. On his retiring, he had the honour to be invited to dine with her the ſame day. The baron gives the following general account of the entertainment.

' The empreſs ſat ſingly at the upper end of a long table, at which about twelve of the nobility were gueſts. The entertainment conſiſted of a variety of excellent diſhes, ſerved up after the French manner, and was concluded by a deſert of the fineſt fruits and ſweetmeats, ſuch as I little expected to find in that northern climate. Moſt of theſe luxuries were however the produce of the empreſs's own dominions : pine apples indeed are chiefly imported from England, though thoſe of the growth of Ruſſia, of which we had one that day, are of good flavour, but generally ſmall. Water melons and grapes are brought from Aſtracan ; great plenty of melons from Moſcow, and apples and pears from the Ukraine.

' But what enlivened the whole entertainment, was the moſt unaffected eaſe and affability of the empreſs herſelf. Each of her gueſts had a ſhare of her attention and politeneſs ; the converſation was kept up with a freedom and chearfulneſs to be expected rather from perſons of the ſame rank, than from ſubjects admitted to the honour of their ſovereign's company.'

After baron (at that time only doctor) Dimſdale had performed inoculation on the empreſs and the grand duke of Ruſſia, a nobleman of the firſt diſtinction acquainted him with the generous manner in which her majeſty propoſed to reward his ſervices. It was told him, that he ſhould be created a baron of the Ruſſian empire, and appointed actual counſellor of ſtate, and phyſician to her imperial majeſty, with an annuity of five hundred pounds a year, to be paid him in England ; beſide ten thouſand pounds, which he immediately received ; and alſo that he ſhould be preſented with a miniature picture of the empreſs, and one of the grand duke, as a memorial of his ſervices to the imperial crown of Ruſſia. Her ma-

majefty was alfo pleafed to exprefs her approbation of his fon's conduct, by conferring on him the fame title, and ordering him to be prefented with a fuperb gold fnuff-box, richly fet with diamonds.

After the narrative of the author's journey, and a general account of his practice in Ruffia, we meet with a minute detail of the inoculation of the emprefs, and of the grand duke.

Next follows, a fhort account of regulations in the Medical College of St. Peterfburg, in 1768 ; with a defcription of the methods propofed for extending the falutary practice of inoculation through the Ruffian empire ; and an eftimate of the number of thofe who die of the natural fmall-pox, with a view to demonftrate the advantages that may accrue to Ruffia from the practice of inoculation.

The fecond chapter contains additional obfervations to the author's treatife on the method of inoculation for the fmall-pox. The additional obfervations, which are intermixed with the original treatife, are, for the fake of diftinction, printed in *Italics.* We fhall extract from this chapter one paffage, relative to a method of inoculation ; prefixing to the additional obfervation fo much of the original treatife as is neceffary for connexion.

‘ The blifter plaifter being removed, the part is to be dreffed with a little unguent. Bafilic. flav. on a pledget of lint, and the whole covered with a little cerate epulotic of the fame difpenfatory, fpread on a foft linen cloth ; and this cerate, I think, is always preferable to any other application that has been, or is now in common ufe for dreffing blifter plaifters.

‘ I do not know that any perfon has ever practifed this method of applying blifter plaifters on the inoculated parts, except myfelf, and thofe who have received this information from me ; but its effects are fo fpeedy and falutary, as to render it worthy of general ufe on fuch occafions. It likewife gives much lefs trouble than the application of large blifter plaifters upon other parts of the body, which are not only more painful, but lefs efficacious. It is indeed attended with fo little uneafinefs, that even children feldom complain of it.

‘ It may perhaps be imagined, that from this application the fore may afterwards become troublefome to the patient ; but experience is againft this fuppofition ; for when I have inoculated in both arms, and bliftered only one, the bliftered incifion has moft commonly healed fooner than the other.

‘ *Under this head I have alfo to add, that in fome cafes, particularly of young children, it happens that the inoculated part,*

even

even early in the diſeaſe, inflames conſiderably, ſo as to occaſion great reſtleſſneſs and fever, although the puſtules on other parts are very few, and of a good kind; in this ſtate I apply a common cataplaſm of bread and milk to the part, which, with certainty, gives relief.

' *Some reſpectable practitioners having expreſſed their ſatisfaction with that part of the chapter of anomalous ſymptoms, &c. where the eryſipelatous raſh that had ſometimes been miſtaken for a confluent ſmall-pox, was ſhewn to be inoffenſive; I am encouraged to mention another complaint that has ſeveral times diſtreſſed me greatly, and I make no doubt has alſo occurred to others in the courſe of their practice, with what I eſteem to be the cauſe, and beſt manner of treating it.*

' *Sometimes a patient who has paſſed through the eruptive fever, in the uſual manner, with moderate ſymptoms, and been relieved from every complaint by the eruption of a few puſtules, has, after all apprehenſions of future illneſs ceaſed, been unexpectedly attacked with a ſmart, and even alarming degree of fever, accompanied with great reſtleſſneſs, and very frequently in children with uncommon fits of crying. Not being able to account for this complaint from any circumſtances belonging to this diſeaſe, I, for a time, attributed it to ſome unknown cauſe, independent of the ſmall-pox; but obſerving that ſeizures of the ſame kind happened in ſeveral inſtances, my attention was excited to inveſtigate its true cauſe, which I am now convinced originates from puſtules ſituated on the internal part of the mouth, or on the membranous parts of the noſe or œſophagus. I have always treated this complaint ſucceſsfully, by moderate cordials, ſufficient to produce a ſlight perſpiration, by which means, the whole diſturbance has generally been over in twenty-four hours, and no further inconvenience has been ſuffered from it; this ariſes from the abatement of the tenſion; for it is obſerved, that the puſtules on thoſe parts, which are conſtantly hot and moiſt, come to maturity much earlier than thoſe on the ſkin.*'

The third chapter treats of the epidemic ſmall-pox; the fourth contains obſervations in favour of the opinion, that the true ſmall-pox attacks the ſame perſon but once; the fifth compriſes obſervations to prove, that ſome perſons paſs through life, without appearing to be capable of receiving the ſmall-pox; the ſixth preſents us with obſervations to prove, that, though a perſon has been expoſed to the natural ſmall-pox, if he is inoculated in time, the inoculation will ſuperſede the natural diſeaſe; and the ſeventh chapter delivers conjectures on the probable cauſes of the different kinds and degrees of natural ſmall-pox, and on the different ſucceſs of the methods adopted in the practice of inoculation. In thoſe several treatises, whatever opinion may be entertained respecting the justness of baron Dimsdale's theoretical sentiments, the facts which he adduces may be considered as incontestible, and must therefore merit the attention of all medical readers.

Twelve Discourses introductory to the Study of Divinity, in which the Principles of the Christian *Religion are attempted to be laid down with Plainness and Precision. By* Edward Tatham, *M. A.* 8vo. 5s. *boards.* Richardson *and* Urquhart.

THE author of these Discourses seems to think, that he should have gained more reputation, as a writer, if he had adorned his compositions with oratorical embellishments. He supposes, ' that an easy descant on a few select and unconnected texts, the effusions of a flowery imagination, a studied modification of sentences, an exact and varied modulation of periods, pleasing metaphors, and fine allusions, are more acceptable to a polished ear,' than a discourse, which is destitute of these ornaments.

This may be true. The effusions of a flowery imagination are captivating: but they are too frequently accompanied with affectation. Simplicity and perspicuity of language, solidity of reasoning, purity of sentiment, and a pathetic application to the understanding and the passions of mankind, are the principal characteristics of sacred eloquence. Splendid epithets, poetical phrases, and florid descriptions, in a sermon, are disgusting to every judicious reader. They degrade the character of the preacher into that of a coxcomb, and are fitter for such oratorical societies, as lately appeared in this metropolis, than for the pulpit.

Upon reading the preface to these Discourses, where the author speaks so favourably of oratorical embellishments, we began to suspect, that he would endeavour to amuse us with flowers of rhetoric. But we must do him the justice to observe, that, though he possesses a warm imagination, he *generally* keeps it under the restrictions of reason and good sense.

These Discourses are thrown into a regular series, and exhibit a summary view of the Christian system, or what is supposed to be the Christian system, under certain general heads, which the author has pointed out in the following recapitulation.

' Happiness in a future life is the end of religion. The human soul is the subject, which is to enjoy it. God is the object from whom it must proceed. And the means of obtaining it, is

to

to pleafe Him by doing his perfect will.—We traced the will of God by the lights of confcience, reafon, and revelation; and by the fame lights difcovered man's native inability to perform it. God created him originally able both to know and to do his duty, and engaged to make him happy on the performance of it; this is the covenant of works. His deprivation was derived from the voluntary difobedience of his primitive parents, whence fin and death enfued, with lofs of happinefs.—The love of God interpofed and projected the plan of man's redemption, by which his immortal attributes are reconciled, and our title to happinefs founded anew. He gave his eternal Son to take upon him our nature, and to difcharge the condition of the covenant of works, by perfect obedience to his will. This is the foundation of the covenant of grace.—Chrift is the mediator of this new covenant, which office divides into three branches; that of prophet, to teach men its condition, and to give them the law of the gofpel; that of prieft, to atone for their fins; and that of king, to fupport them by his grace here, and to reign over them in glory hereafter.—Thefe extraordinary truths were communicated to the world by revelation, of which prophecies, miracles, &c. are the infallible teft. The patriarchs and ancient Jews had them by promife divinely afcertained: Chriftians have them in actual enjoyment confirmed by ftronger evidences.—The Holy Scriptures, which contain this revelation, are proved to be ancient, authentic, and uncorrupted; and the writers of them to have been capable and credible witneffes, and honeft relators, of what they have advanced.—The condition of the covenant of grace, I mean the part incumbent on men, is divided into faith —obedience—and repentance.—And fince thefe cardinal duties are above the capacity of our native powers, our Saviour hath promifed to affift our endeavours by the influence of divine grace, and to intercede with his Father in heaven.—He hath farther appointed efficacious means, by which we may apply for this fpiritual affiftance, by the inftitutions of a holy worfhip—baptifin —and the eucharift.—Such are the extraordinary means, through which we are to advance to the end of our religion,—a refurrection, a future judgement, and the kingdom of the juft.'

In treating on thefe fubjects the author purfues the beaten track; but he purfues it with caution; and though he leans towards Calvinifm, he avoids the groffer abfurdities of that fyftem.

It has been ufual with thofe authors, who have reprefented human nature as utterly corrupted by the Fall, to declaim againft reafon in matters of religion. This writer however gives her a more honourable treatment, and allows her a more extenfive province.

' Though reafon can never afpire to be the companion of religion, fhe is its moft ufeful friend and hand-maid. But, when
fhe

she enters into its service, let her contemplate with serious attention its sublimity and divine extraction. Let her confider, that, however she may be the glory of man, she is herself no more than human; and let her tread on hallowed ground with humble and cautious step. By attending to the nature of religion, she will learn how far her affistance will be useful, and where her operations ought to stop. Here let her draw the line, and at her peril dare to pass it.—Religion is the immediate offspring of heaven; its nature is divine, and fingular. With its nature and doctrines human reason has no concern, only to acquiesce in reverential silence. Its fingularity, also, excludes experience, the only foundation on which she proceeds in her operations. What can she find in the compass of nature to compare it with, in order to judge and to refolve? All those regions of knowlege which are placed on the side of immortality, are forbidden ground. The holy Scriptures are a detachment from the eternal councils, to be the guide of our conduct, and the rule of our faith. Let reason content herself to enquire—When and by whom the several books were written—Whether they are the genuine and uncorrupted works of those whose names they bear—Whether the writers had a full knowlege, and were competent judges, of the facts which they relate—Whether their integrity can be relied on, as honeft and faithful hiftorians—Whether the facts, tranfactions and evidences, which they record, are fufficient credentials of a divine revelation; and whether they prove the doctrines which they fupport to be fealed by fupreme authority. And, laftly, let her inveftigate the true and diftinct meaning of thefe facred records, by comparing phrafes with phrafes, paffages with paffages, and profane with facred writings of the fame date. With confcious fallibility, she may deduce the expedience of revelation from the corruption of our nature, and from the attributes of God; she may illuftrate the œconomy of the divine difpenfations by arguments drawn from the nature of that œconomy itfelf; and she may evince fcriptural truths on fctiptural principles, as she accounts for natural phænomena by experimental obfervations. Reafon and philofophy thus employed cannot poffibly differve the caufe of religion. Thus directed in their refearches, they furnish abundance of inconteftable evidence in fupport of revelation. They bear witnefs to the miffion and divine authority of Jefus. They difmantle infidelity from the iron throne it had erected in the heart, banish error and fuperftition from brooding on the facred pavilion of religion, and rejoice to place faith, the fair offspring of heaven, on the immoveable feat of the underftanding.

'Thus reafon leads us through the mazes of teftimony divine and human to the temple of faith, and leaves us on the facred threfhold, faith receives us under her aufpice, and, if we obey her voice, she will conduct us fafely to the eternal fountain of happinefs and life. Though the credentials of faith are amenable

to

to an earthly tribunal, yet, when these are once adjuſed, ſhe ſoars above the higheſt ſtretch of reaſon in certainty, in ſublimity, and in power. She extends our hopes beyond the limits of human life, and opens an enlivening view into the ſcenes of a future world ; and though her objects be denied the intercourſe of our ſenſes, becauſe too big for our capacities to comprehend, yet are they determined as to their reality, and will be certain in the event.'

Our author is deceived, when he ſuppoſes, that ' reaſon has no concern with the *doctrines* of religion.' She is, on the contrary, very deeply and eſſentially concerned. It is incumbent on her to examine, with the utmoſt attention, whether thoſe notions, which are ſaid to be the doctrines of divine revelation, are really ſuch, or only the miſinterpretations of men. Without this, faith herſelf may be groſsly deluded, may take a dream for inſpiration, and the jargon of an enthuſiaſt for the word of God.

Our author proceeds to diſplay the glorious privileges and advantages, which the Chriſtian derives from faith.

' Above all, what divine ſupport and conſolation does it adminiſter to the ſoul ! when ſhe is oppreſſed by the cares, and ſtung by the arrows, of the world, faith can infuſe an aſſuaging and a healing balſam. Weighed down by the ſeverity of pain, affliction, and diſeaſe, ſhe looks up to faith as her deliverer. When that body, which once gloried in its vigour and beauty, is enfeebled and defaced, when the bright ſcenes of life are diveſted of their gaiety and become dull and chearleſs, when they put off the drapery of youth to take the wintry coat of age ; under all theſe temporary decays and dreary proſpects, faith can ſupport the falling fabric and the feeble knee, by directing us to look forward to a diſtant country, where brighter ſcenes will open, and perpetual youth enſue. Raiſed above the world upon the impregnable rock of faith, the ſoul looks down with indifference on the variable tumultuous tide of human things, and, in venerable dignity, ſtands unruffled by the ſtorms and tempeſts which diſturb this viſionary ſcene. Without faith ſhe is doubtful, bewildered, perplexed, unhappy. By faith her doubts are all removed, her fears are all diſpelled, her deſires are all awakened, her hopes are all confirmed. In her laſt and ſevereſt conflict with human nature, when ſhe languiſhes amidſt the ruins of her falling habitation, faith is her ſhield and buckler, her iron pillar and her wall of braſs. And when ſhe ſtands upon the brink of the vaſt ocean of eternity, without turning her eye to leave one lingering wiſh behind, ſhe is looſed as a ſhip from her cables, repoſing all her confidence on faith, as an infallible pilot to ſteer her into the harbour of ſafety, into the joy of endleſs ages.'

He

He then addresses himself to unbelievers in the following terms :

'You, whose pride, prejudice, singularity, the coldness or inhumanity of whose hearts, or whatever cause, excludes the virtue of faith—you, who reject the truths of the Bible under a pretence that they are contrary to your reason and above your understanding, pause a moment to reflect whether you have made a right use of that reason and understanding. Have you, instead of meddling with what it was never intended you should know, laid the evidences of a divine revelation before you in one collective view, and deduced the general argument? Have you considered the vast chain of prophesies, and the stupendous miracles by which it is supported, the amazing progress of the Christian profession, and the illustrious society of saints and martyrs who died to attest its truth? Have you contemplated the sublimity of its doctrines, the purity of its precepts, and the perfect sanctity of its Author? Have you canvassed the pretensions of those Scriptures by which it is transmitted to you, their antiquity, authenticity, and integrity? Have you run through the annals of Europe, and traced back the history of the church? You who ignorantly demand, in every age, the evidence of your senses to convince you, have you thoroughly weighed the evidence of testimony, and suffered it to have its force? Have you applied for the assistance of wise and learned men, and wished to be helped to proper books? Have you read the defences of Christianity, as well as the attacks upon it ; and, when you had drank the deadly poison, did you take care to apply the antidote? In short, have you done all that was in your power, with a sincere and honest intent? If you can ask your heart all these questions, and answer them truly in the affirmative, there is little danger of dying within the gloomy pale of infidelity. Or : do you vainly persuade yourselves that you will be protected from the terrors of another world by the barrier of wilful ignorance, which you are at so much pains to erect against them ?— You sceptic, you free thinker, you minute philosopher, you libertine, you profane jester, you infidel of every denomination, in a word, you who are against the gospel, because its purity, and punishments are against you, take courage and acquit yourselves as men. Dare to look through the cloud of vice, and vanity, and folly, by which conviction is shut out. You, who delight to be borne down the stream of life, whose brinks are enamelled with pleasures, and lusts, and false illusive flowers, with a smooth enchanting gale, shake off your lethargy, and cast one look forward, before you are irrecoverably swept into the dead sea. Your salvation is an affair of no trifling concern ; it demands seriousness and attention. In your religious enquiries, therefore, be sober, be candid, be impartial. Divest yourselves of passion, prejudice, and every evil affection. Reject the world and the world's law. Retire into yourselves. Consult

U 4

the

the heart. Appeal to the conscience. They will guide you more infallibly than the head alone. And remember, that if you remain obstinate against reasonable conviction, if you sin wilfully, after that you have received sufficient knowlege of tho truth—there remains no more sacrifice for sin, but a fearful looking for of judgment and fiery indignation, which shall devour the adversaries.'

There is an energy, a warmth, an animation, in this address, which incontestibly proves, that the author possesses very considerable abilities. As to some of his theological notions, we can say nothing in their favour; and therefore we cannot but think, that he acquits himself to the greatest advantage on practical subjects.

Before Mr. Tatham publishes a second edition of these Discourses, we would recommend to his consideration Taylor's Key to the Apostolic Writings, or Ben Mordecai's V. VI. and VII. Letters; and these performances may probably induce him to alter his opinion, relative to several passages of Scripture, which he has quoted in support of his theological system.

An Essay on the Right of Property in Land. 8vo. 3s. 6d. boards. Walter.

THE subject of this volume is one of the most important pertaining to human affairs; and the author has treated it with a freedom of philosophical discussion, unrestrained by the municipal laws of every country of Europe, and by the universal prejudices of mankind. He begins with delineating the right of property in land, as derived from the laws of nature.

' All right of property, says he, is founded either in occupancy or labour. The earth having been given to mankind in common occupancy, each individual seems to have by nature a right to possess and cultivate an equal share.—This right is little different from that which he has to the free use of the open air and running water; though not so indispensibly requisite at short intervals for his actual existence, it is not less essential to the welfare and right state of his life through all its progressive stages.

' No individual can derive from this general right of occupancy a title to any more than an equal share of the soil of his country.—His actual possession of more cannot of right preclude the claim of any other person who is not already possessed of such equal share.

' This

' This title to an equal fhare of property in land feems original, inherent, and indefeafible by any act or determination of others, though capable of being alienated by our own. It is a birth-right which every citizen ftill retains.—— Though by entering into fociety and partaking of its advantages, he muft be fuppofed to have fubmitted this natural right to fuch regulations as may be eftablifhed for the general good, yet he can never be underftood to have tacitly renounced it altogether ; nor ought any thing lefs to eftablifh fuch alienation than an exprefs compact in mature age, after having been in actual poffeffion, or having had a free opportunity of entering into the poffeffion of his equal fhare.

' Every ftate or community ought in juftice to referve for all its citizens, the opportunities of entering upon, or returning to, and refuming this their birth-right and natural employment, whenever they are inclined to do fo.

' Whatever inconveniences may be thought to accompany this refervation, they ought not to ftand in the way of effential juftice.

' Although at firft fight fuch refervation may appear incompatible with the eftablifhed order of focieties, and the permanent cultivation of the earth, yet ought it on the other hand to be prefumed, that what is fo plainly founded on the natural rights of men, may by wife regulations be rendered at leaft confiftent with the beft order and profperity of focieties, and with the progrefs of agriculture ; perhaps, very beneficial to the one, and the higheft encouragement to the other.

' In many rude communities, this original right has been refpected, and their public inftitutions accommodated to it, by annual, or at leaft frequent partitions of the foil, as among the ancient Germans, and among the native Irifh even in Spenfer's time.

' Wherever conquefts have taken place, this right has been commonly fubverted, and effaced.

' In the progrefs of commercial arts and refinements, it is fuffered to fall into obfcurity and neglect.'

He afterwards proceeds to fhew that fpeculative reafoners have confounded this equal right with that which is founded in labour, and afcertained by municipal law : that the right of a landholder to an extenfive eftate muft be founded chiefly in labour : that the progrefs of cultivation gives an afcendant to the right of labour, over that of general occupancy : but the public good requires, that both fhould be refpected and combined. He obferves that fuch combination is difficult, and has rarely been eftablifhed for any length of time ; but that it is the proper object of agrarian laws ; and that effectual

fectual means of establishing it may be devised. He distinguishes the value of an estate in land into three parts; the original, the improved, and the improveable value. He remarks that the original and the improveable value of a great estate still belong to the community, and the improved alone to the landholder : that the original value is the proper subject of land-taxes ; that the improveable value may be separated from the improved, and ought to be still open to the claims of the community.

In section second, he considers the right of property in land, as founded on public utility. He sets out upon the principle, that public happiness is the object of good government ; and he endeavours to prove that this is most effectually promoted by independent cultivation of the ground.

In section third, he treats of the abuses and pernicious effects of that exorbitant right of property in land, which the municipal laws of Europe have established. He observes that the oppression proceeding from this right debases the spirit, and corrupts the probity of the lower ranks ; that it checks the progress of agriculture ; and that under the influence of this territorial monopoly, the increase of population tends to diminish public happiness.

In section first of part second, the author considers the circumstances and occasions favourable to a complete reformation of the laws respecting property in land, by the legislative power. In section second, he enumerates the circumstances and occasions favourable to a partial reformation of such laws ; and in section third, he investigates the circumstances which might induce the rulers of a state to direct their endeavours towards the accomplishment of such a change. The four remaining sections of the work are occupied with the consideration of the methods by which this end might be effected. Those are, public institutions, calculated for promoting a gradual and salutary change in the state of property in land ; the generous efforts of private persons acting singly for this purpose ; the united endeavours of private persons ; and a progressive Agrarian law, which might be made the basis of all partial and occasional reformation, respecting property in land.

Such are the principles and suggestions of this speculative Essay, which aims at a reformation never to be expected in any country where the right of territorial property has once been established. The author, however, displays ingenuity ; and the force of his reasoning will be less disputed, than the practicability of the problem which he endeavours to recommend.

A View

A View of Society and Manners in High and Low Life; being the Adventures in England, Ireland, Scotland, Wales, France, *&c. of Mr. G. Parker. In which is comprised a History of the Stage Itinerant. 2 Vols. 12mo. 6s. sewed.* Whieldon.

THESE two volumes contain the adventures of an unfortunate itinerant player, who passed through a series of distresses too often, we believe, experienced by the lower orders in that profession. As the incidents and circumstances which he relates have nothing striking or uncommon in them, the account of his peregrinations, though not ill-written, has nothing in it very interesting or amusive. The hero of the tale, Mr. G. Parker, calls his book A View of Society and Manners (in imitation, we suppose, of Dr. Moore) in *High* and *Low* Life; though, on inspection, we find it entirely confined to the latter, with which he seems indeed to be intimately acquainted. The greater part of the second volume is employed in delineating the characters of every species of thieves and pick-pockets that abound in and about this great metropolis; and is filled with such names as our readers, we may venture to answer for them, never heard of before, such as *chaunter-culls, kiddy-nippers, carrier-pigeons, lifters, jigger-dubbers, knuckles, stoop-knappers, shove-tumrils, morning sneaks, evening sneaks, lumpers, reader-merchants,* and fifty or sixty more of the same kind. These, it seems, are the *cant* names for various sorts of cheats and sharpers, whose occupation, tricks, and frauds, this *ingenious* traveller most accurately describes and exposes.

As there is something curious and uncommon in this part of the work, we shall lay two or three of the characters before our readers.

'CARRIER PIGEONS.

' This is one of the most curious species of villainy that ever was put in practice. It is the grand *arcanum*, the *secret of secrets*, because it takes in the deepest set of scoundrels that ever robbed a generous public; —— I mean lottery-office keepers.

' This is practised by three men and a woman.

' One of the men gets into Guildhall on a morning the moment the lottery commences drawing, and takes down on a split card the second or third number drawn, then runs to the second at the corner of a street, who is termed the *pigeon,* and gives him the number.

' The pigeon being mounted on a very good horse, flies directly to the west end of the town, where a third man on foot meets him, takes the number from the pigeon, and goes into the lottery-office.

' Here

‘ Here there has been a decent looking-woman fitting in the office some twelve or fourteen minutes before his entrance.

‘ He enquires the price of tickets, or examines a number; then flips the card, unperceived by the office-keeper or his clerks, into the woman's hand, and quits the office.

‘ The woman is now left in poffeffion of the fecret to work upon. She afks the office-keeper to infure, and he knowing how long fhe has been in the office, even before the lottery began to be drawn, infures without a queftion.

‘ The woman calls at night, and is told by the office keeper, that fhe has been very lucky to-day, for her ticket is come up; they wifh her fuccefs, and fhe receives the money immediately.’

‘ L I F T E R S.

‘ Is a fpecies of theft executed in the following manner: a genteel-looking woman goes into a large fhop, and afks to look at fome of the neweft-fafhion lace; fhe has a fmall fifh-hook in her hand, which fhe fixes in a piece of lace, and then lets it flip down between her and the counter, at the fame time covering it with her coats: this done, fhe buys a yard of lace, and then in putting her hand into her pocket, pulls a ftring which is fixed to the hook and communicates with her pocket, into which fhe lifts the lace by it. This completed, off fhe fets, with thanks for being a cuftomer, who has *done them upon the lift.*’

‘ R E A D E R - M E R C H A N T S.

‘ Reader is cant for a pocket-book. This bufinefs is practifed by young Jews, who ply only at the Bank and the Royal Exchange.

‘ When you go through the Jews Walk at this laft place, it is more than probable that you are *done* for your pocket-book.

‘ The reader-merchants are particularly watchful of people coming out of the Bank; who if they take coach, as they ftep into it, are almoft fure to be *done.*

‘ If a-foot, they contrive to attract their attention by a number of ways, of which the following is an inftance. In going over any of the Bridges, one of them runs before the perfon into whofe pocket they intend making the *dive,* and cries out, “ There, there, they will be all drowned!” As foon as the gentleman puts his head through the baluftrades to fee the horrible fight, and leaves his pockets expofed, they *work* for his pocket-book, which is done in fo clever a manner, that even fhould the actual pickpocket be perceived by you, yet he has handed it away in fuch a clever manner, that in lefs than twenty minutes it is in Duke's Place, from whence it may be faid to be irrecoverable; for they generally fend the notes to Holland, where they are immediately difpofed of.’

While

While we lament the extreme corruption and depravity of an age that can produce such characters as these, we cannot but acknowlege the utility that may arise from exhibiting them to public view ; to put us upon our guard against their fraud and iniquity.

Nôffe omnia hæc falus eft adolefcentibus.

FOREIGN ARTICLES.

Defcription des principales Pierres gravées du Cabinet de S. A. S. Mfgr. le Duc d' Orleans, &c. Tome 1. *Folio.* 303 *Pages. Paris.*

THE firft fund for this very capital and famous collection, was brought by the fifter and heirefs of Charles II. Elector Palatine, from Heidelberg to Paris. This fund was afterwards increafed by the purchafe of P. Crozat's great and celebrated cabinet. The prefent defcription is a joint performance of Meffieurs l'abbé de la Chau, the infpector of the cabinet l'abbé le Blond, and l'abbé Arnaud. The whole work is to be comprifed in two volumes ; the firft contains one hundred of the fineft antiques, defigned and engraved in a moft elegant and mafterly ftyle, by M. St. Aubin ; who as well as the authors of the text, has been ftudioufly intent on difplaying the characteriftics of each particular piece, the beauties or defects of the performance or drawing of the ancient artift. And upon the whole, in point of plan, arrangement, critical erudition, tafte, and elegance of execution, both on the fide of the authors and of the engraver, the prefent work is by far fuperior to the Monumenta Matthæana.

The preface contains a fevere but judicious review of former works on ancient gems. The plan of the work itfelf, and the arrangement of the gems are nearly the fame as that in Winkelmann's defcription of Baron Stofch's cabinet. The firft volume relates entirely to mythology ; beginning with a fine head of Ifis, and a ftill finer cameo of Harpocrates ; thefe are fucceeded by mafterly performances of Grecian artifts ; a Jupiter ; a Titan ; a Leda ; a Ganymede ; a Minerva ; a Ceres ; a Proferpine ; a Diana ; the whole feries of heathen divinities, and a few heroes. The volume is befides decorated with a moft excellent frontifpiece, exhibiting the portrait of the duke of Orleans, and a number of attributes : and with fifty-one elegant head and tail pieces.

This firft volume fells for feventy-two livres. The fecond which is to appear in 1782, and to contain fubjects from the Grecian and Roman hiftory, will coft only forty-eight livres.

Hiftoire générale de Provence, *dédiée aux Etats. Vol.* 1 and 2. *Quarto. Paris.*

BY Mr. Papon, a member of the academy, and prieft of the oratory at Marfeilles, who with great labour and induftry, has collected both known and unknown materials, and warmly commends the readinefs of moft of the keepers of records and magiftrates

trates of his native country; and of several learned men, to affist
him with their labours in the execution of his plan. The oldeft
inscriptions have been explained by M. Seguier de Nimes: the lite
rary history of the middle ages was furnished by abbé de Capris de
Beauvezet. M de S. Palaye had communicated to our author the
MS. of his well known work on the Troubadours; as were the valuable collections made on the general and particular administration of Provence, by the late M. de Monclar, procureur-general
du parlement, and the accounts which others sent him by the command of the procureur du-Pays, enabled him to draw up a complete geographial description of Provence. For his accounts of its
natural history, he was furnished with Dr. de Lieutaud's MS. Zoology, and D. Gerard de Cotignac's Botany of Provence. The
beft histories hitherto published of Provence, by Messieurs Ruffi
and Bouché contain indeed excellent materials, but are poorly
written. Our author, therefore, availed himself of them as compi-
lations, for compofing a history alike valuable for critical fagacity,
tafte, learning, and fpirit; abounding in facts and obfervations interefting to philofophers and lawyers, and free from needlefs and
tedious digreffions.

The firft volume contains, in fix hundred and eighty-nine pages;
firft, a chorography; then, the firft book of the hiftory, which begins with the foundation of the city of Marfeilles, nearly five hundred and ninety-nine years before the Chriftian æra, and concludes
with the introduction of Chriftianity, in the year 300; and finally
four differtations: 1. On the learned men in Provence, anterior to
the year 100, of the Chriftian æra; 2. On the age in which Pytheas
flourifhed (three hundred and twenty-two years before Chrift;)
and on Thule, which our author finds in Iceland; 3. On the fabulous
tradition of St. Trophimus, who, though he came not into Provence till about the middle of the fecond century, has yet been
pretended to have been a difciple of St. Paul. On fome grand Roman monuments, among which the famous triumphal arch at
Orange, feem to have been defigned for a memorial of the fix great
battles, by which Provence was reduced into a Roman province;
and on the moft ancient coins of Marfeilles, feveral of thefe coins
are exhibited on three copper-plates; four other plates contain a
head of Diana; fome Provençal civil and military ftatues, and two
maps, one of ancient Roman, and another of modern Provence.
The chorography treats of the nature of the foil, the air, its temperature, the quantity of rain between 1770 and 1775, and plants
and animals. The firft book of the hiftory is interfperfed with accounts of the trade and manners of the Grecian colonifts at Marfeilles, and the number of colonies pretended to have been fettled
by that city is greatly reduced. Our author thinks that the Greeks
imported polytheifm, human facrifices, and many fpecies of trees,
fuch as olive, plums, apple, pear, mulberry, vine, cherry, fig, nut,
and chefnut trees, into Marfeilles.

The fecond volume contains, in feven hundred and thirty pages;
the fecond, third, and fourth book of the hiftory, or the times,
from the third century, to the year 1257, when Charles of Anjou
obtained peaceable poffeffion of Provence. The lawlefs meafures
repeatedly taken by the popes and the Gallic clergy, in order to
ufurp the fovereignty of the country, are here minutely related, and
many cruelties committed againft the Albegeois, are juftly and fe-
verely cenfured. Neither are the hiftories of religion, of political
con-

conftitutions, of arts, of fciences, and manners, neglected. The difference between the Gallic, the Roman, the Provençal, and the Franconian nobility, is exactly noticed. The counts of Provence, and fome of the bifhops, are here faid to have rendered themfelves already independent during the laft year of the Burgundian king. Rodolphus; though the archbifhop, and the city of Arles, continued a long time after faithful to the emperor.

Gallantry was imported from Greece and Italy into France, by Conftantia, princefs of Touloufe and Provence, who in 998, married Robert, king of France.

In 1136, king Fulco, of Jerufalem, granted to the citizens of Marfeilles, the mercantile confular in the Levant, which they ftill poffefs. In 1774, the wealth of Provence, and its attendant wantonnefs, were rifen to fuch a degree, that at a meeting at Beaucaire, a gentleman ordered the equivalent of 100 000 livres of the prefent French money, to be diftributed among fuch as happened to be prefent: that another caufed 30,000 fols to be fown, in deniers, on a ploughed field; and that a third, in mere wantonnefs of expenfive cruelty, cauſed thirty of his fineſt horſes to be burned alive. (The wretch deferved to be thrown into the fame fire!)

In 1298, the citizens in Provence, proved, that, though they were not nobles, they were yet capable of being received chevaliers, and of enjoying all the honours belonging to that fpecies of knighthood.

The firft troubadour, was William, count of Poitou, who died in 1122, and is alfo faid to have been the inventor of the tales of the fairies. The poems of thefe troubadours, to whom the author has allotted a whole fection, are not fo ancient as it has been pretended by Noftradamus and others, and are liable to difpleafe by their famenefs, and an exceffive affectation of tendernefs.

The code of Juftinian was already introduced into Provence, in 1253, and taught by a profeffor at Aix. In 1172, the Jews had a college or fchool at Arles, and enjoyed a jurifdiction of their own, which was confirmed to them by the archbifhop, in 1215.

Kermes was gathered in the twelfth century; and fo early as 1209, the wearing of filk ftuffs was become fo general, as to require limitations. Gold and filver were melted down, and preferved in the treafuries in ingots: and though coin was fcarce, the prices of commodities were very high; for a horfe, that is now fold for four marcs of filver, was in 1202, purchafed for thirteen and a half marcs of filver; and in 1155, for five flaves.

M. de St. Vincent has fubjoined a very learned differtation on the coins of the counts of Provence, Touloufe, and Rouergues, of the lords of Andufe, and of many archbifhops and bifhops; enriched with feven copper-plates, and a table of reductions of all the coins between 973 and 1272, to their intrinfic value. From this differtation we obferve that moft of them had obtained the right of coining from the German emperors, and that the bifhop of Melgueil ufed Arabic characters on his coins, probably in order to promote their circulation among the Saracens in Spain. A fecond differtation treats of the origin, formation, and extenfion of the Provençal tongue: and a third relates to the genealogical tables of the counts of Provence, of Forcalquier, and of Weftern Provence, and of the vifcounts of Marfeilles. The fecond volume concludes with a fmall collection of records.

Voyage

Voyage Littéraire de Provence; *contenant tout ce qui peut donner une Idée de l'Etat ancien & moderne, des Villes; les Curiosités quelles renferment; la Position des anciens Peuples, quelques Anecdotes, Litteraires, l'Histoire Naturelle, les Plantes, le Climat, &c. et cinq Lettres sur les Trouveres et les Troubadours. Par* M. P. D. L.   12mo.   Paris.

THE desire of informing and entertaining both travellers and such readers as read chiefly for their amusement, has induced M. Papon, the author of the history of Provence, just noticed, to collect and compress into a small volume many interesting objects dispersed, both in the volumes of his history of Provence, which are already published and in those, which are still to follow, to diversify the abstract by another arrangement calculated for his present purpose, and to improve it by the addition of many articles not to be met with in his larger work.

In the present volume we accordingly find ancient history and geography joined to modern, spritely Latin and French verses to ancient inscriptions, and the curiosities of art to those of nature, in the accounts of the cities of Avignon, Arles, Aix, Marseilles, Toulouse, of the fountains of Vaucluse, of Sainte Beaume, of the Crau, and the Camargue; of the isle of St. Margaret, and the famous man with the iron mask; of the organization of mountains, the indigenous and exotic plants growing in Provence, its fossils, its real or probable physical revolutions; its most remarkable fishes and birds; its climate, winds, and rain; a short treatise on the peculiar administration of Provence, the number of post stages on the high roads; the most remarkable and picturesque views: and, finally, five curious letters, in which father Papon asserts, against the author of the Recueil des Fabliaux, who had maintained that the trouveres, or northern French poets, were not only anterior in point of time, but superior in point of poetical merit to the Eastern or Provençal troubadours); that these Provençal poets, or troubadours, have in fact been the inventors of modern poetry, and the models on which the poets of other nations have formed themselves: that the trouveres had by no means that original character, with which the editor of the Fabliaux had complimented them, but that they are almost always imitators and copyists of the troubadours, and even of the Italian poets, who themselves consider the Provençal troubadours as the fathers of modern poetry:

Mémoires sur l'ancienne Chévalerie, considerée comme un Establissement politique et militaire; par M. de la Curne de Sainte, Palaie, &c. *Nouvelle Edition; augmentée d'un Volume*   3 *Vols.* 12mo. *of which the additional third is sold separately.*   Paris.

IT is on account of this third and additional volume, that we here take notice of this new edition. It contains some curious, and interesting pieces: such as an odd short poem, entitled: le Voeu du Heron, or rather, the Vow on the Heron. " The count of Artois, banished from France, and retired to London, resolves on instigating the king and all the barons of England, to a war against France.   For this purpose he avails himself of an opportunity when that monarch happened to be surrounded by his whole court; the count puts a roasted heron between two plates, carries it himself round the assembly, and forces the king, the queen, and all
the

the lords, to vow on that bird with the moft dreadful imprecations, to do every poffible mifchief to France; and at laft by way of fealing this fatal vow, cuts up the heron, and makes the whole affembly eat of it,' &c. Of all thofe who fwore upon the heron, not one was, unfortunately for France, more faithful to his vow than Gautier de Mauny, one of the moft diftinguifhed knights errants; whofe principal atchievements are by M. S. Palaie collected from Froiffard into a diftinct memoir; as the characters of the other perfonages concerned are exhibited in notes.

The fecond piece is entitled, la Canife, ou la Camife; and ftill more extravagant. It reprefents a lady mad enough to appear in the midft of a grand entertainment, and in the prefence of her hufband, in a fhirt died with the blood of her lover, and rent by the multitude of wounds he had received in the fingle combats which he had fought by her commands. M. de S. Palaie is apt to confider this poem as a mere fiction, as one of thofe literary extravagancies which prove that the enthufiafm of chivalry operated then as powerfully on the brains of the poets as on thofe of the knights; that is, that it turned them all together fomewhat mad: it may be fo; yet when we recollect numbers of fallies, to the full as extravagant, produced by wantonnefs, prompted and influenced by wine and vanity, the contagion of licentioufnefs and debauchery in ancient and modern times, among ladies as well as men, we are lefs confident that the extravagance exhibited in the poem was not founded on fome extravagance really difplayed by fome lady, and encouraged by men.

The third memoir, which, at the fame time, is alfo the longeft and moft interefting in the whole volume, contains an hiftorical delineation of the chace, from the firft ages of the French monarchy to the prefent times. It is divided into four parts, and each of thefe illuftrated with notes; and abounds with many curious and amufing anecdotes.

Summandrag af Swea-Rikes Hiftoria, Ifran de Aldfta til de nyafte Tider. Til Ungdomens Tienft upfatt af Swen Lagerbring, *Cancellie Raid och Hiftorifka Profeffor* Lund, &c. &c. *or, A Sketch of the Hiftory of the Kingdom of* Sweden, *from the earlieft to the prefent Times, drawn up for the Ufe of Youth, by* Swen Lagerbring, *Counfellor of the Chancery, and Profeffor of Hiftory at* Lund, &c. Paris *and* Stockholm. (Swedifh.)

PRofeffor Lagerbring, who has written a great and celebrated Hiftory of Sweden, for which he has been ennobled, has drawn up this concife furvey of the hiftory and ftate of that kingdom, at the requeft of Mr. Gjoerwel, and for the elementary inftruction of youth. Mr. Gjoerwel, librarian to his Swedifh majefty, informs his readers, that from a defire of improving the public inftruction of the Swedifh youth in hiftorical knowlege, he had refolved on the publication of elementary hiftories, both of ancient and modern ftates. Among thofe of the modern, that of Sweden was publifhed firft; it has fince been fucceeded by that of Denmark; which will be followed by the hiftories of Ruffia and Poland, written by Mr. Erl. Samuel Bring. The fketch of the ftate of Sweden is the moft interefting part of the performance. The author treats, in his preface, of the great ufe of hiftorical knowlege, of the poffibility of compofing an authentic and practical hiftory, even though the writer himfelf might not have had any fhare in the adminiftration, or councils. or fecrets of the ftate; and proceeds then to an enumeration of the main fources of hiftory and political knowlege of the ftate of Sweden, in general.

The treatife itfelf gives an account of the fize of the kingdom, the contents of the furface; its productions, corn, forefts, rural oeconomy; of the population of the kingdom in general, and of each province in particular; with fchemes for improving that population, and the decaying towns; of its home trade, external commerce, quantity of exports and imports, manufactories, Eaft India trade; its mines; the feveral boards and departments; the land forces, fortifications, fleet, and maritime regulations; orders of knighthood, and ecclefiaftical ftate.

Since 1618, no corn has been exported from Sweden; on the contrary 500,000 tuns of corn are now annually imported into that kingdom, chiefly, or perhaps even merely, for the confumption of the ftill. From Charles the Twelfth's death to 1769, the number of people in Sweden and Finland has been doubled; in 1769, it amounted to 2,571,825 perfons, which gives to a Swedifh fquare-league no more than 267 perfons; whilft Denmark contains not lefs than 1210 perfons to every one of its fmaller leagues. Stockholm contains 80,000 perfons. The labours on the grand projected canals have ceafed for fome time. From 1770 to 1774, the gold mines of Smaland afforded gold for 4130 ducats. The mines of Salberg yielded in 1773, 1817 marks of filver. The profits on the Eaft India commodities amounted in 1776, to 5,115,473 Swedifh dollars of filver coin. The exports confifts in metals, wood, fifh, Eaft Indian articles, ftuffs, leather, lime, China, furniture, books (to the value of 18,907 Swedifh dollars of filver coin), corn, drugs, falt, hemp, indigo, coffee, and fome other fmaller articles.

Sammandrag of Swea Rikes Hiftoria, &c. *Part III. and IV.* by the fame author are now likewife publifhed. The third part contains the hiftory of Sweden from Guftavus I. to Chriftina; and the fourth, which is again fubdivided into feveral fections, concludes with the death of Charles XII. The hiftory of the wars before Charles XI. is very fhort: but the author's account of the political conftitution, the adminiftration, the national manners, the arts, and efpecially learning, are more minute and full, and fometimes interfperfed with hints advifing the re-eftablifhment of fome neglected, though ufeful, regulations. The author approves of the famous executions of Paikul and Patkul: but has not neglected the apology for baron Goertz, publifhed of late years, and noticed in our Review, in judging of the actions and conduct of that celebrated and unfortunate minifter. Though the fufpicion that Charles XII. may have fallen by the hands of Siquier, is here greatly ftrengthened, Mr. Lagerbring thinks it yet improbable, that a king's officer could have been guilty of that affaffination.

Hiftorifka Uplyfningar om Tilftændet i Swerrige under Konung Fredric *den Foerftes Regering.* 8vo. Stockholm. (Swedifh.)

THE journal of a Swedifh politician, which has a long time been circulated in MS. among Swedes and foreigners, and is now firft publifhed with feveral alterations and improvements: in fome places it has been fhortened, in others, weeded of difgufting

gufting partiality, and in fome illuftrated with interefting notes.
The moft remarkable paffages relate to the refolutions of the Swedifh
generals, immediately after the death of Charles XII. to the ftill
more important diets which fucceeded that cataftrophe ; to baron
Goertz's bold and extravagant fchemes of getting at the fame time
Germany, Great Britain, Poland, and Norway, conquered for the
Pretender, for Peter I. Charles XII. and king Staniflaus ; to king
Frederick's connexions with the countefs Taube; to the war between
Sweden and Ruffia ; to the execution of Loewenhaupt, which is
here cenfured ; to the infurrection of the Dalecarlians ; and, in general, to many of the more ftriking events and tranfactions under
the reign of Frederic I. hitherto not yet fufficiently known to foreigners.

De l'Etat du Sort des Colonies des Anciens Peuples. 8vo. Philadelphia.

THE author of this inftructive and entertaining performance is
said to be one M. de Sainte Croix, a native of Canada. His
purpofe is to difpute the rights of mother countries over their colonies ; and efpecially to confute the Hiftory of Colonizations, originally publifheu in Englifh, and fince tranflated, with various additions, into French and German ; and the affertions of M. de Bou-
gainville.
  The author's plan is very extenfive. Not contented with treating
of the conftitutions of colonies, and of their relations to their refpective mother countries, he takes in the whole hiftory of colonies and even of their mother countries, and the refpective conftitutions of both : but his very digreffions are valuable. He takes
the word colonies, in its moft comprehenfive fenfe, including in it
all forts of emigrations ; and begins with the Phœnicians, their
trade and colonies in Cyprus, Thafos, on the coafts of Thrace, in
Bœotia, Spain, Gades, and Carthage. He then proceeds to the
hiftory and conftitution of Carthage ; whofe colonies confifted
chiefly of Liby-Phœnicians, or defcendants of Phœnician emigrants
who had fettled along the coafts of Africa, mixed with the Li-
byans, and probably degenerated : and had been fubdued by the
Carthaginians, and treated on the fame footing on which fubjects
of an ariftocracy are generally treated, and with that additional contempt, which is now experienced by the Meftices in America. From
the furvey of Carthage and her colonies he comes to that of Greece
and her colonies: here he likewife touches on the origin of the
Grecian tribes ; their culture by Phœnician and Egyptian emigrants ; on the revolutions and unions of feveral people ; on the
Amphictyons, and on the internal conftitutions of fo many different ftates ; and at length on their colonies; on the conftitution
of Athens ; on her conduct towards her colonies; on the hiftory
of her wars; on the oppreffion of her colonies, whom fhe counted
as her allies, and, like her other allies, held under the hardeft
yoke. In her continual wars with her neighbours, and efpecially
with Sparta, thefe allies, and her colonies among the reft, fometimes from neceffity or defpair, took part with her enemies ; and
were, of courfe, treated like faithlefs allies.
  The book concludes with a chapter on the modern colonies of
the Europeans, and with a declamation againft the rapacity, ty-

ranny,

ranny, and false politics exercised against the colonies, in order to keep them, by jealousies and internal dissensions, in slavery. It is easy to conceive that on this occasion the English are much more severely treated by our author, than the French; though he also bitterly complains of the former conduct of the French, towards his countrymen, the inhabitants of Canada.

Beytræge zur Geschichte der Erfindungen; or, Contributions to the History of Inventions; by Professor John Beckmann, *of* Goettingen. 8vo. Leipzig. (German.)

THE first article in this instructive and entertaining publication contains the history of Italian book keeping. The first who taught that art in professed treatises, was the celebrated mathematician Lucas Paciolus de Burgo S. Sepulchri, a Minorite, of whose scarce works notice is here occasionally interspersed.

This history is succeeded by that of odometers, beginning with the notices collected from Vitruvius, and carried down to the latest improvements, of which that made by the late Mr. Hohlfeld, is the most interesting. The life of that excellent and very ingenious artist is here inserted, as drawn up by professor Muller, of Berlin.

The history of brandy distillery follows next: then that of the separation of gold and silver by means of mercury, and of gilding, by amalgama; that of the improvement of lighting streets, where we learn that Antioch, Cæsarea in Cappadocia, and several other cities, of ancient times, had their streets regularly lighted, but not Rome. In modern times that useful institution was first introduced at London and Paris. Here we are told that Paris is now lighted by 6233, London by about 15,000, Venice by 3000, Berlin by 2354, Vienna by 3000, Cassel by 1013, and Goettingen by 400 lamps.

The author proceeds to an historical account of privileges against pirating books, and of the censure of books, previous to their impression and publication. There are instances of authors submitting their performances to the judgement of their governments, even before the discovery of the art of printing.

Some account of the oldest printed almanacs; their progress and successive improvements since the discovery of the art of printing. The oldest almanac calculated for one year, known to professor Beckmann, is one of Hamburgh, for the year 1546.

Some account of the mill for weaving ribbon, follows. It was contrived either in the Netherlands or in Germany, towards the end of the sixteenth or beginning of the seventeenth century; but Dantzick is said to have had one so early as the year 1579. In the Netherlands it was known and used about the year 1621, and prohibited by the States general, in 1623.

Some account of the scarce book of pyrotechnia, by Vanuccio Biringoccio, the oldest Italian work on metallurgy, and very interesting for the history of that art.

This first part of Mr. Beckmann's book will be followed by some more.

FOREIGN

FOREIGN LITERARY INTELLIGENCE.

Déscription et Usage de quelques Lampes à l'Air inflammable. Par F. L. Ehrmann. Strasburg.

MR. Ehrmann describes four lamps for inflammable air, of which the first has been contrived by Mr. Fürstenberger, at Basil; the second, by Mr. Brander, at Augsburg; the third, by Mr. De Gabriel; and the last, and simplest, by Mr Ehrmann himself, and his younger brother. His description is very minute, and illustrated with a copper-plate; and he has subjoined an account of Mr. Neret's warming-pan.

Nouvelle Methode d'extraire la Pierre de la Vessie urinaire par dessus le Pubis sans le Sécours d'aucun Fluide dans la Vessie. 8vo. Paris

A new and valuable improvement made by the famous Fr. Côme.

Chr. Godof. Schütz, *Eloq. & Poës. Prof P. O. in Acad* Jenensi, *Commentationum in* Æschyli *Tragœdiam, quæ inscripta est* Agamemnon, *Libellus primus.* 96 *Pages in Quarto.* Jena.

The learned author begins his commentary on Agamemnon, the most difficult of the Greek tragedies, with developing the fable, and the conduct of the poet; and then proceeds to a very full and very judicious critical illustration of the first act to verse 265.

Nuove Sperienze Idrauliche fatte ne' Canali e ne Fiumi, *per verificare le principali Leggi & Fenomeni delle Acque correnti*; dell' *Abate* Leonardo Ximenés, *Matematico di S. A. R. &c. &c.* 1 vol. in 4to with *Plates.* Siena.

The author, a skilful engineer, had continual opportunities for making observations, and all the theory necessary for drawing general and useful inferences from his observations. He describes a machine of his own invention, with which he has made several experiments on the canal of the lake of Castiglione, and on the river Arno. He explains all the deductions which must be made from the experiments; and the method of determining from thence the swiftness and the strength of the fluid. He gives tables of the various degrees of rapidity, observed at different depths of the water; and shows the falsity of the rules hitherto adopted in these matters. He also calculates the diminution of that rapidity which takes place towards the banks of a river. He concludes with applying the experiments to the measurement of the velocity of winds, so difficult to be known, and to that of the wake of a ship.

Stephani Salagii, *Presb.* Quinque Ecclesiensis *S. D. de Statu Ecclesiæ* Pannonicæ *Libri VII. Liber Primus, de Statu Civili* Pannoniæ; *Liber secundus, de Initiis Religionis Christianæ in* Pannonia; *Liber Tertius, de Antiquis Episcopatibus in* Pannonia. *Gr. Quarto.* Quinque-Ecclesiis. (*or* Five-Churches, *an Episcopal City in* Hungary.)

This work was undertaken by the command and under the auspices of the late learned George Klimo, bishop of Five churches, and its publication afterwards procured by count Joseph Garampi, the pope's nuncio at Vienna.

The first book contains a full and accurate account of the political state of Pannonia, during the five periods anterior to Dioclesian, to the extinction of the Western Empire, to Charlemagne, to

the

the arrival of the Huns, and to the reign of king Stephen the Saint.

In the second book, the author enquires for the first Christian teachers of the Pannonians, Huns, and Sclaves; and thinks it not improbable that St. Peter had been in Sirmium, and the centurion Cornelius, the first Heathen who was christened, in Siscium, or Sissec, &c. &c.

In the third book, he examines the various accounts of the most ancient bishopricks in Pannonia, those of Sirmium, Mursa, Cibalis, Bassiana, Siscia, and Petabio.

Adumbratio Eruditorum Basileensium, *Meritis apud exteros olim hodieque celebrium. Appendicis loco* Athenis Rauracis *addita.* 8*vo.* Basil.

A valuable accession to literary history, as it gives an account of fifty four learned natives of Basil, of the principal incidents of their lives, and of their works. Several of them may justly be ranked among the most eminent in their respective professions: such as, John Bernoulli, at Berlin ; Leonbard Euler, Charles Euler, John James Huber, John Bernhard Merian, Leonhard Thurneiser, Bernhard Verzaska.

La Navigation, Poeme en quatre Chants. 175 *pages.* 8*vo.* Paris.

The subject of this poem is indeed very interesting, and at the same time susceptible of poetical embellishments ; but the author's poetical performance wants spirit, and a plan ; and even the notes subjoined to each of its four cantos are deficient in point of instruction and precision.

Mémoire sur cette Question : combien dépensera un Canal à point de partage pour le Passage d'un Bateau. Dans lequel on examine l'Etat présent du Canal de Briare, en indiquant les Moyens de perfectionner sa Navigation, après avoir préalablement démontré l'inconvenient des Ecluses accolées & des grandes Ecluses en général. D'ou l'on conclud les Regles à suivre pour déterminer la Grandeur et le Placement des Ecluses dans tout Canal de Navigation, dont il est essentiel de menager les Eaux. Par M. de Fer. *Quarto.* Paris.

The views and means hinted at in the title of this memoir are interesting, and their discussion contains new and valuable observations on the subject.

Memorabilia circa Aërem, Vitæ genus, Sanitatem, et Morbos Clausthaliensium *Annorum* 1774—1777. *Aut.* Lebrecht Frid. Benj. Lentin, *Phys.* Clausthal. 144 *Pages in Quarto.* Goettingæ.

This excellent publication opens with an account of the local situation, the nature of the air, the weather, the diet, the employments, and the health of the inhabitants of the mine-town of Clausthal, on the Hartz ; and this is succeeded by a very concise but masterly account of the nature, causes, and variations of the epidemical diseases which prevailed there from October 1774 to the end of the year 1777.

Nicol. Jos. Jacquin *Miscellanea* Austriaca, *ad Botanicam, Chemiam, & Historiam Naturalem spectantia, cum Figuris partim coloratis. Vol.* I. *Quarto.* Viennæ.

A collection of seven valuable treatises on several subjects, illustrated with twenty-one accurate copper-plates, finely coloured after nature.

Editiones

Lectiones Mosquenses. *Edit.* Cbr. Fred. Matthæi, *Prof. & Rect. Gymn.* Mosq. *Vol. I.* 8*vo.* 120 *Pages.* Lipsiæ.

Containing an homily or sermon of John Chrysostom, never before published; a fragment on the twenty-six chapters of St Matthew, from the Catena in IV. Evang. which is attributed to Euthymius Zigabenus; some fragments of a physical book; specimens from the Alphabetical Grammar of George Lecapenus, a writer of the fourteenth century; an account of a MS. of Columella, in the possession of a M. de Demidow; some various readings or variantes, from a MS. of Aratus, with the interlinear glosses; extant in the library of the holy synod, &c. &c. M. Mathei would oblige the public by selecting and publishing only the most interesting parts of the treasures of Greek MSS. in Moscow.

Μωριας Εγκωμιον, *five Stultitiæ Laus,* Def. Erasmi Rot. *Declamatio: cum Commentariis* Ger. Liftsii, *ineditis* Ofwaldi Molitoris, *et Figuris* Jo. Holbenii. *Denuo Typis mandavit* Guil. Gottl. Becker. 8*vo.* Bafil.

An elegant edition of that famous declamation, illustrated with some additional notes, and eighty-three humorous figures copied from those drawn by Holbein, and neatly cut in wood.

De Dictione tropica etiam Scripturæ Sacræ Libri III. Aut. Tob. Gottfr. Hegelmater. *Theol. D. &c.* 8*vo.* Tubingæ.

The doctrine of the tropes is here treated on the principles of the ancient and best modern rhetoricians, and applied to the explanation of a great variety of obscure or disputed passages of the Bible.

Patriotifche Nachrichten und Anweisung zu dem einträglichen Tabacksbau, und zwar des fogenannten Afiatifchen *Tabacks;* or, *Patriotical Accounts and Instructions concerning the profitable Culture of Tobacco, and more especially, of that called* Afiatic *Tobacco; by* J. L. Christ. 8*vo.* Francfort on the Mayn. (German.)

The author warmly recommends the easy and profitable culture of a species of tobacco lately imported from Holland to Hanau, but has not given a botanical description of it. It seems, however, to be a kind of Nicotiana ruftica.

MONTHLY CATALOGUE.
POETRY.

Oenone to Paris: *an Epistle, translated from* Ovid. 4*to.* 6*d.* Law.

THIS is one of the best of Ovid's Epistles, and, perhaps, for that reason, the most difficult to translate. It has already been attempted by several hands, but none have yet done complete justice to it. The author of this informs us, that he translated it for his amusement during a long and tedious voyage. —As he had time enough, he might have afforded a little more care and attention than seems to have been exerted upon his performance; for though the version is by no means contemptb, it wants in some places, correctness and elegance of ex-

Preſſion.   A few lines may ſuffice to give our readers a proper idea of its merit.

> ' Haſt thou forgot ? yet ſhall theſe woods proclaim
> Thy falſehood growing with Oenone's name ;
> Yon poplar, imag'd in the glaſſy wave,
> Thy faithleſs rhimes ſhall from oblivion ſave ;
> " His ſtreams ſhall Xanthus to their ſource reſtore,
> When Paris for Oenone lives no more."
> Ye ſtreams of Xanthus to your ſource return !
> Oenone lives her perjur'd ſwain to mourn.'

Nothing can exceed the beauty of thoſe lines in the original, where Ovid ſays :

> ' Cum Paris Oenone poterit ſpirare relictâ
>   Ad fontem Xanthi verſa recurret aqua :
> Xanthe, retrò propera, verſæque recurrite lymphæ,
>   Suſtinet Oenonen deſeruiſſe Paris.'

Ovid ſays the waters of Xanthus ſhall run back to their fountain— *To their ſource reſtore* does not fully expreſs the ſenſe, and is, beſides, ſtiff and unpoetical.   In the laſt line, the repetition of Paris's name, which has a particular beauty in it, is loſt.   The following line is, we think, indefenſible,

> ' Nor deem me *worthleſs* of a royal bed.'

on account of the word *worthleſs,* which we do not remember ever to have met with followed by the prepoſition *of—Indignus* governs a genitive caſe, but *worthleſs of,* is ſeldom, we believe, uſed in Engliſh.

Speaking of Theſeus, our author ſays :

> ' This youthful ſoldier, amorous, bold, and rough,
> Found Helen's heart *impenetrable ſtuff.'*

This is certainly rather too *familiar* for elegiac verſe, and almoſt deſcends to vulgarity.—Many parts, however, of this tranſlation, are executed with eaſe and ſpirit, as the reader will perceive by the following lines :

> ' When diſtant yet from yonder rocky height
> Thy well-known enſigns ſtruck my watchful ſight,
> Scarce could my feet, impatient of delay,
> Forbear to meet thee thro' the wat'ry way,
> 'Till, on the deck, then firſt, alas ! I fear'd !
> Unlike thy own, a purple dreſs appear'd ;
> Now near and nearer, by the breeze impell'd—
> O fears too juſt ! a woman I beheld !
> What farther madneſs fix'd my ſteps to ſee
> A woman led—ſuſtain'd—embrac'd—by thee !
> Yes ! on thy neck the wanton ſtranger hung !—
> What horrors chill'd me ! and what anguiſh ſtung !
> By piercing ſhrieks my grief I firſt confeſs'd,
> Tore my looſe hair, and ſmote my ſwelling breaſt,

Call'd

Call'd every object to attest my moan——
Then sought my native rocks, and wept alone.
In justice, gods! deserted in her turn,
An equal loss let perjur'd Helen mourn!'

We do not much admire *attest my moan*——All the rest is animated and poetical. If this gentleman proceeds with the Epistles, we would advise him to read over the original very carefully, and adhere to it as closely as possible.

Epistle to Sir John Dalrymple, *Baronet.* 4*to.* 1*s.*

A complimentary poem, written in honour of sir John Dalrymple, by a young Scotchman, who has taken care to inform us (we suppose by way of excuse for his bad verses) that he is but *three and twenty:* if he had shewn us this Epistle before publication, we should have whispered in his ear the Roman bard's excellent advice of

Nonum prematur in annum.

It might then, possibly, have been more worthy of himself and his Mæcenas. In the present state of the poem, we cannot say much in its commendation. In answer to the plea concerning his age, our *young* author will be pleased to remember, that Pope wrote his Essay on Criticism when he was but twenty.—— Amongst many other strange observations in this performance, we meet with the following :

' 'Tis odd in rhyme that *twenty* shou'd excell
For *one* historian that composes well,
The fact no man of learning will deny.'

This, however, is not altogether so clear as our author seems to think it : excellence is as seldom attained in poetry as in history : *twenty* very good poets are not easily found ; and the author of this Epistle, may, perhaps, never be of the number ; though he tells us,

' That Homer shews us how to *live* and *die* ;
That Fingal's tale is *studied in the sky.*'

What he means by Fingal's tale being *studied in the sky,* we cannot comprehend ; nor do we remember that Homer, though he might teach his readers a great many things, was ever considered as a moral writer, like Addison, teaching men to live or, like our Taylor or Sherlock, teaching them to die : but this may be one of Homer's perfections which we never yet had sagacity enough to discover. Speaking of historians, this gentleman says :

' The hireling of the Walpole of the day,
Who one bold truth——nor says, nor dares to say,
Who never ventur'd on one Spartan thought,
Whose quill and conscience by the lump are bought,

All,

> All, at the second page, indignant drop,
> And wish him in the galleys or a rope.'

To condemn a man to the *gallies*, or, according to this elegant mode of expression, to wish him *in a rope*, because we do not admire his history, is rather cruel; the historian might with equal justice inflict the same punishment on our poet for his bad rhymes of *drop* and *rope*, *own* and *crown*, *roam* and *tomb*, *climb* and *dim*, &c. &c. which occur in this Epistle.

After comparing Plutarch and Dalrymple, our author says:

> ' In thee we trace the biographic sage,
> His native beauties blossom in thy page.
> When offer'd empire, William, in reply,
> Reminds his uncle, that the brave can die ;
> And, when half buried in an Irish fen,
> The monarch drinks cold water with his men ;
> His greatness, rather than his cause, endears,
> And those who can bestow them, are in tears.'

To imitate those whom we praise and admire, is certainly the highest compliment which we can pay them ; this young gentleman might, therefore, think that a panegyric on a prose-writer, though in verse, could not be too *prosaic* ; he descends, for that reason, to the familiar, and tells us plainly that

> ' ———— in an Irish fen,
> The monarch drank cold water with his men,'

And, for the very same reason, that he may accommodate his style to the person of whom he speaks, he acquaints us that

> ' ——— each low wretch the *dart* of scandal flings,
> And *squirts* his venom at the first of kings.'

This *low wretch*, we see, is doubly armed against the poor king, he first *flings* his dart, and then *squirts* his venom at him.—A little farther on in the poem he assures us that

> ' Whatever praise is due to those who *write*,
> Superior praise is due to those who *fight*.'

This is another assertion that sounds rather problematical ; Milton was, perhaps, as great a man as Wolfe.

> ' Though while Canāda trembled and admir'd,
> Wolfe, like the Theban, conquer'd and expir'd.'

Here Cānada, by a new poetical licence, is called Canāda ; we wonder that, after the words,

> ' ——— Canāda trembled and admir'd'

he did not add :

> ' And Quebec all his martial ardour fir'd.'

He tells us afterwards, what we very well knew before,

What

' What fame at Cambden brave Cornwallis won,
And how Monro completes what Clive begun ;
How from an army's heart was Maitland torn,
How Fraser fell for Britons yet unborn ;
How gen'rous Campbell paid a soldier's debt,
And shew'd the mercy which he had not *met*.'

We suppose he means *met with*.—Of such couplets as these consists the whole poem : by which our readers will learn what they have to expect from it ; and that, to conclude, in our author's own words, see page 9,

' While sense and knowlege in his trammels creep,
The reader pities them, and falls asleep.'

POLITICAL.

Authentic Rebel Papers, seized at St. Eustatius, 1781. 4*to.* 1*s*. Lambert.

The valuable prizes taken in the port of St. Eustatius have not more enriched the captors, than the letters intercepted in that island have afforded useful information to government. The first of these letters, dated at Edentown, in North Carolina, and addressed to Mr. Beaumarchais at Paris, exhibits, in the strongest colours, not only the deplorable state of the rebel provinces in America, but the avarice, the duplicity, and perfidious policy, of the French court. Other letters are subjoined, containing a similar representation of the distresses of the province of Virginia in particular. We are informed, that papers were also found, which discovered the secret treasons of men in this country, whose fortunes and situations render their guilt more atrocious. If such criminals should be allowed to escape with impunity, it is to be hoped at least, that the dread arising from their detection, will deter them henceforth from those practices. The best effects may therefore be expected, from this fortunate discovery of French politics, and of our domestic enemies.

DIVINITY.

The Evangelical Believer's Confession of the Son of God ; *or* Christ *acknowledged in the Ordinances of the Gospel.* By John Johnson. 8*vo.* 1*s.* 6*d.* Law.

The author explains what he means by ' the evangelical believer's confession of the Son of God ;' and then proceeds to point out what he supposes to be the spiritual intention of the following ordinances, baptism, the Lord's supper, laying on of hands, hearing the word of truth, prayer, praise, fasting, and keeping the sabbath.

In the preface he declares, that he is neither a mystic, a Calvinist, nor an Arminian. The first, he says, ' under pretence of spiritualizing, turns the word of God into fancy and conjecture.' The second ' mixes the glorious truth of the Gospel

with

I

with the doctrines of men, and the feductions of devils.' The third ' is a stranger to the riches of divine grace.' In short, he tells us, ' the time is come, when men will not endure found doctrine:' which is a strong intimation, that *found doctrine* is only to be found in this tract. Of what persuasion then, the reader will ask, is the author? we answer, a baptist; a little opinionated, as we have observed, but evidently actuated by a serious and devout sense of religion, and, in many respects, a rational believer.

Fifty-fix Forms of Morning and Evening Prayers, for the Use of Christian Families, &c. 8vo. 4s. Johnson.

Rational forms of devotion, expressed in clear and unaffected language.

Evangelical Sermons. By Thomas Adam. *8vo. 6s. Buckland.*

By the title, *Evangelical* Sermons, the discerning reader will at once perceive, what theological system this writer has adopted. His discourses however are full of pious instruction and affectionate advice to his parishioners, delivered in plain and familiar language, on the Fall of Man, the Damnableness of Sin, Faith in Christ, the Renunciation of our own Righteousness, a New Birth, and other similar subjects.

A devout Soldier. A Sermon, preached before the North Battalion of Gloucestershire *Militia, encamped on* Roborough Down, *near* Plymouth, August 5, 1781. *By the Rev.* Rob. Hawker. *4to. 1s. Law.*

The author has chosen for his text these few, but expressive words: ' A DEVOUT SOLDIER.' Acts x. 7. from which he takes occasion to shew, ' that devotion, far from being incompatible with the most independent ideas of the army, on the contrary, is a principle every way expedient to the perfection of a military character; and that in every point of view, in which it can be considered, whether imparting dignity to the profession, steadiness to virtuous actions, giving strength to the arm, or inspiring the mind with fortitude, a devout soldier is a distinction of character worthy of the highest emulation.'

This is an excellent discourse, recommending a steady and manly piety, without the least tincture of fanaticism.—The author might have mentioned the conduct of Henry V. before the battle of Agincourt, with great propriety. The king's devotion contributed, perhaps not a little, to that heroic ardour, with which his soldiers fought, and obtained the most extraordinary victory recorded in the English history.

A Sermon preached before the Guardians and Governors of the Asylum, May 19, 1781. *By* S. Glasse, *D. D. 8vo. 6d.* Rivington.

In this discourse the author applies these words, ' I was a stranger and ye took me in, naked and ye clothed me,' to the orphans at the asylum. From thence he takes occasion, in the
usual

usual strain of charity sermons, to set forth the excellence of the institution, the piety and benevolence of the founders and benefactors, and the duty of the children, who enjoy the benefit of such a happy establishment.

CONTROVERSIAL.

A scriptural Refutation of the Arguments for Polygamy, advanced in a Treatise entitled Thelyphthora. By T. Haweis, LL.B. Rector of All Saints, Aldwinckle, Northamptonshire. 8vo. 1s. 6d. Dilly.

We remember the time, when the rector of Aldwinckle had no objections to the orthodoxy of Mr. Madan's decisions. But the case is altered : the wife and respectable counsellor is now become a backslider ; and his notions, instead of being the dictates of piety, and a superior understanding, are ' the reveries of a disordered head, or the more pitiable delusions of a disordered heart.' Pref. p. ix.

Mr. Haweis's maxim, we suppose, on this occasion is, ' Amicus Plato, sed magis amica veritas.' He therefore attacks the doctrine of Thelyphthora with a pious indignation ; and, as we have just observed, aims some oblique strokes at the head and the heart of the author.

In the prosecution of this design he examines all the passages, relating to the subject, in the Old and New Testament ; and proves, in a very plain and satisfactory manner, without any verbal criticisms, that the doctrine of polygamy has no foundation in scripture.

MISCELLANEOUS.

Linguæ Hebraicæ *Studium Juventuti Academiæ commendatum, Oratione* Oxonii *habita in Schola Linguarum* xvi *Kalend.* Decemb. A. D. 1780. *A* Georgio Jubb, S. T. P. *Linguæ* Hebraicæ *Professore Regio Ædis* Christi *Canonico.* 4to. 1s. 6d. T. Payne.

The Hebrew seems to be the parent of most languages in the world. But as the likeness of men of the same family is less in a lateral and remote, than in a lineal and near descent, the vestigia of the original language, in very distant removes, are not easily discoverable. The Chaldee, Syriac, Arabic, &c. are only so many dialects of the Hebrew. The radical words are almost the same in all of them. A great part of the Greek language is evidently derived from the oriental dialects. The alpha, beta, gamma, delta, and the other letters of the Greek alphabet, are the aleph, beth, gimel, daleth, &c. of the Hebrews. The Latin and all the modern languages of Europe are derived from the same source. ' Grammatica, says Roger Bacon, in lingua Latinorum tracta est à Græco & Hebræo *.

Upon these principles alone the knowlege of the Hebrew is of the greatest utility in the study of languages, the compilation of dictionaries, the etymological investigation of words, &c.

---

* Bac. Op. Maj.

But

But there are other reasons, which render it highly expedient for men of letters, especially divines, to make themselves masters of Hebrew. It is the language of an essential part of divine revelation, and of all those books, to which the evangelical and apostolical writers constantly appeal, and from which they borrow an infinite variety of terms, phrases, figures, and images.

The learned author of this dissertation observes, that the books, which are transmitted down to us in Hebrew, are far superior, in point of antiquity, to any productions, that we have in any other language; that their contents are extremely curious, interesting, and important; that a knowlege of this language is highly necessary for every one, who wishes to understand the Scriptures; and that the Hebrew writers and the ancient Greek classics, especially Homer, mutually throw a light on one another; which he demonstrates by several examples.

There is not, as he justly remarks, any difficulty in acquiring a competent knowlege of the Hebrew tongue. Its structure is easy and simple; its anomalies and its radical words are few in number.—F. Lamy tells us, that it has but one thousand and twenty-two roots †.

The professor, in the course of his observations, passes some deserved encomiums on the learned and indefatigable collator of the Hebrew Manuscripts, and the excellent translator of Isaiah.

An Essay on Female Education. By George Hawkins, *Esq.* Small 8vo. 1s. 6d. Wilkie.

This writer declaims with great vehemence against the present management of female boarding-schools in and near the metropolis, and against the ignorance of the governesses. But indiscriminate invectives are unjust. Many of these schools are conducted on the most liberal plan. The author's remarks are chiefly applicable to those of a lower class. He seems to think, that the governess should personally instruct her pupils in every branch of their education. This, in large schools, is impossible. But supposing it otherwise, it is much more effectually performed by proper masters. The author's advice concerning reading, writing, arithmetic, French, geography, music, dancing, and oeconomy, may be very just; but the principal part of it, we make no doubt, is practised in every reputable boarding-school in the kingdom.

A most easy Guide to Reading and Spelling English, *for the Use of Schools.* By John Sharp, *M. A.* 12mo. 1s. Law.

No writer, in composing a spelling book, has taken more pains than Mr. Sharp appears to have done, in collecting words, and ranging them in different classes, in order to lead the young reader, step by step, through the perplexities of ' orthoepy'.

There are two points, which we would submit to his consideration: the first, concerning one of his rules for dividing syllables; the second, concerning his lessons.

---

† Apparat. Biblic. lib. v. cap. 5.

' Rule

' Rule 1. A single consonant between two vowels goes to the last, except x : it always goes to the first vowel.' Examples : a-cid, ba-nish, dra-gon, fla-gon, pa-lace, pa-late, to-pic, &c. This is calculated to introduce a vicious pronunciation. The best rule for dividing syllables in spelling, is to divide them, as they are naturally divided in a right pronunciation.

Our author's lessons contain good moral instruction. But they are composed of such long sentences, that a child will naturally fall into a drawling tone of voice, before he can reach the period. Short sentences are absolutely necessary for children, who are only beginning to read, and can scarcely support their voice through four or five monosyllables.

An Examination of the first Six Books of Euclid's Elements. *By* William Austin, *M. A. Fellow of* Wadham College, Oxford. 8vo. 2s. 6d. Rivington.

A suspicion has often been entertained that the existing copies of the Elements of Euclid contain many alterations and additions introduced since that work issued from the father of geometry. A work which has been two thousand years in the hands of masters in that science, of all nations, must have found many copiers of different opinions, disposed to make innovations, according to their own sentiments, which might arise sometimes from their misapprehensions, besides adding what appeared to them useful properties, or the vanity of making alterations in so celebrated and universal a work. Such alterations are now generally acknowledged to exist ; and several eminent masters have laboured to reform those abuses with much ingenuity and industry, particularly Dr. Isaac Barrow, and Dr. Simson of Glasgow.

With the same laudable design Mr. Austin has, in this short essay, given several ingenious hints and animadversions on our present copies of the Elements, with the view of rendering them more pure, and also easier and shorter ; a circumstance he thinks highly necessary in this age, when education takes in so many objects, and the field of mathematical learning is so much enlarged. Therefore, considering those Elements as an introduction to the science of geometry ; and that the more concise they are made, consistently with perspicuity and the principles of abstract reasoning, the more advantageous they must be to the geometrical student, Mr. Austin previously made several alterations and corrections, for his own use in college. On consulting Euclid's Elements in their original language, he found them, according to his idea, in several places more perfect than the modern translations. In some passages, particularly the definitions of the first book, he conceived that the translator had not fully comprehended Euclid's meaning. It also appeared that many additions had crept in, contrary to the nature of the work, and detrimental to the science. By examining the corollaries with a good deal of care, he found little or no reason to think that any of them were inserted by Euclid ; and he endeavours to prove that they are unnecessary in the Elements. In this, and many

many other inﬆances, he found that commentators and tranﬂlators have all affected to add ſomething of their own, by which the Elements are rendered more tedious and difficult than they originally were.—Euclid's Elements had ſuffered very conſiderable alterations in the hands of the Greeks. Towards the latter end of the ſixth book, five propoſitions, the utility of which has long been queﬆioned, are ſhewn, both from the connection of the ſubject, and the language in which they are expreſſed, to be ſpurious.

Theſe are ſome of the principal points in which Mr. Auﬆin endeavours to reﬆore Euclid to his original degree of perfection. He likewiſe makes a few attempts to reform his author. In examining the axioms he endeavours to explain, in a more diﬆinct manner than has hitherto been done, the nature of a geometrical definition, ſhewing that it ought to contain an equation, without which he thinks no deductions can be made from it. And on this principle he thinks he is enabled to deliver the doctrine of parallel lines in a more ſcientific manner than Euclid or any other geometrician has done. Many other alterations, of leſs conſequence, are made in this examination. Several of Euclid's demonﬆrations are abridged, and ſome propoſitions ſhewn to be unneceſſary. Finally, the author modeﬆly adds, ' It is not preſumed that this examination is in any degree a perfect execution of the plan here propoſed. The author is conſcious of his own inſufficiency for ſuch a work ; and would wiſh to have better qualified himſelf by a longer perſeverance in theſe purſuits. But engagements of a different nature oblige him to deſiﬆ from an undertaking, which he thinks worthy the attention of ſome perſon of more leiſure, learning, and abilities.'

The Hiﬆory of the Chevalier Bayard. *By the Rev.* Joſeph Sterlings. 8vo. 2s. Robinſon.

The chevalier Bayard was born at the caﬆle of Bayard, in Dauphiny, about the end of the year 1469. Though chiefly celebrated for the numerous ſingle combats which he fought, he was alſo diﬆinguiſhed for his military talents as a general, and for many of the moﬆ amiable virtues and accompliſhments of civil life. He has therefore been juﬆly regarded as an ornament of the age in which he lived. The anecdotes preſerved of him are faithfully related by the biographer, and introduced with a differtation on chivalry, illuﬆrating the genius of that inﬆitution, ſo famous in Europe during ſome centuries.

An Account of a Voyge to the Spice Iﬂands, *and* New Guinea. *By* M. P. Sonnerat. *Small 8vo.* 2s. 6d. White.

An abﬆract and tranſlation of the recital of a voyage performed in the South Seas by Mr. Sonnerat, about ten years ago. The tranſlator has ſelected the moﬆ intereﬆing parts of the narrative, and illuﬆrated the ſubject ſo copiouſly, that the additions and remarks are more than equal in quantity to the abﬆract. As accounts of later voyages have been publiſhed, this work cannot claim much novelty ; but it may prove acceptable to thoſe readers who are deſirous of all the information that can be collected.

THE

CRITICAL REVIEW.

For the Month of *November,* 1781.

Philofophical Tranfactions, of the Royal Society of London. *Vol.* LXX. *For the Year* 1780. *Part II.* 4to, 7s. 6d. *fewed.* L. Davis.

ARTICLE XVII. Theorems for computing Logarithms. By the Rev. John Hellins; communicated by the Rev. Nevil Mafkelyne, D. D. F. R. S. and Aftronomer Royal.—There are fome ingenious improvements in the computation of thofe ufeful numbers, fomewhat fimilar to the methods formerly fuggefted by Halley, Sharp, and Simpfon.

Art. XVIII. (printed XVII.) Connoiffances effentielles pour juger de quelque Efpéce nouvelle de Moulin à Cannes qu'on puiffe propofer. Par Monfieur Cazaud, Membre de la Societé Royale.—M. Cazaud, à Weft-Indian planter, eftimates great advantages attending his mill for bruifing the fugar canes, and gives other remarks which may be ufeful in that bufinefs.

Art. XIX. Account of an Offification of the Thoracic Duct. By Richard Browne Chefton, Surgeon to the Infirmary at Gloucefter; communicated by Mr. Henry Watfon, Surgeon to the Weftminfter Hofpital.

Art. XX. An Account of the Effect of Electricity in fhortening Wires. By Mr. Edward Nairne, F. R. S.—By thefe curious experiments Mr. Nairne fhews that the charges of electricity directed lengthways through wire, fhorten it very fenfibly, but without diminifhing its weight, fo that it gains in thicknefs what is loft in length. A piece of iron wire of 10

Y   inches

inches long, and $\frac{1}{16}$ of an inch thick, loft by each electric stroke about $\frac{1}{4}$ of an inch in length, so that by 15 such strokes it was reduced by an inch and $\frac{1}{16}$.

- XXI. Aftronomical Obfervations on the periodical Star in Collo Ceti. By Mr. William Herfchel, of Bath; communicated by Dr. Watfon, jun. of Bath, F. R. S.—This wonderful ftar, we are told, ' was firft obferved by David Fabricius, the 13th of Auguft, 1596, who called it the ftella mira, or wonderful ftar; which has been fince found to appear and difappear, periodically, feven times in fix years, continuing in the greateft luftre for 15 days together, and is never quite extinguifhed.' Mr. Herfchel's obfervations on this wonderful ftar are but few; however, they fufficiently verify the furprifing appearances that have been afcribed to it.

XXII. An Account of a new and cheap Method of preparing Pot-afh, with Obfervations. By Thomas Percival, M. D. F. R. and A. S. Member of the Royal Society of Phyficians at Paris, &c.

' The agriculture fociety at Manchefter has long recommended the making of refervoirs for the water which flows from dunghills in farm yards. This water is ftrongly impregnated with the falts and putrid matter of the dung-hill, and by ftagnation it acquires a much higher degree of putrefcence, and probably becomes proportionably more replete with falts. When thus collected and improved, it is pumped into an hogfhead, which being drawn upon a fledge, or fmall cart, is conveyed into the meadows, for the purpofe of fprinkling them with this rich manure. This important improvement in rural oeconomy, I apprehend, has not been extended much beyond the diftrict of our fociety; and it feems to be unknown to one of the lateft and moft intelligent writers on hufbondry: for lord Kaims, in a recent work on this fubject, of which he has favoured me with a copy, has not even mentioned it.

' But thefe refervoirs may be applied to a purpofe ftill more fubfervient to public utility than that above defcribed. Jofiah Birch, efq. a gentleman who carries on an extenfive manufactory, and bleaches his own yarn, about fix months ago, was induced, by a happy turn of thought, to try whether the dung-hill water might not be converted into pot-afhes. He accordingly evaporated a large quantity of it, and burnt the refiduum in an oven; the product of which fo perfectly anfwered his expectations, that he has ever fince continued to prepare thefe afhes, and to employ them in the operations of bucking. A ftranger to that narrownefs of fpirit which feeks the concealment of a lucrative difcovery, he is defirous that it fhould be communicated to the Royal Society.'

An

An example of the process is then described, and an estimate made of the profits, which are very considerable. Dr. Percival adds many useful and learned remarks on the uses and properties of the same substance.

Art. XXIII. On the Degree of Salubrity of the common Air at Sea, compared with that of the Sea-shore, and that of Places far removed from the Sea. By Dr. Ingen Housz. On this subject the author makes the following deductions.

' It appears from these experiments, that the air at sea and close to it is in general purer and fitter for animal life than the air on the land, though it seems to be subject to the same inconstancy in its degree of purity with that of the land ; so that we may now with more confidence send our patients, labouring under consumptive disorders, to the Sea, or at least to places situated close to the sea, which have no marshes in their neighbourhood.

' It seems also probable, that the air will be found in general much purer far from the land than near the shore, the former being never subject to be mixed with land air.

' It appears also, that the air in frosty weather is in general wholesomer than it is in winter when it does not freeze ; and that uncommon warm weather, happening in the winter season, is apt to render the atmosphere very unwholesome : the reason of which I apprehend to be, that the frost totally checks that general tendency to corruption, which being revived by warmth again increases the infection of the common air, which at that time is so much the greater, because the plants (which are deprived of their leaves in winter) have no power in them to counteract it.

' It seems also probable, that those countries which are by their local situation, exposed to noxious exhalations, are in general much wholesomer in the winter ; and that it is much safer to cross such countries in summer time when it is windy weather than in a calm, &c.

' How far these deductions are founded upon experience may appear by applying them to such places as they may be found to have a relation to.

' My old friend Dr. Damman, an eminent physician and professor royal in midwifery at Ghent, told me, that when he was formerly a practitioner at Ostend, during seven years, he found the people there remarkably healthy ; that nothing was rarer there than to see a patient labouring under a consumption or asthma, a malignant, putrid, or spotted fever : that the disease to which they are the most subject, is a regular intermittent fever in autumn, when sudden transitions from hot to cold weather happen.

' People are in general very healthy at Gibraltar, though there are very few trees near that place ; which, I think, is ow ing to the purity of the air, arising from the neighbourhood of the sea.

‘ Most small islands are very healthy.

‘ At Malta people are little subject to diseases, and live to a very advanced age.’

Art. XXIV. The principal Properties of the Engine for turning Ovals in Wood or Metal, and of the Instrument for drawing Ovals upon Paper, demonstrated. By the Rev. Mr. Ludlam, Vicar of Norton, near Leicester ; communicated by the Astronomer Royal.

Art. XXV. Of Cubic Equations and Infinite Series. By Charles Hutton, LL.D. F. R. S — An elaborate tract on this difficult subject, treated in a new manner, with very considerable and ingenious improvements.

Art. XXVI. An Account of a most extraordinary Degree of Cold at Glasgow in January last ; together with some new Experiments and Observations on the comparative Temperature of Hoar-frost and the Air near to it, made at the Macfarlane Observatory belonging to the College. In a Letter from Patrick Wilson, M. A. to the Rev. Nevil Maskelyne, D. D. F. R. S. and Astronomer Royal.—From these curious experiments it appears that the degree of cold immediately on the surface of the snow is much greater than at a little distance above it. For when a thermometer hung up in the open air at 2 ½ feet above the surface of the snow descended to the great degree of 13 or 14 below 0, another laid on the snow descended to 22 or 23 degrees below 0 !

Art. XXVII. (misnumbered XXVI.) Abstract of a Register of the Barometer, Thermometer, and Rain, at Lyndon, in Rutland, 1779. By Thomas Barker, Esq. Communicated by Thomas White, Esq. F. R. S.—The numbers expressing the mean degrees for the whole year, are for the barometer 29,514 inches, thermometer in the house 52,71, and the thermometer without 50 ¼. The whole quantity of rain 19,878 inches. Observations on the weather are added, and diseases in the several seasons.

Art. XXVIII. (misprinted XXIX.) Journal of the Weather at Senegambia, during the Prevalence of a very fatal putrid Disorder, with Remarks on that Country. By J. P. Schotte, M D. communicated by Joseph Banks, Esq. P. R. S.

‘ The island St. Lewis, otherwise called Senegal, is situated in 16° north latitude, and 16° west longitude. It is separated from the island of Soar on the east by the main river, which, on account of the smallness of the creek by which it is formed, is esteemed a part of the continent. It has the Atlantic Ocean on the weft, from which it is feparated by a fmall neck of land, or more properly fand, called Barbary Point. This neck of land is in feveral places not above five or fix hundred yards broad. A branch of the river runs between it and the ifland itfelf, communicating with the main river above and below the ifland. It is about a mile in length, feven hundred feet in breadth, and contains five or fix thoufand black inhabitants. In the months of Auguft, September, and October, it is ufually about two or three feet above the level of the river at high water; but there are years in which the whole ifland is overflowed; in the other months of the year it may be about five or fix feet above its level in the higheft places. The continent and iflands near, it are as low, and in many places much lower, being overflowed for the moft part during the rainy months; the latter are formed by creeks communicating with the main river, and thickly befet with mangroves. The water of the river is frefh during the rains, but very thick and troubled, the current being fo rapid and ftrong as to ftop the flood-tide; but in the dry months the river water is falt, and no other water is to be had, but fuch as is procured by digging a pit into the fand more or lefs deep according to the height of the ground into which the water filtrates from all fides, and gathers up to the level of the river. This water is brackifh, but as no better is to be had thereabouts, the garrifon, as well as the inhabitants, make ufe of it, except when the river is frefh.

‘ The year is commonly divided by the Europeans as well as the inhabitants into two feafons; viz. the rainy and dry; by others called the fickly and healthy feafon. The rainy or fickly one generally begins about the middle of July, and ends about the middle of October; during this time the wind is generally between the points of caft and fouth, the quarter from which the tornados come. It has been obferved, that this feafon is more or lefs unwholefome in proportion to the greater or leffer quantity of rain that falls. A tornado is preceded by a difagreeable clofenefs and weight in the air, (which feems to be much hotter than the thermometer fhows it to be); and it is known to come on by the rifing of the clouds to the fouth-eaft, which by joining grow darker, fo as to make the horizon look quite black, accompanied with lightning and thunder at a diftance. The breeze dies away by degrees as the tornado advances. and an entire calm fucceeds; the air grows yet darker; animals and birds retire and fhelter themfelves; every thing is filent, and the afpect of the fky, from whence the tornado approaches, is moft dreadful. A violent ftorm comes on all at once, which is fo cold as to occafion the thermometer to fall feven or eight degrees in a few minutes, and ftrong enough to overfet negro huts and veffels, or drive the latter from their anchors, and throw them on fhore. The ftorm abates, and heavy rain follows accompanied with much lightning and ftrong claps of thunder. Sometimes tornados happen without rain, or at leaft with very little, but then

the

the storm is more violent and lasts longer. It has been imagined by some, that this kind of storm brings some pestiferous quality with it, because they had observed, that out of a number of people several fell sick in one night after a tornado.

' This I have in some degree experienced myself; for in the month of September, 1776, feeling myself very well, and having dined as usual, the storm of a tornado suddenly tore down the window-shutters, and blew into the room where I was: about an hour after I had rigors, and in the evening I had a high fever, which turned out to be a very severe bilious one; but notwithstanding this, it has, in my opinion, no such ill quality; and the above phenomenon may be attributed to the change it produces on the air, and of consequence on the body; it may therefore be considered as the occasional cause of a disorder to which the body was pre-disposed long before.

' The dampness of the atmosphere during this season is so great that it is more or less perceptible in every thing. Leather, wearing apparel, and books, grow mouldy. Polished metals grow rusty. Sea salt, sugar, and other saline substances, which were perfectly dry before, melt; and the meat of cattle killed in the evening is spoiled the next morning, so as not to be fit for use.

' Calms are very frequent and disagreeable on account of the musquetoes and other insects, which then quit their retreats from among the mangroves and marshes, and spread over the face of the country.

' The dry or healthy season begins commonly about the middle of October and lasts to the middle of July. It is called dry, because then it hardly ever rains, or at least but very seldom; and healthy, in opposition to the sickly one: for though pleurisies and peripneumonies will happen in the months of December and January, and fluxes in the months of April, May, and June, few people die, which, when compared with the numbers that die in the other season, justifies the denomination. When the rains cease, the wind shifts its quarter, and is for the most part east or north-east in the morning; but as the sun rises on the horizon, the wind changes more and more towards the north, till about noon, sooner or later, it gets to the west or north, which is called sea-breeze, and is very refreshing, though it happens sometimes, that as the sun falls again on the horizon, the wind will shift again towards the east, and continue there all night. This wind blows sometimes very strong, and is always excessively hot, drying up the lakes and pools, which had been formed by the heavy rains and the overflowing of the river, and producing in such as partake of sea water, a fine sea salt in large crystals, not unlike fossil salt. In the months of February, March, April, May, and June, the wind blows almost constantly from between north and west, called sea-breeze, except now and then a day or two it will be east, which when it happens in April makes it excessively hot, the sun being then in and

about

about the zenith of Senegal, heating the vast plains of sand over which this wind is to pass before its arrival there, which, reverberating the received heat, may contribute to increase it; for I have observed, that the same month in the river Gambia was not hotter than than any other wind, owing in all appearance to the difference of the soil of the country, which is not sandy like that of Senegal. I think it is the dust of the sand raised by this wind which makes the atmosphere look hazy. I myself saw, in the year 1775, in the month of April, in a morning preceded by an easterly wind, such a dust imitating a fog in the air, that one could not see above twenty yards.

‘ The weather grew calm, and about eleven o’clock in the forenoon the atmosphere grew clear by depositing a brownish impalpable dust, which covered every thing near a line in thickness. The same thing I observed at sea, from on board of a vessel in the month of March 1775, at the distance of about five or six leagues from the land near the latitude of Senegal. The wind having blown east in the night, I found in the morning the sails, shrouds, and deck, covered with an impalpable dust. The description given by the learned Dr. Lind of the Harmattans of the Coast of Guinea, seems to agree with the east wind at Senegal in almost every respect, except that the damp vapour in the former is not perceptible in this, for it dries every thing that will admit of it. Water poured on the floor of a room for the purpose of cooling the air, is dried up in an instant, and there is some effect on the thermometer placed in such a room. Salt, sugar, and the like substances, which are half melted by the damp air during the rainy season, dry again in a few days into hard lumps. Such houshold furniture as is made of wood, though it has been ever so well seasoned, shrinks and grows loose where joined, or splits and cracks where glued. It dries and parches the skin of the white people as well as the blacks, and makes it sometimes as rough as any clear frosty weather in Europe would. The sky is commonly clear and without clouds; but the atmosphere is hazy, which, in my opinion, as I have already observed, is occasioned by the dust, perhaps in conjunction with vapours arising from the surface of the earth and waters. These vapours, though not to be seen in the open air, I have perceived by their shadows upon white walls, arising from pools which were close to them; but the air being so dry they are absorbed by it, and no more perceptible as vapour. That the evaporation must be very great when this wind blows, the method the blacks have of cooling water will evince. They fill tanned leather bags with it, and hang them up in the sun; the water oozes more or less through the leather, so as to keep the outward surface of it wet, which, by its quick and continued evaporation, occasions the water within the bag to grow considerably cool.

‘ This wind is in general not reckoned unwholesome, either by the inhabitants or Europeans, though it feels very disagreeable,

and

and by depriving the body of its thinner fluids may be looked upon as the immediate cause of some diseases, and the pre-disposing one to others. When it sets in sooner or later in the month of October, it is considered by the inhabitants as producing a cessation of the sickly weather, and the beginning of healthier. In the months of December and January, when the sun is at its greatest distance, it makes the weather feel very cold in the nights and the mornings.

' The putrid disorder, which proved so fatal to the garrison and the inhabitants of Senegal, made its appearance in the beginning of August. The preceding month of July had been remarkably healthy; though the weather was very hot and sultry, there were only three soldiers in the hospital for slight venereal disorders; but we learnt by some black messengers, who came from Goree, that there was a fever raging there, which had carried off numbers of the French garrison and inhabitants of the island, and we thought ourselves very happy not to partake of their fate. On the second of August one of the soldiers, who was in the hospital for a gonorrhea, being cured, was discharged. The fourth of August he was again reported to me as very sick in the barracks. I went to see and found him in a high fever with the worst symptoms. I ordered him to be carried to the hospital, where he died the third day, with all the symptoms of the greatest putridity. The orderly man of the hospital was seized on the sixth of August with the same disease, and died the ninth. One of the venereal patients, who remained still in the hospital, was taken with the same fever, and died a few days after. Some of the soldiers of the fort, having access to the hospital to visit their sick comrades, took the contagion, and spread it through the whole garrison. I am apt to believe, that the disorder was brought to Senegal by the black messengers from Goree; for I understood that one of them had died soon after his arrival in Senegal, and it may be, that the soldier who died first of it got the infection from them; for it is probable, that being discharged the hospital on the second of August, and having leave to take a walk on the island on the third, he had been in company with some of these black messengers, or in the huts where they resorted, for the sake of hearing some news from Goree, where he was acquainted. It may perhaps be observed, that the soldier taking the contagion on the third of August, it could not make so rapid a progress as to manifest itself the next morning in the highest degree; but this I intend to support by the following cases. One of the surgeon's mates dressed a blister on the back of a soldier, ill of the disorder, with a digestive softened with oil of turpentine : having done, he came into the surgery, and looked quite pale, telling me, that the soldier's back had smelled so putrid and offensive, that it had made him quite faint and sick at the stomach. He took some tincture of bark and bitters, and went home, when a fever, with a train of the worst symptoms, made its appearance in the evening,

and

and he died the third day. Another gentleman, who was sent for by the said surgeon's mate in the morning of the second day of his illness, and requested to draw up a will for him, arrived while I was present. He spoke with the patient for a few minutes, and then took me aside, saying, that there was a certain smell about the room, which made him faint and sick at the stomach, and that he should be obliged to retire; he did, but in the evening was seized with the fever and all its bad symptoms, went through several of its stages, but recovered. A black boy, who had been waiting on the said surgeon's mate during his illness, was taken with the same disorder, and died of it in a few days. I could produce several other cases to strengthen what I have advanced concerning the quick appearance of the disorder itself after the contagion had taken place, but I think the three related ones sufficient.

'The cessation of this contagious disease may be dated from about the middle of September. Governor Clarke, who died the 18th of this month, concluded the dreadful scene. He had avoided the communication with all sick people, but did not hesitate in admitting my company. I was the only one who dined with him for several weeks; and as I was continually among the sick in the hospital and on the island (of the former of which I gave him a return every morning) I might probably have conveyed the infection to him in my cloathing, though I was not affected myself. A few people died in the months of October, November, and December; some of relapses of the same fever, and others of severe fluxes and abscesses in the liver, in which the disorder had terminated. It is remarkable, that a fleet of merchant-men, under convoy of a sloop of war, which left Senegal on the fourth of August, and sailed for England, had, by what I could learn, been entirely free from this disorder; neither did it reach as far as the river Gambia, for the garrison at Fort James in that river enjoyed a pretty good state of health during all this time, and lost only two men, who died of fluxes.'

Then follows the journal of the thermometer, wind, and weather; which is very copious, being generally marked three or four times each day.

Art. XXIX. Astronomical Observations relating to the Mountains of the Moon. By Mr. Herschel of Bath. Communicated by Dr. Watson, jun. of Bath, F. R. S.—By Mr. Herschell's observations, the height of the lunar mountains appears to be much less than it has ever been made by former astronomers, the highest according to his computations being little more than 1 ½ miles.

Art. XXX. Account of an extraordinary Pheasant. By Mr. John Hunter, F. R. S.—This article treats of the curious circumstance of a hen pheasant that had assumed the plumage of the cock. Similar instances are related of other birds; and

and ingenious obfervations are interfperfed through the paper.

Art. XXXI. A Letter to Jofeph Banks, Efq. Prefident of the Royal Society, &c. from Daniel-Peter Layard, M. D. Fellow of the Royal Societies of London, Antiquaries, and Gottingen, &c. relative to the Diftemper among the horned Cattle,—contains a fhort hiftory of that diforder, with methods of prevention and cure.

Art. XXXII. An Inveftigatiou of the Principles of progreffive aud rotatory Motion. By the Rev. S. Vince, A. M. of Sidney College, Cambridge. Communicated by George Atwood, A. M. F. R. S.—This article contains a new inveftigation of fome of the firft principles and effects of motion arifing from the impulfe of bodies. The memoir was honoured with the annual prize medal of the Royal Society.

Art. XXXIII. Continuation of the Cafe of James Jones. By Richard Browne Chefton, Surgeon to the Gloucefter Infirmary. Communicated by Mr. Henry Watfon, Surgeon to the Weftminfter Hofpital.

Art. XXXIV. Thermometrical Experiments and Obfervations. By Tiberius Cavallo, F. R. S. who was nominated by the Prefident and Council to profecute Difcoveries in Natural Hiftory, purfuant to the Will of the late Henry Baker, Efq. F. R. S.

Collections for the Hiftory of Worcestershire. *Volume the Firft. Folio.* 2l. 12s. 6d. *boards.* Payne and Son.

THE author of this vaft collection is Treadway Nafh, D. D. rector of St. Peter's in Droitwich, and proprietor of Bevereye, in the county of Worcefter. This gentleman, who appears to be actuated with a laudable zeal for the interefts of his native county, informs us, he has often wifhed that fome perfon would write the hiftory and antiquities of Worcefterfhire. He propofed the undertaking to feveral individuals, offering them all the affiftance in his power; and he even invited the Society of Antiquaries to choofe a proper perfon; promifing to open a fubfcription with three or four hundred pounds. But failing of fuccefs in all his applications, he refolved to undertake the work himfelf, which he knew would be facilitated by materials that had been collecting for almoft two hundred years.

• The firft collector, he informs us, was Mr. Thomas Habington of Hinlip. This unfortunate gentleman, bigoted to his religion, and pitying the hard fate of Mary Queen of Scots, engaged

gaged in defigns for releafing her, which had nearly coft him his life; he was however pardoned, and permitted to retire to Hinlip, which was fettled upon him by his father, in confideration of his marriage with Mary, eldeft daughter of Edward lord Morley, by Elizabeth his wife, daughter and fole heir of fir William Stanley, kight, lord Monteagle. Notwithftanding this efcape, Mr. Habington could not help engaging in the gunpowder-plot, wherein if he was not directly concerned, yet for entertaining Garnet, Oldcorn, and others, he was committed to the Tower, and condemned to die; but by the interceffion of his wife's father, lord Morley, and being queen Elizabeth's godfon, he was reprieved, and pardoned on condition that he fhould retire to Hinlip, and never again ftir out of Worcefterfhire. In this retirement, he gave himfelf up entirely to ftudy the Antiquities of the county.' He died October 8, 1647, aged 87. His portrait is fketched under the article Hinlip.

' His papers were tranfcribed by his fon William Habington, who made fome few additions to them, though his ftudies were chiefly in the poetic line. The hiftory of Edward IV. written and publifhed at the requeft of Charles I. was chiefly compiled from his father's papers. He died November 30, 1659, leaving his collections to his fon Thomas Habinton, of Hinlip, who dying without iffue left his eftate to fir William Compton.

' The MSS. luckily fell into the hands of Dr. Thomas, the induftrious antiquary of Worcefter, the publifher of Dugdale's Warwickfhire, the Survey of Worcefter Cathedral, and many other pieces. He died July 26, 1738, without iffue male, after having taken much pains in collating the regifters of the bifhops, and dean and chapter, and making many other valuable additions to Habington's papers. A mezzotinto portrait of him is annexed.

' After Dr. Thomas's death, all the papers were purchafed by Dr. Charles Lyttelton, late bifhop of Carlifle, and prefident of the Society of Antiquaries, who made many additions to them from the Old Chapter-houfe Weftminfter, the Tower Records, and other public offices. He died 1768, and by will left his collections to the Society of Antiquaries of London; in whofe library they remained till the year 1774, when they were entrufted to me for the purpofe of revifing and publifhing.'

The account of the collection is followed by various particulars relative to the ancient hiftory of the county, its geography, political and ecclefiaftical ftate, and natural hiftory; which are fucceeded by a curious *fac fimile*, in thirteen plates, of the Domefday furvey of the county. The reverend author acknowleges, with a modefty which does him honour, that this work can be confidered only as parochial collections for a hiftory; obferving at the fame time, as an apology for the minutenefs of detail, that ' a county hiftorian is by profeffion a dealer in fmall ware.'

2

Dr. Nash has, with great propriety, arranged the materials in alphabetical order ; a method which he was induced to adopt, from a confideration of the irregular fhape of the county, and the disjointed manner in which the parifhes lie.

The materials of this vaft collection confift of a general account of the refpective manors, as delineated in Domefday-book ; copies of ancient grants and other deeds ; number of families, genealogical tables, armorial bearings, patrons of benefices, lifts of incumbents, monumental infcriptions, the rate of land-tax, the ftate of the poor, with a variety of occafional particulars.

In compiling a work of this kind, the author is naturally expofed to peculiar difficulties. If he be minute, in the account of local circumftances, he is liable to be cenfured, by thofe who confider the public utility as the moft indifpenfable object of the hiftorian : while, on the other hand, if he facrifice the general tafte, to the gratification of provincial attachments, he runs the hazard, not only of fruftrating the principal end of his literary refearches, but of extinguifhing thofe incitements which contribute moft to fupport him in the profecution of fo laborious a work. We have the pleafure to obferve, that Dr. Nash has, as much as poffible, reconciled thofe oppofite difficulties.

In treating of a monument at Alvechurch, the author makes the following remarks, which may not be unacceptable to antiquaries.

' It is an opinion which univerfally prevails with regard to thefe crofs-legged monuments, that they were all erected to the memory of Knights Templars. Now to me it is very evident, that not one of them belonged to that order ; but, as Mr. Habingdon, in defcribing this at Alvechurch, hath juftly expreffed it, to the Knights of the Holy Voyage. For the order of Knights Templars followed the rule of the Canons Regular of St. Auftin, and as fuch were under a vow of celibacy. Now there is a fcarce one of thefe monuments, which is certainly known for whom it was erected, but it is as certain that the perfon it reprefents was a married man. The Knights Templars always wore a white habit, with a red crofs on the left fhoulder. I believe not a fingle inftance can be produced of either the mantle or crofs being carved on any of thefe monuments, which furely would not have been omitted, as by it they were diftinguifhed from all other orders, had thefe been really defigned to reprefent Knights Templars. Laftly, this order was not confined to England only, but difperfed itfelf all over Europe. Yet it will be very difficult to find one crofs-legged monument any where out of England ; whereas no doubt they would have abounded in France, Italy, and elfewhere, had it been a fafhion peculiar to that famous order.

But

But though for these reasons I cannot allow the cross-legged monuments to have been erected for Knights Templars, yet they had some relation to them; being the memorials of those zealous devotees, who had either been in Palestine personally engaged in what was called the Holy War, or had laid themselves under a vow to go thither, though perhaps they were prevented from it by death. Some few indeed might possibly be erected to the memory of persons who had made pilgrimages thither, merely out of private devotion. Among the latter probably was that lady of the family of Mepham, of Mepham in Yorkshire, to whose memory a cross-legged monument was placed in a chapel adjoining to the once collegiate church of Howden in Yorkshire, and is at this day remaining, together with that of her husband, on the same tomb. As this religious madness lasted no longer than the reign of our Henry III. (the tenth and last crusade being published in the year 1268) and the whole order of Knights Templars was dissolved 7 Edw. II. military expeditions to the Holy Land, as well as devout pilgrimages thither, had their period by the year 1312; consequently none of these cross-legged monuments are of a later date than the reign of Edward II. or beginning of Edward III. nor of an earlier than that of king Stephen, when these expeditions first took place in this kingdom.'

Under the article of Hales-owen, we meet with an account of the late Mr. Shenstone, which, as being furnished by one or two of his intimate friends, we shall lay before our readers.

' The grandfather of this gentleman, who was named like himself William Shenstone, lived at Ylley in this parish, where he occupied a considerable farm of his own, and afterwards purchased that of the Leasowes. He had two sons, Joseph and Thomas: to the elder of these he assigned over the farm and lands at Ylley; although he still continued to reside there, together with his youngest son Thomas. But Joseph, being now independent and master, treated his father with great disregard, and by his ungrateful behaviour forced him at length to leave the house. The old gentleman retired to the Leasowes, with his son Thomas, which they jointly managed, chiefly as a grazing farm. Here Mr. Thomas Shenstone married Anne Penn, the eldest of the three daughters of William Penn of Harborough, gent. which lies chiefly in the parish of Hagley. By her he had two sons, William our poet, and Joseph. The latter was bred an attorney at Bridgnorth, but never practised; and died unmarried at his brother's house in 1751. William, the subject of this account, was born at the Leasowes on or about the 18th of November, 1714; and baptized on the 6th of December following. In his earliest infancy he was remarkable for his great fondness for reading, so that when any of his family went to distant markets or fairs, he constantly importuned them to bring him presents of books; which, if they returned home later than his

usual

usual hour of going to rest, were always taken up to bed to him; and sometimes when they had been forgotten, his mother had no other means to allure him to sleep, but by wrapping a piece of wood in paper like a book; which he would hug to his pillow, till the morning discovered the deception. He received the first tincture of learning under a school-dame near the Leasowes, whose memory he afterwards immortalized in his poem of the School-mistress, and whose name he has recorded in one of his letters. He for a short time attended the grammar-school at Hales-owen; whence he was removed to Solihull in Warwick-shire, under the care of the rev. Mr. Crumpton; who had the tuition of many children, sons of the neighbouring nobility and gentry. Here he made a quick progress in the Latin and Greek classics; till, on the 24th of May, 1732, he was admitted a commoner of Pembroke College, in Oxford. Of this college he continued a member near ten years, having at the end of the first four years put on a civilian's gown, but with what design does not appear, for he never took any degree, and apparently never intended to follow any profession, as he had long before succeeded to his paternal estate. His father had died in June 1724, and his grandfather in August 1726, before he was twelve years old, leaving him and his brother under their mother's care, who continued to superintend them till her death in 1732, a short time before he removed to Oxford. At her death, the guardianship of her two sons devolved on the rev. Mr. Thomas Dolman, rector of Brome, in this neighbourxood, but in the county of Stafford, who had married Mary Penn, their mother's sister; of whose paternal care, Mr. Shenstone often spoke with great respect.

'About the time that Mr. Shenstone was a member of Pembroke College, that little seminary was distinguished for the great number of men of genius and learning with which it abounded, and who have since reflected such honour on this their original place of education. With these Mr. Shenstone spent several years in a most pleasing society, and contracted friendships which only terminated with his life. While he was at college, he printed without his name, a small volume of juvenile verses, with the following title: "Poems upon various occasions, written for the entertainment of the author, and printed for the amusement of a few friends prejudiced in his favour. Contentus paucis lectoribus. Hor. Oxford, printed for Leon. Litchfield, &c. 1737." 12mo.

'About the year 1739, he was much resident in London; and for some years following he divided his time between the metropolis, Bath, and Cheltenham, occasionally visiting the university. In the spring of the year 1740, he published his poem of "the Judgement of Hercules;" and in 1742, his "School-mistress;" both separately, in 8vo. In 1745 his uncle Dolman died, who had chiefly managed his estate; which had been occupied by Mr. John Shenstone of Perry Hill, in this parish, a

distant

distant relation, who, with his sons John and Thomas Shenstone rented the farm as tenants. Mr. Shenstone began now to be more resident at the Leasowes, and at first boarded with his tenants; but not liking the restraint he was under, at length took the farm into his own hands; and soon began to display that genius and taste, which at length made the Leasowes to be so much admired and celebrated. The manner of laying out ground in the natural style was quite in its infancy when Mr. Shenstone began his improvements, and, excepting the walk through the High Wood (which was his earliest attempt), very little of what was executed at first now remains unaltered. By degrees he brought these delightful scenes to their present perfection; and long before he died, they had attracted the notice and procured him the friendship of persons the most distinguished for rank or genius. A description of the Leasowes, as left at his death in 1763, by Robert Dodsley, may be seen at the end of the second volume of his works; a poetical description of it is printed in Woodhouse's Poems, and in Giles' Miscellaneous Poems, revised and corrected by Mr. Shenstone himself. This villa has been improved by a plain elegant house built in 1775, by Edward Horne, esq. a gentleman of taste, who is the present possessor, and who has preserved all the rural scenes unaltered.

' As for Mr. Shenstone's moral character, it had all the virtues, and all the imperfections which attend a generous, easy, indolent disposition: with a strong glow of benevolence, and a readiness to serve his friends, he had an equal disinclination to inspect and regulate his own affairs. This, with a total want of frugality, and the expence of keeping up the beauty of his extensive walks, out of an income never more than 300 l. per annum, occasioned often inconveniences extremely distressing to a man of fine sensibility; and sometimes ruffled a temper naturally mild and placid. As a writer his merit is sufficiently ascertained; simplicity, delicacy, and tenderness, characterize his poems more than strength and fire. Yet many of the feebler performances, that clog his works and abate our reverence for his genius, are well known to his friends to have been dragged into notice contrary to his own intention or judgment, being either juvenile, or unfinished escapes, which he never would have suffered to be printed, had he lived to publish his works himself; as he often expressed great concern at the previous insertion of them in Dodsley's Miscellanies, to whom all his manuscripts had been sent, while he was disabled by a severe fit of illness from making a proper selection. Poor Shenstone wanted for his posthumous works such a friend and corrector as Parnell had in Pope. Yet, under all this disadvantage, he ever will deserve a place among our English classics.

' Mr. Shenstone was never married, but acknowledged it was his own fault, that he did not accept the hand of the lady whom he so tenderly loved, and whose charms he had so affectingly sung in his celebrated pastoral ballad, which is among the most
ad-

admired of all his poems. Having, as hath been before obferved, impaired his fortune, not only by his tafte for rural improvements, but by an unfortunate law-fuit, in which he was involved with a near relation ; he was upon the point of being made eafy in his circumftances by a penfion of 300l. per ann. which fome powerful friends were procuring for him, when he was feized with a putrid fever, which put a period to his life at the Leafowes, about five o'clock on Friday morning the 11th of February, 1763. He was buried near his brother under a plain flat ftone, infcribed with his name, on the fouth-fide of Halesowen church-yard.'

The plan of this great undertaking is fo extenfive, that the prefent volume, though containing upwards of fix hundred pages, in large folio, proceeds no farther than the letter H ; and therefore, probably, comprifes not more than a third part of the work. This volume, however, is not more confpicuous, either in point of fize, or the multiplicity of materials, than for the number of beautiful engravings, of manfion-houfes, portraits, monuments of the dead, landfcapes, and objects of natural hiftory, which it contains ; making, in the whole, a work worthy of the liberal motives, and extraordinary attention, with which it has been conducted by the reverend author.

✓ *Phyfiological Difquifitions ; or, Difcourfes on the Natural Philofophy of the Elements.* By W. Jones, F. R. S. [*Concluded from p.* 281.]

THE feventh difcourfe of Mr. Jones's work is on *Foffil Bodies, with fome Obfervations introductory to a Theory of the Earth.* He begins with defining the fcience and fhewing the ufe of it ; how it was improved by Woodward, and the ftudy of it encouraged by Newton. Till the beginning of this century it was but little underftood, but is now in a flourifhing ftate in the chief cities and univerfities of Europe. This part of the work, from the method of it, has the appearance of a courfe of lectures, and has probably been delivered to explain a collection of foffils, to which the author had referred : on which account it may be of great ufe to thofe who are ftudying this fafhionable part of natural hiftory. The difcourfe confifts of three parts ; the firft of which treats of *native foffils*, the fecond of *extraneous foffils*, the third contains fome *general obfervations* and directions for a farther underftanding of the fubject. Under the firft head are comprehended *earths, ftones, gems, cryftals, falts, bitumens, minerals* and *metals*. The native foffils are not fo

par-

Particularly confidered by the author as thofe comprehended under the fecond head, which are called *extraneous,* and fuppofed by him to be the remains of the Deluge. Thefe are Petrified wood, and vegetables of various kinds ; among which the *piped waxen vein,* perforated by fea worms, and the petrified fruits of Sheepy Ifland, fome of which are figured in the plates, are the moft remarkable. The petrified corals have the next place, with the *afteriæ* and *entrochi,* which connect the vegetable and animal kingdoms. From thefe he proceeds to foffil fea fhells, and thence to the petrifactions of fquamous fifh, of which he has figured a fine fpecimen lately difcovered in England, and preferved at Cambridge. He has difcuffed the origin of the *belemnite*; and in treating of foffil bivalvular fhells has noted that fingular circumftance, firft obferved by Woodward, of their retaining the perforation made by the *purpura*. The teeth and bones of fea animals give him occafion to introduce fome learned and ufeful remarks of that eminent naturalift fir Hans Sloane. But there is nothing more obfervable than the petrified human bones with which he has concluded this- head of his difcourfe. Thefe are found in aftonifhing quantities in hard rocks of the colour of a brick, on the coaft of Dalmatia, the rocks of Gibraltar, and other places near the fhores of the Mediterranean.

His general obfervations relate to the circulation of moifture through the ftoney parts of the earth, and the effects of it ; to the diffolution of ftoney matter at the flood, according to Woodward's fcheme ; the overflowing of the earth ; the providential diftribution of its materials ; all of which particulars are preparatory to a theory of the earth in the next difcourfe. To thefe obfervations he has fubjoined practical directions to ftudents in natural hiftory, with figures and defcriptions of the principal claffes of foffils, and concludes the whole with critical remarks on Mr. Lhywd's fanciful account of the *origin of marine foffils,* which we think he has effectually confuted.

His next difcourfe has the title of *Phyfical Geography* ; the earth being here confidered, not as it is the object of geography, but of philofophy. The fubject is introduced with fome remarks on the theories advanced by Burnet, Whifton, and Halley. The earth is then confidered under the three ftates it is fuppofed to have undergone at the creation, called *chaotic, intermediate,* and *habitable* ; and the author thinks the Mofaic account authorifes him to affert, that it went through three fimilar ftages at the flood, and that its reftitution was a *reformation*. But here different theorifts, we apprehend, in a matter of fuch obfcurity, will incline to different fides. That the poft-diluvian earth, as he fays. was inferior in many refpectsnto the Adamitic, is very probable; and agrees with the doctrine of the longevity of the ante-diluvian patriarchs. He appeals to the form of the earth's furface, as a proof that it received its cavities and flexures from vaft currents of defcending waters; and has given two views of a rude valley in Derbyfhire to illuftrate his meaning. From this principle he derives the beauty of our profpects, and all the prefent water-courfes of the earth, from the higheft mountains of inland countries, down to the level of the fea. He argues that the earth's diameter ought to be fhorter at the poles than the equator, from the ftate of the elements, as well as other confiderations: and here he makes a reflexion on the incommenfurability every where obfervable in nature. In treating of the internal difpofition of the earth, he obferves, that the matters it contains are no where difpofed in the order of their gravities; and fhews how the ftrata of the earth are broken for the lodgement of metals, the formationof caverns, with the horizontal expofure of a tract in Caldy Ifland, in Pembrokefhire. From the folids of the earth he proceeds to the fluids, and enquires into the origin of fprings, which, as he contends, are not to be accounted for from falling vapours, but rather from an internal heat fimilar to that which produces perfpiration. This leads him to *fire-damps, volcanoes,* and *earthquakes,* the caufes and effects of which are copioufly treated of; with the ftrange phænomenon of the *flickenfide*-ftones in Derbyfhire.

He next recounts the changes the earth has undergone from different caufes; particularly the feparation of America; and concludes with the evidences, facred, profane, and philofophical, of the farther change which yet awaits it. Philofophical arguments have been taken from the ftate of things in the earth to fhew its antiquity; thefe Mr. Jones confiders, and makes fome ufeful remarks on the hiftory of language and letters. In the diftribution of the land and fea over the globe, he has found that fea on one fide has land in the antipodes: but what is moft obfervable in this difcourfe is the fuperiority of the northern hemifphere compared with the fouthern: 'It has more land, more fun, more heat, more light, more arts, more fenfe, more learning, more religion;' and he goes regularly through all thefe articles of the comparifon, fhewing at leaft how this difference agrees with the defigns of Providence.

Under every divifion of his work, that will admit of it, he introduces the ancient mythology; but here he gives a more extended view of the heathen cofmogonies, and endeavours to
fhew

ſhew how they have preſerved the tradition of the Moſaic. The mundane egg, and the trinity of Hermes, make a conſiderable figure, and are commented upon at large from the ſtores of mythology.

The laſt diſcourſe of this work is on the *Appearances, Cauſes, and prognoſtic Signs of the Weather*. In this ſubject all men pretend to ſome degree of ſkill, and therefore every reader will find ſome trite obſervations which he knew before. But the weather is not a low ſubject : it affords an agreeable and uſeful walk in philoſophy ; it has an important relation to the health of man and the buſineſs of life. ' The changes of the elements, as the author truly obſerves, preſent us with all that is great and wonderful in nature.' When we follow the weather into different regions of the world, we find many curious phænomena, which a pen with the power of deſcription may dwell upon to advantage. Mr. Jones firſt examines into the cauſes of the riſing and falling of vapours, the ſuſpenſion of the clouds, thunder-ſtorms, the aurora-borealis and its kindred meteors. He thence proceeds to the origin of the winds ; and ſhows, by many examples and authorities, that thoſe aerial currents iſſue from the body of the earth. Boerhaave and Woodward had two different theories to account for the changes of the weather, which are here explained. Other cauſes of the weather are the ſun and moon ; hence the trade-winds, tide, weather, &c. The arctic weather near the pole exhibits ſome wonderful ſcenery ; from which the author conducts us to the weather of the torrid zone, and deſcribes the waterſpout, &c. He ſhews how the weather is affected by tracts of mountains, woods, and foreſts ; how blaſting winds are derived from ſandy deſarts ; and how the air is tempered by the waters of the ocean ; which gives a phyſical reaſon why there is ſo large a proportion of ſea in the globe.

The ſigns of the weather, as Mr. Jones has collected them, are from the barometer, vapours, clouds, dew, the face of the ſky, the ſun, moon, and ſtars, the winds, meteors, and the motions of animals. The relation of the weather to the human body is a matter of great concern to the comfort of life, and is here particularly conſidered. The whole is concluded with a moral reflexion, by the obſervation of which thouſands might have been ſaved who have died prematurely. Having deſcribed the circumſtances moſt neceſſary to form a wholſome ſituation, the author ſubjoins : ' There may health fix her ſeat : but let no man think that his ſituation will preſerve him, unleſs he has the prudence to preſerve himſelf. All the varieties of the weather, all climates, all

the

the seasons, and all the elements, are, at war with the indolent and the intemperate.'

In our account of this publication we have confined ourselves to the principal contents of it, without deviating into questions concerning the orthodoxy of the author's philosophical opinions, some of which cannot easily be admitted; though his general principle of the agency of the elements seems clear enough. Upon the whole we may venture to say, that Mr. Jones has offered to the public a work, in a style and method which has given a new face to natural philosophy, and made it more interesting as well as more intelligible to readers of a liberal education.

Experiments and Observations made with a View to point out the Errors of the present received Theory of Electricity, and which tend in their Progress to establish a new System, on Principles more conformable to the simple Operations of Nature. By the Rev. John Lyon. *4to. 12s. in Boards.* Dodsley.

MR. Lyon begins his work with an explanation of the technical terms used by electricians; he then proceeds to give an account of the different systems advanced by philosophers, to account for electric attraction and repulsion: this part of his work he concludes with Dr. Franklin's theory of the Leyden phial, from which he argues, that the whole system depends on the impermeability of glass to the electric fluid, and the impossibility of the fluid's passing over the surface of glass. He proceeds with giving two experiments, to prove the absurdity of the latter supposition. As to the first of these, when we consider how much of its accuracy depends on the dryness of the air, and the glass he made use of, we think it affords no testimony in his favour. In respect of the second, where he makes use of a tube, and a pair of pith balls at the bottom of it, we are convinced, from our own experience, that the phenomenon depends not on the power of the glass to convey the fluid over its surface, but on a quantity of moisture, which it is almost impossible to remove from the inside of a tube. We would recommend to Mr. Lyon the use of a glass stem wiped very dry, by which alteration in his experiment, it is probable he will find a result very different from what he has described; we would advise him likewise to take care that the atmosphere of his conductor does not extend as far as his pith balls, which we have found to be affected at a very great distance from the conductor, when the cylinder we employed was not of very considerable magnitude.

The

The author proceeds to give experiments, shewing that glass is permeable by the electric fluid—' Take, says he, a pane of glass, ten or twelve inches diameter, more or less, according to the size of your jar, and place it upon a wire, under the end of the conductor, where you fix your jar. Let the end of the wire be hooked to a sharp pin, placed perpendicularly to the horizon, with the point close to the under surface of the pane, and opposite to another sharp point upon the upper surface of the glass, upon which also the phial or jar is to be placed, so as to be in contact with the last mentioned point. Fix one end of a large conducting bow, with a glass handle, to the other end of the wire lying under the glass, and, when the jar is charged, if you suddenly touch the knob of the jar with the other end of the conducting bow, the jar will be discharged with a spark, and a snap.'

We cannot coincide with Mr. Lyon in regard to the result of this experiment: we have often tried it without even a semblance of what he describes. We always took care to have the glass well dried, a circumstance which Mr. Lyon seems to have industriously excluded from his electrical ceremonies. Indeed, by blowing with the breath only on the glass, the operator may communicate a shock to it, and we must suppose that something of this kind deceived Mr. Lyon. To set the matter, however, beyond all doubt, we used a fine lamen of talc, instead of the pane of glass, as we knew this substance to be incapable of attracting much moisture from the air; in this case, the shock struck through, but there was always a perforation just opposite to the points; we also discovered, that a single spark from a very small conductor would have the same effect: hence, nothing can be clearer than the impossibility of passing the least portion of the electric fluid through glass, without breaking it. This chapter contains many other experiments, which, in our opinion, when divested of all obscurities, may with the greatest ease be accounted for, on the principles of Franklin's theory.

The fourth chapter contains an examination of the present theory of electric attraction and repulsion: the author examines the several particulars of this theory; and professes to prove by experiment, that they are erroneous through the whole. Nothing, however, is combated but the received mode of accounting for one experiment. We are far from agreeing with him, that this single experiment is the basis, or the key, to what he calls the present hypothetical system of attraction and repulsion; we would recommend to him to read and consider some curious facts on this subject in lord Mahon's work; and not to be so much out of humour with the prevail-

ing

ing hypothesis, till he has by his own accounted for those phenomena.—We have not sagacity enough to see, or conjecture, what Mr. Lyon means by the long quotation from the Principia, which he has given in this chapter. We wish he had been less profuse of his splendors, in other cases where they are not so much wanted as in the present.

Chapter fifth gives a description of the author's apparatus, which we think harmonizes most admirably with his experiments and speculations. He seems to be ignorant of the very simple machines used by modern electricians, and from the representation given, we have reason to believe that he does not make use of some very important improvements in the mode of exciting glass.

Chapter sixth is designed to overturn Dr. Franklin's method of accounting for the Leyden phial : ' which, the author says, depends wholly on the supposition, that when any additional quantity of the fluid is thrown into the inside, an equal quantity must be lost from the outside of the phial,' and vice versa. But, says he, those who favour this system ' have stumbled at the threshold, and have not hit upon the principle on which the phials act. Experiment : take two jars, charge them by their knobs, at the positive conductor. While they are standing with their knobs in contact with the conductor, and at some distance from each other, form a communication between the outside of one of the jars and the inside of both of them, and both the jars will be discharged. How, continues the author, is the equilibrium restored in this experiment to that jar whose inside has no communication with its outside ? The jars are both apparently in the same state after the discharge was made, as they were before they were charged.' We are amazed at the want of sagacity which Mr. Lyon displays in this experiment, and the subsequent remarks : it is wonderful that a man, who has thought at all upon the subject, should not perceive the cause of what he has described in the preceding quotation. The absence of the fluid on the outside of both the jars, depends on the additional quantity which is thrown on both their insides : this is the only cause which operates here ; and, we think, when this cause is removed, the effect can no longer exist : the inside is in this case discharged ; for, agreeable to Dr. Franklin's theory, the outside is supplied with what it wants from the table and other bodies connected with the jar; if the jar were insulated, the phenomenon would be wholly different from that described by Mr. Lyon, the charge would exist in the insulated phial, notwithstanding a thousand phials in contact with the same conductor were charged and discharged,

Experi-

Experiment sixth, of chapter sixth, is, in our opinion, a strong confirmation of the Franklinian theory, instead of being, as the author designs it, a confutation: his only objection is, how comes it to pass that there is a condensation upon the outside of an insulated jar applied to a conductor charged negatively? This will depend upon a variety of circumstances; his want of cleanliness and accuracy, the size of his knob, and the state of the air at the time. We have often found, after much wiping has been employed, that a knob would, in a case similar to what the author has described in this experiment, discharge a brush almost with every turn of the cylinder into the air; it is true the quantity is but small, and, in our opinion, this is the very cause why the jar at the positive conductor is not wholly discharged. Had there been a better conductor to carry it off from the inside of the second jar, all the phenomena Mr. Lyon describes would have been shewn in much greater perfection, and the whole of his experiment would be nothing more than one of the most antiquated facts relating to the Leyden phial. We would farther observe, that the author seems to have thought that the insulated table itself took away none of the fluid from the jar at the prime conductor. We are inclined to think, that if, instead of this clumsy method of insulation, he had made use of dry glass only, or wood well baked, he would not have discovered so much, either to puzzle or lead him astray; indeed the impertinent incumbrance of appendages to his apparatus in this experiment would alone lead us to suspect his accuracy.

Chapter seventh begins with a declamatory Philippic against the Franklinian theory, as substituting in several places ' supposition for demonstration, and as twisting and torturing experiments to correspond with the hypothesis, rather than the hypothesis being proved by experiments to be sufficient to pass for a general law.' Concluding this exordium with a bold metaphor, he proceeds to prove by experiment, that the brush, which appears at the point of a charged conductor, is no proof that the fluid passes out of that point, nor the star, as generally believed, of its entering into it. If we repeat the experiments of this chapter, we must repeat our accusations of inaccuracy, inattention to the insulators which are employed, with various other sources of error, which this author has the talent of exemplifying and diversifying in a most copious manner. We cannot, however, pass over the singular degree of confidence which is displayed in experiment fifth, and the singular manner with which it is supported. To the end of an insulated metal rod he cements a dry globe of glass; by a point which terminates the rod he conveys the

fluid

fluid on the inner surface of the globe: during the operation, he desires you to ' present your finger, or the back of your hand, to the external surface of the globe ; and, he says, that you may both see and feel the electric effluvia passing from the wire through the glass to your finger.' It cannot be supposed, continues the author, in this experiment, that the fluid passes from your finger through the glass to the point of the rod, ' *at such a supposition, the most sanguine advocate for the positive and negative electricity would blush.*' , The author does not consider that the globe, in this experiment, acts as a Leyden phial, is negative on the outside, and of course must appear to emit some of the fluid from the surface to his hand. If he is disposed to feel whether this be true, we would advise him, whilst one hand is applied to the external surface of the globe, with the other hand to touch the insulated rod. Before he assumes the peremptory style of his remarks on this and the following experiments, in which he is misled by the same fallacy, he must account for the possibility of charging any piece of dry glass, in the circumstances in which a globe is placed.

Chapter eighth contains a set of experiments, to shew the similarity of the magnetic to the electric attraction and repulsion. Our remarks on some preceding experiments will affect his deductions from *some* of these ; as to the author's application of the rest, both the poignancy and aptitude seem to be equally invisible. He lays no claim to novelty in most of what he produces in this chapter : the new part, in our opinion, is the only doubtful one; but as to the conclusion drawn from the whole, what it means, or what it is designed for, is totally involved in obscurity. ' From the similarity, says he, there appears to be between these electric and magnetic experiments we may reasonably *conclude,* for there is rather more than a probability, the effluvia of both act from one principle, and that *there is a polarity* in these infinitely and inconceivably small particles of matter. We find, in certain cases, the electric particles as well as the magnetic attract each other, and they will unite with an inconceivable velocity ; and in other cases they as powerfully repel. This cannot be done without some *inherent* and *innate* property in the particles of the electric effluvia — I imagine this property may exist in the first particles of matter, without a directive tendency to one particular point of the horizon. Nature seems to favour this doctrine in a variety of instances, as will be shewn in a *proper place* *. As I believe it will be a difficult, if not

---

* This proper place we have not been able to discover throughout the whole quarto.

an

an impoffible tafk to draw rational and confiftent conclufions from many electric appearances without the affiftance of this theory, I fhall endeavour to fupport it in preference to any other.'

Chapter tenth is faid to contain ' an analyfis of the Leyden phial, with a variety of experiments, to fhew the difcharging of it depends, moft probably, upon an attractive and repulfive property inherent in the particles of the electric effluvia; and that this wonderful phial may act from the fame principle as the magnet, or the loadftone.'——This chapter is in truth a curiofity; it claims our admiration of Mr. Lyon's talents, not only as an experimentalift and a fpeculatift, but as a moft. defcriptive declaimer. Let his fixth experiment be read as one felected from many, equally expreffive of the author's talents. —' Fill a coated jar, *with boiling water up to the top of the infide coating of the jar,* place it in a glafs veffel, and fill the veffel with *boiling water,* till it rifes as high on the outfide as it is in the infide of the jar. Place this veffel upon a ftool with glafs legs, with the knob of the wire of the jar in contact with the conductor of the electrical machine; while the jar is charging, prefent a conducting rod to the outfide of the glafs veffel, and when charged, take the difcharging bow, and form a communication between the outfide of the glafs veffel upon the ftool and the knob of the wire of the jar, and if you darken the room, you may fee the electric effluvia fhoot upon the outfide of the glafs veffel, into beautiful ramifications, from the knob of the difcharging bow. Some of the largeft branches fometimes fhoot between two and three inches long, *and fhow, in miniature, the zig-zag and forked lightning, which ftrike fuch terror into the breaft of the bewildered traveller in a dark and tempeftuous night.* No words can convey an adequate idea of this experiment.'

We affent to the juftice of this concluding paragraph; the experiment, as he calls it, bids defiance to all the feverity of criticifm; it is one of thofe originals which the moft malignant fatirift cannot carricature.——We claim to ourfelves great merit for the patience which has carried us through the remainder of this volume; but we have no right to expect the fame patience from our readers; efpecially when, from woeful experience, we are able to inform them that the firft ten chapters are not the moft abfurd in the book. Like feveral of his betters, Mr. Lyon is *phlogifton mad* towards the conclufion of this volume. All the phænomena in nature are traced ultimately to the fame principle, which is employed by Mr. Lyon to account for fome of the difficulties in the Mofaic account of the creation. In this particular, however, and in a variety of others, which

may

may be pointed out, we would recommend a philofophical part-
nerfhip between Mr. Lyon and Mr. Harrington; a fpecimen
of whofe uncommon abilities may be feen in the following
article.

---

*A Philofophical and Experimental Enquiry into the firft and gene-
ral Principles of Life: likewife into Atmofpherical Air. By*
Robert Harrington. 8*vo.* 6*s.* Cadell.

MR. Harrington, in his introduction, gives a catalogue of
his accomplifhments as a philofopher; he feems afraid
to truft the fagacity of the reader in this particular, and exhibits a daubing as a reprefentation of himfelf, in which a
group of features are jumbled together, not one of which could
have been difcovered from any part of his work. Accipe
digni pauca notanda viri.

' A young man, when he takes up fo learned and extenfive
a fubject, and when he has to combat with the opinions of the
greateft men, requires a deal of refolution; but I hope my
readers will give an impartial canvas. *It is a work* of indefatigable labour, *where* you are to build a fyftem of your own;
a fyftem which comprehends all the different fciences, viz.
natural philofophy, anatomy, phyfic, chemiftry, mathematics,
&c. and not only to be well acquainted with thefe, but even
to correct their errors, and make new improvements in each; otherwife I could not have eftablifhed this extenfive doctrine. And to
do all this myfelf, without having any perfon to affift me, or to afk
a fingle queftion of; being tenacious about difcovering any
part; having, from experience in one or two inftances, found
my confidence betrayed in my philofophical enquiries.' We
affure our readers that this quotation has been made with all
poffible accuracy, and, we think, to render it complete in its
kind, nothing is requifite but a little falfe fpelling.

We no fooner begin to examine the book, than we find ourfelves furrounded with fuch abfurdities, that we know not which
to fix upon as the moft glaring and extravagant. Hear him
' premife (what he calls) the hiftory of *the animal.* There are
two genera in nature which make up the principal part of the
creation upon the globe, being the animal and vegetable kingdoms; we evidently obferve they both enjoy life.——Life is a
very vague term, when applied in this philofophical fenfe;
but what I imply by it is, *a body* having a power of extenfion
within itfelf, being produced from an ovum, by *copulation of
the fexes,* which generates to maturity, and being then capable of propagating its fpecies.' We are inclined to think
that Linnæus himfelf would be puzzled to find what animal
this

this curious defcription refers to; this is the firft inftance in which we have heard the appellation of *genera* given to *king-doms*, and of life being a body produced from an egg, and that the prolific egg is laid long before the parents have copulated.

The author's definition of air is not lefs curious than his hiftory of the animal: ' Air, fays he, is an æthereal, fubtle, and elaftic fluid, *univerfally* difperfed over the *whole* face of the earth, ftrikingly reprefented by the *down of the peach*, for fo does the air cover the furface of the globe, as the down does the peach.' We rather think Mr. Harrington fuppofes that the air is like a goat's beard, for as the beard covers the chin of the goat, fo does the air cover the furface of the globe. Through the whole of this work the author mif-takes phlogifton for heat, and heat for phlogifton; he confe-quently afcribes the fluidity of water to a principle, to which (if there be any truth in chemiftry) water has no affinity; he talks, likewife, of determining the quantity of phlogifton in a body by the thermometer, and gives us the following ac-count of the caufe on which elafticity depends! ' Let us enquire upon what elafticity depends. All fluids have this property in fome degree; but it will be found, that thofe which poffefs moft phlogifton have it moft fenfibly*; fpiritu-ous fluids, for this reafon, poffefs it more confiderably than water; but even water, by giving it a large quantity of phlo-gifton, can poffefs this quality in a very eminent degree; take a few drops of water, place them in *vacuo*, and throw into them a *large quantity of phlogifton*, and their elafticity will overcome the *greateft* force.' Such is the wonderful penetra-tion of Mr. Harrington, that he affures us, ' that, if the whole atmofphere could be decompounded at once, *the phlogifton* that would be let loofe, would be fuch an immenfe *proportion*, as to fet the *whole world* on fire: we often fee, fays he, when there is too *ftrong a folution of phlogifton* in the atmofphere, that it *purges* itfelf by lightning; and in hot climates, it will tear up trees, *caftles*, *nay rocks*; for, agreeable to the laws of nature, whenever there is an overproportion of phlogifton in the air, *fhe* takes that method to *unload herfelf*.' What an un-civil lady is dame Nature, to *unload* herfelf in this *rude, ob-ftreperous*, and *public* manner!

The great ufe of refpiration is one of the moft curious dif-coveries of Dr. Prieftley; who fays, that the lungs are em-ployed in this operation to carry off that fuperabundant quan-tity of phlogifton from the blood, which, if not thus dif-

---

* If this be true, why have oils fo little elafticity?

charged,

charged, would become noxious and fatal.   Mr. Harrington treats all this theory as a complication of the moft egregious blunders.   Phlogifton, according to him, fo far from being hurtful, is abfolutely the nourifhment of the human frame. Blood, he fays, is hardly any thing but phlogifton, and lo! the wonderful experiment, which, in the twinkling of an eye, is to overturn the whole Prieftleyan fyftem.   ‘ I took (fays the wonderful Mr. Harrington) a dog, and after making him very hungry, he *ferocioufly devoured* two quarts of blood, drawn warm from an ox, when thofe poifonous fumes (agreeable to the doctor) were exhaling rapidly ; yet he breathed them, and, inftead of killing the dog, they fenfibly cherifhed him, making him *eat with greater glee and rapidity.’*   Query, which of the two philofophical prodigies is the greateft ? He who proved to the Royal Society that a fifh could live in water ; or Mr. Harrington, who has difcovered that a dog will live upon blood ? But, Mr. Harrington flies from one favage to another, and carries us from his experiments on the dog, to his obfervations on a butcher ; where we behold another wonder from this man of wonders, ‘ What, fays he, muft a butcher fuffer, who is conftantly expofed to thofe fumes ? Why, with reflection we fhould fay, he would not live five minutes, he being fo immediately expofed to the exhalations of the fluids * of whole oxen ; yet fo far from *killing* him, it makes him *thrive and grow fat.*   It is a juft obfervation, that butchers *are fatter* than the generality of mankind ; thofe fumes which fly from warm blood, on expofure to the air, being remarkably nutricious and invigorating.’   Thefe fingularities in the hiftory of a butcher, we muft take entirely on Mr. Harrington’s authority, as we do not pretend to vie with him in the acquaintance he may have amongft the fraternity at Whitechappel ; between whom, and the fraternity who meet in the Old Baily, fome ill-natured fnarlers may trace a moft intimate connexion.   But, the author’s courage is not lefs wonderful than his penetration ; ‘ fo fenfible, fays he, of the folidity of my theory, and the fallacy of the doctor’s, I was determined to give it a fair trial, *at the hazard of my health.*   Having got a large veffel of bullock’s blood, drawn warm from the animal, *I introduced* my head *over* it, and that my lungs might collect as much of the effluvia as poffible, I inclofed my head within the mouth of the veffel, *with all the addrefs I was able,* with a motive that the atmofphere fhould not fteal the vapour from me.’   This experiment he ‘ tried without any dread, nobody being at hand to drag him from the pernicious fumes in cafe he had been

---

* We fuppofe he means the fumes.

con-

convulfed: but, fays he, inftead of *its* having this ferious confequence, I found not the leaft bad effects from *it* ; but, on the contrary, I found the living principle *entertained by it, feeding its appetite.'*

After all thefe wonderful efforts, and many more equally extraordinary, the author takes breath, paufes, and then re-capitulates fome of his difcoveries. ' I have, fays he, not only proved that phlogifton makes up the greateft part of the animal, it being laid up as a refervoir, in the form of fat, againft an emergency of either want of food, or extreme cold ; which I fhould prefume no one will deny : but I have likewife proved that this phlogifton, either in the form of fatted globules, *or any other*, which the animal poffeffes, may be received into the ftomach of another animal, and fo far from being pernicious to the animal, is *immediate* to its life.'

We prefume our readers muft by this time be very well fa-tisfied with the great philofophical talents of Mr. Harrington. We affure them that the paffages we have quoted are not given. as the moft extraordinary, but as the firft that ftruck us in re-viewing his book. We fhould not have been fo free in ex-preffing our difapprobation, if we had not been alarmed by a menace, which we read with great concern ; where he tells us he has another work *in hand*.——Heavens forbid ! If, how-ever, the cacoethes fcribendi fhould, in fpite of every wholefome caution, continue to tyrannize over Mr. Harring-ton, we would advife him once more to attend another courfe of Dr. Black's lectures, whofe name he quotes with great triumph, as that of the profeffor who honoured him with his inftructions in chemiftry.

Sketches of the Lives and Writings of the Ladies of France. *By* Ann Thickneffe. *Vol. II. and III.* 12mo. 5s. *fewed.* Dodfley.

THE firft volume of this work commenced with the cele-brated Heloife, the miftrefs of Abelard, and concluded with Madame de Maintenon *. The next lady mentioned by Mrs. Thickneffe, in the continuation of the narrative, is Ma-dame de Houlieres, the daughter of Melchoir du Ligur, a gentleman of good family, but fmall fortune. She was born at Paris in 1633, and contracted an early tafte for poetry, in which fhe afterwards difplayed confiderable talents. Of the

---

* See Crit. Rev. vol. xlv. p. 218.

perfon

perfon and fortune of this lady Mrs. Thicknefse gives the following account.

' The charms of her perfon bore a kind of fimilitude with thofe of her mind; fhe was perfectly elegant, with a foftnefs of manners, which rendered her a moft agreeable companion; but the beft panegyric we can give of this celebrated lady, is exprefsed in the following lines which are at the bottom of her portrait engraved by Vanfchuppen, and placed at the head of the firft edition of her works.

' Si corine en beauté fut célebre autrefois,
Si des vers de pindare elle effaca la gloire,
Quel rang doivent tenir au temple de memoire
Les vers que tu vas lire, & les traites que tu vois ?

' But with all thefe advantages, Madame des Houlieres was far from being happy. Her works breathe every where, murmurs againft fortune. At the age of eighteen, fhe married Monfieur des Houlieres, an officer in the fervice of the prince of Condé, who was obliged, fhortly after their marriage, to accompany that prince in his expedition to Rocroi, which was attended with fuccefs; and by which, Monfieur des Houlieres was raifed in the army; but being led into extraordinary expences to fupport his new acquired honours, his affairs were thrown into the utmoft embarrafsment, and moft of his effects were feized: to add to his misfortunes, his pay was alfo ftopped; upon which, Madame des Houlieres went in perfon to court, and prefented a petition on behalf of her hufband, but no notice being taken of it, fhe made loud complaints, which was looked upon as a crime, and for which fhe was arrefted, and conducted a prifoner to the caftle de Vilverden, two leagues from Brufsels.

' As foon as Monfieur des Houlieres was informed of his wife's confinement, he folicited for her being fet at liberty; but finding there were but little hopes of obtaining it, he marched to Vilverden with fome foldiers, forced the fortrefs, and brought off his wife in triumph; but he would undoubtedly have fuffered for this refolute action, had it not been that a general pardon was at that very time proclaimed, and of which he very opportunely took advantage. He, however, obtained foon after, employment in the king's fervice, and his wife purfued her ftudies and tafte for poetry.'

The fpecies of poetry for which Madame de Houlieres was chiefly diftinguifhed, was that of the paftoral kind. She had the honour of being admitted into the academy of Arles in Provence, and in that of Ricovrate at Padua; and at length
fhe

she obtained a pension from the crown; which enabled her to spend the evening of her days in tranquillity, until a cancer put a period to her life, in 1695.

The lady immediately succeeding is the marchioness de Villars, mother to the celebrated Louis Hector, marshal duke de Villars. Her maiden name was Marie de Bellefonds; and she was remarkable, not only for her beauty, but for her wit and conversation. The chief productions of this lady are her letters, which were written from Madrid, while her husband, the marquis de Villars, was ambassador at that court. Those letters, as the biographer observes, are written with great spirit, though not in the most elegant style; and contain a great number of curious anecdotes, as well as observations on the manners and customs of the Spanish court.

Madame de Villedieu was born at Alençon in 1640. Her father, M. des Jardins, was provost of the Maréchaussée in that town, and her mother had been waiting-woman to the duchess de Rohan. She was considered as a woman of great literary abilities, and of a lively turn of wit; but, unfortunately, indulged herself in the immoderate use of spirituous liquors, in consequence of which she died at the age of forty-three. One of her first productions is a romance, or rather a collection of several, entitled, Les Desordres de l'Amour.

The marchioness de Lambert was the only daughter of M. de Marguenat de Courcelles, who died when she was but three years of age.

' Her mother, says the historian, married the celebrated Monsieur Bachaumont, a man of great learning, who perceiving the genius of his daughter-in-law, took infinite pains to cultivate it, by which means, she soon caught the habit of thinking deeply.—Her style of writing is noble, pure, and elegant, adorned with all the graces of the French language, and though she may have a few equals, she had no superior in a delicate and sentimental manner of expressing her thoughts. In February 1666, she married Henry de Lambert, marquis de Saint Bris, who died a lieutenant general, leaving her a son and daughter, whom she educated with the utmost care: her house was considered as a kind of academy, where persons of the first genius assembled. Her works, which are in the highest esteem, are, Avis d'une mere à son fils, (Advice of a mother to her son) and Avis d'une mere à sa fille, another to her daughter; both which, are wrote in an elevated style, and abound with solid sense. She died at Paris the 12th of July, 1733, in the eighty-sixth year of her age, highly regretted by men of letters, and infinitely beloved by all ranks and orders of people.'

From

From the two above mentioned works of this lady, Mrs. Thickneſſe afterwards gives ſeveral extracts, accompanied with ſenſible obſervations.

Madame Guyon was born at Montargis, of illuſtrious parents, in 1648. She was chiefly remarkable for piety, which is alſo the principal merit of her writings.

Madame de Saliez was born at Alby, in Provence, where ſhe married a magiſtrate of that city, who ſoon after left her a widow. She was reputed a woman of excellent underſtanding, which ſhe took great pains to cultivate, both by ſtudy and converſation. She eſtabliſhed in the place of her birth an agreeable ſociety, under the name of Societé de Chevalieres de la Bonne Foi ; and ſhe formed the project of eſtabliſhing alſo a new ſet of female philoſophers. She lived to a great age, highly eſteemed and honoured ; and died in 1730, at Alby, the place of her nativity.

Mademoiſelle de Roſilli was deſcended from the noble and ancient family of Touraine. She was celebrated for her poetical compoſitions, which were eſteemed for the elegance of their ſtyle, and delicacy of ſentiment. She died at Paris in 1704, at the age of eighty-three ; diſtinguiſhed by the appellation of Calliope, becauſe ſhe treated only of heroic ſubjects.

Mademoiſelle Cheron was born at Paris in 1648. She was the daughter of Henry Cheron, an eminent painter in enamel, in which art he inſtructed his daughter. The celebrated Le Brun procured her the ſingular honour of being admitted a member of the Royal Academy of Painting and Sculpture. She was no leſs diſtinguiſhed for poetry and muſic than for painting, and obtained from Lewis XIV. a penſion of five hundred livres.

After ſeveral ladies of inferior note, Mrs. Thickneſſe mentions Mademoiſelle Deſcartes, niece to the celebrated philoſopher of that name. Her principal writings were two compoſitions, one entitled, La Relation de la Mort de Deſcartes, part written in verſe, and part in proſe ; the other entitled, L'Ombre de Deſcartes.

The next lady with whom Mrs. Thickneſſe preſents us is the counteſs D'Aulnoy, author of the Lady's Travels into Spain. From this work the biographer has, for the entertainment of her readers, extracted ſeveral paſſages ; as ſhe has done from the romances of Mademoiſelle de la Force.

After mentioning a few other ladies, our authoreſs introduces an account of the celebrated Mad. Dacier. The maiden name of this lady was Le Fevre. She was born in 1651, at Saumur, in the academy at which place her father was profeſſor of the belles lettres. He inſtructed his daughter in the Latin,

Greek,

Greek, and Italian ; and fhe was able, very early in life, to underftand and relifh all the beauties of the beft writers in thofe languages. She married Mr. Dacier, a young pupil of her father's, and who was the fon of a proteftant gentleman in Languedoc. Mrs. Thickneffe gives an account of the different productions of this literary heroine, who died in 1720, univerfally efteemed for her uncommon learning and abilities.

For the gratification of our readers, we fhall prefent them with an extract from thofe fketches, on a character which has fo much, and fo defervedly, attracted public notice.

' Mademoifelle le Fevre, (who we fhall in future, call madam Dacier,) fome time after the death of her father, came to Paris—where fhe renewed thofe ftudies, by which fhe gained the higheft reputation. The firft thing fhe applied herfelf to, was to give a tranflation of Callimachus, which fhe fhewed in manufcript to the dauphin's fub-governor, (fince bifhop D' Avranches,) and to many other learned men, who exceedingly applauded her undertaking, among which number, was the duke de Montaufier, who earneftly recommended it to her, to tranflate fome Latin authors for the ufe of the young prince. In 1674, fhe publifhed Le Florus, which was foon followed by another work, intitled Eutrope. Thefe performances proved fufficient to fpread the fame of madam Dacier, throughout Europe. Queen Chriftina of Sweden expreffed her admiration of her fuperior talents in a very polite letter, in which that princefs made her the moft advantageous offers to induce her to fettle at her court, at the fame time expreffing her wifhes that madam Dacier would embrace the catholic religion.

' Her fhining talents received ftill greater luftre from her amiable virtues. Her piety, modefty, courage, and fortitude, made her revered by all ranks of people. Her charity towards the poor was fo unbounded, that fhe often fuffered great inconvenience, and denied herfelf many of the comforts of life, that fhe might be enabled to fuccour thofe who were unfortunate and diftreffed.

' Monfieur Dacier, one day reprefenting to her the neceffity there was in being lefs liberal towards others, confidering the narrownefs of their circumftances, fhe replied :

    `` Ce n'eft pas les biens que nous avons qui nous
       Feront vivre ; ce font les charités que nous
       Ferons ; elles nous rendront amis de Dieu, & elles
       Contribueront à effacer nos péchés,''

' She was as modeft as fhe was wife, for fhe feldom or ever converfed upon any topic by way of fhewing her erudition ; and particularly in the company of her own fex, was ever cautious of difplaying her fuperior knowledge, but adapted herfelf to the capacities of thofe with whom fhe converfed. They report a fingular anecdote of her, which is a convincing proof not only of her modefty, but her judgment. In the age fhe lived, it was cuftomary it feems for men of learning to carry a book with them when they travelled, and whenever they vifited fuch perfons who were diftinguifhed for their learning, they ufed to entreat the favour of them to write their name down in the book, and to add alfo a fentence to it. One time when a learned German went to madam Dacier, he prefented her his book, and begged fhe would do him the honour to write her name, and alfo a fentence; but when fhe beheld the names of moft of the learned men in Europe, fhe was ftartled, faying, fhe fhould blufh to think of puting her name among thofe of fo many illuftrious men. The German would not be refufed, the more fhe endeavoured to excufe herfelf from complying with his requeft, the more he preffed her, till at laft, being prevailed upon by his importunities, fhe took the pen and wrote down her name, to which fhe added the following line from Sophocles.

" Le filence eft l'ornement des femmes."
Silence is the ornament of women.

' In 1680, fhe publifhed Dictys Cretenfis, and Dares Phrygius. In 1681, fhe gave Aurelius Victor, and alfo a tranflation of Anacreon, which met with the greateft fuccefs. This was foon followed by three comedies tranflated from Plautus, with remarks, which did her the higheft honour. She was foon after received as a member of the academy at Padua. The fame year, fhe gave a tranflation of Homer, with remarks on the fuperior beauties of that great poet. This performance gave rife to that famous difpute between her and that celebrated writer, Monfieur de la Motte. Never was any literary difpute carried to fuch lengths, or had made fo much noife in the world. Each had their partifans, and each maintained their caufe with uncommon fpirit, wit, and erudition. This literary quarrel produced another compofition from the pen of madam Dacier, intitled, Des Caufes de la Corruption du Goût. In 1711, fhe finifhed the Iliad; and the Odyffey, appeared in 1716, and was thought by the beft judges equal to the Iliad. She alfo tranflated Ariftophanes, Terence, and Callimachus: her comparifon between Plautus and Terence is drawn in a mafterly manner.

' Amidft thefe occupations, madam Dacier did not omit that important and material duty, the education of her own children—whofe natural genius gave her every reafon to believe

the

that they would have been an ornament to fociety. But while fhe fondly indulged herfelf with the pleafing idea of enjoying the fruits of her labour, death put a period to all her hopes.——Her lamentation for the lofs of a favourite daughter, who died at the age of eighteen, is written in the moft pathetic ftyle. In her, fays madam Dacier, were united all thofe virtues and talents, which can render a woman truly amiable. This inconfolable mother has immortalized her own grief and the merit of her daughter in her preface to the Iliad, in which fhe has raifed a monument to her memory, more durable than either bronze or marble. This elogium has been efteemed as a chef-d'œuvre, not inferior to any thing of the kind, either ancient or modern.'

Next follow, Mademoifelle Catherine Bernard, the countefs de Murat, Madame Dunoyer, and feveral others of inferior reputation, with whom concludes the fecond volume of thofe Sketches.

The third volume opens with Mademoifelle Heritier, who was born at Paris in 1664. She is celebrated, not only for poetical talents, but for beauty of perfon, and elegance of manners. This lady is fucceeded by Madam Durand, who compofed a number of novels, which were much admired in France. She alfo wrote a little hiftory, entitled, Les Belles Grecques, or the Grecian Beauties; confifting of anecdotes collected from Greek and Latin authors.

We are afterwards prefented with the Marchionefs de Vielbourg, Madame de Rochechouard, Madame de Gomez, Madame de Staal, the countefs de Fontaines, and a number of other ladies, who are all more or lefs diftinguifhed as writers of romance, memoirs of their own times, or poetical compofitions.

From the great number of literary ladies mentioned by Mrs. Thickneffe, one would almoft be inclined to imagine, that the ladies in France were diftinguifhed by the peculiar privilege of being born writers. But there feems ftrong reafon to conclude, that this has been more owing to the fafhion of affecting mental accomplifhments, than to the real endowments of nature: and it is obfervable, that the fucceffion of literary ladies in France has declined in the fame proportion in which that of England has advanced.——Whether this proceeds from the fuperior abilities of fome Englifh ladies, whom our neighbours on the continent have defpaired of rivalling, we fhall not determine. If fuch a multitude of examples, however, can excite emulation, Mrs. Thickneffe may have the merit of rouzing all the latent ta-

lents

lents of her sex; and of inspiring her contemporaries with an euthusiasm for that literary fame, which she has endeavoured to perpetuate, by this ingenious and pleasing monument erected to the memory of the French ladies.

Miscellanies by the Honourable Daines Barrington. 4to. 18s. White.

THIS volume contains a variety of miscellaneous essays on geographical discoveries, ornithology, and other curious and useful subjects.

Some of the first articles are tracts on the possibility of reaching the North Pole; first published in 1775 and 1776, and now reprinted with additional observations.

Navigators have penetrated into the arctic circle, and acquired some knowledge of Nova Zembla, West Greenland, and Spitzbergen or East Greenland. But their navigation has terminated at a considerable distance from the pole; and it is generally supposed, that the greatest efforts of human industry can never surmount the barriers, with which nature seems to have encircled those regions. But a true philosopher will never despair of making farther advances. Every attempt for this purpose is laudable, and may be attended with no inconsiderable advantage with respect to navigation and geography. There is a spacious field for investigation. A very considerable part of our hemisphere is yet unknown. We may still say with Seneca,

——— Venient annis
secula seris, quibus oceanus
· Vincula rerum laxet, et ingens
Pateat tellus, Tiphysque novos
Detegat orbes *. Sen. Med. v. 374.

---

* Seneca adds:
——— Nec sit terris
Ultima Thule.

Our author, having occasion to mention Thule, supposes it to be Ireland; and endeavours to support his opinion by a passage in Statius, Sylv. v. 317. But this notion is utterly inconsistent with the account, which is given of Thule, and of Ierne, Juverna, or Hibernia, by Strabo, Pliny, Mela, Solinus, Dionysius, and other Greek and Roman writers. Some take Thule to be Iceland, and others Schetland. From the fabulous and contradictory accounts of the ancients, it is probable, that this famous island was with them a sort of poetical region, or a terra incognita, like the Insula Atlantica of Plato.

Not.

Notwithſtanding our modern diſcoveries, which have amply verified this remarkable prediction, many more will certainly be made by future navigators, of which we have at preſent no idea. And an accident may bring us to the knowlege of what could never be ſuggeſted by arguments à priori.

The ingenious author of theſe tracts appears to be a zealous advocate for proſecuting our geographical reſearches, eſpecially towards the north pole.

Among other general reaſons, which he produces in favour of his opinion, that the polar ſeas are navigable, or not covered with perpetual ice, he mentions the following :

‘ Nothing has been ſuppoſed to ſhew more ſtrongly the wiſdom of a beneficent Creator, than that every part of this globe, ſhould (taking the year throughout) have an equal proportion of the ſun's light.

‘ It is admitted, that the equatorial parts have rather too much heat for the comfort of the inhabitants, and thoſe within the polar circles too little ; but as we know that the tropical limits are peopled, it ſhould ſeem, that the two polar circles are equally deſtined for the ſame purpoſe ; or, if not for the benefit of man, at leaſt for the ſuſtinence of certain animals.

‘ The largeſt of theſe, in the whole ſcale of creation, is the whale, which, though a fiſh, cannot live long under water, without occaſionally raiſing its head into another element, for the purpoſe of reſpiration * : moſt other fiſh alſo occaſionally approach the ſurface of the water.

‘ If the ice therefore extends from N. lat. 80 ½ to the pole †, all the intermediate ſpace is denied to the Spitzbergen whales, as well perhaps as to other fiſh : and is that glorious luminary, the ſun, to ſhine in vain for half the year upon ten degrees of latitude round each of the poles, without contributing either to animal life or vegetation ? For neither can take place upon this dreary expanſe of ice.

. . . ‘ I beg leave alſo to rely much on the neceſſity of the ice's yielding to the conſtant reciprocation of the tides ; becauſe no ſea was ever known to be frozen but the Black Sea, and ſome ſmall parts of the Baltic ; neither of which have any tides ; at the ſame time, that the waters of both contain much leſs ſalt, than thoſe of other ſeas, from the great

---

* ‘ Sometimes the ice is fixed, where there are but few whales ſeen ; for underneath the ice they cannot breathe ’ Martens's Voyage to Spitzbergen.

† The limits of the voyage towards the North Pole, performed by captain Phipps, now lord Mulgrave, in 1773, if we rightly recollect, were 80° 48'.

influx of fresh water rivers : for this last reason it may likewise be presumed, that the circumpolar seas are very salt, because there are probably no such influx beyond N. lat. 80, Spitzbergen itself having no rivers.'

A writer, in the Swedish Transactions of 1752, says, ' There are three kinds of ice in the northern seas. The first is like melted snow, which is become partly hardened, is more easily broken into pieces, less transparent, is seldom more than six inches thick, and when dissolved, is found to be intermixed with salt. This first sort of ice is the only one, which is ever formed from sea water.

' If a certain quantity of water, which contains as much salt as sea water, is exposed to the greatest degree of cold, it never becomes firm and pure ice, but resembles tallow, or suet, whilst it preserves the taste of salt ; so that the sweet transparent ice can never be formed in the sea. If the ice of the sea itself therefore, confined in a small vessel, without any motion, cannot thus become true ice, much less can it in a deep and agitated ocean.' The author hence infers, that all the floating ice in the polar seas comes from the Tartarian rivers and Greenland. Mr. Barrington is of the same opinion.

In the Philosophical Transactions for the year 1776, there is an experiment for parting fresh water from salt by freezing. If, upon this principle, the frost detaches as much water from saline particles, as is sufficient to form an incrustation, may not we suppose, that a much larger body of ice may be gradually superadded by the freezing of the rain and sleet in the polar regions ? Or if the basis of the ice is formed by large floats, which come from the Tartarian rivers and Greenland, may not those floats be rendered permanent by the constant addition of ice, formed out of dews, fogs, rain, &c. ? This point, we apprehend, deserves some consideration.

The author, having made some other previous remarks, produces several instances of navigators, who have penetrated beyond 80 $\frac{1}{2}$.

In this detail he mentions a great number, who have proceeded to 81, 82, and 83 ; and some, who are *said* to have advanced as far as 86, 88, and 89 ; but the latter were chiefly Dutchmen, and their relations cannot perhaps be sufficiently authenticated. In Harris's Voyage is the following passage : ' By the Dutch journals they get into N. lat. 88° 56', and the sea open.'

From a variety of instances, which our author has collected, of Greenland ships advancing into very high latitudes, from much conversation with the officers of the royal navy, and with intelligent seamen, both in England and Holland, who

have

have been many years concerned in the whale fishery, he infers, that an attempt to fail to the north pole is by no means that chimerical project, which some may imagine.

The reason why none of our Greenland whale ships have ever made the attempt is this : they are all insured ; if therefore they were to go beyond the common fishing latitudes, it would be such a departure from the voyage insured, that they would not be able to recover, if accidents happened in such a deviation.

Yet in a little time this scheme will most probably be tried : for by a late act of parliament a reward of 5000l. is offered to such of his majesty's subjects, as shall first penetrate beyond the 89 degree of northern latitude ; and a reward of 20,000l. to such as shall first discover a communication between the Atlantic and the Pacific oceans, in any direction whatsoever of the northern hemisphere.

The late captain Pickersgill, who commanded the Lion armed brig, on the coast of West Greenland in 1776, in his Journal, which was laid before the Royal Society in 1778, says :

' I shall conclude with a few observations on this part of the world (Greenland) so terribly represented by people, who, in order to raise their own merit, make dangers and difficulties of common occurrences, merely because the places are unknown, and there is little or no probability of their being ever contradicted. I do not mean this as a personal reflection ; but having discoursed with many of the masters of Greenland vessels, as well as their employers, and heard such dreadful stories of these countries, I cannot help remarking it, as tending to mislead those, who, from a laudable principle, would be benefactors to their country, but are deterred from it by these misrepresentations. I shall communicate observations on the ice, the atmosphere, the land of Frobisher, and the *probability* of a N. W. passage, in a short time.'

This however has unfortunately been prevented by the captain's death ; but the Astronomer Royal, who communicated his Journal to the Royal Society, informed Mr. Barrington by letter, ' that he had often heard this navigator express himself as well assured of a N. W. passage ; adding, that he received accounts of it from the inhabitants on the side of Davis's Straits, and that it was directly N. W. very different from Baffin's track.' Captain Pickersgill likewise thought, ' that the best method to find the passage was to get out early, before the ice broke away in the upper part of Davis's Straits.'

From many other reports, which the author has collected, he infers, that the polar voyage should be attempted early in the feafon. ' For if, fays he, I am right in what have fuppofed, that the ice, which often packs near the coafts of Spitzbergen, comes chiefly from the rivers, which empty themfelves into the Tartarian fea, it feems highly probable, that this is the proper time of pufhing to the northward, as the ice in fuch rivers cannot be then completely broken up. What other ice therefore may be feen at this time is probably the remains of what was difembogued, during the preceding fummer.

' Another proof of this arifes from what happened in 1773; for the Carcafe and Race-horfe were obftructed at 80° and a half, by an immenfe bank of ice, during part of the months of July and Auguft; but four Greenland mafters were a degree farther to the northward during the months of May and June, in the fame year.

' No one winters in Spitzbergen, but fome few Ruffians; from whom however we have not been informed, what happens during that feafon, though it fhould feem from the obfervations of Barentz, thofe of the Ruffians in Maloy Brun, and a fhip having pufhed into the Atlantic from Hudfon's Bay, during the midft of December *, that the northern feas are then navigable.

' For the fame reafon probably Clipperton, who paffed the ftraits of Magellan in the midft of winter, faw no ice, which is fo frequently met with at Midfummer by thofe, who fail to the fouthward of Cape Horn.

' — If the ice however fhould pack in April or May (which I conceive it would not, as little muft be left to float from the preceding fummer) yet as the warm weather is then increafing from day to day, the navigator would wait with fome degree of patience, till his fhip may be releafed from this temporary obftruction. The fituation of the difcoverer under thefe circumftances, may be compared to a traveller, paffing over a large tract of fea-fand, when the tide is flowing or ebbing. In the firft inftance he fpurs his horfe, becaufe the fea may be expected at his heels; in the latter he proceeds with great compofure, as every inftant he lofes in point of time, the fea is farther removed.'

But the greateft difficulty attending a navigator in very high latitudes is *revocare gradum,* how to get back again; for, fhould he be befet there in the ice, his fituation would be very dangerous; as he might be detained a long time, if not for the whole winter.

---

* For thefe and other facts, alluded to in the foregoing extracts, we muft refer the reader, who wifhes to know them, to Mr. Barrington's Tracts.

In order to obviate, as much as possible, this and some other objections, our author recommends the following precautions:

' The ship should be such as is commonly used in the Greenland fishery, or rather of a smaller size, as it works the more readily, when the ice begins to pack round it.

' There should, on no account, be a larger complement of men than can be conveniently stowed in the boats, as it sometimes happens, that the Greenland vessels are lost in the ice; but the crews generally escape by means of their boats. The crew also should consist of a larger proportion of smiths and carpenters, than are usually put on board common ships.

' As it may happen, that the crews in the boats may be kept a considerable time, before they can reach either ship or shore, there should be a sort of awning, to be used occasionally, if the weather should prove very inclement.

' As it is not necessary, that the boats should last many years, it is advised that they should be built of the lightest materials, because on this account they are more easily dragged over the packed ice.

' —— The Dutch, vessels on the Greenland fishery have three boats fastened on each side of the ship, which may be sufficient to contain the whole crew, in case of accidents. The early discoverers had always what was called a ship in quarters on board, which might be put together, when a creek, &c. was to be explored.'

Here it may not be improper to take notice of some observations communicated to the author by captain Ford of the Manchester, a Greenland vessel.

' The only precaution, says the captain, to be taken, in order to proceed towards the pole, is to fit out two strong ships, that are handy and sail fast, well equipped, and secured in the manner of those that are generally sent to Greenland on the whale fishery. Such ships should be manned with about forty able seamen in each, and victualled for eighteen months, or two years, and be entirely under the command of some expert, able, and experienced seaman, who has frequented those seas for some time past. They should sail from England about the middle of April, in order to be in with the edge of the ice about the 10th of May, when it begins to separate and open. There is not the least reason to suppose, that the seas to the west, north-west, and north of Spitzbergen are covered with permanent and perpetual ice, so as never to be opened by the operation of the winds; for daily experience shews us, that a northerly wind, when of any long duration, opens and separates the ice, so as to admit of ships
going

going amongft it, in fundry places, to a very high latitude, if attempted.'——

To return to Mr. Barrington's remarks :——' As it is pof-fible alfo, that the crew may be obliged to winter within the arctic circle, it is recommended, that the fhip fhould be ba-lafted with coals. That there fhould be a framed houfe of wood on board, to be made as long as poffible, for the oppor-tunity of exercife within doors ; and that there fhould be a Ruffian ftove, as a fire in a common chimney does not warm the room equably.——On the Labrador coaft the furriers raife a wall of earth about three feet thick, all round their huts, as high as the roof, which is found to contribute much to warmth within doors, fo as to want little more heat than arifes from the fteam of lamps.

' It appears, by the accounts of the Dutch, who wintered in Nova Zembla, as well as the Ruffians, who continued fix years in Maloy Brun, that during this feafon there are fome-times days of a tolerable temperature ; fnow fhoes therefore fhould be provided, as alfo fnow eyes, not to lofe the benefit of the air and exercife, during fuch an interval. The beard likewife fhould be fuffered to grow, on the approach of win-ter, from which the Ruffian couriers are enabled to fupport the feverity of the open air.'

The author farther recommends Ruffian boots, the winter cap of the furriers of North America, leads for the hands, and dumb bells for exercife ; the ufe of the flefh brufh, in order to prevent the fcurvy, and fome very ufeful precautions with regard to clothing and provifions.

Thefe are *fome* of the moft material obfervations, which this very ingenious and public fpirited writer has advanced, with refpect to the poffibility of reaching the North Pole. We have extended our account of thefe tracts to a confider-able length, as we entirely agree with the author, that it is rather a reflection upon a fcientific nation, which has long taken the lead in geographical difcoveries, and fent out fhips which have penetrated into the antarctic circle, that more is not known, with regard to the circumpolar regions of our own hemifphere, than can be collected from maps, made in the time of Charles I. efpecially when the run from the mouth of the Thames to the North Pole is not a longer one, than from Falmouth to the Cape de Verde iflands,

The fecond article in this volume is an enquiry, whether the turkey was known before the difcovery of America.

The earlier writers on ornithology, as Belon, Ray, and Willoughby, fuppofe, that the turkey was introduced into
Eu-

Europe from Afia. But Mr. Buffon maintains, that we owe this bird to America. His principal arguments in favour of this opinion are the following :

1. Hernandez, about the year 1576, has mentioned this bird, in his Natural Hiftory of Mexico, as indigenous in that country.

2. Sperlingius, in his Zoologia Phyfica, printed in 1661, fays, ' Ante centum, et quod excurrit, annos, delata hæc avis ex Novâ Indiâ in Europam.'

3. Travellers affirm, that few or no turkies are found in Afia.

Our author anfwers each of thefe arguments in their order. Some of his remarks are to this effect :

Cortez returned from the conqueft of Mexico in 1528. This then is the earlieft period, which can be affigned for the introduction of the turkey into Europe from America.

Four *young* turkies (confequently bred in England) were dreffed at a ferjeant's feaft in 1555 *. And I fufpect, fays Mr. Barrington, that I find a ftill earlier mention of thefe birds in England : for capons of *Greafe,* made part of an entertainment in the year 1467 †.

' With regard to their being firft known in England, during the reign of Henry VIII. this depends upon the following old diftich :

> ' Turkies, carps, hops, pickarel, and beere,
> Came into England in one yeare.

' Thefe lines are certainly erroneous with regard to fome of the particulars ; but *are* generally *agreed* to have been made from the tenth to the fifteenth year of Henry VIII. or from 1519 to 1524 ; the lateft of which is before Cortez's firft return into Spain ; and confequently, we muft have been fupplied with thefe birds from fome other quarter than that of Mexico. It is to be obferved alfo, that they are thus early called Turkies.' [Hops were firft brought into England in 1525, and ufed in brewing ; but the phyficians reprefented to parliament, that they were unwholefome ; upon which the ufe of them was prohibited, 1528. Anderfon.]

The name of this bird in moft of the European languages muft afford a ftrong intimation of the country, from which it was originally brought.

' The Spanifh word is not, pavon de las Indias, as Mr, Buffon ‡ ftates ; but fimply pavo, and formerly pago.' If

---

* Dugdale's Orig. Jur. p. 105.
† Leland's Itin. vol. vi. p. 5.
‡ This is the Spanifh name given by Minfhew.

however,

however, the name were pavon de las Indias, this term would not fignify the Weft Indies; for in all European languages the addition of Weftern is neceffary.' In France the name is, coq d'Inde; in Italy, gallo d'India & gallinaccio; in Germany, Indianifchir hahn, the cock of India, and Kalekutifcher hahn, the cock from Calecut. The Englifh name is a prefumptive proof, that thefe birds were brought into England from Turkey. In all thefe terms, and others, which our author mentions, there is not the leaft allufion to their firft coming from America.

We fhall add an authority to thofe, which Mr. Barrington has produced, (though we make no doubt, but that much earlier ones may be eafily found) and that is, the following account of the turkey in Minfhew's dictionary : ' A turky cocke, or cocke of India ; avis ita dicta, quod ex Africâ, et ut nonnulli volunt alii, ex Indiâ vel Arabiâ ad nos allata fit.— Minfhew's dictionary was publifhed in 1625; and in this article he gives us the fentiments of preceding writers.

But this point, we apprehend, will admit of no difpute, if this bird was the meleagris of the ancients. .Moft of the early writers on ornithology have fuppofed, that they are the fame : but M. Buffon contends, that the meleagris was the peintade or Guinea-hen. Our author fays, he will not pretend to pronounce with any pofitivenefs on this point ; but he thinks, that neither of them was commonly known to the ancients. at leaft to the Romans, nor perhaps ufed by them as poultry ; firft, becaufe it is fcarcely to be conceived, how thefe very ufeful birds, having been once introduced into Italy, could have been loft, as both turkies and guinea-hens were undoubtedly for many centuries : whereas the peacock, by no means fo neceffary as either of them, was continued from the time of the Romans to the prefent century ; fecondly, becaufe none of the Roman writers allude to the difagreeable noife, or to the quarrelfome difpofition of the Guiney-hens ; and thirdly, becaufe they have defcribed the meleagris with great uncertainty. For thefe, and fome other reafons, he concludes, that when the Romans fpeak of volucres Libycæ, or Numidicæ, they only refer to a variety of the common fowl, the plumage of which might fomewhat refemble that of the Guiney-hen, as we now diftinguifh them by the name of Bantam, &c.

On this point we fhall content ourfelves with one or two quotations. Varro, no incompetent judge of thefe matters, gives an account of three forts of fowl, the villaticæ, the rufticæ, and the Africanæ. Of the laft he fays : ' Gallinæ Africanæ funt *grandes*, variæ, *gibberæ*, quas meleagridas appellant Græci. Hæ noviffimæ in triclinium ganearium [genia-

num

rum Seal.] introierunt è culinâ, propter faftidium hominum ; veneant propter penuriam magno. De tribus generibus, gallinæ faginantur maxime.' He then proceeds to tell us, how they are to be chosen and fattened. Var. de Re Ruft. l. iii. 9. Columella fays : ' Africana eft, quam plurique Numidicam dicunt, meleagridi fimilis, nifi quod rutilam galeam & criftam capite gerit, quæ utraque funt in meleagride cærulea.' De Re Ruft. l. viii. c. 2. In this paffage Columella tells us, that thefe two birds differed only in the *colour* of their creft and comb. If fo, the gallinæ Africanæ and the meleagrides, mentioned by Varro, were birds of the fame fpecies, the one properly called meleagris by the Greeks; the other, gallina Africana, or the meleagris of Africa.

The avis Afra was a delicacy at Rome, in the time of Horace [*]. And the authority of Varro fufficiently proves, that the meleagris was introduced into the Roman entertainments before the Auguftan age. There certainly can be no doubt, but that the latter was a fpecies of our turkey. The foregoing defcriptions can fcarcely be applied to any other bird. Salmafius, who difcuffes this point very learnedly, fays, ' Meleagrides veterum noftræ funt gallinæ Indicæ : nullo modo fuper hoc fas eft ambigere.' Salm. Plinian. Exer. p. 872.

From thefe confiderations we conclude, with our author, that, whether turkies were found in America by the firft difcoverers or not, the Europeans are chiefly indebted to Afia, and perhaps Africa, for this valuable addition to our tables.

[*To be concluded in our next.*]

Cardiphonia : or, the Utterance of the Heart; in the Courfe of a real Correfpondence. 2 vols. 12mo. 7s. Buckland.

THESE letters, as the author affures us, were publifhed with no other aim, ' but that of promoting the good of mankind, and being fubfervient to the gracious defigns of God in the gofpel;' and a defign fcarcely could be more laudable than fuch a defign. It was viewed in this light by his correfpondents ; and they generally returned him his letters. For this piece of politenefs they will be amply rewarded ; for inftead of two or three fugitive manufcripts, each of them will now receive two fubftantial volumes ; not filled with

---

[*] Hor. Epod. ii. 53. Afra avis deceptat palato. Petron. Numidicæ, meleagrides, phafianæ, were facrificed to Caligula. Suet. Cal. § 22.
Vid. Boch. Hieroz. l. 1. 19. Hofm. Lex. Martinii Etymol. &c.

empty

empty compliments, or trifling anecdotes; but with pious observations, and spiritual instructions, seasoned with a holy
'unction,' or to use our author's expression, 'drops of grace [*].'

As we seldom have it in our power to give our readers any
thing, but the fragments of profane and secular learning, we
shall now, for once, endeavour to oblige them with something
more 'sound and savory.'

A fable :—' I have an imperfect remembrance of an account
I read, when I was a boy, of an ice palace, built one winter at Petersburg. The walls, the roof, the floors, the furniture, were all of ice, but furnished with taste; and every
thing, that might be expected in a royal palace, was to be
found there; the ice while in the state of water being previously coloured, so that to the eye all seemed formed of the
proper materials; but all was cold, useless, and transient.
Had the frost continued till now, the palace might have been
standing; but with the returning spring it melted away, like
the baseless fabric of a vision. Methinks there should have
been one stone in the building, to have retained the inscription, Sic transit gloria mundi; for no contrivance could
exhibit a fitter illustration of the vanity of human life. Men
build and plan, as if their works were to endure for ever;
but the wind passes over them, and they are gone. In the
midst of all their preparations, or, at farthest, when they
think they have just completed their designs, their breath goeth
forth, they return to their earth, and in that very day their
thoughts perish.

'How many sleep, who keep the world awake.' Vol. I. p. 89.

A caution against the wiles of the devil.—' Satan will
doubtless watch you, and examine every corner of the hedge
around you, to see if he can find a gap, by which to enter.'
p. 271.

A paradox.—' If I had a proper call, I would undertake to
prove, that to exhort and deal plainly with sinners, to stir
them up to flee from the wrath to come, and to lay hold of
eternal life, is an attempt not reconcileable with sober reason,
upon any other grounds than those doctrines, which we are
called Calvinists for holding; and that all the absurdities,
which are charged upon us, as consequences of what we teach,
are indeed truly chargeable upon those, who differ from us in
these points...As to myself, if I *was* not a Calvinist, I think
I should have no more hope of success in preaching to men,
than to horses and cows.' vol. ii. p. 69.

---

[*] Vol. II. p. 293.

Ad-

Advice to a young divine, on preaching without notes.—— ' A written fermon is fomething to lean upon ; but it is beft for a preacher to lean wholly upon the Lord,' p. 77.

Learning unneceffary.—' A few minutes of the fpirit's teaching will furnifh us with more real, ufeful knowlege, than toiling through whole folios of commentators and expofitors. .. There is nothing required but a teachable humble fpirit ; and learning, as it is commonly called, is not neceffary, in order to this.' p. 91.—What occafion then for thefe two volumes ?

Death a gentleman-ufher.—' We are cafed up in vehicles of *clay*, and converfe together as if we were in different *coaches*, with the blinds clofe down round. We fee the carriage, and the voice tells us, that we have a friend within : but we fhall know each other better, when death fhall open the coach doors, and hand out the company fucceffively, and lead them into the glorious apartments which the Lord hath appointed to be the common refidence of them that love him.' p. 122.

Offers of fervice to Jefus Chrift, as a lackey, a journeyman, or in any other capacity.—' I am willing to ferve him for the fake of ferving him, and to follow him, as we fay, through thick and thin. I want to live with him by the day, to do all for him, to receive all from him, to poffefs all in him, to leave all to him, to make him my hiding-place, and my reft-ing-place.' p. 171.

The Lord a match-maker.—' You were fent into the world for a nobler end than to be pinned to a girl's apron-ftring ; and yet if the Lord fees it not good for you to be alone, he will provide you a helpmeet. I fay, if he fees the marriage ftate beft for you, he has the proper perfon *already* in his eye ; and though fhe were in Peru, or Nova-Zembla, he knows how to bring you together.' p. 173.

Notwithftanding this, many a good man is deceived.—— ' In Captain Cook's Voyage to the South Sea, fome fifh were caught, which looked as well as others ; but thofe who eat them were poifoned : alas, for the poor man, who catches a poifonous wife. There are fuch to be met with in the ma-trimonial feas, that look paffing well to the eye ; but a con-nection with them proves baneful to domeftic peace, and hurt-ful to the life of grace. I know two or three people, per-haps a few more, who have great reafon to be thankful to Him, who fent the fifh, with the money in its mouth, to Pe-ter's hook. He fecretly inftructed and guided us where to angle.' p. 192.

Good reafons for being thankful.—' Surely I have reafon, in my worft times, to be thankful, that I am out of hell, out of Bedlam, out of Newgate.'

Thankf-

Thanksgiving for *smaller* mercies.——' I believe I had naturally a turn for the mathematics, and dabbled in them a little way : and though I did not go far, my head sleeping and waking was stuffed with diagrams and calculations. Every thing I looked at, that exhibited either a right line or a curve, set my wits a wool-gathering. I bought my name-sake's [Newton's] Principia, but I have reason to be thankful, that I left it, as I found it, a sealed book.' p. 232.

A sketch of the author's character.——' I think my sentiments and experience are as orthodox and Calvinistical as need be ; and yet I am a sort of speckled bird among my Calvinist brethren ... It is impossible I should be all of a colour, when I have been a debtor to all sorts ; and like the jay in the fable, have been beholden to most of the birds in the air for a feather or two. Church and meeting, methodist and Moravian, may all perceive something in my coat taken from them. None of them are angry with me for borrowing from them, but then why could I not be content with their colour, without going among other flocks and coveys to make myself such a motley figure ? Let them be all angry ; if I have culled the best feathers from all, then surely I am finer than any.' p. 344, 346,

These extracts will be sufficient to give our readers a competent idea of this work. It is written in the canting strain ; and will probably be read with avidity by the groaning brethren of the tabernacle.

An Essay on Inspiration : considered chiefly with respect to the Evangelists. By Gilbert Wakefield, *B. A.* 8vo. 2s. sewed. Johnson.

INspiration is generally supposed to be such a supernatural illumination of the mind, as prevents all error and misconception.——The design of the present Essay is to refute this notion : for which purpose the author endeavours to prove,

1. That inspiration, in this sense, is unnecessary.——The only qualifications, he thinks, which are requisite to establish the authenticity of any historical narration, are a sound understanding, competent information, and integrity of heart ; and these qualifications the gospel-historians eminently possessed, ' Why then, he says, should we superinduce an unnecessary succedaneum ?'

2. That it is inexpedient and improbable.

3. That it is disclaimed by the sacred writers themselves.—— On this head he observes, that St. Luke's expressions, in the introduction to his evangelical history, are in effect a positive
                                                        and

and literal difavowal of all extraordinary affistances, and appear to be decifive in the prefent queition ; and that St. John fpeaks of what he had teftified of Jefus, and his achievements, as of things, which were tranfacted in the prefence of the difciples ; as objects therefore of ocular infpection, not of intuitive difcernment.

An objection to this opinion is ufually drawn from John xvi. 13, which the author ftates and folves it in this manner :

' This is part of our Saviour's laft addrefs to his difciples, and was defigned to confole them under their forrow at his departure. It is an inference from the preceding verfe, which will conduct us to a true interpretation

' I have yet many things to fay unto you, but ye cannot bear them now.

' But when He, the Spirit of the Truth is come, He will guide you into all the truth.

' As if he had faid, " Ye have many things to learn, and much to rectify, with refpect to your notions of my character, and that of my difpenfation. But your prefent mifconceptions and inveterate prejudices incapacitate you for a circumftantial and unreferved reprefentation of the true ftate of thefe important matters. When the Holy Spirit, whom I fhall be authorifed to fend after my afcenfion, fhall come unto you, he will gradually enlighten your underftandings, and purge the groffnefs of your conceptions. He will take you by the hand, and conduct you to the knowlege of thofe gofpel-truths, which are now fo imperfectly apprehended by you, or are contrary to your perfuafions."

' What relation this paffage has to a permanent and plenary infpiration refiding in the evangelifts, though ufually alledged in fupport of this doctrine, I confefs myfelf unable to difcover. The bufinefs of the Holy Spirit, we fee, was to expand their hearts to more liberal conceptions, to correct their prejudices, and to remove their ignorance : to inftruct them, in fhort, in what they did not feel and know, and had therefore no concern with matters of actual experience and obfervation.'

Here, we prefume, the author makes fuch conceffions as would fatisfy a reafonable opponent.

He proceeds to fhew,

4. That the foregoing doctrine of infpiration is inconfiftent with the writings of the evangelifts. Under this head he points out two or three paffages, which he thinks are contradictory. The firft concerning the death of the daughter of Iairus ; the fecond relating to the account of the two malefactors ; and our Saviour's promife to one of them, in St. Luke.

5. That it is detrimental to the cause of revelation—' Because this opinion places the credibility of the gospels upon a foundation very different from that of every other authentic and accepted history, by superinducing an extraneous motive of belief, which evacuates at once every species of attestation, historical, prophetical, and moral.'

In the last section he considers the character and pretensions of St. Paul.

The result of his observations is this :

' When St. Paul speaks and directs in his own apostolical character, his word is of the highest possible authority, and is impressed with more marks of credibility and of a divine origin, than any other writings of the New Testament : and that his epistles, as far as they have been transmitted to us entire and uncorrupted, contain truth, evangelical truth, without any mixture of error.

' But facts are of more importance in authenticating the Christian revelation, than arguments and opinions, though advanced by apostles themselves : and the contracted plan of epistolary writings, and their unavoidable defects, arising from our ignorance of the complicated circumstances under which they might be composed, and from many other particulars, render the gospel histories, which exhibit the life of Jesus, as they are a more exact and copious delineation of Christianity, a more secure and eligible rule of conduct.'

In discussing this point of theological controversy, our author has made several new and ingenious remarks, though the subject has been anticipated by Le Clerc, and other eminent writers.

The passages however, which he has produced, do not sufficiently support the doctrine, for which he contends. There is no occasion to give up any of them, as inconsistencies. Satisfactory answers have been, or may be, given to his objections. For instance : with respect to the pretended contradiction between the evangelists, relative to the two malefactors, it has been very properly observed, that the plural number is frequently employed for the singular. Thus Matt. xxi. 7. They brought the ass and the colt, and they set him, επανω αυτων, upon *them,* instead of επανω ενος εξ αυτων. Vide Glassii Gram. 3. 17.

In many cases, it is very difficult to determine, what is a contradiction in two different writers. We may be easily deceived by figurative expressions, but more especially by the representation of different circumstances, attending the same events.

1   Be

Be this as it may, it seems inconceivable, that the apostles should be endowed with the gift of tongues, miracles, and prophecy, and yet not have sufficient illumination to avoid absurdities and contradictions, in composing those important writings, which were to be the comfort and edification of all Christians to the end of the world.

A general Essay on Tactics. With an introductory Discourse, upon the present State of Politics, and the Military Science in Europe. To which is prefixed, a Plan of a Work, entitled, the Political and Military System of France. Translated from the French, of M. Guibert. 8vo. 14s. in Boards. Millan.

IT may justly appear surprising that, though tactics, or the art of war in general, be one of the first sciences with which mankind became acquainted, yet its principles have hitherto hardly ever been established with any tolerable degree of certainty or precision. But many are the causes which have contributed to retard the progress of this art. The great variety of weapons, armour, and instruments of war, the customs, and even the particular physical qualities of different nations, the genius or prejudices of commanders, the fluctuation of manners, the diversities of climate, and a number of other circumstances, have all had more or less influence on the discipline and regulation of armies. And to those rather than to sentiments of universal benevolence, is it owing, that a science, which has for its object the destruction of the human species, should be later in attaining perfection, than those which are calculated for the preservation or convenience of it.

This work is introduced with a preliminary discourse, consisting of two parts. The former contains a review of modern politics, their parallel with those of the ancients, their defects, and the obstacles which they occasion to the grandeur and riches of a state. In this discourse, the author discovers a clear and penetrating judgment, and establishes his observations with sentiments that are liberal, and with a force of argument peculiarly striking and persuasive. For the satisfaction of our readers, we shall present them with the following passage.

' Let us cast our eyes over Europe, and view more in detail those pernicious effects. The ministers of Spain extirpated the Moors. They forgot that they were men, and without a numerous population a kingdom could not prosper. They invade a new world, possess themselves of rich mines, and never perceive all the while that Spain remains desolate and her lands uncultivated. They are tyrants over the Low Coun-

tries

tries; they foresee not, that they are going to revolt, and how much it is out of their power to make them return to their yoke. An error in calculating, that beyond certain circumscribed limits the greatness of a state is but defenceless and weak; an error in not knowing where to fix the boundary to what may be animated and defended; they would throw their arms over all, the Low Countries, Franche Comté, Rouiſſillon, Italy, Portugal, and all escape them.

' Let us come nearer to our own time. The ministers are not more skilful. Richelieu was desirous to extend the power of his master, or more properly speaking his own. He was urgent to depress the nobility and to destroy their prerogatives, which made them more the vassals than the subjects of the sovereign. Let him, if he meant to effect that, have applied vigorous methods; let him openly have attacked those pretensions, which the nobility might have employed as restraints to the strength and happiness of a monarchial system; let him have extended authority by authority, I should have admired, I should have extolled his genius. But in order more effectually to destroy that nobility, he corrupts it, he degrades it, he forces it to quit its residence; because he is sensible that its poverty and simplicity supports its vigour; he lures it to the court, where he foresees it will shortly ruin itself by luxury, and that afterwards it will be dependant on the sovereign, by the favours it will be necessitated to supplicate. This fatal system was put in practice by Louis XIV. and his ministers. The manners of the kingdom were changed. The degradation of the nobility brought on the slavery of the subjects. The burthen of that nobility corrupted and kept in pay once more falls on a languishing people, which ought to have been supported by it. Soon, there remained nor national spirit, nor energy, nor virtue; was this the Richelieu, whose splendid pompous monument adorns our temples; of whom the frenzy of our eloquence is continually resounding the unmerited praise; and history, where sacred truth should find a sanctuary, instead of proving that statues and panegyrics are almost always the monuments of prejudice or flattery, eternizes his unjust reputation, it gives the appellation of sublime, to a system of politics, of that ambitious man, who enfeebled his country in hopes of adding strength to its government: as if a good and sane government, instead of debasing its country and being burthensome to her, ought not, on the contrary, by the self-same motion, attempt to exalt herself, when she rises, even above her.

' Colbert, with a happy gift of great genius, mistook the true interests of France. He turned it into a mercantile state.

He

He perceived Holland rising up from the midst of her bogs act a principal part in Europe. Thus he reasoned, " Money and commerce is the perpetual motion of public prosperity. I am the minister of the finances, it is in my power to increase the revenues of the state ;" in the twinkling of an eye granaries are changed to manufactories, our husbandmen to artificers. One branch of administration revives and flourishes, while the body of the tree decays and dries up.

' Lovois pants for war, because Colbert is desirous of peace ; the interest of a minister for war is to embarrass the minister who has the management of the finances. He fires the ambition of his master ; he tells him that France wants only armies by land, by whose means Europe would sink under the laws they might impose. Soon all maritime power is neglected, the sea-ports are shut, all other parts of administration are sacrificed to the splendor of one sole department.

' Louis XIV. adds by his conquests some few provinces to France. He conceives, because his kingdom is increased in surface, it must of course be augmented in strength. He takes, for sure signs of a nation's power and riches, the produce of his manufactories and the wealth of his merchants. He rises to a pitch of luxury which his revenue is not great enough to support ; like another Cadmus, he thinks his orders for supplies will raise out of the earth men ready armed ; he obliges all his subjects to take the field ; he drains France at the time she is victorious ; in the midst of her misfortunes, he sets her on the very verge of her ruin ; dies, and leaves behind him nothing but immense debts and famine, with a method of making war, less decisive, and more expensively ruinous.

' Let us reflect on the epocha of this prince ; hurried away by his example all the governments of Europe, strained every nerve to force their expedients, increasing their armies, augmenting their duties, extend, in emulation of one another, their possessions, draw campaigns into towns, provinces into capitals, capitals into courts, mistake bombast for actual power, luxury for riches, splendor for real glory ; in short, make the nation groan, for the sake of grasping at a fatal shadow of grandeur and supremacy ; wretched system of politics, and which brings to mind that instrument of torture, in the shape of a horse, on which Busirus had the victims stretched, where their limbs were to be broken.

' The maritime powers fall into an epidemical disease, in regard to commerce, which is not by any means less fatal. They fain would clasp the poles, sail on every sea, hoist their standard on every coast. There arises between them a system of politics, unknown until that æra, and only worthy of a

bar-

barbarous age. They reciprocally shut up their ports, or only open them on certain terms, or for the acquisition of certain commodities. They forget that mankind is but a vast family, subdivided into many others, called French, English, Dutch, Spanish, &c. none of which can be completely happy and powerful, without a free and entire correspondence in receiving reciprocal exchanges, assistances, kindnesses and instructions.'

The second part of this discourse contains a review of the art of war since the beginning of the world; the present situation of that science in Europe; its parallel with what it formerly has been; the necessary relation of military establishments with political constitutions; the defects of all our modern governments in this particular. Those different subjects are treated by the ingenious author in a comprehensive and masterly manner, and abound with remarks which highly merit the attention of a philosophical reader.

The preliminary discourse is followed by the plan of a work, entitled, 'France political and military.' This extensive plan contains nothing less than a history of the civil and military constitutions of almost all the states in Europe; detailed at greater length in proportion as they are more connected with France. The compiling materials for this great work, has employed M. Guibert many years; and he reckons that many more will be requisite for the completion of his purpose. But for the benefit of his country during the present war, he has now published such parts of his intended work as are more immediately useful, under the title of a General Essay on Tactics. This essay is also divided into two parts; one comprehending elementary tactics, and the other the great tactics. In the former he treats of all the variety of arms requisite for the infantry, cavalry, light-troops, and artillery. In the other, he gives a theory, adapted to practice, of every movement which an army is capable of executing. He afterwards examines the various relations which fortification, and the knowledge of the ground, can have with tactics; concluding with an account of the present method of subsisting armies, and pointing out what improvements may be made in this particular. The whole is illustrated with a number of engravings, explanatory of the various movements described in the work.

From the apparent abilities of M. Guibert, there is reason to expect, that, when he has accomplished his great undertaking, it will be a work of uncommon merit; and, if we be not mistaken, prove yet more interesting as a political than a military production.

A System

A System of Tactics, practical, theoretical, and historical. Translated from the French *of M.* Joly de Maizeroy, *by* Thomas Mante, *Esq.* 2 *vols.* 8vo. 13s. *boards.* Cadell.

THIS system is divided into four parts. The first treats of the arms, military operations and customs, of the ancients; which the author confiders under diftinct heads, namely, the tactics of the ancient people of Asia; the regulation and difcipline of the Greeks; the Roman tactics; a comparifon of the phalanx with the legion; the fhouts of the ancients, and their inftruments of war. In the inveftigation of all thofe fubjects, the author fhows great acquaintance with the writings of antiquity; which he appears to have examined with uncommon attention and care.

The fecond part defcribes the different orders of battle among the ancients. It begins with the battle of Thymbræa; on which we are prefented with many obfervations, which appear to be made with judgment, and an accurate knowlege of the principles of the fcience. Next follows a defcription of the battle of Pharfalia, with obfervations; and a parallel between the difpofition of the armies, and the conduct of the generals, in thofe two celebrated actions of antiquity.

The author afterwards treats of the oblique order; defcribing the battle of Arbela, and alfo giving obfervations upon it. He examines the different cuftoms relative to orders of battle; the intermixing infantry with cavalry; of corps in ambufh; of armies in poft, entrenched camps, and lines. He next recites inftances of actions, that refemble the oblique order, applied to the fecond and third difpofition of Vegetius; and defcribes the movements of the king of Pruffia to form the oblique. The author then defcribes the battle of Leuctra, and gives obfervations upon it; treating in the fame manner of the battle of Mantinea, of the paffage of the Hydafpes, and of the battle of Alexander with Porus. What follows of the ancient tactics relates to the war of Eumenes and Antigonus, the battles of Gabena and Marathon, with obfervations and parallels.

The third part of the work defcends to the military operations of modern times. The firft object of the author's remarks is the Crefcent Order, and that of the three feparate bodies, which are ufually oppofed to it. In this part, he defcribes the battles of Zaldarana, Aleppo, Alcazar; on all which he makes judicious and pertinent obfervations. Subfequent to thofe, is an account of ambufcades in battle; and of the order of attack by the centre; which the author illuftrates by the battle of Hochftet, and that of Modin. He

like-

likewife delivers obfervations and theory concerning the intermixing of cavalry and infantry : treats of armies engaging with a river behind them ; of corps de referve ; with a differtation on the wedge, and an examination of the chevalier de Folard's column.

The fourth part treats of the application of the double cohort to the different operations of war ; of the paffage of defiles and rivers ; of defcents ; fieges ; the attack and defence of entrenchments ; of the attack of armies pofted behind redoubts ; of the different kinds of camps ; of foraging ; of winter quarters, the fuccouring of places, the furprifing of places ; of fquare orders ; of the plefion or long fquare ; of the conduct of convoys ; of the return of pounded armies ; and of the order of marching ; the whole concluding with maxims of general importance in the art of war.

As a fpecimen of this work, we fhall prefent our readers with a part of the differtation on the wedge.

' The wedge is an evolution, concerning which opinions have ever been, and are ftill, very much divided. The chevalier de Folard feems to doubt of its reality ; as does likewife M. Guifcard, much better verfed than the chevalier in the ancient tactics. The new tranflator of Elian thinks otherwife, and has exerted himfelf to prove the affirmative. But, notwithstanding all the paffages with which he endeavours to fupport himfelf, we may eafily difcover the excefs of his partiality ; not that his reafons are always ill founded, in any other refpect than this, that they are not unanfwerable, and the contrary authorities are in ftill greater number. It is to the different application of the fame terms, the little dependence which we can have on fuch an author as Elian, the miftakes into which even Vegetius himfelf has often fallen, we are to afcribe that irreconcileable variety of fentiments. It muft be allowed, that by taking fome paffages according to the letter, we fhall be fure to find in them the true wedge ; but we fhould compare thefe paffages with others, and make proper allowances for the circumftances, in which the terms embolos and cuneus are employed. To begin with the Greeks.

' Xenophon, it is true, fays, word for word, in his account of the battle of Mantinea, that "Epaminondas formed an embolon of infantry, with which he advanced to fhock the enemy, as one galley does another with its beak." But this is no proof, that the embolon was fharp at the head, and broad at the bottom. This corps marched in front of the line, which followed ; in which fituation, an oblong might reprefent the beak of a galley, as well as a triangle could. In the fame action, Epaminondas is likewife faid to have made

a very

a very strong embolon with all his cavalry. Surely nobody
will say, this was a wedge. But, allowing that the Greeks
formed their squadrons into a wedge or lozenge, it is highly
improbable, that the whole of the Theban cavalry should
have been formed into one single wedge. I cannot think of
more than two ways to understand this passage. One is, that
the line was broken, and bent back in the form of a V;
the other, that the general, designing to hide part of his
forces, had shortened his line, and doubled his squadrons behind one another; and this is the interpretation I adopted in
describing the battle of Mantinea. I rest my interpretation on
the custom of the Greeks, who took this disposition in cases,
in which they did not chuse to expose their whole strength;
such, for instance, as those, in which they could not extend
themselves. Elian, who has placed it among his evolutions
of cavalry, is not against me. In this passage, I cannot think
the word embolon means any more than a vast squadron of
great depth; and what should hinder our understanding it,
when spoken of infantry, in the same sense?

' Nor have we any reason to think, that Epaminondas
formed a triangle at Leuctra. Xenophon says, that the Lace-
demonians were twelve deep, and that the Thebans formed a
corps, of no fewer than fifty ranks. If the latter had been
disposed in a triangle, why did not the historian express their
disposition in the same terms, he did that at Mantinea? He
contents himself with taking notice, that the Thebans were
drawn up very deep. When we say, that a corps is formed
of such a depth, and mention the number of ranks, it is the
same thing, as if we were to say, that the ranks are of an
equal length; and that, of course, the whole forms a square.
It had been ridiculous enough to say of a triangular corps,
which had one or two men at its point, and fifty at its base,
that it had fifty ranks. Plutarch's words concerning this affair cannot be made to suggest any other idea, than that of a
great body of infantry; and Diodorus speaks of nothing but
a dense and compact body. The expression obliquam phalan-
gem formavit (he disposed his phalanx obliquely) signifies nothing but the order of attack; a man, in my opinion, must
be greatly prejudiced, to conclude from these words, that the
order here used was the wedge.

' When Alexander attacked the Taulantines, who occupied
a defile which he wanted to pass, he made divers manœuvres
to induce them to weaken the body they had there; then,
suddenly forming an embolon of his phalanx, he threw himself into it. Nothing here can be made to signify a wedge,
rather than a column. Thus, too, in the chapter on the battle
of

of Arbela; where it is said, that Alexander formed a wedge of the cavalry of his right wing, and the infantry nearest to it, in order to throw them rapidly into the chasms he might perceive in the Persian line; it is still less probable, that he should have formed a wedge of all his royal companies, than that Epaminondas should have done it with regard to his left wing, at Mantinea; the object of the latter, as I have already said, was to hide part of his forces; and this he might have done by breaking his line, and making them form an angle, with its point foremost. Alexander had not the same motives for this disposition at Arbela; all he wanted was to throw himself directly into the chasms of the enemy's line; and this he did in the order of march; that is to say, in column, which is the disposition nearest akin to it. The term embolos, employed in this place by Arrian, does not signify the same thing that Xenophon means by it, when speaking of Mantinea. Here then we have already a strong proof, that the Greeks used this word in different senses.

'But supposing us still very much in the dark, with regard to the true sense of this term; to understand it of the angular disposition, we should be first convinced, that the angle is easier to form than the full square, of greater depth than front; that its march must be more rapid; and its shock more impetuous. Let us examine this one moment. The strength of the Grecian order depended on the pressure of its ranks; and the degree of this pressure, on the number of them: it is on this principle the column ought to act. For this purpose, all the parts of it should unite their strength, to carry it, in concert, against the same point. The ranks and files, therefore, should be all parallel and perpendicular, to the end, that the weight of every man falling directly on the man before him, may give those in the front such an impulse, as the enemy shall not be able to withstand. Now, a real impulse of this kind can only be found in a square body; since it is in a square body alone, the motion of every part is direct; and each communicates, as much as possible, to the other, the entire mass of its own motion.'

This work may not only be read with great advantage by the military gentleman, but with pleasure by the antiquary. For beside a judicious system of modern tactics, the author has given an ingenious and instructive commentary on the tactics of the earlier ages, particularly of the Greeks and Romans. His theory is drawn from practice; his precepts confirmed by apposite examples; and he has illustrated the whole with plates, exhibiting the various subjects in a clear, accurate, and scientific view.

Tactics.

Tactics. By Lieutenant Colonel William Dalrymple, *of the Queen's Royal Regiment of Foot.* 8vo. 5s. *in Boards.* Faden.

IT affords me pleasure to find, that, while some French writers are exerting all their ingenuity to improve the tactics of their own nation, Great Britain has also her men of science, who cultivate the same subject, and are no less ardent for aggrandizing the military fame of their respective country. Of this work, which is dedicated to his majesty, we shall lay before our readers the introduction.

' It is a melancholy reflection, that the speculations of men should tend to the improvement of an art for the destruction of their own species ; but till the bounds of ambition be more justly ascertained, and legislatures refine on government, a great part of every community must be employed in the profession of arms.

' On taking a view of the different states of Europe, it is surprising to behold the number of men engaged in this honourable service: the British army, like others, has increased to a most enormous magnitude ; but it has not made an equal progress in its regulations and tactics.

' Confining my observations to the field discipline, it must have been obvious, that the troops at our several encampments, have appeared the armies of different states : there are not two regiments that form column from line, or line from column alike ; we see one battalion taking up its ground in front, and another in flank ; some regiments march on their front rank, and others on their rear in the same manœuvre ; the commanding officer of one corps prefers open, another close files ; and this irregularity must prevail, till an universal tactical system be established, and the whole army trained upon the same plan : the mechanical operations of troops once ascertained, a more ample field in the great theatre of war would be opened to our officers, who are now to study the common rules of their profession when they should enter on the practice : Sir William Howe says in his narrative, " that the troops at Halifax, in 1776, received great benefit from being exercised in line, a very essential part of discipline, in which they were defective till that time."

' These considerations, and my remarks on the progress of military science in other countries, have led me to enter into the minutiæ of forming troops for service ; and I have here detailed it in such a manner, as would serve for a basis, upon which the field discipline of the army might be regulated : but before I make any observations on the subject, I must take notice of what has fallen from a very eminent military author;

that

that " land forces are nothing in this country, and that marines are the only species of troops." If we were never to be engaged in any offensive land war beyond the desultory attacks on an enemy's coast, or if our enemies were never to make any serious attempts upon us, such an idea would be very just, and our tactics might be confined to the mere use of the firelock; to prime and load; present and fire; but whilst there is a possibility of more extensive employment, our troops should not move in such a circumscribed sphere: it would be very useful for both officers and soldiers to have a little knowledge of naval affairs, as every operation of war in which we may be engaged from this island, must be connected with the sea; but if they were fixed to that service, we should be totally unacquainted with the sublimer branches of our profession, which require an education different from the marines.

' In America, it has been the practice to adopt the formation of two deep; but as troops may be employed in different countries and situations, we should have an establishment calculated accordingly; whenever the depth of our battalions is reduced, the extent must be increased, and the column of march being lengthened considerably, the movement of great bodies becomes more difficult; besides, in an open country, the fire of three ranks must give a manifest superiority over the feeble efforts of two ranks.

' The system of formation I have here established is three deep, conformably with the European school; the hint is taken from the Memoires Militaires de Guischardt, Preface du Traducteur sur la Tactique d'Arrien, tom. 2de p. 111. It is calculated principally for an open country, and supposed to be the most perfect arrangement for troops armed as we are at present; but to act in an enclosed, woody, or mountainous country, it may be not only necessary to reduce the formation to two deep, or even to one rank, but to open the order considerably; for as irregular fortification is to regular, so is this irregular kind of formation, to that of three deep, the primitive and supposed most perfect arrangement; whenever the country permits the use of the primitive formation, it is to be preferred; but in situations where a change may be necessary, it must be left to the genius and skill of those who command.

' In a neighbouring nation, there has been much controversy about formation; I shall venture to say, that our tactics must be subservient to the arms, not the arms to the tactics; and I am of opinion, that impulsion by close combat, in the manner of the ancients, is inconsistent with our present mode of arming.

                                               ' The

' The clothing I have proposed is for actual service ; when troops are not immediately employed, dress and parade produces cleanliness and favours subordination.

' As I have not introduced grenadiers or light infantry into my establishment, I thought it necessary to give some reasons for rejecting them.

' Much more might have been said on arms and accoutrements, I have only made some general observations on those subjects.

' The mode of training has been practised, and attended with success in the queen's regiment, which I have had the honour to command ; I have endeavoured to introduce what is only essentially necessary.

' The movement is combined with the French ordonnance of 1776 : I have made it subservient to my own establishment ; but the principle will answer for any establishment or body of men whatever.

' To spare criticism, I shall again observe, that the fabric is not altogether of my own construction ; it would have been impossible to have kept clear of the works of others, there having been already so much written on the subject ; nay it would have been absurd to have attempted it, for a military point once settled, becomes permanent, and cannot be reversed by opinion. I have endeavoured at mathematical correctness to produce conviction.

' There may be many military sentiments taken from other authors, and, though not marked as such, I shall most readily acknowledge them ; for wherever I have found an idea that corresponded with my own, I have adopted it.

' The absolute necessity of a military code to regulate the field discipline of the army, induced me to offer my aid towards so essential a point ; there is still, no doubt, much room left for improvement, and I trust a more able pen will complete what I have only begun.'

The author of this treatise considers the subject under the following heads, viz. dress, arms, accoutrements, the espontoon and halbard, officers, training, exercise, march, march of route, march of manœuvre, points of view, points of alignment, from line to break and form column, march of the column, the open column to form line, close column, deployments from close column, to march en echellon, to march by divisions in file, to march in front, to march to the rear, passing a defile, on the attack of infantry, on the defence of infantry against cavalry, of the different positions that a line in order of battle can take up, central movements, some general rules for the movement of second lines.

This

This treatife is confined to infantry, relative to which it is both explicit and practical; with the additional merit, that colonel Dalrymple appears to have drawn many of his rules from perfonal obfervation and experience.

FOREIGN ARTICLES.

Des koeniglich Preuffifchen *Feldmarfchalls Grafen von* Schwerin *Gedanken über einige militærifche Gegenflænde; or, Thoughts on fome military Subjects, by the late Count* Schwerin, *Field-Marfhal of the Armies of the King of* Pruffia. 8vo. Vienna *and* Leipzig. (German.)

WE are not indeed informed to whom we owe the publication of this very interefting and inftructive performance; but it has been judged worthy of the famous commander under whofe name it appears. It evinces an intimate acquaintance with the conftitution of armies, with their former defects, and the diforders arifing from them, and with the moft effectual remedies. The greater part of the author's reflections are illuftrated and confirmed by real ftriking facts, judicioufly felected, and accurately ftated.

The reflections treat of the following fubjects: 1. Of marches, and the methods of fhortening the way. ' We have feen, fays the author, that wherever the king was prefent, marches were always conducted with greater rapidity, and advantage for the troops. A meadow or foft ground are often confidered as impracticable, merely on the affertion of interefted country people. Generals alfo keep often too ftrictly to the orders received, and rather chufe to lofe an opportunity than to fwerve from an order, given merely by the infpection of a map. Marches are often obftructed, when orders are not given with fufficient diftinctnefs; or when, from partiality or other private views, they are mifinterpreted; when on any thing's lagging behind, a whole column ftops; when the generals always continue in the van, without caring for the progrefs of the columns; finally, when the commanders of battalions or fquadrons do not ftop at every narrow paffage, and endeavour to get their corps quickly paft it.' The bridge-waggons, a contrivance for paffing brooks and ditches, are here greatly commended, and fully defcribed. 2. Of the marching into camps and quarters. What diforders muft, in the author's time, have ftill prevailed on fuch occafions, when we are told, that villages were plundered, that half of the provifions were fpoiled and trod into the mire; that furniture was broken; that wells were exhaufted and fpoiled; that the general's own quarters and property were plundered, that officers were infulted, and that no quarters were provided for prifoners and for fick people? The noble author propofes remedies, which promife to prevail on the country people to ftay at their homes, and to benefit the army. 3. Of the means of guarding camps from the entrance of fpies: the inconveniences of the propofed means will be greatly outweighed by their advantages. 4. Of the meffengers, and majors of guides: a very ufeful inftitution, as guides and meffengers, forced into the fervice by chaffeurs, huffars, and blows, are apt to betray officers themfelves into the hands of enemies. 5. Of main quarters; they ought by all means to be ftrong. 6. Of pro-

provisos and stipulations to be inserted in cartels, concerning the treatment of prisoners of war; that, if officers are to be plundered, they ought at least not to be stripped of their coat, waistcoat, and breeches, hat, shirt, and boots. 7. Of plundering, and the easiest means for preventing it. The author begins with settling the true sense of the word; and then remarks, that not only common soldiers, servants, and women are apt to plunder, but that even distinguished generals are sometimes guilty, by appropriating corn magazines to themselves, by getting corn and malt brewed into beer, and that beer sold by their footmen. He observes, that even the severest prohibitions avail little against such disorders, if means are not found for eradicating them altogether; and that it is better to cause ten innocent people to be punished than to suffer one guilty to escape *. 8. Of the means of preserving plenty in armies, by passports, convoys, entrepots, purchases, and insuring. The author proposes to raise, at every four leagues, entrenchments spacious enough for sheltering one thousand waggons, and to protect each of them with two or three battalions. The commissariate ought then to keep a hundred thousand dollars in its hands, for the purpose of insuring convoys. 9. Of a better provision for subaltern officers, lieutenants, ensigns, &c. by boarding, &c. with the captain. 10. Of the officers in waiting, and the chasseurs employed in conveying orders. 11. Of the means of keeping up the spirits of a regiment; that the men are not so much disgusted even by severe punishment, as by being wronged. The regiments in which the greatest number of desertions happen, are those commanded by disgusted or over-anxious officers. A few officers of an unhappy temper are sufficient to render a whole regiment miserable. 12. Of spies. 13. Of hussars, and their excursions. 14. Of the qualifications of a commander in chief. He ought not to be under thirty, nor past fifty years of age. That it is an erroneous idea to require too great a length of service; that an officer of capacity and inclination for the service will learn as much in six campaigns as another in thirty-six. He ought not to be distracted by domestic or family cares; not to be overladen with correspondence, nor troubled with the details of the army. He must be allowed to give the general orders, and to leave the arrangement of the details of their execution to subalterns. To comprise the whole by his commands, with all the state affairs and the intrigues of foreign courts, to extricate himself from the most critical situations, not by holding councils of war, but by his own strength of mind; this, the author thinks, no one except his own king yet able to perform. 15. What better methods ought to be taken by captains for the conservation of their men : and what the king can do towards effecting that purpose. 16. Of the baggage. It cannot farther be lessened (in the Prussian army), but it is still susceptible of a better disposition. Five different sorts of carriages are here proposed; the duties and business of all the people employed with them are minutely described, and the whole expence calculated 17. Of convoys, which the author endeavours to reduce to a regular system. 18. Of adjutants, or aid de camp generals, and of the sons of generals. 19. Of the precautions to be employed by troops quartered over-night in villages.

---

* The English laws adopt a contrary maxim; that it were better ten guilty persons escape, than one innocent suffer.

Mémoire

*Mémoire Physique et Médecinal, montrant des Rapports évidens entre les
Phénomenes de la Raguette divinatoire, du Magnétisme, et de l'Elec-
tricité; avec des Ecclaircissemens sur d'autres Objets non moins im-
portans qui y sont rélatifs; Par M. T***, (Thouvenel) Docteur en
Médécine de* Montpellier, &c. 8vo. Paris.

DR. Thouvenel, the author of this singular and remarkable performance, has already distinguished himself by several instructive memoirs and dissertations on various medical subjects, such as:
on the Product of Sanguification; on Medical, or reputed Medical
Substances of the Animal Kingdom; on the Nature, Use, and Effects of Air, Food, and Physic, and their Relations to Animal
Oeconomy; de Corpore Mucoso; an Analysis of the Mineral Waters of Contrexeville, in Lorrain, &c. which have been generally
well received both by his countrymen and foreigners.

His present publication begins with a string of general and very
just observations on the abuse and danger both of excessive credulity and incredulity in physical matters; and with applying them to
the singular and striking phenomenon of the divinatory wand or
rod, used by certain individuals, whom he calls sourciers, or discoverers of sources, to point out the existence and direction of the
course of subterraneous springs, or running-waters.

By these sourciers he means certain human individuals, whose
corporeal frame is so singularly constituted as to render them sensible of the impression of subterraneous, and especially running-waters; not only by means of a wand, or rod which they hold in their
hands, but sometimes even without it: as is the case with a certain
Bleton, a plain, simple man, closely observed and examined by the
author, and by many other sensible persons; and whose operations
have prompted Dr. Thouvenel to his present attempt towards accounting for so strange a phenomenon, the reality of which has been
so often disputed or denied by almost all philosophers and physiolo-
gists. It is considered, however, by Dr. Thouvenel, from his own observations and experiments, as entirely ascertained and indisputable.

He attempts to explain it, by supposing certain emanations, or effluvia of the electrical kind, operating on certain particular and determined emunctories existing in the bodies of the sourciers. To a
similar kind of emunctories he refers the ' pretendedly magical and
empirical method of curing by touching the patient, &c.' the diseases and powers mistaken for effects of sorcery or supernatural
agency: and so far is he from denying the reality of such facts, that
he endeavours to account for them from the operation or influence
of electrical, or magnetical matters, and other fluids perhaps still
more subtle and unknown, because their effects are not perceptible
in the ordinary course of nature, and never become so but by a
concourse of certain very rare and extraordinary circumstances.

In the second section Dr. Thouvenel gives an ample and minute
detail of all the observations and experiments which he himself has
made on Bleton, and by which he has been fully convinced of the
reality of the action of subterraneous waters on that singular man,
one of the most astonishing sourciers that has ever appeared.

' Bleton is a poor peasant, neither an impostor nor a quack, and
surely not fit to be either. He has been brought up by charity in
one of the Carthusian convents of the province of Dauphiné: and
the occasion of his becoming sensible of his talent, if it be one, says
the author, was as follows:

' As the age of seven years, when he carried a dinner to some labourers,

bourers, he sat himself down on a stone, where he was seized with an ague; the labourers made him sit down by them, and the ague ceased: he returned several times to the stone, and each time the ague returned. The story was told to the prior of the Carthusian convent; who was curious to see the experiment; after being convinced of the fact, he ordered to dig under the stone; and found there a spring, which, as the author of the relation has been told, now turns a mill.

' As for Bleton, he is entirely ignorant of the cause which enabled him to feel when he is on running-water ... for it must be running: he uses a rod or wand, merely for satisfying the spectators; and it matters not of whatever species of wood, green or dry, it be, &c.'

Dr. Thouvenel has observed, that they are nervous, spasmodic, and convulsive symptoms, which arise in this torpillo individual, as he calls him, on the water: but not on all sorts of subterraneous water, not on superficial water; that the motions of the wand, of whatever sort of wood, happen on his fingers, and on those of other people, merely by his touching them; that the direct rotation, that is forwards, of this wand on its axis, indicates the spring head and course of the sources; that the retrograde motion at a distance of those sources, in whatever line, indicates their depth, is the most amazing phenomenon of this physical wonder. Dr. Thouvenel thinks it bears some relation to positive and negative terrestrial electricity, of which the trains of water are the conductors, as in the atmosphere, and which by their communication rouse the animal electricity. He has made ' physical isolements, and chemical electres, which have suspended the motions of the body and those of the wand; and he points out the experiments which still remain to be made, in order still better to ascertain the nature of the emanations, and the mechanism of their operation on the fourciers and on their wand.

In the third section, Dr. Thouvenel has collected all the verbal processes, reports, certificates, &c. which have been received by him in consequence of a circulatory letter sent by him into all the provinces, and to all the persons for whom Bleton has operated: these reports, certificates, &c. he calls, ' preuves de surérogation & inutiles aux physiciens,' on account of the most perfect conviction which he himself has acquired by his own observations. This section contains also analogous facts observed on other similar individuals, who, says the author, are, and will be more common than it is thought, though most of them subaltern, and far from coming up to Bleton. From those stories it appears that the talents of these sort of people have long been employed for discovering mines and metals, as well as water. [The Reviewer of this article recollects to have often heard in several parts of Germany, of certain people, called hoard-diggers, who, by means of the direction of a similar wand, pretend to discover treasures concealed in fields, in forests, under the ruins of old castles; but generally cheat such weak people as engage in their adventures.]—The author draws inferences, and makes applications of the talent of the individuals in question. He calls that talent a real gift of nature, and points out its affinities, which he always considers as more and more evident and numerous, with the electrical and magnetical phenomena.

The stories, attestations, and certificates subjoined to this third section are very numerous. The first, is the account of a learned and respectable countryman of Bleton's, a prior of a convent at the foot of a very high mountain, called Autum, in Dauphiné, respected and beloved by all his acquaintance, about sixty-five years old, plain in his manners, full of candour, and learned, and withal a noted four-cier, like Bleton. The author of the relation paid him a visit, dissembled his having heard any thing of his talent, and spoke to him of Bleton as of a cheat, like J. Aymar, and Parangue, two other fourciers. ' You are mistaken, Sir, answered he, I know him (Bleton) well; he is an honest man, whom I esteem: and I have the same sensations as he, &c. Jacques Aymar and Parangue have the same talent, but they have abused it in an odious manner. Consider, Sir, that the part of a mean impostor does not suit my condition and character. Do not doubt then, I beseech you, of what I am going to tell you. Bleton and I have often operated on the same spots, and it has never yet happened that we should not have hit together on the spots under which there are waters running: we cannot be mistaken in that respect.

' As for the depths, an infinite variety of circumstances can betray us into errors; and I confess, that in this respect, Bleton has more experience and skill than myself. You consider the motion of the wand as a juggling trick; but it turns really. I protest to you, that when I am on a spring, and hold a willow twig, strong as my fist is, it is in vain I grasp it, the twig overpowers the resistance. Bleton will sometimes be mistaken in assigning the depths, because the sensations we feel vary according to the greatness of the current, and, I add, according to its rapidity: but surely he shall never be mistaken as to the existence of the water. I will not attempt to explain to you, why I feel the emanations of subterraneous waters, and why you do not feel them; why stagnant waters affect me much less; why a river produces weaker sensations than a spring in the bowels of the earth; why a source, in ascending, gives me an illness I cannot endure, whilst, when descending, I follow her without fatigue. I know that in the chain of causes and effects there are points marked out by the Supreme Being, where philosophy and ignorance are confounded. The fact exists; I will prove it to who ever doubts its existence; but I leave reasonings on it to people more learned than I am.' This honest prior, adds M. C. (from whom this and many other accounts are borrowed by Dr. Thouvenel) wants nothing; he operates gratis, and he operates often. He has had the mortification of being summoned before his bishop, by highland priests, believing in sorcery .. I have had the satisfaction, says the same M. C. to see him operate and argue with Bleton, &c. &c.

This relation we have selected from among many others, because the prior makes no trade of his talent, and because, from his reasonings, he appears to be a man of sense and integrity, and there-fore to deserve the more credit.

An essential objection, however, still occurs, which Dr. Thouvenel will, no doubt, remove in the next edition of his curious and well written book. In all the histories, certificates, and attestations, he has printed only the initial letters of names, with points and asterisks. Dr. Thouvenel says: that ' though the names of the respective persons are written at full length in Mr. C's memoir, and in his correspondence, yet for fear of disobliging some of them, he has chosen to quote all of them only by their initial letters, but to let the names of the places where the experiments have been made, stand at full length ... d'autant qu'en matiere de physique les noms ne sont rien aux faits.'

To this it has very justly been answered, that when the question is of facts of whatever kind, it is always highly essential to know the names of those who attest such facts as ocular witnesses; because this knowledge of their names has a great influence on their credibility; and this the rather, as in an affair like this, where no man needs to blush for attesting what he has seen, Dr. Thouvenel might easily have obtained leave to publish at full length the names of almost all the persons who have communicated and attested the curious and interesting facts he relates. Nor can we conceive for what use the names of witnesses can be signed at full length to certificates, if they would shrink from the eyes of the public.

Till this essential difficulty shall be entirely removed, we must, therefore, content ourselves with suspending our opinion as to the credibility, probability, and nature of the whole, and think, *non liquet.*

FOREIGN LITERARY INTELLIGENCE.

Traité de la Construction des Vaisseaux; avec des Eclaircissemens et des Démonstrations touchant l'Ouvrage intitulé, Architectura Navalis Mercatoria, &c. Par Frederic Henri de Chapman, *Chevalier de l'Ordre Royal de l'Epée, prémier Constructeur des Armées Navales de* Suede, *&c. Traduit du* Suedois, *publié avec quelques Notes & Additions pour entendre la Lecture indépendemment du grand Ouvrage en Planches du même Auteur; par* M. Vial de Clairbois, *Sous-Ingenieur, &c.* Brest & Paris.

THE author of the Swedish original of this treatise published, in 1768, a great work, consisting chiefly of a number of large copper-plates, and intitled, Architectura Navalis Mercatoria: this was, in 1775, succeeded by the present treatise on the construction of ships. Mr. Vial, who is himself a skilful naval architect, thought the Swedish work, on account of many valuable and original hints and views, worthy of a French translation, which he accordingly undertook and executed, by the assistance of M. de Lowenorn, a Danish naval officer, serving in the French fleet.

Lectiones Theologicæ de Ecclesiâ. Auctore uno è P. R. *12mo.* Rothomagi.

By the rev. M. Baston, a zealous partisan of the Gallican church, whose tenets he strenuously maintains against the pretensions of the Roman court. He accordingly asserts, that the pope is by no means infallible, even when he pronounces ex cathedra; that he is subject to œcumenical councils; that he must moderate the exercise of his authority by that of the holy canons; that neither he nor the church have any direct or indirect power over the temporalities, either of kings or private persons. The author decides also, without hesitation, that the Bible is not the supreme judge of disputes on matters of faith; but that these must be decided by the church: and this, says he, because, 'Ecclesiæ autoritas per scripturam quatenus authenticam; et scriptura quatenus inspirata per autoritatem ecclesiæ, probatur. Nullus proinde circulus (vitiosus in demonstrando): certissima est hæc solutio.' We congratulate him and his church on the discovery of this fine distinction. Qui bene distinguit, bene docet!

Ces.

Lectiones

Lectiones Theologicæ de Matrimonio. Auctore uno è P. R. 12mo. Rothomagi, & Parisiis.

By the same ingenious writer; who has treated the subject of matrimony after the scholastic method, without, however, entangling himself in a labyrinth of subtle but useless questions. In examining the question often agitated by catholic divines, concerning the minister of that sacrament (marriage), he contents himself with relating the various arguments adduced by the different contending parties, without declaring for either of them; and concludes the discussion in a manner somewhat pleasant and unexpected: ' Legentium erit aut unam selegisse, aut *omnes suspiciosas* habere: modo tamen crediderint veritatem apud eas (sententias) latenter hospitari.' *Then truth must keep a very strict incognito indeed!*

Beskrivelse over den Opmaalings Methode, &c. or, an Account of the Method of Mensuration employed in levying the geographical Maps of Denmark. *By* Thomas Bugge, *Prof. of Mathematics and Astronomy at* Copenhagen. 132 *Pages in Quarto, with three Plates.* Copenhagen. (Danish.)

In 1768, a regular instruction was drawn up, a number of land surveyors appointed, and accurate instruments procured for the above purpose. The first result of their skillful and instructive application was a valuable map, entitled, ' Kortover Siælland og Moen' ... which exhibits the Danish islands of Sealand and Moen, with the neighbouring coasts of Schonen, Falster, Laaland, Langeland, Thorsinge, Fyen, Samsoe, and Jutland; and has been drawn up under the direction of the Royal Danish Society of Sciences.

Historia Literaturæ Græcæ *in* Suecia *ab ejus initiis ad Annum* 1650. *Auctore* Erico Michaele Fant. Aman. *Reg. Biblioth. Acad. et Eloq. Doct.* 4to. Upsalæ & Lipsiæ.

The study of the Greek language began in Sweden as in many other countries, at the Reformation, and especially with the translation and explication of the New Testament. The famous queen Christina learned and read Greek; but the most eminent Greek scholars in Sweden, during the period here treated of, were Meursius, Scheffer, and John Gezelius.

Cosmographie Elémentaire divisée en Parties Astronomique & Géographique. Ouvrage dans lequel on a tâché de mettre les Verités les plus interessantes de la Physique céleste, à portée de ceux même qui n'ont aucune Notion de Mathématiques, &c. Par M. Mentelle, *&c.* 8vo. *with Cuts and Maps:* Paris.

This very useful elementary cosmography is intended for an introduction to Mr. Mentelle's great and valuable work of geography. The first part of this introduction treats of the mundane system; and the second, of general geography.

Mes Loisirs, ou Poësies diverses. Par M. L. Pons, *de Verdun, Avocat au Parlement.—' Les longs Ouvrages me font peur.'—*119 *Pages in* 12mo. Paris.

Short and pretty trifles.

Les Ellipses de la Langue Latine, *précédées d'une courte Analyze des différens Mots appelés Parties d'Oraison. Ouvrage destiné aux jeunes Humanistes. Par M.* Fargoult, *Prof. Emerite de l'Univ. de* Paris. 249 *Pages in small* 8vo. Paris.

A learned and instructive performance.

L'Apolo-

L'Apologétique et les Préscriptions de Tertullien. *Nouvelle Edition revue & corrigée d'après les MSS. les Editions & différens Ouvrages de* Tertullien, *avec la Traduction & les Remarques. Par M. l'Abbé de* Gourcy, *Vicaire Général du Diecese de* Bourdeaux, &c. 12mo. Paris.

Two of the beſt treatiſes of Tertullian, an ardent, and forcible, but ſometimes obſcure, incorrect, barbarous, or taſteleſs writer, are here publiſhed, with many critical corrections of the text, and a very elaborate tranſlation, greatly ſuperior to the original, in point of taſte and perſpicuity.

Lettres de M. de Voltaire à M. l'Abbé Mouſſinot *ſon Tréſorier, écrites depuis 1736 juſqu'en 1742. pendant ſa Rétraitte à* Cirey, *chez Madame la Marquiſe du* Châtelet, *& dans leſquelles on voit quelques Détails de ſa Fortune, de ſes Bienfaits; qu'elles furent alors ſes Etudes, ſes Querelles avec des* Fontaines, *&c. Publiées par* M. L'Abbé D***, *244 Pages in* 8vo. Paris.

The contents of theſe poſthumous letters of M. de Voltaire, appear from the title. They are written on familiar domeſtic concerns; yet often entertaining, and may ſometimes prove even inſtructive.

La Muſica, Poëma por D. Thomas de Yriarte. 166 *Pages in* 8vo. *En* Madrid, *with Plates.*

A didactic poem, highly eſteemed in Spain, and very elegantly printed.

El ingenioſo Don Quixote *de la* Mancha, *compueſto por* Miguel de Cervantes Saavedra; *nueva Edition, corregida por la Real Academia* Eſpanola. 4 *Vols in Quarto, with many fine Plates. En* Madrid.

A maſterpiece of Spaniſh typography, and for the beauty of its types, paper, and ink, equal at leaſt, if not ſuperior, to the moſt beautiful editions of Baſkerville's.

MONTHLY CATALOGUE.

POETRY.

An Ode to the Genius of Scandal. 4to. 1s. Kearſly.

THE editor of this Ode informs us, in an advertiſement prefixed, that the author intended it ſolely for the amuſement of his intimate acquaintance; but that he, the editor, who was favoured with the poem, thought a more enlarged publication would be *beneficial to mankind,* and that moreover (for which he ſuppoſes we ſhall certainly take his word) that ' the *ſpirit* and *elegance* of the compoſition, and the philanthropy it breathes, muſt recommend it to encomium, and ſecure the applauſe it ſo juſtly merits.'

When a truſty eſquire promiſes and vows ſo much for his knight, it may perhaps be thought impertinent in critics to call in queſtion his veracity, or to find any fault with a work ſo meritorious. We ſhould otherwiſe perhaps have been induced to obſerve, that we do not find any ſuch extraordinary ſpirit and ele-

gance

gance in this compofition, which, in our opinion, has nothing in it very new, ftriking, or poetical; nor do we fee how it can turn out fo *beneficial to mankind*, being nothing more than a ftring of common-place thoughts on a hackneyed fubject, which have been repeated by various writers, at all times and in all places, without making mankind a jot the better, or lefs inclined to fcandal and defamation.——After enumerating the ill effects of calumny, our author fagaciously obferves that

> ' Thefe are the triumphs Scandal claims—
> Triumphs deriv'd from ruin'd names—
> Such as, to generous minds unknown,
> An honeft foul would fcorn to own.
> Nor think, vain woman, while you fneer
> At others faults, that you are clear;
> No! - turn your back—you undergo
> The felf-fame malice you to others fhow.'

To which might be added—to continue the rhyme,

> That, thus it is, without your verfe we know,
> And thus it was a thoufand years ago.

There is nothing new in all this, nor indeed in any part of the poem; nor is the manner of expreffing known truths agreeable enough to attract our attention; though the meafure is fufficiently varied; for the author has treated us in this fhort Ode with every kind of verfe which the English language affords. He fets out with the folemn lyric.

> ' Oh! thou, whofe all-confoling pow'r
>   Can foothe our cares to reft:
> Whofe touch in Spleen's moft vap'rifh hour
>   Can calm each female breaft;

and a few lines after changes the chord, and gives us a fing-fong,

> ' Teach me, powerful genius! teach
>   Thine own myfterious art,
> Safe from retaliation's reach,
>   How I may throw detraction's dart,'

Here the fourth line does not anfwer as it fhould to the fecond; befides that the word *retaliation* is enormoufly long, and ill-adapted to the meafure. He endeavours, however, foon to make us amends by a little familiar jigg, and exclaims thus, in dancing rhyme,

> ' The firft informations
> Of loft reputations
> As offerings to thee I'll confign,
> And the earlieft news
> Of furpriz'd billet-doux
> Shall conftant be ferv'd at thy fhrine.'

Then comes the flow and folemn heroic meafure,

> ' Now,

' Now, now indeed, I burn with sacred fires—
Indeed !

      'Tis Scandal's self that ev'ry thought inspires !
      I feel, all potent genius, &c.'

And the moment after we begin to be arch and comical : a lady
cries out,

      ' Each fool of Delia's figure talks,
        And celebrates her fame ;
      But, for my part, whene'er she walks,
        I think she's rather lame.
      And mind ma'am Chloe toss her head !
        Lord ! how the creature stares !
      Well !—I thank God it can't be said
        I give myself those airs.'

Then we return to the elegiac strain, and the weeping maid,

      ' Beside a mournful willow
      Ev'ry night *forlórnly* pining,
      Mute on her lilly hand reclining,
      Bedews her *waking* pillow.'

Forlornly is, we believe, quite a new word, and *waking* pillows
are things very seldom to be met with. But lest we should be
too deeply affected with the melting strain, the author relieves
us immediately with,

      ' Sweet girl, she was once most enchantingly gay,
      Each youth felt her charms, and acknowledg'd their sway.'

With about twenty more tit-up-a-tit verses, that run glibly off
with very little meaning. In this manner he goes on, skipping
through all the varieties of versification, to the end of the poem,
which concludes with the following advice to the ladies, in the
true odaic measure.

      ' — when from those sweet lips we hear,
      Ill-nature's whisper, Envy's sneer,
        Your pow'r that moment dies.
      Each coxcomb makes your name his sport,
      And fools when angry will retort
        What men of sense despise.
      Leave, then, such low pursuits as these,
      And take a nobler road to please—
        Let Candour guide your way—
      So shall you daily conquests gain,
      And captives glorying in your chain,
        Be proud to own your sway.'

The reader will judge by the above quotations what reliance
is to be placed on the editor (not improbably the author also)
of this poem, who boasts so much of its wonderful elegance and
spirit ; though it appears to us, and we believe will to the public,
as a very indifferent composition.

The Cheltenham *Guide; or, Memoirs of the* B-n-rd *Family continued. Small 8vo. 2s. sewed.* Harrison and Co.

What a heap of vile pictures of himself has the ingenious Ansty lived to see just looked at, and then thrown by, like old family portraits, amongst the lumber of modern literature!

O imitatores, servum pecus!

Of all the aukward pretences to the wit, humour, and poetry of the *Bath Guide* that have appeared, this is one of the worst. For a specimen of this author's style and manner, take the following extract from the first letter of Tristram B-n-r-d, esq. to Rantum Squash, gent.

    ' At present we lodge at the sign of the Swan,
But intend soon to move on a much cheaper plan,
To very good rooms, well furnish'd and near,
Where weekly the dancers and fidlers all meet.
At the inns here each article's sold very dear,
From the sparkling Champaign, to the blood-colour'd beer;
From the ven'son that's kept till it stink by degrees,
To the rasher of bacon, or slice of green cheese:
Nor improper—where water is drank, to charge high
(As the less is your custom) for what you must buy.
    ' For the first time, next Monday, we go in a party,
First to suck at the pump, then to eat breakfast hearty.
For the company meet ev'ry Monday, I'm told,
Both the young and the gay, and the ugly and old,
To drink tea together, stare hard, and talk news,
In a room near as long as his Majesty's Mews.'

These are some of the best lines in the whole collection of fine poems, which, if we are to credit the title-page, is already arrived at the honour of a—*fifth edition.*

D R A M A T I C.

The Critic; or, a Tragedy Rehearsed. A Dramatic Piece in three Acts; as it is Performed at the Theatre Royal in Drury-Lane. *By* Richard Brinsley Sheridan, *Esq.* 1s. 6d. Becket.

This piece has been seen and admired by every body; and the oftener it is seen, and the oftener it is read, the more will it be applauded. Hypercritical remarks on it would therefore be totally unnecessary. There is, indeed, more true wit and humour crouded into this little performance, than has, perhaps, appeared since the days of Wycherley and Congreve. The impartiality of cool reflection obliges us, at the same time, to condemn that which we cannot but admire. Ridicule is a dangerous and destructive weapon, which, Drawcansir like, destroys every thing before it, without mercy and without distinction. Wantonness of wit, and exuberance of fancy, have carried the ingenious author of the Critic beyond the limits of reason, justice, and impartiality. Not content with lashing the false sublime, bombast,

baft, and all the ftage-trick of modern tragedy, he has attacked
tragedy itfelf, and endeavoured, but too fuccefsfully, to render it
an objeð of ridicule and farcafm. How far it may be confiftent
with the charaðer of a manager of a theatre to weaken one of its
beft fupports, we leave Mr. Sheridan to determine. Certain however it is, that fince the exhibition of the Critic, tragedy, which
a celebrated writer has declared to be one of. the greateft
exertions of the human mind, is fallen into contempt; it will be
fome time at leaft before fhe can recover the blow. We hope,
notwithftanding, for the credit of a Britifh audience, that they
will not be laughed out of their feelings, or fuffer themfelves to
be deprived of that pleafure, not to mention the profit and inftruction, which may arife from the exhibition of a good tragedy well performed, for any thing that fuch a wicked wit as our
author can fay againft it.

A Trip to Scarborough. *A Comedy. As performed at the Theatre*
    Royal in Drury Lane. *Altered from* Vanbrugh's *Relapfe; or,*
    Virtue in Danger. By Richard Brinfley Sheridan, *Efq.* 8vo.
    1s. 6d. Wilkie.

The ingenious Mr. Horace Walpole has obferved, in his
Memoirs of Hogarth, that when this excellent artift was
employed, in the early part of his life, on the works of *others,*
as in prints for Hudibras, &c. he fhewed very few marks of
that genius and humour which fo eminently diftinguifhed his
own. The celebrated Mr. Brinfley Sheridan, in the dramatic
performance before us, feems to ftand nearly in the fame pre-
dicament : he has altered Vanbrugh's Relapfe, and given it the
title of *A Trip to Scarborough*; but in the alteration we find not
a fpark of that lively wit and eafy dialogue that fhines forth in
the School for Scandal. Some of Vanbrugh's indecencies are
taken away, and, in that refpeð, the play is mended; but
what is added is neither like Vanbrugh nor Sheridan. The
play, however, is in poffeffion of the ftage, and we fuppofe muft
ftand as it is; it would anfwer no purpofe, therefore, to point
out its deficiencies. We hope the author of the Critic will employ his time better for the future than in altering Vanbrugh, or
any other writer, and entertain us with compofitions of his own.

Duplicity : a Comedy. As it is Performed at the Theatre-Royal in
    Covent-Garden. *By* Thomas Holcroft. 8vo. 1s. 6d. Ro-
    binfon.

This Comedy is written with a good defign, and the moral inftruction naturally arifing from it is one of the beft that can be
drawn in the prefent age from any dramatic exhibition, viz. an
utter abhorrence of the fafhionable vice of gaming, fo univerfally prevalent amongft us. The gamefter's narrow efcape from
ruin, by the amiable and artful conduð of his friend, which is
the ground-work of the fable, is well conceived, not badly executed, and in confequence of it the cataftrophe in the fifth að is remarkably interefting. It had likewife all the ftage-effeð which
                                                            the

the author or actors could expect from it. The under-plot and the characters concerned in it are, on the other hand, totally uninteresting, and, in many scenes, even disagreeable and disgustful. 'Squire Turnbull and Miss, speaking in the Zomerzetshire dialect, may, for aught we know to the contrary, be drawn exactly after nature; but there are parts of human nature, as well as of the human body, that should rather be concealed than exposed. Where we feel little pleasure from the object itself, we shall find still less from the representation of it.—The outline, of the dramatic picture before us is well drawn, but the intermediate parts are not well filled, and the colouring of the whole too faint and languid to ensure fame to the artist.

The Marriage Act: a Farce, in Two Acts, as it is performed at the Theatre-Royal in Covent-Garden. 1s. Kearsly.

Why this farce is entitled the Marriage Act, we cannot discover, as it might, with equal propriety, have been called by any other name. This however is a matter of very little consequence, as the piece is, with regard to the plot, songs, and dialogue, entitled to very little consideration.

The Divorce: a Farce, as it is performed at the Theatre-Royal, Drury-Lane. 1s. Kearsly.

This farce is entirely calculated for stage-effect; and must, for success, depend in a great measure on the acting. Those by whom it is *read* will, we apprehend, wish to *see* it; and those who *see* it will not wish to *read*, but to *see* it again.

√ M E D I C A L.

Some Observations on the Origin and Progress of the atrabilious Constitution and Gout. Chap. V. containing the irregular and complicated Gout. By William Grant, M. D. 8vo. 1s. 6d. Cadell.

These observations, which constitute a fifth chapter of Dr. Grant's treatise on this subject, are divided into three parts. In the first, he treats of the irregular gout in general, improper regimen in the intervals, errors during the fit, want of vigour, complication. The second contains the division of irregular gout into classes; namely, unformed gout, wandering gout, redundant gout, internal gout, feeble gout of old age, or of debilitated habits. The third part treats of the complicated gout, gout with inflammation, coughs in a gouty habit, spring-gout, with synochus non putris, synochus putris in a gouty habit, cholera morbus in gouty habits, bilious fever in a gouty habit, atrabilious fever in a gouty habit, malignant fevers in gouty habits, special method of cure for the lues. All those subjects, though sometimes, perhaps, unnecessarily discriminated, are treated by the author in a clear and practical manner.

As

An Account of the Nature and Medicinal Virtues of the principal Mineral Waters of Great Britain *and* Ireland, *and of those most in repute on the Continent. By* John Elliot, *M. D. 8vo.* Johnson.

Prefixed to this account of mineral waters, is a republication of Dr. Priestley's pamphlet on the impregnating of water with fixed air. This subject is introduced with the history of the discovery; which is followed by directions for performing the impregnation. Those are immediately succeeded by Dr. Nooth's objections to that method; and a comparison of it with his own, both as published by himself, and as improved by Mr. Parker, Mr. Magellan, &c. To the foregoing articles, Dr. Elliot has subjoined a method of imitating the sulphureous mineral waters, by impregnating water with sulphureous air; and also of imitating more exactly the several mineral waters.

The account of the various mineral waters is arranged in alphabetical order; and contains not only their virtues, but the method and reason of using them, so far as could be learnt from the authors who have been consulted on the subject. This treatise being intended for the use of the public, as well as of the faculty, Dr. Elliot has, with great propriety, drawn it up in such a manner as may be understood by those who are unacquainted with the art of physic. We have the satisfaction also to observe, that he has given an account of many waters, which have hitherto been very little known beyond the narrow sphere of their own neighbourhood. The whole may be justly considered as a comprehensive and useful treatise on medicinal waters.

The Medical Pocket-Book. 12mo. Johnson.

This abstract, compiled by the ingenious and indefatigable Dr. Elliot, contains a short, but plain account of the symptoms, causes, and methods of cure of disorders; including such as require surgical treatment; with the virtues and doses of medicinal compositions and simples; all digested into alphabetical order.

DIVINITY.

A Sermon preached at St. Dunstan's in the West, *on Sunday April 29, and at* St. Mary Abbots, Kensington, *on Sunday* July 15, 1781, *for the Benefit of the Humane Society, instituted for the Recovery of Persons apparently dead by drowning. By* Jacob Duché, *M. A. 8vo. 1s.* Rivington.

The author takes his text from the prayer of Jonah, 'The waters compassed me about,' &c. ch. ii. 5, 6. and applies some of the circumstances, in the case of that prophet, to those persons, who have been apparently drowned, and recovered by the medical assistance of the Humane Society.

By the account annexed to this discourse, it appears, that since the first establishment of this society, in 1774, 319 persons, who were apparently dead, have been restored to the community.

As

As this excellent institution has been attended with so much success, the directors are extremely desirous of improving their plan, by appointing medical assistants in every part of the country, and by extending their rewards to those, who shall be so happy as to restore any one to life, in other cases of sudden death. They wish likewise to enlarge the distribution of the pamphlets, which contain the most useful and approved directions on this subject, and to present a Bible, with some little book of spiritual instruction and advice, to each recovered person, as a perpetual memorial of the mercies such person has received. —These improvements Mr. Duché very properly recommends to the consideration and the patronage of the subscribers and the public.

Advice addressed to the Clergy of the Diocese of Carlisle, *in a Sermon, preached at a general Ordination, holden at* Rose Castle, *on* Sunday, July 29, 1781. *By* W. Paley, *M. A.* 4to. 1s. Faulder.

This discourse contains some excellent advice to young clergymen, respecting their moral conduct.

MISCELLANEOUS.

Elements of Geometry, translated from the French of J. J. Rossignol, *Professor of the Mathematics in the University of* Milan. 3s. 6d. *boards.* Johnson.

This work is the production of a learned professor in one of the most respectable universities in Europe, and is ' the result of numberless efforts, observations, and corrections, continued through twenty years.' The manner in which the elements are here treated is in a great degree new as well as useful. Not only the principal propositions of real use in mathematics or in practical arts are arranged in an orderly and dependent series, adapted to the author's mode of demonstration, but also the mode of demonstration itself is considerably out of the common way of treating this difficult subject.

In order to render the elements of geometry short, easy, and familiar to the generality of capacities, the author has taken some liberties not allowed of in the Euclidean method of demonstration; and, without indulging an affectation of novelty, remarks that he has often been under the necessity of striking out into unbeaten paths; by which, he continues, obstacles have sometimes perhaps been avoided, which had before frequently embarrassed both the pupil and the teacher. To make the selection of the chief properties, and new-model them to advantage, we must acknowlege, required judgment, experience, and attention.

The version is well executed, in the pure geometrical style; and, in apology for rendering the work into our language, the translator observes, that it seems to be one of the most successful attempts which have ever been made to facilitate the study of geometry. Originality of plan, clearness of arrangement, simplicity of demonstration, and elegant concifeness of expression, will

will, he apprehends, be found to be the leading characters of these elements.

Those who know where the difficulties of an undertaking of this kind principally lie, will perhaps easily pardon the liberties which the author has taken, in making use of numbers in the doctrine of proportion, and, in employing the methods of exhaustions and indivisibles, in demonstrating the properties of solids, where they perceive that by these means he has enabled the learner to make himself master of the principal elementary propositions, with the most perfect facility, and, at the same time, with a degree of accuracy, sufficient for every purpose of practice. Nor will it, remarks the translator, be thought too bold an innovation, that, in a mathematical work, the author makes use of *physical prints*, and these too of different magnitudes ; if it be observed, that he always expresses this term by the idea commonly affixed to *aliquot parts*, and that he only applies it to commensurable lines or figures actually existing.

It is not to be expected that this work can supersede the use of the elements of Euclid, which have a strictness of proof, and universality of application, of which none of the more easy methods of demonstration, invented by the moderns, can boast. But it is presumed, that it may enable those, who are employed in the practical use of the mathematical arts, at an easy expence of time and attention, to acquire a general knowledge of the theory on which they are founded ; and that it may be of great benefit to young geometricians, in introducing them to a ready acquaintance with the terms and principles of this difficult science, and preparing them for making farther advances in mathematical knowledge.

The Life of Mr. Thomas Firmin, *Citizen of* London. *By* Joseph Cornish. 12mo. 2s. 6d. Johnson.

Mr. Thomas Firmin, girdler and mercer, of the city of London, though a private man, was eminently distinguished by his truly patriotic virtues. His charity was extended to persons of all parties and persuasions. He was a liberal benefactor to distressed families, to imprisoned debtors, and to the French and Irish refugees. He set up several manufactories for the employment of the poor, and was a zealous promoter of every humane and charitable institution. His excellent character procured him the friendship of bishops Wilkins, Fowler, Tillotson, and other eminent men. He died in 1697, aged 66. Some account of his life is inserted in most of our biographical publications.

The author's principal design, in this work, is to set before the reader, and especially the young tradesman, a pattern of imitation, with respect to industry, prudence, integrity, charity, and all those virtues, which appeared with so much lustre in this worthy citizen.

The compiler of this work is the author of ' A Letter to the Right Rev. the Lord Bishop of Carlisle,' mentioned in our Review for Jan. 1778, of ' A brief and impartial History of the Puritans,' and some other religious tracts.

Proposed Form of Register for Baptisms. 4to. 5s. *Boards.* Nichols.

Proposed Form of Register for Burials. 4to. 5s. *Boards.* Nichols.

Parish registers are said to have been first introduced by the direction of Cromwell, vicar-general, in the year 1538. The great convenience, arising from this ordinance, occasioned its being farther enjoined in the reigns of Edward VI. Elizabeth, and James I. In the reigns of king William and queen Anne they became the objects of parliamentary consideration. Still however they are not kept as they should be. The entries are frequently irregular, confused, and defective.

The forms here proposed are excellently contrived to answer every useful purpose. The book for baptisms has distinct columns for the date, the age, the name of the child, and the names of the father and mother, with the profession of the former, and the maiden name of the latter. The register for burials has separate columns for the name of the deceased, the names of father and mother, age, supposed cause of death, and a specification of the place of interment. At the end some pages are reserved for memorandums of any interesting or remarkable occurrence in the parish.

The utility of all such entries is evident. They may be of singular service in genealogical and topographical disquisitions, in shewing the healthiness of the parish, and ascertaining the increase or decrease of population. In short, if properly managed, they will form a parochial history.

The preface contains some useful hints relative to churchyards.

The Cheltenham *Guide : or useful Companion in a Journey of Health to* Cheltenham Spa. 8vo. 1s. 6d. Johnson.

In this pamphlet the author presents us with a description of the town of Cheltenham, and the country adjacent ; beside a particular account of the nature and virtues of the Cheltenham Spa, and a variety of other circumstances. The whole forms a useful companion to those who visit that place, for the purpose either of pleasure or health.

Sentimental Excursions to Windsor, *and other Places.* 12mo. 2s. 6d. *sewed.* Walker.

Imitations of the inimitable *Tristram* are become so frequent as to render the perusal of them to the last degree tedious and disgusting : not a month passes wherein we are not pestered with sentimental journeys, adventures, &c. in the *Shandean* style and manner. Amongst these the author of *Excursions to Windsor* stands forth an avowed disciple of the *Sternian* school ; and seems, by mere dint of extraordinary diligence and attention, to have imitated his master with some degree of success, as our readers will perceive by the following short extract.

' THE

'THE POCKET HOOP.

' It is aftonifhing, that women will encumber their perfons fo as to alter the elegant fymmetry of the human frame !—The perfon of a fine woman is the moft beautiful edifice in nature ! — True beauty confifts in fimplicity, and the figure of a well-made female always fhews to the beft advantage when its ornaments are fimple—it fhould never be embellifhed in the *compofite* order.—— From the days of *fig-leaves* to the prefent time, *art* has only laboured to difguife nature. ——

' Hiftory informs us, that queen Elizabeth was remarkable for the protucburance of *the rotundo*; and this, fay the antiquarians in drefs, firft introduced the fashion of hoops. But whether this *rotundo* was a *permanent rotundo behind*, natural to the make of her majefty, or a *temporary* rotundo *before*, arifing from a *natural caufe*, authors are filent.

' A hoop, fays an old writer, is an airy cool drefs. That may be, anfwers a modern writer, arguing on the fame fubject—but how comes it to pafs that queen Elizabeth, who was a *virgin* queen, and her *maids* of *honour*, who were *virgins* by *virtue* of their office, fhould require more cooling than their grandmothers ? Now the queftion is very eafily anfwered—Queen Elizabeth and her *maids* of honour were *virgins*—their grandmothers certainly were not.

' I suppofe, fir, faid my fellow-traveller, we fhall breakfaft here, as the coach ftopped at the *Star and Garter* at Kew-bridge. I leaped out and gave the lady my hand :—fhe fprung forward ; but the reacherous hoop croffing the door of the coach, gave fo fudden a jerk to the lady, that as fhe fprung fhe fell, and as fhe fell, of courfe the hoop became inverfed, as you may have feen an umbrella, or *parafol*, on a windy day—fhe flipped from under her garments. —— Heaven preferve us !

' I fixed my eyes upon the *fign*.—It is the *Star and Garter*, faid I to myfelf, in an under voice, and in the fame tone I read the motto —— "HONI SOIT QUI MAL Y PENSE."

' I kept my eyes fixed upon the *fign*, without once attempting to extricate the lady. Had it been the fign of the *Gorgon's* head, I could not have been more *petrified* ;—but my man, who had now defcended from the roof of the coach, having more prefence of mind, entered the coach at the oppofite door, and taking the lady by the fhoulders, gently pulled her backwards, while I fmoothed her cloaths, and brought the villainous hoop to its primitive fituation.

' The lady, having adjufted her drapery, came out fideways.

' I led her into the houfe, and being fhewn into a room—fhe curfed her hoop in a tone of bitternefs infinitely more vindictive than the curfe itfelf—but how could I fay *Amen*?—I confidered myfelf under fome obligations to the object of her curfes, " fo *amen* ftuck in my throat."

' It was my own fault, faid the lady ; I fhould have come out fideways at firft.—But the way you attempted to come, madam, faid I, was moft *natural*.—True, fhe replied, but not the moft

fortunate ;

fortunate; our *natural* movements feldom are, faid I—till this inflant I confidered *hoops* as protections from fuch accidents, replied the lady, but I now perceive they render one's *motions* very *unnatural*—fo faying, fhe retired.—Breakfaft was ferved in:—the lady returned divefted of her hoop—her dimity jacket fitted her fhape exactly—her petticoat hung in folds—an elegant *neglegee* appearance marked her perfon—the confcious tint upon her check indexed the continuance of her confufion.——We breakfafted, and having afcended the carriage with caution, and taken our feats, without further accident, we purfued our journey.——

'The fcene at the inn-door, when I innocently gazed upon the *Star and Garter*, was frefh in my memory.——Not an aftronomer of them all, from Ptolemy the Egyptian, down to Copernicus the German, and from Copernicus the German, down to Newton the Englifhman, had ever fo ftrong a conception of the *hirfute* conftellation, called by *ftar-gazers Berenice's locks*, as I had of the *fign* at Kew-bridge.—— Every object was painted upon my imagination in the moft lively colours.'

This, confidered merely as an imitation of *Sterne*, has its fhare of merit ; our regard to decency and good manners obliges us, at the fame time, to remark, that it is a pretty exact copy of one of the worft of *Triftram's* features, and imitates but too well that *pruriency* of fancy, and *falacious* love of *afterifms*, for which the *Shandys* were fo eminently diftinguifhed.—The reader, however, who has a tafte for this fpecies of the defultory and digreffive, and wifhes more for entertainment than inftruction, will find in thefe Excurfions fome fprightly fallies of imagination, fome amufing incidents, and fenfible obfervations on men and manners, which in his own excurfion to Windfor or elfewhere, if he has not the good fortune to meet with *an agreeable companion in a poft-chaife*, may ferve inftead of one, to amufe and divert him.

Profody made eafy. By the Rev. W. Nixon, *A. B. Mafter of the endowed School, at* Youghal, 8*vo.* 2*s.* Buckland.

The author lays down and illuftrates the common rules of profody, points out the manner of fcanning the odes of Horace, gives an account of the different forts of verfe ufed by the Roman poets, and makes fome obfervations on their beauties and defects.

This tract is extremely proper for fchool-boys, and all others, who wifh to know the ftructure of Latin verfe, or even to read that language with propriety.

In the Latin poets there are innumerable verfes, in which the general rules of profody are violated. Many of thefe are probably nothing more than inadvertencies in the authors themfelves, or errors in our prefent copies. In a treatife on this fubject, the groffer anomalies, we apprehend, fhould be reprefented, not as precedents, but as defects.

THE
CRITICAL REVIEW.

For the Month of *December*, 1781.

Philosophical Transactions, of the Royal Society of London. *Vol.*
LXXI. For the Year 1781. *Part* I. 4*to.* 7*s.* 6*d. fewed.*
L. Davis.

PRefixed to this part of the Philosophical Transactions is a
Speech, delivered to the Royal Society, on the 30th of
November, 1780, by their prefident, fir Jofeph Banks. The
incident which gave occafion to this addrefs, was the Society's
having that day affembled, for the firft time, in the new apartments, which have been granted it by his majefty. Sir Jofeph
celebrates the royal munificence with great zeal, in a ftrain
of merited panegyric, intermixed with fome reflexions tending
to animate the Royal Society in the profecution of fcience.
The Speech, being but fhort, we fhall infert it, for the gratification of our readers.

' The emotions of gratitude infpired by the very place in which,
by the munificence of our Royal Patron, we are now for the firft
time affembled, render it impoffible for me to neglect the opportunity which this feafon, when ye have been ufed to hear yourfelves addreffed from the chair, affords me, of offering my fmall
tribute of acknowledgement for a benefit fo eminently calculated to promote the honour and advancement of this fociety.

' Eftablifhed originally by the munificence of a royal founder !
foftered and encouraged fince that time by every fucceffive monarch who has fwayed the Britifh fceptre, ye have ever proved
yourfelves worthy the favour of your royal Protectors. A Newton, who pruned his infant wing under your aufpices, when his
maturer flights foared to worlds unmeafurably diftant, ftill thought

a place among you an honourable diftinction. A Newton's immortal labors, a Boyle, a Flamftead, a Halley, a Ray, and many others, of whom I truft it is needlefs to remind you, have made ample returns for the patronage of former monarchs.

'But bountiful as the encouragement ye have received from former patrons has ever been, the favors which fcience has, through your interceffion, received from his prefent majefty (whom God long preferve!) have eminently outdone their moft extenfive ideas of liberality. Ample funds, by him provided, have enabled you to reward men of extenfive knowledge and ability, for fpending whole years in the fervice of fcience; obferving twice the tranfit of the planet Venus over the difk of the fun. At your requeft, the publick defrayed the expence of conveying them to the moft diftant parts of the globe we inhabit, where the purpofes of their miffion, fo important to the fcience of aftronomy, could beft be fulfilled; while ye alone enjoy among your fellow-academies the reputation of having both fent and rewarded them.

'And more; thofe very donations were fo liberally planned by that attention to fcience which has ever diftinguifhed his prefent majefty's reign, and will for ever bear teftimony of his enlarged mind, and difpofition favorable to the advancement of true knowledge, that the furplus alone enabled you, with his royal approbation, to inftitute experiments on the attraction of mountains, amidft the barren and bleak precipices of the Highlands of Scotland, which then, for the firft time, beheld inftruments of the niceft conftruction tranfported to the fummits of their pathlefs crags, and men, ufed to other habitations, voluntarily refiding in temporary huts, eager to exprefs a grateful fenfe of their royal patron's liberality, by thus promoting to the utmoft the caufe of fcience, in which they were, under his protection, embarked.

'Gifts like thefe, unfolicited and unconditionally beftowed, might have fatisfied the impulfes even of a princely munificence; but not fo with our royal patron. Amply informed in every branch of real knowledge, he refolved to beftow a ftill more diftinguifhed mark of his favour on fcience which he loved, and in this his laft beft gift has fulfilled his royal refolution.

'Such a donation, fo fuited to our prefent profperous and flourifhing condition under his royal patronage and protection, is admirably calculated to increafe the refpect, great as it is, which ye have ever received from the learned of all Europe, placing you at once, in every point of fplendid accommodation, as much above all foreign academies, as the labors of your learned predeceffors had raifed you above them in literary reputation.

'Let then gratitude to a fovereign, from whom ye have received fuch confpicuous encouragement, engage you, by an application to a promotion of the fciences ye feverally poffefs, to

de-

deserve a continuance of his royal favor; to measure your future exertions by the standard of his princely liberality; and thus shew the world, that ye still are, as ye always have been, worthy the patronage of your king!'

The first article presents us with the Natural History and Description of the Tyger-cat of the Cape of Good Hope. By John Reinhold Forster, LL.D.—Dr. Forster distinguishes the genus of cat into three subdivisions. The first comprehends such as have long hair or manes on their necks: the second such as have remarkable long tails: and the third those which have a brush of hair on the tips of their ears, with shorter tails than the second subdivision. The doctor informs us, that after a minute examination of a tyger-cat, which was brought him at the Cape of Good Hope, he found its manners and economy perfectly analogous to those of our domestic cats. The description of this cat is accurately delivered in Latin, in the manner of Linnæus.

Art. II. Experiments and Observations on the specific Gravities and attractive Powers of various saline Substances. By Richard Kirwan, Esq. F. R. S.

Art. III. Account of the violent Storm of Lightning at East-bourn, in Sussex, Sept. 17, 1780; communicated by Owen Salusbury Brereton, Esq. F. R. and A. S.

Art. IV. An Account of the Harmattan, a singular African Wind. By Matthew Dobson, M. D. F. R. S. communicated by John Fothergill, M. D. F. R. S.—The harmattan is a periodical wind, which blows from the interior parts of Africa towards the Atlantic Ocean. It rises indiscriminately at any hour of the day, at any time of the tide, or at any period of the moon. It continues sometimes only a day or two. sometimes five or six days; and has been known to last fifteen or sixteen days. It blows with a moderate force, not quite so strong as the sea-breeze. Of the peculiar qualities of the harmattan, Dr. Dobson, who had his first information from Mr. Norris, gives the following account.

' A fog or haze is one of the peculiarities which always accompanies the harmattan. The gloom occasioned by this fog is so great, as sometimes to make even near objects obscure. The English fort at Whydah stands about the midway between the French and Portuguese forts, and not quite a quarter of a mile from either, yet very often from thence neither of the other forts can be discovered. The sun, concealed the greatest part of the day, appears only about a few hours about noon, and then of a mild red, exciting no painful sensation on the eye.

' As the particles which constitute the fog are deposited on the grass, the leaves of trees, and even on the skin of the negroes, so as to make them appear whitish, I recommended to Mr. Norris the ufe of a good microfcope, as this might poffibly difcover fomething concerning the nature of thefe particles. " I was prevented, fays Mr. Norris, by the bad ftate of my health from availing myfelf of the microfcope; neither could I difcover any thing by the tafte, or by expofing plates covered thinly with melaffes, for when I had dropped an acid or alkali into the water in which I had diffolved the melaffes, nothing followed to enable me to judge of the nature of the particles. Surely they cannot be infects, or animalculæ of infects? for we have no appearance of any thing produced from the myriads of them which are depofited on the earth. They do not flow far over the furface of the fea: at two or three miles diftance from the fhore the fog is not fo thick as on the beach; and at four or five leagues diftance it is intirely loft, though the harmattan itfelf is plainly felt for ten or twelve leagues, and blows frefh enough to alter the courfe of the current."

' Extreme drynefs makes another extraordinary property of this wind. No dew falls during the continuance of the harmattan; nor is there the leaft appearance of moifture in the atmofphere. Vegetables of every kind are very much injured; all tender plants, and moft of the productions of the garden, are deftroyed; the grafs withers, and becomes dry like hay; the vigorous ever-greens likewife feel its pernicious influence; the branches of the lemon, orange, aud lime trees droop, the leaves become flaccid, wither, and, if the harmattan continues to blow for ten or twelve days, are fo parched as to be eafily rubbed to duft between the fingers: the fruit of thefe trees, deprived of its nourifhment, and ftinted in its growth, only appears to ripen, for it becomes yellow and dry, without acquiring half the ufual fize. The natives take this opportunity of the extreme drynefs of the grafs and young trees to fet fire to them, efpecially near their roads, not only to keep thofe roads open to travellers, but to deftroy the fhelter which long grafs, and thickets of young trees, would afford to fkulking parties of their enemies. A fire thus lighted flies with fuch rapidity as 'to endanger thofe who travel: in that fituation a common method of efcape is, on difcovering a fire to windward, to fet the grafs on fire to leeward, and then follow your own fire. There are other extraordinary effects produced by the extreme drynefs of the harmattan. The covers of books, Mr. Norris informs me, even clofely fhut up in a trunk, and lying among his cloaths, were bent as if they had been expofed to the fire. Houfhold furniture is alfo much damaged: the pannels of doors and of wainfcot fplit, and any veneered work flies to pieces. The joints of a well-laid floor of feafoned wood open fufficiently to lay one's finger in them; but become as clofe as before on the ceafing of the harmattan. The feams alfo in the fides and decks of fhips are much injured and become very leaky, though the planks are two or three inches in thicknefs. Iron-bound cafks require the hoops to be frequently driven tighter; and a cafk of rum or brandy, with wooden hoops,

can

can scarcely be preserved; for, unless a person attends to keep it moistened, the hoops fly off.

' The parching effects of this wind are likewise evident on the external parts of the body. The eyes, nostrils, lips, and palate, are rendered dry and uneasy, and drink is often required, not so much to quench thirst, as to remove a painful aridity in the fauces. The lips and nose become sore, and even chapped; and though the air be cool, yet there is a troublesome sensation of prickling heat on the skin. If the harmattan continues four or five days, the scarf skin peels off, first from the hands and face, and afterwards from the other parts of the body, if it continues a day or two longer. Mr. Norris observed, that when sweat was excited by exercise on those parts which were covered by his cloaths from the weather, it was peculiarly acrid, and tasted, on applying his tongue to his arm, something like spirit of hart's-horn diluted with water.'

Art. V. Essay on a new Method of applying the Screw. By Mr. William Hunter, Surgeon; communicated by Lieutenant General Melville, F. R. S.—This new method of applying the screw consists in making a male screw move in a female one, there being one thread to the inch more in one than in the other, and is something similar in principle to Nonius's division of lines. The effect is, that for each turn of the handle, or of the male screw, the female screw will advance forward, only by the small fractional part of an inch, whose numerator is 1, and denominator the product of the two numbers of threads to an inch. Thus, if the former screw has 10 threads to an inch, and the latter 11; then each turn will advance the latter screw only ($\frac{1}{10} \times \frac{1}{11}$ or) $\frac{1}{110}$ of an inch. This contrivance may sometimes be useful, either in cases of great accuracy, or to raise very heavy weights to small heights. But the machinery will generally be complex, cumbersome, and expensive.

Art. VI. An Account of the Turkey. By Thomas Pennant, Esq. F. R. S. communicated by Joseph Banks, Esq. P. R. S.—After describing the turkey with great exactness, Mr. Pennant proves, by a variety of authorities, that it is a native of America.

Art VII. Account of a Nebula in Comâ Berenices. By Edward Pigott, Esq. In a Letter to Nevil Maskelyne, D. D. F. R. S. and Astronomer Royal.—The mean place of this new nebula is here determined to be in 191° 28′ 38″ declination, and 22° 53′ north declination, for April 20, 1779.

Art. VIII. Double Stars discovered in 1779, at Frampton-house, Glamorganshire. By Nathaniel Pigott, Esq. F. R. S. Foreign Member of the Academies of Brussels and Caen, and

Cor-

Correspondent of the Royal Academy of Sciences at Paris; communicated by Nevil Maskelyne, D. D. F. R. S. and Astronomer Royal.

Art. IX. An Account of the Ganges and Burrampooter Rivers. By James Rennel, Esq. F. R. S. communicated by Joseph Banks, Esq. P. R. S.—The Burrampooter has been but lately known in Europe as a capital river, yet it is here represented as longer and wider than the Ganges, to which it is very similar, both arising from the same mountains, and uniting a little before they enter the ocean at the bay of Bengal.

'The Ganges and Burrampooter rivers, together with their numerous branches and adjuncts, intersect the country of Bengal in such a variety of directions, as to form the most complete and easy inland navigation that can be conceived. So equally and admirably diffused are those natural canals, over a country that approaches nearly to a perfect plane, that, after excepting the lands contiguous to Burdwan, Birboom, &c. (which altogether do not constitute a sixth part of Bengal) we may fairly pronounce, that every other part of the country has, even in the dry season, some navigable stream within twenty-five miles at farthest, and more commonly within a third part of that distance.

'It is supposed, that this inland navigation gives constant employment to 30,000 boatmen. Nor will it be wondered at, when it is known, that all the salt, and a large proportion of the food consumed by ten millions of people are conveyed by water within the kingdom of Bengal and its dependencies. To these must be added, the transport of the commercial exports and imports, probably to the amount of two millions sterling per annum; the interchange of manufactures and products throughout the whole country; the fisheries; and the article of travelling.

'These rivers, which a late ingenious gentleman aptly termed sisters and rivals (he might have said twin sisters, from the contiguity of their springs), exactly resemble each other in length of course; in bulk, until they approach the sea; in the smoothness and colour of their waters; in the appearance of their borders and islands; and, finally, in the height to which their floods rise with the periodical rains. Of the two, the Burrampooter is the largest; but the difference is not obvious to the eye. They are now well known to derive their sources from the vast mountains of Thibet; from whence they proceed in opposite directions; the Ganges seeking the plains of Hindoostan (or Indostan) by the west; and the Burrampooter by the east; both pursuing the early part of their course through rugged vallies and defiles, and seldom visiting the habitations of men. The Ganges, after wandering about 750 miles through these mountainous regions, issues forth a deity to the superstitious, yet gladdened, inhabit-

ant

ent of Hindooftan. From Hurdwar (or Hurdoar) in latitude 30°, where it gufhes through an opening in the mountains, it flows with a fmooth navigable ftream through delightful plains during the remainder of its courfe to the fea (which is about 1350 miles) diffufing plenty immediately by means of its living productions; and fecondarily by enriching the adjacent lands, and affording an eafy means of tranfport for the productions of its borders. In a military view, it opens a communication between the different pofts, and ferves in the capacity of a military way through the country; renders unneceffary the forming of magazines; and infinitely furpaffes the celebrated inland navigation of North America, where the carrying places not only obftruct the progrefs of an army, but enable the adverfary to determine his place and mode of attack with certainty.

'In its courfe through the plains, it receives eleven rivers, fome of which are equal to the Rhine, and none fmaller than the Thames, befides as many of leffer note. It is owing to this vaft influx of ftreams, that the Ganges exceeds the Nile fo greatly in point of magnitude, whilft the latter exceeds it in length of courfe by one-third. Indeed, the Ganges is inferior in this laft refpect, to many of the northern rivers of Afia; though I am inclined to think that it difcharges as much or more water than any of them, becaufe thofe rivers do not lie within the limits of the periodical rains.

'The bed of the Ganges is, as may be fuppofed, very unequal in point of width. From its firft arrival in the plains at Hurdwar, to the conflux of the Jumnah (the firft river of note that joins it) its bed is generally from a mile to a mile and a quarter wide; and, compared with the latter part of its courfe, tolerably ftraight. From hence, downward, its courfe becomes more winding, and its bed confequently wider, till, having alternately received the waters of the Gogra, Soane, and Gunduck, befides many fmaller ftreams, its bed has attained its full width; although, during the remaining 600 miles of its courfe it receives many other principal ftreams. Within this fpace it is, in the narroweft parts of its bed, half a mile wide, and in the wideft, three miles; and that, in places where no iflands intervene. The ftream within this bed is always either increafing, or decreafing, according to the feafon. When at its loweft (which happens in April) the principal channel varies from 400 yards to a mile and a quarter; but is commonly about three quarters of a mile.'

The whole courfe of the river is then particularly defcribed, with its bed, the velocity of its current, its windings, and the caufes of them, &c. The curious particulars of the annual fwelling and overflowing of the Ganges are thus defcribed.

'It appears to owe its increafe as much to the rain water that falls in the mountains contiguous to its fource, and to the fources of the great northern rivers that fall into it, as to that which

falls

falls in the plains of Hindooftan ; for it rifes fifteen feet and a half out of thirty-two (the fum total of its rifing) by the latter end of June : and it is well known, that the rainy feafon does not begin in moft of the flat countries till about that time. In the mountains it begins early in April ; and by the latter end of that month, when the rain-water has reached Bengal, the rivers begin to rife, but by very flow degrees ; for the increafe is only about an inch per day for the firft fortnight. It then gradually augments to two and three inches before any quantity of rain falls in the flat countries ; and when the rain becomes general, the increafe on a medium is five inches per day. By the latter end of July all the lower parts of Bengal, contiguous to the Ganges and Burrampooter, are overflowed, and form an inundation of more than a hundred miles in width ; nothing appearing but villages and trees, excepting very rarely the top of an elevated fpot (the artificial mound of fome deferted village) appearing like an ifland.

‘ The inundations in Bengal differ from thofe in Egypt in this particular, that the Nile owes its floods entirely to the rain-water that falls in the mountains near its fource ; but the inundations in Bengal are as much occafioned by the rain that falls there, as by the waters of the Ganges ; and as a proof of it, the lands in general are overflowed to a confiderable height long before the bed of the river is filled. It muft be remarked, that the ground adjacent to the river bank, to the extent of fome miles, is confiderably higher than the reft of the country, and ferves to feparate the waters of the inundation from thofe of the river until it overflows. This high ground is in fome feafons covered a foot or more ; but the height of the inundation within, varies, of courfe, according to the irregularities of the ground, and is in fome places twelve feet.

‘ Even when the inundation becomes general, the river ftill fhews itfelf, as well by the grafs and reeds on its banks, as by its rapid and muddy ftream ; for the water of the inundation acquires a blackifh hue, by having been fo long ftagnant amongft grafs and other vegetables : nor does it ever lofe this tinge, which is a proof of the predominancy of the rain water over that of the river ; as the flow rate of motion of the inundation (which does not exceed half a mile per hour) is of the remarkable flatnefs of the country.

‘ There are particular tracts of land, which, from the nature of their culture, and fpecies of productions, require lefs moifture than others ; and yet, by the lownefs of their fituation, would remain too long inundated, were they not guarded by dikes or dams, from fo copious an inundation as would otherwife happen from the great elevation of the furface of the river above them. Thefe dikes are kept up at an enormous expence ; and yet do not always fucceed, for want of tenacity in the foil of which they are compofed.

‘ During

' During the fwoln ftate of the river, the tide totally lofes its effect of counteracting the ftream ; and in a great meafure that of ebbing and flowing, except very near the fea. It is not un-common for a ftrong wind, that blows up the river for any con-tinuance, to fwell the waters two feet above the ordinary level at that feafon : and fuch accidents have occafioned the lofs of whole crops of rice. A very tragical event happened at Luckipour in 1763, by a ftrong gale of wind confpiring with a high fpring tide, at a feafon when the periodical flood was within a foot and half of its higheft pitch. It is faid that the waters rofe fix feet above the ordinary level. Certain it is, that the inhabitants of a confiderable diftrict, with their houfes and cattle, were totally fwept away ; and, to aggravate their diftrefs, it happened in a part of the country which fcarce produces a fingle tree for a drowning man to efcape to.

' Embarkations of every kind traverfe the inundation : thofe bound upwards, availing themfelves of a direct courfe and ftill water, at a feafon when every ftream rufhes like a torrent. The wind too, which at this feafon blows regularly from the fouth-eaft, favours their progrefs ; infomuch, that a voyage, which takes up nine or ten days by the courfe of the river when con-fined within its banks, is now effected in fix. Hufbandry and grazing are both fufpended ; and the peafant traverfes in his boat, thofe fields which in another feafon he was wont to plow ; happy that the elevated fite of the river banks place the herbage they contain, within his reach, otherwife his cattle muft perifh. '

' The following is a table of the gradual increafe of the Ganges and its branches, according to obfervations made at Jellinghy and Dacca.

	At Jellinghy.		At Dacca.	
	Ft.	In.	Ft.	In.
' In May it rofe	6	0	2	4
June	9	6	4	6
July	12	6	5	6
In the firft half of Auguft	4	0	1	11
	32	0	14	3

' Thefe obfervations were made in a feafon, when the waters rofe rather higher than ufual ; fo that we may take 31 feet for the medium of the increafe.

' The inundation is nearly at a ftand for fome days preceding the middle of Auguft, when it begins to run off ; for although great quantities of rain fall in the flat countries, during Auguft and September, yet, by a partial ceffation of the rains in the mountains, there happens a deficiency in the fupplies neceffary to keep up the inundation. The quantity of the daily decreafe of the river is nearly in the following proportion : during the latter half of Auguft, and all September, from three to four inches ; from September to the end of November, it gradually leffens from three inches to an inch and a half ; and from November to the

the latter end of April, it is only half an inch per day at a medium. These proportions must be understood to relate to such parts of the river as are removed from the influence of the tides. The decrease of the inundation does not always keep pace with that of the river, by reason of the height of the banks; but after the beginning of October, when the rain has nearly ceased, the remainder of the inundation goes off quickly by evaporation, leaving the lands highly manured, and in a state fit to receive the feed, after the simple operation of plowing.'

The course of the Burrampooter is next described; in the other circumstances of its overflowing, &c. it is perfectly similar to the Ganges.

' On tracing this river in 1765, I was no less surprised, at finding it rather larger than the Ganges, than at its course previous to its entering Bengal. This I found to be from the east; although all the former accounts represented it as from the north: and this unexpected discovery soon led to enquiries, which furnished me with an account of its general course to within 100 miles of the place where Du Halde left the Sanpoo. I could no longer doubt, that the Burrampooter and Sanpoo were one and the same river: and to this was added the positive assurances of the Assamers, " That their river came from the north-west, through the Bootan mountains." And to place it beyond a doubt, that the Sanpoo River is not the same with the river of Ava, but that this last is the great Nou Kian of Yunan; I have in my possession a manuscript draught of the Ava River, to within 150 miles of the place where Du Halde leaves the Nou Kian, in its course towards Ava; together with very authentic information that this river (named Irabattey by the people of Ava) is navigable from the city of Ava into the province of Yunan in China.

' The Burrampooter, during a course of 400 miles through Bengal, bears so intimate a resemblance to the Ganges, except in one particular, that one description may serve for both. The exception I mean is, that, during the last 60 miles before its junction with the Ganges, it forms a stream which is regularly from four to five miles wide, and but for its freshness might pass for an arm of the sea. Common description fails in an attempt to convey an adequate idea of the grandeur of this magnificent object; for,

" ————— Scarce the muse
Dares stretch her wing o'er this enormous mass
Of rushing water; to whose dread expanse,
Continuous depth, and wond'rous length of course,
Our floods are rills ————
Thus pouring on, it proudly seeks the deep,
Whose vanquish'd tide, recoiling from the shock,
Yields to this liquid weight ————"   Thomson's Seasons.

' I have

' I have already endeavoured to account for the singular breadth of the Megna, by supposing that the Ganges once joined it where the Issamutty now does ; and that their joint waters scooped out its present bed. The present junction of these two mighty rivers below Luckipour, produces a body of running fresh water, hardly to be equalled in the old hemisphere, and, perhaps, not exceeded in the new. It now forms a gulf intersperfed with islands, some of which rival, in size and fertility, our Isle of Wight. The water at ordinary times is hardly brackish at the extremities of these islands ; and, in the rainy season, the sea (or at least the surface of it) is perfectly fresh to the distance of many leagues out.

' The bore (which is known to be a sudden and abrupt influx of the tide into a river or narrow strait) prevails in the principal branches of the Ganges, and in the Megna ; but the Hoogly River, and the passages between the islands and sands situated in the gulf, formed by the confluence of the Ganges and Megna, are more subject to it than the other rivers. This may be owing partly, to their having greater embouchures in proportion to their channels, than the others have, by which means a larger proportion of tide is forced through a passage comparatively smaller ; and partly, to there being no capital openings near them, to draw off any considerable portion of the accumulating tide. In the Hoogly or Calcutta River, the bore commences at Hoogly Point (the place where the river first contracts itself) and is perceptible above Hoogly Town ; and so quick is its motion, that it hardly employs four hours in travelling from one to the other, although the distance is near 70 miles. At Calcutta, it sometimes occasions an instantaneous rise of five feet : and both here, and in every other part of its track, the boats, on its approach, immediately quit the shore, and make for safety to the middle of the river.

' In the channels, between the islands in the mouth of the Megna, &c. the height of the bore is said to exceed twelve feet ; and is so terrific in its appearance, and dangerous in its consequences, that no boat will venture to pass at spring tide. After the tide is fairly past the islands, no vestige of a bore is seen, which may be owing to the great width of the Megna, in comparison with the passages between the islands ; but the effects of it are visible enough, by the sudden rising of the tides.'

Art. X. Astronomical Observations on the Rotation of the Planets round their Axes, made with a View to determine whether the Earth's diurnal Motion is perfectly equable. In a Letter from Mr. William Herschel of Bath, to William Watson, M. D. F. R. S.—These observations, of the planets Jupiter and Mars, are very curious, and seemingly accurate. They succeed very well for the latter planet, whose rotation on its axis is determined within 2 or 3 seconds of time. Mr. Herschel intends to continue those observations, which will enable

enable him to ascertain the point with a still greater degree of accuracy. After which he intends to make use of the resulting time of revolution, to examine the equability of the earth's rotation, which is made the standard for all other motions.

Art. XI. Some Account of the Termites, which are found in Africa and other hot Climates. In a Letter from Mr. Henry Smeathman, of Clement's Inn, to Sir Joseph Banks, Bart. P. R. S.——The termites are insects, called by most travellers white ants, and hitherto very imperfectly described. Mr. Smeathman observes, that Linnæus has classed this genus erroneously; placing it among the aptera, or insects without wings; though, in its perfect state, it has four wings without any sting. The author's description is curious, and seems to have been obtained by very attentive observation.

Art. XII. An Account of several Earthquakes felt in Wales. By Thomas Pennant, Esq. F. R. S. in a Letter to Sir Joseph Banks, P. R. S.

' Dear Sir,   Downing, Dec. 12, 1781.

' On Saturday last, between four and five in the evening, we were alarmed with two shocks of an earthquake; a slight one, immediately followed by another very violent. It seemed to come from the north-east, and was preceded by the usual noise; at present I cannot trace it farther than Holywell.

' The earthquake preceding this was on the 29th of August last, about a quarter before nine in the morning. I was forewarned of it by a rumbling noise not unlike the coming of a great waggon into my court-yard. Two shocks immediately followed, which were strong enough to terrify us. They came from the north-west; were felt in Anglesea, at Caernarvon, Llanrwst, in the isle of Clwyd south of Denbigh, at this house, and in Holywell; but I could not discover that their force extended any farther.

' The next in this retrograde way of enumerating these phenomena was on the 8th of September 1775, about a quarter before ten at night, the noise was such as preceded the former; and the shock so violent as to shake the bottles and glasses on the table round which myself and some company were sitting. This seemed to come from the east. I see in the Gentleman's Magazine of that year, that this shock extended to Shropshire, and quite to Bath, and to Swansea in South Wales.

' The earliest earthquake I remember here was on the 10th of April 1750. It has the honour of being recorded in the Philosophical Transactions, therefore I shall not trouble you with the repetition of what I have said.

' Permit me to observe, that I live near a mineral country, in a situation between lead mines and coal mines; in a sort of neutral tract, about a mile distant from the first, and half a mile from the last. On the strictest inquiry I cannot discover
that

that the miners or colliers were ever senfible of the fhocks under ground: nor have they ever perceived, when the fhocks in queftion have happened, any falls of the loofe and fhattery ftrata, in which the laft efpecially work; yet, at the fame time, the earthquakes have had violence fufficient to terrify the inhabitants of the furface. Neither were thefe local; for, excepting the firft, all may be traced to very remote parts. The weather was remarkably ftill at the time of every earthquake I have felt.'

Art. XIII. Extract of a Letter from the Right Honourable Philip Earl Stanhope, F. R. S. to Mr. James Clow, Profeffor of Philofophy in the Univerfity of Glafgow. Dated Chevening, February 16, 1777.—The chief improvement his lordfhip makes by this method [*], is to 'approximate to two roots at once, by one and the fame feries, continued backwards as well as forwards.'

Art. XIV. Extract of Two Meteorological Journals of the Weather obferved at Nain in 57° North Latitude, and at Okak in 57° 20/ North Latitude, both on the Coaft of Labradore. Communicated by Mr. De la Trobe.

This firft part of the volume concludes with the ufual Meteorological Journal kept at the Houfe of the Royal Society, by Order of the Prefident and Council, for the year 1780. From which it appears that the means of the whole year were as follows, viz. thermometer without 51,7; thermometer within 52,8; barometer 29,91; variation of the needle 22° 41' weft; and the whole quantity of rain 17¼ inches.

/ *Miscellanies by the Honourable* Daines Barrington. (*Concluded, from p.* 365.

IN our laft Review we gave our readers the fubftance of Mr. Barrington's tracts on the poffibility of reaching the north pole; and an account of his enquiry, whether the turkey was known before the difcovery of America: we now proceed to the remaining part of this publication, which confifts of the following mifcellaneous articles.

Effay II. On the Rein-Deer. [Rennthier, which is ufually pronounced rein-deer, fignifies an animal formed for running, from the Teutonic word *rennen, to run*. Bufching's Geog. vol. I. p. 345.]

It has been a generally received opinion, that the rein-deer will not live for any time fouth of Lapland, or that part of

---

[*] Concerning the roots of adfected equations.

North America, which, though of a more fouthern latitude, equals Lapland in the rigour of its climate. Our author produces feveral inftances to prove, that this is a vulgar error. He particularly mentions a buck-rein, which was kept near three years by Mr. Heyne, a merchant, in a clofe at Homerton near Hackney, and died fuddenly, having been in perfect health the preceding day, in 1773.

All defcribers of the rein-deer take notice of the cracking noife, which they make, when they move their legs. Hoffberg attributes this noife to their feparating, and afterwards bringing together the divifions of their hoofs : but he does not affign the caufe of their fo doing. Our author thinks, that, as thefe animals live in a country, which is covered with fnow for a great part of the year, they naturally feparate their hoofs, when their feet are to touch the ground, fo as to cover a larger furface, to prevent their finking ; and that when the leg of the animal is raifed, the hoof is immediately contracted ; and, by the collifion of its parts, occafions the fnapping, which is heard upon every motion of the rein.

Le Brun relates, that the chiefs of the Samoieds have fometimes fix or eight of them to draw their traineaus, and that they never fweat, notwithftanding their being often much preffed ; but pant with their tongues out, juft as grey-hounds do after a fevere courfe.

The lichen is their favourite food. Our author procured fome of it ; and conceives that it may be nourifhing either for man or beaft. We have much of the fame, he fays, on our own heaths.

III. On the Bat, or Refe-Moufe.

The moft interefting circumftance, relating to this animal, is its ftate of torpidity, during the winter. Mr. Cornifh, a gentleman whom our author mentions, at Totnes in Devonfhire, is, we are told, perfectly well acquainted with the lurking places of bats ; and can find them, at any time during the winter, particularly in a large cavern near Torbay.

A dozen of thefe bats were fent up, in their ftate of torpidity, to Mr. John Hunter, for diffection ; but they were unfortunately killed before they reached London, either by the motion of the carriage, by their not hanging in their ufual attitude, or by their being deprived of their proper temperature of air.

They were kept for fome time by Mr. Hunter, before he would abfolutely pronounce them to be dead ; and afterwards at fir Afhton Lever's, before they were *fet up*. But though they never fhewed any figns of life, yet their bodies did not putrify. The fame thing, fays our author, I had occafion to ob-

obferve, with regard to fome torpid martins, which were fent to me from Somerfetfhire, and which I wifhed Mr. Hunter to diffect. Thefe birds alfo did not revive, but no figns likewife of putrefaction appeared, though they were kept a confiderable time.

'Here it may be obferved, that a moderate heat, fuch as that of the bofom or hand, is the moft likely to bring torpid animals to life, which are often killed by being placed too near the fire, from the common prejudice, that one cannot have too much of a good thing.

'For a more immediate teft of life in the animal, it will fhrink either upon the touch, or holding a lighted candle near it.'

IV. On the fudden Decay of feveral Trees in St. James's Park.

It is well known, that Rofamond's Pond, as well as fome fmaller ones within the ifland of St. James's Park, have lately been filled up : and it is obferved, that every tree, which grew very near to their margins, has died within the enfuing year.

For this decay Mr. Barrington affigns the following reafons :
'When a tree is planted at a diftance from water, the roots fpread equally in every direction in order to receive the moifture, which is neceffary to carry on its growth and vegetation. When it is however placed very near to the water's edge, the roots on that fide are chiefly protruded, to meet with the nourifhment fo immediately at hand, and for the fame reafon, become vaftly larger than thofe, which are extended in any other direction. If therefore in procefs of time the water is dried up, the tree is left without any other fupply than that which is commanded by one which is furrounded with a dry foil, at the fame time that the principal roots are only to be found on one fide ; fo that the tree is deprived of at leaft half the nourifhment, which was neceffary for its fupport. But it is not only where ponds or ditches have been filled, that the trees in St. James's Park have fuffered, for many of the limes on the fides of the Mall are decaying very faft, and that from year to year, when they were before in a moft flourifhing ftate. I fhould fuppofe, that this alteration arifes from the central walk becoming convex inftead of concave, by a vaft quantity of frefh gravel, which has alfo been laid on the two fide walks. The confequence of which is, that almoft all the rain which falls never reaches the roots, having fo much a thicker furface to penetrate through, than when the limes were originally planted, as alfo by being carried off immediately to the fide drains, by the convexity of the Mall, in

its

its prefent ftate. Even under the moft favourable circumftances much rain muft fall to moiften an inch of foil, from
which the capillary parts of the roots are far removed, being
probably more than twelve times that depth.'

The decay of the limes in St. James's Park may perhaps
be owing to thefe caufes. But there is another circumftance,
which will have a very confiderable effect on the growth of
trees ; and it is this : when trees, efpecially large ones, are
planted, the workmen, who are employed in this bafinefs,
generally dig a hole in the ground to the depth of half a
yard, or more. And here the tree is fixed, with its roots
very near a dry, impenetrable gravel. In a courfe of years
the roots are at the ne plus ultra of all nourifhment, and neceffarily decay.——This abfurd mode of planting fruit-trees is
very often the caufe of their rufty appearance, and their early
decay ; which would be prevented, if the young trees were
planted on the furface, and a proper quantity of mould
thrown around them to cover the roots. The danger of their
being blown down by the wind may be eafily obviated by
ftakes, or fupporters, proportionable to the fize of the trees ;
and thefe fupporters would not be wanted for any confiderable
time, as the roots would foon extend themfelves through a
fertile foil.

V. On the periodical appearing and difappearing of certain Birds, at different Times of the Year.

In this tract the author does not pretend to deny, that a
bird or birds may fometimes fly from Dover to Calais, or over
any other fuch narrow ftrait ; or that there may be a periodical
flitting of certain birds from one part of a continent to another : the Royfton-crow, and rock-ouzel, furnifh inftances of
fuch a regular migration. What he chiefly contends for is,
that it feems to be highly improbable, birds fhould at certain
feafons, traverfe large tracts of fea, or rather ocean, without leaving any of the fame fpecies behind, but the fick or
wounded.

We fee certain birds in particular feafons, and afterwards
we fee them not : from this circumftance it is inferred, that
the caufe of their difappearance is, their having croffed large
tracts of fea.

Our author replies, that no well-attefted inftances can be
produced of fuch a migration. They who fend birds periodically acrofs the fea, being preffed with this very obvious
anfwer, have recourfe to two fuppofitions, by which they endeavour to account for their not being obferved by feamen during their paffage.

The

The first is, that they rise so high in the air that they become invisible. But unfortunately the rising to this extraordinary height, or the falling from it, is equally destitute of any ocular proof, as the birds being seen whilst crossing an ocean.

There is an objection to the hypothesis of birds passing seas at such an extraordinary height, arising from the known rarefaction of the air, which may possibly be inconvenient for respiration, as well as flight. If this were not really the case, one should suppose, says Mr. Barrington, that birds would frequently rise to such uncommon elevations, when they had no occasion to traverse oceans.

It has been urged by some, that the reason, why seamen do not regularly see the migration of birds, is, they choose the night and not the day for the passage.

Mr. Barrington answers: ' Though it may be allowed, that possibly birds may cross from the coast of Holland to the eastern coast of England, for example, during a long night, yet it must be dark nearly as long as it is within the Arctic circle to afford time for a bird to pass from the line to many parts of Europe, which M. de Buffon calculates may be done in about *eight* or *nine* days.

' If the passage happened in half the nights of the year which have the benefit of moon-light, the birds would be discovered by the sailors almost as well as in the day time, to which we may add that several supposed birds of passage (the fieldfare in particular) always call when on their flight, so that the seamen must be deaf, as well as blind, if such flocks of birds escape their notice.

' Other objections however remain to this hypothesis of a passage during the night.

' Most birds not only sleep during that time, but are as much incapacitated from distinguishing objects, as well as we are, in the absence of the sun: it is therefore inconceivable, that they should choose owl-light for such a distant journey.'

In this question the ornithologist ought to consider, that a journey of a night is as much as can well be allowed for one *stage* in the migration of birds. For birds want *food* and *rest*, as much as other animals ; and it seems impossible to conceive, that they should be able to support a constant exertion of their wings, for any longer space of time, without refreshment.

Our author proceeds to consider all the instances, which he has been able to meet with, of any birds being actually seen, whilst they were crossing any extent of sea.

Sir Peter Collinson, in a letter printed in the Philosophical Transactions (1760) says : ' Sir Charles Wager had frequently informed him, that in one of his voyages home in the spring, as he came into soundings in our channel, a great flock of swallows almost covered his rigging; that they were nearly spent and famished, and were only feathers and bones ; but being recruited by a night's rest, they took their flight in the morning.'

Mr. Barrington answers, 1. If these were birds, which had crossed large tracts of ice in their periodical migrations, the same accident must happen eternally, both in spring and autumn, which is not however pretended by any one. 2. The swallows are stated to be spent both by famine and fatigue ; and how, he asks, were they to procure any flies or other sustinence on the rigging of the admiral's ship, though they might indeed rest themselves.

Sir Charles informs us, that he was in the channel, and within soundings. These birds therefore were probably only passing from head-land to head-land ; and, being forced out by a strong wind, were obliged to settle upon the first ship they saw, or otherwise must have dropped into the sea ; which I make no doubt happens to many unfortunate birds, under the same circumstances.

These observations are applicable to every other instance of the like nature.

Having shewn the improbability of the foregoing hypothesis, with respect to swallows and other birds, the author endeavours to prove, that they remain in a torpid state during the winter.

But it may be said, that as the swallows have crowded the air during the summer, in every part of Europe, since the creation, and as regularly disappear in winter, why have not the instances of their being found in a sleeping state been more frequent ?

To this he answers, 1. that mankind have scarcely paid any attention to the study of natural history, till within these late years ; 2. that the common labourers, who have the best chance of finding torpid birds, have scarcely any of them a doubt, with regard to this point ; and, consequently, when they happen to see them in this state, make no mention of it to others, because they consider the discovery as neither uncommon, nor interesting to any one ; 3. that the instinct of secreting themselves, at the proper season of the year, likewise suggests to them its being necessary to hide themselves in such holes and caverns, as may elude the search of men, and every other animal, which might prey upon them.

Mr,

Mr. Barrington refers the reader to several well authenticated instances, mentioned in the Philosophical Transactions, Birch's History of the Royal Society, &c. from whence the fact seems to be fully ascertained ; and allowing this to be the case, he appeals to the partizans of migration, whether any instance can be produced, where the same animal is calculated for a state of torpidity, and, at the same time of the year, for a flight cross the ocean.

It may be objected, that, if swallows are torpid when they disappear, the same thing should happen with regard to other birds, which are not seen in particular parts of the year.

To this he replies, that some other birds, which are conceived to migrate, may be really torpid, as well as swallows. However, he supposes, that the notion, which prevails with regard to the migration of many birds, may most commonly arise from the want of observation, and ready knowlege of them, when they are seen on the wing, even by professed ornithologists. Thus the supposition of the nightingale being a bird of passage arises from not readily distinguishing it, when seen in a hedge, or on the wing.

In opposition to the opinion of those who contend for the migration of this bird, he observes, that it is scarcely ever seen to fly above twenty yards ; that though common in Denmark, Sweden, and Russia, as well as in England, it is never seen or heard in Scotland * ; that it can have no inducement for crossing from the continent to us ; and lastly, that it has been often seen in the winter.

There are certain birds, such as the snipe, woodcock, redwing, and fieldfare, which appear during the winter, but disappear during the summer ; and it may be asked, where such birds can be supposed to breed, if they do not migrate from this island.

In answer to this objection our author alleges, that the snipe constantly breeds in the fens of Lincolnshire, Wolmar forest, and Bodmyn downs ; that woodcocks, for reasons which he assigns, may not only continue with us during the summer, but also breed in large tracts of wood or bog, without being observed ; and that the fieldfare and redwing may probably remain with us in summer, without being attended to ; and particularly the redwing, which scarcely differs at all in appearance from the thrush.

The landrail is commonly supposed to migrate across the seas. But this, he thinks, is impossible. For when put up

---

* Q. Is this a fact ?

E e 2

by

by the fhooter, it never flies 100 yards ; its motion is exceffively flow, whilft the legs hang down like thofe of the water fowls, which have not web-feet, and which are known never to take longer flights. This bird is not very common with us in England, but is exceffively fo in Ireland, where it is called the corn-creak.

Now they who contend, that the landrail, becaufe it happens to difappear in winter, muft migrate acrofs oceans, are reduced to the following dilemma : they muft either fuppofe, that it comes from America, which is impoffible ; or, that it muft pafs over England in its way to Ireland, from the continent of Europe ; and if fo, no reafon can be given, why more of them are not obferved in this country.

VI. On the Torpidity of the Swallow-tribe when they difappear.

In this tract the author produces many well attefted inftances, in order to prove, that fwallows pafs the winter in a torpid ftate under water in ponds, rivers, &c. To thefe inftances we fhall add (as we happen to have the book before us) the teftimony of the celebrated Huetius, who afferts, that fwallows have been found in a torpid ftate, in hollow rocks, on the banks of the river Orne, near Caen in Normandy, ' immani numero,' in vaft numbers, hanging like clufters of grapes on a vine. Huet. de Reb. ad eum pertin. p. 98.

VII. On the prevailing Notions with regard to the Cuckow.

The principal notion here *controverted* is, that the cuckow neither hatches nor rears its young. Ariftotle feems to have been the author of this opinion. De Hift. Anim. ix. 29. There cannot, fays the author, be a ftronger proof, that the general notion about the cuckow arifes from what is laid down by Ariftotle, than the chapter which immediately follows, as it relates to the goatfucker, and ftates, that this bird fucks the teats of that quadruped. From this circumftance the goatfucker hath obtained a fimilar name in moft languages, though probably no one, who thinks at all about matters of this fort, continues to believe, that this bird fucks the goat, any more than the hedgehog does the cow.

By the way it may be obferved, that the notion of the porcupine fhooting its quills, the poifonous effect of the tarantula, and ants hoarding for winter, are errors of the fame nature.

The hedge-fparrow is generally fuppofed to be the fofter-parent of the cuckow. But the bare fact of a young cuckow being fed by a hedge-fparrow, or other bird, is, our author thinks, no proof, that the egg was hatched by fuch a dam ; becaufe, fays he, if fhe has young ones of her own, it appears

from

from many inftances of fociality in the brute creation, that fhe will probably take to this large foundling ; and much more fo, if fhe hath loft her own brood, or if they have forfaken her on being completely fledged.

' If the hedge-fparrow is a complete mother to the young cuckow, fhe muft not only difregard the removal of her own five eggs, but the colour of them ; for the cuckow's egg is not only much larger, but is of a dirty yellow, fpotted with black, whereas her own are of a fine pale blue.

' Again, all other neftlings, whilft callow, want to be covered by the plumage of the dam ; but how can this gigantic orphan receive fuch warmth from a hedge-fparrow ?

' The time moreover of the egg's being hatched is commonly in proportion to its fize ; the hedge-fparrow therefore would probably abandon it, fuppofing it to be addled.

' It will undoubtedly be urged, that all reafons from analogy are of little weight againft pofitive facts ; to which I moft readily affent. But though I have made many enquiries about this extraordinary notion, I never could hear evidence of any other circumftance to fupport it, except that the young cuckow had been fed by a fmall bird, which is by no means fufficient to prove, that it was alfo hatched by the hedge-fparrow. On the contrary, I have received feveral well attefted inftances of cuckows hatching and feeding their own neftlings.'

VIII. On the Linnæan Syftem.

In this tract Mr. Barrington takes notice of fome defects in the works of Linnæus, at the fame time acknowledging the diftinguifhed abilities, and the great merit of this celebrated naturalift.

He obferves, that his defcriptions are frequently obfcure, and fometimes unintelligible ; that by comprifing the animal kingdom of the whole globe, except infects, viz. beafts, birds, reptiles, and fifhes, in 532 pages, octavo, he has given us very little more than a mere vocabulary, that too much time is taken up in maftering the elements of this fyftem ; that a young fimpler cannot eafily find out the name of an unknown plant by the directions of Linnæus ; that plants can only be diftinguifhed, on his fyftem, while they are in flower ; that the chives and pointals are too minute, too uncertain in their number, and feldom in a ftate proper to be examined ; that his directions are ufelefs in a collection of dried plants, that his new appellations are perplexing to the difciples of all former botanifts, &c.

Moft of thefe remarks are certainly juft. The Linnæan fyftem has been admired, more on account of its novelty, than its utility. There is something curious in the idea of distinguishing plants by the organs of generation; but it is a provoking circumstance, that sometimes these organs cannot be distinguished without a careful dissection, and a microscope. Ease and simplicity are excellencies, to which the Linnæan system has no pretensions. Plants should be distinguished into classes by those parts, (their petals especially) which are large and plain.—There is not perhaps a better book for an English botanist than Hill's British Herbal.

IX. Particulars of an Agreement between the king of Spain and the Royal Society, for an Exchange of Natural Curiosities.

The animals of Hudson's Bay can only be procured by the king of Spain from England; and the natural productions of Peru, Chili, Buenos Ayres, and the Philippines, from the Spaniards. The Royal Society transmitted a considerable number of specimens to Madrid in 1773, but no return has yet been made to the Society on the part of his Catholic majesty.

X. An Account of Mozart, a very remarkable young Musician, Mr. Charles Wesley, Master Samuel Wesley, little Crotch, and the Earl of Mornington.

XI. Of the Deluge in the Time of Noah.

Objections to the supposition of an universal deluge:

'He must be a more ingenious architect than even bishop Wilkins, who can contrive a single vessel large enough for Noah and his family, the beasts, fowls, reptiles, and insects, of the whole globe, together with provisions for their sustenance, during the space of a twelvemonth; whilst the lives of each animal, in this confined state, must also have continued for that time, otherwise some genus or species must have been intirely destroyed, without a new creation.

' If we are to understand likewise the expression literally of *all*, the extirpation of the web-footed fowls would not have followed; nor of the water reptiles and insects.

' On the other hand, there must have been a new creation of either the salt or fresh-water fish, supposing the fluid which covered the face of the globe to have been either salt or fresh, as the former could not have lived a twelvemonth in water so much freshened, or the latter in an element become so much salter.

' How could the animals, almost peculiar to the arctic circle (a rein-deer for example), or those only found in America at present, have been procured for the ark, or insects in their different metamorphoses? How was the proper food also to be supplied for the animals of the whole globe, for a year, when many of them, particularly insects, only feed upon peculiar plants,

plants, which therefore muſt have continued to vegetate in part of the ark deſtined for a conſervatory. The animals again are directed to be male and female ; many of which, within the twelvemonth, would have procreated ; and from what ſtores on board the ark was this numerous offspring to be ſupported ?

' The deluge, if univerſal, likewiſe continuing for a twelvemonth, all the annual plants of the globe muſt have been deſtroyed, not to mention both ſhrubs and trees, many of which would have loſt all vegetative power, after they had been covered ſo long by water, either freſh or ſalt.'

The advocates for a general deluge, urge, that ſhells of marine animals are found on the tops of mountains, which could not be conveyed thither by any other method.

Our author anſwers, firſt, that ſuppoſing the whole globe to be covered with water, what could have been the inducement to the ſhell-fiſh, many of which perhaps cannot move, to deſert their proper habitation in the bed of the ſea, in order to tranſport themſelves to the top of an inland mountain, where they muſt immediately ſtarve for want of their uſual nouriſhment ?

2dly. That ſuch foſſils in the cabinets of virtuoſi are often reported by the ſeller to have been found in ſuch places, contrary to the real fact, as the ſpecimen, with many collectors, is on that account more valued.

3dly. That the ſuppoſed ſhells, impreſſions of plants, &c. are not always examined with ſufficient candor and accuracy.

And, laſtly, that ſubterraneous inſects may have occaſioned many of theſe ſtrong reſemblances to plants, or luſuſes, either by their claws, or antennæ, or perhaps by emitting a liquor, which may both excavate and diſcolour the ſtone, or other body, on which they may happen to work.

This hypotheſis, though our author has taken ſome pains to ſhew its probability, will certainly be reckoned among the ' luſuſes' of ingenious men.

The latter part of this tract is an explanation of the Moſaic account of the deluge. The point in controverſy depends principally upon the ſignification of the word *earth*. Our author ſuppoſes, that this term is to be confined to the country, where Noah lived ; and very rightly obſerves, that it is uſed in this limited ſenſe by many other writers, both ſacred and profane.

XII. The Hiſtory of the Gwedir Family, by Sir John Wynne, the firſt baronet of that name, who was born in 1553.

What

What feems to be moft interefting in this piece are fome anec-dotes and circumftances, which relate to the more immediate anceftors of the author, as they are ftrongly characteriftic of the manners and way of living in the principality, during that period. In other refpects, it has only the merit of a Welch pedigree.

XIII. A Letter intended for Dodfley's Mufeum, on the Englifh and French writers. The plan of this piece is taken from The Battle of the Books.

XIV. A Dialogue on the Ancient Tragedies, written at Oxford in 1746.

XV. Ohthere's Voyage, and the Geography of the 9th Century illuftrated.

Ohthere's Voyage to the Northern Seas is included in the Anglo-Saxon verfion of Orofius, tranflated and publifhed by Mr. Barrington in 1773.

When king Alfred * came to this part of Orofius's Geography, it is fuppofed, that he confulted Ohthere and Wulf-ftan, who had lived in the northern parts of Europe, which the ancients were little acquainted with, and took down this account from their own mouths.

This is a curious relique of antiquity. But the geography is obfcure and uncertain. And our northern travellers moft probably amufed his majefty with ftories of their own invention, the known privilege of travellers.

XVI. The Journal of a Spanifh Voyage, in 1775, to explore the Coaft of America, northward of California.

This account of an eight months navigation on the unfrequented coaft of America, to the latitude of 57° 57' will be a ufeful addition to geography, efpecially as Capt. Cook had fo few opportunities of examining the fame continent, having, it is faid, been prevented by unfavourable winds.—

In the courfe of thefe differtations the learned and ingenious author has taken occafion to explode feveral vulgar errors; for which he particularly deferves the thanks of every philofophical reader.

Hiftory of Quadrupeds. In two Volumes. 4to. 1 l. 11 s. 6 d. White.

IT cannot but afford great fatisfaction to all the lovers of natural knowledge, to fee a general Hiftory of Quadrupeds executed by fuch a mafter in that fcience as the author of Bri-

---

* See Crit. Rev. July, 1773.

tish Zoology. The work which he now prefents to the public, we are informed, was originally intended for private amufement, and as an index, for the more ready turning to any particular animal in M. De Buffon's voluminous Hiftory of Quadrupeds: but as it fwelled to a fize beyond the author's firft expectation, he was induced to communicate it to the world.

Though Mr. Pennant has erected his fyftem chiefly on the bafis of that of M. De Buffon, he is far from reftricting his refearches to the information delivered by that ingenious and agreeable author. For, by his own obfervations, as well as by thofe which have been communicated to him by his numerous friends, he has made great additions to the fubject. With how much judgment he has arranged the materials of this great work, will appear from his remarks on the fyftems of preceding naturalifts, and the particular method which himfelf has followed. Of the various fyftems which have been invented, he thus delivers his fentiments.

'The Synopfis of our illuftrious countryman, Mr. Ray, has been long out of print; and though, from his enlarged knowledge and great induftry one might well fuppofe his work would for fome time difcourage all further attempts of the fame fort, yet a republication of that Synopfis would not have anfwered our prefent defign: for, living at a period when the ftudy of natural hiftory was but beginning to dawn in thefe kingdoms, and when our contracted commerce deprived him of many lights we now enjoy, he was obliged to content himfelf with giving defcriptions of the few animals brought over here, and collecting the reft of his materials from other writers. Yet fo correct was his genius, that we view a fyftematic arrangement arife even from the chaos of Aldrovandus and Gefner. Under his hand the indigefted matter of thefe able and copious writers affumes a new form, and the whole is made clear and perfpicuous.

'From this period every writer on thefe fubjects propofed his own method as an example; fome openly, but others more covertly, aiming at the honour of originality, and attempting to feek for fame in the path chalked out by Mr. Ray; but too often without acknowleging the merit of the guide.

'Mr. Klein, in 1751, made his appearance as a fyftematic writer on quadrupeds, and in his firft order follows the general arrangement of Mr. Ray; but the change he has made of feparating certain animals, which the laft had confolidated, are executed with great judgment. He feems lefs fortunate in his fecond order; for, by a fervile regard to a method taken from the number of toes, he has jumbled together moft oppofite animals; the camel and the floth, the mole and the bat, the glutton and apes; happy only in throwing back the walrus, the feal, and the

manati,

manati, to the extremity of his fyftem: I fuppofe, as animals nearly bordering on another clafs.

' M. Briffon, in 1756, favoured the world with another fyftem, arranging his animals by the number or defect of their teeth; beginning with thofe that were toothlefs, fuch as the ant-eater, and ending with thofe that had the greateft number, fuch as the opoffum. By this method, laudable as it is in many refpects, it muft happen unavoidably that fome quadrupeds, very diftant from each other in their manners, are too clofely connected in his fyftem; a defect which, however common, fhould be carefully avoided by every naturalift.

' In point of time, Linnæus ought to have the precedence; for he publifhed his firft fyftem in 1735. This was followed by feveral others, varying conftantly in the arrangement of the animal kingdom, even to the laft edition of 1766. It is, therefore, difficult to defend, and ftill more ungrateful to drop any reflections on a naturalift, to whom we are fo greatly indebted. The variations in his different fyftems may have arifen from the new and continual difcoveries that are made in the animal kingdom; from his fincere intention of giving his fyftems additional improvements; and perhaps from a failing, (unknown indeed to many of his admirers) a diffidence in the abilities he had exerted in his prior performances. But it muft be allowed, that the naturalift ran too great a hazard in imitating his prefent guife; for in another year he might put on a new form, and have left the complying philofopher amazed at the metamorphofis.

' But this is not my only reafon for rejecting the fyftem of this otherwife able naturalift: there are faults in his arrangement of mammalia, that oblige me to feparate myfelf, in this one inftance, from his crowd of votaries; but that my feceffion may not appear the effect of whim or envy, it is to be hoped that the following objections will have their weight.

' I reject his firft divifion, which he calls primates, or chiefs of the creation; becaufe my vanity will not fuffer me to rank mankind with apes, monkies, maucaucos, and bats, the companions Linnæus has allotted us even in his laft fyftem.

' The fecond order of bruta I avoid for much the fame reafon: the moft intelligent of quadrupeds, the half reafoning elephant, is made to affociate with the moft difcordant and ftupid of the creation, with floths, ant-eaters, and armadillos, or with manaties and walrufes, inhabitants of another element.

' The third order of feræ is not more admiffible in all its articles; for it will be impoffible to allow the mole, the fhrew, and the harmlefs hedge-hog, to be the companions of lions, wolves, and bears: we may err in our arrangement,

" Sed non ut placidis coeant immitia, non ut
Serpentes avibus geminentur, tigribus agni."

' In his arrangement of his fourth and fifth orders we quite agree, except in the fingle article noctilio, a fpecies of bat, which hap-

happening to have only two cutting teeth in each jaw, is separated from its companions, and placed with squirrels, and others of that clafs.

' The fixth order is made up of animals of the hoofed tribe ; but of genera fo different in their nature, that notwithstanding we admit them into the fame divifion, we place them at fuch diftances from each other, with fo many intervening links and foftening gradations, as will, it may be hoped, leffen the fhock of feeing the horfe and the hippopotame in the fame piece. To avoid this as much as poffible, we have flung the laft into the back ground, where it will appear more tolerable to the critic, than if they were left in a manner conjoined.

' The laft order is that of whales : which, it muft be confeffed, have, in many refpects, the ftructure of land animals ; but their want of hair and feet, their fifh-like form, and their conftant refidence in the water, are arguments for feparating them from this clafs, and forming them into another, independent of the reft.

' But while I thus freely offer my objections againft embracing this fyftem of quadrupeds, let me not be fuppofed infenfible of the other merits of this great and extraordinary perfon : his arrangement of fifh, of infects, and of fhells, are original and excellent ; he hath, in all his claffes, given philofophy a new language ; hath invented apt names, and taught the world a brevity, yet a fulnefs of defcription, unknown to paft ages : he hath with great induftry brought numbers of fynonyms of every animal into one point of view ; and hath given a concife account of the ufes and manners of each, as far as his obfervation extended, or the information of a numerous train of travelling difciples could contribute : his country may triumph in producing fo vaft a genius, whofe fpirit invigorates fcience in all that chilly region, and diffufes it from thence to climates more favourable, which gratefully acknowledge the advantage of its influences.'

It may next be proper to lay before our readers the plan which Mr. Pennant has followed in the diftribution of quadrupeds.

' I copy, fays he, Mr. Ray, in his greater divifions of animals into hoofed, and digitated ; but, after the manner of Mr. Klein, form feparate genera of the rhinoceros, hippopotame, tapiir, and mufk. The camel being a ruminating animal, wanting the upper fore-teeth, and having the rudiments of hoofs, is placed in the firft order, after the mufk, a hornlefs cloven-hoofed quadruped.

' The apes are continued in the fame rank Mr. Ray has placed them, and are followed by the maucaucos.

' The carnivorous animals deviate but little from his fyftem, and are arranged according to that of Linnæus, after omitting the feal, mole, fhrew, and hedge-hog.

' The herbivorous or frugivorous quadrupeds keep here the

4 fame

fame ftation that our countryman affigned them; but this clafs comprehends befides, the fhrew, the mole, and the hedge-hog. The mole is an exception to the character of this order, in refpect to the number of its cutting teeth; but its way of life, and its food, place it here more naturally than with the feræ, as Linnæus has done. Thefe exceptions are to be met with even in the method of that able naturalift; nor can it be otherwife in all human fyftems; we are fo ignorant of many of the links of the chains of beings, that to expect perfection in the arrangement of them, would be the moft weak prefumption. We ought, therefore, to drop all thoughts of forming a fyftem of quadrupeds from the character of a fingle part: but if we take combined character, of parts, manners, and food, we bid much fairer for producing an intelligible fyftem, which ought to be the fum of our aim.

' The fourth fection of digitated quadrupeds, confifts of thofe which are abfolutely deftitute of cutting teeth, fuch as the floth and armadillo.

' The fifth fection is formed of thofe which are deftitute of teeth of every kind, fuch as the manis and ant-eater.

' The third and fourth orders, or divifions, are the pinnated and the winged quadrupeds; the firft takes in the walrus and the feals, and (in conformity to preceding writers) the manati. But thofe that compofe this order are very imperfect: their limbs ferve rather the ufe of fins than legs; and their element being for the greateft part the water, they feem as the links between the quadrupeds and the cetaceous animals.

' The bats again are winged quadrupeds, and form the next gradation from this to the clafs of birds; and thefe two orders are the only additions I can boaft of adding in this work.'

In this hiftory, Mr. Pennant gives the various fynonyms of each animal, with a concife and accurate defcription, and as full an account as could be collected, of their place, manners, and ufes.

As a fpecimen of the work, we fhall prefent our readers with a few detached paffages. The following is our author's account of the Corfican fpecies of fheep.

' The height of the male, to the top of the fhoulders was two feet and a half: irides a light yellowifh hazel: horns, ten inches and a half long, five and a half round at the bafe, twelve inches diftant between tip and tip: finus lacrymalis very long. Ears fhort and pointed; brown and hoary without, white within. Head fhort and brown; lower part of the cheeks black; fides of the neck tawny: lower part covered with pendant hairs fix inches long, and black. Body and fhoulders covered with brown hairs, tipped with tawny: on the middle of the fides a white mark pointing from the back to the belly. Belly, rump, and legs white; the laft have a dufky line on their infides. Tail

short s

short: scrotum (as common to all) pendulous, like that of a ram.

' The remains of Martino, a male animal of this kind, imported from Corsica by the illustrious defender of the liberties of his country, general Paoli, is now preserved in the Leverian Museum. It was of the age of four years at the time of its decease. Its horns are twenty-two inches long; the space between tip and tip near eleven; the girth near the base the same. This poor animal had the ill fortune to fall, in our land of freedom, into heavy slavery, and hard usage, in the latter part of his life, which stinted its growth, and prevented the luxuriancy of its horns; which ought, at its age, to have had the volutes of a large-horned ram, to have been fifteen inches round at the base, and to have resembled those of the painting by Oudry.

' The colours of this specimen differed a little from the others. On the front of the neck is a large spot of white. The shoulders were covered with black hairs; bright and glossy in a state of vigour. On each side of the back, near the loins, is a large bed of white. The eyes, when in health, large, bright, and expressive.

' The male, in its native country, is called mufro, the female mufra. They inhabit the highest part of the Corsican Alps, unless forced down by the snows into rather lower regions. They are so wild, and so fearful of mankind, that the old ones are never taken alive; but are shot by the chasseurs, who lie in wait for them.

' The females bring forth in the beginning of May, and the young are often caught after the dam is shot. They instantly grow tame, familiar, and attach themselves to their master. They will copulate with the sheep: there is now an instance in England of a breed between the ram of this species, and a common ewe. They are likewise very fond of the company of goats.

' In a wild state, they feed on the most acrid plants: and when tame will eat tobacco, and drink wine.

' Their flesh is savory, but always lean. The horns are used for powder-flasks, slung in a belt, by the Corsican peasants; and some are large enough to hold four or five pounds, of twelve ounces each.

' The Sardinians make use of the skins dressed, and wear them under their skirts, under the notion of preserving them against bad air. They also wear a surtout without sleeves, made of the same materials, which falls below the knees, and wraps close about their bodies. The skin is very thick, and might have been proof against arrows, when those missile weapons were in use. At present these surtouts are worn to defend them against briars and thorns, in passing through thickets. In all probability they are the very same kind of garment as the mastruca fardorum, which the commentators on Cicero suppose to have been

8

made

made of the ſkins of the mufro : and the Maſtrucati Latrunculi the people who wore them. This is in a manner confirmed, as they are ſtill in uſe with the latre or banditti of the iſland ; who find the benefit of them in their impetuous ſallies out of the brakes of the country, on the objects of their rapine.

'The race is at preſent extinct in Spain ; but is ſtill found in Sardinia and Corſica : whether it exiſts ſtill in Macedonia, we are ignorant. It is found in theſe days in great abundance, but confined to the north-eaſt of Aſia, beyond the lake Baikal, between the Onon and Argun, and on the eaſt of the Lena, to the height of lat. 60 ;· and from the Lena to Kamſchatka ; and perhaps the Kurili iſlands. It abounds on the deſert mountains of Mongalia, Songaria, and Tartary. It inhabits the mountains of Perſia, and the north of Indoſtan. The breed once extended further weſt, even to the Irtis ; but as population increaſed, they have retired to their preſent haunts, ſhunning thoſe of mankind.

'It is probable that theſe animals are alſo found in California. The Jeſuits who viſited that country in 1697, ſay that they found a ſpecies of ſheep as big as a calf of a year or two old, with a head like that of a ſtag, and enormous horns like thoſe of a ram ;· and with a tail and hair ſhorter than that of a ſtag. This is very likely, as the migration from Kamtſchatka to America is far from being difficult.

'They were once inhabitants of the Britiſh iſles. Boethius mentions a ſpecies of ſheep in St. Kilda, larger than the biggeſt he-goat, with tails hanging to the ground, and horns longer, and as thick as thoſe of an ox. This account, like the reſt of his hiſtory, is a mixture of truth and fable. I ſhould have been ſilent on this head, had I not better authority ; for I find the figure of this animal on a Roman ſculpture, taken out of Antoninus's wall near Glaſgow. It accompanies a recumbent female figure, with a rota or wheel, expreſſive of a via or way, cut poſſibly into Caledonia ; where theſe animals might, in that early age, have been found. Whether they were the objects of worſhip, as among the ancient Tartars, I will not pretend to ſay : for among the graves of thoſe diſtant Aſiatics, brazen images, and ſtone figures of their argali, or wild ſheep, are frequently found.

'Their preſent habitations, in Sibiria, are the ſummits of the higheſt mountains, expoſed to the ſun, and free from woods. They go in ſmall flocks ; copulate in autumn, and bring forth, in the middle of March, one, and ſometimes two young. At that ſeaſon the females ſeparate from the males, and educate their lambs ; which when firſt dropped are covered with a ſoft grey curling fleece, which changes into hair late in the ſummer. At two months age the horns appear, are broad, and like the face of an ax. In the old rams they grow of a vaſt ſize. They are ſometimes found of the length of two Ruſſian yards, meaſured along the ſpires ; weigh fifteen pounds apiece ; and are ſo capacious as to give ſhelter to the little foxes, who find them accidentally fallen in the wilderneſs.'

The

The subsequent quotation is selected from the account of the antelope, for the sake of the reference which it contains.

' A. with upright horns, twisted spirally, surrounded almost to the top with prominent rings; about sixteen inches long, twelve inches distance between point and point: in size, rather less than the fallow deer or buck: orbits white: white spot on each side of the forehead: colour, brown mixed with red, and dusky: the belly and inside of the thighs white: tail short, black above, white beneath. The females want horns.

' Inhabits Barbary. The form of these horns, when on the scull, is not unlike that of the ancient lyre, to which Pliny compares those of his strepsiceros. The brachia, or sides of that instrument, were frequently made of the horns of animals, as appears from ancient gems. Monfaucon has engraven several.

' To convey the idea of this structure, I caused the figure of one to be engraved, taken from the fifth volume of the Philosophical Transactions abridged, tab. xiv. p. 474. I prefer this to many other figures, as the shell of a tortoise forms the base; which gave rise to the beautiful comment on this passage, in Horace, by Doctor Molyneux.

" O Testudinis auree
Dulcem que strepitum, Pieri temporas !
O mutis quoque piscibus
Donatura cygni, si libeat, sonum."

' The art of giving to dumb fishes the voice of a swan, was thought a strange idea, till that gentleman pointed out that a tortoise made part of the lyre; which animal was by the ancients ranked in the class of fish: and even gave the name of χελυς to that species of musical instrument. Horace again invokes his lyre by an address to the tortoise; which flings light on a seven-stringed one preserved in the supplement to Monfaucon.

" Tuque testudo resonare septem
Callida nervis,
Nec loquax olim neque grata."

Mr. Pennant thus describes the Scythian antelope, which is one of the most remarkable species.

' A. with horns distant at the base, and with three curvatures; the last pointing inward. Stand a little reclining: the greatest part annulated: ends smooth. Colour a pale yellow. Are semipellucid: length about eleven inches.

' Head rather large. Nose in the live animal much arched and thick: very cartilaginous: divided lengthways by a small furrow: end as if truncated.

' Ears small: irides of a yellowish brown. Neck slender: prominent about the throat. Knees guarded by tufts of hair.

' The hair, during summer, is very short: grey mixed with yellow: below the knees darker. Space about the cheeks whitish:

forehead

forehead and crown hoary, and covered with longer hairs. Under side of the neck and body white.

' Winter coat long, rough, and hoary.

' Tail four inches long: naked below; above cloathed with upright hairs, ending with a tuft.

' Size of a fallow-deer.

' Females destitute of horns.

' These animals inhabit all the deserts from the Danube and Dnieper to the river Irtish, but not beyond. Nor are they ever seen to the north of 54 or 55 degrees of latitude. They are found therefore in Poland, Moldavia, about mount Caucasus, and the Caspian sea, and Sibiria, in the dreary open deserts, where salt-springs abound, feeding on the salt, the acrid and aromatic plants of those countries, and grow in the summer-time very fat: but their flesh acquires a taste disagreeable to many people, and is scarcely eatable, until it is suffered to grow cold after dressing.

' The females go with young the whole winter; and bring forth in the northern deserts in May. They have but one at a time; which is singular, as the numbers of these animals are prodigious. The young are covered with a soft fleece, like new-dropt lambs, curled and waved.

' They are regularly migratory. In the rutting-season, late in autumn, they collect in flocks of thousands, and retire into the southern deserts. In the spring they divide into little flocks, and return northward at the same time as the wandering Tartars change their quarters.

' They very seldom feed alone; the males feeding promiscuously with the females and their young. They rarely lie down all at the same time: but by a providential instinct some are always keeping watch: and when they are tired, they seemingly give notice to such which have taken their rest, who arise instantly, and as it were relieve the centinels of the preceding hours. They thus often preserve themselves from the attack of wolves, and from the surprize of the huntsmen.

' They are excessively swift, and will outrun the swiftest horse or greyhound: yet partly through fear, for they are the most timid of animals, and partly by the shortness of their breath, they are very soon taken. If they are but bit by a dog, they instantly fall down, nor will they even offer to rise. In running they seem to incline on one side, and their course is so rapid that their feet seem scarcely to touch the ground.

' They are during summer almost purblind; which is another cause of their destruction. This is caused by the heat of the sun, and the splendor of the yellow deserts they are so conversant in.

' In a wild state they seem to have no voice. When brought up tame, the young emit a short sort of bleating, like sheep.

' The males are most libidinous animals: the Tartars, who have sufficient time to observe them, report that they will copulate

pulate twenty times together; and that this turn arises from their feeding on a certain herb, which has most invigorating powers.

' When taken young, they may easily be made tame: but if caught when at full age, are so wild and so obstinate as to refuse all food. When they die, their noses are quite flaccid.

' They are hunted for the sake of their flesh, horns, and skins, which are excellent for gloves, belts, &c. The huntsmen always approach them against the wind, least they should smell their enemy: they also avoid putting on red or white cloaths, or any colours which might attract their notice. They are either shot, or taken by dogs; or by the black eagle, which is trained to this species of falconry.

' No animals are so subject to vary in their horns; but the colour and clearness will always point out the animal to which they belong.

' This probably was the animal called by Strabo κολος, found among the Scythæ and Sarmatæ, and an object of chace with the ancient inhabitants. He says it was of a size between a stag and a ram, and of a white colour, and very swift. He adds, that it drew up so much water into its head, through its nostrils, as would serve it for several days in the arid deserts: a fable naturally formed, in days of ignorance, from the inflated appearance of its nose.'

We shall next present our readers with the account of the elk, or moose-deer.

' A male of this species, and the horns of others, having been brought over of late years, prove this, on comparison with the horns of the European elk, to be the same animal. But the account that Josselyn gives of the size of the American moose has all the appearance of being greatly exaggerated; asserting, that some are found twelve feet or thirty-three hands high. But Charlevoix, Dierville, and Lescarbot, with greater appearance of probability, make it the size of a horse, or an Auvergne mule, which is a very large species; and the informations also that I have received from eye-witnesses, make its height from fifteen to seventeen hands. The writers who speak of the European kind, confine its bulk to that of a horse. Those who speak of the gigantic moose, say, their horns are six feet high; Josselyn makes the extent from tip to tip to be two fathom; and La Hontan, from hearsay, pretends that they weigh from 300 to 400 lb. notwithstanding he says, that the animal which is to carry them is no larger than a horse. Thus these writers vary from each other, and often are not consistent with themselves. It seems then that Josselyn has been too credulous, and taken his evidence from huntsmen or Indians, who were fond of the marvellous; for it does not appear that he had seen it. The only thing certain is, that the elk is common to both continents; and that the American, having larger forests to range in, and more luxuriant food, grows to a larger fize than the European.

' In America they are found, though rarely, in the back parts of New England; in the peninfula of Nova Scotia, and in Canada; and in the country round the great lakes, almoft as low fouth as the Ohio. In Europe they inhabit Lapland, Norway, Sweden, and Ruffia; in Afia, the N. E. parts of Tartary and Siberia, but in each of thefe continents inhabit only parts, where cold reigns with the utmoft rigour during part of the year.

' They live amidft the forefts, for the conveniency of browzing the boughs of trees; by reafon of the great length of their legs, and the fhortnefs of their neck, which prevent them from grazing with any fort of eafe, they often feed on water-plants, which they can readily get at by wading; and M. Sartafin fays, they are fo fond of the anagyris foetida, or ftinking bean trefoil, as to dig for it with their feet, when covered with fnow.

' They have a fingular gait; their pace is a high fhambling trot, but they go with vaft fwiftnefs; in old times thefe animals were made ufe of in Sweden to draw fledges; but as they were frequently acceffary to the efcape of murderers and other criminals, the ufe was prohibited under great penalties. In paffing through thick woods, they carry their heads horizontally, to prevent their horns being entangled in the branches. In their common walk they raife their fore-feet very high; that which I faw ftepped over a rail near a yard high with great eafe.

' They are very inoffenfive animals, except when wounded, or in the rutting-feafon, when they become very furious, and at that time fwim from ifle to ifle, in purfuit of the females. They ftrike with both horns and hoofs. Are hunted in Canada during winter, when they fink fo deep in the fnow as to become an eafy prey: when firft unharboured, fquat with their hind parts, make water, and then go off in a moft rapid trot: during their former attitude, the hunter ufually directs his fhot.

' The flefh is much commended for being light and nourifhing, but the nofe is reckoned the greateft delicacy in all Canada: the tongues are excellent, and are frequently brought here from Ruffia: the fkin makes excellent buff leather: Linnæus fays, it will turn a mufket-ball: the hair which is on the neck, withers, and hams, of the full-grown elk, is of great length, and very elaftic; is ufed to make matreffes. The hoofs were fuppofed to have great virtues in curing epilepfies. It was pretended, that the elk, being fubject to that difeafe, cured itfelf by fcratching its ear with its hoof.

' The elk was known to the Romans by the name of alce and machlis: they believed that it had no joints in its legs; and, from the great fize of the upper lip, imagined it could not graze without going backward.

' Before I quit this fubject, it will be proper to take fome notice of the enormous horns that are fo often found foffil in Ireland,

and

and which have always been attributed to the moose deer: I mean the moose deer of Joſſelyn; for no other animal could poſſibly be ſuppoſed to carry ſo gigantic a head. Theſe horns differ very much from thoſe of the European or American elk; the beam, or part between the baſe and the palm, is vaſtly longer: each is furniſhed with a large and palmated brow antler, and the ſnags on the upper palms are longer. The meaſurements of a pair of theſe horns are as follow: from the inſertion to the tips, five feet five inches; the brow antlers eleven inches; the broadeſt part of the palm, eighteen; diſtance between tip and tip, ſeven feet nine: but theſe are ſmall in compariſon of others that have been found in the ſame kingdom. Mr. Wright, in his Louthiana, tab. xxii. book III. gives the figure of one that was eight feet long, and fourteen between point and point. Theſe horns are frequent in our Muſeums, and at gentlemen's houſes in Ireland: but the zoologiſt is ſtill at a loſs for the recent animal. I was once informed by a gentleman long reſident in Hudſon's Bay, that the Indians ſpeak of a beaſt of the moofe kind (which they call waſkeſſer) but far ſuperior in ſize to the common one, which they ſay is found 7 or 800 miles S. W, of York Fort. If ſuch an animal exiſted, with horns of the dimenſions juſt mentioned, and of proportionable dimenſions in other parts, there was a chance of ſeeing Joſſelyn's account verified: for if our largeſt elks of ſeventeen hands high carry horns of ſcarcely three feet in length, we may very well allow the animal to be thirty-three hands high which is to ſupport horns of 3 or 400 lb. weight. But from later enquiries, I find that the waſkeſſer of the Indians is no other than the animal we have been deſcribing.'

From Mr. Pennant's accurate and extenſive knowledge of natural hiſtory, and from the information which he has received, not only from preceding writers on that ſubject, but from printed voyages of the beſt authorities, and from living voyagers, foreign and Engliſh; not to mention the Britiſh Muſeum, or that of Sir Aſhton Lever, ſo highly applauded by this ingenious naturaliſt; from all thoſe conſiderations, the preſent work may be juſtly conſidered as the completeſt ſyſtem of the hiſtory of quadrupeds, hitherto publiſhed: and to render it the more uſeful, as well as pleaſing, it is enriched with a great number of beautiful engravings.

Uncertainty of the preſent Population of this Kingdom; deduced from a candid Review of the Accounts lately given of it by Dr. Price, on the one Hand, Mr. Eden, Mr. Wales, and Mr. Howlett, on the other. 8vo. 6d. Richardſon *and* Urquhart.

THE author of this pamphlet founds his opinion upon a review of the accounts lately given by Dr. Price, on one hand; and by Mr. Eden, Mr. Wales, and Mr. Howlett, on

the

the other, respecting the population of this country.   According to Dr. Price's estimate, the inhabitants of England and Wales must be short of five millions; but the other writers on this subject make the number much more considerable. Mr. Howlett, in particular, supposes it to amount to between eight and nine millions.   The author of the present pamphlet expresses a strong suspicion of the accuracy of many of the articles in Mr. Howlett's tables of total and returned houses.   That this apprehension is well-grounded, the very proportion, between the houses said to be returned, and the total number, renders it, he thinks, extremely probable.   For this proportion is not greatly different from that between the number of houses charged at the tax-office, and the whole number returned there; the former being to the latter considerably less than as three to four.

‘ Now, admitting, says he, that some of the articles in Mr. Howlett's tables are correct, authentic, and rightly stated, as they probably are; the proportion, with respect to the remainder, would, I fancy, be nearly the same as that now mentioned.

‘ This striking analogy, however, is not my only ground of suspicion.   I have discovered, with regard to one place, that the fact is really as I have hinted.   The number of houses said to be returned in the parish alluded to is 96, the total 198. A correspondent, on whose veracity I can safely depend, assures me, that these 198 are all in the parish duplicate, and that the 96 are those which are charged or assessed.   As Mr. Howlett has suffered, either his precipitation or his inattention to mislead him in one instance, and as strong marks of suspicion accompany many of his other articles, he will, I presume, readily excuse me, if I either do not admit his very sanguine and flattering conclusions, without great caution and considerable deductions; or if I deny that he has, in particular, here evinced, that our present numbers are between eight and nine millions, or that their increase has been more than one-third since the Revolution.’

The following remarks on the register-evidence, which was adduced by Mr. Howlett, are worthy of attention.

‘ With respect to the proofs of either absolute or relative population derived from parish registers, which are generally deemed so decisive and satisfactory, they appear to me, of all others, the most precarious and uncertain.   The degrees of mortality prevalent at different æras, the number of dissentients or separatists from the state religion, the correctness and fidelity with which the registers themselves are kept; must all be well ascertained before their information can be at all depended

pended upon. The varying ratio of mortality alone may fometimes render all comparifon ufelefs for the purpofe in queftion. When the peftilence raged quite over Europe, and, in the courfe of a year or two, fwept almoft half its inhabitants into the grave, had the annual average amount of births and deaths for ten or fifteen years been taken, and a judgment thence formed of its actual population, we muft have concluded it to have been vaftly greater than it was fifty years before or after; whereas it is indubitably certain that it was on the contrary, prodigioufly lefs. Should we examine the parochial records of mortality in our own country for ten years, in that part of the laft century, in which near fifty-thoufand perfons died of the plague in our metropolis alone, and the fame dreadful diftemper fent death into every quarter of the nation, we fhould be led to imagine that our inhabitants were more numerous than before or fince; as not only the burials were vaftly augmented, but, for obvious reafons, the baptifms likewife. But allowing the ratio of mortality at the two periods between which we want to draw a parallel to remain nearly the fame, yet a further difficulty ftill arifes from the different number of feparatifts from the eftablifhed worfhip, who are feldom entered in the parochial regifters. Carry this refearch into France. You will, perhaps, find the Proteftants not a third part fo many as they were at the Revolution; and I am ftrongly inclined to believe, that that increafed population the French writers, with fuch colour and plaufibility, fo much boaft of, is a mere deception, owing very much, if not entirely, to this circumftance alone. Bring the enquiry back into England; the Papifts are incomparably fewer at prefent than a hundred years ago; and as to the Diffenters, their diminution is fo great and ftriking, that it is even among themfelves a common topic of complaint and lamentation; and with regard to the carelefs inaccuracy with which the regifters were formerly kept, every one that confults them will be immediately convinced.'

One of the arguments advanced by Mr. Howlett, in favour of the rapid progrefs of population in the northern counties, was the vaft number of chapels of eafe, which have been erected within thefe thirty years. But this author affirms, on what he confiders as the moft authentic intelligence, that, in confequence of this multiplication of chapels, it is no uncommon thing for baptifms (and fometimes perhaps burials) to be entered twice; firft in the chapel-regifter, and afterwards, for greater fecurity, in that of the mother church. Hence the aftonifhing excefs of the baptifms over the burials in fome parifhes, frequently even to more than double.

The

The author concludes, as follows, by mentioning the collateral teſtimony, conjunctly with which, he is ready to admit the evidence of parochial regiſters.

‘ That I may not be thought too ſceptical, or diſpoſed to indulge an abſurd degree of incredulity, I ſhall be perfectly ſatisfied with the regiſter-evidence, even though the ſeveral qualifications neceſſary to render it a complete ground to eſtimate our relative numbers, ſhould not be fully attainable, provided it nearly correſponds with the deficiency of the ſurveyors’ returns of houſes, and with the proportion of men allotted to the triennial ſervice of the national militia. This deficiency and this proportion will indeed be extremely different, not only in different counties, but even in different parts and diviſions of the ſame county. The average, however, ariſing from the aggregate of correct and well-authenticated information from two or three principal towns, and thirty or forty villages and country-pariſhes in every province throughout the nation, and taken perfectly at a venture, will aſcertain theſe points with all deſirable preciſion. If the computations fairly formed from theſe two data mutually agree with each other, and with the regiſter teſtimony of advanced population, we may be as fully convinced of our increaſed numbers, and may be nearly as ſure of what is their preſent actual amount, as from the moſt correct and accurate ſurvey. But if, on the contrary, they all totally differ, and if in particular the deficiency in the ſurveyors’ returns does not exceed fifty, or even a hundred thouſand, we muſt be forced to admit the painful idea of depopulation, and ſhall have nothing to do but to make the beſt of it.’

If Mr. Wales and Mr. Howlett continue their reſearches, the remarks thrown out by this writer will be worthy of their notice; and we ſhould be glad to ſee that thoſe gentlemen have evinced, as nearly as poſſible, the accuracy of their general computation, upon principles the moſt fair, unexceptionable, and deciſive.

The Queſtion conſidered, Whether Wool ſhould be allowed to be exported, when the Price is low at Home, on paying a Duty to the Public? By Sir John Dalrymple, *Bart.* 8vo. 6d. Cadell.

THE queſtion agitated by this judicious writer is a matter of great importance in political economy, and merits the moſt deliberate inveſtigation. To determine it with the greater certainty, ſir John Dalrymple ſets out with ſtating ſome general

neral propofitions, apparently juft, and which may ferve as firft principles in the profecution of the enquiry. Thofe propofitions are as follows;

' I. That the exportation of raw materials is a gain to a country, in proportion to the quantity of induftry employed in producing them, of the fhipping employed in exporting them, and of the value got for them in return.

' II. That it is more advantageous to a country, to work up its own raw materials into manufactures, to be confumed at home or exported abroad, than to export them to foreign countries for the ufe of their manufactures; and, confequently, that a wife nation may prohibit the exportation of its raw materials, to the extent of its ability to work them up at home with advantage.

' III. But if, from any circumftances, either of war or of peace, a country cannot, at a particular period, find a vent for the manufacture as it ufed to do, then a continuance of the prohibition to export the raw material feems impolitic; becaufe, if the raw material, which cannot be manufactured at home, be not allowed to be exported abroad, it muft be left to perifh. But this prohibition will be doubly impolitic, if the material thus left to perifh, be of a nature to have coft much money in producing, and be of fo great value, that the profit of the farmer, and the rent-roll of the landlord, depend upon it; and, confequently, the revenue of the ftate, and the induftry of the people, both of which are intimately connected with the greater or lefs quantity of money in the hands of the farmer and landlord.

' IV. If any doubt fhould arife, whether there be fuch a redundancy in the raw material, as difables the manufacturer to work it up with a good profpect of a market, then the infallible teft to find out the truth is, to enquire into the ftate of the price of the raw material. When there is a redundancy, the price will be low; when there is not, it will be high. Thus the barometer of price will eafily and infallibly point out when the raw material fhould, and when it fhould not, be allowed to be exported.

' V. If a nation fhould think of fubmitting to prohibit the exportation of a raw material, left it fhould ferve the manufactures of another country; that is to fay, fhould inflict a certain evil upon itfelf, from the hopes of inflicting a very uncertain evil upon its neighbours; it ought to be very fure that thefe neighbours cannot be fupplied with the raw material elfewhere, either within themfelves or from others.

' VI. If the raw material prohibited to be exported, be in great requeft with other nations, it will be fmuggled abroad,

not-

notwithstanding the prohibition. If the experience of ages has proved that this cannot be prevented, with respect to wool at least, it seems, at the first blush of the proposal, more wise to permit it to be exported, on paying a duty to the state, than to be making daily and vain complaints, that it is exported without paying any. But whether that first impression ought, or ought not to be indulged, will deserve the consideration of every landed and every commercial man in the kingdom, of the meanest beggar, as well as of the king and his parliament.'

The intelligent author next proceeds to give his reasons, why parliament should allow wool to be exported from Great Britain, when the price is low, on paying a duty to the public. That our readers may be the better enabled to judge of the subject, we shall lay before them the whole of those considerations.

' Reason I. The redundancy of wool is at present so great in Britain, that it is sunk in many places 50 per cent. and in very few places less than 30 per cent. If not allowed to be exported, that superfluity must either perish, or, being pressed into a glutted market, must sink still lower the price even of that portion which can be manufactured.

' Reason II. Anciently the English paid their chief attention to the fleece of the sheep, because it was the chief object of price. In ancient records, the value of the whole sheep bears no proportion to his wool. At present, in most countries, people pay attention to the carcase alone, because the fleece is no longer the object of price. But if the value of wool was allowed to be raised, by presenting to it two markets instead of one; that is to say, both the home and foreign, instead of the home alone; the quality of wool, which like other objects of art and of nature is capable of improvement, would be improved. The power of English industry, when not damped by mistaken policies, is beyond that of all nations. The great increase in the length, the weight, and the quality of the fleeces made by the gentlemen of Lincolnshire, even within these thirty years, shews the extent to which the improvement of English wool might be carried. Spanish rams are more easily to be transported from Spain into England, than Spanish horses; and yet these last, though prohibited to be exported, find their way from the one country into the other. At some period, and that not a distant one, the wool of Britain might come to rival the wool of Spain in its quality. It is a mistake to think that all the wool of Spain is fine. We are apt to think so, because all the wool that comes to us from Spain, we see to be fine. But the fact is, that as the

king

king of Spain has a duty of near 18d. upon every pound of wool exported, none but the very finest is sent abroad, often not more than a small part of the very finest of the fleece. In many parts of Spain they are as attentive to the breed of their sheep, as they are to the chastity of their wives, or as we are to the breed of our race-horses. They carry their sheep from province to province for proper food and climate, according to the different seasons of the year. The code of laws concerning the flocks and fleeces of Spain makes a folio volume; and there is a great law officer, with a court of justice, to whom the care of seeing the regulations of that code executed, is intrusted. But in the few parts of Spain, where no attention is paid to the breed, and where the sheep are kept upon the same pasture round the peasants houses all the year, as is done in most parts of Old Castile, the fleeces are as miserable, though in the finest climate of the world, as in the worst hills of Scotland. In ancient times, the wool of England was in as much estimation at European markets as the wool of Spain. But the Spaniards, by allowing their wool to be exported, led their people to improve it; while the English, by prohibiting it to be exported, led their people to neglect it. Remove the artificial obstruction, and nature and industry will bring things to their ancient state again. A tax upon the exportation of English wool will, in one respect, operate exactly in the same manner that a tax upon the exportation of wool from Spain has operated; for, in order to escape the weight of the tax, merchants will export only the finest kinds of wool, and the wool-growers knowing this, will vie with each other who shall produce the finest.

‘ Reason III. The prohibition to export wool defeats its own object. As it confines the wool-grower to one market, it sinks the price; sinking the price, it causes a demand from foreign countries; causing a demand from foreign countries, it tempts the smuggler to export; and, by this circle, it is the real cause of that very thing which it is intended to prevent. But this is not all: the man who smuggles one cargo abroad, will smuggle another home; and to decrease his risk, and increase his profit, his new cargo will be of the least bulk, and the highest value he can get; and consequently will, to a degree not very easily estimable, hurt the industry and the revenue of his country. Let it be inquired, from what coasts the greatest quantity of English wool has been run to France, and to what coasts the greatest quantity of French goods have been run to England, and they will be found to be the same. Is a regulation, which under its wings has fostered up a system of smuggling, and strengthened it by the mutual dependance

of

of an exporting and an importing trade, of no confideratioe
to a nation, whofe old taxes, when defeated, muft be fupplied by new ones, upon manufacture, trade, money, and
land ?

' Reafon IV. Since then it is impoffible to prevent the exportation of our wool, the difpute feems to refolve into this
queftion, whether it be beft to allow the fair trader to export
it, on paying a duty to the public, or to fubmit to the fmuggler
exporting it, without paying any ? If the exportation be permitted, and the duty confequently levied only when the price
is low, the two following confequences will follow :—1ft,
When there is a redundancy of wool, more than is manufactured at home, it will be exported, to the profit of the
landholder ; and 2dly, It will produce a large revenue, to the
profit of the ftate.

' Reafon V. Every argument for encouraging the exportation of corn when price is low, applies equally to the exportation of wool when price is low, with two advantages on the
fide of the laft of thefe mæafures.   For firft, if it be imprudent
to fupply our enemies with a raw material for their manufacture at an advanced price, it feems more imprudent to
fupply them with food, the firft principle of all manufactures,
at a lower price than we eat it ourfelves ; and fecondly, it
feems ftrange that a duty fhould be refufed to be accepted on
the exportation of the one, when a bounty is not fcrupled to
be beftowed on the exportation of the other.'

To the reafons above delivered, the judicious baronet afterwards enumerates a variety of poffible objections, all of
which he endeavours to remove by clear, explicit, and extremely forcible anfwers.   The latter being of confiderable
length, we fhall only fpecify the objections, which are ranked
under five diftinct heads.   ' If there be a redundancy of wool,
the natural remedy is to turn pafture land into corn land.—
A permiffion to export wool, would raife the price of wool
too high ; and confequently, would hurt the manufacturing,
to ferve the landed intereft.—A mixture of Englifh wool is
abfolutely neceffary in the fabric of foreign woollens ; to
fupply them with wool, is therefore to promote their manufactures at the expence of our own.—The woollen manufactures of Spain have been kept down, by the latitude given to
the exportation of wool.—If a tax be laid on the exportation
of wool, it will either continue to be fmuggled, to avoid the
tax, or it will not be exported at all.'

Sir John Dalrymple, in fupport of his reafons, and anfwers
to objections, adduces a number of facts, which tend to confirm the opinion he entertains on this fubject.   From authorities

thorities cited in the pamphlet, he obferves, that before the prohibition to export wool took place in England at the Ref_toration, and in Scotland at the Union, the average price of wool was far higher in both countries than it has been fince the prohibition : that the exportation of woollen manufacture from England has not been greater, all circumftances con_fidered, fince the prohibition took place than it was before; and in Scotland has been lefs : that fince the prohibition took place, the quantity of wool fmuggled abroad has been im_menfe : that in ancient times, the Englifh wool was in as great requeft abroad as the Spanifh : and that, at the clofe of the laft century, it was computed, that one-fifth of the land rents in England was paid by wool.

On a fubject which is liable to be viewed in different lights, by the woollen manufacturers and the landed intereft, it muft give pleafure to all men of public fpirit, to behold this im_portant queftion treated with fuch perfpicuity as it is by fir John Dalrymple ; whofe judicious obfervations will, we hope, conduce to eftablifh a uniformity of fentiment in a matter of great national importance.

A complete Digeft of the Theory, Laws, and Practice of Infurance. By John Wefkett. *Folio. 2l. 5s. in boards.* Richardfon *and* Urquhart.

IN a Preliminary Difcourfe, publifhed a few years fince, Mr. Wefkett delineated the great diforders which prevail in the affairs of infurance, explained their principal caufes, and pro_pofed methods for their better regulation and prevention. The author has now completed his elaborate work, which is conveniently digefted in an alphabetical form, under fuch heads as relate to infurance, in all the variety of circumftances. Mr. Wefkett delivers not only the moft prudential rules and cautions, but reports of decided cafes, with the neceffary forms of obligation, in contracting to infure againft hazards at fea. The fubject being too technical to excite the attention of the greater part of our readers, it may be fufficient to give them, by a fpecimen, an idea of the manner in which it is treated. For this purpofe, we fhall felect the article *Infurance,* as being of a general nature.

‘ The various matters which relate to infurance, being treated of diftinctly under their feveral refpective heads throughout this work, it will fuffice to fpeak here of the fubject in general.

‘ The civilians have laboured much in their enquiries upon the nature of the contract of infurance ; “ whether it be fponfio, con_tractus qui re conftet, ftipulatio, fidejuffio, litterarum obligatio, emptio-

emptio-venditio, locatio, focietas, mandatum, and whether it be contractus innominatus vel nominatus?"—But, all this is frivolous and mere fubtility : it is fufficient to know that infurance is a contract by which the infurer promifes to the infured, or him who hath intereft in the fhip, cargo, or thing which is infured (for otherwife it is not an infurance, but a wager) to guarantee or indemnify him from all the loffes and damages which fhall happen thereto, without fraud or fault of the infured, by unavoidable accidents, or dangers of the fea, during the voyage, or during the time of the rifque, according to the tenor of the contract, or policy; in confideration of a fum, called premium, paid by the infured to the infurer.—I offer this definition of infurance, as more adequate and complete than any I have met with; and as comprehending that of Loccenius, Stypmannus, Straccia, Scaccia, Targa, Kuricke, Bornier, and all the efteemed authors who have treated of it.

' Grotius calls it " Contractus, in facto praeftandae indemnitatis circa cafus fortuitos averfio periculi;" and obferves that it was unknown to the ancients : De jur. bel. & pac. lib. ii. cap. 12. fect. 3.—Gerard Malynes, in his Lex Mercatoria; Molloy, De jure maritimo, and feveral other Englifh authors, feem to favour a contrary opinion, founded on a paffage of Suetonius, in Vita Claudii, cap. 18. which alludes fomewhat to infurance : but the learned civilian and fenator Langenbeck, of Hamburgh, in his annotations on infurances, has very judicioufly and evidently fhewn that the meaning of Suetonius was no more than this; that in time of public danger, whenever any private man's property fhould be made ufe of for the fervice of the commonwealth, the lofs and damage of the private perfon were to be made good by the public : this is founded in juftice and equity; and is followed at this time by all governments that are guided by equitable principles : but it cannot be parallel with the infurance here treated of; which is a matter of choice, and for conveniency, between private perfons.—Concerning infurance of this nature we meet with nothing older than an ordinance made at Barcelona, mentioned in Cafa Regis's Confolato del Mare, or a treatife on the fea-laws of Oleron, which, though without date, by fome facts it recites, feems to have been made about the year 1435; and, by the preamble to this ordinance, it appears that not many others had preceded it, fince it begins with thefe words; " Whereas in times paft but few ordinances of infurance have been made; which defect wanted correction, and amendment, &c." but in 1481, the crown of Arragon being united to the Spanifh monarchy by the marriage of Ferdinand, the Catholic, with Ifabella, heirefs of Caftile, the Catalans became fubjected to the laws of Spain, and therefore no further notice is to be taken of their particular laws at Barcelona.—The next remarkable ordinance is one made at Florence in 1523, which is ftill in force at Leghorn : then follows the celebrated one of Philip II. of Spain. 1556.

                                                            ' Ac-

'According to Stypmannus, Cleirac's Guidon, and many other authors, the contract of maritime insurance, passed from the Italians amongst the Spaniards: afterwards into Holland; and then became in use amongst all commercial nations.

'Monf. Savary says, the Jews were the first who introduced the practice of insurance about 1183.—Being driven from France they made use of this way to avoid the risquing entirely the loss of their effects; but, the current practice of insurance was first established in England.—Dict. du Citoyen.

'Whoever was the first contriver of it, it has for many ages been practised in this kingdom; and is supposed to have been introduced here jointly with its twin brother, exchanges, by some Italians from Lombardy, who at the same time came to settle at Antwerp, and among us; and this being prior to the building the Royal-Exchange, they used to meet in the place where Lombard-street now is, at a house they had, called the pawn-house, or Lombard, for transacting business; and as they were then the sole negociators of insurance, the policies made by others in after times had a clause inserted that " they should be of as much force and effect as those heretofore made in Lombard-street."—As insurances in time grew more general in England, the legislature, by stat. 43 Eliz. cap. 12. erected a court called the Court of Policies of Assurance, for deciding all disputes and differences concerning them in a summary way; with an office for making and registering of policies, which was kept on the west side of the Royal-Exchange; but this did not exclude others from making insurances, in whose policies were added, immediately after the above-mentioned clause, the words following " or in the Royal-Exchange or any where else;" and the whole still remain in the policies now in use.

'This branch of business was originally confined to maritime affairs solely; but by modern laws or customs, insurances are much extended, and may be made as follows, viz.—on divers kinds of merchandises; on ships or part of ships; by the month, or for a time stipulated, or to one single port, or out and home, with liberty to touch at the different places mentioned in the policy, or for a trading voyage; on the freight, or hire of ships; on the money for fitting out of ships: on bottomry, or money borrowed on the keel of a ship, or on the goods to be shipped on board her, called respondentia; on ships and their cargoes jointly;—on the profit expected by the goods; in some places, on interest or no interest, i. e. without further proof of interest than the policy, and on the rise or continuance of the current price of merchandises;—on houses, furniture, warehouses, cellars, and the value of goods laid up therein, against danger from fire (for which purpose there are in London, several societies and offices erected, with a limitation to this branch only) on fisheries, and the bounties to ships employed therein; on the lives of men, and their liberty; on cattle: on lotteries; also on goods sent by land, or by hoys, or lighters, &c. on rivers;—and, in general, on every kind of property or interest, in whatsoever situation, liable to any risque of loss or damage :—the whole according to the circumstances agreed upon and understood by the parties, and under the restrictions of the customs, usages, laws, and ordinances, of the respective countries, in which the contract is made.

'Every person may insure, who by the laws of his country has a right to dispose of his property : but in some places where ordinances relating to insurances are in force, many persons are excepted ; particularly those concerned either in the management or direction of them : as insurance-brokers, commissioners, and secretaries of any chambers, or tribunals, for judging of differences that may arise in this branch of business ; since they ought all to be men strictly impartial : nor in any country, whatsoever, except England, are brokers permitted to insure.

'Notwithstanding all ancient, and some modern ordinances relating to insurance, enjoin the insured, in explicit terms, to run part of the risque themselves ; nay, in some cases, that are likely to give occasion to fraud, forbid insuring at all ; yet such injunctions and prohibitions are commonly evaded, and seldom long complied with : the custom of overlooking or dispensing with the disposition of the law in those respects has crept in every where.

'Insurances promote and support trade and navigation, as thereby the risques of diligent, industrious, and inventive persons, are so lessened, that they may engage even in important undertakings : it is easily understood how the public is benefited hereby : and by taking such precautions, as making insurance, a greater share of confidence is acquired amongst individuals :—but, as the best institutions are subject to abuse, certain bounds and regulations are necessary, which, whilst they give such latitude as may promote and encourage trade, ought not to be so extremely wide as that ill consequences may ensue.   That this consideration should be attended to in enacting all laws and ordinances relating to insurances, is not to be controverted ; nor that it should also be had in view, in the explanation and application of those laws to particular cases.

'The learning relating to marine insurances hath of late years been greatly improved by a series of judicial decisions, which have now established the law in such a variety of cases, that (if well and judiciously collected) they would form a very complete title in a code of commercial jurisprudence : but, being founded on equitable principles, which chiefly result from the special circumstances of the case, it is not easy to reduce them to any general heads in mere elementary institutes : thus much may however be said ; that, being contracts, the very essence of which consists in observing the purest good faith and integrity, they are vacated by any the least shadow of fraud or undue concealment : and, on the other hand, being much for the benefit and extension of trade, by distributing the loss or gain among a number of adventurers, they are greatly encouraged and protected both by common law and acts of parliament.—2 Black. Comm. 451.

'For

' For a more comprehenfive view of this fubject, the nature of divers commercial, maritime, and other matters which have affinity therewith, muft alfo be well underftood ; and indeed, the fenfe of the marine law, as well as the eftablifhed cuftoms and ufages of traders, as they concern owners, freighters, mafters of fhips, mariners, &c.—for there is frequently fo neceffary a dependency and connection between all thefe matters, and fuch an involution of circumftances, that the evidence, in regard to cafes of infurance, cannot be come at, nor a right judgment made, without taking many, and fometimes, perhaps, all of thefe things into due confideration.

' It is notorious to all the mercantile world that, as the Englifh infurers pay more readily and generoufly than any others, moft infurances are done in England : we infure at lower rates than other nations, becaufe we have more bufinefs of this kind, and the fmallnefs of our profit is compenfated by the frequency ; the cheapnefs of infurance, and the eagernefs of foreigners to infure here, reciprocally contribute to each other : we are often applied to, becaufe we infure at an eafy rate ; and we can infure at an eafy rate, becaufe we are often applied to.

' In Holland, France, Sweden, and moft other countries, they may not infure the property of enemies.'

The remark with which this quotation concludes, naturally fuggefts the notice of that important controverfy, ' Whether it be right, advantageous, or even legal, to infure an enemy's fhips, or merchandifes, in time of war or hoftilities ?' Mr. Weſkett prefents us with an abftract of all the arguments which have been urged for and againft the practice, and alfo makes feveral interefting obfervations on this important fubject.

This work has been compiled with great care and induftry, by one who is evidently a mafter of the fubject.—It abounds with proofs of extenfive reading, as well as of mature reflexion, and judicious remarks ; and if the completeft fyftem of infurance, that has hitherto been compofed, be entitled to praife, the prefent ufeful Digeft muft meet with the approbation of the commercial world.

Cui Bono? Or, an *Inquiry, what Benefits can arife either to the* Englifh *or the* Americans, *the* French, Spaniards, *or* Dutch, *from the greateft Victories, or Succeffes, in the prefent War. Being a Series of Letters addreffed to* M. Necker, *late Controllergeneral of the Finances in* France. *By* Jofiah Tucker, D. D. 8vo. 2s. Cadell.

SINCE the commencement of the prefent difpute with America, this ingenious author has often attempted to convince the nation, that the profecution of the war was repugnant to its interefts ; and that Britain ought, in good policy, to permit the independency of her colonies. Having failed in his reiterated applications for this purpose to his own country, he now addreffes the French, whom he would alfo perfuade of their political error, in expecting any beneficial confequences from the adverfity, or even the total fubjection of England. The following extract contains the principal parts of his arguments on this fubject.

'The former letter being only an introduction, we are now coming to the main fubject. Poor England is fubdued by the combined forces of France and her allies. Perhaps, indeed, fhe may not be fo abfolutely conquered, as to be annexed as a province to the French empire,—neverthelefs fo totally ruined as to become a bankrupt, and to make a moft defpicable figure both in the political and commercial world.—Or, if you would chufe an abfolute fubjection rather than a partial one, the difference between the one condition and the other is not fo very material, but that this alfo may be granted for argument's fake. England therefore is no longer an independant ftate, but a province to France, and to be governed by a vice roy of the grand monarch!—can you afk for more?

'What then is to be the confequence of this mighty change?—And what effects are to follow, in the courfe of trade, and in the fyftem of politics, from this grand revolution?—Refpecting trade, it is evident to a demonftration, that were a tradefman, or a fhopkeeper to be afked, whether it is his interest, that his richeft cuftomers and beft paymafters fhould become bankrupts and beggars? he would give you a very fhort anfwer. Perhaps likewife he would be tempted to afk in his turn,—" Do you mean, Sir, to infult my underftanding, or to exprefs your own ignorance by afking fuch a foolifh queftion?" But it feems, public trading nations are to proceed by oppofite methods, and by maxims of trade and commerce, quite contrary to thofe of individuals. Bodies politic are to ufe every effort in their power to beggar their cuftomers firft, and to trade with them afterwards, the wifeft courfe: fo that what would have been the height of folly and abfurdity in the one cafe, not to fay, wickednefs and immorality,—is to be confidered in the other as the depth of prudence, forefight, fagacity, penetration, or what you pleafe.—Here therefore, let us begin our accounts, and open our books debtor and creditor between one commercial nation and another.

'The Englifh, when a great and rich people, bought vaft quantities of the choiceft wines and brandies which France could produce; and they were known to be the beft of cuftomers by paying for them in ready money, and even by advancing fums aforehand!—But when thefe dealers fhall be reduced to the loweft ebb of want and indigence,—they will buy more wines and brandies than ever they did, and become better cuftomers than they were before. This is penetration! this is fagacity!

'Again, the Englifh, when in great profperity, and overflowing

flowing with riches, were remarkably vain and oftentatious: and their females in particular (as it was natural for the fex) vied with each other in all the parade of finery. Hence they were induced, and by their wealth they were enabled to buy the richeft filks and velvets, and the moft elegant gold and filver laces, that could be wrought in France: for nothing was thought to be too coftly, provided it came from your country. In fhort, French fafhions were the ftandards for drefs; French cooks taught the laws of eating; and French milliners, taylors, frizeurs, and dancing-mafters prefcribed the rules of good-breeding and politenefs. But when thofe happy, wifhed for times fhall come, when England is to be ftripped of all its riches, then thefe quondam good cuftomers will buy more filks, mote brocades, more gold and filver lace, and more every thing than ever they did before,—becaufe they will have nothing to pay: and the whole tribe of cooks, milliners, taylors, frizeurs, perfumers, &c. &c. will think themfelves fuperlatively happy in working gratis for beggared Englifh.—This again is another fpecimen of confummate wifdom, and deep penetration!'

In the third letter, the reverend author reverfes his former reprefentation, and having endeavoured to prove, that it is the true intereft of France to have Great Britain a rich cuftomer, *and not a poor one,* he next proceeds to demonftrate that the profperity of France is fubfervient to that of Great Britain. Dr. Tucker labours particularly to expofe the unreafonablenefs of the jealoufy of trade between thofe two nations, and to fhew the inefficacy of that paffion for obtaining any good end. He obferves, that even the pretences for national jealoufies between France and England, are much lefs plaufible than thofe which might have arifen between any two neighbouring countries on the globe.

' Thus, for example, the genius of a Frenchman, nationally confidered, is quick and lively, rapid and defultory; that of an Englifhman penetrating and thoughtful, methodical and correct. In the one fancy is predominant, in the other judgment. The Frenchman's brilliant fancy leads him to excel in almoft all the works of ornament and fhew: the Englifhman's folid judgment may be traced in the manufacture of fuch goods as are fitteft for general ufe and convenience. A Frenchman wifhes to ftrike the eye of the fpectator at the firft glance; an Englifhman ftrives to call forth his attention to examine the goodnefs of the work, and the fkill and contrivance of the workman. Thefe obfervations have been often made: indeed they are very obvious. Why then is not the proper inference deduced from them?—An inference of fo much confequence to the peace and happinefs of mankind? Namely, that fuch different talents and capacities cannot, properly fpeaking, be rivals to each other; for they act in different fpheres, and tend to different ends and ufes. Therefore there is fo much the lefs colourable pretext for national jealoufy between France and England, refpecting trade, inafmuch as there can hardly be a national competition between them.'

In the fifth letter, the author ftates the cafe between England and America, fuppofing the former to be victorious. Three things, he obferves, are the object of the prefent conteft. Firft, we propofe to recover our loft trade with the colonies. Secondly, we hope, that when a reconciliation fhall take place, the Americans will be perfuaded to bear fome fhare in the general expences of the empire. And thirdly, we conceive, that by their fubmiffion we fhall recover our national glory. We fhall lay before our readers the author's arguments on the firft of thofe heads.

' And firft we propofe the recovery of our trade. Trade, Sir, is a very vague term; and may ftand for any commercial intercourfe between nation and nation, or between man and man, however carried on. But, in the place before us, the term muft fignify the exportation of Britifh manufactures into America, and the importation of American produce into Britain. This exportation, and this importation, it feems, we have loft: and war and victory are propofed as the propereft of all meafures for the reparation of our loffes. Now it happens very unluckily for the advocates for the prefent war, that both thefe propofitions are egregioufly falfe;—Falfe, I mean, in the fenfe by them intended. For we have no otherwife loft our trade with America, than as both the Americans, and ourfelves are become much the poorer, and therefore fo much the worfe cuftomers to each other, by reafon of thofe enormous expences, which the war has occafioned:—At the fame time, that the price of the goods and commodities of the refpective countries is prodigioufly enhanced to the confumers;—enhanced, I fay, on account of higher freights, higher infurances, and greater rifques;—and above all on account of thofe vaft profits which foreigners with their neutral bottoms gain at prefent, by being the fole agents, factors, and carriers between the two countries.

' This being the cafe, and fuch the difadvantages on both fides, is it to be wondered at, that the trade between England and America fhould not be at prefent in a flourifhing condition? How indeed could it have been otherwife in fuch a ftate of things?—At the fame time, it is proper to afk, will the continuance of the war, and thofe mutual beggaries and bankruptcies confequent thereupon;—Will thefe things be a means of reviving our trade, and of making either fide the richer, or the better cuftomers?—The man who chufes to maintain fuch a paradox, is not to be envied on account of his logic. He may fay what he pleafes.

' Heretofore it was a kind of unpardonable offence to endeavour to convince the Englifh, that their manufactures had a preference to thofe of other nations in point of cheapnefs. For the

English

English have a most unaccountable propensity towards the gloomy
and the dismal in their prospects concerning trade. And nothing seems to please them better, as the celebrated lord Chesterfield used to say, than gravely to be told, that they are ruined
and undone. Therefore his friend lord Bolingbroke grounded all
his patriotic dissertations on this very basis ;—For which worthy
deeds he, and his brother patriots were held in such high esteem
by the good people of England during the long, pacific, and
wealth-creating reign [if I might use such a term] of Sir R. Walpole, as approached almost to adoration. Indeed, long before
them, ruined and undone was the burden of the song. An author of some repute, one Joshua Gee, was so possessed with this
desponding notion, that he undertook to demonstrate by figures,
and tables of accounts, that the balances of trade were almost
every where prodigiously against us : so that, according to this
comfortable demonstration, there would not have remained one
shilling in Great Britain for these 60 years last past. Yet, Sir,
we have spent and lavished away, since that period, chiefly in
unnecessary and unprofitable wars, upwards of 150,000,000l.
sterling :—A sure proof that he was miserably deceived in his calculations ; though a most melancholly reflection on our own prudence.

'However, that, which reason and argument could not do,
respecting trade, experience itself has at last effected. For now
the English merchants and manufacturers find and feel, that their
goods at an American market (notwithstanding all the present
disadvantages they labour under) are allowed to be better, and
cheaper, than the like articles of other nations, the Americans
themselves being judges. This is a happy omen, which may
tend to many good consequences, if properly improved. For
from hence it undeniably follows, that the Americans will buy our
goods, when it is their interest, and when they are able so to
do, notwithstanding the bitterest antipathy they can conceive
against us. And I defy any man to prove, that they ever did
buy our goods, contrary to their own interests, even during the
most flattering periods of their friendship. [One thing however
I must confess, that heretofore they frequently bought English
merchandise, when they knew they were not able, and never intended to pay for them. And with those very capitals purchased
estates, or carried on a trade to the Spanish main. Therefore if
this be meant by the complainants, when they lament the loss of
the American trade, I hope we shall never recover such a trade
for the future : that is, never trust them to the same amount.
The bad debts of the Americans to this country, long before the
present disturbances, were great beyond imagination ;—much
greater than the sums owing to England from all the world besides.]

' Moreover we now see, and know, that the best produce of
America can find its way into England, if we give the best price,
notwithstanding these obstacles, which civil wars, and national

G g 3   animo-

animofities, accompanied with every other difficulty and difcouragement, can throw in the way. The tobacco of thofe revolted colonies, Maryland, and Virginia, with the valuable productions of other colonies, are now bought and fold as openly and avowedly, even at public auctions, in all our great fea-ports, as before the war. Therefore after fuch proofs, what is it, which we can wifh for, or defire more? And if this be not fufficient to convince us, that the conqueft of America,—fuppofing it ever fo feafible,—can be of no manner of ufe in a mercantile view,—I fhould be glad to know, what kind of proof will, or can be thought fufficient? In a word, if daily experience, and matters of fact are not able to bring us to a confeffion, that our plan is totally wrong, I know not what elfe to have recourfe to, but to declare openly and without referve, that we are determined to act both againft conviction—and againft our own intereft.'

In the fixth letter, the doctor enquires, what benefits will accrue to America, fuppofing her to obtain independence in the profecution of the prefent war : and on this fubject his opinion feems to be perfectly rational.

' As to the future grandeur of America, fays he, and its being a rifing empire, under one head, whether republican, or monachical, it is one of the idleft, and moft vifionary notions, that ever was conceived, even by writers of romance. For there is nothing in the genius of the people, the fituation of their country, or the nature of their different climates, which tends to countenance fuch a fuppofition. On the contrary, every prognoftic that can be formed from a contemplation of their mutual antipathies, and clafhing interefts, their difference of governments, habitudes, and manners, — plainly indicates, that the Americans will have no center of union among them, and no common intereft to purfue, when the power and government of England are finally removed. Moreover, when the interfections and divifions of their country by great bays of the fea, and by vaft rivers, lakes, and ridges of mountains ; —and above all, when thofe immenfe inland regions, beyond the back fettlements, which are ftill unexplored, are taken into the account, they form the higheft probability that the Americans never can be united into one compact empire, under any fpecies of government whatever. Their fate feems to be,—a difunited people, till the end of time. In fhort, the only probable fuppofition, that can be formed of them at prefent is this ;—That being fo very jealous in their tempers, fo fufpicious, and diftruftful of each other, they will be divided, and fubdivided into little commonwealths, or principalities, according to the abovementioned natural divifions, or boundaries of their country ; and that all of them in general, will be more intent on profecuting their own internal difputes and quarrels, than defirous to engage in external wars, and diftant conquefts. They will have neither leifure, nor inclination, nor abilities for fuch undertakings.'——

The

The concluding letter contains a plan for a general pacification; to which indeed the whole of the author's arguments have an obvious tendency.

In those letters, the Dean of Glocester treats his subject with his *usual* vivacity, moderation, and acuteness. He certainly may, in a peculiar manner, claim the privilege of being exempted from national or political prejudices; and though he cannot hope to see his arguments prove effectual against the *ratio ultima regum*, he yet may enjoy the satisfaction to reflect, that he has sincerely urged the cause of mutual benevolence, and endeavoured to extinguish every spark of animosity between the contending nations.

Bibliotheca Topographica Britannica. *No. II. Part II. Containing Reliquiæ Galeanæ, or, Miscellaneous Pieces by the late learned Brothers* Roger *and* Samuel Gale. 4to. 5s. sewed. Nichols.

THE first number of this publication contains the History and Antiquities of Tunstall in Kent, by the late Mr. Mores. The second, among other articles, comprehends the Memoirs of Thomas, Roger, and Samuel Gale. The third, which is now before us, consists of Letters, written by Roger Gale, Esq. Dr. Stukeley, Maurice Johnson, Esq. Sir John Clerk, E. Cony, Esq. the Rev. Mr. Conyers Place, the Rev. Mr. Ella, Thomas Robinson, Esq. Mr. N. Salmon, Mr. R. Goodman, Mr. Beaupré Bell, Dr. C. Mortimer, Sam. Gale, Esq. Dr. Ch. Hunter, Mr. V. Snell, Capt. Pownall, Dr. S. Knight, Ch. Gray, Esq. Dr. Th. Blackwell, Dr. Rawlinson, and some other learned antiquaries.

The subjects are Roman roads, camps, stations, coins, ruins, urns, sepulchres, inscriptions, &c.

From these letters we shall give our readers two or three short extracts.

Sir John Clerk's observations on the British language.

' I must observe, were it doubtful, that the Saxons were not such strangers in Britain as the generality of our historians believe, since they had made us many visits, and the language of the Britons, according to Cæsar and Tacitus, differed very little from the German, and was originally the same, namely, the Celtic. This language was about 17 or 1800 years ago spoken uniformly by five nations, the Germans, Illyrians, Gauls, Spaniards, and Britons; they had very near the same characters, so that what most of our writers call Saxon characters are truly old British characters, and those which were used in the language spoken from the South parts of Britain to the Murray frith in Scotland; that very language, with

gra-

gradual alterations and mixtures, which we fpeak at this day.

‘ I know that a Welfhman will laugh at this doctrine ; for the people of Wales commonly believe, that, upon the inva-fions of the Romans and Saxons, moft of the true Britons re-tired into their country with their language, which continues among them at this time ; but this I can demonftrate to be a miftake, for the language fpoken in Wales and the High-lands in Scotland came from Ireland, and has no affinity with the old Celtic, of which I could give you hundreds of proofs from the ancient remains of the Celtic : in the mean time, I will not fay but that the Irifh language may be as old, and pof-fibly older, than the Celtic, but fure I am the latter was quite different from the former.’

What does this writer mean by faying, ‘ the Saxons had made us many vifits ?’ Every one knows, that they came into Bri-tain in the year 449. But neither the Saxon Chronicle, Bede, nor any other writer, give us the leaft intimation of any earlier vifit.——As there are feveral notions, which feem to be a little problematical, in this extract, it is to be wifhed, that the au-thor had entered into the fubject, and delivered his fentiments with more precifion.

A remarkable circumftance relative to natural hiftory, or the incredible number of hedgehogs in Lincolnfhire, in a letter from Mr. M. Johnfon, jun. to Dr. Stukeley, Oct. 14, 1719.

‘ Your own parifh, Holbeach, affords one remarkable ar-ticle in the parochial charge, where the laft year the church-wardens paid 4l. 6s. for the deftruction of urchins or hedge-hogs, at but one fingle penny a-piece ; and the prefent of-ficers have paid above 30l. on the fame account already. The vaft ftocks of cattle in this noble parifh, and fome coney burroughs, have drawn thofe creatures from all parts hither, as one would think *.’——

According to this account, the number of thefe animals, deftroyed in two years, muft have amounted to 8232 ! Poffibly there might be an overcharge of two or three thoufand in the churchwardens rate.

Dr. Stukeley to Mr. R. Gale, on Sir Ifaac Newton’s Chro-nology.

‘ Mr. Conduit has fent me fir Ifaac Newton’s Chronology. I do not admire his contracting the fpaces of time ; he has purfued that fancy too far. I am fatisfied he has made fe-veral names of different perfons one, who really lived many

---

* See a Vindication of the Hedgehog, Gent. Mag. vol. xlix. p. 395.

ages afunder. He has come pretty near my ground-plot of the Temple of Solomon, but he gives us no uprights. He runs into the common error of making Sefac and Sefoſtris one perſon, with Marſham, and many others : the confequence of which is, that the Ægyptians borrowed architecture from the Jews, when I am fatisfied all architecture was originally invented by the Ægyptians ; and I can deduce all the members and particulars of it from their ſacred delineations, and Vitruvius himſelf was as far to feek in the origin of the Corinthian capital, and other matters of that fort, as a Campbell or Gibbs would be. I judge the late biſhop of Peterborough (Cumberland), in his two poſthumous pieces, has gone further in reſtoring ancient chronology.

‘ Weſt-thorp, where ſir Iſaac Newton was born, is a hamlet of Colſterworth. Sir Iſaac's anceſtors are buried in Colſterworth church. We have got the fineſt original picture of ſir Iſaac by Kneller, at Mr Newton Smith's, his nephew, at Barrowby, a mile from us.’

Extract of a letter from Mr. T. Blackwell, author of An Enquiry into the Life and Writings of Homer, to Mr. R. Gale, concerning Dr. Bentley, dated, Grantham, October 2, 1735.

‘ Dr. Mead having been fo good as to write to his friend Dr. Bentley, that I intended to viſit Cambridge, the old gentleman, who never ſtirs abroad, fent for us, and did us, I am told, unuſual honours. We ſpent fome hours with him, had a deal of converſation about himſelf, and fome about Manilius and Homer. He ſpoke very freely ; fo I found his emendations of the latter ſolely to relate the quantity of the verſe, and ſupplying the lines, where the cæſura cuts off a vowel, which the ancient critics called Μειϸρὸν or Λαϸαϸὸν, as it was in the end or middle of the verſe. This he does by inferting, or, as he fays, by reſtoring the Æolic Digamma F, which ſerves as a double conſonant, and which he pronounces like our W ; thus, ἀυτὺς ϛὲ ἑλώϸια τεύχε κυνέϸϸιν, he reads, ἀυτὺς ϛὲ Fελώϸια τεύχε κυνέϸϸιν, and pronounces *auteus de Wheloria*, &c. So οἶνϐ, Φοινϐ, αϛαινος, wine, — ἰς, Fις, αϛις, which has likewife the found of the Latin *vis* ; fo they faid, according to him, *Wirgilius, Warro, Owidius, wab!* Yet, if you pleaſe to look into the firſt or fecond Book of Dionyſius Halicarnaſſæus's Antiquities, you will find the Digamma explained by a Φ in Greek, and a V in Latin, and the other Greeks faid indifferently Βιϸγιλιϐ and Οὐιϸϛιλιϐ, Βαϸϸὼν and Οὐαϸϸὼν. But the doctor fays, he, and Ariſtarchus, and Demetrius were all dunces, who knew nothing of the Di-

gamma,

gamma, which he himſelf reſtored the uſe of, after it had been loſt 2000 years.'

Though there are ſome remarks, in theſe Letters, which have been thrown out in haſte, and in the latitude of conjecture, yet there is alſo a variety of hints, anecdotes, and obſervations, which are certainly juſt, and cannot fail of being acceptable to the curious reader, but more eſpecially to the antiquary.

The Count of Narbonne, *a Tragedy. As it is acted at the Theatre Royal in* Covent Garden. *By* Robert Jephſon, *Eſq.* 8vo. 1s. 6d. Cadell.

THIS Tragedy, undoubtedly one of the beſt that has appeared for ſome years, is founded on Mr. Horace Walpole's celebrated novel, or romance, called the Caſtle of Otranto, from whence the ingenious Mr. Jephſon has drawn almoſt all the intereſting circumſtances and events that compoſe his drama, very judiciouſly omitting the marvellous part of it, as well knowing that *nodding helmets, waving plumes,* and *walking pictures,* would have made but a ridiculous figure on an Engliſh ſtage. The Fable is artfully conducted throughout; the characters well ſuſtained, and diſcriminated; the ſentiments, for the moſt part, natural, unaffected, and ſuitable to the perſons by whom they are delivered; the ſtyle and diction remarkably correct, elegant, and harmonious; ſufficiently raiſed above vulgar language to become the dignity of the tragic muſe, and at the ſame time without affectation, bombaſt, or puerility. The firſt, third, and fifth acts have ſome ſcenes that are maſterly and pathetic, in which good actors may always appear to great advantage; the ſecond and fourth are rather heavy and unintereſting: every picture however muſt have light and ſhade, and we do not recollect any modern tragedy which has fewer faults and imperfections than the Count of Narbonne.

The following extracts may ſerve to convince our readers that what we have ſaid, with regard to Mr. Jephſon's ſtyle and manner, in this applauded performance, is not more than he deſerves; and will, we doubt not, invite them to a peruſal of the whole drama.

· A C T I. S C E N E VI.

' *Count.*]. Where's my child,
My all of comfort now, my Adelaide?

Counteſs,] Dear as ſhe is, I would not have her all;
For I ſhould then be nothing. Time has been,

When,

When, after three long days of abſence from you,
You would have queſtion'd me a thouſand times,
And bid me tell each trifle of myſelf;
Then, ſatisfied at laſt that all were well,
At laſt, unwilling, turn to meaner cares.

   Count.] This is the nature ſtill of womankind;
If fondneſs be their mood, we muſt caſt off
All grave-complexion'd thought, and turn our ſouls
Quite from their tenour to wild levity:
Vary with all their humours, take their hues,
As unſubſtantial Iris from the ſun:
Our boſoms are their paſſive inſtruments;
Vibrate their ſtrain, or all our notes are diſcord.

   Counteſs.] O why this new unkindneſs? From thy lips
Never till now fell ſuch ungentle words,
Nor ever leſs was I prepar'd to meet them.

   Count.] Never till now was I ſo urg'd, beſet,
Hemm'd round with perils.

   Counteſs.]   Ay, but not by me.

   Count.] By thee, and all the world. But yeſterday,
With uncontroulable and abſolute ſway
I rul'd this province, was the unqueſtion'd lord
Of this ſtrong-caſtle, and its wide domains,
Stretch'd beyond ſight around me; and but now,
The axe, perhaps, is ſharp'ning, may hew down
My periſh'd trunk, and give the ſoil I ſprung from,
To cheriſh my proud kinſman Godfrey's roots.

   Counteſs.] Heaven guard thy life! His dreadful ſummons
     reach'd me,
This urg'd me hither. On my knees I beg,
(And I have mighty reaſons for my prayer,)
O do not meet him on this argument:
By gentler means ſtrive to divert his claim;
Fly this deteſted place, this houſe of horrour,
And leave its gloomy grandeur to your kinſman.

   Count.] Riſe, fearful woman. What! renounce my birth-right?
Go forth, like a poor friendleſs baniſh'd man,
To gnaw my heart in cold obſcurity!
Thou weak adviſer! Should I take thy counſel,
Thy tongue would firſt upbraid, thy ſpirit ſcorn me.

   Counteſs.] No, on my ſoul!—Is Narbonne all the world?
My country is where thou art; place is little:
The ſun will ſhine, the earth produce its fruits,
Chearful, and plenteouſly, where'er we wander.
In humbler walks, bleſs'd with my child and thee,
I'd think it Eden in ſome lonely vale,
Nor heave one ſigh for theſe proud battlements.

   Count.] Such flowery ſoftneſs ſuits not matron lips.
But thou haſt mighty reaſons for thy prayer:
They ſhould be mighty reaſons, to perſuade

                               Their

Their rightful lord to leave his large possessions,
A soldier challeng'd, to decline the combat.
   Countess.] And are not prodigies then mighty reasons?
The owl mistakes his season, in broad day
Screaming his hideous omens; spectres glide,
Gibbering and pointing as we pass along;
While the deep earth's unorganized caves
Send forth wild sounds and clamours terrible;
These towers shake round us, though the untroubled air
Stagnates to lethargy:—our children perish,
And new disasters blacken every hour.
Blood shed unrighteously, blood unappeas'd,
Though we are guiltless, cries, I fear, for vengeance.
   Count.] Blood shed unrighteously! have I shed blood?
No; nature's common frailties set aside,
I'll meet my audit boldly.
   Countess.]   Mighty Lord!
O! not on us, with justice too severe,
Visit the sin, not ours!
   Count.]   What can this mean?
Something thou would'st reveal that's terrible.
   Countess.] Too long, alas 't has weigh'd upon my heart;
A thousand times I have thought to tell thee all;
But my tongue falter'd, and refus'd to wound thee.
   Count.] Distract me not, but speak.
   Countess.]   I must.   Your father
Was wise, brave, politick; but mad ambition,
(Heaven pardon him!) it prompts to desperate deeds.
   Count.] I scarce can breathe. Pr'ythee be quick, and ease me.
   Countess.] Your absence on the Italian embassy
Left him, you know, alone to my fond care.
Long had some hidden grief, like a flow fire,
Wasted his vitals;—on the bed of death,
One object seem'd to harrow up his soul,
The picture of Alphonso in the chamber:
On that his eye was set.—Methinks I see him,
His ashy hue, his grizzled bristling hair,
His palms spread wide. For ever would he cry,
" That aweful form, how terrible he frowns!
See how he bares his livid leprous breast,
And points the deadly chalice!"
   Count.]   Ha! even so!
   Countess.] Sometimes he'd seize my hands, and grasp them close,
And strain them to his hollow burning eyes;
Then falter out, " I am, I am a villain;
Mild angel, pray for me; stir not, my child!
It comes again; oh! do not leave my side."
At last, quite spent with mortal agonies,
His soul went forth; and heaven have mercy on him!

                               Count.]

Count.] Enough. Thy tale has almost iced my blood.
Let me not think. Hortensia, on thy duty,
Suffer no breath like this to pass thy lips :
I will not taint my noble father's honour,
By vile suspicions suck'd from nature's dregs,
And the loose ravings of distemper'd fancy.
  Countess.] Yet O decline this challenge !
  Count.]   That hereafter.
Mean time prepare my daughter, to receive
A husband of my choice.   Should Godfrey come,
(Strife might be so prevented) bid her try
Her beauty's power.   Stand thou but neuter, Fate !
Courage and art shall arm me from * mankind.'

This scene is extremely well written, and must consequently please in the closet ; but those who would wish to feel the
full effect of it on the stage, must see that excellent actress
Miss Young, in the part of the Countess.

Our second quotation shall be taken from the third scene of
the fourth act, where the business and interesting part of the
fable (perhaps unavoidably) standing still, the author seems to
have taken uncommon pains to decorate his piece with rich
imagery and poetical ornament.

' S C E N E   III.

  ' *Countess.*] Will then these dreadful sounds ne'er leave my ears ?
' " Our marriage was accurs'd ; too long we have liv'd
In bonds forbid ; think me no more thy husband ;
The avenging bolt, for that incestuous name,
Falls on my house ; and spreads the ruin wide,
For our offence, o'er this afflicted land."
These were his words.
  Adelaide.]   O ponder then no more !
Lo ! where the blessed minister of peace,
(He whose mild counsels wont to charm your care,)
Is kindly come to cheer your drooping soul ;
And see, the good man weeps.
  Countess.]   What ! weep for me !

---

* We are sorry to observe that this line, which concludes the
act, is unworthy of its author.   The expression of arming *from*
mankind, instead of *against*, is certainly very aukward and
ungrammatical.—We meet also in this tragedy with two words
which we would gladly expunge from it, viz. *interrogatories* in the
first act,
      ' I will cut short thy *interrogatories* ;'
and in the second, *transfer*,
      ' Suffer this hasty *transfer* of your child.'
These would certainly sound better in Westminster-hall and Jonathan's coffee house than on Covent-Garden stage.

                                        Austin.]

Auftin.] Ay, tears of blood from my heart's inmoft core,
And count them drops of water from my eyes,
Could they but wafh out from your memory
The deep affliction you now labour with.
 Countefs.] Then ftill there is fome pity left in man :
I judged you all by him, and fo I wrong'd you.
I would have told my ftory to the fea,
When it roar'd wildeft ; bid the lionefs,
Robb'd of her young, look with compaffion on me ;
Rather than hoped in any form of man
To find one drop of human gentlenefs.
 Auftin. (*approaching her.*] Moft honour'd lady !——
 Countefs.]   ——Pray you, come not near me.
I am contagion all ; fome wicked fin,
Prodigious, unrepented fin, has ftain'd me.
Father, 'twould blaft thee but to hear the crimes,
This woman, who was once the wife of Raymond,
This curs'd forfaken woman here, has acted.
 Auftin.] What flanderous tongue dare thus profane your virtue ?
Madam, I know you well ; and, by my order,
Each day, each hour of your unfpotted life,
Might give as fair a leffon to the world,
As churchmen's tongues can preach, or faints could practife.
 Countefs.] He charges me with all——Thou, poor Hortenfia !
What guilt, prepoft'rous guilt, is thine to anfwer !
 Ade.] In mercy wound not thus your daughter's foul.
 Auftin.] A villain or a madman might fay this.
 Countefs.] What fhall I call him ? He, who was my hufband ;
My child, thy father ;——He'll difclaim thee too,
But let him caft off all the ties of nature,
Abandon us to grief and mifery,
Still will I wander with thee o'er the world :
I will not wifh my reafon may forfake me,
Nor fweet oblivious dulnefs fteep my fenfe,
While thy foft age may want a mother's care,
A mother's tendernefs, to wake and guard thee.
 Ade.] And, if the love of your dear Adelaide,
Her reverence, duty, endlefs gratitude
For all your angel goodnefs, now can move you,
Oh, for my fake (left quite you break my heart,)
Wear but a little outfide fhow of comfort ;
Awhile pretend it, though you feel it not,
And I will blefs you for deceiving me.
 Countefs.] I know 'tis weaknefs, folly, to be mov'd thus ;
And thefe, I hope, are my laft tears for him.
Alas, I little knew, deluded wretch !
His riotous fancy glow'd with Ifabel ;
That not a thought of me poffefs'd his mind,
But coldnefs and averfion ; how to fhun me,
And turn me forth a friendlefs wanderer.

                                                              Auftin.

Auſtin.] Vain were the attempt to palliate injuries,
Too foul in their own nature to receive
Whiteneſs from words ; but, lady, for your peace,
Think, conſcience is the deepeſt ſource of anguiſh :
A boſom, free like your's, has life's beſt ſunſhine ;
'Tis the warm blaze in the poor herdſman's hut ;
That, when the ſtorm howls o'er his humble thatch,
Brightens his clay-built walls, and cheers his ſoul.
You pay the forfeit of the aggreſſor's wrong,
Suffering the pangs, which guilt alone ſhould ſuffer.

  Counteſs.] O father, reaſon is for moderate ſorrow ;
For wounds which time has balm'd ; but mine are freſh,
All bleeding freſh, and pain beyond my patience.
Ungrateful ! cruel ! how have I deſerved it ! —
Thou tough, tough heart, break for my eaſe at once !

  Auſtin.] I ſcarce, methinks, can weigh him with himſelf ;
Vexations ſtrange have fallen on him of late ;
And his diſtemper'd fancy drives him on
To raſh deſigns, where diſappointment made him.

  Counteſs.] Ah no ! his wit is ſettled, and moſt ſubtle ;
Pride and wild blood are his diſtemper, father.
But here I bid farewel to grief and fondneſs :
Let him go kneel, and ſigh to Iſabel ;
And may he as obdurate find her heart,
As his has been to me !

  Auſtin.]   Why that's well ſaid ; —
'Tis better thus, than with conſuming ſorrow
To feed on your own life.   Give anger ſcope :
Time then at length will blunt this killing ſenſe ;
And peace, he ne'er muſt know again, be your's.

  Counteſs.] I was a woman, full of tenderneſs ;
I am a woman, ſtung by injuries.
Narbonne was once my huſband, my protector ;
He was—what was he not ? — He is my tyrant ;
The unnatural tyrant of a heart that lov'd him.
With cool deliberate baſeneſs he forſakes me ;
With ſcorn as ſtedfaſt ſhall my ſoul repay it.

  Auſtin.] You know the imminent danger threatens him
From Godfrey's fearful claim ?

  Counteſs.]   Too well I know it ;
A fearful claim indeed !

  Auſtin.]   To-morrow's ſun
Will ſee him at theſe gates ; but truſt my faith,
No violence ſhall reach you.   The raſh count
(Loſt to himſelf) by force detains me here.
Vain is his force :—our holy ſanctuary,
Whate'er betides, ſhall give your virtue ſhelter ;
And peace and piety alone approach you.

  Counteſs.] O that the friendly boſom of the earth
Would cloſe on me for ever !

                                        Auſtin]

Auſtin.]   Theſe ill thoughts
Muſt not be cheriſh'd. That all-righteous power
Whoſe hand inflicts, knows to reward our patience :
Farewel ! command me ever as your ſervant,
And take the poor man's all, my prayers and bleſſing.'

The colouring of this ſcene our readers will acknowledge to be highly finiſhed. The compariſon * of a clear conſcience to the warm blaze in the herdſman's hut is a very happy one, and finely expreſſed.

This tragedy, with all its beauties, which are numerous, has one capital and eſſential defect, viz. the want of a proper moral leſſon reſulting from the whole.

" I am not blind, (ſays Mr. Walpole, in his preface to the firſt edition of the Caſtle of Otranto) to my author's defects. I could wiſh he had grounded his plan on a more uſeful *moral* than this, that, *the ſins of fathers are viſited on their children to the third and fourth generation.* I doubt whether in his time any more than at preſent, ambition curbed its appetite of dominion from the dread of ſo remote a puniſhment."—The ſame objection which Mr. Walpole made to his own novel, muſt every ſpectator and every reader make to Mr. Jephſon's drama. The Count of Narbonne is judiciouſly painted by the author as paſſionate, ambitious, ſenſual, and revengeful, though guiltleſs of the intended murther of his daughter ; and therefore we do not lament his fate : but what had the wronged mother and the innocent daughter done, that ſhould involve them in the ſame puniſhment with the murtherous Alphonſo, and the falſe, ambitious Narbonne ? Why muſt all poetical juſtice be thus ſacrificed to inculcate an idea that is ſhocking to truth and equity ? Will ſuch a notion, if univerſally received, operate towards rendering mankind more cautious of committing crimes that may be attended with ſuch conſequences ? The effect, as Mr. Walpole properly obſerved, is much too remote, while the undeſerved puniſhment of innocence is to the laſt degree oppreſſive, and muſt tend to diſcourage men from the practice of virtue, not only ſo unjuſtly but ſeverely chaſtiſed.

Our author's fable is liable alſo to this cenſure : the cata-

---

* This ſimile is better timed, and is introduced with much more propriety than that of Narbonne's, in the third ſcene of the fifth act, when he ſays,

' Fame, like water, &c.'

It is entirely out of nature for ſuch a character as the Count, when his mind is agitated by contending paſſions, and in the height of diſtreſs, to be ſearching after compariſons. All that Narbonne ſays on this occaſion is prolix, and ſhould have been omitted.

strophe,

ftrophe, which he has founded on injuftice, is produced by fuperftition; the accomplifhment of a prophecy. What conclufion can be drawn from hence, but that oracles, divinations, and prophecies, fhould be believed, and muft always be fulfilled? Such notions can only tend to enflave the mind, and bring us back to the long exploded errors of ignorance and barbarifm. We wifh therefore to fee a tragedy of Mr. Jephfon's free from thofe objections, and from which a better moral may be drawn than from the Count of Narbonne.

The Fair Circassian. *A Tragedy. As performed at the Theatre-Royal,* Drury-Lane. *8vo.* 1s. 6d. Baldwin.

THOUGH we do not in the Fair Circassian meet with that artful conduct of the fable, and knowlege of ftage-effect, together with that even flow of language, correctnefs, and precifion, which fo eminently diftinguifh the Count of Narbonne; it has, notwithftanding, a fufficient fhare of merit to entitle it to no inconfiderable portion of public applaufe, efpecially when confidered as the ingenious author's *firft* dramatic production. We cannot, at the fame time, compliment Mr. Pratt on the choice of his fubject: which, though well calculated for an Oriental tale, adorned by Hawkefworth with pleafing machinery, fine fentiments, and eafy diction, does not furnifh that chain of interefting events, or that difplay of character which are effentially neceffary to the formation of an affecting tragedy. The rivalfhip of two brothers, without fome very new and ftriking fituations that may deeply intereft the fpectator, is a circumftance too common and familiar to furprife or affect us; not to mention that the author has, by no means, made the beft ufe of the few materials with which Hawkefworth had fupplied him. The ftop put to the celebration of the nuptial rites, in the third act, by the treachery of the prieft, awakens the attention of the audience, and feems to promife an interefting fufpenfe; but this lofes all its effect, and appears flat and infipid from the immediate difcovery of the whole by Omar. The tale is difbelieved by Hamet and Almeida, and every thing is juft in the fame fituation they were before the falfe oracle was delivered. In the two laft acts the plot is intricate and perplexed; the meeting of Almeida and Almoran in the dark, and her miftaking him for Hamet, are aukward and improbable circumftances; and the cataftrophe, not being naturally produced, gives but little fatisfaction.

With

With all thoſe diſadvantages in point of fable, and the in-artificial management of it, there are parts of this tragedy which lay claim to our warmeſt approbation.   The characters of Almoran and Hamet are well contraſted and ſupported ; the ſentiments juſt and noble ; and the diction, in general, eaſy and poetical ; though, in ſome parts, not ſo * chaſte and correct as from a writer of taſte, abilities, and experience might have been expected.

As a ſpecimen of our dramatiſt's ſtyle and manner, we ſhall preſent our readers with the firſt ſcene of the ſecond act, be-tween Hamet and Omar, where the venerable old prieſt ſpeaks with great dignity, and gives his young maſter ſome excellent advice in very good language.

‘ A C T   II.   S C E N E   I.
H A M E T,   O M A R.

Hamet.] Thou good old man—Thou full of days and honours
Guide of my youth, and glory of my crown,
My boſom labours with a friend's impatience
As now I lead thee to theſe ſacred ſeats,—
Theſe awful ſepulchres, where Perſia's kings,
My anceſtors, *repoſe in ſolemn ſilence*—
Oh, my heart throbs till I have told thee all.

Omar.] My prince, my child ! I praiſe thy tender zeal,
And though oppreſſive time upon this head
Hath heavy ſnow'd full many a winter's whiteneſs,
Yet once this heart—the memory ſtill is dear—

---

* Amongſt the inaccuracies of language and expreſſion, in this tragedy, may be reckoned the following, which we would wiſh to ſee corrected in future editions.—One of the lovers talks of drinking
    ‘ — large *draughts* of paſſion ;’
and ſpeaking of his miſtreſs, ſays,
        ‘ her eyes *ſhot ſuns.*’
Almoran ſays,
    ‘ My *defrauded* world's at length reſtor'd.’
A *defrauded* world can never, with any propriety of language, ſignify the world which I have been *defrauded of.*
To *intercede* the merciful—inſtead of to *intercede with.*
Who ſo fit as *thee*—inſtead of *thou.*
Deſcend thy choral choir—inſtead of *make to deſcend.*
    ‘ *Depoſit* lov'd of ev'ry little care.’
    ‘ This is another Caled of the *core.*’
    ‘ —holy men their *ſanctities* prepare.’
Where's *the virtues*—for where *are the virtues.*

Theſe, with ſeveral others equally inelegant, improper, and un-grammatical, ſhould be altered.

Felt

Felt a fond paffion, pure and warm as thine.
To all that rateth high a virgin's worth,
Senfe, beauty, foul, long fince was Omar wed.
   Hamet.] If thou haft lov'd, with unfatigued ear,
Thou wilt allow the fweet prolixity,
Love's foft delay, and tender repetition.
" But, oh! by what fad ftroke of cruel fortune
Fell from thy reverend arms this deareft treafure?"
   Omar.] " Full forty years Olmana to this bofom
Minifter'd every balm of virtuous foftnefs.
Paffion from reafon caught the wifh compos'd,
The hope obedient, and the fteady purpofe,
A life devote to nature and to Heaven.
At length it pleas'd the gods to take her from me,
And pluck this pillow from my aged head;
Her death was fudden, but her life prepar'd.
In my firft widow'd days I felt as man;
At length her facred fpirit feem'd to chide,
And whifper'd that it only went before
To intercede the Merciful for mine.
I left her with the gods, and wept no more."
But come, what fays Almeida?
   Hamet.]   How her name
Like fudden fun-beams darting thro' a cloud,
Lights up an inftant joy in Hamet's bofom.
Oh, had'ft thou feen her all diffolv'd in paffion—
Paffion, tho' yielding, modeftly chaftis'd,
" And fhaded by a delicate referve,
Only to look more lovely thro' the veil"—
Had'ft thou but feen her, eloquently dumb,
Sink in her father's arms, confefs her foftnefs
In all the fweet diforders of the heart,
Then blufht and figh, and even weep for words!—
   Omar.] When does Abdallah's daughter then confent,—
   Hamet.] Hear it, ye favouring heav'ns, and every breeze,
Bear on your viewlefs wings the tender tidings,
I fhall to-morrow claim—
   Omar.]   To-morrow!
Knows royal Almoran this fudden purpofe?
   Hamet.] Ah Omar thou haft fprinkled drops of ice
Cold on my heart, to freeze the flame of love.
Not all the jealous vigilance of fondnefs;
Not the ftill waking eyes of faithful Ali
Can foil the felon arts of wily Caled.
Almoran again hath feen her, friend—and much,
Still much I fear left—
   Omar.]   Oh, forbear;
Wear not a doubtful eye upon a brother,
Nor let fufpicion fear thy generous heart.
   Hamet.] Heaven knows my fondnefs: knows the generous love,
" Refpect fincere, and tendernefs I bear him,

And the foft fhade I caft o'er all his failings :"
Dear is my brother to this faithful heart,
As the warm tide that conftant flows to feed it.

Omar.] The fainted Solyman thou know'ft decreed,
That ye fhould wear his yet unblemifh'd crown
In amity together, wield his fceptre
As brothers and as friends.——Unite to blefs,
By a well-order'd government, the land :
The fmiling arts of peace diffufe around,
Or give——where patriot virtue points the caufe
To be the caufe of heav'n——frefh nerves to war ;
O'er the wide wave to fpread the advent'rous fail,
Lift modeft genius from the lowly vale,
And bid it bloffom in a warmer foil,
More near its native fkies.——

 Hamet.   Dear parent fage,
Deep are thy counfels 'grav'd upon this heart.

 Omar.] Yet fpare a moment to the voice of truth,
Even from the hour of panting foftnefs fpare it.
Oh ne'er forget, thou noble youth, 'tis thine
To tafte with Almoran the blifs fupreme
That flows from all the great, the glorious virtues,
Worthy of kings, on kings alone conferr'd ;
Pity that foftens juftice : merit, guarded
From bolder arrogance, e'en by the fhield,
The temper'd fhield of royalty itfelf.
" Bleffings deriv'd from bleffings well beftow'd,
Delights like thefe——oh, may they long be thine,
Grow greater by divifion." Yet remember
If e'er thou'rt tempted——which the gods forbid——
Should'ft thou, as faction or as favour urges ;
Should private paffions, or domeftick broils,
Frauds of the ftate, or follies of the palace,
A miftrefs or a minifter, e'er lead
Thine eye, thy hand, thy heart from what thou ow'ft,
From what the laws, the land, the people claim——
Claim as a duty from the prince they ferve,
Not Perfia's utmoft pomp combin'd to foothe thee,
" Not all the graces of the lov'd Almeida,
Nor yet the princely pledges of her faith
Climbing thy knee and blooming round thy board,
Not ev'n the hufband's pride, the father's tranfport,"
Can fnatch thee from the fhame referv'd for him,
Who, bafe and lawlefs, wantons with his power:
" Covers with blood his violated country,
To an enfanguin'd fabre turns his fceptre,
And more than traitor defolates the empire.

 Hamet.] Oh, never, never may this breaft, which throbs
With all a patriot's, all a parent's ardour,
To ferve the weal of Perfia, feel a curfe
So charg'd with anguifh, or fo full of horrour !

            With

With my lov'd ſubjects teach me, gods, to ſhare
The plenteous glories of this fertile land,
While royal Almoran partakes the jóy,
And late poſterity atteſts our virtue !
Now, then, my friend, I muſt require thy aid.
  Omar.] What would my gracious prince ?
  Hamet.]   Engage
His ſecond father in an inſtant office
Of tender import—This letter—take it Omar.
Why trembles thus my fooliſh hand to give it ?
'Tis to my brother, and contains—oh heav'ns !
  Omar.] " The tidings of to-morrow. This perchance—
'Tis dangerous ; [*aſide*] ſoft—is there no other way ?
  Hamet.] Why pauſes Omar ?
Why deeply bent to earth his thoughtful eye ?
  Omar.] Thy love hath ſpoke, I doubt not, brotherly.
  Hamet.] Omar, my heart was in it. Take it then,
O take it, friend !" There, in that little ſpace
Are all my future hopes and fears inſcribed ;
It is the hiſtory of a brother's love,
Writ to a brother's friendſhip—Yes, my Omar,
This is the hour which Almoran devotes
To private kindneſs, and unburthen'd freedom :
Upon his ſacred moments thou haſt claim ;
And who ſo fit as thee to grace a meſſage
Where Hamet's happineſs ſo cloſes, centres ?
  Omar.] Dear to this feeble boſom are ye both ;
I honour, love, reſpect—do all but fear you.
The man we dread was never truly lov'd.
  Hamet.] Delay no longer then—oh think a little,
Something allow to ardent love's impatience ;
No reſt ſhall Hamet know till thy return,
But trembling, anxious, wait thy coming, Omar.—
In the bleſs'd grove that ſhades Almeida's chamber,
There will I kneel, there awful bend to heaven,
That all our wiſhes may be crown'd in peace.   [*Exit Hamet.*
  Omar alone.] I would not check his joys too far ; and yet
Too plain, alas, theſe aged eyes can ſee
A train of miſchiefs gathering round our heads.
This letter notes the hour, when to the moſque
Hamet conducts his fair Circaſſian bride.
Ye mighty Powers, who rule the royal ſoul,
And touch the maſter chords that ſway our nature,
Let kindred kindneſs ſave my kings from diſcord,
Preſerve the publick welfare, private quiet :
And theſe old eyes ſhall pour their thanks in tears.   [*Exit.*

    There are many other paſſages in the Fair Circaſſian, which
will give our readers pleaſure in the peruſal. The deſerved applauſe and favourable reception which this tragedy has met with,
will, we hope, encourage the author to produce another ſtill
more worthy of our attention.

FOREIGN ARTICLES.

Séance publique de la Faculté de Médécine de Paris, *tenue le* 9 Decembre, 1779, *dans les Ecoles exterieures de la* Sorbonne. 135 *Pages in* 4to. Paris.

AN interesting collection, beginning with the account given by M. de l'Epine, to the faculty, of the dissertations addressed to him on the question proposed in 1778, for the prize of the session of 1779. The prize has been founded for ever by the late Dr. Malouin; the question for 1779 was: ' Which are the physical, moral, and political advantages of children being nursed by their own mothers, both for the children, and for the mothers themselves?' This question was answered in one memoir, greatly to the satisfaction of the faculty.

II. M. le Vacher de la Feutrie's speech, in which he proposes and explains the subject of the prize for the next year, with the motives of the faculty for proposing it. It is: ' 1. Are there *certain* signs of the presence of worms either in the stomach or in the intestinal canal? 2. Which are those signs? 3. When is the presence of those insects dangerous? 4. Which are the curative means, in the different circumstances?'

III. Relation of the judgements pronounced by the faculty, on the accounts given by the committee, on the eight following objects:

1. On the machine and reservoirs for the filtration and purification of the water taken on the point of the Isle of St. Louis: approved.

2. On proposals for establishing a public infirmary in a place called au Gros Caillou, for receiving and treating patients for a moderate price per day. The faculty has highly approved of the proposal.

3. A memoir returned by the prevôt des marchands, or chief magistrate of Paris, to the faculty, containing complaints of several private individuals, neighbours of the fire machine of the late Mess. Perrier, near la Grille de Chaillot. The plaintiffs were apprehensive lest their health might be injured by the smoke of the coal-fire continually burning there for turning that pump, or water-work. On the report of the committee, who had examined the place, the faculty has pronounced their fears to be groundless.

4. A powder presented by an English gentleman, Mr. Fowler, as fit for stopping external hæmorrhages. After several trials and experiments, successfully made by the committee, on animals and even on men, the powder has been approved. M. Desessarts observes that the judgment of the faculty has since been farther confirmed by the complete success of that powder on a patient whose leg was cut off in the hospital de la Charité: and subjoins, that the faculty keeps in her archives, under the seal of secrecy, the composition of that powder, which its author has communicated to her commissioners.

5. On the dogs-skins dressed by M. Robert, the secret of whose dressing had been purchased by a citizen who had experienced their good effects, and who intended to publish that secret for the benefit of the public. In order to assure himself of the fidelity of the receipt, that philanthrope had requested the faculty to examine it. From the experiments made in consequence of this request by the committee of the faculty, it appeared that the balm with which

these

these skins are dressed, is, in fact, the same which M. Robert had of M. Fagon, first physician to Lewis XIV. And, in order to promote the wishes of the generous purchaser, the faculty has ordered that receipt to be printed and sent to the apothecaries of Paris, to whom alone the preparation and sale of these compositions were to be entrusted.

6. In a considerable town in France, suspicions had arisen and spread, that breweries might be dangerous to the health and lives of their neighbours. These fears, it seems, arose from the experiments which modern physicians had made on *gas*. As the animals exposed to the *gas* of fermenting beer, die very soon, it was but natural for common people to consider those vapours as very pernicious. But they do not know, that the same vapour which when pure, is apt to kill men and beasts instantaneously, does not hurt them in the least, when mixed with a quantity of common air sufficient for respiration: now, as in the neighbourhood of breweries, and even in breweries, when they are not too closely shut, the *gas* of the fermentation is always mixed with a quantity of air continually renewed and abundantly sufficient for respiration, it follows, that there are no dangers to be apprehended from the neighbourhood of breweries, or of cellars where wine, cyder, and other matters are fermenting.

7. A method for tinning copper vessels, presented to the faculty by Madame Dumazis; and after many trials and comparisons, approved of and adopted by the faculty, as preferable to those which had hitherto been employed.

8. A metallic mixture, in which zinc is the chief ingredient, presented by a M Doucet, a founder, for making casseroles, and other kitchen-furniture. This metal, to which the Parisian Academy of Sciences had refused their approbation, for kitchen utensils used in dressing victuals, has here obtained that of the faculty for the same use.

(The Academy had refused her approbation to vessels made of that metal, 1. because when hot, they are liable to break on the least shock; 2. because the acid liquors used in kitchens, yield with the zinc, a metallic salt of a disagreeable taste, and apt to injure the ragoûts, and perhaps even health itself.)

This account of the judgments of the faculty is succeeded by another relation of the same M. Desessarts, containing an interesting and well-written abstract of most of the physical theses defended by the bachelors of physic, during the course of their licence.

This abstract is succeeded by the eulogies of M. Joseph Jussieu, by M. le Preux; of M. Hazon, and of M. Michel, by M. Desessarts.

M. Joseph Jussieu, third brother to Anthony, and to the illustrious Bernard Jussieu, went, in his early youth, with the other academicians, to Peru; and after forty years absence returned to France, absolutely deprived of memory, and property. His case was indeed a lamentable one: ' Je ne veux me permettre aucune conjecture, says M. le Preux, sur la cause de l'infortune de M. Joseph Jussieu; je ferai seulement observer qu'il exerça avec distinction pendant quarante ans la pratique de la médécine, dans un pays riche, et où l'on sçait être reconnoissant; que sans le moindre avis il fut embarqué, transporté ensuite à Paris, et déposé chez son frère, (M. Bernard Jussieu) n'ayant ni papiers ni effets, avec le simple bagage du vrai philosophe, c'est à dire, portant sur lui-même toute sa garderobe, et encore étoit-elle d'une modestie à affliger les regards.'

Reflexions on this tragical incident, and on the singular way of relating it, will rise of themselves in the mind of every sensible reader.

The cause of M. Michel's death was singular, and worth being recorded, as a caution to young and alert people always to walk cautiously. ' He enjoyed, says M. Defessart, perfect health. A false step exposed him to an evident danger. The violent effort he was forced to make to recover his equilibrium, and to prevent his fall, raised through his whole frame a violent commotion, which was soon succeeded by an acute fever and the heaviest symptoms. The stroke of death had been given; no art nor power of physic could save him, and the unhappy youth died on the sixth day.'

After these eulogies follow an account of the means of rearing foundlings; especially of the diet and food fit for them, if destitute of woman's milk; extracts of the different memoirs, and a consultation of the faculty on the same subject; all of them so full and interesting, as to admit of no abstract.

A dissertation, by M. Majault, on the effect of vinegar, which had been recommended as a proper remedy against the deleterious effects of arsenic. Here M. Majault relates a great number of chemical experiments made by himself and M. de la Planche, Doctor of the Parisian Faculty of Physic. The final result of these experiments is, that vegetable acids are by no means to be trusted to as proper remedies against the dreadful effects of arsenic.

A memoir, by Dr. Mallet, on the quinquina of Martinico, known under the name of quinquina piton; so called from the hills in the French West Indian islands on which it grows. This species of quinquina was first brought to France, by M. Badier, a planter of Guadaloupe, and examined by Dr. Descemet, a skilful botanist at Paris. From his account this quinquina is a genuine one, and much like that of Peru. The chemical analysis of this new quinquina, and its comparison with that of Peru, were made by M. de la Planche; from the observations made by several physicians it appears even superior to that of Peru in several respects: because, say they:

' 1. Que le quinquina piton, pris en dedoction à la dose de deux gros, dans une chopine d'eau, et à la dose d'un gros en bol, même de demi gros, est vomitif & purgatif.

' 2. Qu'il guerit les fievres intermittentes récentes; qu'il suspend celles qui sont anciennes, et qui ont résisté longtems à l'action du quinquina du Perou, et qu'il est même à présumer, (continues M. Mallet) qu'il les auroit guéries toutes radicalement, s'il m'eut été possible d'en faire prendre encore deux doses aux malades que j'ai traités, & qui n'ont pas voulu en continuer l'usage.

' 3. Que son action est très-prompte.

' 4. Enfin, que la propriété qu'il a de faire vomir & de purger est un avantage précieux qui doit même lui assurer la préférence sur le quinquina du Pérou, dans le traitement des fièvres intermittentes, puisqu'il réunit à lui seul la faculté d'évacuer copieusement les malades, et celle de guérir la fiévre...

' Si nous considérons maintenant, le quinquina piton sous des vues politiques, nous croyons, qu'indépendamment des avantages dont nous venons de parler, il mérite celui de fixer l'attention du gouvernement ternement en ce qu'il peut devenir pour la France une nouvelle branche de commerce très intéressante.'

Yet we are apt to think that the real value of the new branch of trade must *chiefly*, or rather *entirely*, *depend* on the real *medicinal* virtues of that quinquina piton.

This dissertation is followed by a learned botanical memoir on the chesnut tree, (châteignier) by M. Deltement, who proves that Linnæus has improperly classed Tournefort's Castanea, and the same Botanist's Fagus, under one and the same genus.

The last memoir of this collection, treats of the use of opium in intermitting agues: it is written by Dr. Moriffot des Landes, and designed to prove that opium, though very useful in many cases, is not therefore adviseable in all, as a specific remedy: and that, like every other medicine, it must be administered, cum grano salis, or with judgment and caution.

This short abstract will sufficiently evince the merits and value of the labours of the College of Physicians of Paris.

FOREIGN LITERARY INTELLIGENCE.

Opuscules Mathematices. 8vo. Segovia.

BY Dom Pedro Giannini, Professor of the Royal Corps of Artillery in Spain; the same who has already, in 1773, published in Latin, at Parma, in quarto, Opuscula, on hydraulics, on the cycloids, on the lost work of Apollonius, which Dom Giannini has attempted to restore after the indications of Pappus.

This present valuable publication treats of the chief properties of the cissoid, and of the solution of a problem in mechanics, relating to the curve described by a body tending to a center in a direct ratio of the distance; and on a new species of trajectory, which, turning round a center, is always cut at right angles by a given line.

Méthode nouvelle & générale pour tracer facilement des Cadrans solaires sur toutes Surfaces planes, en Situations quelconques, sans Calculs ni Embarras d'Instrumens, par un seul Problème Geometrique qui fait connoître l'Axe et la Souflylaire, la Latitude du Lieu, la Situation du Plan, la Déclinaison du Soleil, et le Parallele du Jour, lors de l' Opération. Principes et Usage du Comput & de l'Art de Vérifier les Dates. Par M. de la Prife, ancien Architecte, &c. 260 Pages in 8vo. with 23 Plates. Caen.

Containing the description of a solid, by whose means points of shadow are easily taken; and the method of drawing all sorts of dials, by three points of shadow, by means of an hyperbola; the demonstrations and the practice. A treatise of gnomonics, of 150 pages, is here succeeded by an abstract (in 100 pages) of the principles contained in the great work on the art of verifying dates, which has been published by the learned Benedictines, Dom Clemencet and Dom Durand. The abstract shows how to find the epacts, the festivals, the days of the week, of whatever year: the year and the day are to be found by means of the other chronological circumstances.

L'Iliade d'Homere en Vers François. Par M. le Baron de Beaumanoir, Chévalier de l'Ordre de S. Louis, ancient Capitaine de Dragons. 2 vols. 8vo. Paris.

The author confesses, in his advertisement, that ' there may possibly be some temerity in thus presenting to the public a new translation of Homer, after those which have already been so favourably received. But his prevailing taste for poetry, his fancy raised by repeated perusals of the greatest of poets, his very gratitude itself have not permitted him to remain silent. He has indeed perceived in the Iliad long-winded passages, repetitions, too frequent descriptions of battles; he has therefore taken the liberty of retrenching sometimes, but with all possible circumspection, in order to render the perusal (of Homer) more interesting. As for the enumeration which terminates the second canto, he thought it quite sufficient to translate it into prose, though from the easy flow of his versification, he says, he might as easily have translated that passage also into verse. And indeed so far is his poetical vein from being exhausted by this translation of the Iliad, that it has already produced many cantos of the Odyssey too!

Alas, poor blind old Homer has too often been very cavalierly treated by many a knight-errant; and perhaps by no one more so than by this captain of dragoons.

Mémoires sur différens sujets de Literature. Par M. A. Mongez, Chanoine regulier, &c. 95 Pages. 8vo. Paris.

Three dissertations: the first, on the antiquity of hospitals; the second, on the use of lacrymatory vessels; the third, on the Colossus of Rhodes; with a discourse on the study of French literature.

Traité des Eaux Minérales de Chateldon, de celles de Vichy & de Hauterive en Bourbonnois, avec le Détail de leurs Propriétés Médicinales & leur Analyse. Par M. Desbrest, Conseiller du Roi, M. D. &c. Intendant des Eaux Minérales & Médicinales de Chateldon en Bourbonnois. 359 Pages in 12mo. à Moulins & à Paris.

The mineral waters of Chateldon have but lately risen into notice. The author of this work first observed their good effects on himself, and then on many other patients; and does not scruple to place them in the first rank.

L'Art de soigner les Pieds; contenant un Traité de Cors, Verrues, Durillons, Oignons, Engelures, les Accidens des Ongles & leur Difformité. Présenté au Roi, par M. Laforest, Chirurgien PEDICURE de Sa Majesté & de la Famille Royale. 12mo. Paris & Versailles.

One hundred and thirty-nine pages on the various disorders of the feet, enumerated in the title, by a professed surgeon PEDICURE.

Nouvelles Observations & Récherches Analytiques sur la Magnésie du Sel Epsom, suivies de Reflections sur l' Union Chimique, des Corps. Par Prerre Butini. 8vo. Geneva.

A very elaborate and instructive performance.

Essai sur la Minéralogie des Monts Pyrénées; suivi d'un Catalogue des Plantes observées dans cette Chaîne des Moutagnes: Ouvrage enriche de beaucoup de Planches & de Cartes. 4to. Paris.

An important work, the result of great labour and expence; warmly approved of by the Parisian Academy of Sciences, and printed under their privilege.

MONTHLY CATALOGUE.
POLITICAL.

Observations on the natural and civil Rights of Mankind, the Prerogatives of Princes, and the Powers of Government. By the Rev. Thomas Northcote. 8*vo.* 1*s.* Dilly.

IN this pamphlet, Mr. Northcote produces many ingenious and plausible arguments, in support of the universal right of the people to election and representation. It seems to be, in respect of government, as in that of religion, that though the general ideas of both are conformable to the light of nature, certain modifications are necessary, for adapting them, with advantage, to the practice of mankind. While, therefore, we applaud Mr. Northcote's liberal zeal for the universal rights of the people, we cannot help considering the unlimited extention of those privileges as, in effect, injurious to society, and subversive of the public order and general happiness, to maintain which is the object of every well constituted government.

A Letter to the Right Hon. Charles Jenkinson. 4*to.* 2*s.* Debrett.

The author of this Letter, after indulging himself in a vein of petulant scurrility, against a most respectable and respected character, proceeds to arraign, with all the virulence of party-spirit, the conduct of administration, in regard to the American war. He descants much on the efficient and official council : in treating of which, he totally misrepresents the great authority, mentioned in support of that distinction. Towards the conclusion of the Letter, this *modest, independent Whig,* is so obliging as to mention the names of those persons to whom, in *his* opinion, his majesty ought to entrust the direction of public affairs.

A Speech of the Hon. Charles James Fox, *at a general Meeting of the Electors of* Westminster. *A Broad Sheet.* 3*d.* Debrett.

A republication, from the news-papers, of the transactions and harangues, in Westminster-Hall, on the 10th of December : printed on a large sheet of paper, ornamented with an engraving of Mr. Fox.

On the Debt of the Nation, compared with its Revenue ; and the Impossibility of carrying on the War without Public Oeconomy. 8*vo.* 2*s.* Debrett.

In this production we meet with an account of the national debt ; of the annual revenues for the support of government, and the charge of collecting them ; observations on the commissioners reports, and on the expenditures for the civil list ; with strictures on the navy and army expences, compared with their amount in the last war. In respect of those subjects, the author is apparently well informed ; but to render his observations entirely satisfactory, it is necessary that the estimates upon which he proceeds, should be authenticated. Mean while,

while, we may obferve, that the defign of the whole feems to be, to recommend economy in the public finances, upon a plan lefs extenfive than that which was propofed by Mr. Burke, in the laft feffions of the preceding parliament.

The Signs of the Times: or, a Syftem of true Politics. By James Illingworth, *D. D.* 8vo. 2s. 6d. A. Donaldfon.

A rhapfody on original fin, types, oppofition, rebellion, the American war, and a variety of other religious and political fubjects.

Obfervations on a Pamphlet entitled An Enquiry into the Advantages and Difadvantages refulting from Bills of Inclofure. 8vo. 2s. Bew.

The author of this tract is a zealous advocate, as every thinking and philofophical man muft be, for the enclofure of commons. He confiders a bill for this purpofe in the light of ' a petition to fecure the property of certain perfons from depredation, and to put it into their power to enjoy and improve their own, and only their own.' He fhews the abfurdity of leaving a large tract of land unimproved and neglected, merely that a poor man may keep a flock of geefe upon it; when the fame ground, if properly cultivated, would maintain feveral families. He ftates the expences, and other inconveniences, attending the prefent method of carrying bills of enclofure into execution; and lays down the plan of *a general act* of parliament for the enclofure of all the commons in England worth cultivating. This, he thinks, would promote population, and produce fuch additional revenues, as in time would difcharge the national debt.

In the generality of bills of enclofure, it has been the practice to allot a certain proportion in lieu of tithes, as a full equivalent and compenfation for them. Much has been lately faid in the houfe of lords upon this fubject; and it is anxioufly expected, that a bill will yet pafs for an univerfal commutation. Our author freely acknowleges the pernicious tendency of tithes; but infifts, that any allotment of land in exchange, muft injure either the tenants, the landlords, or the clergy. To prove this point, he gives us a variety of calculations, on which he fays : ' By thefe calculations it appears, that a proportion of one-fixth, to one-feventh, will in general be as much, as the laity can give in lieu of tithes, without lofs to themfelves; but it is apparent, that the clergy muft be fufferers, whenever they accept of it. On the other hand, fhould fuch an equivalent be made to them, as appears to me they have a right to expect and demand, containing a quantity of land, the rents of which are equal to the tithe they give up, it follows, that the laity muft be greatly injured by the bargain.'—He therefore propofes a pecuniary compenfation, to be paid out of each titheable farm, of the nature of a rent.

They who wifh to fee the foregoing paradox explained, muft have recourfe to the author's calculations.—Here however we shall

shall beg leave to observe, that, in a scheme of commutation, the clergy may give up a part of their legal demands without any real detriment ; because at present they very seldom, if ever, receive the full value of their tithes.

D I V I N I T Y.

A serious and affectionate Address to all Orders of Men, adapted to this awful Crisis. 8vo. 1s. Robinson.

The author of this Address is Mr. Thomas Mills, bookseller at Bristol, an enthusiastic admirer of the works of the late Wm. Law, which, he tells us, ' bear every internal character of a *divine* original.' The poor man, it seems, ' had been bewildered and lost in the endless mazes of doubt and error,' till he happily met with the works of ' this truly *illuminated* divine.' And now, ' from the love which he bears to his dear fellow-pilgrims, he could not, in the evening of his life, go *home* to his eternal *native* country, well contented, till he had pointed out to those, who may yet be strangers to Mr. Law's works, a treasure of such inestimable value.'

A Sermon preached before the University of Oxford, Nov. 5, 1781. By William Crowe, LL.B. 4to. 1s. Cadell.

From the institution of the passover among the Jews, in remembrance of their deliverance out of Egypt, the author of this discourse takes occasion to shew the propriety of our observing the 5th of November, as a day of public thanksgiving. But the commemoration of this day, he says, may well consist with perfect charity towards the Roman Catholics, and with some relaxation of those penalties, by which their religion has been restrained. We have no occasion at present to be alarmed on account of their numbers, their disposition, or the influence and practice of that church, with which they hold communion. These considerations naturally lead him to a review of those precautions, which the people of this nation were obliged to take, when their civil and religious rights were actually violated in the reign of James II.

M E D I C A L.

An Enquiry into the Nature, Causes, and Method of Cure of Nervous Disorders. By Alex. Thomson, M. D. 8vo. 1s. Murray.

The author of this Enquiry, after giving a brief description of the nerves, and enumerating many symptoms of their morbid affection, endeavours to account for the prevalence of nervous disorders, upon the general principles of idleness and intemperance, independently of any particular species of modern luxury ; and in support of this opinion, he adduces arguments of great weight. Concerning the origin of nervous complaints, he observes, that, for the most part, they may be traced to a weakness of the stomach and bowels ; whence if those disorders do not actually derive their

earliest

earlieſt exiſtence, at leaſt the ſigns of their invaſion are there moſt perceptible.

'That, ſays he, a diſeaſe which depends upon irritability, and is ſupported by a ſympathy in the nervous ſyſtem, derives its origin from the ſtomach and bowels, is an opinion ſtrongly confirmed by the texture and offices of thoſe parts. Furniſhed with numerous branches of nerves, there are extremely ſuſceptible of irritation ; to which they are alſo particularly expoſed from the weight or reſiſtance of the food, its occaſional acrimony, and the ſtimulating nature of the gaſtric fluids, rendered yet more acrimonious by vitiated digeſtion.'

The difficulty attending the cure of nervous diſorders, is placed by our author in a light peculiarly clear and forcible.

'In attempting, ſays he, the removal of the nervous complaint, the greateſt attention is neceſſary to inveſtigate the preciſe origin, whether ſingular or plural, whence it derives its ſupport : for without ſuch knowledge, in vain ſhall we endeavour to prevent the effects of irritation. With every advantage on our ſide, we ſhall often have occaſion to regret the obſtinacy of the diſeaſe. Indeed, that nervous diſorders ſhould prove difficult of cure, will not appear ſurpriſing, when we conſider how much they are diſtinguiſhed by a variety of oppoſite indications and circumſtances, of a poſitive and negative, of a phyſical and moral kind. Amidſt the neceſſity of nouriſhment, is every impediment to digeſtion. The impurity of the blood we find aggravated by great irregularity of the diſcharges. Sleep, however indiſpenſable for recruiting the exhauſted ſtrength, in many caſes comes not ſpontaneouſly ; nor can it be procured by medicine, without increaſing relaxation. Exerciſe, abſolutely neceſſary, is often prevented by a liſtleſſneſs, utterly averſe to motion. In morbid irritability, which requires the moſt ſoothing treatment, the patient is peculiarly liable to perturbations of body and mind. Notwithſtanding incidental or habitual lowneſs of ſpirits, which ſeems to indicate the expedience of ſome exhilirating liquor, even the moderate uſe of cordials may be neither effectual nor ſafe. Anxiety, natural to the complaint, and increaſed by every conſideration, muſt yet be ſupported with patience. And laſtly, though ſo complicated a diſtemper might ſeem to demand the moſt active remedies, it is often obſerved to be aggravated even by thoſe of the gentleſt kind.'

In the courſe of this pamphlet we meet with many judicious remarks on the method by which the cure of nervous diſorders has hitherto been uſually conducted ; as well as with an explicit detail of that which is the moſt rational and moſt ſucceſsful. We would, therefore, recommend this ingenious Enquiry not only to the gentlemen of the medical profeſſion, but to all who are afflicted with any ſymptoms of nervous irritability.

The

The Physician's Vade Mecum; or a concise System of the Practice of Physic. small 8vo. 2s. 6d. Robinson.

The plan of this elegant little volume is to exhibit a system of the medical art, drawn up in the most practical, and, at the same time, in the concisest manner. Such an epitome, it is observed in the preface, is calculated not only to afford, on every occasion, an immediate recourse to the oracular treasures of physic, but to imprint on the mind the most useful and essential precepts of the science. We entirely agree with the author, in respect to the utility of such a work ; as we also do with regard to his opinion, that, notwithstanding the numerous late improvements in physic, nothing is so much wanted as a judicious compendium of practice. He observes that the only treatise of this kind is the PROCESSUS INTERGI of Sydenham ; a work which, however valuable, is now, on account of the progress of observation, become in a great measure obsolete. This treatise, therefore, is intended as a new Processus Integri, extracted not from the writings of one physician, but from those of all the most eminent of the present time. In respect of its more extensive plan, as well as of the select observations, of which it consists, it is evidently superior to the celebrated production above mentioned ; for beside delivering explicitly the most approved rules in practice, attention has been paid to the identifying every disease, and particularly those which are more obscure, or might be confounded with each other ; by always delineating their characteristic and indispensable symptoms. Where prescriptions are given, they have been thrown into notes at the bottom of the page; a method, the editor observes, which places them in a conspicuous view, without interrupting the text. In the arrangement of the diseases, we are first presented with those of a general nature, and afterwards with such as are local. The acute diseases precede the chronical ; and in both classes, the distempers are ranked in regular progression from the head downwards. A system so happily imagined, and executed with so much care ; which delivers essential observation without tedious detail, and inculcates precept without empiricism, must, we are persuaded, prove highly acceptable to the medical faculty.

Some Observations on the present Epidemic Dysentery. By Francis Geach. 1s. Baldwin.

These Observations appear to be drawn from experience, and a careful attention to the sick ; but as they coincide, in general, with the remarks of former writers, they serve to confirm, rather throw any new light on the nature and treatment of the disease.

√ N O V E L S.

The Adventures of a Rupee. 12mo. 3s. sewed. Murray.

This mode of making up a book, and styling it the Adventures of a Cat, a Dog, a Monkey, a Hackney-coach, a Louse, a Shilling, a Rupee, or—any thing else, is grown so fashionable, that
few

few months pass which do not bring one of them under our inspection. It is indeed a convenient method to writers of the inferior class, of emptying their common-place books, and throwing together all the farrago of public transactions, private characters, old and new stories, every thing, in short, which they can pick up, to afford a little temporary amusement to an idle reader. This is the utmost degree of merit which the best of them aspire to; and, small as it is, more than most of them ever arrive at. The flight performance before us is perhaps one of the best of its little species, and may give half an hour's entertainment to a coffee-house critic, or a lounging traveller, as the style is tolerably easy and correct, and some of the materials are not unentertaining. From these we shall select a short story, that may give our readers an idea of our author's manner, and which has some humour in it.

A Rupee, the relater of these adventures, falls into the hands of a Fakir, or Indian priest. These men travel in large troops, and, like some of the monks in Catholic countries, extort charity by a kind of religious robbery. To deceive the vulgar, they inflict on themselves the most severe penances, and for these sufferings pretend that their Brama, or God, admits them to a knowlege of future events. Concerning a company of these, our Rupee tells the following tale.

' In the midst of these pleasures, (says the Rupee), two Fakirs arrived with the news that the illustrious Hyder Alli had given a general invitation to their body, to dine with him on a certain day. The hope of gain prompted some to attend, vanity not a few, and curiosity many. Among the rest, my master resolved to attend; he sewed me up in the lining of his ragged covering, and in company with about four hundred Fakirs, we set out to be present at the feast given to our body by Hyder Alli.

' Hyder at this time was engaged in several wars, in the course of which, he gave many proofs of great generalship and force of mind.

' He could well counterfeit any character, which it was for his interest to assume. The ill qualities of the human mind, which afford the best handle for governing mankind, he could use to much advantage.—War is conducted on different principles in the East, from those by which it is regulated in Europe. If a general, who is dreaded by an enemy, can be carried off by any piece of treachery, it is looked upon as fair as any stratagem in the field. —Hyder was well versed in business of this nature.—He was also skilled in the art of negotiation, and could look with great sagacity into the events of futurity.

' My master and his companions had heard much of this warriour, whose fame spread over all Indostan. They were dazzled with the honour of an invitation from so celebrated a man, and assembled in hundreds from every quarter. — To the number of twelve thousand the Fakirs sat down at table—Dishes succeeded dishes, and dainty dainty; for this was a day, on which, by the

expreſs command of Hyder, they were ſo relax of their ordinary
ſeverity. — Good humour and ſelf importance ſhewed themſelves
over all the tattered aſſembly, which to a diſtant ſpectator, muſt
have appeared not unlike a London rag fair—The intoxication of
honour and good cheer was univerſal, when Hyder makes his appearance—The majeſty of his countenance, in ſpite of the ſmile
that then adorned it, ſtruck terror into the congregation — Silence
and dread were univerſal—The animating principle of a whole
camp, which extended to the boundaries of our viſion, ſtood before us. After looking up three times to heaven, in adoration of
the great Brama, he thus broke ſilence.

‘ Illuſtrious ſervants of the power whom we adore, I come
to return you my thanks for the honour you have done me in
accepting my invitation. I entertain the higheſt veneration
for the ſanctity of your lives, and the ſeverity of your manners. You have ſhewn yourſelves worthy of that maſter you
all worſhip, by deſpiſing all ſenſual comforts. You have even
gone farther: as if you poſſeſſed a mind in a ſtate of perfect
ſeparation from body, you have continually inflicted on
yourſelves the moſt excruciating tortures, and theſe you have
borne without teſtifying any ſenſe of pain. You have rolled
naked in the dirt, while the rude pebbles deprived you of the
ſmall fragments of ſkin your other ſufferings had left behind.
Illuſtrious ſervants of Brama, who ſee the chain of future
events, Hyder Alli pities your ſufferings.—Be not ſeen amongſt
men any more in the mean dreſs in which you now appear.
Lay aſide theſe rags that ill befit the miniſters of heaven. Dreſs
is a mark of diſtinction; and you who hold the firſt rank amongſt
men, ſhould not be diſtinguiſhed by filth. I have prepared
cloaths that will defend you both from the cold and the
heat, for well I know you have no money to purchaſe any for
yourſelves. My ſoldiers ſhall ſee the ſervants of Brama immediately dreſſed in them. Such is the council that Brama puts into
the heart of Hyder Alli—Can I ſay more?

‘ After this ſpeech, he immediately went out. The whole aſſembly ſat in ſilent vexation; for every individual was ſenſible,
that his rags which ſeemed ſo worthleſs, contained great treaſures.
But it would have been in vain to remonſtrate. Hyder's ſoldiers
perform with alacrity the charitable office of cloathing the naked,
and took poſſeſſion of the rags, which were heavy with gold, under the pretence of burying them; for what could be ſuppoſed of
value in the tattered coverings of poor men that practiſed ſelf denial! The operations of war which Hyder carried on at this time
againſt the Britiſh, began to be languid for want of money; he
ſaw the evil, and took this method of providing againſt it. Thus
I eſcaped, with many thouſands of the ſame ſpecies, and found
myſelf in the poſſeſſion of the great Hyder Alli.'

This ſtory is well imagined, and not ill-told. It certainly ſets
Hyder Alli's ſagacity in a favourable light, and marks him out
to

to us as what we have experienced him to be, a most formidable enemy. The part here attributed to him is, at least we may observe, more probable than that which our author has related of him in the sixth chapter of these Adventures, where, in his history of Miss Melville, he has made him a rival of Scipio's in the best part of his character. But for this adventure, and some others equally amusing, we must refer our readers to the book itself, which we may venture to recommend to them as a better entertainment than cards and dice, during the long evenings of the Christmas holydays.

The History of John Juniper, *Esq. alias* Juniper Jack. *3 vols. 12mo.* 10s 6d. Baldwin.

Just before the publication of this work, it was whispered round, that it contained the *true* history of a no less respectable personage than the celebrated John Wilkes, shadowed out under the character of Juniper Jack; a circumstance which naturally raised the curiosity of the public, whose sanguine expectations will be miserably disappointed, when they discover, as we have found by a painful perusal, that, instead of exhibiting any entertaining traits of that great phænomenon, the reader will meet with little more than a series of uninteresting vulgar occurrences, and an aukward affectation of humour. It is said, notwithstanding, in the title-page, to be written by the author of the Adventures of a Guinea; a work we remember to have read with great pleasure, and which displayed indisputable marks of taste and genius. —But, Oh! what a falling-off is here!

The Masqued Weddings. 2 Vols. Small 8vo. 6s. Hookham.

Whether this novel was written in haste, we know not; but from the uninterrupted flow of the language, it must be read with precipitation. To compensate this inconvenience, however, it abounds with vivacity, and cannot fail of affording entertainment.

The Female Monitor, or the History of Arabella *and Lady* Gay. 8vo. 2s. stitched. Richardson.

The title of this production might suggest the idea, that it possesses at least some moral merit; but at the same time that it bears the marks of great affectation, it is far too frivolous to be useful.

Lucinda; *or the Self-devoted Daughter.* Small 8vo. 3s. Hookham.

An extravagant assemblage of terrible incidents, recited in bombastic narrative.

INDEX.

I N D E X.

Theory

INDEX to the FOREIGN ARTICLES.

I N D E X.

END OF THE FIFTY-SECOND VOL.